# A GUIDE TO FREQUENTLY ENCOUNTERED CONSTRUCTION ISSUES


Editors: Fred D. Wilshusen, Eric A. Berg, Terrence L. Brookie, and Carrie Lynn H. Okizaki

# CONSTRUCTION CHECKLISTS: A GUIDE TO FREQUENTLY ENCOUNTERED CONSTRUCTION ISSUES

Editors:
*Fred D. Wilshusen*
*Eric A. Berg*
*Terrence L. Brookie*
*Carrie L. Okizaki*

Cover design by ABA Publishing.



Printed in the United States of America

12 11 10 09 08 5 4 3 2 1

**Library of Congress Cataloging-in-Publication Data**

Construction checklists : a guide to frequently encountered construction issues / editors, Fred D. Wilshusen, Eric A. Berg, Terrence L. Brookie.
p. cm.
Includes bibliographical references and index.
ISBN 978-1-60442-145-3 (alk. paper)
1. Construction industry—Law and legislation—United States. 2. Construction contracts—United States. I. Wilshusen, Fred D., 1957– II. Berg, Eric A. III. Brookie, Terrence L.
KF902.C59294 2008
343.73'078624—dc22

2008030288

Discounts are available for books ordered in bulk. Special consideration is given to state bars, CLE programs, and other bar-related organizations. Inquire at Book Publishing, ABA Publishing, American Bar Association, 321 North Clark Street, Chicago, Illinois 60654-7598.
www.ababooks.org

# Table of Contents

**Trial/Hearing**

## General Lists

# Biographies of Editors

**Fred D. Wilshusen** is a partner in the Dallas, Texas, law firm of Thomas, Feldman & Wilshusen, LLP, a law firm that concentrates in the areas of construction law and related litigation representing all segments of the construction industry. He is a frequent lecturer on construction law issues to trade groups and professional associations. He is the author or co-author of several construction-related publications, including the *Texas Lien and Bonds Claims Handbook,* 5th ed. (2005); "Texas Construction Trust Fund Act and Bankruptcy Preferences," in *The Construction Law Journal,* Winter 2003; and "Construction Law Annual Survey of Texas Law," 44 S.W.L.J. 2101 (1990). Mr. Wilshusen served on the Governing Committee of the ABA Forum Committee on the Construction Industry from 2002 to 2005. He has held several other positions with the ABA Forum, including chair of the Publications Committee of the ABA Forum from 2005 to 2006. He is also a member of the ABA Litigation Section, Construction Litigation Subcommittee. Mr. Wilshusen graduated from Austin College in 1979. He graduated from Texas Tech University School of Law in 1983 (cum laude). He is a member of Phi Kappa Phi and Order of the Coif.

**Eric A. Berg** is a shareholder with Vedder Price PC in its Chicago office. He focuses his practice on construction law, in both litigation and transactional work. As a litigator, he has represented owners, contractors, subcontractors, architects, engineers, and lenders. Mr. Berg also has extensive experience in other areas of commercial litigation and alternative dispute resolution. Mr. Berg's transactional work includes drafting and negotiating contracts for the design, construction, rehabilitation, and construction management of hotels, hospitals, office buildings, apartment buildings, private residences, retail stores, factories, warehouses, and mixed-use facilities. For numerous clients, he has provided counsel on interpretation of and compliance with the Americans with Disabilities Act and other accessibility statutes. In 2006, Mr. Berg was named an Illinois Super Lawyer as the result of a research project conducted jointly by *Law & Politics* and *Chicago* magazines. The respected English publisher Chambers and Partners lists Mr. Berg in *Chambers USA: America's Leading Lawyers for Business.* Mr. Berg is AV® rated by Martindale-Hubbell. He is a 1987 graduate of Yale University and a 1992 graduate of Northwestern University School of Law.

**Terrence L. Brookie** is a partner in the firm of Locke Reynolds LLP in Indianapolis, Indiana, where he is the chairperson of the Construction and Real Estate Group. He concentrates his practice in the area of construction law, fidelity and surety law, and business litigation. He is also a mediator and arbitrator of construction and commercial disputes. Mr. Brookie is a frequent speaker for construction and commercial groups and has lectured and written numerous articles for several industry groups and professional organizations in the construction industry. He is a member of the ABA's Forum on the Construction Industry (Governing Committee Member), TIPS Fidelity/Surety Law Committee, and the Construction Litigation Committee. Mr. Brookie received his B.A. from Denison University in 1978 and his J.D. from Indiana University School of Law in 1981. He is a Fellow of the American College of Construction Lawyers and selected by his peers for inclusion in *The Best Lawyers in America*, 2005–2008.

**Carrie Lynn H. Okizaki** is a partner in Schiff Hardin LLP's Construction Law Group. Ms. Okizaki currently concentrates her practice in advising owners, developers, general contractors, and design professionals in a variety of commercial and litigation matters, including multifaceted, complex disputes involving delays, disruption, and losses of efficiency; breaches of contracts for performance, scope of work, and payment; and multiparty insurance coverage issues. In her transactional practice, she represents owners, architect/engineers, contractors, and energy clients in creating and negotiating contract forms (consulting services, materials, and professional services), as well as project-specific contracts (engineering, procurement, and construction/multi-prime/design-build) for large projects. Ms. Okizaki received her B.S. in Foreign Service from Georgetown University in 1996 and her J.D. from the University of Colorado School of Law in 2000, where she was a casenote and comment editor for the *University of Colorado Law Review*.

# Contributors

**Matthew R. Alter,** Borden Ladner Gervais LLP, Scotia Plaza, 40 King Street West, Toronto, ON M5H 3Y4; (416) 367-6196 (phone); (416) 361-2728 (fax); *malter@blgcanada.com; www.blgcanada.com*

**Michele C. Ammendola,** Becker & Poliakoff PA, Emerald Lake Corporate Park, 3111 Stirling Road, Fort Lauderdale, FL 33312-6525; (954) 364-6023 (phone); (954) 985-4176 (fax); *mammendola@becker-poliakoff.com; www.becker-poliakoff.com*

**Mark I. Anderson,** executive vice president and chief operating officer, Warner Construction Consultants Inc., 2273 Research Boulevard, Suite 500, Rockville, MD 20850-3291; (301) 670-9020 (phone); (301) 670-7977 (fax); (240) 599-7140 (direct); *manderson@warnercon.com; www.warnercon.com*

**Jeremy S. Baker,** Schiff Hardin LLP, 6600 Sears Tower, 233 South Wacker Drive, Chicago, IL 60606-6473; (312) 258-5500 (phone); (312) 258-5600 (fax); *jbaker@schiffhardin.com; www.schiffhardin.com*

**Scott K. Behrendt,** Theodora Oringher Miller & Richman PC, 535 Anton Boulevard, Ninth Floor, Costa Mesa, CA 92626-7109; (714) 549-6200 (phone); (714) 549-6201 (fax); *sbehrendt@tocounsel.com; www.tocounsel.com*

**Eric A. Berg,** Shareholder, Vedder Price PC, 222 North LaSalle Street, Chicago, IL 60601; (312) 609-7635 (phone); (312) 609-5005 (fax); *eberg@vedderprice.com; www.vedderprice.com*

**Paul W. Berning,** Thelen Reid Brown Raysman & Steiner LLP, 101 Second Street, Suite 1800, San Francisco, CA 94105; (415) 369-7229 (phone); (415) 369-8612 (fax); *pwberning@thelen.com; www.thelen.com*

**Shannon J. Briglia,** Briglia McLaughlin, PLLC, 1950 Old Gallows Road, Suite 750, Vienna, VA 22182; (703) 506-1990 (phone); (703) 506-1140; *sbriglia@briglialaw.com; www.briglialaw.com*

**Terrence L. Brookie,** Locke Reynolds LLP, 201 N. Illinois St., Suite 1000, P.O. Box 44961, Indianapolis, IN 46244-0961; (317) 237-3851 (phone); (317) 237-3900 (fax); *tbrookie@locke.com; www.locke.com*

**Christopher R. Bryant,** PSP, executive consultant, Warner Construction Consultants Inc., 2273 Research Boulevard, Suite 500, Rockville, MD 20850-3291; (301) 670-9020 (phone); (301) 670-7977 (fax); *cbryant@warnercon.com; www.warnercon.com*

**Fred J. Bush,** P.E., Esq., Acct., PSP vice president, Warner Construction Consultants Inc., 2273 Research Boulevard, Suite 500, Rockville, MD 20850-3291; (301) 670-9020 (phone); (301) 670-7977 (fax); *fbush@warnercon.com; www.warnercon.com*

**Stephen D. Butler,** Esq., counsel for special projects, former general counsel (retired), Parsons Brinckerhoff Inc., 1 Penn Plaza, New York, NY 10019; (415) 509-4226 (phone); (415) 567-7456 (fax); *butler@pbworld.com; www.pbworld.com*

**Christian A. Carrillo,** Morris Polich & Purdy LLP, 1055 West 7th Street, 24th Floor, Los Angeles, CA 90017; (213) 891-9100 (phone); (213) 488-1178 (fax); *ccarrillo@mpplaw.com, www.mpplaw.com*

**Kristine L. Cato,** McAngus Goudelock & Courie LLC, 700 Gervais Street, Suite 300, Columbia, SC 29201; (803) 227-2277 (phone); (803) 748-0526 (fax); *kcato@mgclaw.com; www.mgclaw.com*

**Christopher S. Dunn,** Waller, Lansden, Dortch & Davis LLP, 511 Union Street, Suite 2700, Nashville, TN 37219; (615) 850-8687 (phone); (615) 244-6804 (fax); *chris.dunn@wallerlaw.com; www.wallerlaw.com*

**Wendy J. Earle,** Borden Ladner Gervais LLP, Scotia Plaza, 40 King Street West, Toronto, ON M5H 3Y4; (416) 367-6186 (phone); (416) 361-2713 (fax); *wearle@blgcanada.com; www.blgcanada.com*

**R. Carson Fisk,** Ford, Nassen & Baldwin PC, 98 San Jacinto Boulevard, Suite 1450, Austin, TX 78701; (512) 236-0009 (phone); (512) 236-0682 (fax); *rcfisk@fordnassen.com; www.fordnassen.com*

**Terry J. Galganski,** JD, director of insurance and risk programs, The Weitz Company LLC, 400 Locust Street, Suite 300, Des Moines, IA 50309; (515) 698-4282 (phone); (515) 471-3953 (fax); *terry.galganski@weitz.com; www.weitz.com*

**Bruce R. Gerhardt,** vice president, senior counsel, HDR Inc. Legal Department, 8404 Indian Hills Drive, Omaha, NE 68114-4098; (402) 399-1055 (phone); (402) 399-1339 (fax); *bruce.gerhardt@hdrinc.com; www.hdrinc.com*

**Peter C. Halls,** Faegre & Benson LLP, 90 South 7th Street, Suite 2200, Minneapolis, MN 55402-3901; (612) 766-6819 (phone); (612) 766-1600 (fax); *phalls@faegre.com; www.faegre.com*

**Troy L. Harris,** King & Spalding, 1180 Peachtree Street NE, Atlanta, GA 30309-3521; (404) 572-2446 (phone); (404) 572-5138 (fax); *tharris@kslaw.com; www.kslaw.com*

**Stephen A. Hess,** Esq., Sherman & Howard LLC, 90 South Cascade Avenue, Suite 1500, Colorado Springs, CO 80903-4015; (719) 475-2440 (phone); (719) 635-4576 (fax); *shess@shermanhoward.com; www.shermanhoward.com*

**Gregg E. Hutt,** Esq., Trenam, Kemker, Scharf, Barkin, Frye, O'Neill & Mullis PA, 2700 Bank of America Plaza, 101 East Kennedy Boulevard, Tampa, FL 33602-5150; (813) 227-7482 (phone); (813) 229-6553 (fax); *gehutt@trenam.com; www.trenam.com*

**Amy Hobbs Iannone,** assistant general counsel and director of risk management, Barton Malow Company, 26500 American Drive, Southfield, MI 48034-2337; (248) 436-5044 (phone); (248) 436-5045 (fax); *amy.iannone@bartonmalow.com; www.bartonmalow.com*

**Paul A. Ivanoff,** Osler, Hoskin & Harcourt LLP, 1 First Canadian Place, P.O. Box 50, Toronto, ON M5X 1B8; (416) 862-4223 (phone); (416) 862-6666 (fax); *pivanoff@osler.com; www.osler.com*

**Edward M. Josiah,** Nautilus Consulting, LLC, 60 Mall Drive, Commack, NY 11725; (631) 891-3040 (phone); (631) 891-3059 (fax); *ejosiah@nautcon.com; www.nautcon.com*

**Jeffrey R. Jury,** Burns, Anderson, Jury & Brenner, P.O. Box 26300, Austin, TX 78759; (512) 338-5322 (phone); (512) 338-5363 (fax); *jjury@bajb.com; www.bajb.com*

**David T. Kasper,** Locke Reynolds LLP, 201 North Illinois Street, Suite 1000, P.O. Box 44961, Indianapolis, IN 46244-0961; (317) 237-3800 (phone); (317) 237-3900 (fax); *dkasper@locke.com; www.locke.com*

**Daniel P. King,** Locke Reynolds LLP, 201 North Illinois Street, Suite 1000, P.O. Box 44961, Indianapolis, IN 46244-0961; (317) 237-3800 (phone); (317) 237-3900 (fax); *dking@locke.com; www.locke.com*

**Clifford F. Kinney Jr.,** Spilman Thomas & Battle PLLC, 300 Kanawha Boulevard East, P.O. Box 273, Charleston, WV 25321-0273; (304) 340-3844 (phone); (304) 340-3801 (fax); *ckinney@spilmanlaw.com; www.spilmanlaw.com*

**Lori Ann Lange,** Peckar & Abramson, Two Lafayette Centre, 1133 21st Street, NW, Suite 500, Washington, DC 20036; (202) 293-8815 (phone); (202) 293-7994 (fax); *llange@pecklaw.com; www.pecklaw.com*

**Steven B. Lesser,** Becker & Poliakoff PA, Emerald Lake Corporate Park, 3111 Stirling Road, Fort Lauderdale, FL 33312-6525; (954) 985-4137 (phone); (954) 985-6805 (fax); *slesser@becker-poliakoff.com; www.becker-poliakoff.com*

**Theodore D. Levin,** P.E., Esq., Morris Polich & Purdy LLP, 1055 West 7th Street, 24th Floor, Los Angeles, CA 90017; (213) 891-9100 (phone); (213) 488-1178 (fax); *tlevin@mpplaw.com; www.mpplaw.com*

**John C. Livengood,** Esq., AIA, associate vice president, PinnacleOne—An Arcadis Company, 9861 Broken Land Parkway, Suite 254, Columbia, MD 21046; (202) 669-1360 (phone, mobile); (202) 291-3481 (fax); *jlivengood@pinnacleone.com; www.pinnacleone.com*

**Fredrick J. Ludwig,** Husch Blackwell Sanders LLP, 720 Olive Street, Suite 2400, St. Louis, MO 63101; (314) 345-6222 (phone); (314) 345-6060 (fax); *fredrick.ludwig@huschblackwell.com; www.huschblackwell.com*

**Erich R. Luschei,** Theodora Oringher Miller & Richman, PC, 535 Anton Boulevard, Ninth Floor, Costa Mesa, CA 92626-7109; (714) 549-6150 (phone); (714) 549-6201 (fax); *eluschei@tocounsel.com; www.tocounsel.com*

**Rashida Y. V. MacMurray,** Attorney at Law, 343 West 145th Street, New York, NY 10031; (212) 283-4870 (phone); *ryvmac@mac.com*

**Alfred A. Malena Jr.,** Thompson, Slagle & Hannan LLC, 12000 Findley Road, Suite 250, Duluth, GA 30097; (770) 662-5999 (phone); (770) 447-6063 (fax), *amalena@tshlawyers.com; www.tshlawyers.com*

**Frank T. Mamat**, Foster, Swift, Collins & Smith, PC, 32300 Northwestern Highway, Suite 230, Farmington Hills, MI 48334; (248) 539-9900 (phone); (248) 851-7504 (fax); *fmamat@fosterswift.com; www.fosterswift.com*

**Daniel D. McMillan,** Jones Day, 555 South Flower Street, 50th Floor, Los Angeles, CA 90071; (213) 243-2582 (phone); (213) 243-2539 (fax); *ddmcmillan@jonesday.com; www.jonesday.com*

**Troy M. Miller,** Bose McKinney & Evans LLP, 2700 First Indiana Plaza, 135 North Pennsylvania Street, Indianapolis, IN 46204; (317) 684-5000 (phone); (317) 684-5189 (direct); (317) 223-0189 (direct fax); *tmiller@boselaw.com; www.boselaw.com*

**Michael G. Murphy,** P.E., Esq., Greenberg Traurig PA, 450 South Orange Avenue, Suite 650, Orlando, FL 32801; (407) 999-2509 (phone); (407) 841-1295 (fax); *murphymg@gtlaw.com; www.gtlaw.com*

**Denise L. Nestel,** Porter & Hedges LLP, 1000 Main Street, 36th Floor, Houston, TX 77002; (713) 226-6612 (phone); (713) 226-6212 (fax); *dnestel@porterhedges .com; www.porterhedges.com*

**W. Samuel Niece,** Thelen Reid Brown Raysman & Steiner LLP, 101 Second Street, Suite 1800, San Francisco, CA 94105; (415) 369-7698 (phone); (415) 371-1211 (fax); *wsniece@thelen.com; www.thelen.com*

**Carrie Lynn H. Okizaki,** Schiff Hardin LLP, 6600 Sears Tower, Chicago, IL 60606-6473; (312) 258-5694 (phone); (312) 258-5600 (fax); *cokizaki@schiffhardin. com; www.schiffhardin.com*

**Robert J. Orelup,** Drewry Simmons Vornehm LLP, 8888 Keystone Crossing, Suite 1200, Indianapolis, IN 46240-4621; (317) 580-4848 (phone); (317) 580-4855 (fax); *rorelup@drewrysimmons.com; www.drewrysimmons.com*

**Melissa A. Orien,** Holland & Hart LLP, 60 East South Temple, Suite 2000, Salt Lake City, UT 84111-1032; (801) 799-5800 (phone); (801) 799-5700 (fax); *morien@ hollandhart.com; www.hollandhart.com*

**José M. Pienknagura,** vice president, risk manager, and general counsel, The Hunt Corporation, Hunt Construction Group Inc., 6720 North Scottsdale Road, Suite 300, Scottsdale, AZ 85253; (480) 368-4740 (phone); (480) 368-4745 (fax); *jmpienknagura@thehuntcorp.com; www.thehuntcorp.com*

**Patrick J. Poff,** Trenam, Kemker, Scharf, Barkin, Frye, O'Neill & Mullis PA, 2700 Bank of America Plaza, 101 East Kennedy Boulevard, Tampa, FL 33602-5150; (813) 223-7474 (phone); (813) 229-6553 (fax); *pjpoff@trenam.com; www .trenam.com*

**John W. Ralls,** Thelen Reid Brown Raysman & Steiner LLP, 101 Second Street, Suite 1800, San Francisco, CA 94105; (415) 369-7210 (phone); (415) 369-8710 (fax); *rralls@thelen.com; www.thelen.com*

**Scott C. Ryan,** general counsel, Perini Building Company Inc., 360 East Coronado Road, Phoenix, AZ 85004; (602) 256-6777 (phone); (602) 256-7547 (fax); *sryan@periniwest.com; www.perini.com*

**E. Jane Sidnell,** Fraser Milner Casgrain LLP, 30th Floor Fifth Avenue Place, 237 4th Avenue S.W., Calgary, AB T2P 4X7; (403) 268-3119 (phone—direct line); (403) 268-3100 (fax); *jane.sidnell@fmc-law.com; www.fmc-law.com*

**George Anthony [Tony] Smith,** Kilpatrick Stockton LLP, 1100 Peachtree Street, Suite 2800, Atlanta, GA 30309-4530; (404) 815-6070 (phone); (404) 541-3208 (fax); *tsmith@kilpatrickstockton.com; www.kilpatrickstockton.com*

**Clark T. Thiel,** Thelen Reid Brown Raysman & Steiner LLP, 101 Second Street, Suite 1800, San Francisco, CA 94105; (415) 369-7480 (phone); (415) 369-8955 (fax); *cthiel@thelen.com; www.thelen.com*

**Patricia H. Thompson,** Carlton Fields PA, 100 S.E. Second Street, Suite 4000, Miami, FL 33131; (305) 539-7239 (phone); (305) 530-0055 (fax); *pthompson@carltonfields.com; www.carltonfields.com*

**William W. Thompson, Jr.,** Peckar & Abramson PC, Two Lafayette Centre, 1133 21st Street, NW, Suite 500, Washington, DC 20036; (202) 293-8815 Ext. 7115 (phone); (202) 293-7994 (fax); *wthompson@pecklaw.com; www.pecklaw.com*

**Donald A. Tobin,** Peckar & Abramson PC, Two Lafayette Centre, 1133 21st Street NW, Suite 500, Washington, DC 20036; (202) 293-8815 Ext. 7107 (phone); (202) 293-7994 (fax); *dtobin@pecklaw.com; www.pecklaw.com*

**John S. Vento,** Trenam, Kemper, Scharf, Barkin, Frye, O'Neill & Mullis PA, 101 East Kennedy Boulevard, Suite 2700, Tampa, FL 33602; (813) 223-7483 (phone); (813) 229-6553 (fax); *jsvento@trenam.com; www.trenam.com*

**Lisa K. Virani,** Eisner & Frank, 9601 Wilshire Boulevard, Suite 700, Beverly Hills, CA 90210; (310) 855-3200 (phone); (310) 855-3201 (fax); *lvirani@eisnerlaw.com; www.eisnerlaw.com*

**Robert W. Wachsmuth,** Glast, Phillips & Murray PC, The Court Building, 219 East Houston Street, Suite 400, San Antonio, TX 78205-2878; (210) 244-2106 (phone); (210) 244-4199 (fax); *rwachsmuth@gpm-law.com; www.gpm-law.com*

**Kenneth K. Wang,** Koenig Jacobsen LLP, Two Park Plaza, Suite 700, Irvine, CA 92614; (949) 756-0700 (phone); (949) 756-2370 (fax); *kkw@kjattorneys.com; www.kjattorneys.com*

**James E. Weatherholtz,** Buist Moore Smythe McGee PA, 5 Exchange Street, P.O. Box 999, Charleston, SC 29402; (843) 720-4628 (phone); (843) 723-7398 (fax); *jweatherholtz@buistmoore.com; www.buistmoore.com*

**Fred D. Wilshusen,** Thomas, Feldman, Wilshusen LLP, 9400 NCX Tower, 9400 North Central Expressway, Dallas, TX 75231; (214) 369-3008 (phone); (214) 369-8393 (fax); *fwilshusen@tfandw.com; www.tfandw.com*

**Ellie B. Word,** Krebs, Farley & Pelleteri PLLC, One Jackson Place, 188 East Capitol Street, Suite 900, Jackson, MS 39201; (601) 968-6710 (phone); (601) 968-6708 (fax); *eword@kfplaw.com; www.kfplaw.com*

**Wm. Cary Wright,** Carlton Fields PA, 4221 West Boy Scout Boulevard, Suite 1000, Tampa, FL 33607-5736; (813) 229-4135 (phone—direct line); (813) 229-4133 (fax); *cwright@carltonfields.com; www.carltonfields.com*

# Introduction

One of the stimulating but challenging features of a construction law practice is that it involves many areas of law. In addition to a heavy dose of contract and general business law, the construction attorney needs, at various times, to be conversant with principal and surety concepts, real estate principles, trial and arbitration law and procedure, labor and employment law, and a variety of specialty laws specific to the construction industry. The foregoing (nonexclusive) list is further complicated by lack of uniformity among the various jurisdictions in which our clients work and that, in the case of international projects, may differ radically from American law and tradition. Our clients frequently customize their relationships between projects, further complicating the analysis of their issues. The typical construction law practice makes an attorney that he or she must be both a jack-of-all-trades as well as a master of all trades.

Attorneys have long used checklists as a quick reference tool when an emergency does not permit patient deliberation regarding a particular issue until a later time. Checklists are also useful to double-check relevant issues for consideration. Recognizing this, the ABA Forum on the Construction Industry has tapped the considerable experience of its members to generate checklists covering a wide array of issues that most construction attorneys will encounter in their practice. This book includes checklists for reviewing a variety of contracts as well as specific contract clauses, checklists for design issues, contract administration issues, pre-litigation and litigation checklists, topical checklists for labor and employment issues, government contracting, international contract issues, and an assortment of other issues.

This book does not attempt to cover every issue a construction attorney will encounter. However, most construction attorneys will regularly encounter numerous issues covered by the checklists in this book. More significantly, many checklists in this book are also available to assist the construction attorney who encounters an area only infrequently and is particularly in need of an outline formulated by attorneys who regularly practice in that area.

This book was designed to be a "desk book"—a practical reference tool to be freely pulled off the shelf to provide guidance on short notice or as a handy tool to double-check your thinking on a particular issue. If in time its cover is creased and worn and the corners of its pages are bent from use, then it has served its purpose. The many authors who have invested the time to draft the checklists included herein hope this book will be a valuable addition to your construction law library.

FRED D. WILSHUSEN

# CONTRACT FORMATION & NEGOTIATION

## General Form of Agreements

# Checklist 1: Stipulated-Sum Contracts—Owner's Considerations

Stipulated-sum construction contracts establish a firm price for the performance and completion of a defined scope of work. The contractor bears the cost risk for the work scope and earns a profit or suffers a loss to the extent its cost of work is less or more than the fixed sum. The owner is obligated to pay the contract price, and the contractor is obligated to complete the work for the contract price, regardless of the contractor's actual cost of completion. This checklist addresses certain essential terms for fixed-sum contracts, but it does not address all of the general and special conditions an owner may wish to include as part of the agreement.

____ 1. **Does the contract clearly and completely identify the work the contractor is required to perform?** A well-defined scope of work is the owner's best protection against changes in the contract price and time. Where the scope of work is not clear, disputes may arise concerning the work the contractor is obligated to perform for the contract price. Work beyond the scope is generally considered extra work for which the contractor may receive additional time and compensation.

____ (a) **How is the scope of work defined?** The scope of work may be defined many different ways. Most commonly, the work scope is defined by incorporating into the contract the plans and specifications, general and special conditions, bid documents, reports, and other matters. Those documents often are specially defined as the "Contract Documents" and, taken as a whole along with the contract for construction, are the integrated final agreement of the parties.

____ (b) **Is the contractor's scope of supply clearly established, and are there owner-supplied items that should be excluded?** Constructing a project requires labor, materials and

**Daniel D. McMillan** is a partner with Jones Day, where he is co-chair of the firm's international construction practice. He represents owners, design professionals, and contractors in litigation, arbitration, and contract negotiations. He litigated the first case in the United States to result in a published decision concerning disputes review boards.

**Erich R. Luschei** is a senior attorney with Theodora Oringher Miller & Richman. He represents owners, design professionals, and contractors in construction disputes and contracting and has represented clients for more than 20 years in complex business and regulatory matters.

equipment—and many other resources as well. The owner may want to broadly phrase the resources the contractor is obligated to supply categorically, by enumeration, or both. A categorical statement, such as "except as specifically provided herein, contractor shall provide, furnish, and supply all things necessary and incidental for the timely performance and completion of the work," may protect the owner against later assertions by the contractor that the contractor is not responsible for procurement of certain items.

____ (c) **Does the contract plug possible holes in the description of the scope of work?** There are a variety of "catch-all" provisions that owners should consider to plug potential holes in the scope of work that may result from incomplete or inaccurate scope definitions. These provisions include: (i) the contractor's representation and warranty that it has thoroughly reviewed the construction documents and there are no errors, omissions, or discrepancies; (ii) advance waivers of claims for extra time and money for conditions the contractor could have ascertained from diligent inspection of site conditions, review of construction documents, etc.; (iii) disclaimers by the owner of implied warranties, and by the contractor of reliance on owner-supplied information concerning conditions of the work; and (iv) catch-all provisions requiring the contractor to perform all work and services and supply all things reasonably related to and inferable from the construction documents.

____ (d) **Does the contract clearly respond to exclusions, exceptions, qualifications, clarifications, and assumptions identified in the contractor's bid?** Contractors often identify several provisions that form the basis for their bids: exclusions, exceptions, qualifications, clarifications, and exceptions. While some of these provisions are innocuous and merely identify basic assumptions concerning the project, others may substantially undermine the scope of work or scope of supply. Such matters should be specifically addressed in negotiations and either negated by an integration clause or built into the contract documents.

____ 2. **Does the contract clearly establish the terms for compensation and payment to the contractor?** The compensation and payment provisions of the contract are essential to the owner's ability to ensure budget control and to ensure that the contractor completes all work for the stated contract price.

____ (a) **Does the contract make clear that the contract price is full and complete compensation for all work and services**

**provided by the contractor?** The price term of the contract needs to be stated broadly to ensure there is no ambiguity about what payment to the contractor represents. The price term should make clear that the price represents full and complete compensation for the timely performance and completion of all work required by the contract documents strictly in accordance with the terms and conditions of the contract documents.

____ (b) **Is the contract price subject to adjustment due to inflation?** Given escalation in construction costs, many contractors are reluctant to contract on a fixed-price basis absent some form of escalator that takes into account increases in the cost of resources needed for construction. To the extent an owner must provide some relief, if only to avoid bids that are heavily laden with contingency, an owner may want to consider using a narrowly tailored price adjustment clause. The owner must be careful in identifying the prices that may be adjusted, the index to be used, the method of adjustment and the process by which the adjustment is effectuated.

____ (c) **Is the contractor required to continue work when payment disputes occur on the project?** Payment disputes often arise on construction projects. It is important to the owner that the contractor not cease work when payment disputes arise. To avoid cessation of work, an owner may want to include a provision that obligates the contractor to continue work in the event of a dispute over payment.

____ (d) **Does the owner have a contractual right of setoff?** An owner may want to include a contractual right to setoff amounts that a contractor owes the owner against payments due to the contractor. Such setoff provisions protect the owner from having to engage in subsequent litigation to recover money for items that are the contractor's responsibility.

____ (e) **Will the contractor be paid on the basis of progress of its work and, if so, what measure of progress should be used?** Owners often compensate the contractor on an incremental basis as the work progresses. The owner must be careful in negotiating progress payments to ensure that payments made reflect the status of completion of the work performed. A contractor may be compensated on the basis of the percentage of the work that is complete, often pursuant to a schedule of values that specifies in advance the payment to which the contractor is entitled for major components of the contractor's work. The amount of the payment is determined on a periodic (usually monthly) basis through inspection of the work and other methods of verification. Progress payments are also an important source of leverage for an owner to ensure that the contractor is in compliance with other terms of the contract documents. An owner may want to condition its obligation to make progress payments on the contractor's submission, at the time of a pay application, of items required of the contractor, such as schedule updates, lien releases. and other documents required under the contract requirements.

____ (f) **Does the contract permit the owner to retain funds to ensure the faithful completion of the work and do the payment provisions comply with statutes requiring prompt payment of progress payments and retention?** Especially when the owner does not require payment and performance bonds, an owner may want to hold retention to ensure the faithful performance and completion of the work and payment by the contractor to its subcontractors and suppliers. The typical retention amount is 10% of the amount otherwise due to the contractor, which retention generally is released following completion of the project and/or expiration of warranty periods. Contractors may want to negotiate alternatives to retention in order to maintain their working capital. A variety of alternatives exist, but the owner should be careful to ensure that any alternative provides comparable assurances of liquidity to the holding of cash retention, such as a demand money guarantee or a sight draft letter of credit.

____ (g) **Does the contract require the contractor to pay its subcontractors and suppliers?** To avoid liens, the owner may want to require that the contractor promptly pay like amounts of charges due to its subcontractors and suppliers in conformance with the terms of their respective agreements.

____ (h) **What conditions does the contract establish for making the final payment?** The owner's obligation to make final payment should be conditioned on the contractor's compliance with all of the contract requirements and the contractor supplying all items required in the form specified, including lien releases, as-built documentation, warranties, product manuals, in-service training, and the like.

____ (i) **Is the contractor required to certify that pay applications are true and correct?** The owner may want to require the contractor to certify with each payment application, including the application for final payment, that all amounts

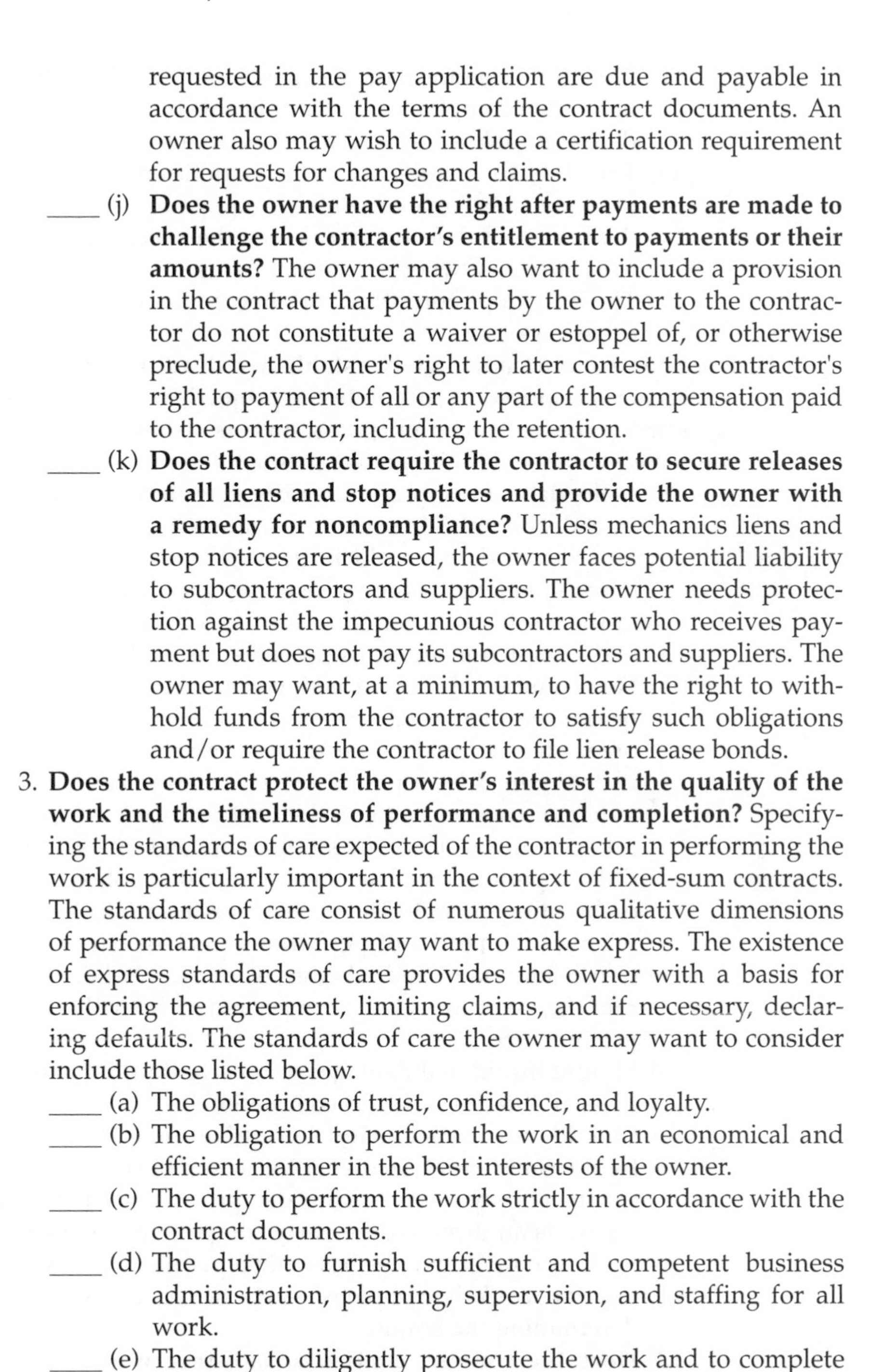

requested in the pay application are due and payable in accordance with the terms of the contract documents. An owner also may wish to include a certification requirement for requests for changes and claims.

____ (j) **Does the owner have the right after payments are made to challenge the contractor's entitlement to payments or their amounts?** The owner may also want to include a provision in the contract that payments by the owner to the contractor do not constitute a waiver or estoppel of, or otherwise preclude, the owner's right to later contest the contractor's right to payment of all or any part of the compensation paid to the contractor, including the retention.

____ (k) **Does the contract require the contractor to secure releases of all liens and stop notices and provide the owner with a remedy for noncompliance?** Unless mechanics liens and stop notices are released, the owner faces potential liability to subcontractors and suppliers. The owner needs protection against the impecunious contractor who receives payment but does not pay its subcontractors and suppliers. The owner may want, at a minimum, to have the right to withhold funds from the contractor to satisfy such obligations and/or require the contractor to file lien release bonds.

____ 3. **Does the contract protect the owner's interest in the quality of the work and the timeliness of performance and completion?** Specifying the standards of care expected of the contractor in performing the work is particularly important in the context of fixed-sum contracts. The standards of care consist of numerous qualitative dimensions of performance the owner may want to make express. The existence of express standards of care provides the owner with a basis for enforcing the agreement, limiting claims, and if necessary, declaring defaults. The standards of care the owner may want to consider include those listed below.

____ (a) The obligations of trust, confidence, and loyalty.

____ (b) The obligation to perform the work in an economical and efficient manner in the best interests of the owner.

____ (c) The duty to perform the work strictly in accordance with the contract documents.

____ (d) The duty to furnish sufficient and competent business administration, planning, supervision, and staffing for all work.

____ (e) The duty to diligently prosecute the work and to complete it by the time specified in the agreement, time being of the essence in contractor's performance and completion of the work.

____ (f) The duty to perform the work in a good workmanlike manner and in compliance with applicable building codes, standards, guidelines, and recommendations.

____ (g) The duty to correct work that is deficient or defective in workmanship, materials, and equipment. For a further discussion of defective work, see the checklist for General Conditions—Owner's Considerations.

____ (h) The duty to perform the work in compliance with all applicable laws.

____ 4. **Does the contract adequately establish a deadline by which the contractor is required to complete the project?** In addition to securing a firm price for budget purposes, owners also want construction completed within a definite period of time.

____ (a) **Is the date of completion readily determined from the contract documents?** In some cases, an owner is able to identify a particular date by which the work must be completed. In other situations, a contingency may exist to commencement of the work and a period of time specified for performance and completion upon the occurrence of that contingency. For example, the construction contract may be executed before the plans and specifications are final or before the owner has secured all permits. When the completion date is determined by a period of performance calculated from a date of commencement, the contract needs to specify the act, circumstance, or event that initiates the contractor's duty to perform, such as the issuance of a notice to proceed or building permit. The owner also needs to be clear on whether the period of performance is based on work days or calendar days, and whether weekends, holidays, and/or rain days are included in or excluded from the period of performance.

____ (b) **Should liquidated damages or reverse liquidated damages be available for delay in completion**?

____ (c) **Should the contract include incentives for early completion by the contractor?** An owner for whom the completion date is critical may want to consider providing a performance bonus as an incentive for early completion of construction. Such incentives may be based on a per diem bonus for each day the work is completed early or other mechanism for determining the bonus.

____ (d) **Does the contract contain an advance waiver of claims for delayed early completion?** Contractors are increasingly asserting claims for delayed early completion. Such claims usually include claims for "extended" overhead and increased direct costs resulting from what the contractor asserts is a prolonged period of performance. Owners may want to include advance waivers of claims for delayed early completion.

____ (e) **Does the contract contain a no-damages-for-delay clause?** Owners who have flexible time requirements, but constrained project budgets, are able to provide more time in those circumstances, but not additional money. In those situations, an owner may want to specify that in the event of an owner-caused delay, the contractor's sole remedy is an extension of time. Statutes in some states prohibit the use of no-damages-for-delay clauses on public contracts, and even in the case of private contracts such clauses are likely to be strictly construed.

____ (f) **Is the contractor required to prepare and submit for owner's approval a project schedule and work plan in sufficient detail for the owner to understand how the project will be constructed and to monitor and enforce time requirements?** Is the contractor required to update the work plan and schedule periodically and when significant changes occur in the planned sequence of work? For a discussion of schedule provisions, see the checklist for General Conditions—Owner's Considerations.

____ (g) **Does the contract identify delays that excuse the contractor's performance and specify the remedy in the event of an excusable delay?** A contractor may have no ability to control certain types of delays and typically expects additional time for performance when unexpected events beyond the contractor's control disrupt the construction schedule. The contract should identify the circumstances under which the owner will provide the contractor with schedule relief; specify the remedy available in the case of an excusable delay; define the contractor's obligations when a force majeure event or other excusable delay occurs, such as notice and mitigation requirements; and exclude events that are not excusable, like the contractor's financial inability to perform.

____ 5. **Does the contract establish a process for the owner to monitor the project status on a regular basis?** An owner needs the ability during the course of construction to monitor the work and should include contract provisions that enable the owner to secure information.

____ (a) **Does the contract require the contractor to appoint and maintain a designated representative?** An owner typically should require that the contractor assign a designated representative to the project. The designated representative should have authority to act and make decisions on the contractor's behalf, be available to the owner at all reasonable times, be competent and experienced, and have a presence at the jobsite (physically or otherwise) at all times that construction is in progress. The owner may want to limit the contractor's ability to replace the designated representative, and may want to retain the right to demand replacement in the owner's sole discretion.

____ (b) **Does the contract contain provisions for regular communication and reporting about the status of the project?** An owner may want to include provisions requiring the contractor to schedule and attend weekly or monthly meetings and special meetings requested by the owner. The owner may also want to require the contractor to provide regular reports concerning issues of special concern and other reports concerning the project as the owner may request. The owner may also want to require the contractor to keep and make available to the owner all of the contract documents, project correspondence, and other information relating to the management and administration of the project.

____ (c) **Does the contract establish terms and conditions under which the contractor may subcontract the work?** An owner needs to consider the effect that subcontracting may have on the project and whether, to what extent, and on what terms and conditions subcontracting should be permitted. The owner may want to retain the right to approve subcontractors, identify specific qualifications that subcontractors must satisfy, and obtain copies of subcontracts. The owner may also want to retain the right to require the contractor to replace a subcontractor at the owner's discretion. The owner may want to specify that the contractor is responsible for all work performed by subcontractors; is not relieved from its contractual responsibilities by virtue of owner's approval of the use of subcontractors; and is responsible for directing, coordinating, administering, supervising, and evaluating the services provided by its consultants and subcontractors. The owner may also want to require the contractor to include certain provisions in subcontract agreements, such as flow-down requirements and the right of the owner to enforce the subcontract as a third-party beneficiary. Care must be taken, however, to consider statutory protections provided to subcontractors, such as subcontractor listing laws that restrict the contractor's ability to substitute subcontractors.

____ 6. **Does the contract reserve to the owner the right to make changes to the contract and establish a process for determining the cost and time impact of changes?** Unless the owner has the right to make changes to the project, the contractor can refuse to perform or condition its performance on price and time concessions by the owner. Provisions for change orders, change directives, and claims relating to asserted changes are essential to the owner's ability to maintain flexibility regarding the project.

____ (a) **Does the contract give the owner the right to make changes to the work?** The owner needs to preserve its right to make changes without invalidating the contract. Absent the reservation of that right, a contractor may take the position it is not required to perform changes directed by the owner, and the project may be adversely affected if the owner needs to bring in another contractor to effect a change.

____ (b) **Is there a method in the contract by which to determine the cost impacts for changes in the work if the owner and contractor cannot agree?** An owner may be able to eliminate uncertainty in the pricing of changes by specifying, in the contract, the method by which compensation for changes will be determined. The method may include unit prices for labor, materials, and construction equipment; cost-plus arrangements; stipulated overhead or general condition rates; or other methodologies.

____ (c) **Is there a method in the contract by which to determine the time impacts for changes in the work if the owner and contractor cannot agree?** An owner may be able to eliminate uncertainty in schedule adjustments by specifying in the contract the method by which extensions or other changes will be determined.

____ (d) **Does the contract contain procedures requiring notification of claims and a process for resolving them?** For a discussion of claims provisions, see the checklist for General Conditions—Owner's Considerations.

____ 7. **Does the contract protect the owner from risk through appropriate insurance?** Project insurance provides financial assurances to the owner against the risk of being sued and/or held liable for personal injuries to construction workers and third persons, property damage, and damage to the construction in process. The most typical types of insurance procured by contractors are worker's compensation insurance, general liability insurance, automobile insurance, and builder's risk insurance. Each of these types of insurance cover different risks and have different exclusions and limitations.

____ (a) **Does the contract require the contractor to provide and maintain worker's compensation and employer's liability insurance to protect the owner against claims by injured workers?** Are the limits sufficient? Do the limits apply to each accident?

____ (b) **Does the contract require the contractor to provide and maintain liability insurance to protect the owner against claims from third parties for bodily injury and property damage?** Is the deductible so high that the owner is at risk if the contractor becomes insolvent? Are the limits high enough for the project on an individual and aggregate basis? Is the coverage based on occurrences or claims made? If a claims made policy is permitted, is the contractor required to supply tail coverage? Do the coverages include or exclude premises liability, completed operations, contractual liability, and other significant policy provisions?

____ (c) **Does the contract require the contractor to provide automobile insurance to protect the owner against claims from third parties for bodily injury and property damage caused by the operation of motor vehicles?** What deductibles, limits, and coverages should the owner require?

____ (d) **Does the owner need the contractor to supply other types of insurance coverage?** Other types of insurance to consider may include builder's risk insurance, which protects *inter alia* against damage to the construction work itself, materials procured for the construction, and materials in transit to the construction site.

____ (e) **Do the insurance provisions address other important issues?** This would include whether the owner is an additional insured, the insurer waives subrogation, or the owner's policy is noncontributing.

____ (f) **Is the owner entitled to notice of nonpayment of premiums or cancellation from the insurer?** Does the contract permit the owner to pay the premium and offset the premium from payments owed to the contractor or to recoupment? Does the owner have the right to request and receive the contractor's insurance policies?

____ 8. **Does the contract require the contractor to indemnify the owner against loss or damage?** It is common in construction contracts for the owner to require an indemnity provision through which the contractor agrees to indemnify, defend, and hold the owner harmless against loss or damage resulting from the contractor's acts or omissions.

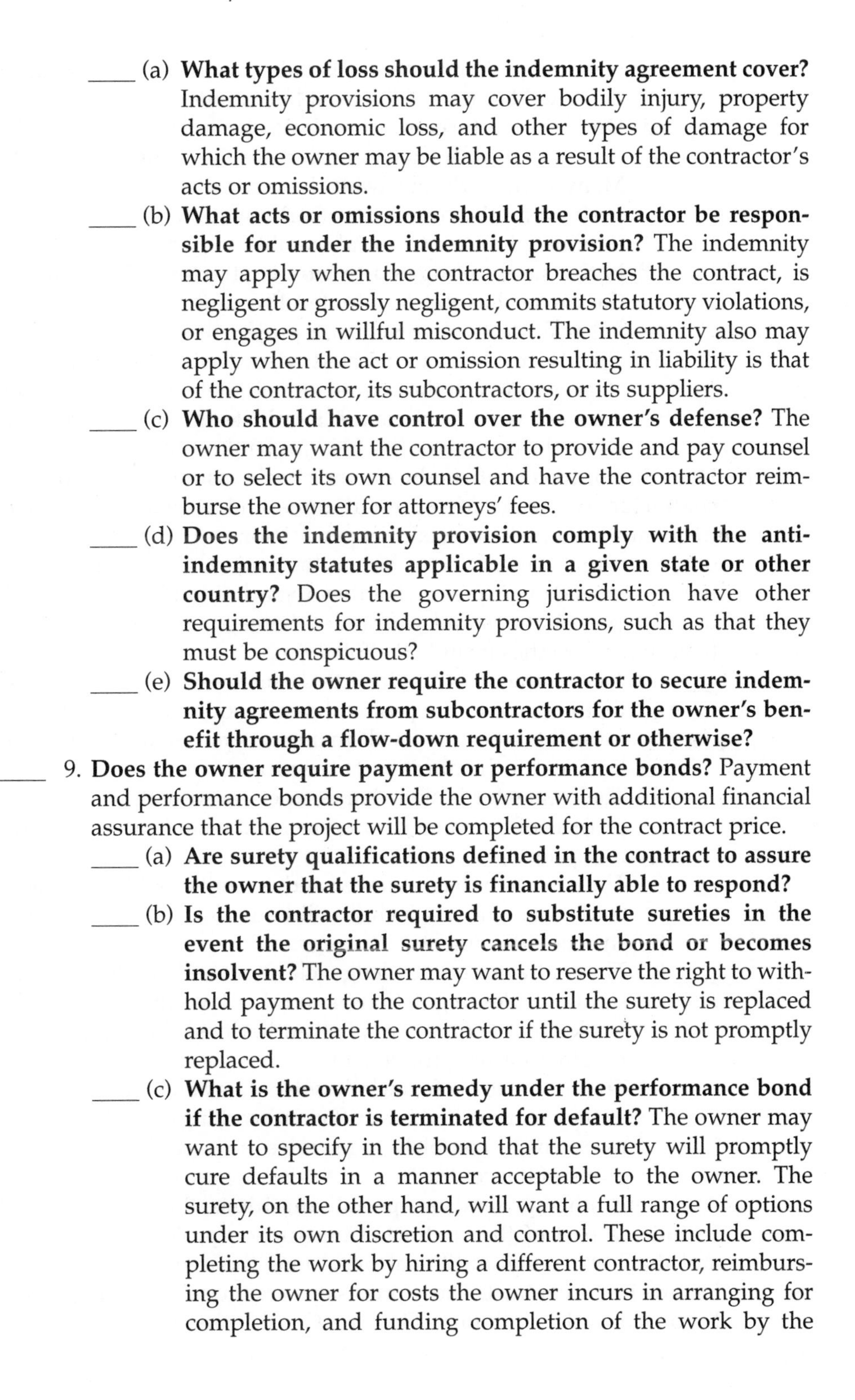

____ (a) **What types of loss should the indemnity agreement cover?** Indemnity provisions may cover bodily injury, property damage, economic loss, and other types of damage for which the owner may be liable as a result of the contractor's acts or omissions.

____ (b) **What acts or omissions should the contractor be responsible for under the indemnity provision?** The indemnity may apply when the contractor breaches the contract, is negligent or grossly negligent, commits statutory violations, or engages in willful misconduct. The indemnity also may apply when the act or omission resulting in liability is that of the contractor, its subcontractors, or its suppliers.

____ (c) **Who should have control over the owner's defense?** The owner may want the contractor to provide and pay counsel or to select its own counsel and have the contractor reimburse the owner for attorneys' fees.

____ (d) **Does the indemnity provision comply with the anti-indemnity statutes applicable in a given state or other country?** Does the governing jurisdiction have other requirements for indemnity provisions, such as that they must be conspicuous?

____ (e) **Should the owner require the contractor to secure indemnity agreements from subcontractors for the owner's benefit through a flow-down requirement or otherwise?**

____ 9. **Does the owner require payment or performance bonds?** Payment and performance bonds provide the owner with additional financial assurance that the project will be completed for the contract price.

____ (a) **Are surety qualifications defined in the contract to assure the owner that the surety is financially able to respond?**

____ (b) **Is the contractor required to substitute sureties in the event the original surety cancels the bond or becomes insolvent?** The owner may want to reserve the right to withhold payment to the contractor until the surety is replaced and to terminate the contractor if the surety is not promptly replaced.

____ (c) **What is the owner's remedy under the performance bond if the contractor is terminated for default?** The owner may want to specify in the bond that the surety will promptly cure defaults in a manner acceptable to the owner. The surety, on the other hand, will want a full range of options under its own discretion and control. These include completing the work by hiring a different contractor, reimbursing the owner for costs the owner incurs in arranging for completion, and funding completion of the work by the terminated contractor (usually where the contractor defaulted because of financial limitations).

____ (d) **Does the performance bond allow the surety to hire the terminated contractor to undertake the completion work?** Many owners do not want the contractor they terminated performing the completion work unless the contractor was terminated due to financial inability to perform.

____ (e) **Is the surety obligated to cure contractor defaults where the owner has not terminated the contractor?** Sureties do not want to be involved in a project unless the contractor already has been terminated. However, there are circumstances in which the contractor is in default, but the owner does not want to or cannot terminate the contract, such as when the contractor has filed for bankruptcy protection.

____ 10. **Does the contract confirm the owner's basic assumptions about the contractor by means of representations and warranties?** Owners frequently assume that certain representations are implicit by virtue of the fact that the contractor bid on the project. Owners may want to consider making express what they regard as implied through the use of representations and warranties. Some suggested representations and warranties include the following:

____ (a) The contractor is qualified to do business in the jurisdiction that is home to the project, has all required licenses to perform the work, and will maintain such qualifications and licenses for the duration of the project;

____ (b) The contractor is skilled and experienced with constructing projects of the same nature, size, and complexity as the current project;

____ (c) The contractor has reviewed and is familiar with the project, conditions under which it will be performed, and the construction documents;

____ (d) The contractor is knowledgeable about and familiar with the statutes, rules, regulations, and other laws applicable to the work, and the processes of all authorities whose approval is required for the project; and

____ (e) The contractor is financially solvent, is able to pay its debts as they mature, and has sufficient working capital and other resources to complete the services in accordance with the terms of the contract.

____ 11. **Are there other general or special conditions the owner should include as part of the contract?** Construction projects are complex and there are many additional provisions the owner may want to include in the contract. Those provisions are the subject of the checklist on General Conditions—Owner's Considerations.

# Checklist 2: Stipulated-Sum Contracts—Contractor's Considerations

Contracts between owners and contractors are often divided between the principal agreement itself, which contains the chief negotiated terms between the parties, and a separate set of "standard" terms and conditions. The following checklist is focused on drafting the terms of the principal agreement between the owner and the contractor where the price term is stated as a "stipulated sum"; that is, the contractor performs the work for a fixed price. Where the contract sum is based on the cost of work plus the contractor's overhead and profit, see the "Cost-Plus Contacts—Contractor's Considerations" checklist. Where the contract price is a stipulated sum, but the contract sets out a "guaranteed maximum price," both checklists should be consulted.

This checklist is intended to be used in conjunction with the "General Conditions—Contractor's Considerations" checklist to constitute a complete review of the contract.

____ 1. **Identification of Owner.**

____ (a) Determine the type of entity and the status of the owner's registration with the Secretary of State or other responsible business registration office.

____ (b) Determine whether the owner is a governmental or quasi-governmental agency. Special contracting rules may apply to such entities, and it may not be apparent from the name of the entity whether the entity is a government agency or not. As some examples, the enforceability of a pay-if-paid clause, an indemnification clause, or a no-damages-for-delay clause may turn on whether the owner is a governmental entity. In addition, procurement statutes and regulations may apply to government entities, and bonding, claims, and payment rules may be specified by statute.

____ (c) Where appropriate, determine whether the owner is a subsidiary, parent, or other affiliate of the real party in interest that has been created so as to shield the real party in interest from liability.

**Stephen A. Hess** is with Sherman & Howard and practices construction law and litigation. His writings have appeared in numerous national construction law treatises and journals. He is an adjunct faculty member of University of Denver's Sturm College of Law, where he created and teaches the school's Construction Law Seminar.

____ 2. **Property Issues.**

____ (a) Confirm that the owner with whom the contractor is contracting is the record owner of the property.

____ (b) Ensure that the property described in the contract as the location of the project is described in sufficiently detailed legal terms to enable the contractor to file liens or otherwise utilize the property as security.

____ (c) When the "owner" is a tenant, confirm the contractor's ability to lien the property; this may include ensuring that the owner of the property has consented to the improvements or has not posted or otherwise protected the property against liens.

____ 3. **Defining the Contract Documents.**

____ (a) Ensure that the enumeration of the contract documents includes all documents on which the contractor has relied in agreeing to terms with the owner and includes exceptions, where necessary, to cover incomplete or variable documents whose terms may not be defined at the time of contracting. In addition, ensure that the contract documents are defined to encompass clarifications or additions during the contracting process (a common occurrence, for example, in response to bid queries where such additional or clarifying terms are added as addenda). Many contracts are written in such a manner that the "Contract Documents" section includes (or can be read as implying) a merger clause, under which all previous representations, promises, negotiations, and terms are merged into the written contract.

____ (b) Assess the extent to which bid documents should be (or will be) included as part of the final Contract Documents. In particular, identify "requests for bid" or "requests for proposals" and the relevant portions within those documents that are to be incorporated into the contract. Bid documents can add unexpected terms to the contract, and should be reviewed in connection with the final contract to ensure consistency. This is especially true with respect to government projects where an apparent successful bidder has an opportunity to negotiate the terms of the contract.

____ 4. **Contract Time.**

____ (a) Ensure that the stated date of completion is fixed from an express or definable time of commencement. If the time of commencement is to be fixed by the future issuance of a "notice to proceed," the contract should not state a specific date for completion. By using a floating and indeterminate

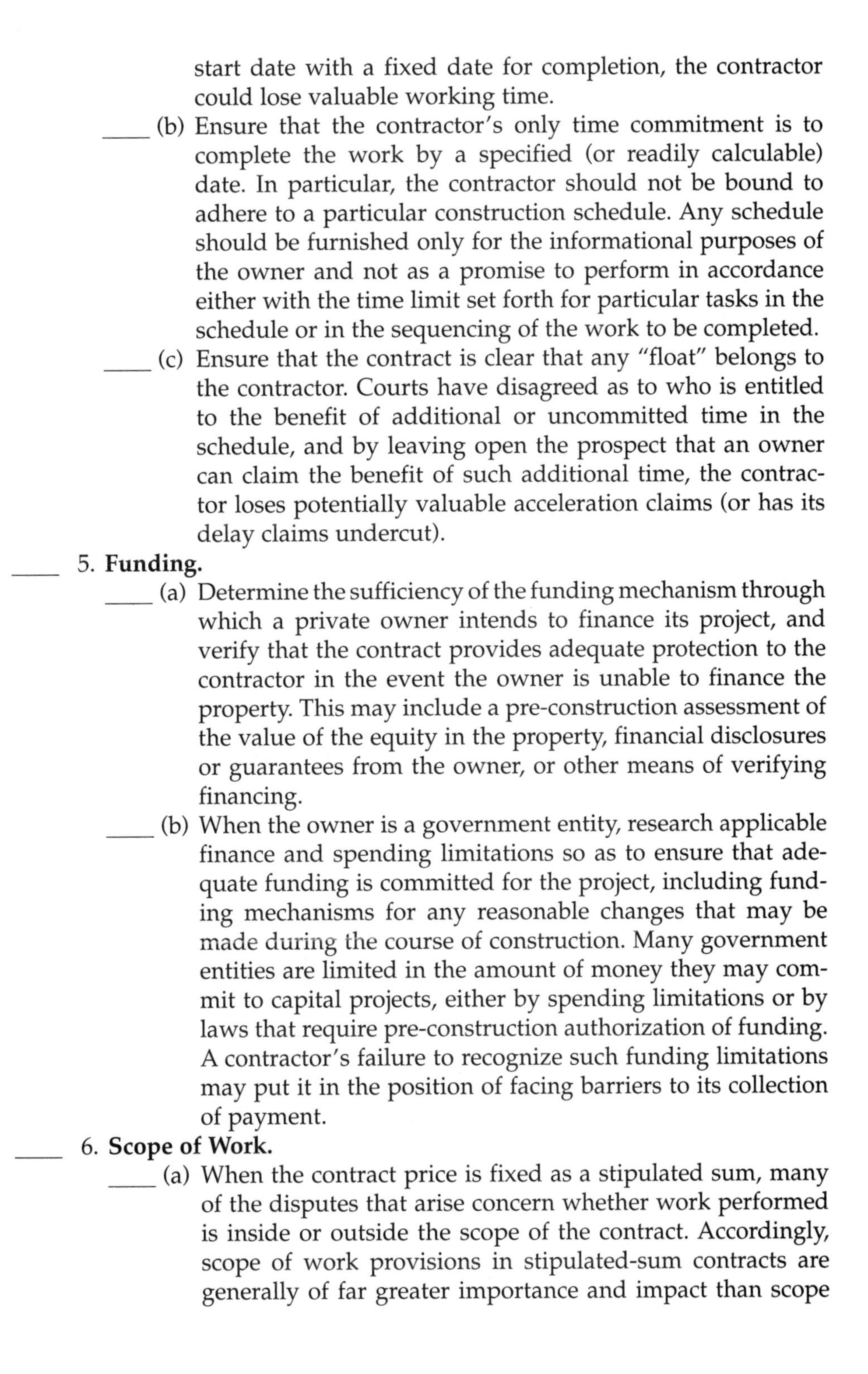

start date with a fixed date for completion, the contractor could lose valuable working time.

____ (b) Ensure that the contractor's only time commitment is to complete the work by a specified (or readily calculable) date. In particular, the contractor should not be bound to adhere to a particular construction schedule. Any schedule should be furnished only for the informational purposes of the owner and not as a promise to perform in accordance either with the time limit set forth for particular tasks in the schedule or in the sequencing of the work to be completed.

____ (c) Ensure that the contract is clear that any "float" belongs to the contractor. Courts have disagreed as to who is entitled to the benefit of additional or uncommitted time in the schedule, and by leaving open the prospect that an owner can claim the benefit of such additional time, the contractor loses potentially valuable acceleration claims (or has its delay claims undercut).

____ 5. **Funding.**

____ (a) Determine the sufficiency of the funding mechanism through which a private owner intends to finance its project, and verify that the contract provides adequate protection to the contractor in the event the owner is unable to finance the property. This may include a pre-construction assessment of the value of the equity in the property, financial disclosures or guarantees from the owner, or other means of verifying financing.

____ (b) When the owner is a government entity, research applicable finance and spending limitations so as to ensure that adequate funding is committed for the project, including funding mechanisms for any reasonable changes that may be made during the course of construction. Many government entities are limited in the amount of money they may commit to capital projects, either by spending limitations or by laws that require pre-construction authorization of funding. A contractor's failure to recognize such funding limitations may put it in the position of facing barriers to its collection of payment.

____ 6. **Scope of Work.**

____ (a) When the contract price is fixed as a stipulated sum, many of the disputes that arise concern whether work performed is inside or outside the scope of the contract. Accordingly, scope of work provisions in stipulated-sum contracts are generally of far greater importance and impact than scope of work provisions in cost-plus contracts, where the owner bears the ultimate cost of the project regardless of the scope. In a cost-plus contract that includes a guaranteed maximum price, the same concerns arise. Accordingly, the contractor should verify that the scope of work is precise, the plans and specifications are complete, and that the contract documents are clear enough that disputes over what work is in the scope of work and what work is outside the scope of work are not likely.

____ 7. **Material Price Escalation Clause.**

____ (a) Include a clause that permits the contractor an increase in the contract price for material price increases that are not reasonably anticipated by the contractor. Such a clause is necessary, as courts may not be inclined to grant relief on the basis of price increases absent truly extraordinary circumstances unless the parties have specified in the contract an allowance for such increases.

____ 8. **Budget Estimate.**

____ (a) Ensure that the budget estimate does not become a binding term under the stipulated-sum contract. An owner might reasonably ask for a budget estimate for purposes of financial planning, and where financing of the project is provided by a lender, the lender may request a budget in advance of construction for purposes of regulating disbursements under the loan and for serving as a basis for estimates in payment applications. Although these uses are perfectly appropriate, the owner should understand that a stipulated-sum contract fixes the price at which construction will be completed and that any budget provided for planning purposes cannot be used to vary the stipulated sum. In particular, owners should understand that any savings in individual line item costs do not give the owner additional money to spend, just as any cost overruns in individual line items are never borne by the owner.

____ (b) When a budget is provided that contains an express contingency, ensure that the owner understands and acknowledges that the contingency is a planning tool for the contractor, that the contractor is not obligated to account to the owner for expenditure of the contingency, and that the contingency is not an "allowance" that the owner may spend as part of the stipulated sum in the event that the contractor does not exhaust the contingency. If the parties want to include variable payment terms in the contract (such as a contingency), it should be defined as an owner

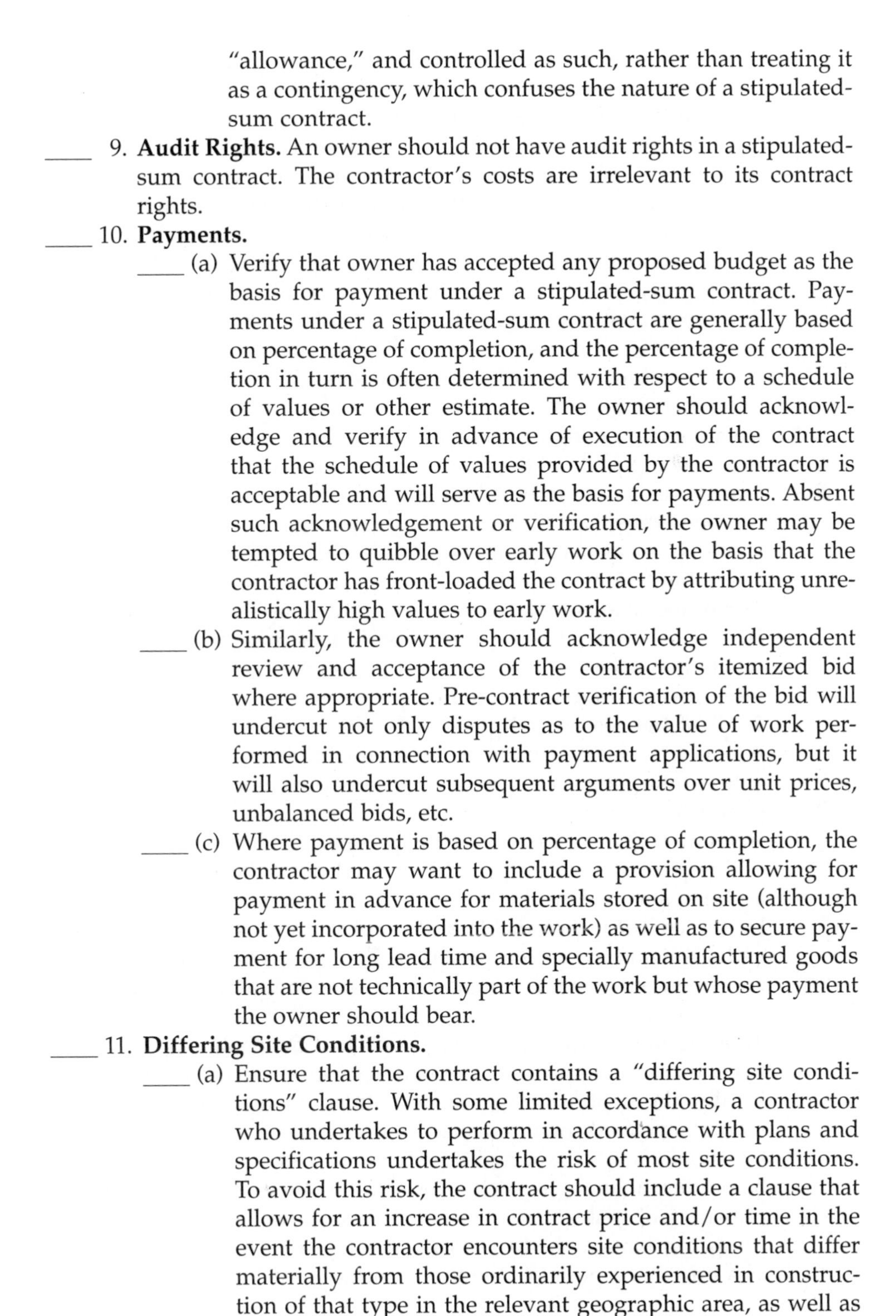

"allowance," and controlled as such, rather than treating it as a contingency, which confuses the nature of a stipulated-sum contract.

____ 9. **Audit Rights.** An owner should not have audit rights in a stipulated-sum contract. The contractor's costs are irrelevant to its contract rights.

____ 10. **Payments.**

____ (a) Verify that owner has accepted any proposed budget as the basis for payment under a stipulated-sum contract. Payments under a stipulated-sum contract are generally based on percentage of completion, and the percentage of completion in turn is often determined with respect to a schedule of values or other estimate. The owner should acknowledge and verify in advance of execution of the contract that the schedule of values provided by the contractor is acceptable and will serve as the basis for payments. Absent such acknowledgement or verification, the owner may be tempted to quibble over early work on the basis that the contractor has front-loaded the contract by attributing unrealistically high values to early work.

____ (b) Similarly, the owner should acknowledge independent review and acceptance of the contractor's itemized bid where appropriate. Pre-contract verification of the bid will undercut not only disputes as to the value of work performed in connection with payment applications, but it will also undercut subsequent arguments over unit prices, unbalanced bids, etc.

____ (c) Where payment is based on percentage of completion, the contractor may want to include a provision allowing for payment in advance for materials stored on site (although not yet incorporated into the work) as well as to secure payment for long lead time and specially manufactured goods that are not technically part of the work but whose payment the owner should bear.

____ 11. **Differing Site Conditions.**

____ (a) Ensure that the contract contains a "differing site conditions" clause. With some limited exceptions, a contractor who undertakes to perform in accordance with plans and specifications undertakes the risk of most site conditions. To avoid this risk, the contract should include a clause that allows for an increase in contract price and/or time in the event the contractor encounters site conditions that differ materially from those ordinarily experienced in construction of that type in the relevant geographic area, as well as for conditions that differ from those represented in any pre-construction documents such as soil reports.

____ (b) Where an owner insists on a stipulated-sum contract without a differing site conditions clause, the contractor should ensure that its price and pre-construction investigation accommodate the fact that the contractor will bear all responsibility for site conditions. There is nothing objectionable about an owner's insistence that a differing site conditions clause be deleted, especially in light of the desire of many owners to have an absolutely guaranteed contract price. However, an owner's insistence on deletion of a differing site conditions clause should be priced to reflect the risk involved.

____ 12. **Retainage.** Although most contracts allow for the retention by the owner of a portion of the contract price until substantial completion, many jurisdictions impose limitations on the amount of retention that can be withheld by the owner. Any retainage set out in the contract should be measured against applicable statutes to ensure consistency. These limitations or qualifications may include a statutory elimination or reduction of retainage after partial completion (typically after 50% of the contract price), exclusion of fees from retention requirements, and release of the retention upon such events as the architect's interim certification of a limited punchlist (retaining, for example, 200% of the cost to complete such items). In addition, ensure that retention is released upon substantial completion, less any reasonable withholding necessary to satisfy any punchlist obligations of the contractor.

____ 13. **Insurance.** During the contracting process, it is likely that the owner will request status as a primary insured or, at the very least, as an additional named insured. Verify that insurance coverage as required by the contract is available and in place, and that any requested endorsements have been procured. The contractor's failure to procure required insurance may expose the contractor to substantial additional damages.

____ 14. **Termination for Convenience.** Ensure that the contractor is entitled to compensation for early termination for convenience by the owner. Ideally, the contractor would be entitled to recover any profit it would have made on unfinished work. At the very least, the contractor should not be expected merely to recover its costs into the job before termination, as such a term leaves the contractor subject to unreasonable risk of loss of its anticipated profit. The amount of such compensation may be fixed as a percentage of actual costs to date or as a prorated amount of the total contract profit, although the latter raises difficult accounting and bidding questions that may make determination of profit difficult.

____ 15. **Standard of Care.** It may be advantageous in the agreement to specify that the contractor's standard of care for performance of work is to perform all work in accordance with the standards prevalent in the community in which the project is being built, or some similar standard. The purpose for providing an express standard of care in the contract is to take advantage of those jurisdictions in which the economic loss rule bars a party from seeking tort remedies where a contract between the parties expresses or implies a particular standard of care. Or course, the standard of care should be no more expansive than the standard that would be implied by the law in the absence of any express statement thereof.

# Checklist 3: Cost-Plus Contracts—Owner's Considerations

Parties to a cost-plus agreement, such as the American Institute of Architects' (AIA) A111 (2007) Agreement, are attempting to establish the three most important parameters of an owner–contractor agreement: scope, schedule and budget. Each one of these parameters is important, and within each are myriad possibilities for detail and hence negotiation; often the three are interrelated. The following is a checklist for owners to consider when creating a cost-plus agreement, focusing primarily on scope, schedule, and budget and on other miscellaneous project-related elements that should be covered in the agreement.

____ 1. **What is the scope?** An owner must decide what it is hiring the contractor to perform. Are pre-construction services included, such as working with the architect to find ways to value-engineer the project? Are other contractors working on other aspects of the project, and, if so, how are the lines between the two scopes being drawn?

____ (a) **How well developed are the plans and specifications?** If they are well developed, then they can be identified as the basis for the scope of the work. Owners should also attempt to get the contractor to agree to be responsible for elements of the work that are inferable from the plans and specifications. If the plans and specifications are not well defined, then the agreement should contain a more elaborate verbal description of what the scope includes. A contractor's proposal may be attached as an exhibit, but only with caution, as—in most instances—it will have been drafted by the contractor with its (and not the owner's) best interests in mind. Furthermore, there may be terms in the contractor's proposal that may conflict with negotiated terms in the main body of the contract.

____ (b) **Is the owner undecided as to alternates and allowances?** There may be many elements to a project about which the owner is undecided and will need to identify with placeholders in the agreement. Alternates are variations in the scope for which there is a specific price tag assigned. Allowances

**Eric A. Berg** is a shareholder with the law firm of Vedder Price PC in its Chicago office. He represents owners and developers in drafting and negotiating cost-plus contracts.

are items of the scope of work that are exempt from the guaranteed maximum price. An amount may be given as an estimate, but the contractor will not be held to it in case of price increases.

____ (c) **Has the contractor submitted clarifications, qualifications, and assumptions?** The contractor may have a certain set of assumptions as to what is and what is not included in its scope of work. For example, many contractors will exclude the cost of winterizing the project so as to permit year-round construction. These assumptions should and often are set out by the contractor as part of the guaranteed maximum price-development process. The assumptions should be reviewed carefully by an owner and its representatives to avoid future scenarios in which a contractor is requesting additional payment for extra work that the owner believed was part of the original scope.

____ 2. **What is the schedule?** Key in any project is a set timeframe in which the contractor is expected to complete the project.

____ (a) **How is the project completion timeframe to be measured?** This can be based on a specific number of days or a specific calendar date by which the project must be completed. If a specific number of days is used, the timeframe should be measured from a particular commencement date: the date on which the agreement is executed, the date on which the owner issues a notice to proceed, or some other prearranged date. The commencement date can take on critical importance, particularly if it is used as the initial starting point for calculating the project duration—for example, "Contractor shall achieve substantial completion within 365 days of the date of commencement."

____ (b) **How is completion defined?** Most projects will have two definitions for project completion: substantial completion and final completion. Both definitions should have specific descriptions. Substantial completion is generally defined as the date on which the owner can use the project for its intended purpose. This can be a vague marker, though, if the project is multi-use or a multi-unit luxury apartment building. Some contractors assume that substantial completion is co-extensive with issuance of a certificate of occupancy. If this is accurate and the owner agrees to it, then the agreement should specifically link the two.

____ (c) **What happens at substantial completion?** The agreement should list what takes place upon substantial completion. Typically, this includes release of retainage to the contractor and the creation of a list ("a punchlist") of items to be completed within a specific period of time. A pre-agreed percentage of payment should be withheld to incentivize the contractor to complete the punchlist. A set time period for completion of the final punchlist is also advisable.

____ (d) **What should the schedule look like?** Schedules are typically the province of the contractor, as they reflect the means and methods for completing the work. However, owners may require that schedules contain particular information and that the contractor provide the owner with copies of the schedules and regular schedule updates that accurately reflect the owner's progress. First, schedules should be required to be prepared using a critical-path methodology, the industry-recognized method for letting the most important aspects of construction "drive" the schedule. Owners should also work with the contractor to pull milestone dates from the schedule and make them obligations under the agreement. Thus, failure to reach a milestone date (and not an immaterial schedule deadline) may be cited as grounds for terminating the contract for cause. For larger or more complex projects, the owner may also require that the contractor provide the information required to allow the owner to track the contractor's progress using an earned value management system. This includes a work breakdown structure (WBS) and the contractor's planned, actual and earned hours for each schedule activity.

____ (e) **Is there a penalty for late completion?** Owners should refrain from using the word "penalty": penalties are disfavored in the law, and courts will not enforce them. Courts will enforce liquidated damages provisions, which assess a predetermined amount to be imposed on the contractor for project delay. Liquidated damages are discussed in more detail in another checklist in this book. Owners should know, though, that liquidated damages provisions act as a substitute for the exercise of proving actual out-of-pocket and other consequential losses suffered by an owner as a result of the contractor's delay. (Keep in mind, too, that liquidated damages do not presuppose that all delay is due to forces beyond the contractor's control. Such elements still need to be pleaded and proven before an owner can recover liquidated damages from a contractor.) In negotiating liquidated damages provisions with a contractor, the owner should anticipate the contractor's requesting a cap.

____ 3. **What is the budget?** In most circumstances, an owner and a contractor will reach an agreement on the total project cost. As stated elsewhere herein, this usually can only take place when the plans and specifications are sufficiently well developed to permit this determination. Otherwise, the agreement should set forth a mechanism by which the parties will agree at a later date that the scope of the work has reached such a level of definition that an upper-limit figure is ascertainable.

____ (a) **Is there an upper-limit project sum, otherwise known as a guaranteed maximum price?** Cost-plus agreements compensate the contractor by reimbursing the contractor for the costs incurred in the (proper) performance of the work. The "plus" part of the term "cost-plus" refers to the mark-up charged by the contractor. Preferably for the owner, the project scope will be sufficiently developed so as to permit a maximum ceiling, or "guaranteed maximum price," beyond which the sum of the cost of the work and the contractor's fee will not exceed. Many in the construction industry use the terms "guaranteed maximum price," "GMAX," and "GMP" interchangeably.

____ (b) **What is the cost of the work?** As one might anticipate, if the basis of the contractor's payment is the cost of the work, the definition of the cost of the work is of paramount importance. Most cost-plus contracts, such as the AIA A111, contain multi-page descriptions of what constitutes a recoverable cost. Broadly speaking, all costs incurred in providing labor and materials to the project, including subcontractors' labor and material and certain jobsite overhead costs, are compensable out-of-pockets costs. Most contract negotiations will center on fine distinctions of recoverable costs, for example, whether a contractor has the right to payment for costs of correcting nonconforming work. In this portion of the agreement, parties often establish a pre-agreed "burden rate," that is, a per-hour mark-up for insurance, pension, worker's compensation, and other benefits for each laborer working on the project.

____ (i) **What are the general conditions?** General conditions (not to be confused with the ancillary contract document that details the parties' legal rights and obligations during the project, also known as the "general conditions") are the jobsite overhead expenditures, oftentimes expressed in a monthly lump-sum amount. Because owner-caused delays will usually result in additional jobsite overhead expenses, it is important to establish what the owner receives in return for the monthly charge.

____ (c) **What is the contractor's fee?** The contractor's fee is usually a percentage mark-up on the cost of the work. As may be expected, this gives the contractor little incentive to bring in the cost of the work for well below the guaranteed maximum price. One way of avoiding this problem is to establish a lump-sum fee, fixed at a predetermined number regardless of the underlying cost. To incentivize the contractor to bring in the project below the guaranteed maximum price in those circumstances, the parties may establish a savings ratio—for example, for every dollar the cost of the work plus the contractor's fee comes in below the guaranteed maximum price, the owner gets 50 cents and the contractor gets 50 cents.

____ (i) **Upon what is the contractor's fee based?** Some owners will permit a mark-up on only some portions of the cost of the work, such as labor and materials only. Is this primarily a function of what the contractor's fee is meant to compensate? Is it solely limited to the contractor's profit, or is it meant to reimburse certain noncompensated elements of the contractor's overhead, such as home office (that is, non-worksite) overhead? Depending on the business deal struck by the parties, sometimes elements of the contractor's jobsite overhead—"general conditions"—may be exempt from a contractor mark-up.

____ (ii) **How will the contractor keep the owner's interests in mind?** Cost-plus agreements should contain in them a commitment by the contractor to complete the project scope with the owner's best interests in mind. This will prevent a guaranteed maximum price contract from turning into what some refer to as a guaranteed *minimum* price contract.

____ (d) **Is there a contingency?** Just as certain elements of the work scope are covered by allowances and alternates, the parties may wish to set aside a lump sum in the contract sum as a contingency. A contingency fund is just that: money dedicated to cover unanticipated circumstances. It is best to think of a contingency on a spectrum: at one end, it is a slush fund for the contractor's unfettered use, which the owner should entirely write off as a lost expense; at the other end of the spectrum, it is a rigidly proscribed line-item cost of the work that requires owner pre-approval before it is used.

____ 4. **When and how will the contractor be paid?** The agreement should contain details for the date on which the contractor's pay application is due; the required degree of documentation of the contractor's costs; the time for review, approval, and payment on the pay applications; and whether an escrow will be used.

____ 5. **What if there are changes?** Changes will occur on every project. Although the change-order process is best described in the agreement's general conditions, the agreement is the best place to establish a pre-agreed mark-up for the contractor's profit and overhead on increases in the scope of work.

____ 6. **Who speaks for the owner and the contractor?** Owner's and contractor's representatives should be identified, along with the scope of their authority.

____ 7. **What insurance is the contractor required to carry?** This, too, is key. Owners should discuss the required policy coverages and limits with their insurance agent or risk-management consultant. An owner should do more than obtain a certificate of insurance; acquiring an endorsement identifying the owner as an additional insured on the contractor's policy will afford a greater degree of protection for the owner. Moreover, if the contractor asks to limit its liability to its amount of available insurance coverage (not recommended), the insurance limits will gain in importance.

____ 8. **Does the owner have an audit right?** With a cost-plus contract, the entire contract sum is predicated upon the contractor billing actual costs as permitted under the agreement. Consequently, the owner's right to audit the contractor's costs is of paramount importance, along with a parallel obligation to maintain project records for a certain number of years.

____ 9. **Are there any project-specific requirements to include in the agreement?** Is the owner developing property as a part of a redevelopment agreement or other municipal ordinance? Are there minority-owned or women-owned business requirements, local-hiring targets, or prevailing-wage obligations that have to be passed along to the contractor?

# Checklist 4: Cost-Plus Contracts—Contractor's Considerations

Contracts between owners and contractors are often divided between the principal agreement itself, which contains the chief negotiated terms between the parties, and a separate set of "standard" terms and conditions. This checklist focuses on drafting the terms of the principal agreement between the owner and the contractor when the contractor is paid the cost of the work plus a fee for overhead and profit (commonly called a "cost-plus" contract). This checklist is intended to be used in conjunction with the "General Conditions—Contractor's Considerations" checklist to constitute a complete review of the contract.

Also note that there are special considerations related to "stipulated-sum" or "fixed-price" contracts that are outlined in another checklist. If the cost-plus contract you are reviewing also includes a guaranteed maximum price, it is essential that the review include both this checklist and the checklist for stipulated-sum contracts (together with the checklist for general conditions).

____ 1. **Identification of Owner.**

____ (a) Determine the type of entity and the status of the owner's registration with the Secretary of State or other responsible business registration office.

____ (b) Determine whether the owner is a governmental or quasi-governmental agency. Special contracting rules may apply to such entities, and it may not be apparent from the name of the entity whether the entity is a government agency or not. As some examples, the enforceability of a pay-if-paid clause, and indemnification clause, or a no-damages-for-delay clause may turn on whether the owner is a governmental entity. In addition, procurement statutes and regulations may apply to government entities, and bonding, claims, and payment rules may be specified by statute.

____ (c) Where appropriate, determine whether the owner is a subsidiary, parent, or other affiliate of the real party in interest that has been created so as to shield the real party in interest from liability.

**Stephen A. Hess** is with Sherman & Howard and practices construction law and litigation. His writings have appeared in numerous national construction law treatises and journals. He is an adjunct faculty member of University of Denver's Sturm College of Law, where he created and teaches the school's Construction Law Seminar.

____ 2. **Property Issues.**

____ (a) Confirm that the owner with whom the contractor is contracting is the record owner of the property.

____ (b) Ensure that the property described in the contract as the location of the project is described in sufficiently detailed legal terms to enable the contractor to file liens or otherwise utilize the property as security.

____ (c) When the "owner" is a tenant, confirm the contractor's ability to lien the property. This may include ensuring that the owner of the property has consented to the improvements or has not posted or otherwise protected the property against liens.

____ 3. **Defining the Contract Documents.**

____ (a) Ensure that the enumeration of the contract documents includes all documents on which the contractor has relied in agreeing to terms with the owner, and include exceptions where necessary to cover incomplete or variable documents whose terms may not be defined at the time of contracting. In addition, ensure that the contract documents are defined to encompass clarifications or additions during the contracting process (a common occurrence, for example, in response to bid queries where such additional or clarifying terms are added as addenda). Many contracts are written in such a manner that the "Contract Documents" section includes (or can be read as implying) a merger clause, under which all previous representations, promises, negotiations, and terms are merged into the written contract.

____ (b) Assess the extent to which bid documents should be (or will be) included as part of the final contract documents. In particular, identify requests for bid or requests for proposals and relevant portions thereof that are to be incorporated into the contract. Bid documents can add unexpected terms to the contract and should be reviewed in connection with the final contract to ensure consistency. This is especially true with respect to government projects, where an apparent successful bidder has an opportunity to negotiate the terms of the contract.

____ 4. **Contract Time.**

____ (a) Ensure that the stated date of completion is fixed from an express or definable time of commencement. If the time of commencement is to be fixed by the future issuance of a notice to proceed, the contract should not state a specific date for completion. By using a floating and indeterminate start date with a fixed date for completion, the contractor could lose valuable working time.

____ (b) Ensure that the contractor's only time commitment is to complete the work by a specified (or readily calculable) date. In particular, the contractor should not be bound to adhere to a particular construction schedule. Any schedule should be furnished only for the informational purposes of the owner and not as a promise to perform in accordance either with the time limit set forth for particular tasks in the schedule or in the sequencing of the work to be completed.

____ (c) Ensure that the contract is clear that any "float" belongs to the contractor. Courts have disagreed as to who is entitled to the benefit of additional or uncommitted time in the schedule, and by leaving open the prospect that an owner can claim the benefit of such additional time, the contractor loses potentially valuable acceleration claims (or has its delay claims undercut).

____ 5. **Funding.**

____ (a) Determine the sufficiency of the funding mechanism through which a private owner intends to finance its project, and verify that the contract provides adequate protection to the contractor in the event the owner is unable to finance the property. This may include a pre-construction assessment of the value of the equity in the property, financial disclosures or guarantees from the owner, or other means of verifying financing.

____ (b) When the owner is a government entity, research applicable finance and spending limitations so as to ensure that adequate funding is committed for the project, including funding mechanisms for any reasonable changes that may be made during the course of construction. Many government entities are limited in the amount of money they may commit to capital projects, either by spending limitations or by laws that require pre-construction authorization of funding. A contractor's failure to recognize such funding limitations may put it in the position of facing barriers to its collection of payment.

____ 6. **Price ("Cost-Plus" Term).** The contract price is the cost of the work plus an allowance for the contractor's overhead and profit (together forming the "plus" portion). In a cost-plus contract, the principal goal should be to draft clear terms defining the costs that may be charged to the owner. Several specific terms deserve special attention:

____ (a) **Self-performed work.** When the contractor contemplates performing a portion of the underlying scope of work with its own forces, the contract should be clear in allowing the costs associated with such self-performed work to be recovered as part of the contract costs (as opposed to being

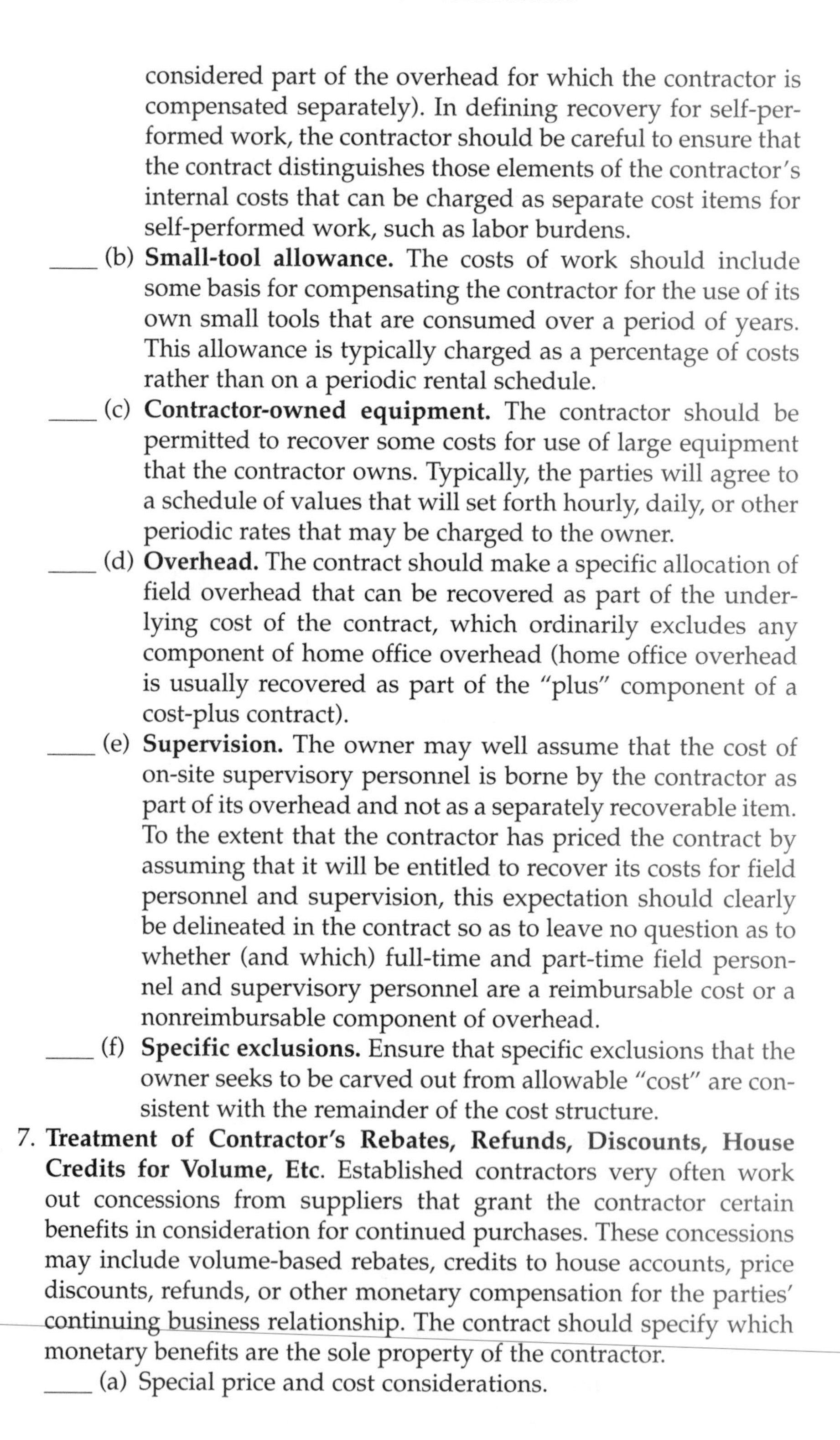

considered part of the overhead for which the contractor is compensated separately). In defining recovery for self-performed work, the contractor should be careful to ensure that the contract distinguishes those elements of the contractor's internal costs that can be charged as separate cost items for self-performed work, such as labor burdens.

____ (b) **Small-tool allowance.** The costs of work should include some basis for compensating the contractor for the use of its own small tools that are consumed over a period of years. This allowance is typically charged as a percentage of costs rather than on a periodic rental schedule.

____ (c) **Contractor-owned equipment.** The contractor should be permitted to recover some costs for use of large equipment that the contractor owns. Typically, the parties will agree to a schedule of values that will set forth hourly, daily, or other periodic rates that may be charged to the owner.

____ (d) **Overhead.** The contract should make a specific allocation of field overhead that can be recovered as part of the underlying cost of the contract, which ordinarily excludes any component of home office overhead (home office overhead is usually recovered as part of the "plus" component of a cost-plus contract).

____ (e) **Supervision.** The owner may well assume that the cost of on-site supervisory personnel is borne by the contractor as part of its overhead and not as a separately recoverable item. To the extent that the contractor has priced the contract by assuming that it will be entitled to recover its costs for field personnel and supervision, this expectation should clearly be delineated in the contract so as to leave no question as to whether (and which) full-time and part-time field personnel and supervisory personnel are a reimbursable cost or a nonreimbursable component of overhead.

____ (f) **Specific exclusions.** Ensure that specific exclusions that the owner seeks to be carved out from allowable "cost" are consistent with the remainder of the cost structure.

____ 7. **Treatment of Contractor's Rebates, Refunds, Discounts, House Credits for Volume, Etc**. Established contractors very often work out concessions from suppliers that grant the contractor certain benefits in consideration for continued purchases. These concessions may include volume-based rebates, credits to house accounts, price discounts, refunds, or other monetary compensation for the parties' continuing business relationship. The contract should specify which monetary benefits are the sole property of the contractor.

____ (a) Special price and cost considerations.

____ (b) The contract should be clear as to for what the "plus" portion of the contract is intended to compensate the contractor, so as to avoid disputes about recoverable costs versus non-recoverable overhead. As noted earlier, questions concerning these issues may arise in connection with home office overhead, field personnel of the contractor, supervisory personnel, etc. There is no "right" allocation of items, but it is important that the parties understand and agree at the outset of the contract with respect to what is separately compensable and what is not.

____ (c) **Price: guaranteed maximum price (GMP).** When the cost-plus contract includes a term that fixes the maximum cost that the contractor will be entitled to recover, such a GMP shifts much more emphasis into the drafting of the scope of work than might otherwise be necessary in a cost-plus contract. The reason for this is simple: the owner will benefit by construing as many items as being within the scope of work as possible, while the contractor will benefit from construing as many items as possible as falling outside the initial scope of work as the actual cost of construction reaches and exceeds the GMP, and pressure for the parties to do so will increase. Accordingly, a GMP contract leaves open the prospect that there will be substantial disagreements concerning the contractual scope of work. An attorney reviewing a cost-plus contract that also includes a GMP should be careful to review the checklist related to stipulated subcontracts.

____ 8. **Scope of Work.** In a contract in which compensation is fixed solely by reference to the contractor's out-of-pocket costs and the contractor's allowance for overhead and profit, there may be less reason to spend much time reviewing the project scope of work. In the end, whether the scope of work is expanded or narrowed and whether work is technically within or outside the initial scope of work proves to be irrelevant; the contractor's compensation is determined with no reference to the scope of work, and disputes over scope of work are relatively rare in cost-plus contracts.

____ 9. **Payments.**

____ (a) Interim payments are typically based on costs expended: payment terms for a cost-plus contract should be scheduled so as to permit the earliest possible reimbursement to the contractor. The contract should not envision any payment schedule that is based on a percentage-of-completion method.

____ (b) In addition to reimbursing the contractor for actual costs expended, the contractor may wish to include advance payment for specially manufactured items and items for which there are long lead-times for delivery. This ensures that the contractor does not end up financing the project by coming out of pocket for expenses that it may not be able to bill to the owner until later in the contract period.

____ (c) Ensure that the contract specifies the manner and timing in which the contractor will recover its overhead and profit for the project.

____ 10. **Retainage.** Although most contracts allow for the retention by the owner of a portion of the contract price until substantial completion, many jurisdictions impose limitations on the amount of retention that can be withheld by the owner. Any retainage set out in the contract should be measured against applicable statutes to ensure consistency. These limitations or qualifications may include a statutory elimination or reduction of retainage after partial completion (typically after 50% of the contract price), exclusion of fees from retention requirements, and release of the retention upon such events as the architect's interim certification of a limited punchlist (retaining, for example, 200% of the cost to complete such items). In addition, ensure that retention is released upon substantial completion, less any reasonable withholding necessary to satisfy any punchlist obligations of the contractor.

____ 11. **Insurance.** During the contracting process, it is likely that the owner will request status as a primary insured or, at the very least, as an additional named insured. Verify that insurance coverage as required by the contract is available and in place, and that any requested endorsements have been procured. The contractor's failure to procure required insurance may expose the contractor to substantial additional damages.

____ 12. **Standard of Care.** It may be advantageous in the agreement to specify that the contractor's standard of care for performance of work is to perform all work in accordance with the standards prevalent in the community in which the project is being built, or some similar standard. The purpose for providing an express standard of care in the contract is to take advantage of those jurisdictions in which the economic loss rule bars a party from seeking tort remedies when a contract between the parties expresses or implies a particular standard of care. Of course, the standard of care should be no more expansive than the standard that would be implied by the law in the absence of any express statement thereof.

# Checklist 5: General Conditions—Owner's Considerations

An owner should consider many issues when drafting the owner/general contractor agreement. The following checklist of questions and issues, although not exhaustive, should be helpful in highlighting some of the important provisions that an owner should consider when drafting such an agreement.

____ 1. **Does the contract specify the terms and responsibilities for project submittals?** Clearly specifying the terms and responsibilities for project submittals can provide increased certainty that the work will be performed correctly and in a timely manner.

____ (a) Is the contractor required to submit each shop drawing, sample, product data, and/or material list based on a specified time and/or schedule so that the owner and architect will have ample time to review, approve, and/or request revisions?

____ (b) Does the contract expressly state that owner review and approval of submittals does not include review and approval of (and does not relieve the contractor from responsibility for) means, methods, techniques, sequences, or procedures of construction, or to safety precautions or programs incidental thereto?

____ (c) Is it clear that the owner review and approval of shop drawings does not relieve the contractor from any of its responsibilities or obligations under the contract and shall not constitute a waiver or create an estoppel as to whether the contractor has complied with the contract?

____ 2. **Does the owner have the right to perform audits?** Most contracts give the owner certain limited rights to perform audits regarding contractor financial information. An owner should consider expanding the right

**Daniel D. McMillan** is a partner with Jones Day, where he is co-chair of the firm's international construction practice. He represents owners, design professionals, and contractors in litigation, arbitration, and contract negotiations. He litigated the first case in the United States to result in a published decision concerning disputes review boards.

**Scott K. Behrendt** is an attorney at Theodora Oringher Miller & Richman PC, a full-service business litigation and transactional law firm with offices in Los Angeles and Costa Mesa, California. His practice involves a wide range of complex commercial litigation, with an emphasis on private and public sector construction litigation and advisory matters.

to audit to provide a more effective means to monitor performance and control project costs.

____ (a) Does the contract provide that the owner shall have the right to review, obtain, inspect, audit, and copy all written and electronically stored records of the contractor pertaining to the contract and/or work, including nonfinancial project documents?

____ (b) Is there a specified time within which all records requested pursuant to an audit shall be provided to the owner, for example, within 10 days of the request?

____ (c) Is the owner expressly allowed to have access to project staff and employees of the contractor to interview in connection with an audit?

____ (d) Does the right to audit include a "flow-down" right to audit all of the contractor's subcontractors and suppliers of every tier?

____ (e) Will the owner be reimbursed for the costs of the audit in the event overpricing or overcharges of any nature are uncovered by the owner as a result of the audit?

____ 3. **Does the contractor have a "continuing duty to perform the work" (that is, waiver of contractor's right to terminate)?** Where the time deadlines for completion of the project and interim milestones are of the essence, an owner may want to include a requirement that a contractor continue the work, even during a dispute.

____ (a) Does the contract expressly state that all time deadlines under the contract are of the essence?

____ (b) Is the contractor required to proceed with the work even if the contractor contends that the owner has materially and/or otherwise breached the contract? (Such a provision effectively amounts to a waiver of the contractor's right to terminate the contract subject to any limitations on the enforceability of such provisions.)

____ (c) If there is an existing dispute, disagreement, or a claim by the contractor pending, is the contractor required to proceed with the work, which shall not be stopped, delayed, postponed, and/or otherwise suspended by the contractor pending the resolution of the same?

____ 4. **Does the owner have the right to terminate the contract for convenience?** A right to terminate for the owner's convenience provides the flexibility to end a contract without cause (that is, without having to establish a default by the contractor or breach that would justify termination).

____ (a) Does the contract specifically allow the owner the right to terminate for convenience?

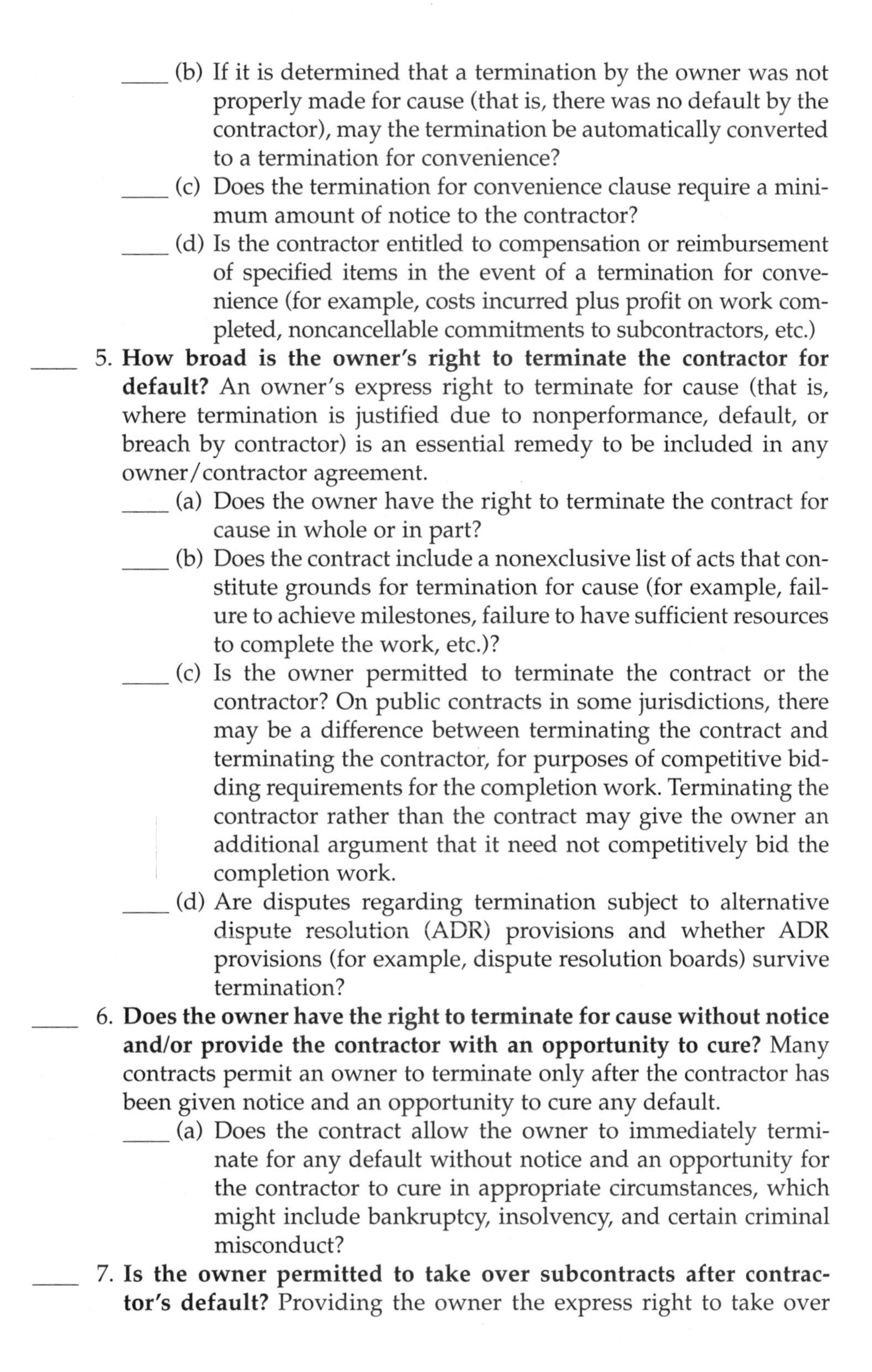

____ (b) If it is determined that a termination by the owner was not properly made for cause (that is, there was no default by the contractor), may the termination be automatically converted to a termination for convenience?

____ (c) Does the termination for convenience clause require a minimum amount of notice to the contractor?

____ (d) Is the contractor entitled to compensation or reimbursement of specified items in the event of a termination for convenience (for example, costs incurred plus profit on work completed, noncancellable commitments to subcontractors, etc.)

____ 5. **How broad is the owner's right to terminate the contractor for default?** An owner's express right to terminate for cause (that is, where termination is justified due to nonperformance, default, or breach by contractor) is an essential remedy to be included in any owner/contractor agreement.

____ (a) Does the owner have the right to terminate the contract for cause in whole or in part?

____ (b) Does the contract include a nonexclusive list of acts that constitute grounds for termination for cause (for example, failure to achieve milestones, failure to have sufficient resources to complete the work, etc.)?

____ (c) Is the owner permitted to terminate the contract or the contractor? On public contracts in some jurisdictions, there may be a difference between terminating the contract and terminating the contractor, for purposes of competitive bidding requirements for the completion work. Terminating the contractor rather than the contract may give the owner an additional argument that it need not competitively bid the completion work.

____ (d) Are disputes regarding termination subject to alternative dispute resolution (ADR) provisions and whether ADR provisions (for example, dispute resolution boards) survive termination?

____ 6. **Does the owner have the right to terminate for cause without notice and/or provide the contractor with an opportunity to cure?** Many contracts permit an owner to terminate only after the contractor has been given notice and an opportunity to cure any default.

____ (a) Does the contract allow the owner to immediately terminate for any default without notice and an opportunity for the contractor to cure in appropriate circumstances, which might include bankruptcy, insolvency, and certain criminal misconduct?

____ 7. **Is the owner permitted to take over subcontracts after contractor's default?** Providing the owner the express right to take over subcontracts upon termination for default helps ensure continuity of performance after termination of the contractor.

____ 8. **Under what circumstances does the owner have the right to suspend work?** This provision gives the owner the discretion and flexibility to suspend the work as deemed necessary by the owner, without cause (that is, any reason, including due to loss of funding, safety issues, investigations, etc.), either for such period of time as may be necessary or convenient for the owner (or for a specified fixed period of time). Usually, such provisions provide that the owner is to pay the contractor certain amounts for overhead and may give the owner the right to terminate the contract in the event that the suspension continues for a certain period of time.

____ 9. **Does the owner have the right to perform the work itself?** If so, under what circumstances? Reserving for the owner the right to perform the contractor's work with its own forces and/or pursuant to separate work contracts provides added flexibility to the owner in ensuring the timely performance and completion of the work.

____ 10. **What are the responsibilities of the contractor for the management and superintendence of the work?** Clearly delineating these responsibilities can help eliminate disputes as well as promote the efficient and timely completion of the work.

  ____ (a) Does the contract provide that it is the contractor's duty to supervise and direct all aspects of the work?

  ____ (b) Is the contractor solely responsible for, and required to exercise full control over, construction means, methods, techniques, sequences, procedures, and coordination of all portions of the work with that of all other contractors and subcontractors in a manner that will facilitate the efficient and timely completion of the work?

  ____ (c) Is the contractor required to ensure competent adequate staff and force of skilled workers on the project site to complete the work in accordance with all requirements of the contract?

  ____ (d) Does the contract provide that the contractor shall provide a qualified full-time superintendent, acceptable to the owner, and assistants, as necessary, who shall be physically present at the project site while any aspect of the work is being performed? Does the contract provide that key personnel shall be fluent in a specified language?

____ 11. **What are the contractor's scheduling requirements?** Requiring the contractor to submit its schedule and schedule updates in a format acceptable to the owner will allow the owner to better monitor progress of the project.

____ (a) Does the contract require the submission of an initial construction schedule, as well as any updates, by a specific date?

____ (b) Is the failure to submit schedules and required updates a breach of contract by the contractor?

____ (c) Does the contract require the contractor to make changes to the schedule as requested by the owner?

____ (d) Is the contractor required to show the logic or methodology of the critical path scheduling? (Note: This and the preceding section could potentially be considered interference by the owner with the contractor's means and methods of construction.)

____ (e) What scheduling software should be used? On larger projects, an owner may want to specify the scheduling software to be used (for example, Primavera, Microsoft P3, etc.) and the format of the schedule and updates.

____ (f) Must schedule updates include plans or proposals for making up delay?

____ (g) Does the contract specify that the "float" is owned by the owner?

____ 12. **Is the contractor required to meet specific dates in the schedule identified as "milestones"?** Including a specific milestone schedule can provide increased certainty as to the completion time for individual portions of the work, which can assist an owner in monitoring and ensuring completion of the contract as a whole.

____ (a) Does the contract specify a construction milestone schedule and require the contractor to proceed expeditiously, not only in accordance with the initial construction schedule and as amended from time to time, but also to achieve all milestones as set forth in the milestones schedule?

____ (b) Is the contractor required to furnish and maintain sufficient forces to ensure completion of all work in accordance with the milestones schedule?

____ (c) Does the contract provide that any proposed adjustments to the milestone schedule that change and/or amend the milestones schedule, contract amount, and/or contract time must be submitted and approved pursuant to the change order procedures of the contract in order to have effect?

____ 13. **What are the owner's options with respect to remedying defective work?** The owner should retain the flexibility to require the correction of defective work either by the contractor or the owner itself at the contractor's expense.

____ (a) If there is any work, material, equipment, or other items that do not conform to the contract requirements or that may be deemed defective by the owner, does the contract provide that such defective items must be removed and replaced by the contractor upon notice from the owner at the contractor's expense? Does the owner have the right to remedy defective work at the contractor's expense in the event the contractor does not do so within a contractually specified period of time (or some other reasonable period of time as may be agreed upon by the parties) and by whatever method the owner deems most expedient?

____ (b) Does the contract provide that the contractor shall be responsible for all delays to the milestones and/or contract time caused by the contractor's removal and replacement of defective work, etc.?

____ 14. **Is the contract clear that payment and/or occupancy by the owner does not constitute acceptance of defective work?** Specifying that the owner's approval of a payment application, or the partial or entire use of occupancy of the work, does not constitute acceptance of work not in accordance with the contract ensures that the owner does not inadvertently acquiesce to defective work.

____ 15. **What are the procedures that must be utilized by the contractor in order to make a claim?** By specifying the procedures for the submission of contractor claims and the required supporting documentation, an owner can better regulate the claims process.

____ (a) What is the required timing and content of any claims submitted by the contractor? Does the contract require that the contractor provide a statement justifying its claim and provide supporting documentation? Must the contractor provide documents and information supporting its claim for compensation? Must the contractor provide a scheduling analysis supporting any asserted delay claim or time impact?

____ (b) Does the contract provide that any failure by the contractor to comply with the claims procedures amounts to a waiver, release, and forfeiture of the claim? An owner should understand the extent to which such provisions will be enforced under local law and draft language to increase the likelihood of enforceability.

____ (c) What are the applicable dispute resolution procedures? Does the contract provide for alternative dispute resolution (e.g., mediation, disputes review boards, binding arbitration, etc.), and does it specify whether any types of claims are not subject to the ADR procedures? Prior to the initiation of ADR or litigation, are there required negotiations that must occur between the executives (or other identified representatives) for the owner and the contractor?

____ 16. **What are the procedures for documenting contract changes and change order proposals?** Detailed procedures for changes, construction directives, and change order proposals can provide the owner the flexibility to direct changes to the work while controlling costs.

____ (a) Does the owner have the right to direct additions, deletions, and/or revisions to the work?

____ (b) Does the contract provide that any changes to the contract can only be approved in writing?

____ (c) Are there specific procedures for owner additions, deletions, and/or revisions resulting in changes to the contract amount, time, and/or milestones pursuant to requests for clarifications, change order proposals, construction directives, and change orders?

____ 17. **Does the owner have the right to assess costs, expenses, and/or damages (including liquidated damages) against contract funds, contractor, or security provided by the contractor such as a performance bond?** By specifying that the owner has a right to assess not only against the existing contract funds otherwise due and payable to the contractor, but also against the contractor and its performance bond, the owner increases its avenues and options for recovery.

____ 18. **What are the certification requirements?**

____ (a) Does the contract require certification of progress pay applications (for example, "contractor certifies under penalty of perjury that the work for which payment is sought in this progress pay application complies with the requirements of the contract and that all such work has been performed and amounts billed by contractor are due")? Doing so may decrease the incidence of false pay applications.

____ (b) Does the contract require certification of potential claims, change orders, and pricing information (for example, "The undersigned originator [contractor or subcontractor as appropriate] certifies under penalty of perjury that the above statements made in connection with this potential claim are true.")? Doing so may decrease the likelihood of falsified information submitted by the contractor.

____ 19. **Does the contract provide limitations on liability to the owner?**

____ (a) **Delay damages.**

____ (i) Is there a no-damages-for-delay provision? (This type of provision may not be enforceable on public works projects in certain jurisdictions.)

____ (ii) Alternatively, does the contract specify that the contractor is not entitled to recover damages for delays that are not the fault of the owner?

____ (b) Is there a mutual waiver of consequential damages? Is the concept of consequential damages defined in the contract or is it being left to interpretation?

____ 20. **Is the contractor barred from recovering delay damages where there is a concurrent delay?** The owner may want to include a provision that expressly provides that the contractor is not entitled to recover delay damages when the delay at issue is concurrent with other delays that are not caused by the owner.

____ 21. **Does the contract contain a "no third-party beneficiary" clause?** An owner should consider specifying that the contractor is not a third-party beneficiary of any contracts to which the owner is a party, including those entered into with design professionals, (for example, architects, engineers, etc.), and that the contractor has no direct right of claims regarding the design of the project. Such a clause eliminates the contractor's right to proceed directly against the owner's design professionals, and others that the owner may want to protect, as a third-party beneficiary. The owner may wish to add other provisions that make it more likely that a court will bar direct claims by a contractor against the owner's design professionals under the economic loss doctrine or otherwise.

____ 22. **Does the contractor have a right to early completion?** Does the contract provide that the contractor has no right to bring an early completion claim or seek delay damages where the project is completed on time?

____ 23. **What are the contractor's requirements with respect to pre-construction review of site conditions, plans, and specifications?**

____ (a) Is the contractor required to perform a thorough pre-construction survey of the project site to ascertain and document all existing actual conditions that may affect the work? Doing so will make it more difficult for a contractor to later claim during construction that it encountered an unknown site condition for which it is entitled to a contract adjustment.

____ (b) Does the contract require the contractor to thoroughly examine pre-construction all plans and specifications for any perceived errors or ambiguities and to file any needed requests for clarification prior to commencement of any work? This requirement will allow the owner the opportunity to correct any such problems in the plans and specifications prior to commencement of construction.

____ 24. **What are the contractor's indemnity obligations?** Does the contract require the contractor to defend, indemnify, and hold the owner harmless from and against any and all claims arising out of or resulting from the contractor's performance of the work? The broader the indemnification, the more protection that is afforded to the owner.

____ 25. **Does the contractor warrant and guarantee to the owner that all work will be performed in compliance with the contract and be free of defects?** To increase the owner's protection, the contract should provide that the contractor's obligations are absolute, that is, they are not released as a result of, among other things, any acceptance of work by the owner, any inspection of the work, or any observation by the architect.

# Checklist 6: General Conditions—Contractor's Considerations

This checklist is intended to guide the user in drafting the "General Conditions" portion of a general contract. The project-specific terms will ordinarily be included in a stipulated-sum or cost-plus contract, and the reader should consult the checklists related to each of those contracts in conjunction with the drafting of the general contract.

____ 1. **Are the contract documents ranked by order of precedence?** In addition to a complete specification of the contract documents, the general contractor may consider including a clause that ranks the documents by order of priority in interpretation for the purposes of resolving any conflicts among the various contract documents.

____ 2. **What is the architect's role?** Ensure that the architect's role and responsibilities are defined clearly. In particular, there should be no doubt as to when the architect is entitled to issue directions binding the contractor, and it should further be clear when the architect is acting as a neutral party with responsibilities of fairness and neutrality to both sides.

____ 3. **What are the contractor's responsibilities with respect to reviewing the plans and specifications?** Ensure that any obligation on the part of the contractor to review plans and specifications in advance of the contract is solely for the purpose of the contractor's familiarizing itself with the work to be performed and does not constitute an affirmation, warranty, or other obligation on the part of the contractor to guarantee the constructability of the project or that the plans and specifications are error-free.

____ 4. **Site Investigation.** To protect the contractor's rights under a differing site conditions clause, ensure that any site investigation required of the contractor only requires the contractor to perform a "reasonable" investigation and does not have the effect of shifting the risk of all subsurface conditions to the contractor. If a differing site conditions clause excludes compensation for any conditions that a *thorough* inspection or investigation would reveal, the contractor bears

**Stephen A. Hess** is with Sherman & Howard and practices construction law and litigation. His writings have appeared in numerous national construction law treatises and journals. He is an adjunct faculty member of University of Denver's Sturm College of Law, where he created and teaches the school's Construction Law Seminar.

a substantial responsibility to investigate the site and the differing site conditions clause may prove unhelpful. Moreover, in a stipulated-sum contract that does not include a differing site conditions clause, the contractor will suffer *all* the costs of adverse subsurface conditions, and accordingly a much more extensive pre-construction investigation is prudent.

____ 5. **What is the contractor's responsibility with respect to coordination among multiple primes?**

____ (a) When the contractor is one of two or more of many prime contractors, the general contract should specify in detail the precise manner in which the owner will coordinate work among the different primes and should further identify each of the specific tasks for which the owner is responsible under the general parameters of coordination. A general clause requiring the owner to accept responsibility for coordination with a concomitant obligation on the part of each contractor to "cooperate" with such coordination may be too general to resolve disputes over particular coordination tasks.

____ 6. **Price.**

____ (a) Where the underlying contract price is calculated in whole or in part with respect to unit prices, consider whether the contract should include adjustment of unit prices where estimated quantities vary from the quantities that served as the basis for the bid. Such a clause is necessary to protect the contractor's pricing when actual units are substantially fewer than the units bid.

____ 7. **Warranty Clauses.**

____ (a) **Disclaimer of express or implied warranties.** Ensure that all disclaimers of express or implied warranties satisfy the state law requirements, and in particular satisfy the Uniform Commercial Code (UCC). The UCC requires specific language to disclaim warranties (especially the warranties of merchantability and fitness for a particular purpose), and if the disclaimers do not satisfy the relevant state's particular requirements, the disclaimers will be futile. Although construction contracts are typically regarded as service contracts rather than sale contracts, warranties related to individual items within a project may be held to the UCC's standards regarding disclaimer of warranties.

____ (b) **Transfer of subcontractor/manufacturer warranties.** General conditions ordinarily require warranties that run from the general contractor to the owner. With respect to equipment and work furnished by others under warranty to the contractor, the contractor should assign these warranties to the owner in full and complete satisfaction of any warranty obligation the contactor would otherwise have to the owner. This has the effect of putting the owner directly in line with the guarantor to make claims handling more efficient, and it limits the contractor's liability.

____ 8. **Limitation on Remedies.**

____ (a) **Mutuality.** Ensure that the contractor is not exposed to consequential damages if the owner is protected from consequential damages. For example, the contractor does not want to be exposed to potential damages for lost rent as a consequence of delayed completion, yet be unable to recover for delays caused by the owner. Of course, it is always nice for the contractor to have recourse to consequential damages while limiting the owner, but as a practical matter the best the parties should hope for is mutuality of their respective obligations. A clause like this appeals to the basic fairness of the relationship, and consequential damages should either be waived by both or accepted by both.

____ (b) **Legality.** Ensure that any limitations on remedies are consistent with state law. There are several types of limitations that are typically invoked in construction contracts, including limitation of damages to fees earned (usually in construction management or design professional contracts), the limits of insurance liability, or stated dollar caps.

____ 9. **No-Damages-for-Delay Clause.**

____ (a) **Enforceability.** Assess and advise contractor with respect to enforceability of a no-damages-for-delay clause, as the contractor should make a conscious business decision as to the acceptability of such a clause in the face of its possible enforcement. The numerous exceptions to the general enforceability of no-damages-for-delay clauses mitigates against their threat to the contractor, but ultimately the acceptance of such a clause is a business decision and not a legal decision.

____ 10. **Liquidated Damages.** Where the contract does not exclude damages for delay, consider the use of a liquidated damage clause to make sure owner does not acquire a runaway lost profits or other delay claim. Liquidated damage clauses are regularly enforced so long as the amount of damages is reasonable at the time of contracting, the parties intend for the liquidated damages to compensate losses rather than punish the contractor, and it is difficult to calculate actual damages arising from delay. It is always more favorable for the contractor not to face any damages for delay, but liquidated damages are often

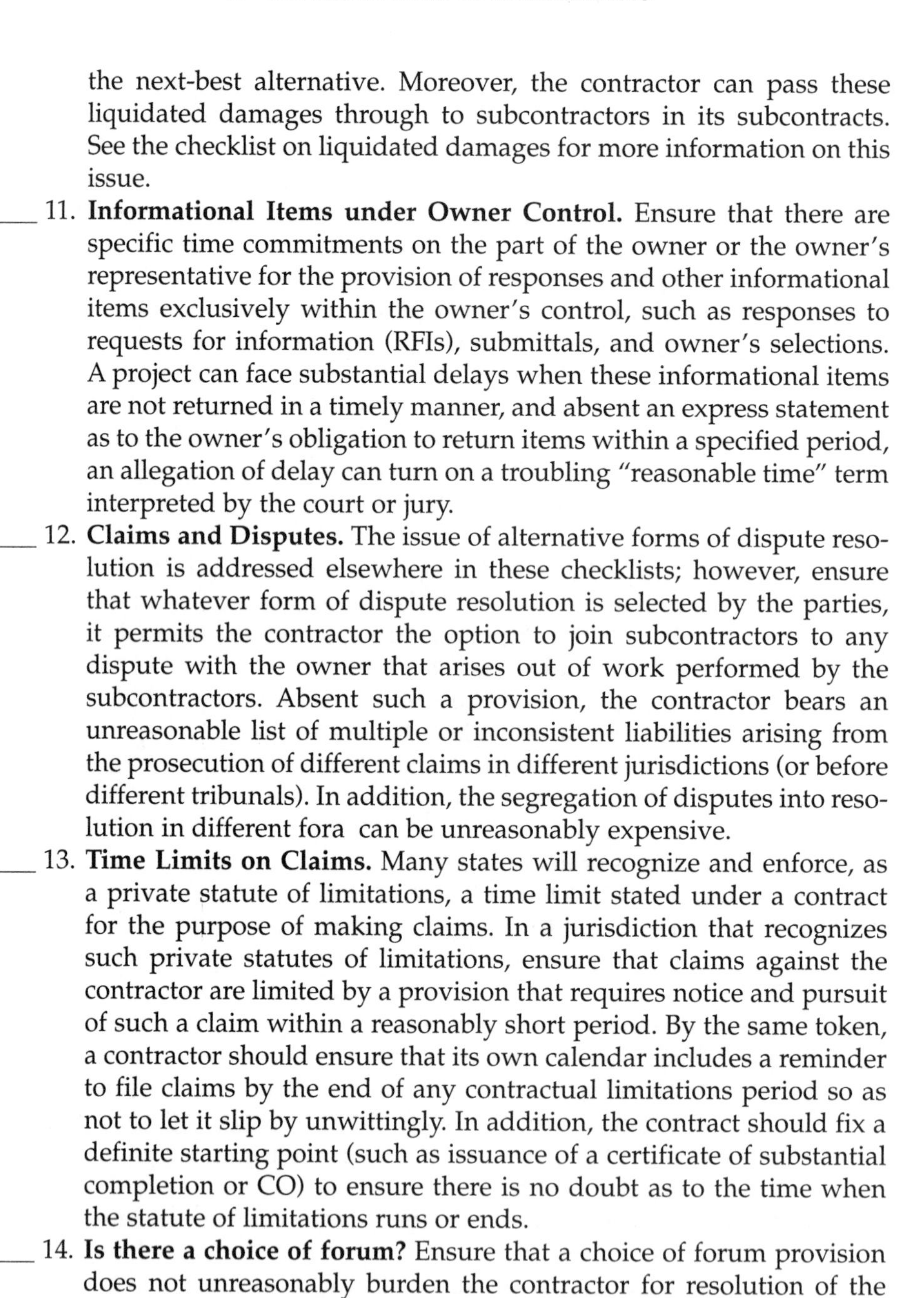

the next-best alternative. Moreover, the contractor can pass these liquidated damages through to subcontractors in its subcontracts. See the checklist on liquidated damages for more information on this issue.

____ 11. **Informational Items under Owner Control.** Ensure that there are specific time commitments on the part of the owner or the owner's representative for the provision of responses and other informational items exclusively within the owner's control, such as responses to requests for information (RFIs), submittals, and owner's selections. A project can face substantial delays when these informational items are not returned in a timely manner, and absent an express statement as to the owner's obligation to return items within a specified period, an allegation of delay can turn on a troubling "reasonable time" term interpreted by the court or jury.

____ 12. **Claims and Disputes.** The issue of alternative forms of dispute resolution is addressed elsewhere in these checklists; however, ensure that whatever form of dispute resolution is selected by the parties, it permits the contractor the option to join subcontractors to any dispute with the owner that arises out of work performed by the subcontractors. Absent such a provision, the contractor bears an unreasonable list of multiple or inconsistent liabilities arising from the prosecution of different claims in different jurisdictions (or before different tribunals). In addition, the segregation of disputes into resolution in different fora can be unreasonably expensive.

____ 13. **Time Limits on Claims.** Many states will recognize and enforce, as a private statute of limitations, a time limit stated under a contract for the purpose of making claims. In a jurisdiction that recognizes such private statutes of limitations, ensure that claims against the contractor are limited by a provision that requires notice and pursuit of such a claim within a reasonably short period. By the same token, a contractor should ensure that its own calendar includes a reminder to file claims by the end of any contractual limitations period so as not to let it slip by unwittingly. In addition, the contract should fix a definite starting point (such as issuance of a certificate of substantial completion or CO) to ensure there is no doubt as to the time when the statute of limitations runs or ends.

____ 14. **Is there a choice of forum?** Ensure that a choice of forum provision does not unreasonably burden the contractor for resolution of the dispute. Choice of forum provisions are generally enforceable, especially in the commercial context, and should not unduly hinder the contractor from making or defending a claim. Some contracts permit either party to file in its own forum, or more commonly (where a single forum is not specified), clauses discourage recourse to formal dispute resolution by vesting venue in the defendant's forum.

____ 15. **Who pays attorneys' fees?** At the very least, attorneys' fee clauses should provide mutuality; that is, the contract should not permit only the owner to recover attorneys' fees in the event of a dispute between the parties. More important, the contractor should bear the decision of whether to include an attorneys' fee clause as a matter of business judgment. As a general rule, prevailing party attorney fee clauses increase the total exposure to each side for losing, while allowing each side at least some hope of being kept whole. On the other hand, the absence of an attorneys' fee clause reduces the potential recovery by a prevailing party (by the amount of its fees), and reduces the median value of any dispute, thereby promoting settlement. There is no general rule as to whether it is "better" to have an attorneys' fee clause or not, except perhaps that a party whose only potential default is a payment default can feel more comfortable with such a clause than a party who might predictably get into a performance dispute.

____ 16. **Can the contractor recover costs for suspension?** Ensure that the contractor is entitled to recover costs for any period of suspension by the owner. In particular, ensure that the suspension clause is harmonized with any no-damages-for-delay clause so that the contractor is not precluded from recovery.

____ 17. **Termination for Default.** Ensure that any termination for default by the owner must be preceded by reasonable notice and an opportunity to cure. Termination itself is a dramatic remedy that is discussed elsewhere in these checklists. At the very least, however, the contractor should protect itself against a precipitous invocation of termination as a remedy by ensuring that the contractor has the opportunity to remedy any asserted defects in performance after due notice so as to allow some opportunity to mitigate against the dire consequences of a termination.

____ 18. **Changes.**

____ (a) **Pricing of directed changes.** A directed change requires the contractor to perform work different from the work defined in the contract, even without a contemporaneous agreement as to price. Ensure that any pricing or default mechanism for the pricing of directed changes in the face of a dispute is reasonable and does not put the contractor at unnecessary risk of loss with regard to directed changes.

____ (b) Require the owner to make some partial payment with respect to directed changes in circumstances in which the parties do not come to agreement as to the price of the changes. Because most directed change clauses require the contractor to continue working even when the price of the change is in dispute, the contractor does not want to leave itself in a vulnerable position in which it is required to perform additional or changed work with no prospect of payment until an elaborate pricing dispute resolution mechanism is completed.

____ (c) Ensure that the contractor is allowed to contest any "field order" or "no-cost change order" where the owner reserves the right in the contract to order no-cost changes to the contract.

____ 19. **Indemnification.**

____ (a) Verify that the scope of the indemnification provided in the contract is legal under state law. Many states bar indemnification in whole or in part, primarily where the indemnitee seeks indemnification regardless of its own fault in causing the loss or damage at issue. In some states, an illegal indemnification clause will void the entire contract; in other states, a void indemnification clause may be stricken, leaving the remainder of the contract enforceable. Finally, some states bar indemnification provisions in government contracts only but allow enforcement of such provisions in private contracts.

____ (b) Ensure that the indemnification provision is mutual; that is, ensure that each party has the obligation to indemnify the other for any losses the other suffers that are caused by the indemnitor. Such cross-indemnification clauses need to be drafted carefully, of course, so they do not effectively cancel each other out in the event of a dispute.

____ (c) Ensure that any indemnification obligation undertaken by the contractor is covered adequately by the contractor's insurance. As a practical matter, this may mean limiting the indemnified risks to bodily injury and property damage, although most ordinary liability policies exclude the "work" being performed from liability coverage and consign the allocation of such risk to a builder's risk policy.

____ (d) Where indemnification is required, the contractor may also request as a condition of indemnification that defense against the alleged claim be tendered to the contractor as a means of allowing the contractor to control both the risk of exposure and the expense of providing a defense. When the contractor is required to bear the owner's cost of defense through separate counsel, such cost of defense may easily approach the ultimate liability, making any defense on the merits ultimately ineffective. The mechanism by which such defense is ensured is by conditioning any indemnification obligation on the tender of the defense through such a clause as the following: "Owner recognizes and agrees that as a condition precedent to any indemnification rights hereunder, it shall be required to give notice of any claim covered by this indemnification clause to contractor immediately, and shall allow contractor to represent owner's interests in defending and settling such claim. In the event owner refuses to tender the defense of any claim to contractor, this indemnification shall be null and void."

____ (e) Ensure that any indemnification right is conditioned on timely notice from the owner of the claim being asserted.

# Checklist 7: EPC Contracts—Owner's Considerations

The engineer, procure, and construction (EPC) contractor is responsible for design, execution, and completion of the work so that the work is fit for its intended purpose. Additionally, the EPC contractor may have commissioning and start-up responsibilities and shall remedy any defects.

____ 1. **The Tender.**

____ (a) Preparing a tender for the type, size, and complexity of EPC projects results in an expensive and time-consuming bid process. To encourage bidders, the owner may consider paying a portion of the preparation costs.

____ (b) The owner, its engineer, or consultant, needs to provide a conceptual framework to all bidders relative to the budget, the duration, the size, and the equipment to be involved.

____ (c) The owner may decide the tender will include design and performance only or may include contract terms.

____ (d) If terms and conditions are included in the tender documents, the owner should specify the priority among the tender documents.

____ 2. **Pricing Structure.**

____ (a) EPC contracts may be fixed price, cost plus, or cost plus with a guaranteed maximum price.

____ (b) Does the owner have the resources to audit expenses on an ongoing basis? If not, a fixed-price contract is less expensive for the owner to administrate because it requires less oversight of payment. Both the cost-plus and cost-plus guaranteed maximum requires oversight to ensure that the owner is not being charged for defective materials, for design defects or inadequacies, or for other ineligible costs. The cost-plus contract is typically the most expensive to administer.

____ (c) Does the owner intend to motivate the EPC with a combination of economic incentives and disincentives? If so, the owner may consider providing a bonus if the project is

**Denise L. Nestel** practices construction law, including the drafting of EPC contracts. She is a member of the ABA Construction Law Industry Forum and has served as chair of the Construction Law Section of the Houston Bar Association from 1997 to 1998 and has written numerous publications.

completed early or the costs were maintained. Conversely, the owner may consider decreasing any fee or eliminating any fee for costs in excess of the targeted costs.

____ (d) Will the owner make any advance payments, typically for the purchase of equipment?

____ (e) Will the owner assess liquidated damages? If so, what triggers liquidated damages: the failure to meet substantial completion for all or part of the project or the failure to meet start-up or commissioning deadlines?

____ 3. **Lender Concerns.**

____ (a) Given the costs and risk involved, the lender will want to protect its interests.

____ (i) What form of security does the lender want from the EPC?

____ (ii) What degree of payment oversight does the lender require?

____ (iii) Does the lender insist on incentives for early completion?

____ (b) In the event of EPC default, does the lender want the right to step into the EPC's shoes and complete or cause the project to be completed?

____ (i) What is the lender's position on financing of cost overruns?

____ 4. **Licensing.**

____ (a) The owner needs to be sure the EPC is licensed in that jurisdiction.

____ (i) Will the EPC be a contractor with a designer as a subcontractor? Will the engineer take prime responsibility? Or, will the contractor and engineer form a joint venture? Not all jurisdictions allow all of these options.

____ (ii) If the EPC is a joint venture, are both entities jointly and severally liable? Does the security cover both entities? Does the insurance cover both entities?

____ 5. **EPC's Security.**

____ (a) The owner will need to consider how much security it will require from the EPC and the form of the security.

____ (b) Whatever form the owner selects should be included in the tender documents.

____ (c) If the owner elects to go with a bond, unlike commercial projects where the penal sum of the bond is typically the contract price, in EPC contracts, the penal sum is typically a percentage (such as 10% or 15%) of the contract.

____ (d) The owner may also agree to accept a letter of credit for security or a parent guarantee. In any case, the owner will want to have an attorney review the guaranty and letter of credit to make sure that funding is available for the necessary duration and at minimal effort to obtain it.

____ 6. **Owner's Representative.**

____ (a) Does the owner want an employee, such as an engineer, to be the representative for owner? If so, is the employee intended to be neutral or a true agent of the owner?

____ (b) If the owner hires a third-party representative, the authority of the representative needs to be determined.

____ (c) Does the owner want the right to stipulate the EPC contractor use certain subcontractors or only the right to veto?

____ 7. **Dispute Resolution.**

____ (a) The owner needs to decide what form and procedures it wishes to use to resolve disputes. Many owners chose dispute adjudication boards (DABs) or dispute review boards (DRBs). If an owner decides to go with a DAB or DRB, the owner needs to make the following initial decisions:

____ (i) Does the owner want a single arbitrator or a panel?

____ (ii) Does the owner want to have the arbitrator or standing panel appointed at the outset of the contract or use an ad hoc panel?

____ a. The larger the project, the more attractive the standing panel is and the more easily its cost can be absorbed. Often, better rates for an arbitrator or panel can be negotiated if it is done pre-dispute or at the start of the contract.

____ (iii) Does the owner want the arbitrator panel's decision to be final or just an interim step on the way to arbitration or litigation?

____ a. Does the owner want to consult the arbitrator or panel in an advisory role to prevent disputes prior to putting a formal issue before the arbitrator or panel?

____ (iv) Does the owner wish to use an engineer, compensated by the owner, to resolve disputes in a fair and impartial manner? Or, should the engineer be the owner's representative?

____ (v) The owner needs to decide whether the decision of the arbitrator or panel will be executed immediately or whether it is an interim decision with a nonbinding effect.

____ 8. **Consultants.**

____ (a) The owner also may need to hire experts or consultants in the fields of federal regulation.

____ (b) If the project is international, the owner needs to consider hiring local consultants and experts to handle the international contracts and legal issues as well as political and governmental issues.

____ 9. **Confidentiality.**

____ (a) Confidentiality may become an issue. What rights and licenses will the owner and EPC have in the contract documents? The owner will want to maintain its proprietary interests in any processes, but at the same time the designers will want to retain rights in their instruments of service.

____ 10. **Indemnification and Limitations of Liability.**

____ (a) Owner may also need to consider the indemnity clause and whether or not the jurisdiction allows a complete transfer of risk or types of risk. Is there an anti-indemnity statute?

____ (b) Although most EPC contractors will ask for limitations of liability, not all jurisdictions allow it.

# Checklist 8: Joint Venture Agreements

A joint venture is an enterprise between two or more entities to conduct a business together for one or more limited purposes, such as to complete a construction project.

____ 1. **Considerations before Forming a Joint Venture.** Forming a joint venture should not be undertaken lightly. There are serious legal, financial, and operational issues to consider before deciding that a joint venture is the optimal organizational choice. These issues should be explored before a marketing proposal or discussion with the client commits one or more entities to a joint venture.

____ (a) **Advantages of a joint venture.** A joint venture structure can have several benefits.

____ (i) A joint venture makes all members[1] more prominent in their association with the project and creates a better ability to sell the client the expertise and capabilities of each firm. This may be beneficial for taking credit for the project in future marketing.

____ (ii) A joint venture allows firms to participate in an equal manner, so that no firm is perceived as being a superior "prime" or inferior "sub."

____ (iii) The client may be more comfortable with the combined capabilities (and liability) of the entities.

____ (iv) The sharing of risk allows the joint venturers to pursue larger projects and obtain greater bonding capacity.

____ (v) A local partner or one with special connections to the owner may allow a nonlocal partner access to a project it normally could not obtain, and the larger nonlocal partners allow the smaller access to a project it might not otherwise be able to obtain with limited resources and capabilities.

____ (vi) If performing government work with minority- or woman-owned business enterprises (MBE/WBE)

**Bruce R. Gerhardt** is senior counsel and vice president at HDR Inc., an engineering and architecture firm with headquarters in Omaha, Nebraska. HDR is a frequent joint venturer with other design firms and with contractors for design-build projects.

requirements under a prime/sub relationship, a major subcontractor would make it more difficult to meet an MBE/WBE percentage requirement. If the prime and major subcontractor instead create a joint venture, the MBE/WBE subcontractor will have a larger percentage participation.

____ (b) **Disadvantages of a joint venture.**

____ (i) Joint venturers are partners, and typically have joint and several liability. See Uniform Partnership Act (1997) § 306(a).

____ (ii) Joint venturers may have fiduciary duties to each other as partners. See *id.* at § 404.

____ (iii) A joint venturer will be bound by the acts of the other venturers acting within the scope of the joint venture. See *id.* at § 301.

____ (iv) Negative publicity to a joint venture may impugn both firms even if attributable only to the conduct of one.

____ (v) There are practical difficulties in controlling the actions of the various parties to a joint venture.

____ (vi) A joint venture exists as a separate legal entity, and a considerable amount of time must be dedicated to organizational, financial, tax, and legal issues while operating a joint venture.

____ (vii) Integrating the operations of the venturers, especially foreign entities or entities with unique cultures, can be very difficult.

____ (viii) Because the joint venture is a separate legal entity, it may be necessary to retain counsel for the joint venture separate from the joint venture partners.

____ (c) **Alternatives to a joint venture.** Before deciding to form a joint venture, each potential member should consider if an alternate structure would better serve the parties or project.

____ (i) **Prime/sub relationship.** This traditional structure is well understood by all participants in the construction industry and the easiest to establish. The parties will not have joint and several liability.

____ (ii) **Limited liability company.** An LLC could be either for the limited duration for the project only, or an ongoing entity to pursue multiple projects. This entity entails more structure but limits the liability of the participants for the actions of each other. However, the owner may not be receptive to this structure or may require contractual commitments from the parties similar to partnership liability.

____ (iii) **Multiple primes.** Each prime contractor separately contracts with the owner. Coordination becomes much more difficult, but there will not be joint and several liability or fiduciary duties.

____ (d) **Legal status of a joint venture.** A joint venture is typically defined as a legal entity, in the nature of a partnership, but generally created for a specific transaction rather than continuing business, between an association of persons or companies. Joint ventures are treated for all practical purposes as partnerships and are subject to the laws governing partnerships. If enacted by the applicable state, the Uniform Partnership Act will be applied to joint venture matters. This includes a fiduciary duty to the other joint venturers.

____ (e) **Pre-formation/teaming agreements.** In situations in which two or more parties wish to pursue a project, but are not assured of being awarded the project, they may want to consider executing a teaming agreement for the solicitation phase rather than creating a joint venture prior to being awarded (or not awarded) the project. If the parties are not successful in obtaining the project, the creation of a joint venture would have been wasted. The teaming agreement can provide that, if successful, the parties will create a joint venture.

____ (f) **Insuring a joint venture.** Before establishing a joint venture, all parties should ensure that they are adequately covered for their participation in a joint venture and that the joint venture is adequately insured.

____ (i) Professional liability policy forms typically do not cover a professional's participation in a joint venture. Coverage may be negotiated and added by endorsement covering an individual entity's interest in the joint venture for claims arising out of its scope of work. Such coverage would not cover any loss caused by another party, even if the insured party has liability as a partner. All professional joint venturers should individually have this coverage. As an alternative or in addition, the joint venture could obtain a project specific policy. Cross-indemnification for each participant's scope of work is also common in a nonintegrated joint venture [see 2(e)].

____ (ii) The members should share insurance certificates with each other annually to ensure that each is maintaining the required insurance to protect itself (and thus the other members).

____ (iii) The members should name each other additional insureds on commercial general liability, automobile liability, and any applicable umbrella or excess policies.

____ (iv) The members should each have their worker's compensation policies waive subrogation as to the joint venture and other members.

____ (v) The joint venture should consider purchasing a commercial general liability policy for the joint venture. This policy would cover claims made against the joint venture by employees of an individual member, as well as third-party claims. The policy would defend and appoint counsel for the joint venture, avoiding the conflict of interest that can arise from representation by one of the parties' individual counsel.

____ (vi) For any insurance obtained in the name of the joint venture, consider how the deductible will be paid. Will it be paid by all parties on a pro-rata basis, or be completely paid by the party causing the claim? If there are multiple claims, what will be the priority of coverage?

____ 2. **Structuring the Joint Venture.** Before creating a joint venture, consideration should be given as to how the venture should be structured to meet the needs of the parties and the project to be performed.

____ (a) **Parties.** A joint venture could consist of an unlimited number of parties. However, not all partners are equal, and not all participants in a project may be well suited to participate as a partner in the joint venture. An analogy to marriage, and taking the same care one would in entering into marriage, is appropriate.

____ (i) Financial resources are important. Each joint venturer will be liable for the joint venture and the other venturers. A party that cannot meet its financial obligations exposes the other members to vicarious liability.

____ (ii) The partner should bring some component of expertise, and that expertise will need to be managed and integrated into the joint venture activities. Consider naming "key personnel" in the joint venture agreement and requiring that the member commits for the duration of the project.

____ (iii) The culture of each party needs to be compatible. Operational or financial conflicts can be very difficult to resolve, and the fiduciary duty each owes to the other makes removing a party very difficult.

____ (b) **Control.** Control of the joint venture can be one of the most problematic issues. Two parties with equal control can create a stalemate if they do not agree on any given issue. With more than two parties, any individual party may be concerned that their legitimate issues can be overridden by the others. Operation of a joint venture may not allow sufficient time to engage in prolonged dispute resolution procedures.

____ (c) **Jurisdiction and governing law.** It is likely that the joint venturers may be domiciled in different states from each other and that the project may be in an entirely different state. The parties should make an informed decision regarding the law that shall govern the joint venture and agree on the place where litigation or arbitration would occur. The agreement should state the principal place of business for the joint venture, with the expectation that jurisdiction over the joint venture will be established in that state.

____ (d) **Integrated versus nonintegrated.** In an integrated joint venture, the parties determine a percentage that each will share of profits and losses. Even if one party's efforts contribute all the profits, the parties will share according to the established split. Typically, the resources and personnel are combined into one effort—creating the essence of a stand-alone business formed for purposes of the project. In a nonintegrated joint venture, each party assumes a specific scope of work and the associated profit or loss with that scope. The parties do not integrate personnel and resources for the project, but perform individually. Nonetheless, in either situation the parties retain joint and several liability for the obligations of the joint venture. See Uniform Partnership Act § 306 (1997). Some joint ventures may combine aspects of integration and nonintegration for different parts of the project.

____ (e) **Indemnification.** Although the partners are jointly and severally liable, the agreement should contain a mechanism for indemnification between them. In an integrated joint venture, the parties are typically allocated the same percentage of a loss as they would be allocated a profit. In nonintegrated joint ventures, or when the loss is caused solely by a member, the member causing the loss is responsible and indemnifies the others. As between the members, a waiver of consequential damages should be considered.

____ (f) **Scope division and changes.** Assuming that the joint venturers can agree to a division of the scope and fee, changes during the project frequently cause additional issues over scope division. Initially, the parties may agree to a generalized split of scope on a percentage basis. Frequently, that percentage may be difficult to achieve when actual activities are allocated. Change orders during the project may increase or decrease the scope of the project. One party may be more affected or benefited by the change. Disputes frequently arise over these issues. During the project, some parties may believe that one party is performing poorly, or the owner may ask for removal of a party. The joint venture structure makes altering scope or participation difficult without the consent of the affected party. It is impossible to spend too much time trying to allocate scope as specifically as possible.

____ (g) **Intellectual property.** In design joint ventures, the agreement should address the ownership of any intellectual property created during the project. It is common in an integrated joint venture to provide that any intellectual property will be owned by the joint venture, with each member having a license to use and reproduce. No further transfer of the copyright ownership is allowed without the consent of all the members. Under nonintegrated joint ventures, the party creating the intellectual property owns the intellectual property and provides the joint venture with a license.

____ 3. **Operating the Joint Venture.** While creating a joint venture is often seen as critical to the marketing effort and winning of projects, participants frequently underestimate the amount of work involved to operate a joint venture. A joint venture creates a distinct legal entity that must be administered by the parties. The joint venture agreement should detail these issues and assign responsibilities to the various parties.

____ (a) **Creation.** Partnerships (and joint ventures) can arise by conduct whether or not the persons intend to form one. See Uniform Partnership Act (1997) § 202(a). Joint ventures should be documented by a joint venture agreement setting forth the rights and responsibilities of the members. In some states, a Statement of Partnership Authority may be filed to establish authority of certain members to execute instruments transferring real property or to limit the authority of certain partners to enter into transactions on behalf of the partnership.

____ (i) **Licensing.** Depending on the services to be performed by the joint venture, the members should determine whether the entity will need to be licensed under applicable state law. In some states, joint ventures must be licensed even prior to bidding.

____ (b) **Management.** As a threshold issue, the drafter should consider the executive management of the joint venture as opposed to the operational (project) management. The entities participating may wish to create a "Policy Board" or "Board of Control" to manage the business of the joint venture. The Board then typically appoints a Project Manager, Assistant Project Manager(s), and others to operate the project for the joint venture. In a small joint venture, these roles could be combined into one Board that manages all aspects of the joint venture.

____ (i) The duties and authority of the Board should be set forth in the agreement, along with any special matters that might require unanimity or a supermajority for approval.

____ (ii) The duties and authority of the Project Manager should be set forth in the agreement, including the form and timing of reporting to the Board.

____ (iii) Will the joint venture need to retain independent legal counsel to provide services to the joint venture, independent of any relationship with the individual members?

____ (c) **Meetings.** Communication is critical to a successful joint venture. The parties should consider holding regular meetings, whether in person or by teleconference, and a provision for allowing the calling of special meetings when needed. The Board should also be regularly updated by the Project Manager of the status of the project. Minutes should be taken and actions of the Board documented. A key consideration will be whether the Board may act only upon the unanimous approval of the Board (which creates the possibility of deadlocks) or upon a majority vote (which creates the fear that a party will be taken advantage of by the others). Another key decision will be whether each party has an equal vote or whether voting is weighted by financial participation. In any cases where the parties may deadlock, it is critical to create a quick dispute resolution procedure [see 3(e)].

____ (d) **Finances.** Management of the finances of the joint venture will be a primary interest to every participant. Consideration should be given to the following:

____ (i) **Initial capitalization.** Will it be necessary for the members to each contribute a certain amount of capital to meet initial joint venture expenses?

____ (ii) **Checking.** Should a checking account be established by the joint venture to allow for the deposit of receipts and the payment of expenditures? Who will be the signatory(ies) on the account?

____ (iii) **Financial statements.** Who will prepare the financial records for the joint venture, and how often will they be distributed to the members? Will an accounting firm be retained to handle the joint venture accounting needs?

____ (iv) **Taxes.** Who will prepare the necessary income tax statements for the joint venture and distribute to the members?

____ (v) **Invoicing and collections.** Who will prepare invoices for the client, what information is necessary from each member, and how will payments from the client be distributed? Payment for joint venture costs should be made before profits or fees are distributed to the members.

____ (e) **Dispute resolution.** As in a marriage, the members of a joint venture should anticipate and prepare for dispute resolution. Divorce is typically not an option while the project is proceeding. Dispute resolution procedures will need to be quick and responsive so that services for the project are not jeopardized during a dispute.

____ (i) Should there be a mandatory meeting of the members prior to instituting formal mediation? This typically may involve member executives (above the Board of Control level) who attempt to resolve disputes for which the Board is deadlocked. In the alternative, if there are an even number of members, an independent member could be appointed in advance. This member would be asked to vote when the parties are deadlocked on a particular issue.

____ (ii) Should there be mediation prior to initiation of litigation or arbitration? Because time is typically of the essence as the project is proceeding, mediation is a standard requirement in most joint venture agreements. Many details should be established to avoid wasting time arranging a mediation rather than mediating. Consider establishing in advance applicable rules, locations, mediators, notice provisions, costs, and minimum times by which the mediation must be held.

____ (iii) After mediation, should there be litigation or arbitration? Consider agreeing in advance to mechanisms to simplify and accelerate the process. Use of default rules (that is, AAA) should consider associated procedural rules and steps, cost, and time to implement.

____ (f) **Default.** Procedures to handle a default by a member should be included in the agreement. This could include failure to make a required capital contribution, other breach of the joint venture agreement, and failure to remain a solvent business. Procedures for removing the member upon a default should be established.

____ (g) **Drafting.** Few attorneys will draft a joint venture agreement from scratch. Sample joint venture documents provide a good checklist of issues to consider and allow the parties to concentrate on those issues most in need of customization and consensus. Parties may also be more receptive to using an industry standard template than using a document prepared by one member's attorney. Documents available that are specific to the construction industry include the AIA C801 (Joint Venture Agreement for Professional Services), EJCDC E-580 (Standard Form of Joint Venture between Engineers for Professional Service), and AGC 299 (Standard Form of Project Joint Venture Agreement between Contractors).

____ 4. **Closing Out the Joint Venture.** Once a project is completed and the purposes of the joint venture are accomplished, the members should properly "wind-down" the joint venture and perform any necessary tasks to end the joint venture. Failure to terminate the joint venture could leave members exposed to claims for the continued activities of some other member, if some member purports to be operating as the joint venture.

____ (a) **Organizational/tax filings.** Joint ventures are treated as partnerships for tax purposes and must report their income and expenses annually. See IRS Form 1065. Schedule K-1 of Form 1065 must be provided to each member of the joint venture annually. This income must then be reported on each member's individual or corporate tax return.

____ (i) In some states, a "Statement of Dissolution" may be filed that cancels any filed Statements of Partnership and limits the authority of any former member from continuing to bind the other partners. See Uniform Partnership Act (1997) § 805.

____ (b) **Document archiving.** The members should agree on the member that will retain the joint venture records and the time period that such records will be maintained. Each partner will want to retain its own records pursuant to its document retention policy. Joint venture records should be maintained for at least the period of the applicable statute of repose for the project location.

____ (c) **Residual liabilities and insurance.** The dissolution (by whatever means) of a joint venture does not end the liabilities of the members. A joint venture or partnership only terminates once the affairs of the partnership are wound up. Because the partners are individually liable, termination of the joint venture does not terminate the liability of each member. See Uniform Partnership Act (1997) § 307(b).

____ (i) For claims made insurance policies (such as professional liability), consideration should be given to an appropriate extended reporting period or the purchase of additional "tail" coverage. Members may also want to require the providing of insurance certificates to each other for a certain number of years after dissolution.

## *Note*

1. The participants in the joint venture will sometimes be called "participants," "venturers," "members," or "partners." This checklist uses these terms interchangeably. Regardless of the term used, it is most critical to remember that the law will treat every participant as a partner for liability and duty purposes.

# Specific Clauses

# Checklist 9: Drafting Dispute Review Board Provisions

Dispute review boards (DRBs) are a specialized form of alternative dispute resolution (ADR) developed for use on large construction projects. DRBs have been used on both public and private projects ranging from subway tunnels to airport terminals. In the event a DRB is used on a project, this checklist should be helpful when considering how to adapt the DRB process to fit the project.

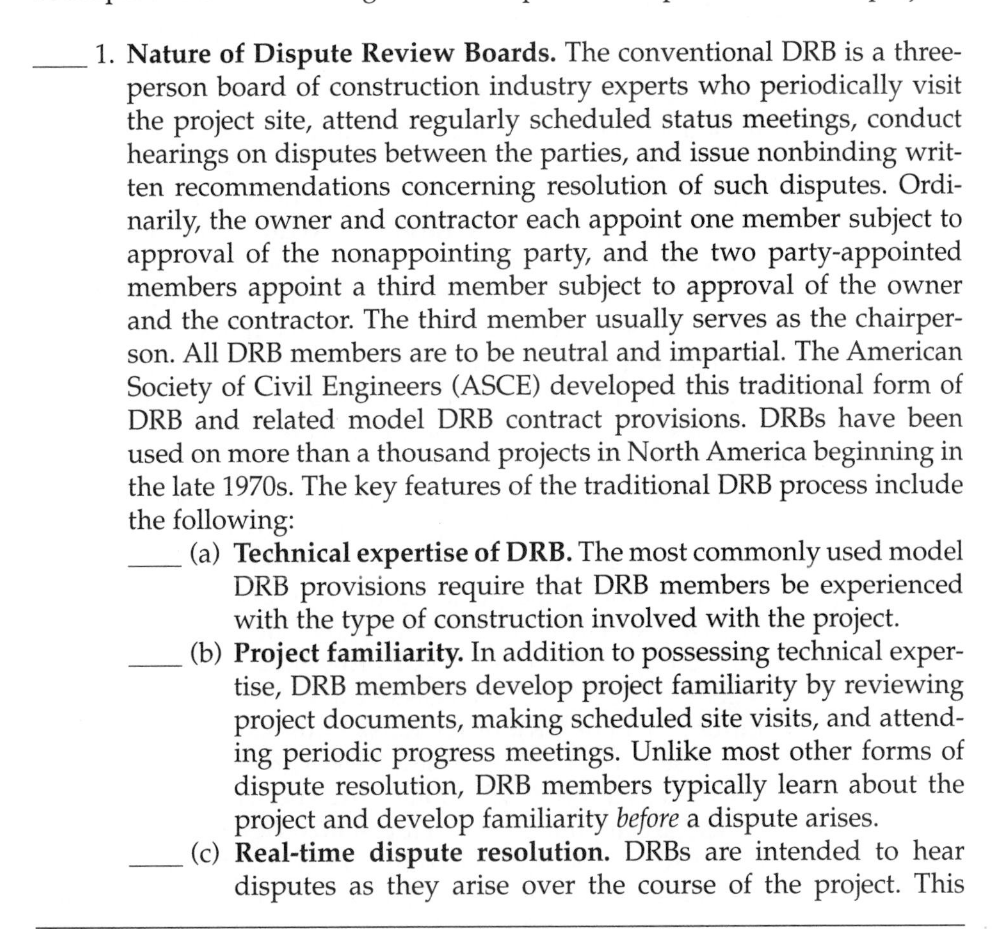

____ 1. **Nature of Dispute Review Boards.** The conventional DRB is a three-person board of construction industry experts who periodically visit the project site, attend regularly scheduled status meetings, conduct hearings on disputes between the parties, and issue nonbinding written recommendations concerning resolution of such disputes. Ordinarily, the owner and contractor each appoint one member subject to approval of the nonappointing party, and the two party-appointed members appoint a third member subject to approval of the owner and the contractor. The third member usually serves as the chairperson. All DRB members are to be neutral and impartial. The American Society of Civil Engineers (ASCE) developed this traditional form of DRB and related model DRB contract provisions. DRBs have been used on more than a thousand projects in North America beginning in the late 1970s. The key features of the traditional DRB process include the following:

____ (a) **Technical expertise of DRB.** The most commonly used model DRB provisions require that DRB members be experienced with the type of construction involved with the project.

____ (b) **Project familiarity.** In addition to possessing technical expertise, DRB members develop project familiarity by reviewing project documents, making scheduled site visits, and attending periodic progress meetings. Unlike most other forms of dispute resolution, DRB members typically learn about the project and develop familiarity *before* a dispute arises.

____ (c) **Real-time dispute resolution.** DRBs are intended to hear disputes as they arise over the course of the project. This

**Daniel D. McMillan** is a partner with Jones Day, where he is co-chair of the firm's international construction practice. He represents owners, design professionals, and contractors in litigation, arbitration, and contract negotiations. He litigated the first case in the United States to result in a published decision concerning dispute review boards.

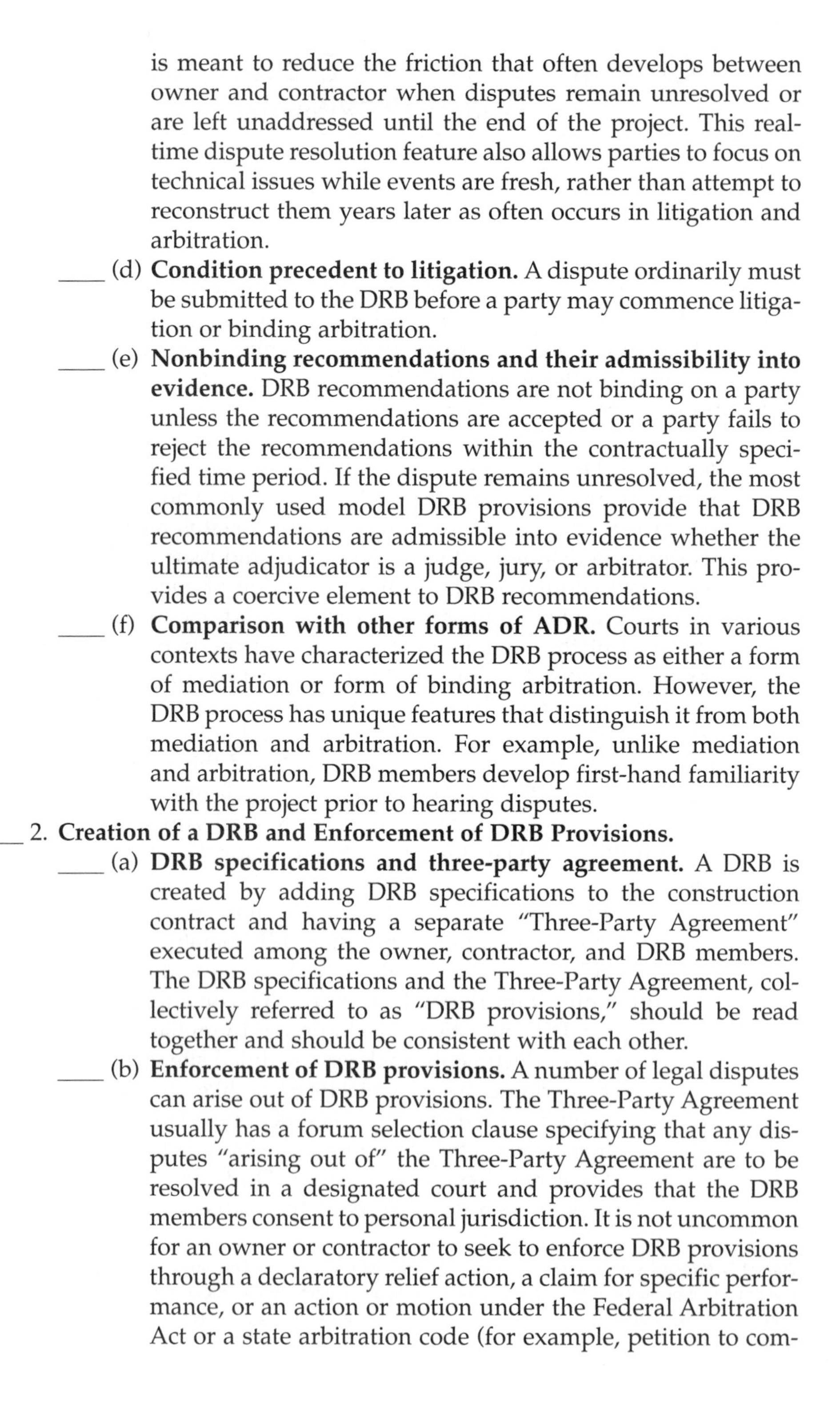

is meant to reduce the friction that often develops between owner and contractor when disputes remain unresolved or are left unaddressed until the end of the project. This real-time dispute resolution feature also allows parties to focus on technical issues while events are fresh, rather than attempt to reconstruct them years later as often occurs in litigation and arbitration.

____ (d) **Condition precedent to litigation.** A dispute ordinarily must be submitted to the DRB before a party may commence litigation or binding arbitration.

____ (e) **Nonbinding recommendations and their admissibility into evidence.** DRB recommendations are not binding on a party unless the recommendations are accepted or a party fails to reject the recommendations within the contractually specified time period. If the dispute remains unresolved, the most commonly used model DRB provisions provide that DRB recommendations are admissible into evidence whether the ultimate adjudicator is a judge, jury, or arbitrator. This provides a coercive element to DRB recommendations.

____ (f) **Comparison with other forms of ADR.** Courts in various contexts have characterized the DRB process as either a form of mediation or form of binding arbitration. However, the DRB process has unique features that distinguish it from both mediation and arbitration. For example, unlike mediation and arbitration, DRB members develop first-hand familiarity with the project prior to hearing disputes.

____ 2. **Creation of a DRB and Enforcement of DRB Provisions.**

____ (a) **DRB specifications and three-party agreement.** A DRB is created by adding DRB specifications to the construction contract and having a separate "Three-Party Agreement" executed among the owner, contractor, and DRB members. The DRB specifications and the Three-Party Agreement, collectively referred to as "DRB provisions," should be read together and should be consistent with each other.

____ (b) **Enforcement of DRB provisions.** A number of legal disputes can arise out of DRB provisions. The Three-Party Agreement usually has a forum selection clause specifying that any disputes "arising out of" the Three-Party Agreement are to be resolved in a designated court and provides that the DRB members consent to personal jurisdiction. It is not uncommon for an owner or contractor to seek to enforce DRB provisions through a declaratory relief action, a claim for specific performance, or an action or motion under the Federal Arbitration Act or a state arbitration code (for example, petition to compel submission of a dispute to the DRB). The applicability of arbitration statutes may itself be the subject of disagreement between the parties given the differences between arbitration and the DRB process.

____ 3. **Model DRB Provisions.** Drafting DRB provisions need not be a made-from-scratch endeavor. There are two basic sources of sample DRB provisions: (1) model DRB provisions prepared by organizations like the Disputes Resolution Board Foundation, the ASCE, the American Arbitration Association, and the International Chamber of Commerce; and (2) DRB provisions from prior projects. Some organizations make model DRB provisions and related guidance available on their websites. See, e.g., the Dispute Resolution Board Foundation website at http://www.drb.org/manual_access.htm; American Arbitration Association website at http://www.adr.org/index2.1jsp. A number of publications discuss differences between available model DRB provisions and serve as a useful resource when drafting DRB provisions.

____ 4. **Drafting Issues.** The drafting issues discussed here are among those that warrant consideration when preparing DRB provisions.

____ (a) **Admissibility of DRB recommendations.** The parties should evaluate whether to modify model DRB provisions to specify that DRB recommendations shall *not* be admissible into evidence. Conventional wisdom holds that a party is more likely to accept unfavorable DRB recommendations or otherwise settle a dispute knowing that unfavorable recommendations would be admissible in subsequent proceedings. On the other hand, the admissibility of DRB recommendations may cause DRB proceedings to become more adversarial, with parties "lawyering up" for DRB hearings. Similarly, a party who believes that the DRB is disposed in its favor may rush to have the DRB hear disputes, not for purposes of attempting to resolve the disputes, but to gain an advantage in litigation. This sort of strategic conduct may be inconsistent with the spirit of the DRB process. Parties should consider these potential trade-offs.

____ (b) **Right to remove DRB members and standards for removal.** At times, a DRB member may lose the respect or confidence of the owner or the contractor. In these circumstances, the owner or contractor may seek to remove one or more members of the DRB to restore confidence in the board. Because a DRB's recommendations are not binding on the parties, it is important that both the owner and the contractor trust and respect the DRB. Otherwise, the DRB's recommendations are less likely to be accepted by the parties and the DRB's effectiveness will suffer. Model DRB provisions vary when it comes to removal of DRB members, however, and should be modified as appropriate.

____ (i) **Contractual right to remove DRB members.** Differences exist among model DRB provisions when it comes to the express right to remove a DRB member. Some model provisions provide that a party-appointed member may be removed only by the party who appointed that member, provide no express right to remove the appointee of the other party, and allow removal of the chairperson only with the concurrence of the two party-appointed members. The parties should consider modifying model provisions to permit the owner or the contractor to remove any of the three DRB members. Doing so permits replacement of any of the DRB members so that mutual confidence in the DRB can be more easily restored.

____ (ii) **Standard for removal of DRB members ("for-cause" versus "at-will").** Some model DRB provisions permit a party to remove its appointee "for cause," while others permit removal "for or without cause." Both of these standards have advantages and disadvantages. The for-cause standard reinforces that DRB members should not be removed blithely, because DRB members build up project familiarity—one of the features of the DRB process that allows for efficient consideration of disputes. When DRB provisions have a for-cause standard, however, the other party may seek to block removal of a DRB member, leading to collateral litigation over the right to remove a DRB member.[1] For this reason, parties may want to ensure that the DRB provisions provide that a party may remove not only its appointee but any of the DRB members "for or without" cause. The risk of this approach is that it can lead to strategic behavior when it comes to replacing DRB members, and replacement of members results in the board's loss of historical knowledge of the project. Of course, if there is a loss of confidence in the DRB, adverse DRB recommendations invariably will be rejected, so it may be better to allow for removal of DRB members without having to show "cause."

____ (c) **DRB qualifications—attorney or retired judge.** None of the model DRB provisions require that a DRB member have any legal training. Instead, DRB members must have technical expertise or experience. A misconception exists that DRBs do not deal with legal issues. In fact, DRBs deal with a host of legal issues. DRBs address contract interpretation questions and elements of claims (for example, differing site condition claims, delay claims, defective specifications, etc.). The parties should consider whether one member of the panel, possibly the chairperson, should be an experienced construction lawyer or retired judge familiar with construction law.

____ (d) **Binding effect of DRB recommendations.** Several drafting points related to the binding effect of DRB recommendations should be considered.

____ (i) **Extending the time to respond.** Although recommendations issued by a traditional DRB are not automatically binding, the recommendations can become binding in the event that a party does not reject the recommendations within the contractually specified time limits. Consider whether the time period for a response should be longer than specified in the model provisions. Many model DRB provisions allow only 14 days to respond to DRB recommendations. Absent a response, the DRB recommendations are deemed to have been accepted by the nonresponding party. Many public agencies cannot accept DRB recommendations that obligate them to increase the contract value without obtaining approval of the agency's board, and the board may not be able to meet within the 14-day window for responding to the recommendations. As a result, the public agency must protect itself by rejecting the DRB recommendations or ask for agreed-upon extensions to respond to the recommendations.

____ (ii) **Hybrid DRBs that issue binding recommendations.** Some owners have modified the conventional DRB process to provide that DRB recommendations are to be automatically binding on certain types of disputes, or disputes below a certain dollar value. This fundamentally changes the role of the DRB and the dynamics of a hearing because the DRB essentially functions as a binding arbitration panel. When a DRB's decisions are to be binding based on a certain dollar threshold, one or the other party may disagree about how to aggregate or disaggregate the value of the claims for purposes of applying the threshold. Careful drafting is required to minimize disputes over whether a "hybrid" DRB is to act in its capacity to issue binding or nonbinding recommendations. The preferred practice is to not authorize DRBs to issue recommendations that are automatically binding.

____ (e) **Limitations on the DRB's jurisdiction and other jurisdictional issues.** Most model DRB provisions do not limit the types of disputes the DRB may consider. This may come as a surprise to a public or even private owner, who simply uses "off-the-shelf" model DRB provisions. Parties should carefully consider whether any express limitations should be placed on the DRB's jurisdiction or the type of disputes that may be heard by the DRB. Even though limiting the DRB's jurisdiction may give rise to disputes over the scope of jurisdiction, it is advisable to consider the "jurisdictional" issues identified here when drafting DRB provisions and modify form agreements as appropriate.

____ (i) **Subject matter carve-outs.** Consideration should be given to whether certain issues should be carved out from the DRB's jurisdiction, including disputes concerning: (a) terminations for cause, (b) project labor agreements, (c) owner-controlled insurance programs, (d) certain statutory claims (for example, prevailing wage claims, violations of a state's false claims act), and (e) other issues that an owner may or may not want to have heard by a DRB (for example, owner's right to direct removal of contractor personnel for safety violations). Drafting clear carve-outs from a DRB's jurisdiction can be easier said than done. For instance, consider an exclusion from jurisdiction for violations of a state's false claims act. If a contractor asserts a differing site condition claim and the owner believes the claim constitutes a "false claim," an issue may arise as to whether the DRB can consider the contractor's differing site condition claim or whether the DRB is only precluded from considering the owner's affirmative claim for violation of the false claims act.

____ (ii) **Dollar limitation on DRB's jurisdiction.** Some owners have modified DRB provisions to limit the jurisdiction of the DRB or alter the role of the DRB, depending on the dollar value of the claim. For example, an owner might limit the DRB's jurisdiction to claims with dollar values below $1 million. Or DRB recommendations, as discussed earlier, might be binding only on claims below a threshold amount. Disputes can arise over (a) how the value of claims are determined, (b) the authority of the DRB to recommend an award in excess of any limitation on its jurisdiction, (c) how a claim is defined and the aggregation or disaggregation of claims for purpose of any dollar limits on jurisdiction, (d) the value (if any) of time only claims (that is, claims seeking an extension of contract completion dates or milestone dates), and (e) who resolves these disputes. Clear drafting can minimize, but may not eliminate, disagreements on such matters.

____ (iii) **Exhaustion of contractual claim procedures.** Parties sometimes disagree over whether contractual claim procedures must be completed prior to a DRB hearing. The DRB provisions should clearly indicate whether there are any preconditions to initiating a DRB hearing and whether the DRB has jurisdiction to consider whether those preconditions have been satisfied or excused.

____ (iv) **Jurisdiction to conduct a hearing in the absence of a party.** Most model DRB provisions do not expressly address whether a DRB may conduct a hearing in the absence of a party. This may create uncertainty about how to proceed should a party refuse to attend a DRB hearing. Model DRB provisions can be clarified in either of two ways. First, model provisions can be modified to make clear that the DRB provisions are "self-executing," in that the DRB may conduct a hearing in the absence of a party, provided adequate notice of the hearing has been given to the party. This has the advantage of not requiring court intervention. Second, model provisions can be modified to require that a court order first be obtained on the propriety of conducting a DRB hearing, when a party refuses to attend. There is no perfect solution to this problem. By not expressly addressing this issue in the DRB provisions, however, the resolution of such standoffs becomes less predictable.

____ (v) **Duration of DRB's operation.** Most model DRB provisions provide that the DRB is to continue to function until the contractor receives final payment. In addition to excluding from the DRB's jurisdiction disputes over termination, drafters of DRB provisions should consider whether the DRB should automatically cease to function where the owner terminates the contract or the contractor. A DRB is designed to ensure prompt resolution of disputes without litigation, to help maintain positive relations between owner and contractor, and to facilitate successful completion of the project. A default termination often signifies a complete breakdown in relations between owner and contractor and frequently yields high-stakes litigation. The propriety of the termination becomes an issue of overriding concern. Thus, it may be advisable, depending on the project, to provide that the DRB is to cease to function upon termination of the contract or the contractor.[2]

____ (vi) **DRB jurisdiction over subcontractors and subcontractor claims.** The traditional DRB only considers subcontractor "pass-through claims" that are asserted by the general contractor against the owner. Some owners have expanded the DRB's jurisdiction to disputes between subcontractors and contractors and between subcontractors and owners. This has been accomplished in a variety of ways, such as specifying in the prime contract that the DRB provisions are to "flow down" to the subcontracts and that subcontractor claims are to be submitted to the DRB. Before expanding the DRB's jurisdiction in this manner, careful consideration needs to be given to how this is to be accomplished. Applying the doctrine of unconscionability, at least one California case has held that the DRB process, as structured and applied to subcontractors who had no role in selecting DRB members, was "presumptively biased and unenforceable as a condition precedent to [a] subcontractor pursuing litigation."[3] An earlier decision of the Southern District of New York, without discussing issues of unconscionability, stayed a subcontractor's claims, holding that the subcontract required that the subcontractor submit claims to the DRB before initiating litigation.[4]

____ (vii) **Who decides the scope of the DRB's jurisdiction?** If a dispute arises between the owner and the contractor over the scope or nature of the DRB's jurisdiction, one party may seek to present the issue to the DRB and another party may seek to have the matter adjudicated by a court. The outcome will depend on the law of the local jurisdiction and the language of the contract. Because DRBs are creatures of contract, drafters of DRB provisions can expressly address this issue or leave it indeterminate, recognizing that doing so may invite collateral litigation over who decides the scope of the DRB's jurisdiction.

## *Notes*

1. See, e.g., *Los Angeles County Metro. Transp. Auth. v. Shea-Kiewit-Kenny,* 59 Cal. App. 4th 676 (1997).

2. See *El Dorado Irrigation Dist.* v. *Traylor Bros., Inc.,* No. CIVS03-949 LKK/GGH, 2006WL 902561, at *9 (E.D. Cal., Apr. 5, 2006) (public owner not required to submit termination dispute to DRB because DRB provisions provided "following termination, the DRB would cease to function").

3. *Sehulster Tunnels/Pre-Con* v. *Traylor Bros. Inc./Obayashi Corp.,* 111 Cal. App. 4th 1328, 1332 (2003).

4. *BAE Automated Sys., Inc.* v. *Morse Diesel Int'l., Inc.,* No. 01 Civ. 0217 (SAS), 2001 U.S. Dist. LEXIS 6682, at *1 (S.D.N.Y. May 21, 2001).

# Checklist 10: Contractors Taking an Assignment of a Trade/Supply Contract from Owner

For contractors faced with a construction contract that requires taking assignment of an owner-held construction or supply agreement, this checklist raises some of the issues necessary for consideration in accepting the assignment and also provides suggestions for minimizing contractor risks when taking such an assignment.

____ 1. **Does the construction contract contain an assignment of a trade/supply agreement?** In the design-bid-build delivery model, a project owner hires an architect or engineer to complete the drawings and specifications before it brings a contractor on board to construct the project. In these situations, in order to maintain the scheduled completion date of the project, the owner oftentimes enters into direct contracts with certain long-lead trade contractors, material suppliers, and/or equipment suppliers, with an eye to assigning such contracts to the general contractor chosen at a later date.

____ 2. **Does the assigned trade/supply agreement pose a risk to the contractor?** As part of an assignment of trade/supply agreements, most owners require the assignee contractor to take full responsibility and liability for the assigned contract. This is risky for the contractor that has no input into the terms and conditions of the assigned contract. Prior to accepting an assignment, the contractor should carefully review any assigned trade or supply agreement for proper allocation of risks and determine whether the terms of the assigned contract provide the contractor with adequate control over the trade contractor/supplier such that it is able to perform its obligations under the construction contract.

____ (a) **Is the trade contractor/supplier creditworthy?** Before going too far down the assignment path, the contractor should conduct a credit check of the company that is proposed to be assigned to it. If the trade contractor/supplier is in a precarious financial position, it may fail to perform. If there are

**Amy Hobbs Iannone** is assistant general counsel and director of risk management for Barton Malow Company, a nationally recognized construction services provider with headquarters in Southfield, Michigan, and regional offices throughout the country. As part of her construction practice, she frequently reviews and negotiates owner–contractor agreements, contractor–subcontractor agreements, and contractor–supplier agreements.

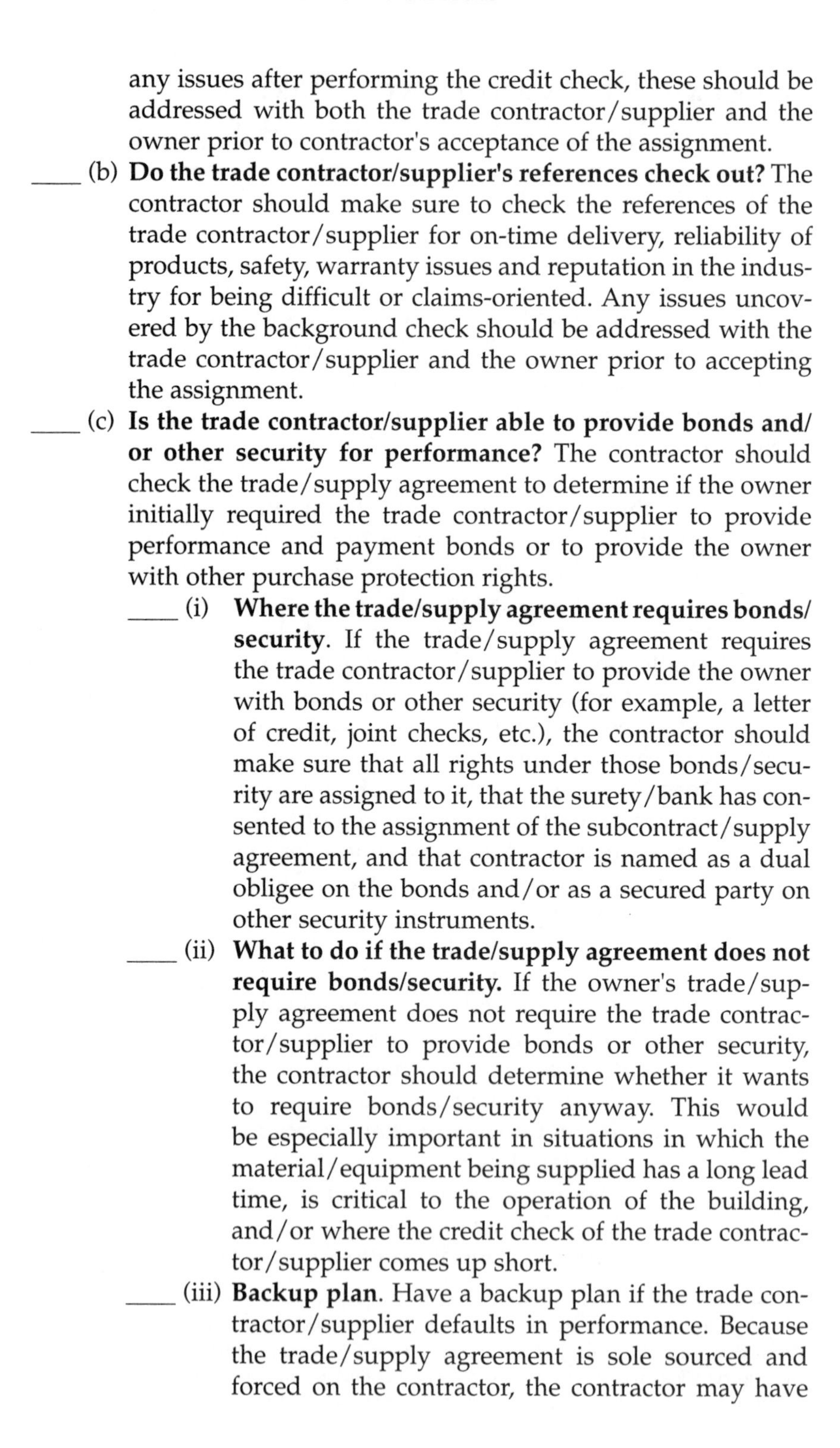

any issues after performing the credit check, these should be addressed with both the trade contractor/supplier and the owner prior to contractor's acceptance of the assignment.

____ (b) **Do the trade contractor/supplier's references check out?** The contractor should make sure to check the references of the trade contractor/supplier for on-time delivery, reliability of products, safety, warranty issues and reputation in the industry for being difficult or claims-oriented. Any issues uncovered by the background check should be addressed with the trade contractor/supplier and the owner prior to accepting the assignment.

____ (c) **Is the trade contractor/supplier able to provide bonds and/or other security for performance?** The contractor should check the trade/supply agreement to determine if the owner initially required the trade contractor/supplier to provide performance and payment bonds or to provide the owner with other purchase protection rights.

____ (i) **Where the trade/supply agreement requires bonds/security**. If the trade/supply agreement requires the trade contractor/supplier to provide the owner with bonds or other security (for example, a letter of credit, joint checks, etc.), the contractor should make sure that all rights under those bonds/security are assigned to it, that the surety/bank has consented to the assignment of the subcontract/supply agreement, and that contractor is named as a dual obligee on the bonds and/or as a secured party on other security instruments.

____ (ii) **What to do if the trade/supply agreement does not require bonds/security.** If the owner's trade/supply agreement does not require the trade contractor/supplier to provide bonds or other security, the contractor should determine whether it wants to require bonds/security anyway. This would be especially important in situations in which the material/equipment being supplied has a long lead time, is critical to the operation of the building, and/or where the credit check of the trade contractor/supplier comes up short.

____ (iii) **Backup plan**. Have a backup plan if the trade contractor/supplier defaults in performance. Because the trade/supply agreement is sole sourced and forced on the contractor, the contractor may have an argument that such default is an excusable delay under the prime agreement. The contractor should review the prime agreement and prevailing laws carefully for provisions that would assist in arguing excused performance.

____ (d) **Is there a promise of indemnification in the trade/supply agreement to the benefit of the contractor?** Most contractors impose strict defense and indemnification requirements on their subcontractors/suppliers. Such requirements are an important risk-transfer device, and the contractor should make sure that where the assigned agreement does not contain an indemnification/defense clause in its favor, that such clause is added to the agreement in the process of assignment.

____ (e) **Does the trade/supply agreement contain adequate insurance requirements?** Most contractors have strict minimum insurance requirements that they expect their subcontractors/suppliers to meet, including providing worker's compensation, business automobile liability, and standard commercial general liability insurance naming the contractor as an additional insured. If the trade/supply agreement does not require adequate limits or coverage, the contractor should make sure that these provisions are modified in the process of assignment.

____ (f) **Is the trade contractor/supplier bound to a schedule that is compatible with the contractor's schedule?** Because time is typically of the essence in a construction contract, the contractor must be assured that the assigned trade/supply agreement requires the trade contractor/supplier to deliver in a timely manner such that contractor can deliver its services in accordance with the schedule it promised in the prime agreement. If there are any differences between the assigned trade contractor's/supplier's schedule and the contractor's schedule, these need to be addressed and resolved prior to taking the assignment.

____ (g) **Are the warranties contained in the trade/supply agreement compatible with the warranties in the prime agreement?** It is very important to compare the warranties provided in the trade contract/supply agreement with the warranties in the contract documents that bind the contractor. Oftentimes, the trade contractor's/supplier's warranty obligations are not as broad as the contractor's warranty obligations to the owner. If, after review, the contractor

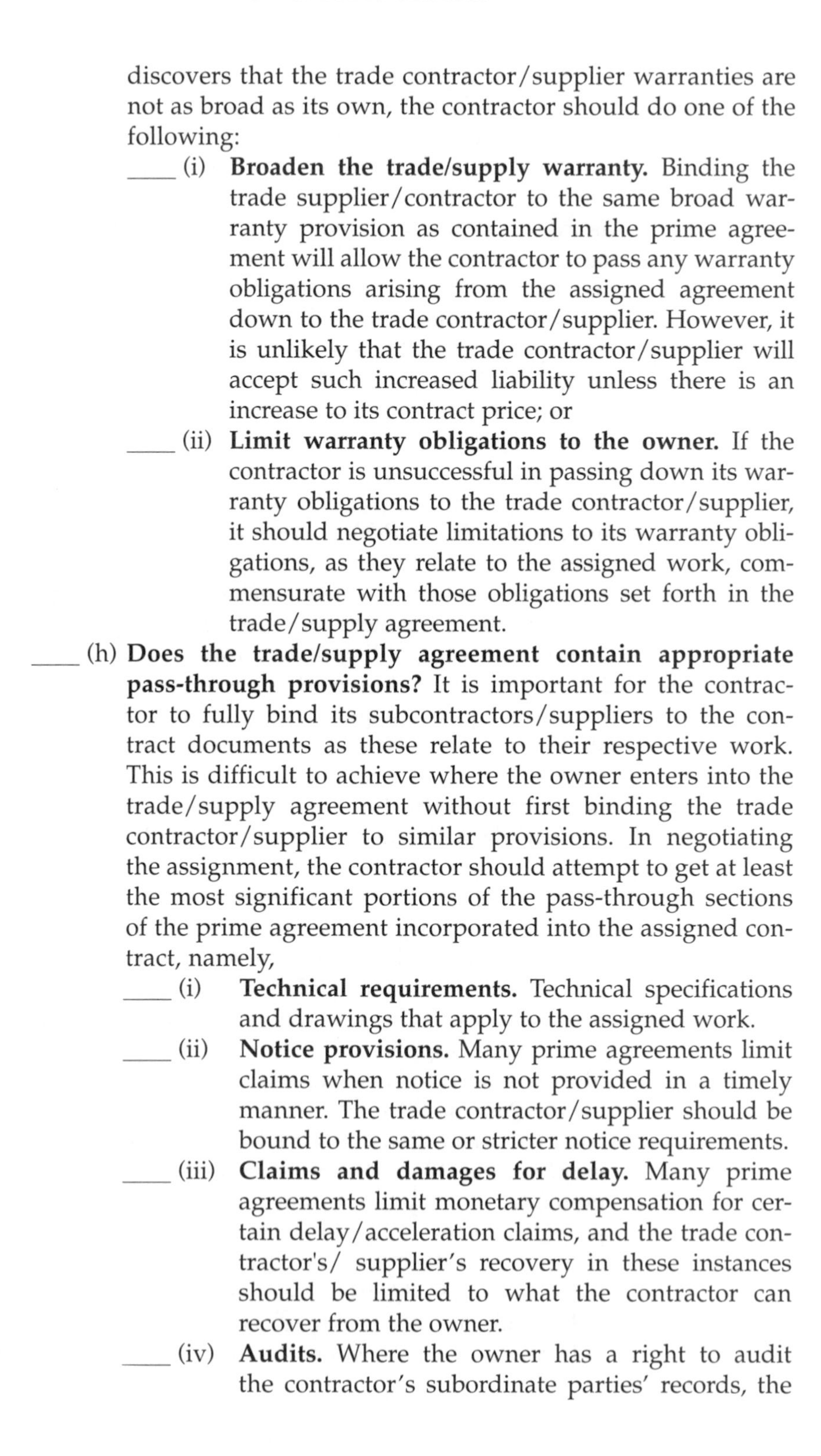

discovers that the trade contractor/supplier warranties are not as broad as its own, the contractor should do one of the following:

____ (i) **Broaden the trade/supply warranty.** Binding the trade supplier/contractor to the same broad warranty provision as contained in the prime agreement will allow the contractor to pass any warranty obligations arising from the assigned agreement down to the trade contractor/supplier. However, it is unlikely that the trade contractor/supplier will accept such increased liability unless there is an increase to its contract price; or

____ (ii) **Limit warranty obligations to the owner.** If the contractor is unsuccessful in passing down its warranty obligations to the trade contractor/supplier, it should negotiate limitations to its warranty obligations, as they relate to the assigned work, commensurate with those obligations set forth in the trade/supply agreement.

____ (h) **Does the trade/supply agreement contain appropriate pass-through provisions?** It is important for the contractor to fully bind its subcontractors/suppliers to the contract documents as these relate to their respective work. This is difficult to achieve where the owner enters into the trade/supply agreement without first binding the trade contractor/supplier to similar provisions. In negotiating the assignment, the contractor should attempt to get at least the most significant portions of the pass-through sections of the prime agreement incorporated into the assigned contract, namely,

____ (i) **Technical requirements.** Technical specifications and drawings that apply to the assigned work.

____ (ii) **Notice provisions.** Many prime agreements limit claims when notice is not provided in a timely manner. The trade contractor/supplier should be bound to the same or stricter notice requirements.

____ (iii) **Claims and damages for delay.** Many prime agreements limit monetary compensation for certain delay/acceleration claims, and the trade contractor's/ supplier's recovery in these instances should be limited to what the contractor can recover from the owner.

____ (iv) **Audits.** Where the owner has a right to audit the contractor's subordinate parties' records, the

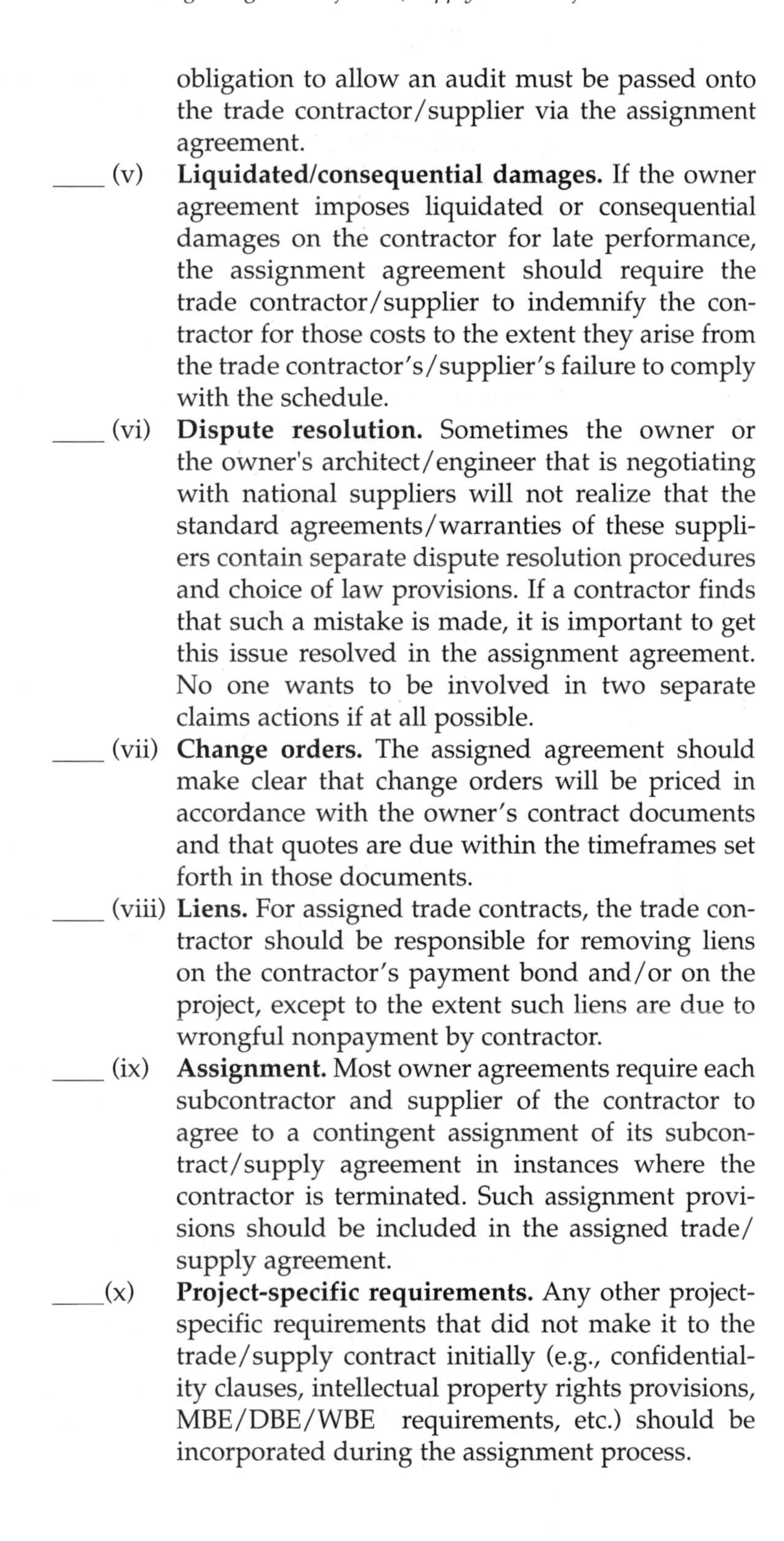

obligation to allow an audit must be passed onto the trade contractor/supplier via the assignment agreement.

____ (v) **Liquidated/consequential damages.** If the owner agreement imposes liquidated or consequential damages on the contractor for late performance, the assignment agreement should require the trade contractor/supplier to indemnify the contractor for those costs to the extent they arise from the trade contractor's/supplier's failure to comply with the schedule.

____ (vi) **Dispute resolution.** Sometimes the owner or the owner's architect/engineer that is negotiating with national suppliers will not realize that the standard agreements/warranties of these suppliers contain separate dispute resolution procedures and choice of law provisions. If a contractor finds that such a mistake is made, it is important to get this issue resolved in the assignment agreement. No one wants to be involved in two separate claims actions if at all possible.

____ (vii) **Change orders.** The assigned agreement should make clear that change orders will be priced in accordance with the owner's contract documents and that quotes are due within the timeframes set forth in those documents.

____ (viii) **Liens.** For assigned trade contracts, the trade contractor should be responsible for removing liens on the contractor's payment bond and/or on the project, except to the extent such liens are due to wrongful nonpayment by contractor.

____ (ix) **Assignment.** Most owner agreements require each subcontractor and supplier of the contractor to agree to a contingent assignment of its subcontract/supply agreement in instances where the contractor is terminated. Such assignment provisions should be included in the assigned trade/supply agreement.

____ (x) **Project-specific requirements.** Any other project-specific requirements that did not make it to the trade/supply contract initially (e.g., confidentiality clauses, intellectual property rights provisions, MBE/DBE/WBE requirements, etc.) should be incorporated during the assignment process.

____ (i) **Are the payment provisions in the trade/supply agreement compatible with the payment schedule in the prime agreement?** Where the owner enters into the trade/supply agreement directly, it will typically promise to pay the trade contractor/supplier within a reasonable number of days of owner's receipt and approval of the trade contractor's/supplier's invoice. However, where the contractor takes assignment of that agreement, it may not be able to honor such payment provisions (because similar timeframes for payment to the contractor will likely be included in its agreement with owner). As such, it is important for the contractor to modify the trade/supply agreement's payment provisions in the process of the assignment. Ideally, these provisions will be replaced with a typical pay-if-paid arrangement, where payment to the subcontractor/supplier is conditioned upon contractor's payment from the owner. In an assignment situation, the contractor has very good argument back to a complaining trade contractor/supplier that by its agreement to enter into the direct agreement with the owner in the first place, it already consented to relying "solely" on the owner's credit for payment.

____ (j) **Does the trade/supply agreement contain similar default and termination provisions as those contained in the prime agreement?** Sometimes owner-direct agreements do not contain the same type of default and termination provisions that the contractor expects to be included in its subcontracts or supply agreements. The contractor should review the trade/supply agreement for missing default and termination terms. Terms that are often missing are details of the contractor's remedies for a default, including supplementing workforce, letting portions of the work to others, termination for convenience, demands for adequate assurances of future performance, and waivers of profit and overhead mark-ups on uncompleted work. The contractor should also make sure that time periods for declaring default and curing default are consistent between the trade/supply agreement and the prime agreement. So, for example, if the owner may declare the contractor in "default" for failure to perform after 7 days' notice and opportunity to cure, the trade/supply agreement should contain a provision requiring the trade contractor/supplier to cure the default in at least the same time period.

____ 3. **How can the contractor minimize the risks of taking an assignment of trade/supply contracts in a competitive bidding situation?** Competitive bidding situations pose unique risks where an assignment of a trade/supply contract is contemplated. Sometimes contractors in competitive bidding situations do not have the luxury of actually reviewing and/or negotiating a trade/supply agreement that is proposed to be assigned. In these situations, it is important for the contractor to consider the following methods of minimizing its exposure:

____ (a) **Qualify the bid.** The contractor should qualify its bid by making clear that its acceptance of the proposed assignment is based on its review and approval of the terms and conditions of the trade/supply agreement and the assigning language. In the alternative, the contractor could qualify its bid by stating that "the contractor's obligations to the owner for the assigned trade/supply scope of work shall be no broader than the obligations set forth in the contract to be assigned." Or, a third alternative would be for the contractor to qualify its bid disclaiming all liability or responsibility for the assigned trade/supply agreement. This option is desirable where the assigned equipment/trade is of a high-risk nature. Of course, the contractor needs to weigh the risk of taking on the assignment versus the possibility of being disqualified from the competitive bidding process for submitting a qualified bid.

____ (b) **Contact the trade contractor/supplier.** In the alternative, the contractor could contact the owner's trade contractor/supplier directly to try to negotiate reasonable terms for the assigned contract, prior to submitting the bid, eliminating the need to qualify the bid.

____ (c) **Factor the costs of the assignment into bid.** When determining general conditions budgets and mark-ups, the contractor should not forget to include the price of the assigned trade/supply agreement in its bid. Because the contractor has to manage the work of the assigned contract, it should be paid for doing so.

____ 4. **What techniques should be used by the contractor in negotiating the assignment?** Once the strengths and weaknesses of the underlying trade/supply agreement are assessed, the contractor should either (a) negotiate the important provisions back into the trade/supply agreement, using the assignment agreement as the mechanism of incorporating these provisions, or (b) negotiate the risky provisions out of the prime agreement.

____ (a) **Important points of negotiation.** In addition to including/negotiating the subcontract/supply provisions listed earlier, other important issues to address in the assignment agreement include:

____ (i) **Risks prior and subsequent to the assignment.** It is important for the assignment to make clear which party (owner or contractor) takes responsibility for the work performed by the trade contractor/supplier prior to the assignment, including determining which party will pay any pending invoices and which party is responsible for paying the retention to the trade contractor/supplier.

____ (ii) **Allowances.** The parties need to define how allowances, unit prices, and other changes that were initially included in the trade/supply agreement will be handled post-assignment.

____ (iii) **Limitations of liability.** The assignment agreement should include any appropriate releases of liability as the parties have negotiated and agreed upon.

____ (iv) **Controlling document statement.** The assignment agreement should make clear that it modifies both the prime contract and the trade/supply agreement, and its provisions control over any contrary provisions contained in either of those agreements.

____ (v) **Proper execution.** The assignment agreement should be executed by authorized representatives of the owner, the contractor, and the trade contractor/supplier.

# Checklist 11: Warranties—Creation, Enforceability, and Assignability

The following is a checklist for negotiating or enforcing a warranty provision by contractors. The checklist identifies many issues that should be considered related to warranties. In addition, many of the points raised in this checklist will assist subcontractors, suppliers, and vendors negotiating or enforcing warranties.

____ 1. **Creation: What is warranted?** A warranty is generally intended to address the issues owners encounter in convincing the contractor to return to the project and remedy defective work after final payment. Basically, all that is required in a warranty is that the contractor's work will conform to the requirements of the contract documents.

____ (a) **Contractor's qualifications.** Contractors will want to qualify that the work only has to "substantially" conform to the contract documents to avoid the owner's insistence on strict compliance.

____ (b) **Avoid warranty for defective work.** Contractors should avoid broadly warranting against "defective work," or risk inviting responsibility for all defects on the project, regardless of whether the owner can establish that the contractor actually caused the defect.

____ 2. **What is not warranted?** Take time to specifically define what is not warranted.

____ (a) **Contract documents.** Contractors will want to include two exclusions premised on the owner's implied warranty of the sufficiency of the contract documents (Spearin Doctrine) and correspondingly exclude responsibility for design errors. Contractors should endeavor to exclude warranty for issues caused by owner-furnished or -specified equipment or materials.

____ (b) **Owner's use.** Contractors should exclude the obligation to remedy damage or defect caused by owner abuse, modifications not executed by the contractor, improper or insuffi-

---

**Troy Michael Miller** is a partner in the litigation and construction section of Bose McKinney & Evans LLP, Indianapolis, Indiana. His practice focuses on representing various participants in the construction process, including design professionals, owners, general contractors, and subcontractors related to warranty and other issues.

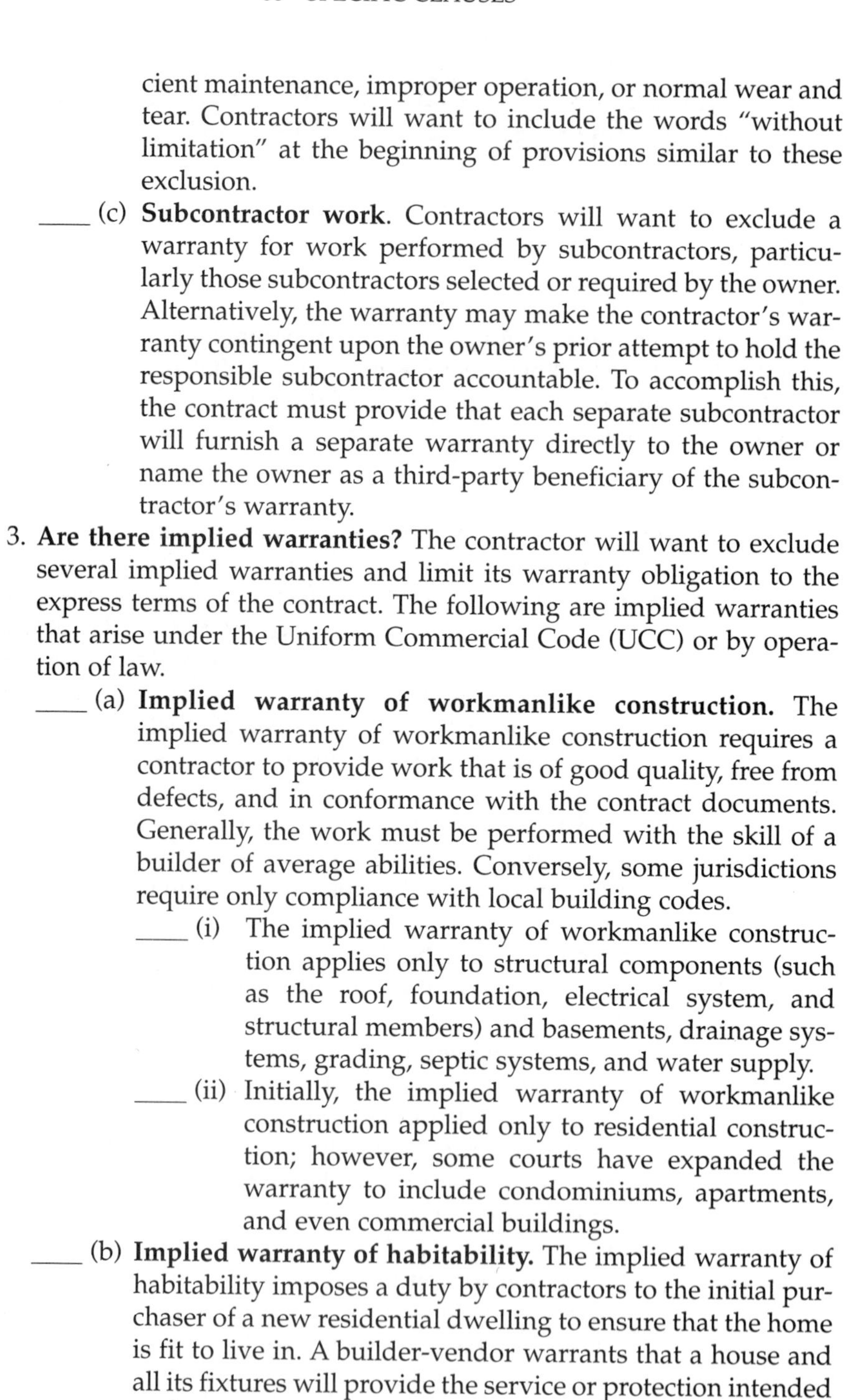

cient maintenance, improper operation, or normal wear and tear. Contractors will want to include the words "without limitation" at the beginning of provisions similar to these exclusion.

____ (c) **Subcontractor work**. Contractors will want to exclude a warranty for work performed by subcontractors, particularly those subcontractors selected or required by the owner. Alternatively, the warranty may make the contractor's warranty contingent upon the owner's prior attempt to hold the responsible subcontractor accountable. To accomplish this, the contract must provide that each separate subcontractor will furnish a separate warranty directly to the owner or name the owner as a third-party beneficiary of the subcontractor's warranty.

____ 3. **Are there implied warranties?** The contractor will want to exclude several implied warranties and limit its warranty obligation to the express terms of the contract. The following are implied warranties that arise under the Uniform Commercial Code (UCC) or by operation of law.

____ (a) **Implied warranty of workmanlike construction.** The implied warranty of workmanlike construction requires a contractor to provide work that is of good quality, free from defects, and in conformance with the contract documents. Generally, the work must be performed with the skill of a builder of average abilities. Conversely, some jurisdictions require only compliance with local building codes.

____ (i) The implied warranty of workmanlike construction applies only to structural components (such as the roof, foundation, electrical system, and structural members) and basements, drainage systems, grading, septic systems, and water supply.

____ (ii) Initially, the implied warranty of workmanlike construction applied only to residential construction; however, some courts have expanded the warranty to include condominiums, apartments, and even commercial buildings.

____ (b) **Implied warranty of habitability.** The implied warranty of habitability imposes a duty by contractors to the initial purchaser of a new residential dwelling to ensure that the home is fit to live in. A builder-vendor warrants that a house and all its fixtures will provide the service or protection intended under normal use.

____ (c) **Implied warranty of fitness for a particular purpose.** This UCC implied warranty imposes a warranty where the seller,

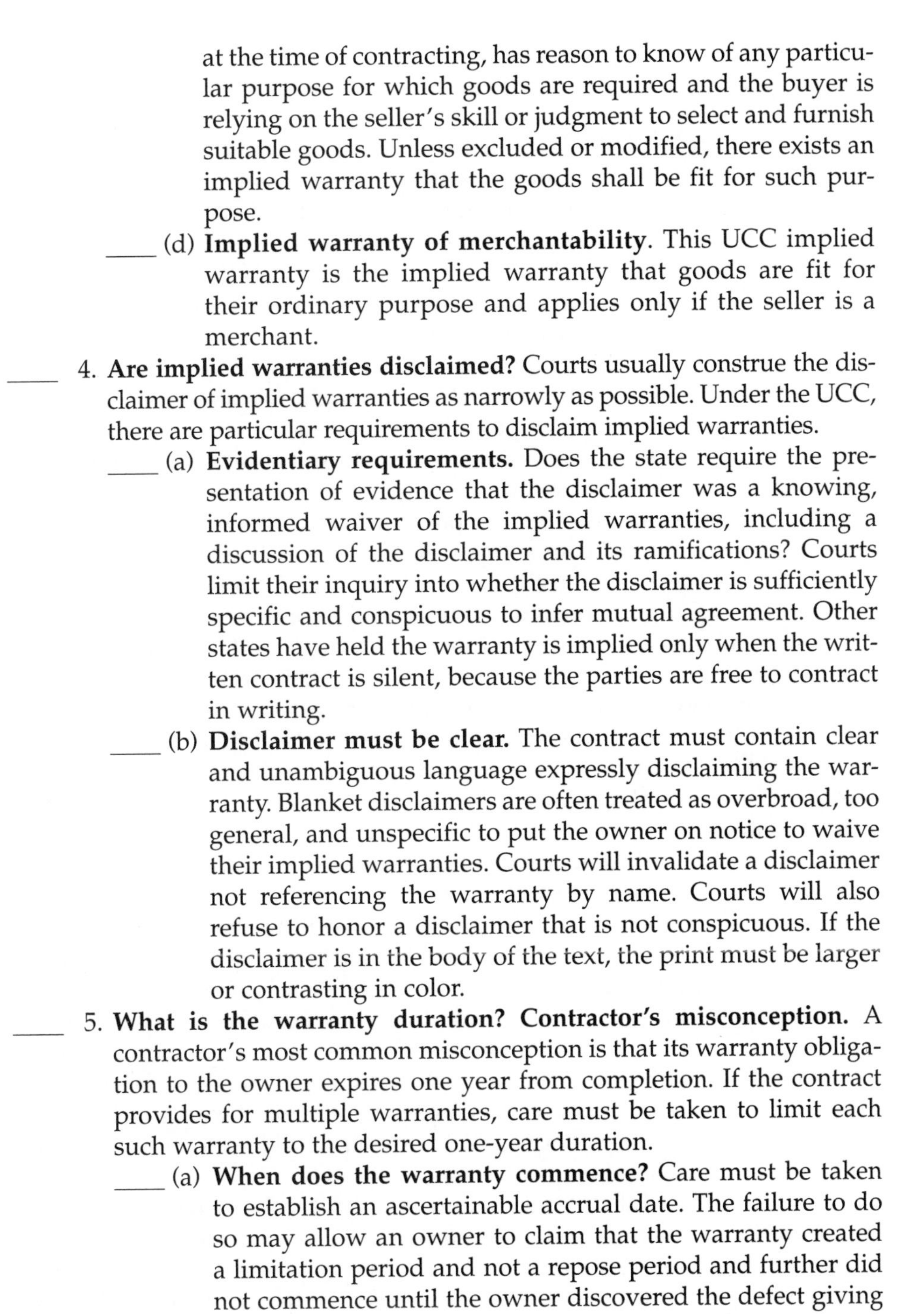

at the time of contracting, has reason to know of any particular purpose for which goods are required and the buyer is relying on the seller's skill or judgment to select and furnish suitable goods. Unless excluded or modified, there exists an implied warranty that the goods shall be fit for such purpose.

____ (d) **Implied warranty of merchantability**. This UCC implied warranty is the implied warranty that goods are fit for their ordinary purpose and applies only if the seller is a merchant.

____ 4. **Are implied warranties disclaimed?** Courts usually construe the disclaimer of implied warranties as narrowly as possible. Under the UCC, there are particular requirements to disclaim implied warranties.

____ (a) **Evidentiary requirements.** Does the state require the presentation of evidence that the disclaimer was a knowing, informed waiver of the implied warranties, including a discussion of the disclaimer and its ramifications? Courts limit their inquiry into whether the disclaimer is sufficiently specific and conspicuous to infer mutual agreement. Other states have held the warranty is implied only when the written contract is silent, because the parties are free to contract in writing.

____ (b) **Disclaimer must be clear.** The contract must contain clear and unambiguous language expressly disclaiming the warranty. Blanket disclaimers are often treated as overbroad, too general, and unspecific to put the owner on notice to waive their implied warranties. Courts will invalidate a disclaimer not referencing the warranty by name. Courts will also refuse to honor a disclaimer that is not conspicuous. If the disclaimer is in the body of the text, the print must be larger or contrasting in color.

____ 5. **What is the warranty duration? Contractor's misconception.** A contractor's most common misconception is that its warranty obligation to the owner expires one year from completion. If the contract provides for multiple warranties, care must be taken to limit each such warranty to the desired one-year duration.

____ (a) **When does the warranty commence?** Care must be taken to establish an ascertainable accrual date. The failure to do so may allow an owner to claim that the warranty created a limitation period and not a repose period and further did not commence until the owner discovered the defect giving rise to the claim.

____ (i) Provisions such as AIA A201 Article 13.7 attempt to establish accrual dates; however, the language

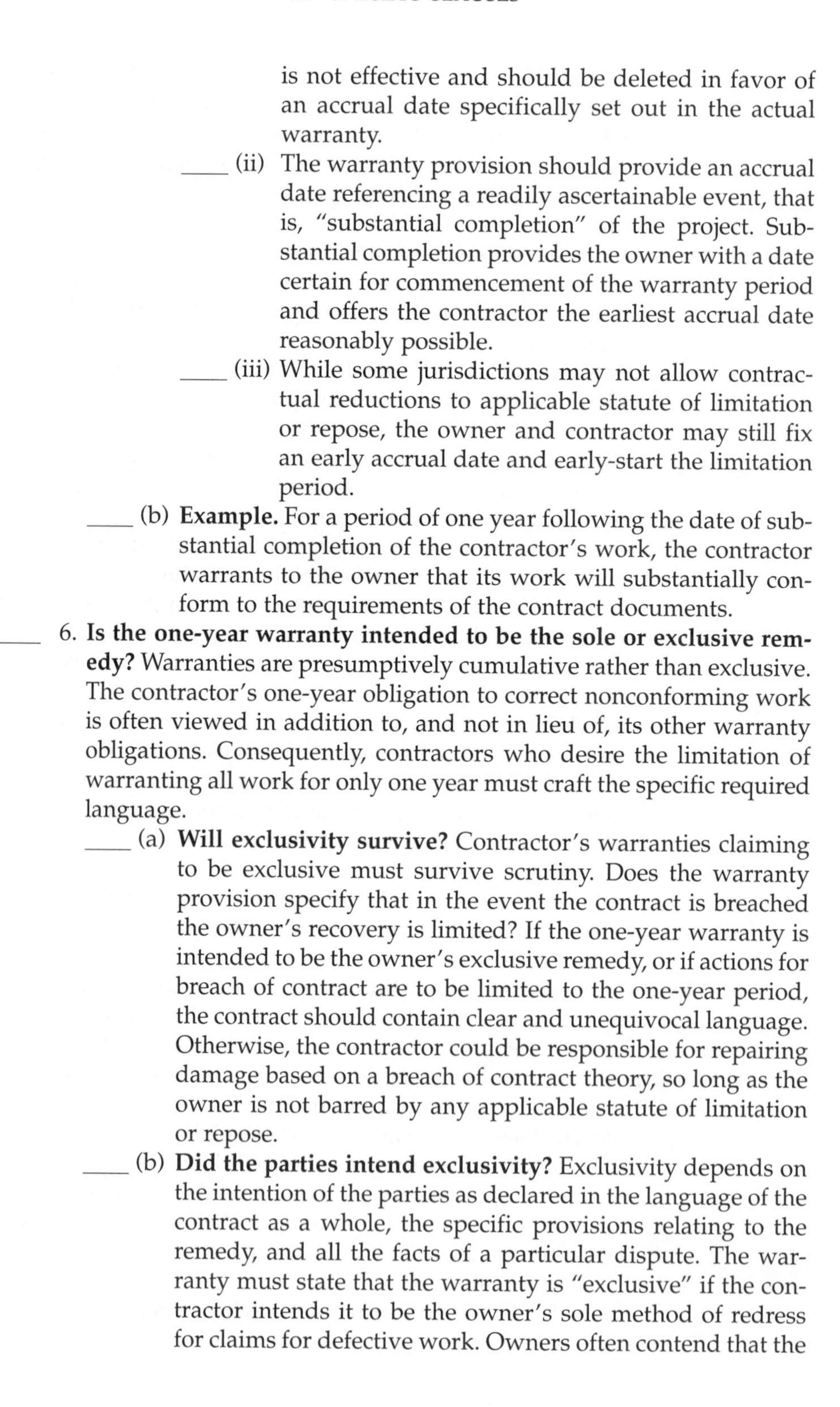

is not effective and should be deleted in favor of an accrual date specifically set out in the actual warranty.

____ (ii) The warranty provision should provide an accrual date referencing a readily ascertainable event, that is, "substantial completion" of the project. Substantial completion provides the owner with a date certain for commencement of the warranty period and offers the contractor the earliest accrual date reasonably possible.

____ (iii) While some jurisdictions may not allow contractual reductions to applicable statute of limitation or repose, the owner and contractor may still fix an early accrual date and early-start the limitation period.

____ (b) **Example.** For a period of one year following the date of substantial completion of the contractor's work, the contractor warrants to the owner that its work will substantially conform to the requirements of the contract documents.

____ 6. **Is the one-year warranty intended to be the sole or exclusive remedy?** Warranties are presumptively cumulative rather than exclusive. The contractor's one-year obligation to correct nonconforming work is often viewed in addition to, and not in lieu of, its other warranty obligations. Consequently, contractors who desire the limitation of warranting all work for only one year must craft the specific required language.

____ (a) **Will exclusivity survive?** Contractor's warranties claiming to be exclusive must survive scrutiny. Does the warranty provision specify that in the event the contract is breached the owner's recovery is limited? If the one-year warranty is intended to be the owner's exclusive remedy, or if actions for breach of contract are to be limited to the one-year period, the contract should contain clear and unequivocal language. Otherwise, the contractor could be responsible for repairing damage based on a breach of contract theory, so long as the owner is not barred by any applicable statute of limitation or repose.

____ (b) **Did the parties intend exclusivity?** Exclusivity depends on the intention of the parties as declared in the language of the contract as a whole, the specific provisions relating to the remedy, and all the facts of a particular dispute. The warranty must state that the warranty is "exclusive" if the contractor intends it to be the owner's sole method of redress for claims for defective work. Owners often contend that the contractor's one-year warranty supplements the contract's other warranties and that a claim for breach of the contract warranty is only one of several actions that an owner can pursue for the contractor's defective work.

____ (c) **Does the warranty include an order of precedence clause?** The warranty must contain an order of precedence clause, which mandates that, in the event of a claimed defect, the one-year warranty provisions control over any other potential warranty found elsewhere in the contract.

____ (d) **Exclusivity example.** For a period of one year following the date of substantial completion, the contractor will, at its election, repair or replace defective work unless said repair or replacement would be economically wasteful under the circumstances, in which event contractor shall compensate owner for the diminished value of contractor's work. The contractor's obligation to repair or replace defective work (or, at its election, compensate the owner for the diminished value of contractor's work) provides the *sole* and *exclusive remedy* to, and provides the *sole* and *exclusive damages* of owner for any cause of action asserted against contractor arising out of or relating to contractor's work, whether owner seeks to recover from contractor under the theories of contract, warranty, tort, or any other theory. In no event shall contractor be liable for special, indirect, incidental, or consequential damages.

____ 7. **Is the warranty enforceable?** As stated previously, the warranty correction period is generally intended to address the problem that owners encounter in convincing the contractor to return to the project and repair defective work after final payment.

____ (a) **Who can enforce the warranty?** Contractor should resist extending its warranty to anyone other than owner who is paying for the warranty.

____ (b) **What is the burden to enforce the warranty?** To invoke the correction obligation, the owner need not prove why a particular system failed but only that it did indeed fail. The warranty correction period is an agreement by the contractor to repair or replace the faulty work regardless of the reason for the defect so long it is not due to abuse or neglect by the owner. If the contractor fails to honor its warranty, the owner does not have the burden of proving the cause of the defect.

____ 8. **What action is required to timely assert a claim?** The warranty may be restricted to not only claims arising or discovered within the warranty period but restricted further to those claims made or initiated by the owner within the warranty period. Without this requirement, owners may argue that having discovered the defects within the warranty period, the owner need only to satisfy the applicable statutory limitation period.

____ (a) **What notice is required?** The warranty should require that the owner provide the contractor with timely written notice of any alleged defect and that the provision of written notice is a "condition precedent" to any claim by the owner against the contractor arising out of or related to alleged defective work. The owner's failure to promptly notify the contractor of the alleged defect may result in waiver by the owner of both its right to demand remedial performance under the warranty and to make a claim for damages for its breach.

____ (b) **Right to cure.** The right to cure is a fundamental contractor right. The warranty notice requirement should allow the contractor the opportunity to observe and document the alleged defect before the defective work is corrected.

____ (c) **Extension of the warranty period.** The contractor should add language to the warranty to clarify that the warranty period within which the owner is required to make a claim shall not be extended by contractor's corrective work unless the parties expressly agree otherwise in writing. Some states hold that the statutory period of repose may be "tolled" if the contractor fails to respond to repair requests, promises to make repairs, or is unsuccessful.

____ 9. **Assignability: Is the warranty assignable?**

____ (a) **Manufacturer's warranties.** Owner will want to require that the contractor assign to the owner at the time of final completion of the work any and all manufacturer's warranties relating to materials and labor used in the work. In addition, the contractor should be required to perform work in such a manner so as to preserve any and all such manufacturer's warranties. The owner should receive assignment of warranties upon completion and acceptance of the work, and contractor should do nothing to otherwise invalidate the warranties.

____ (b) **Statutory warranties.** In addition to the contractual warranties provided by the contractor to the owner and from the contractor's subcontractors, vendors, and material suppliers to the contractor and ultimately the owner, the work at the project may be the beneficiary of additional warranties required by statute, including but not limited to subsequent purchasers of the project. The parties should review any statutory warranties related to the work and adjust

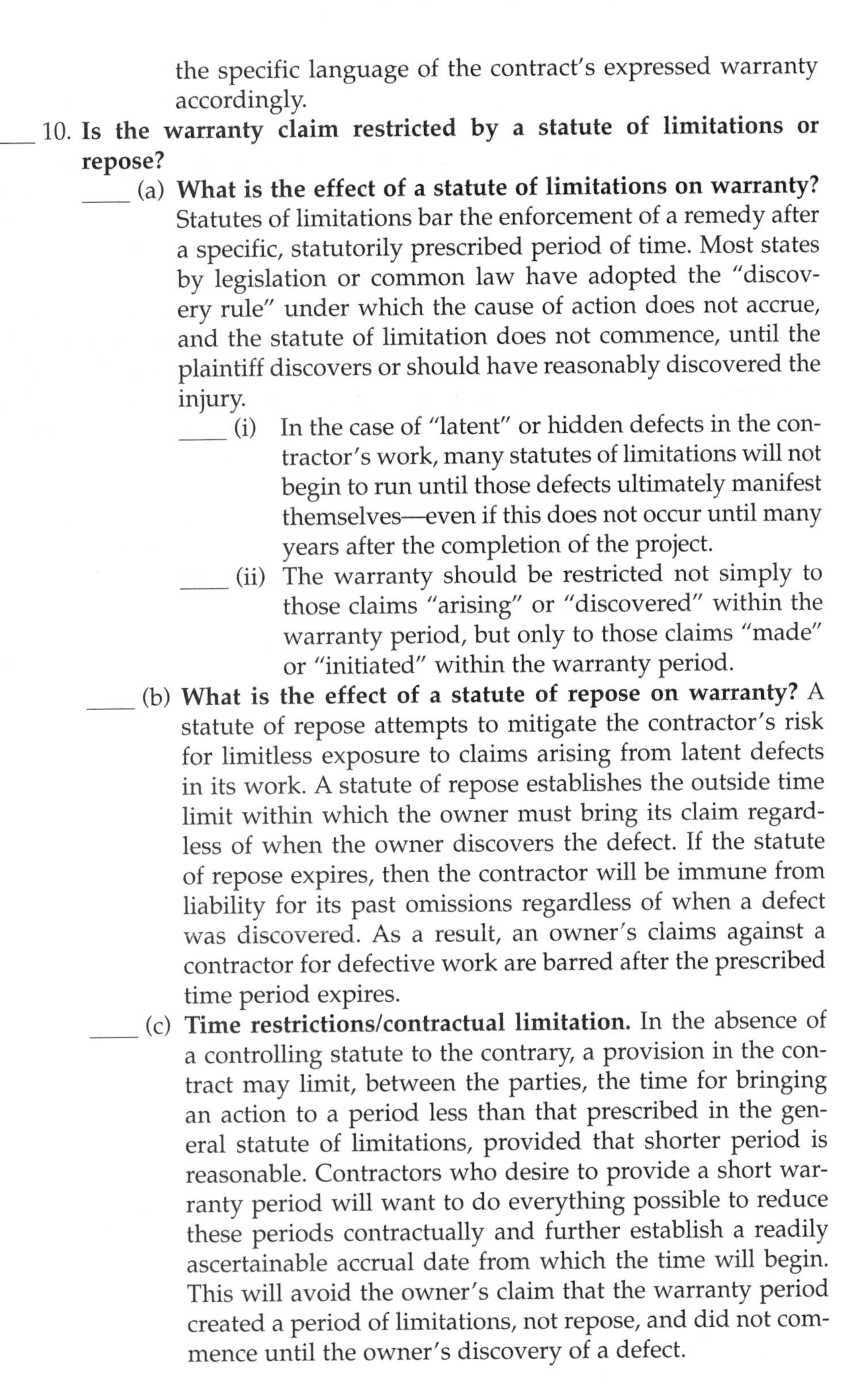

the specific language of the contract's expressed warranty accordingly.

____ 10. **Is the warranty claim restricted by a statute of limitations or repose?**

____ (a) **What is the effect of a statute of limitations on warranty?** Statutes of limitations bar the enforcement of a remedy after a specific, statutorily prescribed period of time. Most states by legislation or common law have adopted the "discovery rule" under which the cause of action does not accrue, and the statute of limitation does not commence, until the plaintiff discovers or should have reasonably discovered the injury.

____ (i) In the case of "latent" or hidden defects in the contractor's work, many statutes of limitations will not begin to run until those defects ultimately manifest themselves—even if this does not occur until many years after the completion of the project.

____ (ii) The warranty should be restricted not simply to those claims "arising" or "discovered" within the warranty period, but only to those claims "made" or "initiated" within the warranty period.

____ (b) **What is the effect of a statute of repose on warranty?** A statute of repose attempts to mitigate the contractor's risk for limitless exposure to claims arising from latent defects in its work. A statute of repose establishes the outside time limit within which the owner must bring its claim regardless of when the owner discovers the defect. If the statute of repose expires, then the contractor will be immune from liability for its past omissions regardless of when a defect was discovered. As a result, an owner's claims against a contractor for defective work are barred after the prescribed time period expires.

____ (c) **Time restrictions/contractual limitation.** In the absence of a controlling statute to the contrary, a provision in the contract may limit, between the parties, the time for bringing an action to a period less than that prescribed in the general statute of limitations, provided that shorter period is reasonable. Contractors who desire to provide a short warranty period will want to do everything possible to reduce these periods contractually and further establish a readily ascertainable accrual date from which the time will begin. This will avoid the owner's claim that the warranty period created a period of limitations, not repose, and did not commence until the owner's discovery of a defect.

____ (d) **Final payment waiver.** Contractors should utilize the contract's final payment provisions to effectuate a waiver of all other potential claims against the contractor, and thereby limit an owner's claims to the limited warranty itself. Form agreements provide that the owner's final payment has no effect on its ability to pursue defects. Contractors will want to modify the contract's final payment provision to waive all other potential claims by the owner.

____ (i) **Example**. The making of final payment shall constitute a waiver of all claims by the owner against the contractor, including but not limited to those alleging negligence, defective work, breach of warranty, or failure to comply with the contract documents, except those brought pursuant to the express terms of the contractor's exclusive warranty.

____ (e) **Bonding considerations.** Bonded contractors must include a specific release of their surety. Even though contractors may initially avoid liability by virtue of the warranty period, the contractor may ultimately remain liable for the defective work as a result of its indemnification obligation to its bond surety.

# Checklist 12: Protecting Intellectual Property Rights

Copyright and patent laws are derived from the U.S. Constitution, Article 1, § 8, cl. 8. Trademarks, however, are created by federal statutes to protect free enterprise.

____ 1. **Protecting Copyrights.** Regardless of a construction project's size and duration, disputes relating to the ownership of the plans and specifications may arise between the owner, the design professional and/or the contractor. These disputes typically arise under copyright law. Determining at the onset which party owns the tangible work product of the collaborative efforts of various parties, who may or may not be in privity, can minimize the adverse impact of costly disputes. Depending on the roles of the parties involved in the project, the ownership of these very valuable documents may vary from project to project. The 1976 Copyright Act, 17 U.S.C. § 101 et seq., created a unified protection system to provide authors with statutory protection at the inception of when the work was reduced to a concrete structure. The act protects all forms of expressions fixed in a tangible medium. The basic concept of copyright law is originality and not the idea itself.

____ (a) **Creation of copyright.**

____ (i) **What is a copyright?** Unlike patents and trademarks, copyrights are not examined as a prerequisite to federal registration. The author obtains the right upon creation, regardless of whether the author subsequently seeks federal protection. Federal registration, however, grants the author additional remedies if the work is infringed. Copyright protection can be extended to anything that can be expressed in a tangible form.

____ (ii) **Who is the author of the work?** An author of a copyright is any person(s) or entity(s) that origi-

---

**Rashida Y. V. MacMurray's** practice includes construction litigation, contract drafting and negotiation, and advising clients on project and contract administration. She has a B.S. in architecture and an M.E. in civil engineering. Before practicing law, she worked as a project engineer and a project manager. She represents a wide array of construction industry professionals and began her legal career prosecuting patent applications, preparing patent opinions, and conducting intellectual property asset evaluation in the mechanical arts technology.

nates and assumes responsibility for an expression or communication. The copyright author can be defined as the original creator of any work; be it written, painted, sculpted, recorded, photographed, or filmed. Copyright protection is self-executing. The author automatically obtains copyright protection when the work is created (that is, fixed in a tangible medium).

____ (iii) **What are the exclusive rights afforded to a copyright owner?** A copyright owner has the exclusive right to do or authorize any of the following: (a) reproduce the copyrighted work in copies; (b) prepare derivate works based upon the copyrighted work; (c) distribute copies of the copyrighted work to the public by sale or transfer of ownership; (d) perform the copyrighted work publicly; (e) include images of the copyrighted work in a motion picture, or display the copyrighted work publicly; and (f) perform a copyrighted sound recording by digital audio transmission. The first two rights are violated regardless of whether the infringing actor does it in public or in private. The remaining four rights constitute infringement of the owner's rights only if the actor does it in public.

____ (iv) **What is fair use?** In limited circumstances, a third party may use the copyrighted work without the permission of the author. Fair use of the copyrighted work, including reproduction, is permitted for criticism, comment, news reporting, teaching, scholarship, or research. For example, a teacher who makes a copy of a copyrighted work to use as a reference to teach his or her class does not violate the author's copyright because the use of the copyrighted work satisfies the definition of fair use. In contrast, a teacher who copies and sells the copyrighted work violates the copyright of the author. In the latter example, the teacher is receiving a profit for the unauthorized use of copyrighted work to the detriment of the author. Fair use is determined on a case-by-case basis using the following factors:

____ a. Is the copyrighted material going to be used for nonprofit educational purposes?

____ b. What is the nature of the copyrighted work? For example, how is the copyrighted work used? In the previously referenced example, the copyrighted work was used to share an important lesson with students.

____ c. What is the amount and substantiality of the portion used in relation to the copyrighted work as a whole?

____ d. What is the effect of the use upon the potential market for or value of the copyrighted work? In other words, does the copying reduce the value of the copyrighted work?

____ (v) **What is a "work for hire"?** A work for hire is defined as a work created by an employee within the scope of employment or specially commissioned. Written agreement, issued by all parties, is a prerequisite to the classification of a work for hire. The default rule is that the original author is the copyright owner.

____ (b) **Subject matter of copyright.**

____ (i) **What is the subject matter of a copyright?** Copyright protection can be extended to any literary work, musical work (including the accompanying words), and dramatic works (including accompanying music); pantomimes and choreographic works; pictorial, graphic, and sculptural works; motion pictures and other audiovisual works; sound recordings; and architectural works.

____ (ii) **What is an "architectural work"?** An architectural work is the design of a building as embodied in any tangible medium of expression, including a building, architectural plans, or drawings. The work includes the overall form as well as the arrangement and composition of spaces and elements in the design but does not include individual standard features. If created on or after December 1, 1990, any architectural work that has not been constructed and/or embodied previously in unpublished plans or drawings is eligible for copyright protection.

____ (c) **Publication.**

____ (i) **Is the work unpublished?** The work is unpublished if it has not been released to the general public.

____ (ii) **Is the work published?** Publication is determined by the first date that the work is offered for sale or other transfer of ownership.

____ 2. **Ownership.**

____ (a) **Can the ownership of copyrighted work be transferred?** A work may be transferred from the author to another party. The transfer may be recorded with the U.S. Copyright Office. The transfer document should include either the actual signature or oath that a true copy was filed in the Copyright Office.

____ (i) **Transfer of ownership via contract?**

____ a. **Is it a preprinted standard agreement?** The American Institute of Architects (AIA) has traditionally provided standard form agreements that address the ownership of intellectual property included in the design professional's plans and specifications. In addition, other professional organizations, such as the Associated General Contractors (AGC) and the Design-Build Institute of America (DBIA), have developed their own series of preprinted contract agreements. Each agreement treats the ownership of certain intellectual property differently.

____ b. **Is it a negotiated contract?** If the parties negotiated the terms and conditions of the agreement, was an explicit provision relating to the ownership of the plans and specifications included?

____ c. **Is there a license?** A license can be either an exclusive or nonexclusive right to use the copyrighted work. A license confers limited ownership rights in the copyrighted work subject to the terms of the license agreement. The licensee, however, cannot prohibit the author from using the copyright work, and the agreement to use the work may be terminated pursuant to the agreement.

____ d. **Is the transfer publicly available?** Prior to starting any project, a request should be made that the owner of the copyright provide written documentation of all transfer of licenses to use any copyrighted work.

The transfer should identify the names of the transferor and the transferee.

____ e. **Is there an indemnity provision in the contract?** A party using copyrighted material created by another should confirm that the party can be indemnified if the original copyright owner asserts that the use was unauthorized.

____ (ii) **Can a transfer be terminated?** An author who sold its rights to others may recapture those rights by serving notice after 35 years from when the rights were sold. This doctrine does not apply to works that were created under the work-for-hire doctrine. The transfer may be terminated during the five-year period beginning 35 years after the transfer was granted.

____ (iii) **Is there a priority conflict between authors of the work?** A priority conflict may arise when two authors working independently or jointly create the same work.

____ (iv) **Is there a notice provision?** A notice provision provides expressed notification to potential infringers that the work is protected and can be used only with expressed permission of the owner. The copyright owner is not required to include the copyright symbol (©) on any of its copyrighted work, but it is prudent to do so.

____ (v) **Is the work jointly owned (that is, are there multiple authors)?** If yes, discuss with at least one of the authors whether the parties have an agreement to require approval from all owners for any use of the work. All joint authors may grant nonexclusive use of the work without the agreement of the co-authors. If there is no agreement from all joint authors, no single author may assign or exclusively license the copyright in the jointly created work.

____ (vi) **Term of copyright.**

____ a. **What is the term of a copyright?** For a work created on or after January 1, 1978, the copyright extends for the lifetime of the author (if the author is defined as a natural person and the work was not the product of a work for hire) plus 70 years. If the work is

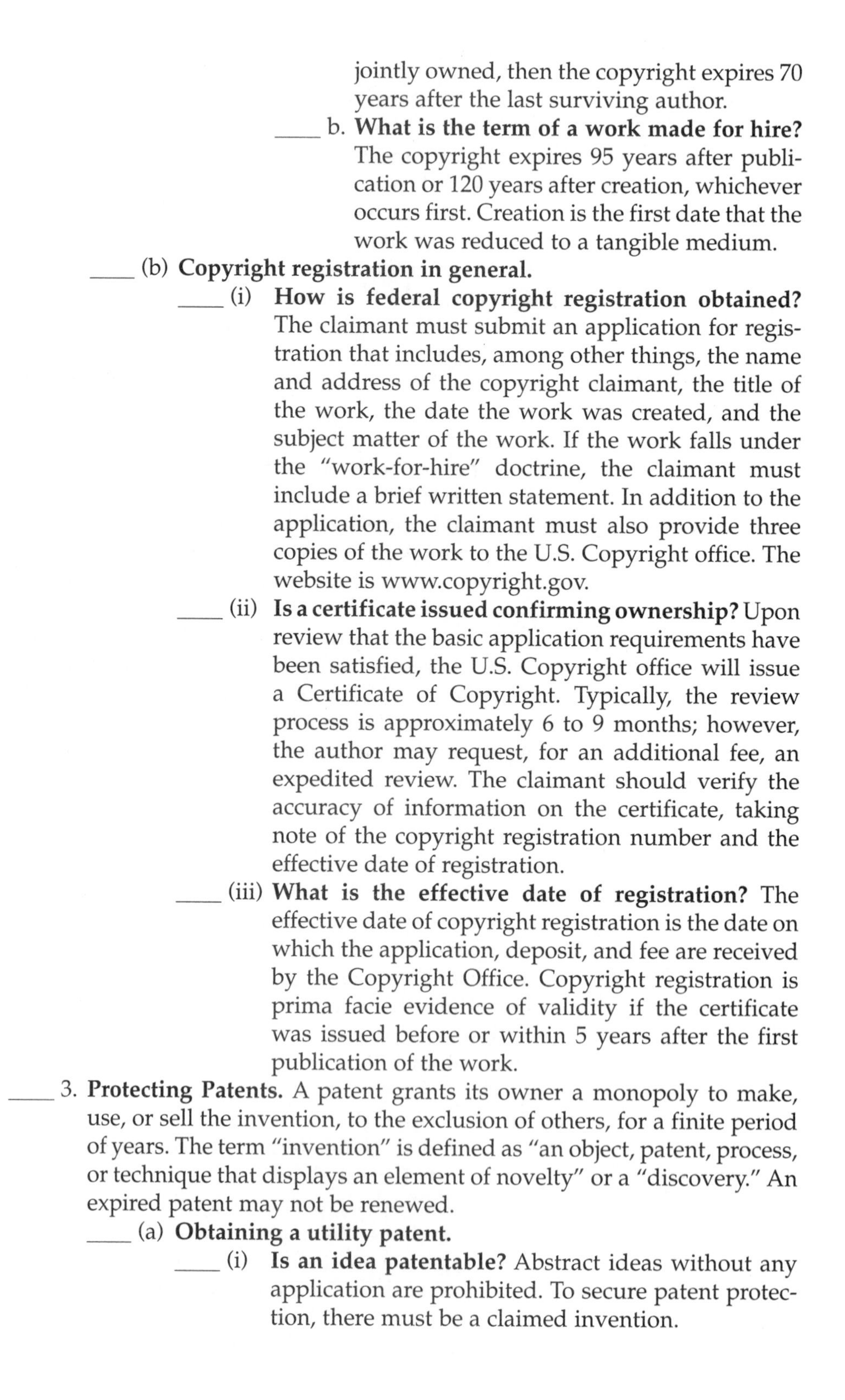

jointly owned, then the copyright expires 70 years after the last surviving author.

____ b. **What is the term of a work made for hire?** The copyright expires 95 years after publication or 120 years after creation, whichever occurs first. Creation is the first date that the work was reduced to a tangible medium.

____ (b) **Copyright registration in general.**

____ (i) **How is federal copyright registration obtained?** The claimant must submit an application for registration that includes, among other things, the name and address of the copyright claimant, the title of the work, the date the work was created, and the subject matter of the work. If the work falls under the "work-for-hire" doctrine, the claimant must include a brief written statement. In addition to the application, the claimant must also provide three copies of the work to the U.S. Copyright office. The website is www.copyright.gov.

____ (ii) **Is a certificate issued confirming ownership?** Upon review that the basic application requirements have been satisfied, the U.S. Copyright office will issue a Certificate of Copyright. Typically, the review process is approximately 6 to 9 months; however, the author may request, for an additional fee, an expedited review. The claimant should verify the accuracy of information on the certificate, taking note of the copyright registration number and the effective date of registration.

____ (iii) **What is the effective date of registration?** The effective date of copyright registration is the date on which the application, deposit, and fee are received by the Copyright Office. Copyright registration is prima facie evidence of validity if the certificate was issued before or within 5 years after the first publication of the work.

____ 3. **Protecting Patents.** A patent grants its owner a monopoly to make, use, or sell the invention, to the exclusion of others, for a finite period of years. The term "invention" is defined as "an object, patent, process, or technique that displays an element of novelty" or a "discovery." An expired patent may not be renewed.

____ (a) **Obtaining a utility patent.**

____ (i) **Is an idea patentable?** Abstract ideas without any application are prohibited. To secure patent protection, there must be a claimed invention.

____ a. **Who is the owner of an invention?** The person claiming the patent must be the original and authentic inventor. The patentee cannot assign the right to pursue a patent in its own name or obtain a patent on an invention created by another person.

____ b. **Is joint inventorship permissible?** If the wrong party claims inventorship or if the patent application includes both incorrect and correct names of the inventors, none of the parties may be able to obtain a patent. If the error was made in good faith, there are some procedures to cure such defects.

____ (ii) **What subject matters are patentable?** The Patent Act, 35 U.S.C. § 101 et seq., enumerates the scope of patent protection, which is a product, a process, or a new and useful improvement of an existing product or process. A process is defined as a means or method of doing something. A product can be defined as a machine, manufacture, or composition of matter. Products of nature are unpatentable.

____ (iii) **Is there a statutory bar for filing a patent application?** In addition to the "novelty" requirement, the patentee must also guard against violating the statutory bar, which prohibits the patentee from obtaining patent protection. The statutory bar puts the patentee on notice that if the patentee does not file a patent application within 12 months of invention, the patentee may lose its rights in the underlying invention.

____(b) **Other types of patents.**

____ (i) **What is a plant patent?** Plant patentability differs from the requirements necessary to secure a utility patent. For plant patents, the utility requirement is replaced by a "distinctiveness" requirement. Therefore, the inventor must demonstrate novelty, distinctiveness, and nonobviousness before obtaining a plant patent. The protection available is limited to the exclusive right to reproduce the plant.

____ (ii) **What is a design patent?** Design patents differ from utility patents because they protect a new, original, ornamental design for an article of manufacture. For design patents, the utility requirement is replaced by an "ornamentality" requirement. The protection afforded design patents is against copying, which

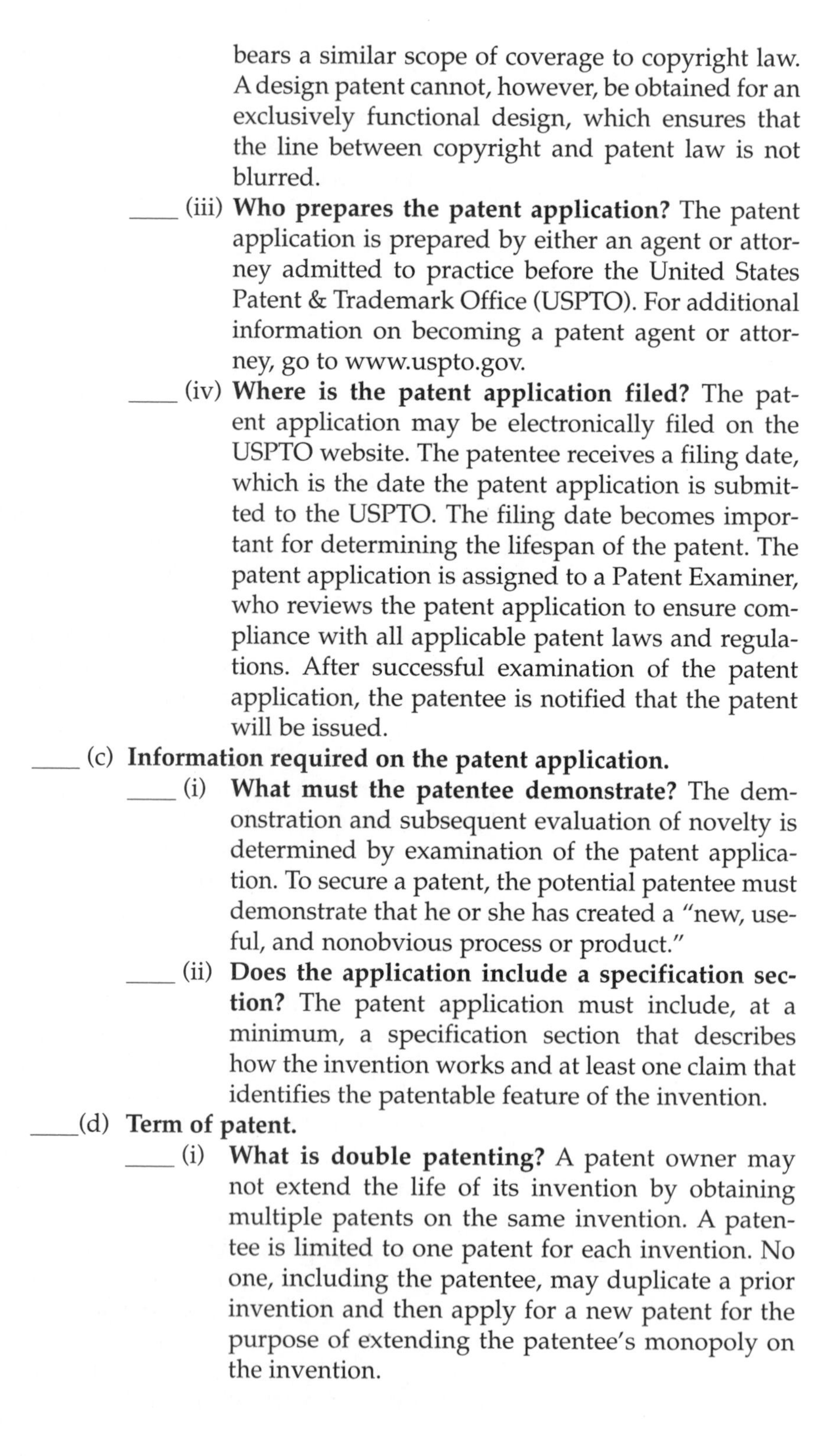

bears a similar scope of coverage to copyright law. A design patent cannot, however, be obtained for an exclusively functional design, which ensures that the line between copyright and patent law is not blurred.

____ (iii) **Who prepares the patent application?** The patent application is prepared by either an agent or attorney admitted to practice before the United States Patent & Trademark Office (USPTO). For additional information on becoming a patent agent or attorney, go to www.uspto.gov.

____ (iv) **Where is the patent application filed?** The patent application may be electronically filed on the USPTO website. The patentee receives a filing date, which is the date the patent application is submitted to the USPTO. The filing date becomes important for determining the lifespan of the patent. The patent application is assigned to a Patent Examiner, who reviews the patent application to ensure compliance with all applicable patent laws and regulations. After successful examination of the patent application, the patentee is notified that the patent will be issued.

____ (c) **Information required on the patent application.**

____ (i) **What must the patentee demonstrate?** The demonstration and subsequent evaluation of novelty is determined by examination of the patent application. To secure a patent, the potential patentee must demonstrate that he or she has created a "new, useful, and nonobvious process or product."

____ (ii) **Does the application include a specification section?** The patent application must include, at a minimum, a specification section that describes how the invention works and at least one claim that identifies the patentable feature of the invention.

____(d) **Term of patent.**

____ (i) **What is double patenting?** A patent owner may not extend the life of its invention by obtaining multiple patents on the same invention. A patentee is limited to one patent for each invention. No one, including the patentee, may duplicate a prior invention and then apply for a new patent for the purpose of extending the patentee's monopoly on the invention.

____ (ii) **When do a patentee's exclusive rights expire?** The patent term is 20 years from the date the application was filed. During this period, a patentee has the exclusive right to make, use, or sell the invention. The right also includes the patentee's right to refrain from making, using, or selling the invention. When the patent expires, the invention is automatically donated to the public domain.

____ (e) **Usefulness of patents.**

____ (i) **What does a patent protect against?** For most construction projects, the patent protection or infringement is rarely a significant issue. A patent protects new and useful processes, machines, articles of manufacture, or composition of matter.

____ (ii) **When do a patentee's exclusive rights expire?** The patent term is generally 20 years from the date the application was filed. During this period, a patentee has the exclusive right to make, use, or sell the invention. The right also includes the patentee's right to refrain from making, using, or selling the invention. When the patent expires, the invention is automatically donated to the public domain.

____ 4. **Protecting Trademarks.** The manner in which a trademark is acquired differs from the acquisition in other intellectual property, such as patents or copyrights. A trademark may not be appropriated without a showing of the use of the trademark in commerce. A trademark can be any word, phrase, mark, or symbol used to identify a specific source of goods. Trademarks also provide protection to the public to assert its purchase preference for a certain manufacturer of goods.

____ (a) **Creation of a trademark.**

____ (i) **What is the function of the trademark?** The purpose of a trademark is to indicate the origin of the goods, guarantee quality of the goods, and serve as a marketing and advertising device.

____ a. **What is first use in commerce?** A trademark owner can acquire rights in the mark by establishing an "intent-to-use" permitted by the statute or actual use of the mark in commerce. A single bona fide offer for sale satisfies the definition of use in commerce.

____ (b) **Federal registration.**

____ (i) **What is the primary purpose of a registered trademark?** To be registered, a trademark must be used to identify and distinguish goods or services. Merely being capable of identifying or distinguishing the goods or services does not automatically qualify the device for federal registration. A device that is solely functional cannot be registered. Color, however, can be a trademark unless the color is used for a purely functional purpose.

____ a. **Where is a trademark application filed?** A trademark owner obtains federal registration. The application must be filed electronically on the USPTO website at www.uspto.gov. The trademark owner must submit an electronic sample of the mark, which is reviewed by a trademark attorney to confirm compliance with all trademark rules and regulations.

____ (ii) **What is the advantage of federal registration?** A national system of trademark registration provides several advantages over state common law trademark rights. The procurement of federal registration affords the registrant the ability to prevail against claims by subsequent good-faith users of the mark. In addition, federal registration serves as constructive notice, regardless of geographic location, of the registrant's trademark rights. Consequently, the registrant can preclude use of the mark in a different geographic location, even where the registrant is not selling goods. Federal registration also gives the registrant its own independent federal cause of action in federal court. Finally, the registrant can acquire statutory rights in the mark such as "incontestability."

____ (iii) **What is distinctiveness?** A trademark must be distinctive either in the inherent nature of the mark itself or the development by the owner through marketing. Distinctiveness permits the original user of a mark to object to a subsequent user on the basis that the subsequent user's mark is not distinctive and closely resembles the original user's mark. In addition, distinctiveness serves to prevent domination of common or descriptive terms in the marketplace as well as to prevent withdrawal of terms in the public domain needed to encourage competition. The four categories of distinctiveness are:

____ a. generic;
____ b. descriptive;
____ c. suggestive; and
____ d. arbitrary or fanciful.

____ (iv) **What subject matter is covered under federal registration?** The Lanham Act is divided into two discrete sections. The first section provides for regulation of the issuance of federal registration to a plethora of marks, words, phrases, and other devices that can satisfy the function of trademark, serve mark, collective mark, or certification mark. The second section, commonly referred to as § 43 of the Lanham Act, codifies the federal law of unfair competition, which forbids false statements in connection with interstate commercial activities, dilution of famous marks, and Internet domain registration of others' marks or personal names.

____ a. **What is a certification mark?** A certification mark is used in connection with goods or services to indicate that those products or services originate in a particular region, or characteristic, or were produced by a member of a particular organization (that is, labor union).

____ b. **What is a collective mark?** A collective mark indicates either that the goods or services are produced by members of a collective group or simply indicates membership in a particular group. A collective mark can be either a collective trade (that is, service mark) or collective membership marks.

____ c. **What is a service mark?** A service mark is a trademark that is used in the sale of services instead of goods. Service marks function identically to trademarks.

____ (c) **Term of trademark.**

____ (i) **Do trademark rights expire?** Trademark rights can only be acquired through use and are a function of commercial reality. Failure to use a mark after the acquisition of legal protection is considered abandonment. A mark is abandoned if the owner discontinues the use of the mark with the intent not to resume use, or the owner must affirmatively do something that causes the mark to lose its distinctiveness.

# Checklist 13: Key Issues for Negotiating a Liquidated Damages Clause

Liquidated damages clauses are common features of construction contracts. Depending on point of view, they can be a carrot-or-stick measure that promotes timely performance or an inflexible boilerplate clause for which there is no practical room to negotiate.

Construction contracts tend to incorporate many other documents by reference. It is important to review all of the referenced terms, specifications, and conditions in other documents to locate potential liability traps, such as a liquidated damages clause, before the contract is signed. While each state will have its particular statutes and case authority regarding the enforceability of a liquidated damages clause, it should be assumed that a court will probably strive to enforce the intention of the parties as expressed by the written document, meaning that there is a high probability that a liquidated damages clause that is not simply a penalty provision will be enforced.

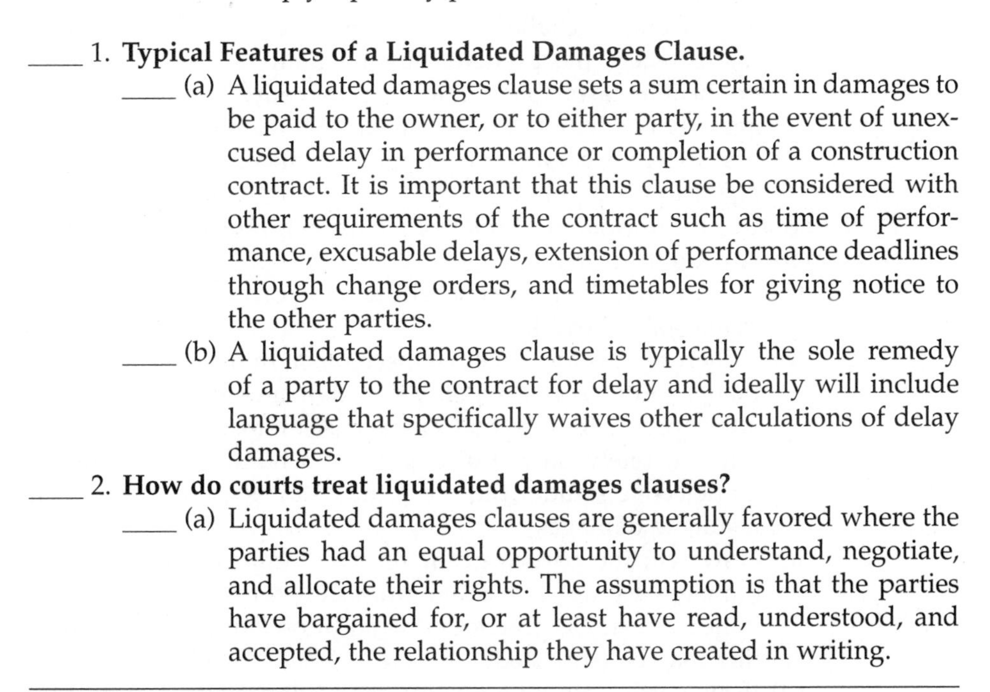

____ 1. **Typical Features of a Liquidated Damages Clause.**

____ (a) A liquidated damages clause sets a sum certain in damages to be paid to the owner, or to either party, in the event of unexcused delay in performance or completion of a construction contract. It is important that this clause be considered with other requirements of the contract such as time of performance, excusable delays, extension of performance deadlines through change orders, and timetables for giving notice to the other parties.

____ (b) A liquidated damages clause is typically the sole remedy of a party to the contract for delay and ideally will include language that specifically waives other calculations of delay damages.

____ 2. **How do courts treat liquidated damages clauses?**

____ (a) Liquidated damages clauses are generally favored where the parties had an equal opportunity to understand, negotiate, and allocate their rights. The assumption is that the parties have bargained for, or at least have read, understood, and accepted, the relationship they have created in writing.

**Jeffrey R. Jury** is a partner in the Austin, Texas, law firm of Burns Anderson Jury & Brenner, LLP. He represents contractors and subcontractors in all types of construction and land use matters and applies the knowledge and experience he has gained to service as mediator and arbitrator of construction disputes.

____ (b) Liquidated damages clauses are generally favored because they provide certainty and expediency in the determination of damages, with an objective of reducing some of the risks and expenses of litigation. These features benefit both parties by providing a certain method of calculating cost, exposure, and damages.

____ (c) Courts typically evaluate liquidated damages clauses along two lines of analysis.

____ (i) Under a prospective approach, the court looks at whether the parties made a reasonable estimate of potential damages that would probably result from breach, with the amount of actual damages from the breach being of minimal or no importance.

____ (ii) Under a retrospective approach, the court considers the reasonableness of the estimated damages compared with the actual damages caused by delay. If the liquidated damages end up being low relative to the actual damages, a court will likely apply the same standard of reasonableness, to see if the clause was the result of what both parties bargained for and chose.

____ (d) The strongest challenge to a liquidated damage clause is made where the predetermined amount of damages does not bear a reasonable relationship to reality. Liquidated damages clauses may not be enforced if they are unconscionable, are merely a penalty for nonperformance, or are otherwise against public policy.

____ 3. **Negotiating a Liquidated Damages Clause—Interests Common to Owners and Contractors.**

____ (a) Be sure that the project schedule and path are realistic, with manageable deadlines.

____ (b) Is there a clear and sensible mechanism in the contract documents to determine when delay damages have accrued to either party? Be sure that any excuses for delays are spelled out concretely, so a judge, jury, or arbitrator can resort to an objective standard to see if the delay is excusable, or if it results in damages.

____ (c) How will the parties evaluate events causing delay before damages accrue? Consider a procedure for the parties to give notice, as early as practical, that additional time or compensation may be requested.

____ (d) If the parties cannot agree upon additional time for completion or compensation, how will that dispute be handled? Will the parties litigate or arbitrate the reasonableness of that decision, or will the issue be carried forward for subsequent determination?

____ (e) A liquidated damages clause may set forth damages for the unexcused failure to meet any milestone on the project, completion of the project as a whole, or both features. Draft the clause that makes the best business sense for your client's interests.

____ (f) The liquidated damages clause should be harmonized with other damages clauses of the contract. If the contract contains any mutual waivers of damages, consider making the liquidated damages clause mutual as well.

____ (g) If standardized form contracts are used, do not assume the boilerplate language reflects an allocation of risk that is desirable, or applicable, to the project. Read the form language carefully, and strike or modify language to fit your client's interests.

____ (h) Identify third parties who may play a role in a delay damages claim, such as an agent or representative of a party to the contract, for the giving of notice or the processing of a claim for extension of time.

____ 4. **Negotiating a Liquidated Damages Clause—Owner's Interest Checklist.**

____ (a) How will the owner be damaged if the project is delayed? Develop a list of how financing, obtaining permits, costs, revenue, and other client interests will be affected if the project is not completed according to schedule.

____ (b) For each category of damages, what is the reasonable, provable amount of damages, expressed per interval of time, that would fairly and reasonably compensate the owner for injuries and damages occasioned by the delay? Even though the liquidated damages clause seeks to predict damages that would be uncertain, the clause must make a reasonable prediction that seeks to compensate the nonbreaching party, rather than penalize the breaching party. The more thoroughly these numbers are considered in advance of contract inception, the more defensible the clause will prove to be.

____ (c) How will requests for additional time be processed for consideration? Most standardized change order forms include a determination of the amount of additional time and expense occasioned by the event. A change order should include language that releases all claims that are not detailed or presented, up to the date of the change order. This will provide additional protection to the owner each time it approves a change order, and encourage the contractor to present its request in a timely manner.

____ 5. **Negotiating a Liquidated Damages Clause—Contractor's Interest Checklist.**

____ (a) How does the contractor assess the reasonableness of the damage estimate? If the contractor believes that the amount of damages is penal, rather than compensatory in nature, further discussion and negotiation with the owner should take place, if it is feasible to do so.

____ (i) Request supporting information and documentation to understand the method of calculation so it can be discussed and negotiated from an informed position.

____ (ii) Some of the basis for the owner's calculation may involve sensitive information, such as lending arrangements and business plans, so be prepared to offer a nondisclosure agreement so you can evaluate the reasonableness of the owner's damage calculation while protecting the owner's interests in keeping competitive information confidential.

____ (iii) Consider requesting a notice provision permitting you to challenge the reasonableness of the imposition or calculation of liquidated damages. This may insert opportunities for dispute, but it can also be viewed as a positive opportunity to have disagreements vetted through a mutually agreeable process before they ripen into conflict.

____ (b) Is the liquidated damages clause of the contract with the owner in harmony with the contractor's subcontract agreements? For example, are delay damages triggered by the same events? As another example, it may be difficult to enforce a delay claim against a subcontractor if the owner has made no delay claim.

____ (c) If the delay damages features of the contract clause are mutual, how will the contractor's damages be calculated? The contractor will have a different set of interests, different cost structure, and different consequences if the project is delayed because of the owner's conduct, and the contractor should consider provisions that make clear how its damages will be determined. For example, what project expenses will be included in the calculation? Will overhead and profit be included in the calculation?

____ (d) How will the progress of the project be monitored, and how will the contractor process and present a request for additional time? Even if the change order requests are on standardized forms, the responsibility for monitoring and presenting documentation should be tasked and followed through accordingly. If presentation of an insurance claim or notice to a surety becomes necessary, a procedure should be in place to avoid a late notice defense.

____ (e) What limits may be imposed on the total amount of damages? Can, or should, the owner's damages be limited to the available insurance policy limits, the amount of profit realized on the project, or some other objective measurement of damages so the project does not become a loss leader?

____ (f) Are there alternatives to a liquidated damages clause that the owner will consider, such as:

____ (i) Limiting liquidated damages to delays caused solely by third parties?

____ (ii) Limiting liquidated damages to delays caused by subcontractors?

____ (iii) Providing incentives to the contractor for early completion?

____ (g) Should the contractor's agreements with subcontractors contain, or incorporate, a liquidated damages clause that flows down to the subcontractor?

____ 6. **Negotiating a Liquidated Damages Clause—Subcontractor Interest Checklist.**

____ (a) If the subcontract contains incorporation language, be sure that all incorporated documents are reviewed. This is the only way to be certain that all potential exposures are identified and considered.

____ (b) Be sure to look for a "flow-down" clause that provides the general contractor's obligations to the owner flow down to the subcontractor, by language such as "the subcontractor is bound to the contractor in the same manner that the contractor is bound to the owner," or similar language. Although state law varies on the language required to make these obligations flow down to the subcontractor, be sure you understand the full extent of the contractor's obligations to the owner. The only way to be thorough and certain about the extent of these obligations is to request a copy of the contract between the owner and the general contractor.

____ (c) Watch for inconsistencies between a liquidated damages clause in the subcontract and the liquidated damages clause in the contract with the owner. Make sure there is no scenario in which you, as subcontractor, could end up paying two sets of liquidated damages.

____ (d) If you are exposed to potential liquidated damages in your contract, add flow-down clauses to contracts with your subcontractors and suppliers. Expect that your suppliers will resist the addition of a liquidated damages clause and will want to rely on their purchase order forms. Remember that the principle that applies here is that if risks and damages can be avoided by one party, the contract should create a structure that allocates the consequences for failure to do so.

____ (e) Once the risks are identified, check with the insurance carrier to determine whether the risks and exposures are within the coverage of the client's applicable insurance policy. The question of whether general liability insurance policies cover this type of defect is a matter of sharp controversy, with frequent changes in the law. A periodic coverage review with counsel is the only way to be assured that insurance coverage will be in place.

____ (f) Follow Contractor's checklist items 5(c)–(e) .

# Checklist 14: Waiver of Subrogation

There are many different types of subrogation interests. This checklist focuses only on the waiver of the right of the property insurer, or builder's risk insurance company, to recover against a potentially negligent party in the event of a claim. This checklist is not an exhaustive summary of the case law governing waiver of subrogation; rather, it is intended to identify issues that should be considered if such an issue develops.

"Subrogation," generally, is defined as "the right of a person to assume a legal claim of another; the right of a person who has paid a liability or obligation of another to be indemnified by that person; an insurer's substitution in place of the insured in regard to a claim against a third party for indemnification of a loss paid by the insurer."

In the context of insurance, subrogation occurs when an insurance company pays its insured and then sues the entity or person responsible for the loss to recover the amounts paid to the insured. The insurance company steps into the shoes of the insured and exercises any rights the insured might have against the responsible party.

To avoid claims by another's insurance company, parties will often contract to waive all rights of subrogation against the other party as part of the contract governing their relationship. The named insured intentionally relinquishes any right to recover damages from another party who may be responsible. While exculpatory, these types of clauses are generally upheld.

____ 1. **Does the contract contain a waiver of subrogation clause?** Without a waiver of subrogation clause in the contract, the parties will be unable to waive subrogation rights.

____ 2. **Is the waiver of subrogation clause in an AIA contract or another contract?**

____ (a) **Source of clause.** The majority of cases interpret AIA language, but, depending on the language, these general principles may be applicable to waiver clauses in custom contracts as well.

---

**James E. Weatherholtz** is a partner in the Charleston, South Carolina, firm of Buist, Moore, Smythe & McGee PA. He regularly represents sureties, contractors, and construction products manufacturers in a variety of construction disputes.

____ (b) **AIA language.** The most common waiver of subrogation clause is found in the AIA General Conditions:

> The Owner and Contractor waive all rights against (1) each other and any of their subcontractors, sub-subcontractors, agents and employees, each of the other, and (2) the Architect, Architect's consultants, separate contractors described in Article 6, if any, and any of their subcontractors, sub-subcontractors, agents and employees, for damages caused by fire or other causes of loss to the extent covered by property insurance obtained pursuant to this Paragraph 11.3 or other property insurance applicable to the Work, except such rights as they have to proceeds of such insurance held by the Owner as fiduciary. The Owner or Contractor, as appropriate, shall require of the Architect, Architect's consultants, separate contractors described in Article 6, if any, and the subcontractors, sub-subcontractors, agents and employees of any of them, by appropriate agreements, written where legally required for validity, similar waivers each in favor of other parties enumerated herein. The policies shall require waiver by endorsement or otherwise.

____ 3. **Whose right is it to waive?** Can an insured waive the right of subrogation without a waiver from its insurance company?

____ (a) **Majority view.** The A201 waiver language bars an insurance company's subrogation claim where the insured had waived its subrogation rights in the construction contract. The insurer, as subrogee, has no greater rights than those possessed by the insured, and has no independent rights apart from the insured. However, the language in the AIA General Conditions states "[t]he policy shall provide such waivers of subrogation by endorsement or otherwise," so the safer course is to obtain the consent of the insurer.

____ (b) **Minority view.** To be effective, a waiver of subrogation clause in a construction contract must require that the party waiving its subrogation rights obtain a written waiver from its insurance company. The reservation of subrogation rights language in the subject policy reserves the insurance company's rights *without limitation*. A key factor is the lack of a requirement in the construction contract that the insured obtain a written waiver of subrogation from the insurance company.

____ (c) **Practice tip.** To gain more protection for the insured, the insurance policy should contain language stating that "coverage will not be prejudiced if the insured has waived, in writing, prior to a loss, any rights of recovery from a party responsible for the loss." This may be effective to combat an insurance company's argument that the waiver is a breach or a failure to cooperate that extinguishes the insurance company's obligation to provide insurance coverage, especially where "reservation of rights" language appears.

____ 4. **What does the waiver cover?**

____ (a) **Losses and damage to real property—even due to a party's negligence**. The waiver of subrogation clause applies when the contractor's carrier pays for a loss due to fire caused by a subcontractor's negligent soldering and then attempts to subrogate against the subcontractor.

____ (b) **Contents of the building.** Is the waiver defined by the scope of work in the contract or the types of risk covered by insurance?

____ (i) **By the risks covered by insurance.** Under Paragraph 11.4.5 and 11.4.7 (AIA A201-1997), the waiver of subrogation applies to personal property. If an owner has an existing policy that covers building contents or personal property and the negligent work of a contractor or subcontractor destroys that personal property, the owner is precluded from pursuing the negligent contractor or subcontractor to the extent there is coverage out there, regardless of whether or not a claim has been made and/or the insurance company made payment.

____ (ii) **By the scope of work in the contract.** The scope of the waiver of subrogation is limited to the value of the work performed under the contract (that is, a new roof), and not applicable to other parts of the building. The waiver only applies to the value of the work performed under the contract (that is, the building addition).

____ (c) **Repair or renovation work.**

____ (i) **Majority view.** For public policy reasons, and because the AIA contract suggests that the parties intended to place all risk on the project on one insurance policy, the waiver applies to all damage, whether to work or nonwork property, to the extent that coverage exists. The scope of the waiver does not depend on the type of policy in place. However, when an owner elects to use insurance broader than that required by the contract, it waives any claims to the extent of that coverage.

____ (ii) **Minority view.**

____ a. **New policy versus existing policy.** When doing repair or renovation work, the owner has the option of purchasing a builder's risk policy for the "new" work, or simply relying on existing property insurance that covers the "nonwork" areas of the building. Where an owner purchases an all-risk policy specifically to cover the new work, and that policy is separate from any existing property insurance policy, then the owner only waives the right to sue for damages arising from the new work. The owner retains its right to sue for damage to nonwork property. If an owner decides to rely on existing property insurance (that covers both the new work and nonwork property), then it waives the right to sue for all damage done as long as the damage is covered by the policy.

____ b. **Endorsement to existing policy.** Where additional insurance is purchased by buying an endorsement to an existing policy, the endorsement is an amendment to, and becomes part of, the existing policy. Therefore, if an owner wants to preserve subrogation rights to sue for damage to nonwork property, the owner must purchase a separate policy, not supplement an existing one.

____ (d) **Adjacent property.** Paragraph 11.4.5 of the AIA A201-1997 contemplates insurance covering real or personal property at or *adjacent* to the site. This paragraph seems to embrace the notion that if renovation or repair work is being done that destroys an existing structure at or adjacent to the site of the repair work, the waiver applies to any property insurance covering the adjacent structure as well.

____ (e) **General liability insurance (CGL policies).** In the same instance, a waiver of subrogation may be construed as a relinquishment of a CGL carrier's right to pursue subrogation.

____ 5. **To whom does the waiver apply?**

____ (a) **Trickle down for subcontractors.** The subcontractor is an "insured" under the policy when an owner is required to purchase insurance to protect the interests of the owner, the contractor, subcontractors, and sub-subcontractors in the work. An insurer cannot recover against an insured because a severe conflict of interest would arise.

____ (b) **Third-party beneficiaries.** Subcontractors who lack privity with the owner may be covered as third-party beneficiaries to the contract. A subcontractor, as a third-party beneficiary, may be able to enforce the waiver of subrogation clause contained within the construction contract.

____ 6. **How long does the waiver last?**

____ (a) The waiver only covers losses during construction. AIA A201-1997 provides in 11.4 that the waiver applies "to the extent covered by property insurance obtained pursuant to the paragraph." The insurance coverage must cover losses until final payment has been made or until no entity other than the owner has an insurable interest, whichever is later. This would preclude the waiver being effective after coverage expires.

____ (b) The waiver may cover all losses covered by insurance, even if the policy is purchased after the completion of construction.

____ (i) If the parties intend to use insurance as the sole source to redress damages, even for policies purchased *after* the completion of the project, the waiver may cover all losses covered by insurance, even if the policy is purchased after completion of construction when the AIA waiver clause applies.

____ (ii) The AIA Comments to the A201-1997 edition indicate that 11.4.5 "extends the provisions for waiver of subrogation to other property insurance the owner may purchase. Such policies may cover property at or adjacent to the project site, or they may replace the property insurance that was in effect on the work during construction." This supports the position that the waiver applies to property insurance supplied after the work was completed.

____ (c) **Warranty work.** Where additional work is being performed pursuant to a modified contract or warranty work, that work is included as part of the original contract work. Therefore, the waiver clause in the contract is effective at the time of the loss, which can occur while this supplemental additional work is performed.

____ 7. **Is your client listed as an additional insured?** Even without an enforceable waiver of subrogation clause, the fact that a contractor or subcontractor is listed as an additional insured may preclude a subrogation lawsuit. An insurance company arguably has no subrogation rights against its own additional insured.

# Checklist 15: Drafting and Negotiating Contractual Indemnity Agreements

Contractual indemnification is a means of shifting risk between the contracting parties for claims made by third persons not a party to the construction contract. A contractual indemnification provision should always be considered in connection with the corresponding contractual insurance obligations. This checklist, while not exhaustive, provides topics useful in drafting and negotiating a favorable and enforceable contractual indemnity clause. The paradigm of indemnity is that of insurance against losses, and not a defense to an action brought by a third person. When negotiating indemnity agreements in construction contracts, the contracting parties should consider the following items.

____ 1. **The Parties to the Indemnity Agreement.**

____ (a) **The Indemnitor.** The "Indemnitor" is the party promising or obligating itself to be responsible for the liability of or the financial losses sustained by the Indemnitee. Generally, the Indemnitor is the party that is best able to control the particular risk that the parties are seeking to shift. For example, contractors, who control the jobsite and the means and methods of construction, often are in the best position to control the jobsite and project risks. Subcontractors are able to control the risk of their discrete portions of the work, and consequently contractors often look to shift certain project risks to subcontractors. Likewise, owners may be in the best position to protect contractors or subcontractors from certain unknown project conditions or risks.

____ (b) **The Indemnitee.** The "Indemnitee" is the party receiving the promise to be free from financial losses associated with certain project risks that either are controlled or accepted by the Indemnitor. Additionally the party in the stronger bargaining position can demand to be the Indemnitee. For this reason and those discussed earlier, there may be several lower-tier Indemnitees. Indemnitees may include multiple people or

**Patrick J. Poff** is shareholder in the Tampa, Florida, office of Trenam Kemker. His practice is predominantly in construction law, representing owners, contractors, and subcontractors in all aspects of construction contract, defect, and insurance claims. He gratefully acknowledges the assistance of **Gregg E. Hutt,** associate of Trenam Kemker, in the preparation of this checklist.

entities who are not parties to the construction contract such as:

____ (i) Companies affiliated with the owner.

____ (ii) Directors, shareholders, representatives, employees, or agents of the owner entity.

____ (iii) Consultants of the owner such as the architect or engineer, including their employees, representatives, or agents.

____ (c) **Lower-tier Indemnitees.** Typically, owners are Indemnitees in the prime construction contracts, and contractors are Indemnitees in subcontracts. Lower-tier indemnification agreements are effective ways contractors can manage and shift their risk as Indemnitors to owners. Either or both parties to an indemnity agreement may want to ensure that all lower-tier indemnity terms and obligations are substantially similar to those in the upper-tier agreements.

____ (d) **Reciprocating Indemnitors/Indemnitees.** Indemnity clauses can be drafted such that only one party indemnifies another (one-way indemnity). However, circumstances may exist in which the parties to a construction contract may consider reciprocal indemnification (that is, mutual indemnity), wherein they indemnify each other for their own conduct with respect to the risks enumerated in the indemnity agreement.

____ 2. **The Source of Legal Rights to Indemnity.**

____ (a) **Contractual indemnity.** Contractual indemnity is based solely on the terms and conditions of parties' written agreement in the construction contract. Whether and when an indemnity obligation is triggered depends on the explicit and unambiguous language of the indemnity terms. Risks, financial losses, and conditions of indemnity not clearly addressed likely will not be enforced. Contractual indemnification may be limited and, in certain instances, altogether prohibited by governing statutory provisions.

____ (b) **Statutory indemnity.** Some states have specific statutory provisions governing indemnity in construction contracts. Statutes, therefore, may provide specific conditions under which certain forms of indemnity can occur. For instance, certain jurisdictions bar contractual indemnity agreements indemnifying an Indemnitee for the Indemnitee's partial or sole negligence.

____ (c) **Common law indemnity.** Common law may imply or permit a right of indemnification based on the relationship of the parties and the factual circumstances of the case. Although this outline focuses on contractual indemnity clauses, parties to indemnity agreements should be aware of the applicable state common law, which may create additional indemnity risk not contemplated by the contractual indemnity agreement in the construction contract.

____ 3. **The Potential Risks to Indemnify Against.**

____ (a) **Owner considerations.** General risks that an owner should consider when seeking indemnification include, but are not limited to:

____ (i) Construction site injuries, which may take the form of sickness, bodily injury, or death.

____ (ii) Defective construction or contractor's failure to materially comply with a product manufacturer's directions or recommendations.

____ (iii) Negligent inspection and observation, which could result from either the contractor's or the design professional's performance.

____ (iv) Nonpayment to subcontractors and suppliers who have furnished labor, services, or materials to the project, including nonpayment for specially fabricated materials that have been ordered but not furnished to the project.

____ (v) Owner's own partial or sole negligent conduct (subject to jurisdictional restrictions).

____ (b) **Contractor considerations.** General risks that a contractor should consider when seeking indemnification include, but are not limited to:

____ (i) Construction site injuries resulting from subcontractors and material suppliers.

____ (ii) Defective design, including insufficient plans or specifications by owner for negligence of owner's consultant(s).

____ (iii) Unforeseen conditions (of site or existing construction, if applicable).

____ (iv) Hazardous or environmental conditions.

____ (v) Negligent inspection or observation by owner's consultant or representative.

____ (vi) Nonperformance by or negligence of subcontractors.

____ (vii) Subcontractor failure to pay lower tier subcontractors or material suppliers.

____ (viii) Contractor's sole or partial negligence (subject to jurisdictional restrictions).

____ (ix) Copyright or patent infringement by owner or owner's consultant.

____ 4. **Forms of Indemnification Sought.**

____ (a) **Limited form.** Under limited-form indemnity, the Indemnitor agrees to hold harmless the Indemnitee from liability or losses caused by the fault of the Indemnitor.

____ (b) **Intermediate form.** Under intermediate-form indemnity, the Indemnitor may also agree to hold harmless the Indemnitee for the Indemnitee's partial fault or negligence.

____ (c) **Broad form.** Under broad-form indemnity, the Indemnitor agrees to hold harmless the Indemnitee for essentially all liability or damages caused by both the Indemnitor and the Indemnitee. Accordingly, under broad-form indemnity, the Indemnitor would be accepting the risk of liability or damages caused by the Indemnitor's sole fault or negligence. Again when considering the use or enforceability of broad-form indemnity, you must consider whether and to what extent state statutes permit or limit such an agreement.

____ 5. **Scope of Indemnification.**

____ (a) **Specifying what the Indemnitor must pay.** The purpose of the indemnity agreement is to protect the Indemnitee from any financial loss associated with specified project risks. The indemnity clause, therefore, should clearly identify from where the financial losses could arise, such as, but not limited to, any or all claims, costs and expenses, demands, liability, damages, or judgments.

____ (b) **Specifying the costs and expenses to be reimbursed.** Typically, when an indemnity provision states "costs" or "expenses," the reference is to court costs and attorneys' fees. However, to ensure that all costs and expenses are covered, the indemnity agreement should expressly include the costs and expenses associated with paralegal fees and expert fees, as well as any other consultant fees that the Indemnitee could incur during in litigation or arbitration.

____ (c) **Defense of the Indemnitee(s).** The indemnity agreement also can include the Indemnitor's obligation to defend the Indemnitee(s) when a claim is presented. The duty to defend can be broader or narrower than the obligation to indemnify. For example, a jurisdiction prohibiting indemnification of the Indemnitee's sole negligence still may enforce a duty to defend arising out of the negligent conduct. Therefore, when negotiating the duty to defend, the parties must define precisely the terms of the defense, which may also include the Indemnitee's selection of counsel and payment to same.

____ (d) **Types of losses to be indemnified.** When drafting and negotiating indemnity agreements, parties should consider the types of losses for which the Indemnitor would be obligated to reimburse the Indemnitee. Losses to protect against should include, but are not limited to, sickness or disease, bodily injury, death and death caused by bodily injury, and property damage (other than damage to the work performed under the construction contract). When including property damage in the indemnity agreement, drafters should determine whether there are other provisions of the construction contract that provide for insurance of property. If such insurance exists, liability for all or part of this damage may be excluded from the indemnity agreement.

____ (e) **Events triggering Indemnitor's obligation.** The obligation to indemnify will depend on whether the event causing the financial loss is clearly expressed by the parties and is intended to be covered by the indemnity agreement. Because indemnity agreements are strictly construed, parties to the indemnity agreement should specify exactly from where or how the loss could arise. As a starting point, drafters should consider the type of construction and the scope of work identified in the construction contract. Toward this end, indemnity obligations may arise during or result from the following:

____ (i) Conduct of the Indemnitor, its employees, representatives, or agents.

____ (ii) Conduct of parties (for example, consultants, subcontractors, or suppliers) working for or through the Indemnitor.

____ (iii) Conduct of the Indemnitee(s), subject to jurisdictional specific limitations or anti-indemnity statutes.

____ (iv) Defects in the work or defects in the equipment and machinery used during performance.

____ (v) Acts, omissions, or material defaults in performance.

____ (vi) Conduct arising out of or in the general or specific location where the work is performed.

____ (vii) Liability of Indemnitor (that is, triggering the duty to indemnify without proof of loss or payment by the Indemnitee).

____ (viii) Sole, partial, or contributory negligence of the Indemnitor or any party for whom it is responsible pursuant to the construction contract.

____ (ix) Strict liability of the Indemnitor or any party for whom it is responsible pursuant to the construction contract.

____ (f) **Exclusions to the events triggering indemnification.** In so much as the indemnity agreement should specify the events triggering the duty of indemnification, the indemnity agreement also may specify events that are excluded. Such events or conditions that should be considered include, but are not limited to:

____ (i) Contributory conduct by Indemnitee(s).

____ (ii) Negligent acts, whether committed in whole or in part of any Indemnitee.

____ (iii) Willful or wanton conduct of Indemnitee(s).

____ (iv) Punitive damages arising from conduct of Indemnitee(s).

____ (v) The area or location where the Indemnitor's work is being performed.

____ (g) **Limitation on the amount of loss.** The scope of indemnity agreements also may address a limitation on the amount of loss sustained by an Indemnitor. Some limitations could include, but may not be limited to:

____ (i) Limits required by statute to an amount that has a commercially reasonable relationship to the cost of the work or the contract sum.

____ (ii) Limits specified by contract to an amount not to exceed the limits of insurance coverage or the cost of the work or the contract sum.

____ (h) **Duration of the indemnity agreement.** The scope of indemnity agreements should also contemplate the duration of the indemnity agreement. Indemnity obligations may survive the completion of work or the project. Parties to the indemnity agreement should consider whether the jurisdiction governing the construction contract adheres to the "completed and accepted" rule, which precludes an Indemnitor's liability for damage where the work is completed and accepted by the owner. Indemnitees, therefore, wanting to extend an Indemnitor's duty of indemnification beyond contract completion, should so clearly specify in the indemnity terms.

____ 7. **Insurance Requirements of the Construction Contract.**

____ (a) **Interpretation of indemnity clause.** Indemnitees must consider whether the Indemnitor's insurance provides adequate protection and will cover the indemnity obligation specified in the indemnity agreement; otherwise, the indemnity obligation could be meaningless. Additionally, coordination between terms of the insurance requirements of the construction contract with terms of the indemnity agreement is essential. A contradiction or inconsistency between the two could create ambiguity and result in an Indemnitee's inability to enforce its indemnity rights. Indemnity agreements, therefore, often are read *in pari materia* with a contractual insurance requirement to construe and apply the Indemnitor's obligations. Parties would be wise to consult with an insurance agent during contract negotiations.

____ (b) **Insurance requirements.** Whether an Indemnitor will be able to honor its indemnity obligation likely depends on whether the Indemnitor has adequate financial assets or insurance resources. When negotiating the terms of the indemnification, the prospective Indemnitee should verify that the Indemnitor's policy is commensurate with its indemnity obligations. Accordingly, construction contracts should contain a clause specifying the Indemnitor's obligation to obtain insurance coverage that not only will cover the contractor's performance, but also have the ability to adequately cover the specific risks and scope of indemnity. In addition, the insurance requirements of the construction contact should consider and possibly include the following:

____ (i) **Additional insureds.** Have the Indemnitor name all Indemnitees as additional insureds in its CGL and other insurance policies.

____ (ii) **Scope of coverage in policy.** Likewise, ensure the contractor's CGL policy covers all risks identified in the indemnity clause. To the extent that certain risks are not covered, the contractor will expose its own assets to fulfill its indemnity obligations.

____ (iii) **Notification of expiring coverage.** Indemnitees should ensure that the terms of either the insurance clauses or indemnity agreements require timely notice of expiring or changing coverage.

____ (iv) **Lower-tier insurance requirements.** The obligation to obtain insurance covering a potential indemnity claim should not be viewed as a single "event" occurring in the prime agreement between the contractor and owner. Rather, insurance covering indemnity risk should be viewed as a "chain of events." Accordingly, Indemnitors should ensure, and Indemnitees should require, contractual terms that all lower-tier parties have adequate insurance that can flow to the upper-tier party. Using subcontractors that cannot obtain the necessary insurance may render an upper-tier Indemnitee's right meaningless.

# Checklist 16: Limitation on Liability Clauses

A limitation on liability clause is a contractual agreement, between the parties to the agreement, that limits liability of one to the other in a way defined by the clause. This limitation may take various forms. It may limit recoveries in terms of monetary amounts, types of actions, the time in which liability exists, or in various other ways. A drafter should consider a variety of practical constraints and the client's objectives when proposing the form of a limitation on liability clause.

____ 1. **Constraints on Limitation on Liability Clauses.** The scope and amount of a limitation on liability clause may be limited by applicable law. The drafter should identify these constraints before crafting a clause so as to ensure the client will receive the benefits of the clause the drafter intends.

____ (a) **Is the limitation on liability clause enforceable?** Most cases hold that, generally, parties may mutually agree to limit to some extent the liability of one party to the other.

____ (i) A court may construe the provision narrowly.

____ (ii) Some state statutes, which limit indemnification for a party's own negligence in construction contracts, have been held to apply to limitation of liability clauses, even if the statute did not expressly mention them.

____ (b) **What are the parties' relative bargaining positions?** The degree to which one party has unequal bargaining power over the other may be considered by the court. If a party has no alternatives in obtaining the contracted services and thus must accept the limitation, the limitation could be found to be contrary to public policy. Evidence that the parties engaged in bargaining over the scope of the clause will support enforcement of the clause. The ability to pay an additional fee in return for an increased limit or additional insurance coverage may support enforcement of the limitation.

---

**Bruce R. Gerhardt** is senior counsel and vice president at HDR, Inc., an engineering and architecture firm with headquarters in Omaha, Nebraska. Limitation on liability clauses are a frequently negotiated provision in agreements with owners and subconsultants.

____ (c) **Who is the client?**

____ (i) **Public entities.** It may be much more difficult to obtain a limitation on liability from a public entity than from a private entity. Public entities can be difficult to negotiate with on issues such as indemnity and may be unreceptive to a limitation on liability.

____ (ii) **Private entities.** The sophistication and size of a private client may affect its willingness to accept such a clause.

____ (iii) **Subcontracts.** If the clause is being negotiated in the context of a subcontract, the parties will need to consider how it will integrate with the prime agreement. The prime will want to avoid agreeing to a limitation on liability with a subcontractor without having the same limitation in the agreement with the owner.

____ (d) **What is the amount of limitation?** A court may look to see whether the limitation shields the breaching party to such an extent that it would remove any incentive to perform. In such a case, the court may find the clause unconscionable.

____ 2. **Interaction with Other Contractual Clauses.** Even with a perfectly crafted limitation on liability clause, other parts of the contract must be considered for the exposure they create and the extent to which they may interrelate with the limitation on liability.

____ (a) **Indemnification.** Although frequently drafted more broadly, indemnification clauses are meant to protect a party (such as the owner) from claims by third parties arising due to the acts or omissions of the other party (such as the contractor or design professional). Is the limitation on liability clause intended to limit liability for indemnification obligations? If so, it should explicitly state this. However, see 1(a)(ii).

____ (b) **Insurance.** A party presented with a limitation on liability clause may note a conflict with other clauses that require a certain level of insurance coverage. A party may argue that if certain amounts of coverage are required, why should it agree to limit liability below that amount? A distinction can be made in terms of coverage available for third-party claims and coverage that would be available to the other party, such as an owner. See 3(c) for using insurance coverages as an amount to limit liability.

____ (c) **Standard of care.** A limitation on liability reduces the exposure a party has for failing to meet the applicable standard of care. The other party may object to a clause that may serve to reduce the incentive to perform quality work or services.

If the contractual standard of care exceeds the customary standard of care, the contract may have created a warranty. In such cases, the limitation on liability would need to expressly cover warranty causes of action.

____ (d) **Accrual of causes of action.** A party's liability can also be limited by restrictions on the time allowed to bring a cause of action. For example, § 1.3.7.1 of the AIA B-141 (1997) starts the accrual of all causes of action at either substantial completion or final completion. The parties could also agree to reduce the statute of limitations and/or statute of repose to a shorter amount of time.

____ 3. **Variations in Structure.** There is room for creativity in determining how a party will have limited liability. While certain structures are more common, other structures may better reflect the needs of the parties or the economics of the project. For examples of various approaches to limitations on liability, see Exhibit H of EJCDC No. 1910-1 (1996).

____ (a) **Ceiling.** Traditionally, a limitation on liability clause will create a ceiling for liability. In this variation, the party's liability will not exceed a certain amount. A very typical clause would provide that the party's liability will not exceed $50,000 or the fees received for the project, whichever is greater. The ceiling could be calculated in many ways, such as a percentage of construction cost, a percentage of fees earned, a flat amount, or any other method that calculates a ceiling.

____ (i) **Joint and several liability.** Consideration should be given as to whether joint and several liability could be imposed. If so, the clause may need to address the possibility that a party is obligated to pay more that its proportionate liability to the other, and whether that will also be subject to the limitation.

____ (b) **Floor.** As opposed to a ceiling, a floor creates a "buffer" amount that will not be the responsibility of a party. It could be considered a contingency amount by which a party, such as the owner, would acknowledge an inherent level of defects or negligence in any construction project. Consider the insurance coverage maintained by the party because liability would continue for amounts above the floor. The floor could also be calculated using a fixed amount, a percentage of construction cost or other amount, or some combination of factors.

____ (c) **Insurance.** Liability could also be limited to insurance coverage maintained by the party and available at the time. In drafting such a clause, consideration should be given to deductibles or self-insured retentions, the effect of a lack of coverage or a reservation of rights, and any erosion or impairment of insurance limits at the time the claim is made. Project policy coverage could be explored as a method for providing an acceptable amount of insurance coverage.

____ (d) **Nonmonetary forms.** Liability can also be limited in other ways. Such clauses can include waivers of consequential damages, waivers of subrogation for insured claims, and waivers of jury trials. Applicable state law must be researched to determine the enforceability of such provisions.

# Design

# Checklist 17: Defining Basic and Additional Services

By clearly defining basic and additional services needed by an owner early, the design professional can objectively determine whether it will be able to meet the owner's needs. This list is intended to provide a framework to use when determining if the firm or design professional is suited for a particular project, and if so, whether a new project should be undertaken. This list is not all-inclusive. Keeping the things in this list in mind when formulating basic and additional services may help avoid claims and disputes during and after a project.

____ 1. **What services are needed for the project?** An owner may not know what services may be required for a particular project. Purchasers of AIA B141-1997 may want to use the list of professional services contained within it as a starting point for discussions with a project owner about what may be required for a project. Fundamentally, the owner's needs must be determined. Moreover, ask the following:
 ____ (a) Why does the owner need any particular service?
 ____ (b) What knowledge, skills, and resources are needed in order to provide the service?

____ 2. **What are the designer's responsibilities?** After a determination is made regarding the professional services that are required for a particular project, the designer and the owner must then determine what work will be the responsibility of the designer and what work will be the responsibility of others.
 ____ (a) At this point, the designer or firm must decide whether or not the owner's needs can be met. This requires attention to several details, including the following:
  ____ (i) Does the designer or firm have the capability to meet the owner's needs?
  ____ (ii) Does the designer or firm have the capacity to handle the work required for the project? If not, can capacity be expanded by new hires, subconsultants, subcontractors, etc.?

**Fredrick J. Ludwig** is an associate in the St. Louis, Missouri, office of Husch Blackwell Sanders LLP. He practices in the firm's Construction & Design group.

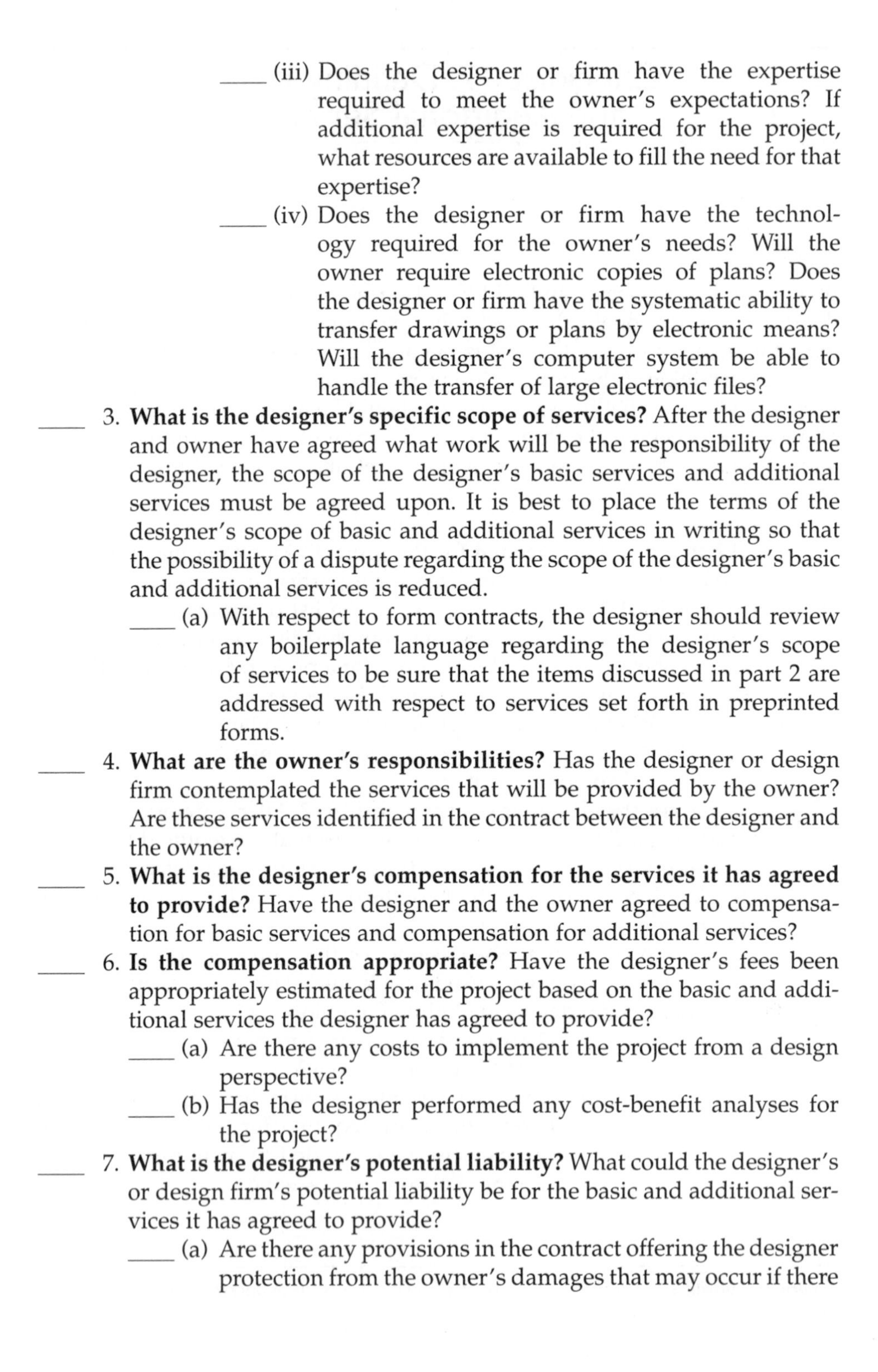

____ (iii) Does the designer or firm have the expertise required to meet the owner's expectations? If additional expertise is required for the project, what resources are available to fill the need for that expertise?

____ (iv) Does the designer or firm have the technology required for the owner's needs? Will the owner require electronic copies of plans? Does the designer or firm have the systematic ability to transfer drawings or plans by electronic means? Will the designer's computer system be able to handle the transfer of large electronic files?

____ 3. **What is the designer's specific scope of services?** After the designer and owner have agreed what work will be the responsibility of the designer, the scope of the designer's basic services and additional services must be agreed upon. It is best to place the terms of the designer's scope of basic and additional services in writing so that the possibility of a dispute regarding the scope of the designer's basic and additional services is reduced.

____ (a) With respect to form contracts, the designer should review any boilerplate language regarding the designer's scope of services to be sure that the items discussed in part 2 are addressed with respect to services set forth in preprinted forms.

____ 4. **What are the owner's responsibilities?** Has the designer or design firm contemplated the services that will be provided by the owner? Are these services identified in the contract between the designer and the owner?

____ 5. **What is the designer's compensation for the services it has agreed to provide?** Have the designer and the owner agreed to compensation for basic services and compensation for additional services?

____ 6. **Is the compensation appropriate?** Have the designer's fees been appropriately estimated for the project based on the basic and additional services the designer has agreed to provide?

____ (a) Are there any costs to implement the project from a design perspective?

____ (b) Has the designer performed any cost-benefit analyses for the project?

____ 7. **What is the designer's potential liability?** What could the designer's or design firm's potential liability be for the basic and additional services it has agreed to provide?

____ (a) Are there any provisions in the contract offering the designer protection from the owner's damages that may occur if there is an alleged breach of contract by the designer, or if there is alleged negligence on the part of the designer?

____ 8. **Can the designer obtain professional liability coverage for the project?** For the services the designer has agreed to provide, is the designer able to obtain professional liability insurance for those services? The designer may want to discuss a potential contract with its professional liability carrier and counsel to determine if the proposed work is covered.

____ 9. **Is the designer offering new services?** Does the designer or firm wish to offer new services with this particular project? If so:
   - ____ (a) What is required to be able to provide these new services?
   - ____ (b) What effect will offering a new service have on the designer's firm?
   - ____ (c) Who within the firm will be responsible for providing any new services?
   - ____ (d) Is there anyone within the firm interested in this particular new area of services?
   - ____ (e) Must new skills be learned in order to provide a new service?
   - ____ (f) Must the firm acquire new technology in order to provide the new service?
   - ____ (g) What is the potential cost versus the potential benefit of offering the new service?
   - ____ (h) Will the new service be a good fit with services currently being offered by the designer or firm?
   - ____ (i) Will the designer or firm be able to offer the new services within the timeframe for any particular project?
   - ____ (j) Is the new service contemplated already a subspecialty? If so, can the designer or firm hire someone with the knowledge and skill in order to immediately provide the new service?

____ 10. **Does the proposed cost fit into the owner's budget?** Does the likely cost of the services the designer is being asked to provide fit within the owner's budget? If not, the designer may wish to be cautious about engaging in the work. The designer may find that this results in the unintentional expansion of the scope of basic and additional services to which the owner and designer originally agreed.

____ 11. **Is the owner realistic?** Are the owner's expectations of the designer or design firm realistic? If not, this may be a red flag. If the owner's expectations are greater than the scope of basic and additional services the designer has agreed to provide, this could result in an increased risk of the owner making a claim against the design professional.

____ 12. **What about services not contemplated in the original agreement?** If any services not contemplated in the original contract are agreed upon, reduce the terms to writing. Not doing so could result in confusion or a dispute regarding the scope of work the designer agreed to perform.

____ 13. **What else can the designer offer?** What additional skills might the designer or design firm want to offer to an owner?

____ 14. **What kind of project is this?** Is the project a design-bid-build project or a design-build project? What impact does this have on the services the designer or design firm is being contracted to provide?

____ 15. **Who else may be needed for this project?** What related disciplines may be required, or will certainly be required?

____ (a) Does the designer or owner have the responsibility for retaining these professionals?

____ (b) If the designer is responsible for these professionals, how does this affect pricing and liability?

# Checklist 18: Common Issues in Program Development

Programming provides valuable resources for both the client and designer. It is considered a critical part of the design process. Programming produces information regarding the interests and requirements of the client and allows the designer to create facilities that would most effectively meet the interests and needs of the client, as well as support the usage and operations of the facilities.

____ 1. **What is programming?** Programming is a process of evaluating and determining the design requirements and parameters of a proposed project. It provides the architect and owner with the necessary information to design and develop a project. Programming varies based on the type of project.

____ 2. **Contractual issues related to program development.**

____ (a) **General contractual consideration.** Programming is not generally included in the design services. AIA B-141 states that programming is the responsibility of the owner. However, the architect should provide a preliminary evaluation of the owner's program as part of the design service.

____ (b) **Factors in setting the fees for programming.**

____ (i) **What is the size of the proposed project?**

____ (ii) **What is the complexity of the proposed project?** The programming fees vary based on the size and complexity of the proposed project. The programming fees are higher for more complex and technical buildings such as sports facilities, hospitals, and laboratories. The programming fees for large-scale projects are also higher.

____ (iii) **What are the applicable codes and standards?** The applicable codes and standards also have an effect on the amount of programming fees. Programming fees are higher if an extensive amount of time is

**Kenneth K. Wang** is an attorney at Koenig Jacobson LLP in Irvine, California, where he represents and counsels design professionals, contractors, and other construction personnel in a variety of claims, including construction disputes, professional liability, and breach of contract claims. He earned his J.D. from Loyola Law School in Los Angeles and undergraduate degrees from University of California, Irvine.

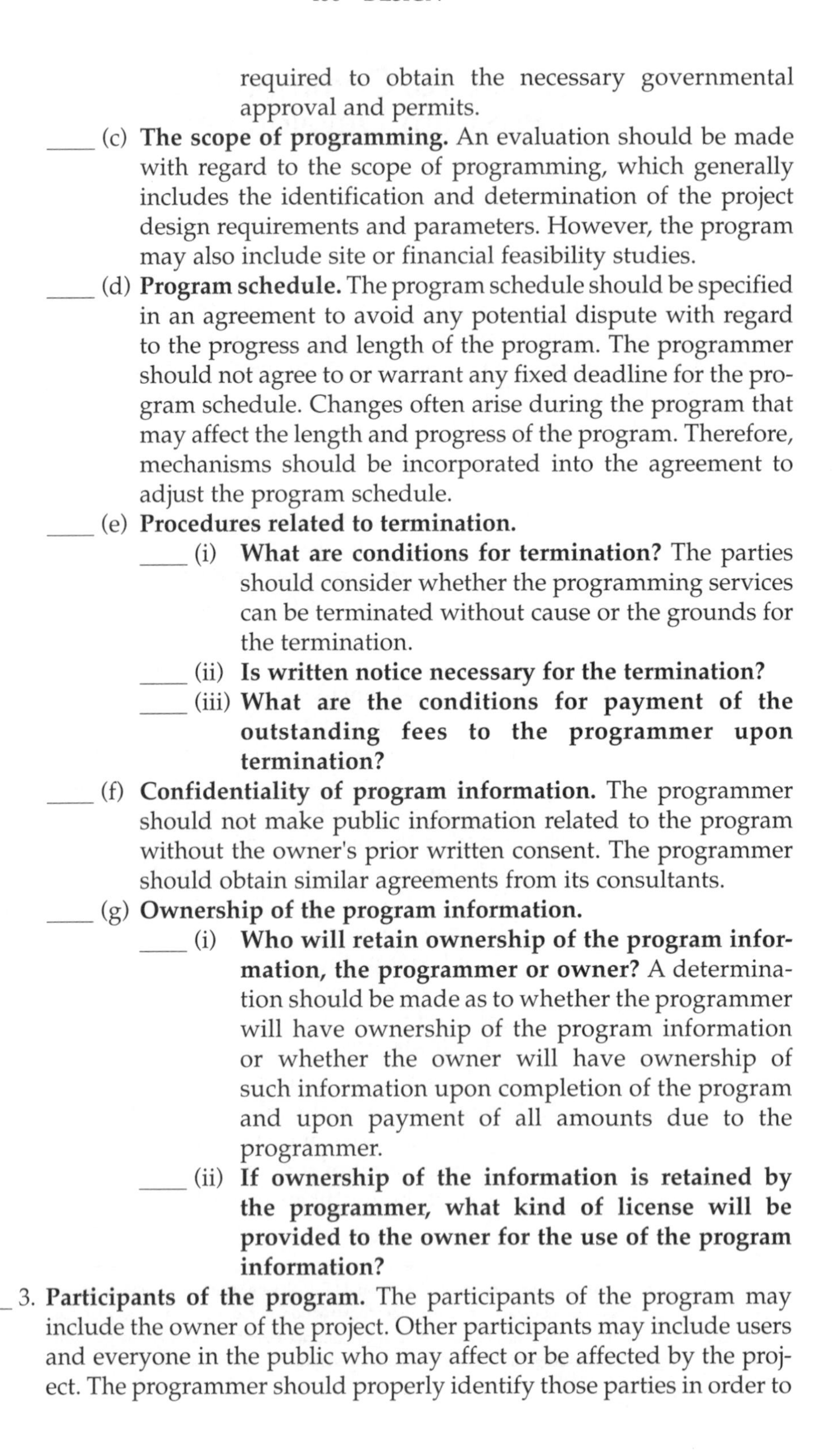

required to obtain the necessary governmental approval and permits.

____ (c) **The scope of programming.** An evaluation should be made with regard to the scope of programming, which generally includes the identification and determination of the project design requirements and parameters. However, the program may also include site or financial feasibility studies.

____ (d) **Program schedule.** The program schedule should be specified in an agreement to avoid any potential dispute with regard to the progress and length of the program. The programmer should not agree to or warrant any fixed deadline for the program schedule. Changes often arise during the program that may affect the length and progress of the program. Therefore, mechanisms should be incorporated into the agreement to adjust the program schedule.

____ (e) **Procedures related to termination.**

____ (i) **What are conditions for termination?** The parties should consider whether the programming services can be terminated without cause or the grounds for the termination.

____ (ii) **Is written notice necessary for the termination?**

____ (iii) **What are the conditions for payment of the outstanding fees to the programmer upon termination?**

____ (f) **Confidentiality of program information.** The programmer should not make public information related to the program without the owner's prior written consent. The programmer should obtain similar agreements from its consultants.

____ (g) **Ownership of the program information.**

____ (i) **Who will retain ownership of the program information, the programmer or owner?** A determination should be made as to whether the programmer will have ownership of the program information or whether the owner will have ownership of such information upon completion of the program and upon payment of all amounts due to the programmer.

____ (ii) **If ownership of the information is retained by the programmer, what kind of license will be provided to the owner for the use of the program information?**

____ 3. **Participants of the program.** The participants of the program may include the owner of the project. Other participants may include users and everyone in the public who may affect or be affected by the project. The programmer should properly identify those parties in order to

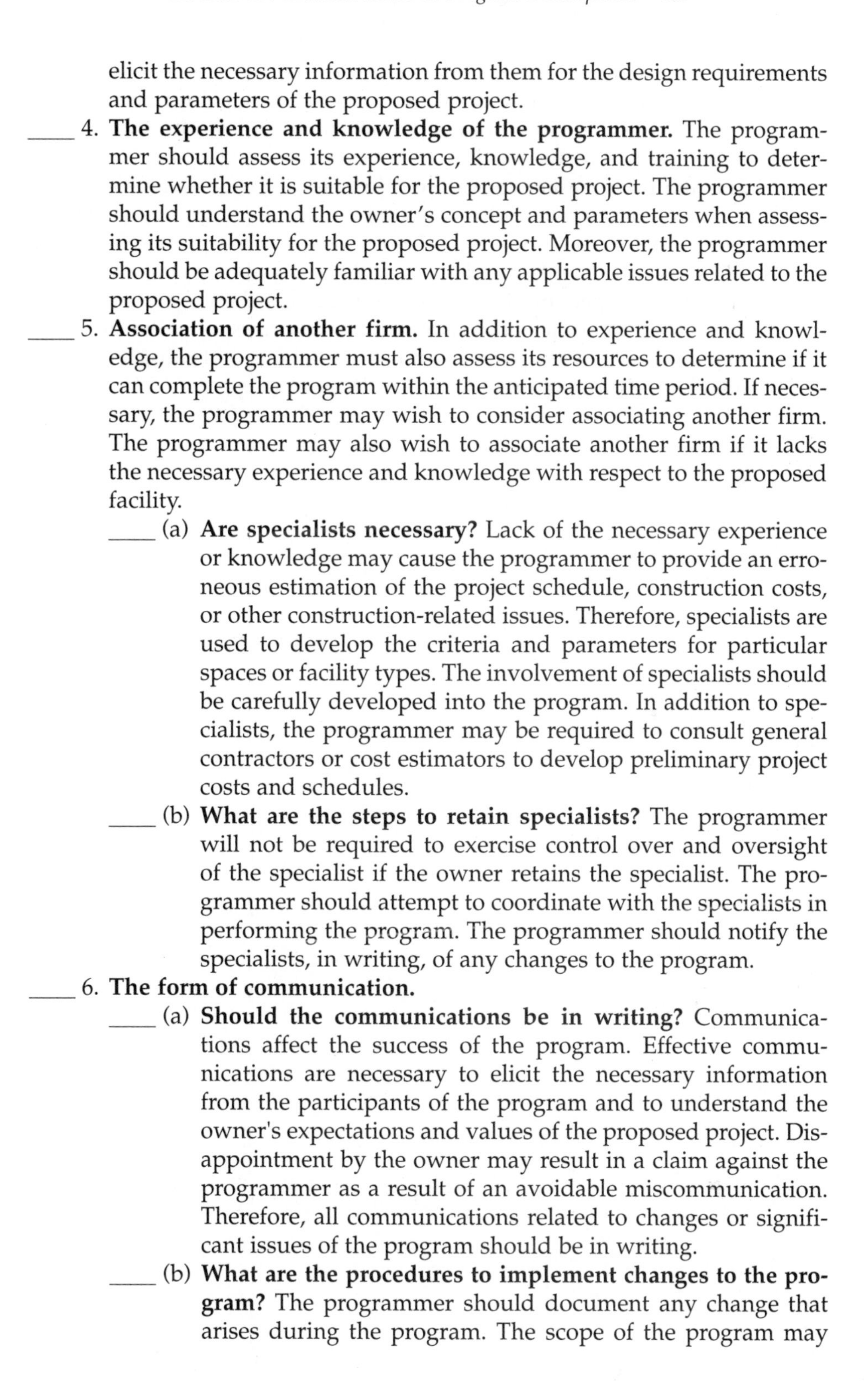

elicit the necessary information from them for the design requirements and parameters of the proposed project.

____ 4. **The experience and knowledge of the programmer.** The programmer should assess its experience, knowledge, and training to determine whether it is suitable for the proposed project. The programmer should understand the owner's concept and parameters when assessing its suitability for the proposed project. Moreover, the programmer should be adequately familiar with any applicable issues related to the proposed project.

____ 5. **Association of another firm.** In addition to experience and knowledge, the programmer must also assess its resources to determine if it can complete the program within the anticipated time period. If necessary, the programmer may wish to consider associating another firm. The programmer may also wish to associate another firm if it lacks the necessary experience and knowledge with respect to the proposed facility.

____ (a) **Are specialists necessary?** Lack of the necessary experience or knowledge may cause the programmer to provide an erroneous estimation of the project schedule, construction costs, or other construction-related issues. Therefore, specialists are used to develop the criteria and parameters for particular spaces or facility types. The involvement of specialists should be carefully developed into the program. In addition to specialists, the programmer may be required to consult general contractors or cost estimators to develop preliminary project costs and schedules.

____ (b) **What are the steps to retain specialists?** The programmer will not be required to exercise control over and oversight of the specialist if the owner retains the specialist. The programmer should attempt to coordinate with the specialists in performing the program. The programmer should notify the specialists, in writing, of any changes to the program.

____ 6. **The form of communication.**

____ (a) **Should the communications be in writing?** Communications affect the success of the program. Effective communications are necessary to elicit the necessary information from the participants of the program and to understand the owner's expectations and values of the proposed project. Disappointment by the owner may result in a claim against the programmer as a result of an avoidable miscommunication. Therefore, all communications related to changes or significant issues of the program should be in writing.

____ (b) **What are the procedures to implement changes to the program?** The programmer should document any change that arises during the program. The scope of the program may be altered by the changes. The changes may also affect the schedule and cost of the program. Clear documentation of the changes would avoid any misunderstanding of the program by the parties.

____ 7. **Has the programmer considered the relevant codes and standards?** The programmer should review the applicable codes and standards for the potential restraints or requirements of the proposed project. The codes, covenants, restrictions, and zoning requirements may have significant impact on the cost and schedule of the project. Therefore, they must be sufficiently identified and addressed in the program. Standards are mandated in certain jurisdictions and must be considered by the programmer for accreditation of the proposed facility.

# Checklist 19: Complying with Licensing and Registration Laws

Following is a checklist for use in evaluating license law issues in the construction industry. These issues arise frequently and must always be considered when a firm undertakes work of a different type, or in a new state. This list tracks the issues in a chronological manner, from identifying potential regulators through keeping existing licenses up-to-date.

____ 1. **Identify the Regulators.** What agency or regulatory body has a licensing or registration requirement that may apply to the firm? In answering this question, be sure to consider:

____ (a) **State level.** State boards of contractor, engineer, and architect licensing or registration must be consulted. The websites of many state licensing boards have the full text of the licensing laws (statutes and regulations).[1]

____ (b) **Local level.** Requirements may be imposed by counties and cities (especially where there is no state licensing requirement).

____ 2. **Is a license required?** Does the work the firm is now performing or is considering performing in the future require it to obtain a contractor's, architect's, and/or engineer's license? In answering this question, be sure to check and consider the following:

____ (a) **Check statutory definitions of key terms.** Identify and review the typically broad definitions of key terms such as "contractor," "practice engineering," and "practice architecture."

____ (b) **An offer to perform work for which a license is required.** Consider whether the license requirement covers work the firm offers to do. This can be an important consideration where the firm is soliciting work in a new state (or in a new discipline) but does not yet have the appropriate license.

____ (c) **An agreement to perform work for which a license is required.** An essential consideration is whether the applicable license requirement covers work the firm has *agreed*

**Paul W. Berning** and **John W. Ralls** are partners in the law firm of Thelen Reid Brown Raysman & Steiner LLP, San Francisco. Both practice construction law, and give advice to contractors, equipment suppliers, and design professionals on licensing issues.

*to do*, even if the work actually will be performed by others. In many jurisdictions, a firm must be licensed if it signs a contract that calls for the performance of construction, architectural, or engineering work, even if all of the work will be performed by licensed professionals in the applicable fields.

____ (d) **Design-build.** Pay special attention to design-build projects. Design-builders may need to have contractor, architect, and engineer licenses.[2]

____ 3. **Nature of the Work Undertaken by Contract.** Even if the firm does not consider itself a construction, architecture, or engineering firm, is the firm performing or undertaking work (including work to be performed by or through others) that requires a license? In answering this question, be sure to consider:

____ (a) **Developers.** Developers may have to be licensed under certain circumstances, especially where they agree or commit to have construction work completed, even if they intend to have the work performed by others.

____ (b) **Construction managers.** The license requirements that pertain to contractors, architects, and engineers often include construction management.

____ (c) **Equipment sales.** Equipment sales contracts that also provide for design and construction as part of installation may require licensing.

____ 4. **Exceptions or Exemptions.** Does the firm fall under any of the exceptions to or exemptions from the pertinent licensing requirement? In answering this question, be sure to consider:

____ (a) **Owner exceptions.** Most jurisdictions recognize that owners may self-perform construction work without a license, although there may be limitations if the owners intend to sell the property within a short time, or for investment purposes.

____ (b) **Utility exceptions.** In some jurisdictions, contractors and design professionals performing work for regulated public utilities may be exempt from licensing requirements.

____ (c) **Federal projects.** Generally, state license laws are preempted by the federal statutes and regulations that pertain to projects performed on federal property.

____ (d) **Cross-over practice.** In many jurisdictions, construction and design professionals may perform work in other disciplines that is ancillary to the primary work performed (for example, architects may be able to perform engineering work that is ancillary to the architectural work).

____ 5. **Who will be the license holder?** Exactly who would be the license holder? In answering this question, be sure to consider:

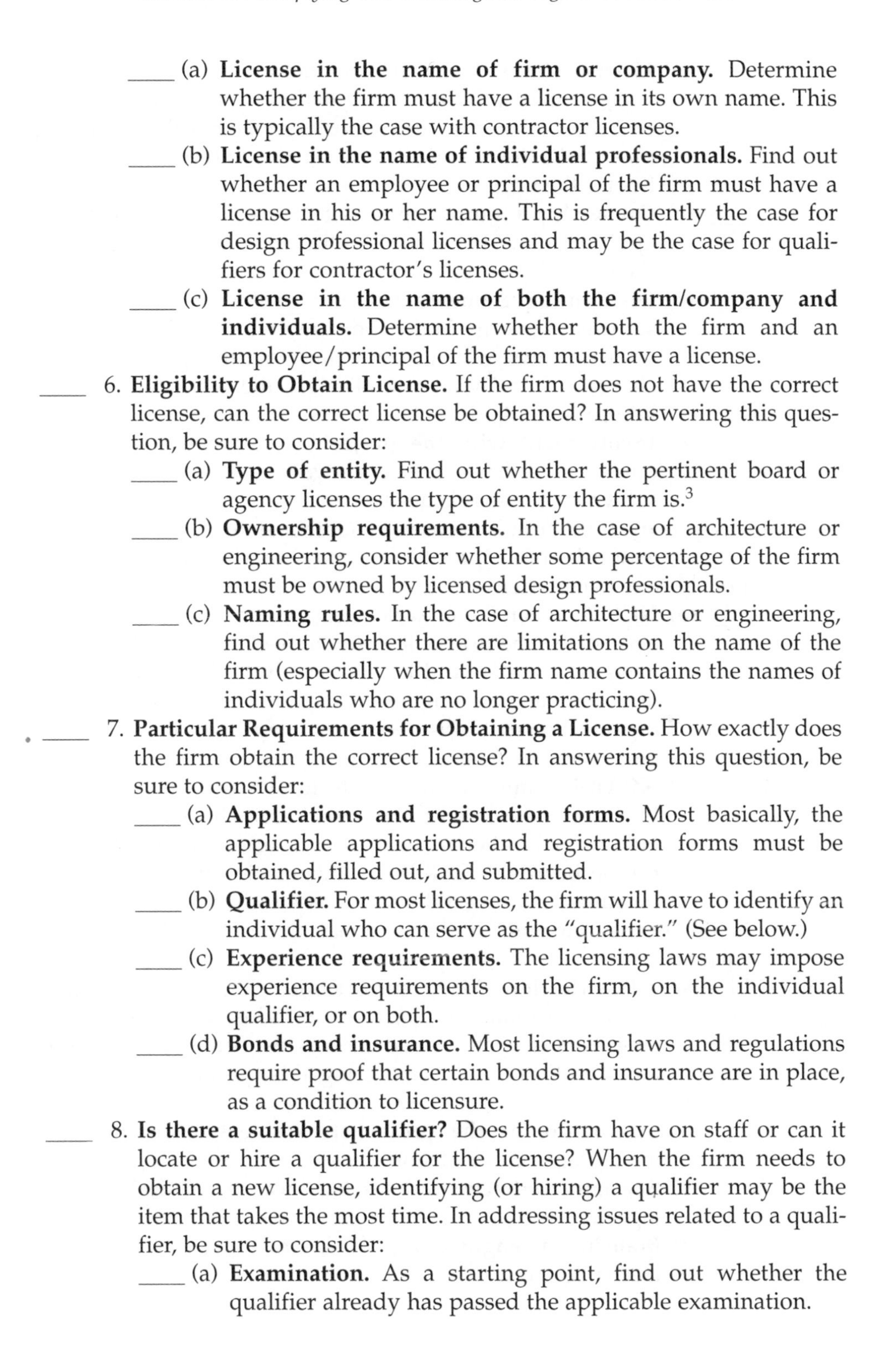

____ (a) **License in the name of firm or company.** Determine whether the firm must have a license in its own name. This is typically the case with contractor licenses.

____ (b) **License in the name of individual professionals.** Find out whether an employee or principal of the firm must have a license in his or her name. This is frequently the case for design professional licenses and may be the case for qualifiers for contractor's licenses.

____ (c) **License in the name of both the firm/company and individuals.** Determine whether both the firm and an employee/principal of the firm must have a license.

____ 6. **Eligibility to Obtain License.** If the firm does not have the correct license, can the correct license be obtained? In answering this question, be sure to consider:

____ (a) **Type of entity.** Find out whether the pertinent board or agency licenses the type of entity the firm is.[3]

____ (b) **Ownership requirements.** In the case of architecture or engineering, consider whether some percentage of the firm must be owned by licensed design professionals.

____ (c) **Naming rules.** In the case of architecture or engineering, find out whether there are limitations on the name of the firm (especially when the firm name contains the names of individuals who are no longer practicing).

____ 7. **Particular Requirements for Obtaining a License.** How exactly does the firm obtain the correct license? In answering this question, be sure to consider:

____ (a) **Applications and registration forms.** Most basically, the applicable applications and registration forms must be obtained, filled out, and submitted.

____ (b) **Qualifier.** For most licenses, the firm will have to identify an individual who can serve as the "qualifier." (See below.)

____ (c) **Experience requirements.** The licensing laws may impose experience requirements on the firm, on the individual qualifier, or on both.

____ (d) **Bonds and insurance.** Most licensing laws and regulations require proof that certain bonds and insurance are in place, as a condition to licensure.

____ 8. **Is there a suitable qualifier?** Does the firm have on staff or can it locate or hire a qualifier for the license? When the firm needs to obtain a new license, identifying (or hiring) a qualifier may be the item that takes the most time. In addressing issues related to a qualifier, be sure to consider:

____ (a) **Examination.** As a starting point, find out whether the qualifier already has passed the applicable examination.

____ (b) **License status.** If the firm identifies an individual who already holds a license (on behalf of himself or herself, or on behalf of another firm), consider whether the qualifying must make the existing license inactive to serve as the qualifier for the firm.

____ (c) **Ownership requirements.** Determine whether under the applicable law, the qualifier must have an equity stake in the company.

____ (d) **Position requirements.** Find out whether the qualifier has sufficient seniority in the company to satisfy the applicable licensing laws, which may require that the qualifier be "in charge" of or "have control" over the work for which a license is required.

____ (e) **Involvement with the projects.** Determine whether the qualifier will have sufficient involvement with the project for which a license is needed.

____ 9. **Reciprocity.** If the firm is licensed in another state, can the firm take advantage of rules of reciprocity or comity? In answering this question, be sure to consider:

____ (a) **NCEES.** When it comes to doing engineering work in multiple states, the firm will likely be well served to hire engineers who are "record holders" with the National Council of Examiners for Engineers and Surveyors (NCEES), an organization that assists with obtaining engineering licenses on a reciprocal basis.[4]

____ (b) **NCARB.** Similarly, for architectural work, the firm will likely be well served to hire architects who are "certificate holders" with the National Council of Architectural Registration Boards (NCARB), an organization that assists with obtaining architectural licenses on a reciprocal basis.[5]

____ 10. **Is the license current?** If the firm has the correct license, is it current?

____ 11. **License Classification.** Many jurisdictions recognize classifications or subclassifications for construction industry licenses. If the firm is doing work in such a jurisdiction, is the firm's license in the appropriate classification? In answering this question, be sure to consider:

____ (a) **Size/nature of the project(s).** Residential, commercial, industrial, number of stories, etc.

____ (b) **Specialty contractor licenses.** Electrical, mechanical, plumbing, etc.

____ (c) **Branches of engineering.** Civil, structural, electrical, and mechanical, etc.

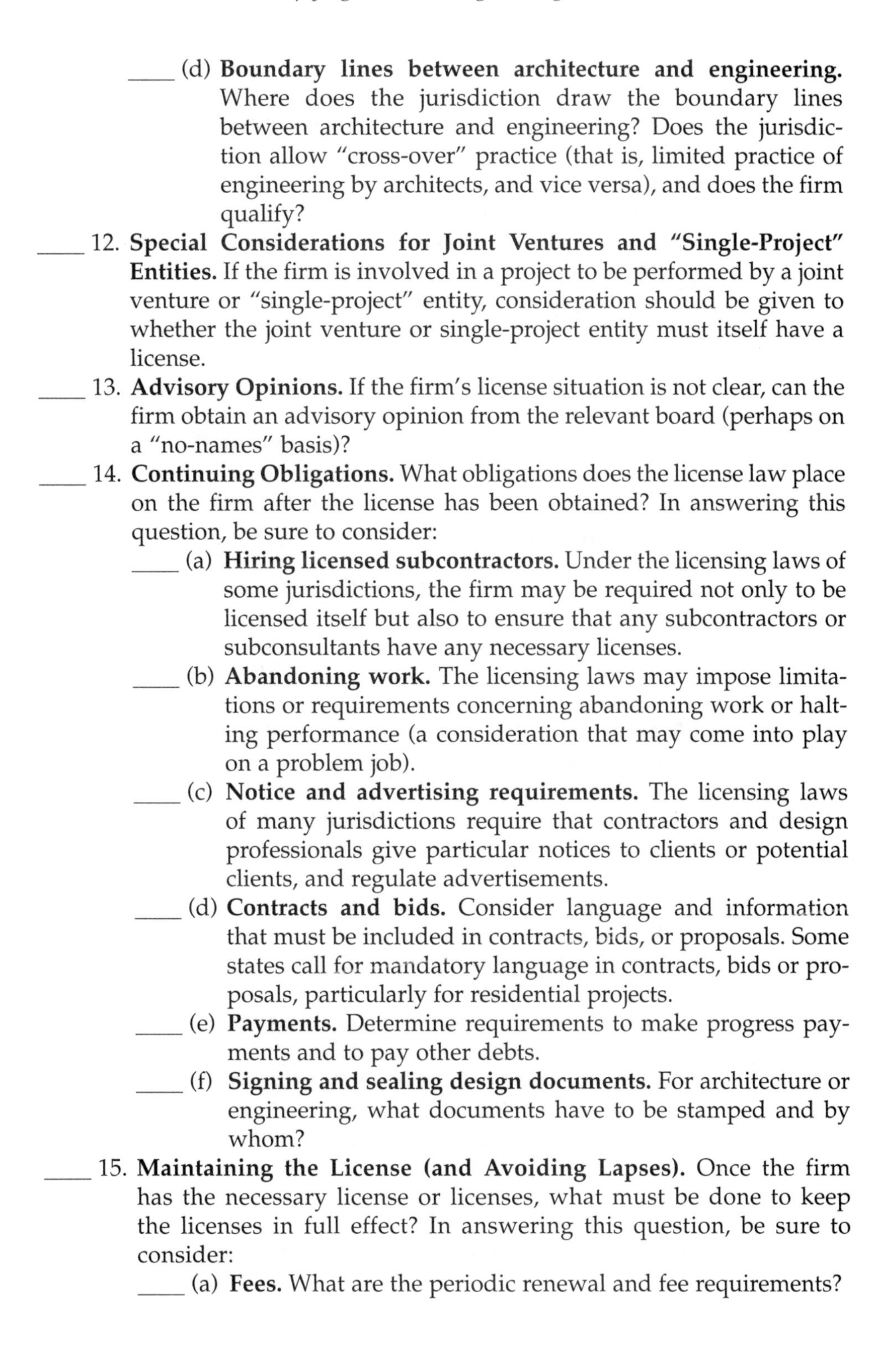

____ (d) **Boundary lines between architecture and engineering.** Where does the jurisdiction draw the boundary lines between architecture and engineering? Does the jurisdiction allow "cross-over" practice (that is, limited practice of engineering by architects, and vice versa), and does the firm qualify?

____ 12. **Special Considerations for Joint Ventures and "Single-Project" Entities.** If the firm is involved in a project to be performed by a joint venture or "single-project" entity, consideration should be given to whether the joint venture or single-project entity must itself have a license.

____ 13. **Advisory Opinions.** If the firm's license situation is not clear, can the firm obtain an advisory opinion from the relevant board (perhaps on a "no-names" basis)?

____ 14. **Continuing Obligations.** What obligations does the license law place on the firm after the license has been obtained? In answering this question, be sure to consider:

____ (a) **Hiring licensed subcontractors.** Under the licensing laws of some jurisdictions, the firm may be required not only to be licensed itself but also to ensure that any subcontractors or subconsultants have any necessary licenses.

____ (b) **Abandoning work.** The licensing laws may impose limitations or requirements concerning abandoning work or halting performance (a consideration that may come into play on a problem job).

____ (c) **Notice and advertising requirements.** The licensing laws of many jurisdictions require that contractors and design professionals give particular notices to clients or potential clients, and regulate advertisements.

____ (d) **Contracts and bids.** Consider language and information that must be included in contracts, bids, or proposals. Some states call for mandatory language in contracts, bids or proposals, particularly for residential projects.

____ (e) **Payments.** Determine requirements to make progress payments and to pay other debts.

____ (f) **Signing and sealing design documents.** For architecture or engineering, what documents have to be stamped and by whom?

____ 15. **Maintaining the License (and Avoiding Lapses).** Once the firm has the necessary license or licenses, what must be done to keep the licenses in full effect? In answering this question, be sure to consider:

____ (a) **Fees.** What are the periodic renewal and fee requirements?

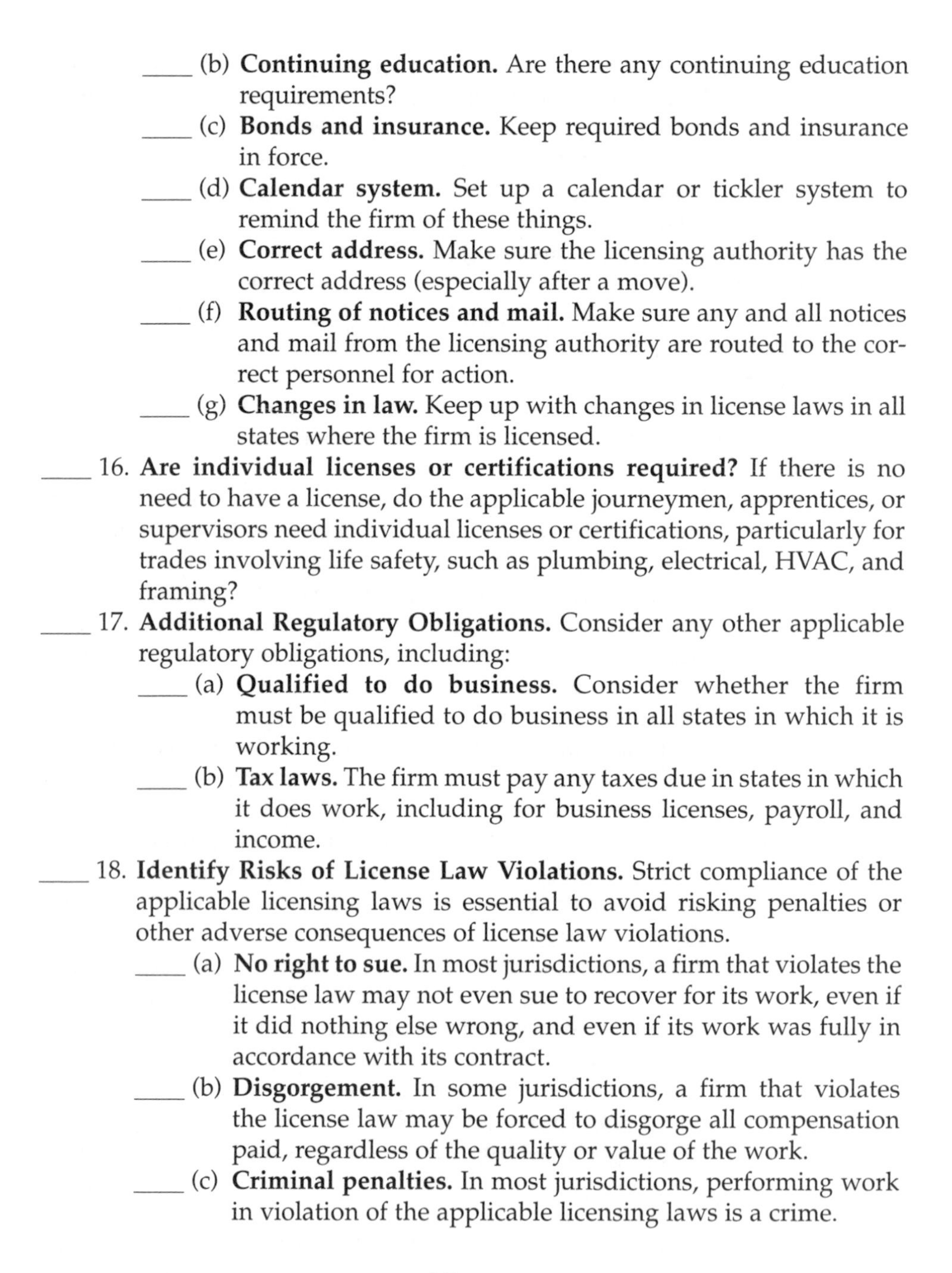

____ (b) **Continuing education.** Are there any continuing education requirements?

____ (c) **Bonds and insurance.** Keep required bonds and insurance in force.

____ (d) **Calendar system.** Set up a calendar or tickler system to remind the firm of these things.

____ (e) **Correct address.** Make sure the licensing authority has the correct address (especially after a move).

____ (f) **Routing of notices and mail.** Make sure any and all notices and mail from the licensing authority are routed to the correct personnel for action.

____ (g) **Changes in law.** Keep up with changes in license laws in all states where the firm is licensed.

____ 16. **Are individual licenses or certifications required?** If there is no need to have a license, do the applicable journeymen, apprentices, or supervisors need individual licenses or certifications, particularly for trades involving life safety, such as plumbing, electrical, HVAC, and framing?

____ 17. **Additional Regulatory Obligations.** Consider any other applicable regulatory obligations, including:

____ (a) **Qualified to do business.** Consider whether the firm must be qualified to do business in all states in which it is working.

____ (b) **Tax laws.** The firm must pay any taxes due in states in which it does work, including for business licenses, payroll, and income.

____ 18. **Identify Risks of License Law Violations.** Strict compliance of the applicable licensing laws is essential to avoid risking penalties or other adverse consequences of license law violations.

____ (a) **No right to sue.** In most jurisdictions, a firm that violates the license law may not even sue to recover for its work, even if it did nothing else wrong, and even if its work was fully in accordance with its contract.

____ (b) **Disgorgement.** In some jurisdictions, a firm that violates the license law may be forced to disgorge all compensation paid, regardless of the quality or value of the work.

____ (c) **Criminal penalties.** In most jurisdictions, performing work in violation of the applicable licensing laws is a crime.

## *Notes*

1. For a list (including contact information) of the pertinent state boards and agencies (including links to websites and contact information), see: *http://www.constructionweblinks.com/Industry_Topics/Licensing__Industry_Topics/ licensing__industry_topics.html.*

2. See generally, J. Heisse & J. Schenck, eds., *The Design/Build Deskbook* (3rd ed., 2004), which has a comprehensive discussion of licensing requirements that pertain to design-build projects in the 50 states and Canada.

3. For an excellent discussion of this issue as it pertains to the licensing of design professionals, see Paul M. Lurie and Hugh Anderson, *The Practice of Architecture and Engineering by Limited Liability Entities Across State Lines*, Constr. Law. 24:1 at 24 (Winter 2004).

4. For additional information on this organization, look at *www.ncees.org*.

5. For additional information on this organization, look at *www.ncarb.org*.

# Insurance

# Checklist 20: Available Insurance and Bonds

The insurance and bonds that may be applicable or necessary for a particular project will vary depending on its inherent risks and how they are assessed by the parties involved in the project, whether they are the owner, designer, or construction contractor. This checklist provides a listing of insurance coverage and bond instruments that may be considered in any project.

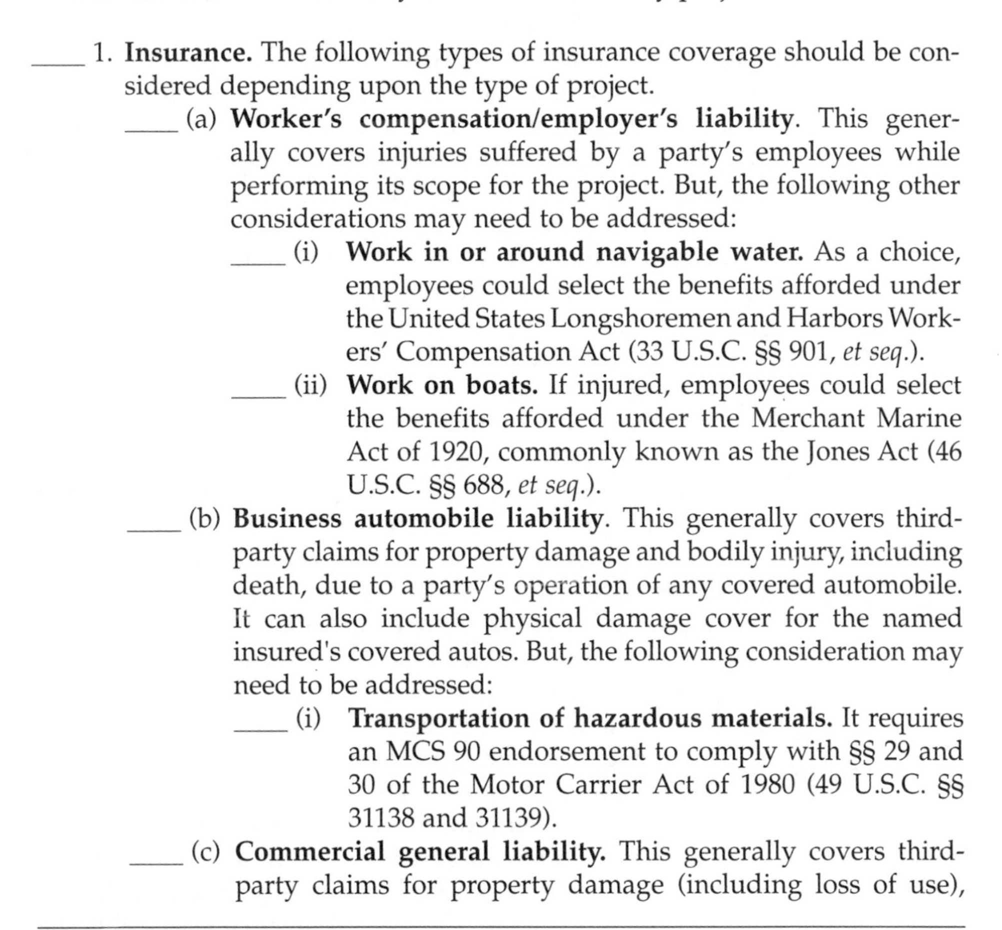

____ 1. **Insurance.** The following types of insurance coverage should be considered depending upon the type of project.

____ (a) **Worker's compensation/employer's liability**. This generally covers injuries suffered by a party's employees while performing its scope for the project. But, the following other considerations may need to be addressed:

____ (i) **Work in or around navigable water.** As a choice, employees could select the benefits afforded under the United States Longshoremen and Harbors Workers' Compensation Act (33 U.S.C. §§ 901, *et seq.*).

____ (ii) **Work on boats.** If injured, employees could select the benefits afforded under the Merchant Marine Act of 1920, commonly known as the Jones Act (46 U.S.C. §§ 688, *et seq.*).

____ (b) **Business automobile liability**. This generally covers third-party claims for property damage and bodily injury, including death, due to a party's operation of any covered automobile. It can also include physical damage cover for the named insured's covered autos. But, the following consideration may need to be addressed:

____ (i) **Transportation of hazardous materials.** It requires an MCS 90 endorsement to comply with §§ 29 and 30 of the Motor Carrier Act of 1980 (49 U.S.C. §§ 31138 and 31139).

____ (c) **Commercial general liability.** This generally covers third-party claims for property damage (including loss of use),

---

**Terry J. Galganski** is director of insurance and risk programs for The Weitz Company, LLC. He has more than 25 years of construction law experience, first in private practice and then in-house with two large engineering firms before joining Weitz. Most of his focus in-house has been on managing Weitz's corporate insurance programs and addressing risk management and insurance issues related to its respective operations.

bodily injury (including death), and personal and advertising injury due to a party's on-site or completed operations or its products. But, the following other considerations may need to be addressed:

____ (i) **Contractual liability.** It provides assurances that the indemnity in the contract will be supported to some extent by this cover afforded under this insurance coverage.

____ (ii) **Limits on a per-project basis.**

____ (iii) **Work using a boat greater than 26 feet.** This situation requires an endorsement under this insurance that provides coverage for boats of longer length or a separate policy, known as protection and indemnity insurance.

____ (d) **Excess or umbrella liability.** It generally provides additional limits (and sometimes additional coverages) beyond what is set forth under the following primary layers of a named insured's corporate liability program: employers' liability, business automobile liability, and commercial general liability.

____ (e) **Professional liability**. It generally covers third-party claims for damages due to a party's negligence in performing its professional services. But, the following considerations may want to be addressed:

____ (i) Specify a retroactive date under the policy that is no later than the date the professional services on the project are to begin.

____ (ii) Because this cover is only claims-made, require that the policy must be renewed a finite number of years following completion of its professional services.

____ (f) **Pollution liability**. It generally covers third-party claims for damages due to pollutant releases due to a party's on-site operations or professional services, as the case may be or as the policy may provide.

____ (g) **Protective liability**. This insurance generally consists of the following coverage types that insure the party usually requesting the cover as the named insured:

____ (i) **Owners' and contractors' protective liability (an OCP policy).** It generally covers third-party claims for property damage and bodily injury, including death, due to the named insured's (usually the owner, but it can be the general contractor) negligent supervision of or its vicarious liability arising out of the designated contractor's ongoing operations.

____ (ii) **Railroad protective liability.** It generally covers third-party claims for property damage and bodily injury, including death, caused by "acts or omissions" at or in connection with the policy's designated job location and physical damage to the railroad company's owned or leased property.

____ (iii) **Owner's protective professional liability.** It generally provides excess cover over any professional liability coverage that is required to be provided by a design professional for the project for the protection of the owner. Unlike the former two protective liability insurance types, the named insured (the owner) procures this cover directly.

____ (h) **Builder's risk**. It generally covers physical damage to the improvements being constructed or installed until their completion, provided they are caused by certain designated perils or all perils, subject to applicable exclusions.

____ 2. **Additional Considerations.** Besides this list of insurance coverage, the following issues should be considered for a project's insurance requirements:

____ (a) Is a controlled insurance program being planned or appropriate? A controlled insurance program generally provides certain insurance coverage, usually workers' compensation/employers' liability and commercial general liability, with some excess or umbrella liability insurance for enrolled participants for a construction project that normally exceeds a construction value of $100,000,000.

____ (b) What are the appropriate limits to request for each applicable cover?

____ (c) What additional insured cover should the party requesting the commercial general and excess or umbrella liability insurance be demanding?

____ (d) How should this same party address the issue of primacy under its and the other party's commercial general liability cover, including any excess or umbrella cover, when it is asking to be named an additional insured under these insurance policies?

____ (e) Should the party include a waiver of recovery rights provision that will cover the damages afforded under any of the listed policies? The following states do not recognize prospective workers' compensation waivers: Kentucky [Ken. Rev. Stat. § 342.700(3)], Maine [See *Fowler v. Boise Cascade Corp.*, 948 F2d 49 (1st Cir. 1991)], Missouri [Mo. Rev. Stat. § 287.150.2(6)], New Jersey (N.J. Stat. Ann. § 34:15-39), Ohio (effective only with the state's permission), Washington (only the state can waive), West Virginia (monopolistic), Wisconsin [see *Campion v. Montgomery Elevator Co.*, 493 NW2d 244 (Wis. 1992)], and Wyoming (monopolistic).

____ (f) What type of certificate of insurance form will be acceptable to verify that the project's insurance requirements are being met?

____ (g) Should certain insurer financial standing requirements be included in the contract?

____ (h) What notice requirements regarding the listed insurance should be demanded from the other party's insurance carriers?

____ 3. **Bonds.** There are several bonds available for a construction project, with the payment and performance bonds being the most commonly used bonds. If the construction project is for a public entity, that entity or state statute may mandate the bond forms that will be acceptable. For private construction projects, the owner may require the bond form that it will accept. With the preceding in mind, the following types of bonds are generally available:

____ (a) **Bid bond.** This bond runs to the benefit of the obligee (most often the project owner) for a penal sum that is usually 5% to 10% of the contract price. It is requested by owners to guarantee the construction contractor (known as "the principal" under this bond) will enter into a contract with the owner for the project. If the construction contractor does not do so, the surety will compensate the owner in the amount of the penal sum listed in the bid bond.

____ (b) **Performance bond.** This bond will generally protect the obligee from the obligor's failure to perform its construction work on the project satisfactorily, which may include any 1-year warranty obligations, subject to any surety defenses.

____ (c) **Payment bond.** This bond will generally protect the obligee from the obligor's failure to pay certain of its project subcontractors appropriately, subject to any surety defenses.

____ (d) **Maintenance bond.** This bond will generally protect the obligee from the obligor's failure to meet its warranty obligations that exceed more than 1 year from project completion, subject to any surety defenses.

____ (e) **Retention bond.** This bond can be generally issued in lieu of holding retainage on a construction contractor. It provides its obligee recourse for the obligor's failure to perform its construction work or pay its subcontractors appropriately up to a penal sum equal to the anticipated retainage.

# Checklist 21: Risk Allocation through Insurance

Construction project risk allocation is best accomplished through judicious implementation of the various strategies and mechanisms to allocate those risks. Among the most common are contractual indemnification provisions, surety contracts, and insurance policies.

Construction form documents implement contractual indemnification and insurance programs in order to allocate risk in owner–contractor and contractor–subcontractor documents or design-build delivery systems. Typically, nonstandard documents also rely on contractual indemnification and a comprehensive insurance program in order to allocate risk. Contract documents usually include provisions relating to the contractor's liability insurance, the owner's liability insurance, and property insurance on the project during construction. This checklist identifies the risks to be addressed by and limitations of those coverages.

____ 1. **Builder's Risk Insurance.** Typically the owner is responsible for purchasing and maintaining property insurance during the construction phase. A builder's risk policy is, effectively, property insurance insuring property at the site and, if properly endorsed, materials stored off site and in transit. The following issues deserve special consideration:

____ (a) **Is the policy written on an "all-risk" or "specified-peril" basis?** The former is more common and usually preferable. Only damage from those risks specifically excluded under an all-risk policy are not covered by the policy.

____ (b) **Does the policy provide for reimbursement of the full replacement cost of the insured property rather than specified or scheduled values?** Replacement cost is the more typical and preferred choice because it avoids the possibility that the cost to replace exceeds the specified scheduled values.

____ (c) **Does the policy include not only the interests of the owner and contractor, but also the interests of all subcontractors and sub-subcontractors?** Failure to include all of the

**David T. Kasper** is a partner with the law firm of Locke Reynolds LLP in Indianapolis, Indiana. He concentrates his practice in litigation, professional malpractice, and insurance services. Representing insurance companies, he advises them concerning coverage, extra-contractual exposure, and litigation.

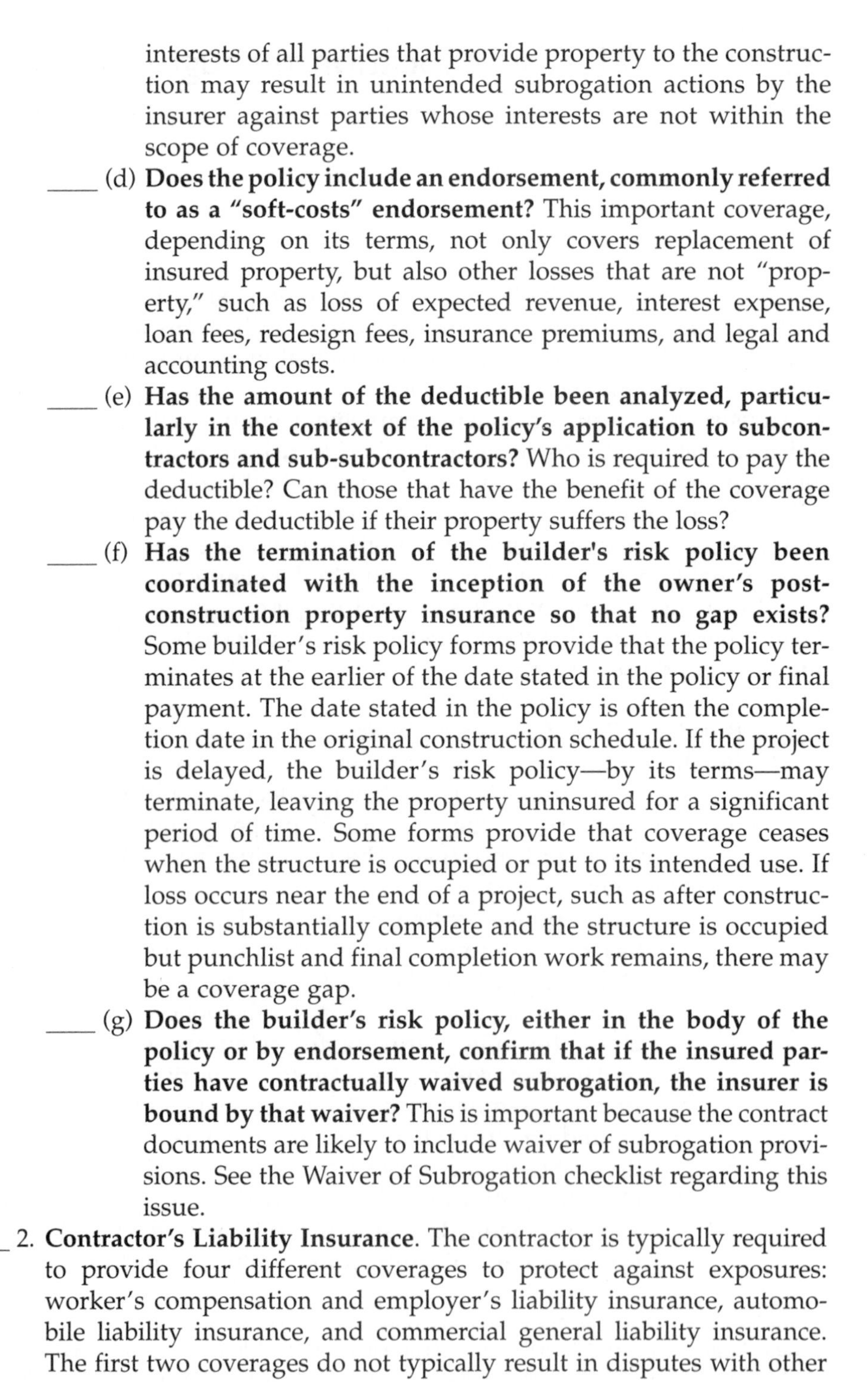

interests of all parties that provide property to the construction may result in unintended subrogation actions by the insurer against parties whose interests are not within the scope of coverage.

____ (d) **Does the policy include an endorsement, commonly referred to as a "soft-costs" endorsement?** This important coverage, depending on its terms, not only covers replacement of insured property, but also other losses that are not "property," such as loss of expected revenue, interest expense, loan fees, redesign fees, insurance premiums, and legal and accounting costs.

____ (e) **Has the amount of the deductible been analyzed, particularly in the context of the policy's application to subcontractors and sub-subcontractors?** Who is required to pay the deductible? Can those that have the benefit of the coverage pay the deductible if their property suffers the loss?

____ (f) **Has the termination of the builder's risk policy been coordinated with the inception of the owner's post-construction property insurance so that no gap exists?** Some builder's risk policy forms provide that the policy terminates at the earlier of the date stated in the policy or final payment. The date stated in the policy is often the completion date in the original construction schedule. If the project is delayed, the builder's risk policy—by its terms—may terminate, leaving the property uninsured for a significant period of time. Some forms provide that coverage ceases when the structure is occupied or put to its intended use. If loss occurs near the end of a project, such as after construction is substantially complete and the structure is occupied but punchlist and final completion work remains, there may be a coverage gap.

____ (g) **Does the builder's risk policy, either in the body of the policy or by endorsement, confirm that if the insured parties have contractually waived subrogation, the insurer is bound by that waiver?** This is important because the contract documents are likely to include waiver of subrogation provisions. See the Waiver of Subrogation checklist regarding this issue.

____ 2. **Contractor's Liability Insurance**. The contractor is typically required to provide four different coverages to protect against exposures: worker's compensation and employer's liability insurance, automobile liability insurance, and commercial general liability insurance. The first two coverages do not typically result in disputes with other parties participating in the construction (that is, owner, subcontractors, design professional, or their insurers).

____ (a) **Commercial general liability insurance.** The contractor's commercial general liability (CGL) policy is a critical component of risk allocation during, and in some instances, after construction. However, both by its terms (including exclusions) and judicial interpretation, the CGL policy does not respond to all risks of loss incurred during the course of construction. The CGL policy protects insureds against loss arising from "bodily injury" or "property damage" caused by an "occurrence" (that is, an accident).

The policy includes personal injury and advertising injury coverage that covers certain intentional torts such as defamation and false imprisonment. The coverages are seldom triggered by typical construction risk. The following issues should be considered:

____ (i) **Do or should the contract documents require the insurer to have a minimum rating?** Services rate insurers by financial strength and size and establish a reasonable minimum rating, which is in all parties' interests.

____ (ii) **Should a standard or manuscript form be used?** Insurers use standardized forms, even if they are developed internally, or prepared by the Insurance Services Office (ISO), an entity that services the insurance industry by developing those forms. A manuscript form is a policy that is drafted for a unique risk not adequately addressed in a standard form.

____ (iii) **If a standard form policy is used but there are unique risks, are there endorsements that should be considered to address those risks?** The agent/broker should be advised in writing of these issues and asked to respond to whether insurance is or is not available.

____ (iv) **Are the required limits of liability, both on a per-occurrence and aggregate basis, sufficient for the exposures?** Requiring unreasonably high limits may limit the number of qualified bidders.

____ (v) **Is this policy written on a location basis?** If so, is there a limitation of liability per location?

____ (vi) **Are the appropriate parties included as named insureds?** Care should be taken that the insured should also include any subsidiaries that may contribute services to the project.

____ (vii) **If the entity to be insured is a joint venture, has appropriate coverage been obtained for the joint venture?** Separate coverage for the participants to the joint venture will not usually cover their joint venture.

____ (b) **Additional insured issues.** Owners and upstream contractors often try to reallocate their risk by having themselves added as insureds on policies of others.

____ (i) **Do the contract documents require additional insured status for certain parties, and, if so, what is or should be the scope of that coverage?** There are a wide variety of additional insured forms that, based on their terms, may provide very limited or very broad coverage.

____ (ii) **What is an acceptable deductible under a policy that grants additional insured status to another party?** Parties contractually seeking to obtain additional insured status should consider specifying the acceptable deductible under the named insured's policy to avoid being confronted with a substantial and unexpected financial obligation.

____ (iii) **Does the additional insured endorsement provide that unless the contract documents require it to be primary and the additional insured's policy is noncontributory, insurance for the additional insured is in excess of any other insurance maintained by the additional insured?** This can defeat the benefit of additional insured status.

____ (iv) **Are there policy forms that accept this requirement included in the policy?** Many standard forms will accept this primary.

____ (v) **Do the contract documents identify by form number the specific additional insured forms that should be used and, if so, have those forms been obtained as part of the policy?** The contract should address this.

____ (vi) **Does the additional insured have coverage only during the construction period ("operations"), or does it provide for coverage after the named insured's operations are completed?** Some ISO endorsements address this.

____ (vii) **Is the insured required to keep the policy in place for a designated period after the completion of construction?** Typically, this should be a requirement in the contract.

____ (viii) **Is there professional services exposure that would not be covered within the general liability coverage, and should a separate professional liability policy be obtained to address it?**

____ (ix) **Is the additional insured entitled to notice of cancellation or nonpayment of premium?**

____ (x) **Is the additional insured coverage illusory?** Because of factors such as limitations in the additional insured endorsement on its scope, or the fact that the construction is in a comparative fault jurisdiction, an additional insured endorsement may not actually provide coverage.

____ (xi) **How can the policy be eroded?** If, under the contractual indemnification provision, the named insured obligates itself to not only indemnify the indemnitee but to also pay its defense expenses, those payments may erode the limit of liability of the policy. Consider the effect of that erosion in specifying the acceptable limit of liability.

____ 3. **Worker's Compensation and Employer's Liability Coverage.** Because it is mandated by statute, few issues arise under worker's compensation coverages.

____ (a) **Should the insurance requirements of the contract documents specify the minimum acceptable rating of the insurer?** Has it been obtained?

____ (b) **Has a policy been obtained that will address certain potential exposures for imputed employer status?** The construction industry has a great variety of employer–employee relationships or regulatory requirements that impute employer status on contractors under certain circumstances.

____ (c) **How does the policy address injury to temporary workers and leased workers?** Does the leasing agency provide coverage for its employees while leased to the contractor? The procurable limit of liability under a primary policy may be inadequate to meet the contract mandated requirements or the risk exposures. Therefore, it may be necessary to obtain one or more layers of excess/umbrella coverage in order to have in place adequate coverage.

____ 4. **Excess/Umbrella Coverage.** Should excess/umbrella liability coverage be required, and, if so, in what amount?

# Checklist 22: Additional Insured Coverage

Generally speaking, requesting additional insured coverage for any project except for an environmental remediation project should focus only on commercial general liability (CGL) and any excess or umbrella liability coverage.

A worker's compensation/employer's liability insurance policy provides cover only for the employer. Its insurers will not allow a third party (that is, a nonemployer) to be included as an additional insured. Albeit limited, a business automobile policy already has certain additional insured coverage built-in. But, due to the frequent request for additional insured coverage, the Insurance Services Office (ISO)[1] developed an additional insured endorsement, CA 20 48, in 1997 to meet this demand. It simply reaffirms the coverage already set forth in the policy: the additional insured is covered for the vicarious acts of the named insured or its permissive users. Therefore, nothing is gained by making the request for additional insured coverage under a business auto policy. Finally, as a matter of long practice by the market, insurance carriers are generally unwilling to provide additional insured coverage to a third party under a professional liability insurance policy. This checklist identifies additional insured coverage that may be available and issues surrounding that coverage.

____ 1. **Available Additional Insured Forms.** Generally speaking, most insurers use one of the CGL form editions promulgated by ISO for its primary layer of this coverage: either its CG 00 01 (occurrence) form or its CG 00 02 (claims made) form. Correspondingly, the following current (but, seemingly ever-evolving) ISO additional insured endorsement forms for the primary CGL coverage (current ISO additional insured endorsement forms) are relevant for this checklist:

____ (a) Additional Insured: Engineers, Architects or Surveyors, CG 20 07 07 04.

____ (b) Additional Insured: Owners, Lessees or Contractors—Scheduled Person or Organizations, CG 20 10 07 04.

____ (c) Additional Insured: Designated Person or Organization, CG 20 26 07 04.

**Terry J. Galganski** is director of insurance and risk programs for The Weitz Company, LLC. He has more than 25 years of construction law experience, first in private practice and then in-house with two large engineering firms before joining Weitz. Most of his focus in-house has been on managing Weitz's corporate insurance programs and addressing risk management and insurance issues related to its respective operations.

____ (d) Additional Insured: Engineers, Architects or Surveyors, CG 20 32 07 04.

____ (e) Additional Insured: Owners, Lessees or Contractors—Automatic Status When Required in Construction Agreement with You, CG 20 33 07 04.

____ (f) Additional Insured: Owners, Lessees or Contractors—Completed Operations, CG 20 37 07 04.

____ 2. **Issues with ISO Forms.** The current ISO additional insured endorsement forms reflect ISO's efforts to narrow the coverage afforded by these forms.

____ (a) **Why?** It is the result of case law that had interpreted many of their earlier additional insured editions more broadly than what ISO had intended.

____ (b) **Manuscripted forms.** In addition to the current ISO additional insured endorsement forms, there are many manuscript additional insured endorsements in circulation too, which generally provide even narrower coverage than that being provided by any of the current ISO additional insured endorsement forms.

____ 3. **General Issues to Consider in Securing Additional Insured Coverage.** The following issues should be considered in any analysis of the additional insured coverage sought for a project:

____ (a) Is it feasible to obtain any former ISO additional insured endorsement forms from another party's insurance carrier beyond the current ISO additional insured endorsement forms?

____ (b) Is the additional insured status requested the broadest coverage that is generally available?

____ (c) Is any excess or umbrella liability cover "following form" in terms of additional insured status?

____ (d) If additional insured coverage is sought for a client, in what order should the following insurance policies apply to a covered claim: the client's primary CGL and excess or umbrella liability insurance (if any) versus the primary CGL and excess or umbrella liability insurance (if any) under which the client is an additional insured? This question is addressing the "primary" requirement that is found in many contract insurance requirements that seek additional insured status by trying to effectively deal with the "other insurance" provisions of these respective insurance policies and the vertical and horizontal exhaustion views articulated by the courts.

____ 4. **Types of Coverage to Specify.** Because of the many ISO and manuscript CGL additional insured endorsements that are out in the marketplace, it is prudent for the party requesting additional insured coverage to specify what kind of coverage the party is seeking and to have, in place, the appropriate support staff to confirm that that coverage has been secured. The most appropriate options available to each of the following contracting parties based solely on the current ISO additional insured endorsement forms are:

____ (a) **Owner.**

____ (i) From designers: CG 20 10 07 04 or CG 20 26 07 04.

____ (ii) From contractors: CG 20 10 07 04 and CG 20 37 07 04.

____ (b) **Designers.**

____ (i) To owner: CG 20 07 07 04.

____ (ii) From contractors via a contractual obligation from the owner to do so in its construction contracts or directly, as the designer assists the owner in preparing these contracts: CG 20 10 07 04 and CG 20 37 07 04.

____ (c) **Contractors.**

____ (i) From its subcontractors: CG 20 10 07 04 and CG 20 37 07 04.

____ (ii) To owner: CG 20 10 07 04 or CG 20 33 07 04.

____ (iii) To designer: CG 20 32 07 04.

____ 5. **Verification of Additional Insured Status.** Besides the requisite additional insured endorsement, each requesting party must determine how it wants to receive verification of this coverage mindful of the usual method to verify it via an Agency-Company Operations Research and Development (ACORD)[2] insurance certificate. The following options can be selected and set forth in the contract to verify additional insured status from most to least effective. These options also go from the least to the most practical in terms of the amount of time and effort to secure them:

____ (a) Provide a manuscript insurance certificate that must be signed by an authorized representative of the insurer, which attaches the requisite additional insured endorsement being demanded by the certificate holder.

____ (b) Provide a manuscript insurance certificate that must be signed by an authorized representative of the insurer, stating the additional insured cover being demanded by the certificate holder.

____ (c) Require an ACORD insurance certificate that must be signed by an authorized representative of the insurer, which attaches the requisite additional insured endorsement being demanded by the certificate holder.

____ (d) Require an ACORD insurance certificate signed by an authorized representative of the insurer, stating the additional insured cover being afforded to the certificate holder.

____ (e) Require an ACORD insurance certificate signed by the other party's insurance broker, stating the additional insured cover being afforded to the certificate holder.

## *Notes*

1. Since 1971, ISO has provided advisory services to more than 1,500 participating insurers and agents, including underwriting, actuarial, and statistical information for and about the property and casualty insurance industry. Its products and services are provided to its participating insurers on an advisory basis. Thus, these insurers can elect to modify, use or reject ISO's forms as each may wish.

2. ACORD is a nonprofit corporation that helped supervise the initial attempt back in 1976 to standardize certificates of insurance by several casualty and property insurers and broker associations. Since that time, ACORD continues to promulgate standard insurance certificate forms and myriad other insurance forms. Its standard casualty insurance certificate is ACORD 25.

# Checklist 23: Builder's Risk Insurance

Builder's risk insurance is designed to cover property loss exposures associated with construction projects, regardless of the insured's fault. Because construction projects often involve unique risks not usually contemplated by standard property insurance coverage forms, a typical construction contract will require that one of the parties obtain builder's risk coverage for the project. The following issues should be considered by owners and general contractors in connection with builder's risk insurance.

____ 1. **Who has responsibility for obtaining builder's risk insurance?**

____ (a) **Owner.** Many standard form contracts provide the owner is the responsible party for obtaining builder's risk insurance.

____ (b) **Contractor.** The owner can vary terms of agreements such that other parties provide the coverage. However, as the owner will ultimately pay for coverage, the owner may deem it feasible to buy and maintain control of the coverage.

____ 2. **Who is covered?** A large number of insurable interests are accommodated by builder's risk insurance. The following should be considered:

____ (a) **Ownership interests of parties.** Ownership of a project during construction is typically more complicated than ownership of a completed structure. While the owner may own the land, the contractor or subcontractor may own the building materials, equipment, and supplies.

____ (b) **Changes in ownership interests.** At any point in time, the ownership interests of the various parties on the project may vary. Also consider whether the owner and the contractor may have rights to different portions of the builder's risk insurance proceeds.

____ (c) **Who should be included as insureds?** Include the owner, the contractor, and all subcontractors as insureds on the builder's risk policy.

____ 3. **What property is covered?** As many different types of property are located on the jobsite, the answer to this question depends on specific coverages stipulated in the policy.

**James E. Weatherholtz** is a partner in the Charleston, South Carolina, firm of Buist, Moore, Smythe & McGee PA. He regularly represents sureties, contractors, and construction products manufacturers in a variety of construction disputes.

____ (a) **Read the policy.** Standard form policies vary significantly with important consequences. What does the policy provide?

____ (b) **Typical policy.** The typical builder's risk insurance policy covers fixtures, materials, supplies, machinery, and equipment that will be integrated into the completed structure. The coverage will also generally include scaffolding, falsework, fences, and temporary structures incidental to the project.

____ (c) **Avoid policies limiting coverage to property located at the job site.** Because it is also common for the owner to be responsible for materials in transit or those stored away from the job, a builder's risk policy that limits coverage to property physically located at the job site should be avoided.

____ (d) **Policies insuring property of all insureds.** Consider, although the most expensive, a policy that insures the property of all insureds at the construction site, whether or not incorporated into the project.

____ 4. **Should subrogation rights be waived?**

____ (a) **AIA provision.** The AIA General Conditions contain a paragraph dealing with waiver of subrogation. Under paragraphs 11.4.5 and 11.4.7 in the AIA A201-1997 (paragraphs 11.3.5 and 11.3.7 in the AIA A201-2007), owners and contractors, by default, agree to waive subrogation rights against one another to the extent a loss is covered by "property insurance applicable to the work."

____ (b) **Can subrogation rights of the insured be waived?** Typically, this does not present a problem because the parties have agreed that builder's risk insurance will cover those risks.

____ (i) A problem can arise, however, where a contractor's negligence causes damage to nonwork areas. This becomes an issue in renovation and expansion projects where a contractor's work can cause damage to existing, attached buildings or other buildings and property on site. As a result, the owner can be bound by a waiver of subrogation even where builder's risk insurance does not cover damage to nonwork areas.

____ (ii) In such cases, owners should consider contract language that protects its right to seek recovery from a negligent contractor who causes damage to nonwork property.

____ 5. **When does the coverage begin and end?** Builder's risk coverage generally applies only to buildings under construction and lapses or is canceled once either the structure is completed or beneficial occupancy occurs.

____ (a) **Does specific language of the policy determine when coverage ends?** Some policies provide that coverage ceases when the building is either occupied or used for its intended purpose. Other policies define specific events that trigger expiration of the policy.

____ (b) **Define the policy term.** Insureds should ensure that their policy adequately defines a policy term and the events that constitute the commencement of construction and termination.

____ (c) **Does coverage apply if the work has not started?** Some courts have found that builder's risk insurance does not apply unless the covered property is in the course of construction or renovation. An intent to start renovations, coupled with the previous owner's renovation work, may not support a finding of coverage under the policy.

____ (d) **When does coverage end?** Typically, coverage ends when construction is completed, the insured no longer has an interest in the property, or the policy expires or is canceled, whichever occurs first. In other cases, policies provide that coverage ceases when the structure is occupied or put to its intended use. That language sometimes leads to disputes over when coverage is actually terminated, especially in cases in which construction is complete and the structure is occupied, but punchlist work remains.

____ (e) **Tip for owners.** Owners may be able to obtain property insurance on the structure at or just before substantial completion or occupancy to avoid gaps in coverage at the end of the job.

# CONTRACT ADMINISTRATION

# Checklist 24: Managing Change Orders

Change orders are a reality on every construction project, regardless of whether the project was bid from 100% construction drawings and is constructed pursuant to a lump-sum contract or if a guaranteed maximum price (GMP) was established from a few sheets of drawings and some general guidelines. A change order is generally defined as "a written instrument prepared by the Architect and signed by the Owner, Contractor and Architect, stating their agreement upon... (.1) [the] change in the Work; (.2) the amount of the adjustment, if any, in the Contract Sum; and (.3) the extent of the adjustment, if any, in the Contract Time" (AIA A201 General Conditions, §7.2.1). Understanding the contractual change order procedure prior to signing a contract and managing to that procedure during construction will help ensure that change orders are identified, priced, and finalized in an efficient manner.

____ 1. **Steps to Take Prior to Contract Execution.**

____ (a) Understand the change order provisions in the contract.

____ (i) Compare the change order procedure set forth in the draft contract with other change order procedures from other projects.

____ (ii) As part of this exercise, evaluate past experiences in relation to the draft change order procedure, and make any necessary modifications. Oftentimes completing this analysis will highlight pitfalls that can be avoided with a little upfront planning.

____ 2. **Understand the Contract Documents.**

____ (a) Establish what contract documents (for example, drawings, specifications, engineer reports, clarifications, addenda) form the basis of the contract price, and list these documents in the contract's exhibits. This is important because these types of documents will form the basis from which a change order will be judged to exist.

____ (b) Train all project personnel on what documents form the basis of the contract.

---

**Scott C. Ryan** is general counsel of Perini Building Company, Inc., a subsidiary of Perini Corp., and is based in Phoenix, Arizona. Perini is an ENR Top 15 contractor and is one of the largest constructors of hospitality and gaming projects in the country.

____ 3. **Is the term "change order" defined, or are there any other pertinent definitions?**

____ (a) Be sure that the project management staff fully understands what is considered a change order. It is also prudent for the owner's and contractor's project teams to meet and discuss what is and is not a change order as early in the project as possible so as to avoid any interpretation-type issues.

____ (b) Consider alternative means to ascertain entitlement to a change order and be sure that the project team is trained on what these different theories are and how to identify them when an event occurs (for example, constructive change such as defective plans and specifications, acceleration, differences in contract interpretation, unreasonable inspections, and acceptance; and cardinal change).

____ 4. **After Contract Execution and During Construction.**

____ (a) In what circumstances is the contractor entitled to a change order?

____ (i) There are many different circumstances that can give rise to a change, but some of the more common reasons include additional scope being added to the contractor's contract, direction by owner to use a subcontractor who is not the low qualified bidder, or the project schedule being affected by an act on the part of one of the project participants.

____ 5. **How can a change be communicated?** Changes can be communicated via change order, construction change directive, supplemental instructions, responses to requests for information (RFIs), shop drawing development, verbal direction, general correspondence, e-mail, etc.

____ 6. **Proceeding with a Change Order.**

____ (a) Review the procedure set forth in the contract.

____ (i) Is a final price for the change required to be negotiated before the contractor is obligated to proceed with the changed work? If so, the contractor may be at risk if it proceeds with the change order work prior to the final settlement of the scope of the change order.

____ (ii) If the contractor does not proceed with the change order work prior to the final settlement of the scope of the change order, there will likely be impacts to the schedule that need to be accounted for in the change order.

____ (iii) In what time period, if any, does a change order have to be finalized and executed? Contractors are sometimes successful in negotiating these types of time periods into the contract along with a restriction on accepting additional change order work should previously issued change orders fail to be resolved in such time period.

____ (iv) Is there a cap on the amount of pending change orders that cannot be exceeded without the contractor having the right to stop work/not accept further change orders? Contractors are sometimes successful in negotiating this type of provision into the contract as a means for mitigating the amount of exposure they will face from unresolved change orders at any given time.

____ (v) Does the sum of all change orders create a situation in which the project is materially different from the project the contractor bargained for (that is, "cardinal change" or "contract abandonment")? Although a difficult argument to assert and prevail on, these types of conditions give a contractor a viable reason for walking off the project and not completing the work.

____ (vi) If the contract contains multiple methods for pricing the change order (for example, lump sum, unit price, time and material), discuss which pricing method will be used with the owner before work commences on the changed work unless the written authorization from the owner establishes which method to use.

____ (vii) In the event of a change to the work, do not proceed without the proper contractual authorization. Contracts usually require written notice delivered via a direction to proceed, a finalized change order, or a construction change directive. It is rare that an owner will consider verbal direction or direction via e-mail to be proper.

____ 7. **Billing for Change Orders.** Billing for completed change order work is fairly straightforward if a change order is executed in a lump-sum amount prior to the completion of the changed work. Change order work may also be billed on a time and material basis with appropriate documentation.

____ 8. **Construction Change Directives.**

____ (a) In the instances in which the contractor is proceeding via a construction change directive or on a unit-price or time-and-material basis, the billing can be more complicated.

For example, if a contractor is proceeding with changes in the work pursuant to a construction change directive, the contractor may be allowed to bill for undisputed amounts monthly upon the presentation to the owner of a completed change order form with the monthly pay application. The drawback is that the contractor may expend a significant amount of resources that the owner may object to, which will likely result in nonpayment of the amounts in dispute.

____ (b) The contractor may not be entitled to bill for any disputed amounts relating to the change order and may be forced to commence the claim procedures set forth in the contract. Be aware that many states will preclude recovery for extra work performed by a contractor if the contractor voluntarily proceeds with the work without first notifying the owner.

____ 9. **Notice Requirements as a Change Order Management and Mitigation Tool.**

____ (a) Identify all notice requirements in the contract, and set up a matrix of the various sections, reason for notice, who the notice has to be served on, in what time period does the notice has to be served, the manner in which notice has to be served, and who will be primarily responsible to send all notices to the owner.

____ (b) Note that if notice requirements are not followed, the party on whom notice was required to be served may have a defense against any claim relating to the assertion of the change order if notice is not given.

____ 10. **Statutory Considerations.**

____ (a) Evaluate any statutory notice requirements that require change orders to be either accepted or rejected as unreasonable within 30 days of receipt of a request for change order. Failure to take one of these actions within the 30-day period results in the requests for change order to be converted to a change to the contract, by law, for which the requesting party is entitled to payment. So, be sure to understand implication of failing to adhere to these notice requirements.

____ (b) These statutes also oftentimes give a contractor stop-work and termination rights, relating to withholdings and delays to the change order process, that are in addition to any rights it may have pursuant to the contract.

____ (c) Note that states do not all enforce these types of statutes and provisions with the same level of strictness.

____ (d) Note that statutes may trump any change order provision to the contrary in the contract. A careful analysis of these types of statutes should be conducted prior to entering into any change order work.

____ 11. **Systems to Manage the Change Order Process.**

____ (a) Establish a project accounting system that will allow costs associated with change orders to be segregated (for example, segregated cost codes). It is very important to keep base contract costs separate from change order costs.

____ (b) Establish a system, or better yet, purchase a project management software package that will track potential change orders as they are identified. This list or change order log of potential change orders should be discussed and formally transmitted to the owner on a regular basis, such as during the weekly project meeting.

____ (c) Establish a reporting structure that will ensure that each project team member understands who to report potential change orders to so that this information will find its way to the person who will be tasked to provide the proper contractual notice to the owner.

____ (d) Establish a filing structure that will allow all documents relating to a change order to be filed together. A problem with getting change orders finalized is that oftentimes the required documentation that substantiates the change order is not organized in one place or in a logical manner. A well-organized filing system will mitigate this problem.

____ (e) Establish a system by which all documentation received subsequent to the execution of the contract is reviewed by competent personnel for any changes to the contract. This documentation includes, but is not limited to, RFI responses, submittal comments, architect's supplemental instructions, meeting minutes, plan review comments, and general correspondence. If a potential change is identified, the change order log should be immediately updated and the proper notification given to the owner.

____ (f) Identify the project team member who will be tasked with notifying the subcontractors and vendors of the potential change order and requesting subsequent pricing information.

____ (g) Train all personnel on the proper identification of change orders and tracking of related costs. A great way to get this training across is to present the change order process in a flowchart format. This is a quick reference tool that is easily understandable.

# Checklist 25: Pitfalls of the Architect as Contract Administrator

An architect performs contract administration services pursuant to the standard AIA B141. There are potential liabilities associated with such services. The following checklist provides some of the pitfalls of architects as contract administrators.

____ 1. **What are the general duties of the architect as a contract administrator?** As the contract administrator, the architect has three principal duties: interpret the construction contract documents, evaluate the nature and quality of work, and resolve interests between the owner and contractor.

____ 2. **What is the applicable standard of care for the architect as the contract administrator?** Unless the contract provides otherwise, the standard of care to be complied with by the architect is based on negligence. The architect is required to exercise reasonable care under the circumstances or to exercise ordinary and reasonable skill and care of the type normally exercised by members of the same profession. The architect as contract administrator is not necessarily liable for any mistake or defect in construction.

____ 3. **What are the sources of liability for the contract administrator?**

____ (a) **Liability assumed by contract.** The legal duties of an architect in a construction project are based primarily on contractual provisions. Despite the standard contractual provisions, the parties may modify the extent and nature of the architect's responsibility with regard to contract administration.

____ (b) **Liability created by conduct.** Liability may be created by the architect's conduct of assuming control and supervision of construction. The contractual language would not shield the architect's liability if created by conduct. The extent of the architect's liability created by conduct varies by the particular facts of each case.

____ (c) **Liability imposed by the courts.** The court does not always limit the liability of the architect based on the contractual

**Kenneth K. Wang** is an attorney at Koenig Jacobsen LLP in Irvine, California, where he represents and counsels design professionals, contractors, and other construction personnel in a variety of claims, including construction disputes, professional liability, and breach of contract claims. He earned his J.D. from Loyola Law School in Los Angeles and undergraduate degrees from University of California, Irvine.

liability limiting language. Some courts have imposed duties on the architect on the grounds that the architect's skill, knowledge, or expertise requires them to act.

____ 4. **Can the architect be held to third parties?** The architect can be held responsible to third parties for personal and economic injury. Whether an architect is responsible for the third party's economic loss varies with different jurisdictions. In certain jurisdictions, the courts have held that the architect is responsible to third parties for the economic loss as a result of contract administration. In other jurisdictions, the courts have struck the third party's economic loss claim on the ground of lack of contractual privity. However, the architect may still be held responsible for the economic loss of the third parties based upon cross-complaints for indemnity.

____ 5. **What is the duty of the architect in interpreting and deciding matters?**

____ (a) **What is the architect's duty in interpreting and deciding matters?** The architect is required to interpret and decide matters concerning the obligations of the owner and contractor on written request of either party. The architect's response to such request must be in writing and within any time limits agreed upon or otherwise with reasonable promptness.

____ (b) **What is the potential liability in interpreting and deciding matters?** The interpretations and decisions of the architect should be consistent with the contract documents, which should be in writing or in the form of drawings. The architect should not show partiality to either the owner or contractor when providing the interpretations or decisions. The architect may be liable if the interpretations and decisions were not rendered in good faith.

____ 6. **What are the duties of the contract administrator in performing site visitations and inspections?**

____ (a) **What is the duty pursuant to AIA contract documents?** Pursuant to Article 2.6.2.1 of AIA B141, the architect should visit the site at intervals appropriate in accordance with the contractor's operations or as otherwise agreed by the owner and the architect, in order to (i) become generally familiar with and to keep the owner informed of the progress and quality of the portion of the work completed; (ii) endeavor to guard the owner against defects and deficiencies in the work; and (iii) determine if the work is being performed in a manner, when fully completed, that will be in accordance with the contract documents. The architect is not required to make exhaustive or continuous on-site inspections to check on the quality or quantity of the work.

____ (b) **What is the potential liability for the failure to discover defective work?** The architect is not required to discover defective work. However, the architect may be held liable for a defect if it is sufficiently apparent or if the architect had actual knowledge of such defect. The architect has a duty to report any apparent or known defect to the owner and see that it is corrected.

____ (c) **What is the potential liability with regard to the dangerous site condition?** The courts have imposed liability upon the architect if he had actual knowledge of an actual dangerous condition or if the architect assumed control of the safety procedures.

____ 7. **Rejection of Work by the Contractors.**

____ (a) **What is the architect's duty to reject work?** AIA B141 provides the architect with the authority to reject work that does not conform to the contract documents. If the architect considers it necessary, he has authority to require inspection or testing of the work to determine whether such work is fabricated, installed, or completed.

____ (b) **What is the potential liability in rejecting work?** The architect must exercise good judgment in evaluating the performance of the contractor and rejecting work. A claim may be filed by the owner or contractor for any wrongful rejection of the work. The architect should provide the basis for the rejection and should render the decisions in that regard as promptly as possible to avoid delay claims.

____ 8. **Resolve Payment Requests by the Contractor.**

____ (a) **What is the architect's duty for resolving payment requests?** AIA B141 requires the architect to review and certify the amounts due the contractor and issue certificates for payment in such amounts. The architect must exercise good faith and act impartially in reviewing and certifying the requested amounts.

____ (b) **What is the potential liability in resolving the payment issues?** The architect may be held responsible to the owner for failure to withhold payment or overpayment. The architect may also be subject to suit by sureties for overpayment to the sureties' principals.

____ 9. **Review of Contractor's Submittals.**

____ (a) **What is the architect's duty in reviewing the contractor's submittals?** AIA B141 requires the architect to review and approve or take other appropriate actions upon the contractor's submittals such as the shop drawings, product data, and samples, but only for the limited purpose of checking of conformance with information given and the design

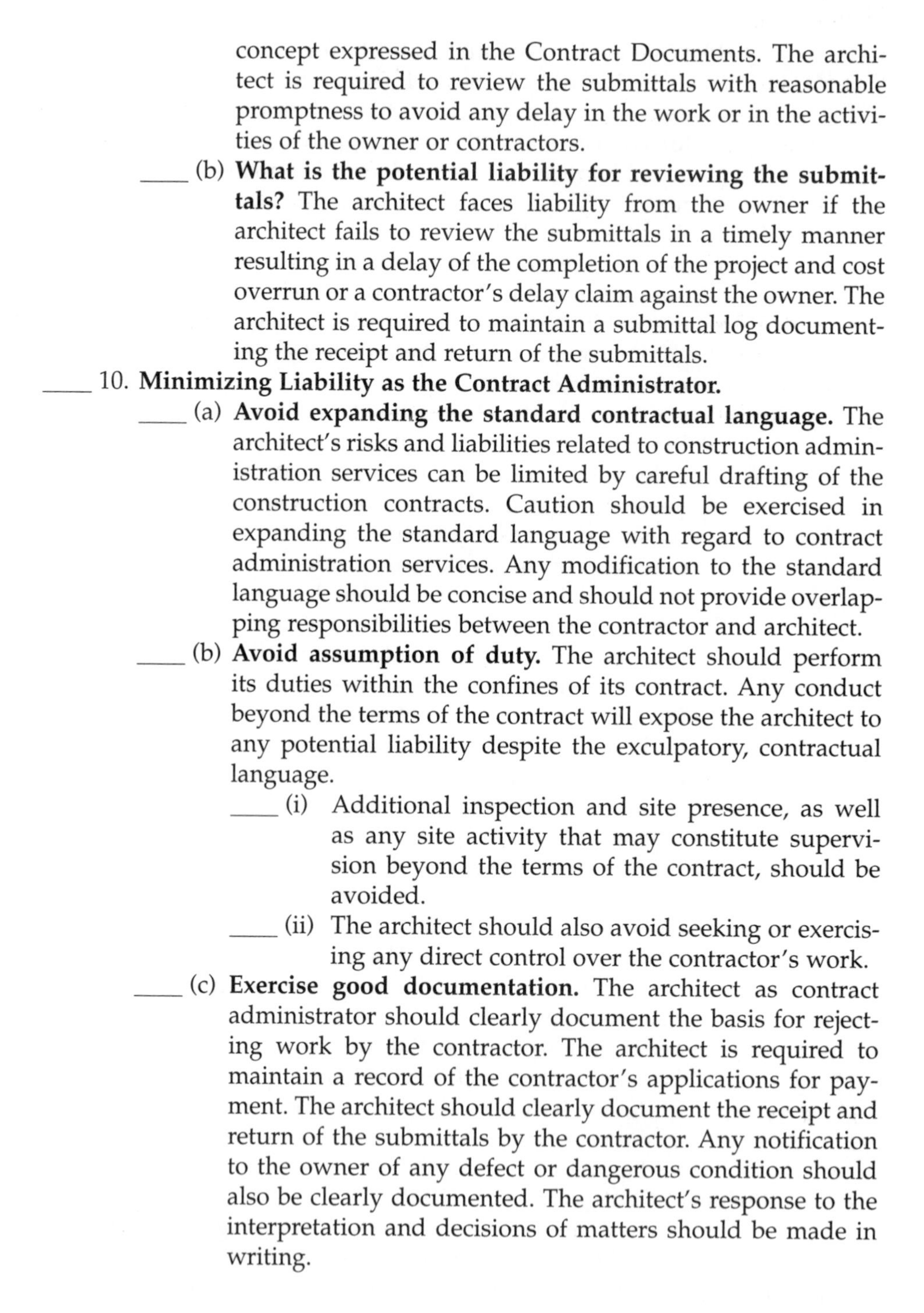

concept expressed in the Contract Documents. The architect is required to review the submittals with reasonable promptness to avoid any delay in the work or in the activities of the owner or contractors.

____ (b) **What is the potential liability for reviewing the submittals?** The architect faces liability from the owner if the architect fails to review the submittals in a timely manner resulting in a delay of the completion of the project and cost overrun or a contractor's delay claim against the owner. The architect is required to maintain a submittal log documenting the receipt and return of the submittals.

____ 10. **Minimizing Liability as the Contract Administrator.**

____ (a) **Avoid expanding the standard contractual language.** The architect's risks and liabilities related to construction administration services can be limited by careful drafting of the construction contracts. Caution should be exercised in expanding the standard language with regard to contract administration services. Any modification to the standard language should be concise and should not provide overlapping responsibilities between the contractor and architect.

____ (b) **Avoid assumption of duty.** The architect should perform its duties within the confines of its contract. Any conduct beyond the terms of the contract will expose the architect to any potential liability despite the exculpatory, contractual language.

____ (i) Additional inspection and site presence, as well as any site activity that may constitute supervision beyond the terms of the contract, should be avoided.

____ (ii) The architect should also avoid seeking or exercising any direct control over the contractor's work.

____ (c) **Exercise good documentation.** The architect as contract administrator should clearly document the basis for rejecting work by the contractor. The architect is required to maintain a record of the contractor's applications for payment. The architect should clearly document the receipt and return of the submittals by the contractor. Any notification to the owner of any defect or dangerous condition should also be clearly documented. The architect's response to the interpretation and decisions of matters should be made in writing.

# Checklist 26: How Owners Can Avoid Litigation on Construction Projects

While it is impossible to completely avoid litigation on construction projects, certain steps can be taken to minimize the potential for litigation. The following checklist addresses these steps.

____ 1. **General Advice.**

  ____ (a) Make sure all contracts for design, project supervision, or construction services are written, as opposed to oral or implied.

  ____ (b) Do not sign the contract until you understand all of its terms.

  ____ (c) Read all exhibits and warranties to a contract before you sign it.

  ____ (d) Review all documents incorporated by reference into the contract before signing it.

____ 2. **Pre-Construction Phase.**

  ____ (a) Determine what permits and approvals are required.

  ____ (b) Meet building officials and other authorities with jurisdiction to clarify code, land use, and zoning issues particular to the state, county, municipality, or city regulations and other local rules.

  ____ (c) Engage in peer review or retain an expert to do the following:

    ____ (i) Identify potential design issues that could result in delays.

    ____ (ii) Identify, avoid, or mitigate construction defects both before and during the project until its completion.

**Steven B. Lesser** is a partner and chair of the Construction Law Group with Becker & Poliakoff PA. He is board certified in construction law by the Florida Bar and devotes his practice exclusively to construction law and litigation. He has substantial experience representing owners, developers, contractors, design professionals, and government entities.

**Michele C. Ammendola** is an associate with Becker & Poliakoff PA's Construction Law and Commercial Litigation practice groups, where she represents owners, developers, contractors, and design professionals in a variety of construction-related claims and disputes.

____ (iii) Make sure the project plans comply with all applicable federal, state, and local laws, rules, codes, ordinances, or regulations.

____ (iv) Make sure that the construction complies with approved design plans, drawings and specifications as well as all applicable federal, state, and local laws, rules, codes, ordinances, or regulations.

____ (d) Determine whether the Americans with Disabilities Act (ADA), environmental laws, and any other federal or state regulations apply.

____ (e) Retain any necessary consultants: land planners, architect, landscape architect, surveyor, engineer, etc.

____ (f) Determine which project delivery method would best benefit the owner for the particular project (for example, fast track, multiple prime, design-build).

____ (i) **Fast track.** Design and construction phases overlap, so excavation and foundation work commences with period when design professionals are finalizing plans and specifications.

____ (ii) **Multiple prime.** Owner enters into several contracts directly with various vendors (for example, direct contracts with electrical, mechanical, plumbing, roofing, or other assorted contractors).

____ (iii) **Design-build.** Owner directly contracts with a single entity that performs all architectural, engineering, and construction functions.

____ (g) Disclose material information to prospective bidders.

____ (h) Notify the contractor if there is a suspicion that an error in the bidding process has occurred.

____ (i) Furnish the contractor with material information that may have a bearing on the contractor's work during the actual performance of the project.

____ (j) "Come clean" with the contractor by disclosing any information that may mislead the contractor in performing its work.

____ (k) Provide accurate plans, specifications, and site information.

____ (l) Document those instances in which the contractor deviates from the plans and specifications to assist in defeating the contractor's claim for additional time and money.

____ (m) Highlight performance specifications in the contract documents and at pre-bid and pre-construction meetings to assist the owner in later defeating claims by the contractor that the specifications are design, and not performance, specifications.

____ (n) Shift the risk of loss onto the contractor through the use of express and specific disclaimers or contractual language making the contractor the explicit guarantor of the adequacy of the plans and specifications.

____ (o) Include a "verification" clause in contracts, which typically requires the contractor to verify the project specifications for accuracy and completeness and serves as a warning to contractors that the drawings and specifications must be reviewed with reasonable thoroughness.

____ (p) Disclose differing site conditions, including geotechnical and other soils reports by consultants or other material information pertaining to subsurface conditions at adjacent sites.

____ (q) Limit the owner's liability for differing or changed site conditions by including a site inspection or investigation disclaimer clause in its contract with the contractor, to shift the burden of risk away from the owner by requiring the contractor to investigate the site prior to submitting a bid for a project. Make sure that general disclaimer clauses are cross-referenced to specific representations elsewhere in the contract documents about the condition of the site.

____ (r) Depending on the project delivery system selected, retain an expert (licensed design professional or general contractor) to act as owner's project representative or construction manager to coordinate each phase and scope of construction directly with the owner.

  ____ (i) Have a design professional prepare all bid specifications, plans, and other documents upon which a contractor would reply when submitting bids for the owner's project.

  ____ (ii) Have a design professional administer the contract until the project's completion (for example, issuance of final approval of work and tendering final payment).

  ____ (iii) Have construction managers assist the owner in obtaining bids.

____ (s) Perform your "due diligence" when selecting a design professional, construction manager, or contractor.

  ____ (i) Check with applicable state and local authorities (for example, state licensing board, secretary of state, better business bureau, applicable building department, department of consumer affairs, etc.).

  ____ (ii) Verify that design professionals and contractors are licensed for the types of work they will be performing under the contract.

____ (iii) Determine whether any administrative or legal action was taken against design professional or contractor.

____ (iv) Determine past performance of contractor bonding capacity.

____ a. Financial solvency.

____ b. Litigation, lien, and default history.

____ c. Ability to obtain necessary types and amounts of insurance for the project.

____ (t) Make sure the owner's construction contracts do the following:

____ (i) Expressly define who is acting as the owner's project representative.

____ (ii) Define the project representative's obligations, duties to the owner for the project, as well as the scope of authority to act on behalf of the owner.

____ (u) Make sure that the owner's contracts with the design professionals are consistent with contracts with owner's general contractor and other parties.

____ (v) Expressly state whether the parties agree to the following:

____ (i) Mediation or arbitration.

____ (ii) Waiver of their right to jury trial (should be conspicuous type and font).

____ (iii) Consolidation.

____ (iv) Indemnification.

____ 3. **Construction Phase.**

____ (a) Avoid creating conditions that may result in project delays.

____ (i) Provide contractor with access to the work site and timely acquire all permits and easements, etc.

____ (ii) Coordinate work among multiple prime contractors to prevent unreasonable project delays.

____ (iii) Use risk-shifting clauses to avoid liability for delays that occur on multiple prime contractor projects.

____ (iv) If furnishing materials or equipment, owners should deliver such materials and equipment in both a timely manner and in a sequence that would reasonably permit the contractor to finish the work on schedule and prevent delays.

____ (b) Avoid ordering fixtures, furnishing, and equipment directly from suppliers.

____ (c) Order materials with enough lead time to mitigate impact of possible delays.
____ (d) Have a list of backup suppliers to contact if materials are delayed due to unforeseen events or if the supplier suddenly goes out of business.
____ (e) Review contractor submittals, change orders, and requests within a reasonable time.
____ (f) Promptly respond to valid requests for time extensions.
____ (g) Make timely inspections.
____ (h) Coordinate with owner-retained inspectors, construction managers, and jurisdictional authorities to avoid project delays.
____ (i) Avoid actions that could be construed as hindering, delaying, or interfering with the timely completion of work.
____ (i) Overzealously inspecting work.
____ (ii) Improperly issuing stop work orders.
____ (iii) Prematurely issuing a notice to proceed.
____ (iv) Inundating the contractor with change orders and clarifications that modify the scope of the original contract.
____ (v) Failing to keep the jobsite clear of obstructions.
____ (vi) Failing to disclose material information to the contractor.
____ (vii) Occupying and using the building prior to completion of the work.
____ (viii) Failing to furnish necessary revisions to plans and specifications, coupled with the failure to make progress payments.
____ (ix) Failing to obtain necessary city approvals.

____ 4. **Time.**
____ (a) Include clear project commencement and completion dates in the contract.
____ (b) Require detailed schedules and updated schedules with each application for payment.
____ (c) Make updated schedules a condition precedent to receiving payment.
____ (d) Be realistic when defining project commence and completion dates.
____ (e) Require inclusion of "time is of the essence" clauses and other contractually mandated time frames.

____ 5. **Payment and Releases.**
____ (a) Make sure contract includes clear payment terms or an objective basis by which to determine payment to ensure contract is legally enforceable.

____ (b) Determine in advance whether the owner should have ability to pay suppliers or subcontractors directly by contract or state law.
____ (c) Include contract terms that allow the owner to withhold retainage for the project.
____ (d) Consider escrowing any funds withheld for project retainage.
____ (e) Make timely payments to contractors to avoid being subjected to a claim of lien or a claim for breach of contract or unjust enrichment.
____ (f) Determine in advance who will pay for escalation costs to avoid disputes with contractor or suppliers.
____ (g) Have the owner or the owner's representative review all payment requests, confirm work is completed, and approve work performed and materials used before issuing payment.
____ (h) Acquire partial lien waivers from all potential lienors for each payment made by the owner.
____ (i) Require a consent of surety to final payment when a payment bond exists.
____ (j) Determine in advance who will cover the costs of permits, government fees, taxes, etc., to avoid disputes with contractor about these costs.
____ (k) Determine in advance which payment methods would work best for the owner.
____ (l) **Fixed sum.** Designate specific amount the owner will pay the contractor for all work described in bid specifications.
    ____ (i) **Cost plus.** Owner pays contractor an unspecified sum computed as all actual costs incurred by contractor plus a previously agreed upon markup amount of each cost to cover the contractor's overhead and profits.
    ____ (ii) **Unit price.** Owner pays lump sum directly to the contractor for each unit of work performed where the project entails repetition of largely identical activities (for example, restoration of balconies at a condominium complex).

____ 6. **Bonds and Insurance.**
____ (a) Require the contractor to obtain payment bond to protect the owner's property from being liened in the event the contractor fails to pay potential lienors.
____ (b) Require the contractor to procure performance bond to ensure the contractor complies with the terms of the contract and any change orders or amendments.

____ (c) Review actual bonds before executing contract to make sure that limiting language is considered.
____ (d) Procure builder's risk insurance.
____ (e) Obtain premises liability insurance.
____ (f) Require contractor to obtain worker's compensation, commercial general liability, automobile liability, and umbrella insurance policies.
____ (g) Require the contractor to name the owner as an "additional named insured" on its liability policies for the project.

____ 7. **Dispute Resolution.**
____ (a) Clearly define the person or entity that will be the "final arbiter" of contract disputes (for example, the owner's project representative).
____ (b) Include provisions for use of notice and right to cure laws in applicable jurisdictions to resolve disputes regarding owner's construction/design defect claims against contractors, subcontractors, design professionals, and other potentially culpable parties.
____ (c) Include provisions for mediation or other forms of alternate dispute resolution (ADR) to resolve claims promptly during construction before they evolve into larger, more complex problems.
____ (d) ADR offers owners the advantage of resolving disputes without the time or expense often associated with traditional litigation.
____ (e) ADR may provide owners with a means to gauge the strengths and weaknesses of their claims or defenses before engaging in formal litigation.

____ 8. **No Damage for Delay and Liquidated Damages.**
____ (a) Require the contractor to give the owner copies of all work schedules to track progress of work and avoid or mitigate delays.
____ (b) Depending on whether the project is located in a state that enforces them, include a "no damages for delay" clause in contracts to shift responsibility of delays caused by the owner onto the contractor.
____ (c) Include liquidated damages clauses that:
____ (i) Charge the contractor a specific sum for each day the project exceeds the anticipated completion date;
____ (ii) Bear a reasonable relationship to anticipated actual damages a nonbreaching party could incur as a result of contemplated delays; and

____ (iii) Are neither arbitrary nor excessive and unenforceable.

____ 9. **Changes to Scope of Work.**

____ (a) Specify all items of work the contractor must perform to avoid change order disputes by requiring the following:

____ (i) All change orders, field orders, and stop orders must be in writing, and signed by the owner and/or its project representative and the contractor, as a condition precedent to payment for any work or materials not covered in the contract.

____ (ii) All change orders or field orders must provide a detailed description of the type of additional work to be performed, the types and quantities of additional or alternate materials to be used, and the costs for the extra labor or materials furnished.

____ 10. **Warranties.**

____ (a) Negotiate with contractors for express written warranties for both labor and materials.

____ (b) Make sure the owner's contract spells out any types of notice or other requirements the owner must comply with to trigger warranty protection.

____ (c) Review jurisdiction and venue for resolution for all disputes that arise out of warranty claims.

____ 11. **Project Wind Up.**

____ (a) Release retainage following final payment, pending completions, and approval of all work, including punchlist items.

____ (b) Acquire final releases of lien from all potential lienors.

____ (c) Obtain copies of all warranties from the contractor, any subcontractors, and all manufacturers contemporaneous with issuing final payment.

____ (d) Make sure the contract requires the contractor to provide the owner with copies of close-out documents such as final releases of lien, as-built drawings, express warranties, and related items.

____ (e) Make sure the contract includes a provision that states that the owner's final payment or occupation of the property does not automatically constitute an acceptance of the work or materials furnished or operate as a waiver of all the owner's claims against the contractor or others for any latent or patent construction or design defects, change to express or implied warranty claims, or claims for violation of any applicable federal, state, or local ordinances or building codes.

# Checklist 27: Key Provisions of a Comprehensive Lien Release

This checklist covers important terms and provisions to include in a comprehensive lien release. For the client or an attorney representing the interests of owners, general contractors, or subcontractors, the complete and appropriate release of lien rights is just as important as the steps taken to create them—and must be treated with equal care.

This checklist cannot cover all of the lien procedure issues that pertain to each state. It is imperative that local law be reviewed for any statutory or administrative rules restricting lien waivers and for specific guidance on the language and forms that are required in the jurisdiction where the lien is being released.

____ 1. **Ultimate Objective of a Comprehensive Lien Release: Finality**. The release should document the conclusion of a transaction in a way that allows the parties to move forward safely. A second, but equally important objective, is to give notice to the world of the conclusion of the transaction and description of the parties' interests. Approach drafting the release from the perspective of making it easy for a title company searching the public records to locate both the claim and the release, and be satisfied that the claim against the property has been extinguished. In all identification and description, it is better to err on the side of more, rather than less, detail.

____ 2. **Identification of the Parties.** Identify which parties are releasing claims and who are obtaining a release of claim. Full identification includes the name, including the correct business name of any entity involved; address; telephone number; and contact information regarding counsel for the party. Remember that you are providing contact information to others who will be reviewing the release later, so be as complete as possible.

____ 3. **Ownership of Lien Rights.** For the releasing party, include language that confirms and certifies that the releasing party owns the lien rights and that the rights have not been assigned or otherwise transferred. This will give the released party the assurance that all of the rights in the "bundle of sticks" are being released.

---

**Jeffrey R. Jury** is a partner in the Austin, Texas, law firm of Burns Anderson Jury & Brenner, LLP. He represents contractors and subcontractors in all types of construction and land use matters and applies the knowledge and experience he has gained to service as mediator and arbitrator of construction disputes.

____ 4. **Consideration.** State the form of consideration for the release, acknowledge the sufficiency of the consideration, and document the manner and timing by which consideration has been exchanged. In your transmittal communication to the adverse party, state that the release is conditioned upon the exchange of consideration, in the event that the consideration fails to transfer.

____ 5. **What work is covered?** Describe the work that is covered by the release, both by reference to the contract under which it was provided and a description of the work performed.

____ 6. **Description of the Property.** The release must accurately and completely describe the property against which the lien rights exist so that anyone searching public records will be able to identify that the lien has been released. Include a street address and any name by which the property is commonly known as an extra precaution, in the event that some aspect of the legal description, such as the metes and bounds, fails to match.

____ 7. **Scope of Release.** Describe the scope of the release with broad language that captures all lien and claim interests that are released, including any bond rights or other unknown potential interests. Use language that is unconditional, stating that the release does not depend on any other performance or occurrence of another event, other than the transfer of the stated consideration.

____ 8. **Effective Date of the Release**. While local law will control when the release becomes effective notice to prospective purchasers, the release should state when, as a matter of the agreement between the parties, the release of the lien interest became effective.

____ 9. **Signature Issues.**

____ (a) Above the signature line, a statement should be included that acknowledges that the signing party has had the opportunity to seek legal advice and counsel of the party's choosing, and that the release was read before signing.

____ (b) If the releasing party is an entity, the release document should state the person signing the lien release has the authority to do so as an official act of the entity. This will provide protection from a contention that the release was not an official act of the entity.

____ 10. **Acknowledgment.** Local law may vary regarding whether the lien release must be acknowledged before a notary public. Require, as a matter of form, that a lien release be so acknowledged. Acknowledgement of the release will also confirm, under oath, that the release is supported by sufficient consideration and that the person signing the release had authority to do so, which makes it easier to prove that the document is authentic in court or during litigation or an arbitration if there is a subsequent dispute.

____ 11. **What issues should be considered if the release covers a lien that has already been filed of record?**

____ (a) If a lien has been filed, be sure to recite the lien by complete recording information, such as the name of the document, the date of recording, the document number, and the location of the filing office.

____ (b) Review the information in the original filing for accuracy and completeness, especially with the correct name of the owner and the claimant. If the original filing omits important information, be sure to include it in the release. Do not assume that the lien on file contains all of the information that needs to be in the release.

____ (c) Determine where the release must be recorded or filed. File the release in all government offices in which the original lien was filed. Normally, this will be in the county in which the property is located, but be sure that the release is transmitted everywhere it needs to appear of record, including third parties who have expressed an interest in the filing, such as a lender, surety company, or contracting officer.

____ 12. **Check All Legal Filing Requirements.** When the comprehensive lien release is ready to be filed, make a final check of the local requirements for filing or recording, especially fees. This will avoid having the filing rejected for noncompliance with technical requirements, with the resulting delays.

# Checklist 28: Navigating the Submittal Process

Submittals are a necessary component of any construction project. Submittals, and the review thereof, help ensure that the contractor and all subcontractors are providing the equipment, materials, and other items that were specified. Submittals also provide for the opportunity to help coordinate different aspects of the work. Also, as part of the submittals necessary to satisfy the contract requirements, the contractor and subcontractors are often required to submit physical specimens to the owner and architect for review. The submittal process is not the most complex process on a construction project and can be easily navigated if the proper amount of work is put in at the beginning of the project.

____ 1. **Responsibility for Management of the Submittal Process.** Assign responsibility to manage the submittal process to the appropriate personnel.

____ 2. **Establishment of a System.** Establish a system, or better yet, purchase a project management software package that will manage the submittal process. This system should track submittals by CSI code and version number.

____ 3. **Understand the Submittal Requirements in the Contract.** Does the contract contain language addressing the submittal process? Oftentimes, the contract will establish what types of documents and samples have to be submitted and in what quantity. The contract may also detail what type of as-built documents will have to be submitted. A matrix of the different submittals required by the contract should be completed at the very beginning of the project.

____ 4. **Understand the Submittal Requirements in the Specifications.** The specifications will likely have a general specification section that sets forth the submittal procedure if it is not included in the text of the contract. The specifications will also have the bulk of the project's specific submittal requirements and will be more detailed than the requirements set forth in the main body of the contract. A matrix of the different submittals required by the specifications should be completed at the very beginning of the project.

---

**Scott C. Ryan** is general counsel of Perini Building Company, Inc., a subsidiary of Perini Corp., and is based in Phoenix, Arizona. Perini is an ENR Top 15 contractor and is one of the largest constructors of hospitality and gaming projects in the country.

____ 5. **Conduct Coordination Meetings.**

____ (a) **Coordination meetings with permitting authorities and inspection agencies.** Coordination meetings to address the following issues should be considered: coordination meetings with the permitting authorities (for example, building inspector), governmental inspecting agency (for example, health inspector, fire marshal, state elevator inspector) and third-party inspectors (for example, testing engineers) should be conducted at the beginning of the project. One of the goals of these meetings is to establish any submittal requirements these entities have and the various reasons they require these submittals (for example, covering work, obtaining certificate of occupancy). A matrix of these different submittal requirements should be completed at the very beginning of the project.

____ (b) **Coordination meetings with certifying agencies.** Coordination meetings with any certifying agencies (for example, U.S. Green Building Council—LEED) should be conducted at the beginning of the project. One of the goals of these meetings is to establish any submittal requirements these entities have and what certifications are required. A matrix of these different submittal requirements should be completed at the very beginning of the project.

____ (c) **Review and coordinate the various matrices.** Clarify any conflicts and document the resolution of any conflict.

____ 6. **Determine Applicable Time Periods.** Do the specifications or other contract documents establish any time periods for submitting the various submittals? Contracts do not usually establish time periods in which the owner/architect has to respond to the submittal. However, contracts usually have general language that requires submittals to be submitted in a timely fashion so as to not delay the project and to allow for a reasonable review time.

____ 7. **Addressing Submittals with the Contract Schedule.** Include all material submittal requirements in the contract schedule.

____ (a) Include all material requirements in the contract schedule to establish when various submittals will have to be submitted and approved so as to not affect the project schedule.

____ (b) Do not just include submittals relating to critical path work items. An activity which was originally noncritical may become critical.

____ 8. **Coordinate Submittal Requirements with the Subcontractors.** Ensure that the subcontractors are not only aware of what is required, but what impact the subcontractor can have on the project should the subcontractor not adequately manage its submittal process, including back-charges for the multiple reviews of rejected submittals.

____ 9. **Establish an Intake Procedure.** An intake procedure for submittals should include procedures to ensure the following:
- ____ (a) Submittals are properly logged into the contractor's tracking system.
- ____ (b) Submittals are reviewed for compliance with the contract requirements.
- ____ (c) Submittals are properly transmitted to the owner/architect.
- ____ (d) The time the submittals have been out for review is being tracked.

____ 10. **Establish Submittals as a Regular Agenda Item.** Submittals should be a standing item to discuss in all owner and subcontractor meetings, including the following:
- ____ (a) Outstanding submittals that are overdue or about to become overdue.
- ____ (b) Rejected submittals.
- ____ (c) Which submittals will be submitted in the next couple of weeks.
- ____ (d) Comments and changes to submittals that will have a time and money impact.

____ 11. **Establish What Documents Must Be Submitted at Project Completion.** The contract documents may identify certain documents and materials that will have to be submitted at project completion. Establish what documents and materials will have to be submitted to the owner at project completion (for example, as-built drawings, equipment warranties, written warranties from subcontractors, attic stock, operation and maintenance manuals, building keys, evidence of training, subcontractor contact list with scope of work identified).

# Checklist 29: Performance Security—Owner

Each party involved in a construction project has an obvious interest in seeing that it receives the benefits it expects from the other parties. From the owner's perspective, the expected benefit is the contractor's timely performance of the work in accordance with the plans and specifications. From the contractor's perspective, the expected benefit is being paid on time. Accordingly, this checklist and Checklist 30: Payment Security—Contractor consider forms of protection of interest to both owners and contractors (of whatever tier) and, within each category, first-party protections (that is, those that can be included in the construction contract itself) and third-party protections (that is, those that involve a contractual relationship with a third party).

____ 1. **First-Party Performance Protection (that is, within the construction contract).** The first line of defense for the owner of a construction project is the power of the purse-strings. This involves assurance that the owner pays only for timely, conforming work; that the contractor has an ongoing incentive to complete its work in accordance with the contract; and that, in the event the contractor fails to do so, the owner has tools at hand to mitigate the resulting damage.

____ (a) **Payment application process.**

____ (i) What documentation (for example, lien and claim waivers on its own behalf and lien and claim waivers from subcontractors and suppliers) must the contractor submit in support of its applications for payment?

____ (ii) If the contractor must submit executed lien and claim waivers with its applications for payment, does the law where the project is located specify the form such documents must take?

____ (iii) Are payments conditioned upon performance by the contractor (for example, is the contractor to be paid on a "milestone" basis or based on a percentage of the work completed)?

---

**Troy L. Harris,** King & Spalding LLP, Atlanta, Georgia, is a fellow of the Chartered Institute of Arbitrators and an adjunct professor at Emory Law School. He is a member of the Steering Committee for Division 8 (International Contracting) of the ABA's Forum on the Construction Industry.

____ (iv) Is a third party, such as the architect or owner's representative, required to certify that the contractor has complied with the contract's payment application provisions and has therefore earned the payment claimed?

____ (v) Does the construction contract include line-item valuations (for example, a "Schedule of Values") to help the owner compare the contractor's claimed progress against the work actually performed?

____ (vi) Is there a "cost-loaded" schedule (that is, one that ties schedule completion to value earned by the contractor)?

____ (vii) Is there a "force account" provision requiring the contractor to perform disputed extras (with a corresponding formula for payment) pending final dispute resolution?

____ (b) **Retainage.**

____ (i) Does the contract permit the owner to withhold a percentage of the earned progress payments until the contractor has completed its work? What is the percentage of retainage? Ten percent is traditional, although lesser retainages are now being agreed to (for example, 10% until satisfactory completion of 50% of the work, at which point retainage is reduced or eliminated until substantial completion).

____ (ii) Is the retainage specified in the contract adequate to provide an incentive to the contractor to complete its work?

____ (c) **Certification of performance quality and progress by third party.**

____ (i) Does the contract require the design professional (architect or engineer) or designated third party to inspect the progress of the work for which the contractor seeks payment?

____ (ii) Is the design professional required to certify that the contractor's application for payment accurately states the amount to which the contractor is entitled, based on the payment provisions of the contract and the work the contractor has performed during the period covered by the application for payment?

____ (iii) Are there other representatives of the owner (for example, a construction program manager) who must review and certify the accuracy of the contractor's application for payment?

____ (iv) What recourse does the owner have against any third parties who wrongly certify a contractor's application for payment?

____ (d) **Time and schedule management.**

____ (i) Is the contractor required to submit updates to its schedule to ensure that the schedule accurately reflects the contractor's progress?

____ (ii) Are the parties required to attend weekly progress meetings to help ensure timely identification of problems?

____ (iii) Must the owner notify the contractor of delays before requiring it to develop a plan for getting a project back on schedule? Does the contractor have a specified amount of time to cure any delays?

____ (iv) Does the owner have a right to supplement the contractor's forces? If so, under what circumstances?

____ (v) Does the owner have the right to terminate the contractor's performance of the work, in whole or in part? For convenience or for breach only?

____ (vi) Is the contractor required to continue performing pending the resolution of any disputes?

____ (vii) Does the design professional have absolute discretion to decide disputed aesthetic issues?

____ (viii) Is there a designated project neutral to resolve performance or scope disputes?

____ (e) **Liquidated damages.**

____ (i) Does the contract permit the owner to assess liquidated damages against the contractor for the contractor's failure of performance (for example, failure to meet completion dates or failure to meet performance standards)?

____ (ii) May the owner withhold accrued liquidated damages from progress payments otherwise due to the contractor?

____ (iii) Has the liquidated damages provision been reviewed for enforceability under the applicable law?

____ (f) **Subcontract issues.**

____ (i) Does the contract require the contractor to assign its key subcontracts to the owner in the event the owner terminates the contractor's performance (either for default or for convenience)?

____ (ii) If the owner takes over subcontracts, will the owner have any exposure to the subcontractors for unpaid work prior to assignment?

____ (iii) If the owner takes over subcontracts, what types of claims may subcontractors have against the contractor or the owner?

____ (iv) Have the subcontractors waived their lien rights against the owner?

____ (v) Is the contractor obligated to discharge, by bond or otherwise, any subcontractor or supplier liens?

____ (vi) Does the owner have the right to withhold from the contractor funds that are attributable to unpaid subcontractors? Can the owner make payments to unpaid subcontractors and suppliers directly or to an express trust for their benefit?

____ 2. **Third-Party Performance Protection.** In addition to the built-in protections of the owner–contractor agreement, the prudent owner will also have required the contractor to furnish some form of protection involving a third party having contractual obligations running directly to the owner. Generally speaking, these protections may be of two kinds, based on whether the third party's obligations to the owner are dependent on the contractor having breached the underlying construction agreement or whether the third party's obligations are independent of the contractor's performance.

____ (a) **"Dependent" protection: performance and payment bonds.**

____ (i) Is the contractor required to furnish performance and payment bonds?

____ (ii) Is the surety financially sound? There are various sources of information regarding a surety's ability to perform its obligations, including ratings from commercial credit rating organizations (for example, A.M. Best Company), information from state insurance boards, and lists of approved sureties maintained by local courts.

____ (iii) Does the surety have a reputation for denying claims?

____ (iv) Does the contractor have problems on other jobs bonded by the surety?

____ (v) What is the penal sum of the performance bond? One hundred percent of the contract price is typical.

____ (vi) What steps does the performance bond require the owner to take before the surety is obligated to perform (for example, must the owner declare the contractor in default or give the surety an opportunity to investigate)?

____ (vii) Must the owner make the balance of the contract funds available to the surety?

____ (b) **"Dependent" protection: parent guaranties.**

____ (i) Is there a parent guaranty?

____ (ii) Are the obligations of the parent coextensive with those of its principal?

____ (iii) What conditions must be satisfied before the parent is required to perform under the parent guaranty? In particular, must the owner declare the contractor in default of its obligations before the guarantor is required to perform?

____ (iv) Does the parent have the ability to satisfy its obligations, or are the assets required to secure the contractor's performance held by a related affiliate (for example, ultimate parent)?

____ (v) Do third parties (for example, subcontractors and suppliers) have any recourse under the parent guaranty? If not, what is the owner's protection against claims by such third parties?

____ (c) **"Independent" protection: standby letters of credit (U.S. banks).**

____ (i) Is the letter of credit "documentary" (that is, requires submission of specified documents before the issuing bank is authorized to honor the letter of credit) or "clean" (that is, requires the bank to honor the letter of credit without submission of documents other than a bank draft)?

____ (ii) If the letter of credit is documentary, what documents must be submitted to the issuing bank to draw on the letter of credit? In particular, does the letter of credit require any statement or certification that the contractor has failed to perform its obligations? Note that improper certification may give the contractor grounds for an injunction against the issuing bank to prevent the bank from honoring the letter of credit. Improper certification may also give rise to a claim by the issuer against the owner for breach of the warranty that the presented documents are not forged or fraudulent [see Uniform Commercial Code § 5-110(a)(1)] or a claim by the contractor against the owner for breach of the warranty that drawing on the letter of credit will not violate the construction contract [see Uniform Commercial Code § 5-110(a)(2)].

____ (iii) In what amount is the letter of credit? Five to 20% percent of the contract value is typical.

____ (iv) Are there any uniform rules [for example, the International Chamber of Commerce Uniform Customs and Practice for Documentary Credits ("UCP 500")] incorporated by reference into the letter of credit?

____ (v) Do any treaties (for example,the UNCITRAL Convention on Independent Guarantees and Standby Letters of Credit) apply to the letter of credit?

____ (vi) What law applies to any dispute over the interpretation or enforcement of the letter of credit? What is the dispute resolution mechanism, including venue for any injunctive relief or seat of any arbitration?

____ (vii) Has local counsel given an opinion concerning the interpretation or enforceability of the letter of credit?

____ (viii) Do third parties (for example, subcontractors and suppliers) have any recourse under the letter of credit? If not, what is the owner's protection against claims by such third parties?

____ (d) **"Independent" protection: bank guaranties (banks outside the United States).**

____ (i) Is the bank guaranty "documentary" (that is, does it require submission of specified documents before the issuing bank is authorized to honor the guaranty) or "clean" (that is, requires the bank to honor the guaranty without submission of documents other than a bank draft)?

____ (ii) If the bank guaranty is documentary, what documents must be submitted to the issuing bank to draw on the guaranty? In particular, does the guaranty require any statement or certification that the contractor has failed to perform its obligations? Note that improper certification may give the contractor grounds for an injunction against the issuing bank to prevent the bank from honoring the guaranty.

____ (iii) In what amount is the bank guaranty? Five to 20% of the contract value is typical.

____ (iv) Are there any uniform rules (for example, UCP 500) incorporated by reference into the bank guaranty?

____ (v) Do any treaties (for example, the UNCITRAL Convention on Independent Guarantees and Standby Letters of Credit) apply to the bank guaranty?

____ (vi) What law applies to any dispute over the interpretation or enforcement of the bank guaranty? What is the dispute resolution mechanism, including venue for any injunctive relief or seat of any arbitration?

____ (vii) Has local counsel given an opinion concerning the interpretation or enforceability of the bank guaranty?

____ (viii) Note that bank guaranties issued by banks outside the United States are not subject to the warranties stated in Uniform Commercial Code § 5-110.

____ (ix) Do third parties (for example, subcontractors and suppliers) have any recourse under the bank guaranty? If not, what is the owner's protection against claims by such third parties?

# Checklist 30: Payment Security—Contractor

The following considerations apply to anyone providing labor or materials to a construction project, whether the prime contractor, subcontractors (of any tier), or suppliers. Because the contractor's right to payment is measured by its performance, a contractor must consider carefully the criteria that it must satisfy before the owner has the obligation to make payment. Generally speaking, it is in the contractor's interest to reduce or, if possible, eliminate the conditions it must satisfy before it is entitled to receive payment.

____ 1. **Payment Application Process.**

- ____ (a) What documentation must the contractor submit in support of its applications for payment?
- ____ (b) Must the contractor include claim and lien waivers when submitting its application for payment? Claim and lien waivers from its subcontractors and suppliers?
- ____ (c) Is the waiver of claims or liens limited to those that have accrued through the date of the payment application? Does the waiver exclude retainage and claims for which notice has been given?
- ____ (d) How are payments conditioned upon performance by the contractor (for example, is the contractor to be paid on a "milestone" basis or based on a percentage of the work completed)?
- ____ (e) Is a third party, such as the architect, owner's representative, or representative of any lender, required to certify that the contractor has complied with the contract's payment application provisions?
- ____ (f) Does the contract contain any conditions precedent to payment other than timely performance in accordance with the contract documents?
- ____ (g) How long does the owner have to make payment? Is the owner obligated to pay interest on late payments?
- ____ (h) Is the owner obligated to pay undisputed amounts?

---

**Troy L. Harris,** King & Spalding LLP, Atlanta, Georgia, is a fellow of the Chartered Institute of Arbitrators and an adjunct professor at Emory Law School. He is a member of the Steering Committee for Division 8 (International Contracting) of the ABA's Forum on the Construction Industry.

____ (i) What is the dispute resolution mechanism applicable to resolving payment disputes?
____ (j) What are the contractor's protections under applicable law?
____ (k) Are there any waivers of applicable "prompt pay" statutes?
____ (l) Does the owner have the right to withhold payments on account of unpaid subcontractors or suppliers?
____ (m) Does the owner have the right to pay subcontractors and suppliers directly?

____ 2. **Positive Cash Flow Arrangements.**
____ (a) Must the owner provide financial data to the contractor?
____ (b) If the owner must provide financial data to the contractor, what right does the contractor have to require updated financial information (for example, upon missed payment by the owner, change in scope or contract price)?
____ (c) Does the contractor have any right to slow or stop work without penalty if the owner's financial condition deteriorates?
____ (d) If the contractor slows or stops work due to the owner's financial condition, does the contractor have any right to recover its demobilization or remobilization costs?
____ (e) Is any third party providing financing to the owner?
____ (f) What conditions must the owner satisfy before it is entitled to disbursement of financing proceeds?

____ 3. **Retainage.**
____ (a) Does the contract permit the owner to withhold a percentage of the earned progress payments until the contractor has completed its work? What is the percentage of retainage? Ten percent is traditional, although lesser retainages are now being agreed to (for example, 10% until satisfactory completion of 50% of the work, at which point retainage is reduced or eliminated until substantial completion).
____ (b) Does the contract require the owner to reduce the amount of retainage as the project progresses?
____ (c) Will the percentage of retention specified in the contract create cash flow problems for the contractor?
____ (d) Will the owner or contractor accept a bond or other security in exchange for payment of the retainage to the contractor or subcontractor?

____ 4. **Certification of Performance by Third Party.**
____ (a) Does the contract require the design professional (architect or engineer) or designated third party to inspect the progress of the work for which the contractor seeks payment?
____ (b) Is the design professional required to certify that the contractor's application for payment accurately states the amount to which the contractor is entitled, based on the payment

provisions of the contract and the work the contractor has performed during the period covered by the application for payment?

____ (c) Is performance "to the satisfaction of the owner" measured by objective or reasonable person standards?

____ (d) Are there other representatives of the owner (for example, a construction program manager) who must review and certify the accuracy of the contractor's application for payment?

____ 5. **Work Scope Requirements.**

____ (a) Is the bid incorporated into the construction contract to ensure that the anticipated scope and exclusions are part of the contract?

____ (b) How does the contract address owner-requested changes to the work?

____ (c) Does the contractor have the right to refuse to perform requested changes?

____ (d) Does the contract require the owner to provide written direction before the contractor is obligated to perform disputed work?

____ (e) Is there a "force account" provision obligating the owner to pay a percentage of disputed items of work?

____ (f) What right to additional payment does the contractor have in the event of owner-requested changes to the schedule?

____ (g) Does the owner have the unilateral right to reduce the scope of the contractor?

____ (h) Can the owner supplement the contractor's forces and back-charge the contractor?

____ 6. **Liquidated Damages.**

____ (a) Does the contract permit the owner to assess liquidated damages against the contractor for the contractor's failure of performance (for example, failure to meet completion dates or failure to meet performance standards)?

____ (b) May the owner withhold accrued liquidated damages from progress payments otherwise due to the contractor?

____ 7. **Unanticipated Events.**

____ (a) Does the contract provide for increases in the contract price based on unusual increases in labor or material costs or other escalations in price?

____ (b) What events amount to a *force majeure* excusing the contractor from further performance?

____ (c) What protection does the contractor have in the event of differing site conditions? What representations or warranties does the contractor make with respect to its inspection of site conditions?

____ 8. **Owner-Created Risks.**

____ (a) If the design and specifications are provided by the owner, does the contractor have an obligation to notify the owner of defects it discovers?

____ (b) Does the applicable law recognize any implied warranties with respect to plans or specifications provided by the owner? If not, which party under the construction contract is liable for defects in the plans or specifications?

____ (c) What right to additional time or money does the contractor have in the event owner-furnished information is inaccurate?

____ (d) Does the contract contain a "no damages for delay" provision?

____ (e) Is the owner required to provide notice prior to incurring clean-up or other nonemergency back-charges?

____ (f) Does the contract require the owner to provide notice prior to performance of work to be back-charged?

____ 9. **Subcontractor Issues.**

____ (a) Is there a labor and material payment bond?

____ (b) What steps are required for a subcontractor or supplier to assert a claim under the bond?

____ (c) Does the jurisdiction in which the project is located permit those who furnish labor or materials to the project to assert liens against the property?

____ (d) If the jurisdiction recognizes lien rights, what steps must be taken to perfect such rights (for example, must notices be posted or served before, during, or after work is performed, or must proceedings to foreclose the lien be commenced within a specified period after the work is performed)?

____ (e) Will failure to file a lien claim at the beginning of work waive all lien rights?

____ (f) What are the monthly notice deadlines for preserving lien rights?

____ (g) Does the applicable law provide that funds received from the owner by the contractor for work performed by subcontractors are held in trust for the benefit of the subcontractors?

____ (h) Does the owner have the right to pay subcontractors directly?

# CLAIMS/DISPUTES

## Pre-Filing Issues

# Checklist 31: New File Intake Issues

This checklist is designed to help a lawyer who has been contacted to represent a client or new client with a claim or dispute.

____ 1. **Run a Conflict Check.** Before the client or potential client has told you any confidential information, have the client identify for you the names of the client or potential clients as well as the adverse parties. On construction projects, identifying the client can sometimes have complications. Many times the owner of a project is a single-purpose entity such as a limited liability company that is a subsidiary of the company that calls the lawyer. Often general contractors are joint ventures or sometimes a special-purpose entity. Subcontractors might be sole proprietorships. Sureties and insurers often select and pay for lawyers to represent their principals or insureds. Because there are so many parties on a construction project, it sometimes happens that factual investigation will implicate potential defendants that were not obvious at first. It is a good idea to inquire as to the identities of significant parties on the project, such as the owner, the general contractor, design-builder, construction manager, architect, engineer, sureties, insurers, and any key subcontractor or subcontractors that may be involved and to review those names for conflicts when there is the potential they will be implicated.

____ 2. **Have a Written Engagement Letter.** If there is representation, the attorney should have a written confirmation of the terms of the engagement. Among other things, the written confirmation of the terms of the engagement should specify the following:

____ (a) The scope of representation and the specific identity of the client. If more than one party is being represented, there should be a careful analysis of potential conflicts and the engagement letter should be addressed to all of the clients. You should address the extent of consents to potential conflicts as well as issues of whether or not any information will be kept confidential from any of the clients or shared with all.

**Peter C. Halls** is in the construction law practice at Faegre & Benson LLP and formerly served as group head. He represents a variety of participants in the construction industry, including architects, engineers, contractors, subcontractors, owners, and sureties.

____ (b) The terms of compensation for fees and disbursements should be addressed as well as specifics regarding who will pay the compensation if more than one party is being represented.

____ (c) Whether there is a retainer and how it will be applied.

____ (d) If there is a contingent fee arrangement, the percentage of the contingency should be specified; what it is calculated upon should be carefully identified; how counterclaims are handled should be considered; any aspects of the matter that will be based on hourly rates in addition to the contingency fee, if any, should be specified; when the fee is due and payable should be stated; and how disbursements are to be financed and paid should be set forth.

____ 3. **Use a Disengagement Letter.** If the lawyer declines representation, or the potential client chooses not to use the lawyer for representation after the initial inquiry, the lawyer should confirm the declination in writing, addressing the following:

____ (a) That there is not and has not been any attorney–client relationship for the matter at issue.

____ (b) That the attorney is not rendering an opinion as to the merits of the matter.

____ (c) That the potential client should seek legal representation as soon as possible because there are potential time deadlines that, if missed, could be extremely harmful to the potential client's rights and claims.

____ 4. **Gather Basic Information about the Factual Background and Claims.** Gather important documents. The client's contract is often the most important document. Make sure you have all relevant documents incorporated into it. The contract is usually the first document to review. Depending on the issues and facts, other important documents to gather and review might include correspondence, notices of claims, lien statements, surety bonds, change orders, daily reports, and other helpful documents.

____ (a) **What are the issues?** What are the client's potential claims, what claims might be made against the client, and what are the potential defenses? In addition to such standard causes of action as breach of contract or negligence, are consumer fraud (some states have very broad consumer fraud statutes that provide for additional remedies such as attorneys' fees and multiple damages), bad-faith surety or insurance practices (some states impose obligations on insurers and sureties to perform good-faith investigations and other responsibilities to respond to a claim and provide causes of action for the failure to do so), defamation (there are often

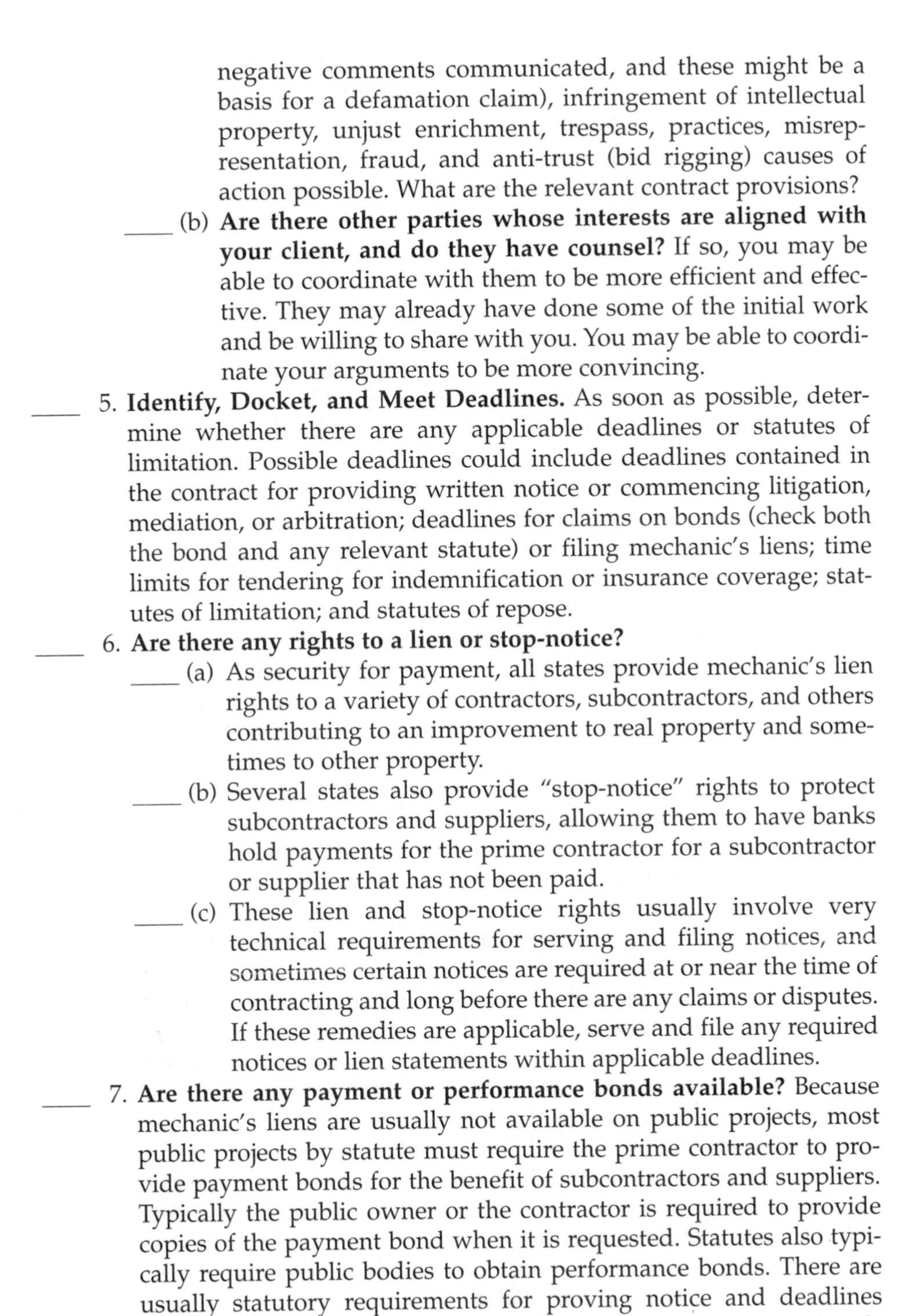

negative comments communicated, and these might be a basis for a defamation claim), infringement of intellectual property, unjust enrichment, trespass, practices, misrepresentation, fraud, and anti-trust (bid rigging) causes of action possible. What are the relevant contract provisions?

____ (b) **Are there other parties whose interests are aligned with your client, and do they have counsel?** If so, you may be able to coordinate with them to be more efficient and effective. They may already have done some of the initial work and be willing to share with you. You may be able to coordinate your arguments to be more convincing.

____ 5. **Identify, Docket, and Meet Deadlines.** As soon as possible, determine whether there are any applicable deadlines or statutes of limitation. Possible deadlines could include deadlines contained in the contract for providing written notice or commencing litigation, mediation, or arbitration; deadlines for claims on bonds (check both the bond and any relevant statute) or filing mechanic's liens; time limits for tendering for indemnification or insurance coverage; statutes of limitation; and statutes of repose.

____ 6. **Are there any rights to a lien or stop-notice?**

____ (a) As security for payment, all states provide mechanic's lien rights to a variety of contractors, subcontractors, and others contributing to an improvement to real property and sometimes to other property.

____ (b) Several states also provide "stop-notice" rights to protect subcontractors and suppliers, allowing them to have banks hold payments for the prime contractor for a subcontractor or supplier that has not been paid.

____ (c) These lien and stop-notice rights usually involve very technical requirements for serving and filing notices, and sometimes certain notices are required at or near the time of contracting and long before there are any claims or disputes. If these remedies are applicable, serve and file any required notices or lien statements within applicable deadlines.

____ 7. **Are there any payment or performance bonds available?** Because mechanic's liens are usually not available on public projects, most public projects by statute must require the prime contractor to provide payment bonds for the benefit of subcontractors and suppliers. Typically the public owner or the contractor is required to provide copies of the payment bond when it is requested. Statutes also typically require public bodies to obtain performance bonds. There are usually statutory requirements for proving notice and deadlines for commencing suit on payment bond claims, and often bonds have notice and deadline requirements. In addition, even on private

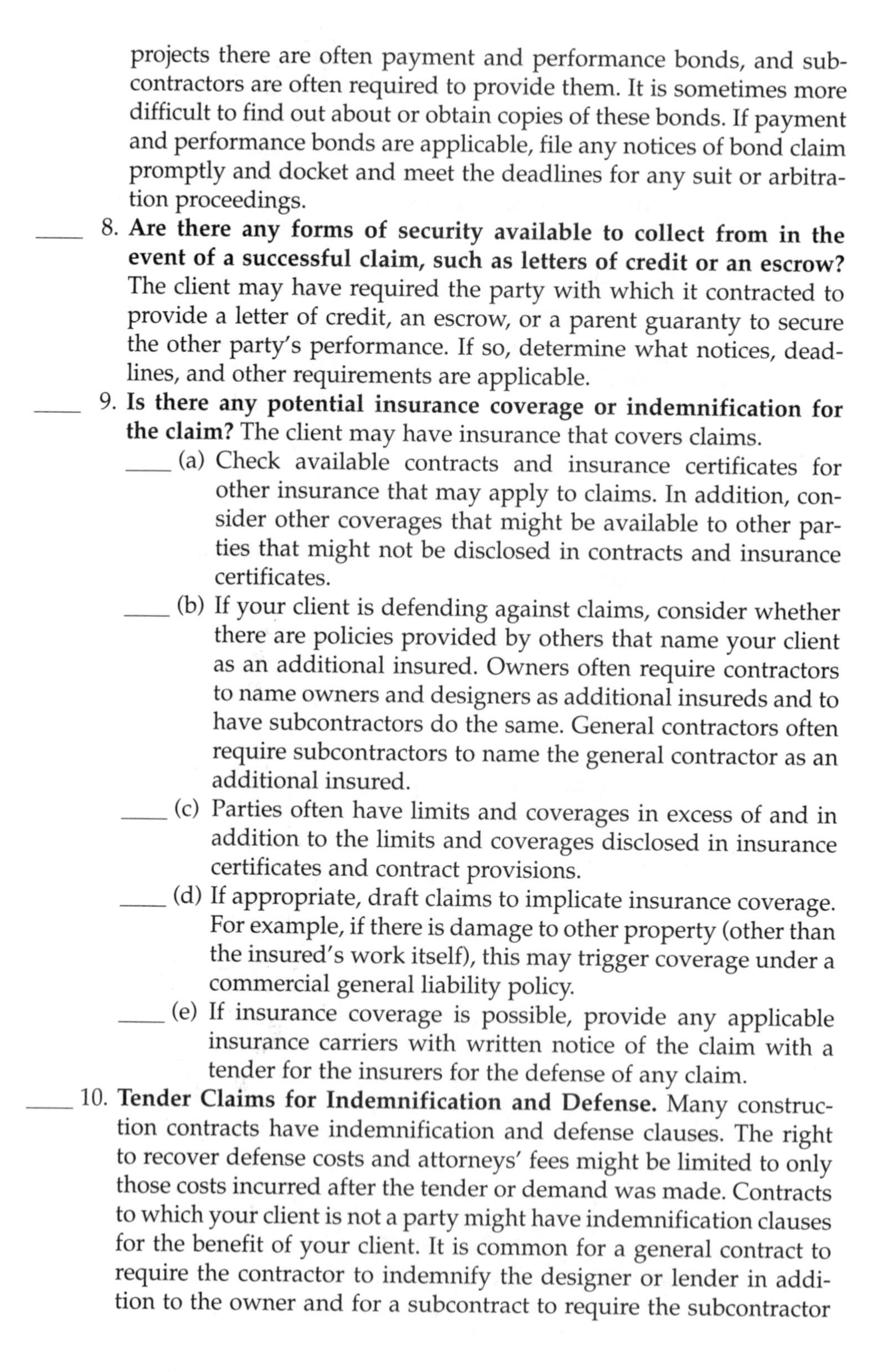

projects there are often payment and performance bonds, and subcontractors are often required to provide them. It is sometimes more difficult to find out about or obtain copies of these bonds. If payment and performance bonds are applicable, file any notices of bond claim promptly and docket and meet the deadlines for any suit or arbitration proceedings.

____ 8. **Are there any forms of security available to collect from in the event of a successful claim, such as letters of credit or an escrow?** The client may have required the party with which it contracted to provide a letter of credit, an escrow, or a parent guaranty to secure the other party's performance. If so, determine what notices, deadlines, and other requirements are applicable.

____ 9. **Is there any potential insurance coverage or indemnification for the claim?** The client may have insurance that covers claims.

- ____ (a) Check available contracts and insurance certificates for other insurance that may apply to claims. In addition, consider other coverages that might be available to other parties that might not be disclosed in contracts and insurance certificates.
- ____ (b) If your client is defending against claims, consider whether there are policies provided by others that name your client as an additional insured. Owners often require contractors to name owners and designers as additional insureds and to have subcontractors do the same. General contractors often require subcontractors to name the general contractor as an additional insured.
- ____ (c) Parties often have limits and coverages in excess of and in addition to the limits and coverages disclosed in insurance certificates and contract provisions.
- ____ (d) If appropriate, draft claims to implicate insurance coverage. For example, if there is damage to other property (other than the insured's work itself), this may trigger coverage under a commercial general liability policy.
- ____ (e) If insurance coverage is possible, provide any applicable insurance carriers with written notice of the claim with a tender for the insurers for the defense of any claim.

____ 10. **Tender Claims for Indemnification and Defense.** Many construction contracts have indemnification and defense clauses. The right to recover defense costs and attorneys' fees might be limited to only those costs incurred after the tender or demand was made. Contracts to which your client is not a party might have indemnification clauses for the benefit of your client. It is common for a general contract to require the contractor to indemnify the designer or lender in addition to the owner and for a subcontract to require the subcontractor to indemnify the owner, lender, or architect. If so, tender defense and indemnification to all appropriate parties.

____ 11. **Is there any evidence that should be preserved?** Is there physical evidence that should be examined or preserved? Are there paper or electronic documents and data in the hands of the client or other parties that should be preserved?

____ (a) **Assist the client with accurate documentation of facts.** The client can take care to note in daily reports and meeting minutes facts relevant to the prospective claims and defenses. The absence of such information is sometimes evidence that such facts or situations did not exist. The client might be able to create and use accurate cost coding and other accounting measures to properly segregate its costs to identify and support damage calculations. Other parties may have sent the client correspondence stating facts that are not accurate and that hurt the client's position. If not objected to or corrected, such letters can often be damaging. If still appropriate, the client should respond to such communications with necessary objections and corrections. The client can send communications to the other parties documenting the facts according to the client, which, if not objected to, will be support for the client. Documenting the condition of the project can be very helpful. Photographs and videotape tours can be very convincing visual evidence of construction defects, problem conditions, and the status of the work at critical junctures such as at the time of termination of a contractor before a replacement contractor begins or at the point a circumstance begins to delay or interfere with work. Videotapes of interviews with witnesses should be considered.

____ (b) **Pay particular attention to electronically stored information.** Companies often have processes in place for the regular destruction of electronically stored information or may do so on an irregular basis. Parties to litigation that have destroyed relevant electronically stored information and their lawyers have been exposed to severe sanctions and malpractice liability. Once a client or its counsel reasonably anticipates litigation, counsel should put a legal hold in place to ensure the preservation of relevant information. A legal hold is a communication from outside or in-house counsel directing employees to preserve potentially relevant information, including e-mails and other electronically stored information. Destruction of electronically stored information or other documents when a legal hold was not issued or was late is potentially per se sanctionable. The legal hold should be issued to any employee with potentially relevant information. Pay special attention to key players, those central to the dispute, to emphasize the obligations of the hold to them and to identify and preserve any electronically stored information they may have. Legal holds should include the following in language easily understood by a nonlawyer: identity of the person issuing the legal hold, brief description of the lawsuit or dispute, instructions about how to preserve information (for example, where to place relevant documents, e-mails, etc.), the effective date of the legal hold, a statement that the legal hold takes precedence over document retention policies, and a list of specific categories of information that are subject to the hold. The client should make sure that it shuts off any program that automatically deletes relevant electronically stored information. Once the legal hold is issued, systems should be put in place to monitor compliance and to periodically remind employees of the hold and to inform new employees. As to the opposing parties, as appropriate issue a preservation letter requesting that any further destruction of electronically stored information or other documents cease immediately.

____ 12. **Are there any witnesses whose interviews should be given priority?**

____ (a) Are any witnesses leaving the jurisdiction or the employment of the client or in ill health?

____ (b) Should the lawyer take early depositions to preserve testimony?

____ (c) Consider using pre-litigation discovery if available in the relevant jurisdiction. Many jurisdictions provide mechanisms for certain types of pre-litigation or nonadversarial discovery.

____ 13. **Check for the Appropriate Dispute Resolution Options and Requirements.**

____ (a) Is mediation available, required, or desired?

____ (b) Is arbitration available, required, or desired? Often mediation is made a condition precedent to being able to demand arbitration or start a lawsuit.

____ (c) Is there a claim procedure that must be followed even before mediation or arbitration or a lawsuit is commenced?

____ 14. **Has any party started an arbitration or lawsuit related to the dispute at issue?** A docket search in likely relevant jurisdictions may be worthwhile. Has the client been made a party to those proceedings and are any pleading deadlines approaching? Does the client want to be a party to such proceedings?

____ (a) If any key party is near insolvency, perform a bankruptcy docket check to make sure that there is not an automatic stay in bankruptcy that would be violated by the assertion of a claim or a lien.

____ 15. **Should experts be engaged immediately?** If it is helpful to examine a project site or physical evidence that may be altered or destroyed, it may be particularly important to engage an expert immediately. Experts that are engaged early may be more credible because they have had a better opportunity to learn the facts or see the evidence when things are fresh. Early experts can help the lawyers identify facts and issues earlier and focus on and preserve evidence and address issues that may have otherwise been overlooked.

____ 16. **Check for Any Impacts on Other Agreements.** A project owner may be obligated to notify its lender of claims or liens. A project "owner" might be a tenant and have requirements to notify the landlord of lien claims, construction defects, or claims. The general contract might require the general contractor to notify the owner of a claim by a subcontractor.

____ 17. **Is there a strategy that can be pursued to resolve the matter short of more expensive litigation or arbitration?**

____ (a) Determine what efforts have been made to date to resolve the dispute and what prevented the dispute from being resolved.

____ (b) Is there more or better information that the client can provide?

____ (c) Has the client made unreasonable claims or provided deficient supporting materials?

____ (d) Has the matter been at an impasse with two project managers that have a personality dispute? Determine if there are other persons that can be engaged in the settlement discussions. For example, can higher levels of management be included in the discussions?

____ (e) Who really has the authority to resolve this matter for the other party or parties? Can other parties be engaged who might have more influence? For example, sometimes a subcontractor whose claim against the general contractor has been ignored can find involvement by the owner or designer helpful. The owner does not want to see a subcontractor dispute turn into a mechanic's lien claim that involves the owner and its lender in litigation.

# Checklist 32: Termination—Owner's Considerations

The following checklist should be helpful for owners that are considering terminating a contractor. It will help when considering some of the issues faced in this important decision. Much of this checklist will work for anyone upstream in the construction chain considering terminating someone "downstream."

____ 1. **Is the termination for convenience?** A termination for convenience is specified in many contracts and does not have to be based on any failure or breach by the other party. If it is a termination for convenience, check your contract to ensure this is allowed and that all proper procedures have been followed.

____ 2. **Is the termination for cause?** A termination for cause must be based on breach that is "material." In other words, the failure must go to the essence of the contract. This usually means that the breach is a substantial one involving one of the major terms of the contract. Usually it involves a failure under the payment provisions for the contract, a failure to timely perform, or a failure to perform in a good and workmanlike manner.

____ 3. **Risk of Continued Performance.** For the owner, continued performance occasionally is more risky than termination. Sometimes a contractor's performance is so poor or slow that the costs of continued performance exceed the potential costs that would arise in the event the termination was found, for whatever reason, to be wrongful.

____ 4. **Risks of Termination.**

____ (a) **Termination.** Termination, except in the most extreme cases, is more expensive in the long run than a negotiated settlement. Completing a terminated scope of work with a different contractor is always more expensive than completing with the first contractor. If the owner has terminated in error, these completion costs will be nonreimbursable. In addition, the owner can face a suit for lost profits by the contractor that was wrongfully terminated. Further, completing with

---

**Fred D. Wilshusen** is a partner in the Dallas, Texas construction law firm of Thomas, Feldman & Wilshusen LLP. As part of his construction practice, he frequently represents construction owners, contractors, and subcontractors facing termination issues.

a different contractor usually delays completion leading to delay-related costs suffered by the owner, such as interest on the interim construction loan or lost rents due to delayed completion of a commercial facility.

____ (b) **Substantial completion.** If the contractor has completed the project except for the minor items, termination will not protect the owner from nonpayment to the contractor.

____ 5. **Options.**

____ (a) **Backcharge.** If you have a contractor that is not performing in a timely or proper manner, is there a less extreme solution than termination? Often, the contract will allow the aggrieved party to supplement the other party's workforce and backcharge the costs if the contractor has fallen behind. There are other less extreme solutions than termination to correct failures by the contractor. If the contractor's work is defective, the contract may allow the owner to use independent contractors to correct defective work and backcharge the contractor for the cost. If the contractor is failing to pay subcontractors or suppliers, the contract may allow the owner to make direct payments to the claimants and credit such payments to amounts due to the contractor.

____ (b) **Arbitration.** Some contracts require continued performance by both parties despite the commencement of arbitration on a disputed issue. Therefore, you might be able to refuse to compromise on a key dispute without having to declare a total termination. Even in the absence of a contractual provision, such an arrangement can be attractive to both parties and be negotiated.

____ 6. **When Termination Is Likely.**

____ (a) **If termination is likely, communicate that clearly.** Follow the provisions in the contract precisely.

____ (i) **Written notice.** If the contract requires 3 days written notice and an opportunity for the contractor to cure, then give the written notice.

____ (ii) **Correspondence.** Any correspondence should be by certified or registered mail to document dates, time, and receipt.

____ (iii) **Additional copies.** It is advisable to send an additional copy by first-class mail or hand delivery so the option of refusing delivery is not available.

____ (iv) **Telegram.** If serving notice is particularly difficult, use a telegram. A telegram carries added psychological impact and can stimulate action when other forms of notice fail to elicit a response.

____ (b) **Review the bond.** If the contractor is bonded, carefully review the bond and send all notices necessary to trigger the bonding company's obligations under the bond.

____ (c) **Dispute resolution.** How are disputes resolved under the contract? Litigation? Arbitration? Administrative law judges? How does the dispute resolution mechanism affect your strategy? Arbitrators will be more knowledgeable about construction issues than juries. They will also be more likely to make a decision based on fairness rather than technicalities. If your position is strong contractually but weak factually, you might want to negotiate a solution rather than force the issue to arbitration by terminating.

____ 7. **Preserving Rights.**

____ (a) **What must be done to preserve your claim?** Do you have to give the architect an opportunity to tender an advisory opinion? Must the contractor protest a decision it disagrees with? In writing?

____ 8. **Review the Contract.** If you are going to terminate, as simple as it sounds, review your contract.

____ (a) **Relevant clauses.** The relevant clauses are usually located under provisions labeled "Owner's Rights and Obligations," "Contractor's Rights and Obligations," "Termination for Convenience," "Conditions of Default," or other similarly worded clauses. Although reviewing the entire contract is always advisable, if practically speaking this is not going to happen, it is easy enough to locate the key paragraphs and review those provisions carefully.

____ (b) **Decision, then action.** Once you have decided to terminate, do it clearly; do it quickly. There is no advantage to be gained by delay at this point. Further delaying the decision to terminate might cause the contract to become tied up in a bankruptcy or an injunction.

____ (c) **Send all notices.** Send all notices and take any other steps required under the contractor's bond to invoke the bonding company's obligations. Often this means sending a written declaration of default by the contractor to the bonding company.

____ (d) **Send notice and itemization.** Take care to send proper notice and itemization of back-charges to the terminated contractor to preserve all rights to recover such damages.

____ 9. **Post-Termination.**

____ (a) **"Unterminate."** Sometimes, declaring termination is the "splash of cold water" that finally stirs the terminated party to action. Occasionally, the parties want to "unterminate"! Practically speaking this is something of a legal "no man's land." Thankfully, on occasion, a practical resolution prevails, and the law is forced to improvise a solution. If the parties want to resume performance with one another, the decision to "unterminate" and "undeclare a default to the bonding company" can be documented with properly drafted and signed declarations exchanged between the parties.

____ (b) **Bad-faith claims.** Investigate any bad-faith claim options you might have with the bonding company for the contractor if it has failed to fully pursue completion of the contract. Many states mandate that the bonding company investigate a default and respond in good faith or face added liability.

____ (c) **Race to the courthouse.** The party that files suit first will have an advantage in the courthouse. When facts are heavily contested, the party who can relate its version of the facts to the jury first has a decided advantage in the subsequent battle at the courthouse.

# Checklist 33: Termination—Contractor's Considerations

This checklist raises some of the issues a contractor must deal with if facing a threat of termination or if considering "walking a job." This list will also work generally for anyone downstream in the construction chain facing a termination with a party "upstream."

____ 1. **Is the termination for convenience?** A termination for convenience is specified in many contracts and does not have to be based on any failure or breach by the other party. If it is a termination for convenience, check your contract to ensure this is allowed and that all proper procedures have been followed. Some termination for convenience clauses require the submission of a damages claim within a specific time period after the termination.

____ 2. **Is the termination for cause?** A termination for cause must be based on a breach that is "material." In other words, the failure must go to the essence of the contract. This usually means that the breach is a substantial one involving one of the major terms of the contract. Usually it involves a failure under the payment provisions of the contract, a failure to timely perform, or a failure to perform in a good and workmanlike manner.

____ 3. **Risk of Continued Performance.**

____ (a) **Cash flow.** For the contractor, continued performance occasionally is more risky than termination. Continued loss of cash flow will force many contractors to cease performance regardless of risk.

____ (b) **Problems with supplementation of labor.** If the owner heavily supplements the contractor's forces, numerous difficult issues make termination almost seem attractive. How do you calculate scope of work completed on a pay application? You almost certainly will not receive your full progress billing or all of your retainage. In addition, how can warranty obligations be separated when another has performed portions of your scope of work?

**Fred D. Wilshusen** is a partner in the Dallas, Texas construction law firm of Thomas, Feldman & Wilshusen LLP. As part of his construction practice, he frequently represents construction owners, contractors, and subcontractors facing termination issues.

____ (c) **Waiver.** If you wish to "walk the job," be careful not to waive your rights. When a party has committed an act that you consider a material breach of your contract, if you continue performance it can constitute a waiver of your right to terminate the contract and obligate you to continue performance and sue for any damages you suffered after completing performance.

____ 4. **Risks of Termination.**

____ (a) **Large completion costs.** For the contractor, termination carries great risks if the contractor has wrongfully walked off the job. The owner will certainly incur greater costs to complete the work with a different contractor. Furthermore, the owner will usually suffer delays to completion of the project, which can involve very substantial damages in the form of additional interest on the interim construction loan as well as lost rents due to the delay in completion. These costs can be very large, and the contractor could be liable if his termination was wrongful.

____ (b) **Reputation.** What effect will termination have on your reputation? A primary sales tool for some contractors is their reputation for completing projects. Walking from even one job can create an image of divisiveness or a lack of team spirit that will follow a contractor for a long while.

____ (c) **Is the job bonded?** Walking the job guarantees a demand on the contractor's performance bond. Almost all such bonds are backed by a general indemnity agreement. The indemnity agreement is signed by the key individuals behind the contractor and their spouses. In the event the bonding company suffers losses, it will look personally to these individuals for reimbursement. Further, the principal often does not remember signing such a document, and it must be obtained from the surety or bonding agent.

____ 5. **Options.**

____ (a) **Temporary suspension.** Does the contractor have a right to cease performance in the event of nonpayment rather than declaring a termination of the contract? "Walking the job" without termination can be the pressure necessary to shake loose payments that have been questionably withheld.

Sometimes the circumstances on the project determine the course of action regardless of the personal desires of participants. For example, if continued performance by a contractor in the face of nonpayment will lead to bankruptcy, then termination is the only answer despite the high risk involved.

____ (b) **Lien and bond rights.** Sometimes aggressively pursuing lien and bond rights can solve a severe nonpayment problem.

____ (c) **Contract requirements.** Some contracts require continued performance by both parties despite the commencement of arbitration on a disputed issue. Therefore, you might be able to refuse to compromise on a key dispute without having to declare a total termination. Even in the absence of a contractual provision, such an arrangement can be attractive to both parties and be negotiated.

____ 6. **When Termination Is Likely.**

____ (a) **Demonstration of good faith.** If the contractor is at fault, the best solution is a demonstration that he will make the maximum commitment to correct the problem. Often, a commitment to work overtime, weekends, or double forces for a short period will convince others of the contractor's good faith. The cost of doing this over a short term would be vastly exceeded by the costs of actual termination, loss of cash flow, and subsequent legal expenses.

____ (b) **Negotiate.** If you want to avoid termination, how can you best negotiate the situation?

____ (i) **Determine who the ultimate complaining party is.** For example, if you are a subcontractor and the real complaints are coming from the owner, with the general contractor simply acting as a liaison, then a settlement will not be negotiated without the participation of the owner. Determine who the true aggrieved party is, and set up a meeting with all parties involved that have important factual knowledge or whose legal rights are involved.

____ (ii) **Persons with knowledge.** If you strongly believe you are not at fault, you need all persons in your workforce who have specific knowledge of the facts you rely on to be present to support your statements.

____ (iii) **Have an agenda.** Have a prearranged agenda distributed for the meeting to avoid unnecessary side issues.

____ (iv) **Understand the dispute.** Make every effort to understand the specific dispute before the meeting commences.

____ (v) **Know your strategy.** Know your strategy before walking into the meeting and stick with it.

____ (vi) **Get everyone in the same room.** Often these meetings are unsuccessful because numerous

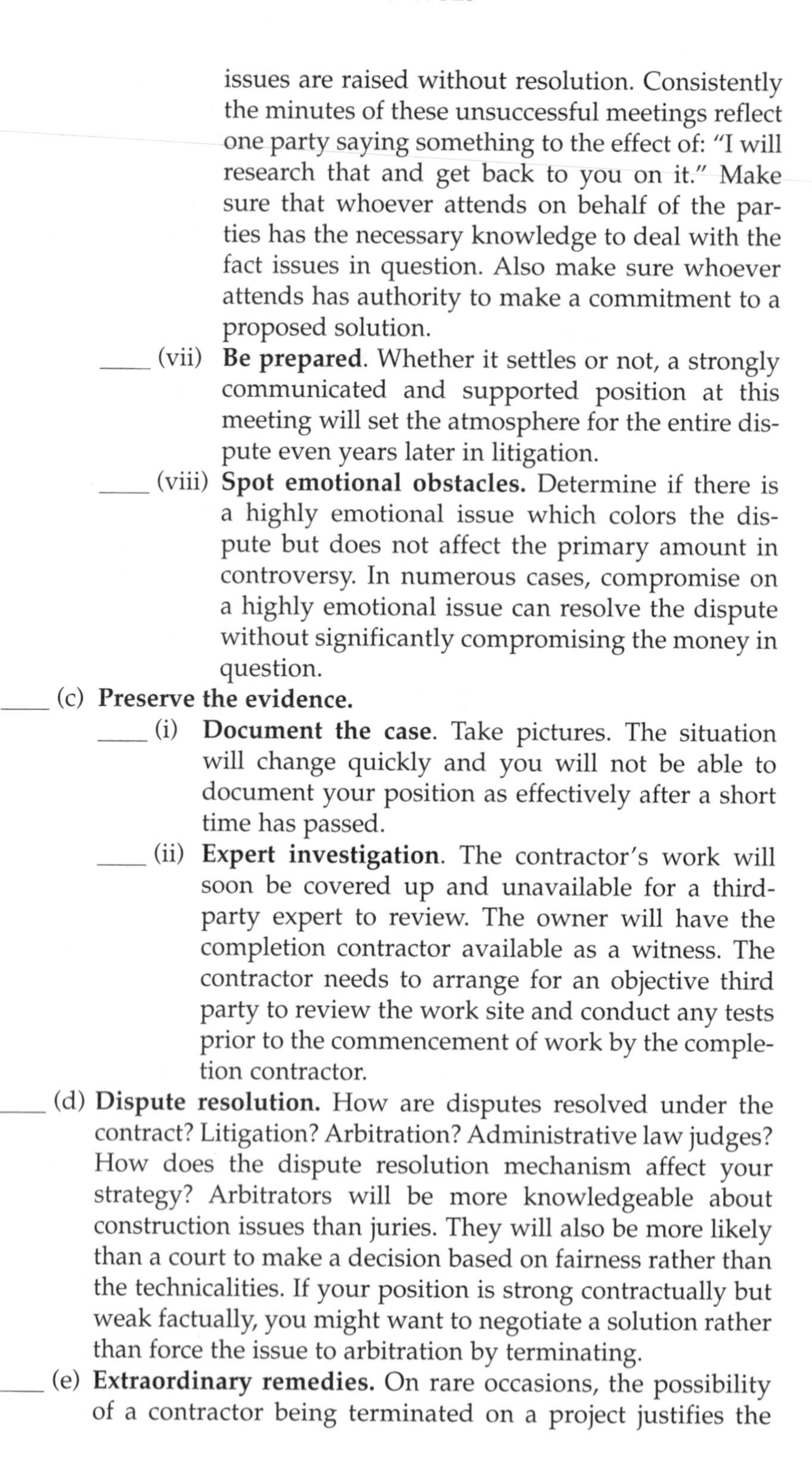

issues are raised without resolution. Consistently the minutes of these unsuccessful meetings reflect one party saying something to the effect of: "I will research that and get back to you on it." Make sure that whoever attends on behalf of the parties has the necessary knowledge to deal with the fact issues in question. Also make sure whoever attends has authority to make a commitment to a proposed solution.

____ (vii) **Be prepared**. Whether it settles or not, a strongly communicated and supported position at this meeting will set the atmosphere for the entire dispute even years later in litigation.

____ (viii) **Spot emotional obstacles.** Determine if there is a highly emotional issue which colors the dispute but does not affect the primary amount in controversy. In numerous cases, compromise on a highly emotional issue can resolve the dispute without significantly compromising the money in question.

____ (c) **Preserve the evidence.**

____ (i) **Document the case**. Take pictures. The situation will change quickly and you will not be able to document your position as effectively after a short time has passed.

____ (ii) **Expert investigation**. The contractor's work will soon be covered up and unavailable for a third-party expert to review. The owner will have the completion contractor available as a witness. The contractor needs to arrange for an objective third party to review the work site and conduct any tests prior to the commencement of work by the completion contractor.

____ (d) **Dispute resolution.** How are disputes resolved under the contract? Litigation? Arbitration? Administrative law judges? How does the dispute resolution mechanism affect your strategy? Arbitrators will be more knowledgeable about construction issues than juries. They will also be more likely than a court to make a decision based on fairness rather than the technicalities. If your position is strong contractually but weak factually, you might want to negotiate a solution rather than force the issue to arbitration by terminating.

____ (e) **Extraordinary remedies.** On rare occasions, the possibility of a contractor being terminated on a project justifies the contractor seeking an injunction or relief in the bankruptcy courts to protect its rights in the unperformed portions of the contract. Only the most extreme cases would justify such extraordinary action. Nevertheless, both legal remedies would give the contractor protection from immediate termination.

____ 7. **Termination.**

____ (a) **Review your contract.** If you are going to terminate, as simple as it sounds, review your contract. Practically speaking, the relevant clauses are usually located under provisions labeled "Owner's Rights and Obligations," "Contractor's Rights and Obligations," "Termination for Convenience," "Conditions of Default," or other similarly worded clauses. Although reviewing the entire contract is always advisable, if practically speaking this is not going to happen, it is easy enough to locate the key paragraphs and review those provisions carefully.

____ (b) **Perfect your rights.** What must be done to preserve your claim? Do you have to give the architect an opportunity to render an advisory opinion? Must the contractor protest a decision he disagrees with? In writing?

____ (c) **Warn your subcontractors and suppliers.** With a little effort, goodwill can be maintained with the people you can least afford to alienate—your suppliers and subcontractors. They will soon find out you are unable to pay. They will be much more tolerant if you assist them in protecting lien and bond rights that are often time-sensitive.

____ (d) **Work with your bonding company.** Likewise, there is nothing to be gained by ignoring your bonding company. The likelihood of the bonding company's sympathy (or at least tolerance) is greatly increased by full disclosure and regular communication. Further, the bonding company has much discretion to settle the owner's claims in good faith and collect the cost under the "Indemnity Agreement" despite your disagreement. Therefore, the race to win the bonding company's loyalty is very important in protecting your claims and defenses.

____ 8. **Post-Termination.**

____ (a) **Revoking the default.** Sometimes, declaring termination is the "splash of cold water" that finally stirs the terminated party to action. Occasionally, the parties want to "unterminate"! Practically speaking this is something of a legal "no man's land." Thankfully, however, a practical resolution often prevails and the lawyer is forced to impose a solution.

If the parties want to resume performance with one another, the decision to "unterminate" and "undeclare a default to the bonding company" can be documented with properly drafted and signed declarations exchanged between the parties.

____ (b) **Demand from the bonding company.** Expect a demand letter from the bonding company indicating that it will seek reimbursement for its expenses in completing the project.

____ (c) **Race to the courthouse.** The party that files suit first will have an advantage in the courthouse. When facts are heavily contested, the party who can relate its version of the facts to the jury first has a decided advantage in the subsequent battle at the courthouse.

# Checklist 34: Enforcing a Liquidated Damages Clause

Liquidated damages clauses are prepared to avoid the difficulty of estimating damages caused by a delay to a construction project. Actual delay is necessary to recover liquidated damages. While liquidated damages clauses are a useful tool, these clauses are not enforceable if they are used as a penalty. Once generally disfavored, most jurisdictions now generally enforce them. The rules for enforcing liquidated damage clauses vary greatly from jurisdiction to jurisdiction, but this list outlines guiding principles to consider when trying to enforce a clause.

____ 1. **General Test of Enforcement.** In general, most jurisdictions look at some variation of the following three factors:

____ (a) The liquidated damages must be a reasonable estimate of actual damages and not a penalty.

____ (b) The owner's claimed damages must be foreseeable—those types of damages that normally arise from breach of a contract.

____ (c) Actual damages must be difficult to prove with certainty.

____ 2. **Is it reasonable?** There are two primary approaches:

____ (a) **"Single-look" approach.** Reasonableness is determined at the time of contracting.

____ (i) Avoids the problems associated with hindsight and not being able to determine what the parties were thinking at the time.

____ (ii) More accurately reflects the expectations of the parties at the time of contracting.

____ (b) **"Second-look" approach.** If the actual damages are significantly less than the liquidated damages, then the clause can be determined to be unreasonable.

____ 3. **What is the scope of the clause?** By its terms, a liquidated damages clause can limit only one type of damages, such as loss of use of the project, or they can quantify the total damages suffered from delay.

____ (a) Types of damages that liquidated damages generally seek to remedy include construction loan financing, budget

**Melissa A. Orien** is in the Salt Lake City office of Holland & Hart LLP. Her practice focuses on construction, design, and real estate litigation. She represents owners, contractors, and subcontractors on a variety of public and private construction-related disputes.

revisions, extended construction management services, extended inspection services as jobsite overhead, extended rental payments while owner awaits occupancy of new facility, unrecouped costs of idle workforce, additional fixed costs at old site, and lost profits.

____ (b) Unless the clause has specific language stating that it only liquidates one aspect of the damages, the clause is likely a bar to recovering any other damages.

____ 4. **Default Termination/Project not Substantially Completed.**

____ (a) In some jurisdictions, contracts must expressly reserve the right to apply the clause during procurement of a replacement contractor or until successive completion of the project.

____ (b) Absent an express reservation, these jurisdictions award liquidated damages for delays up until the date of material breach or abandonment but not after the contractor abandons the project.

____ 5. **Liquidated Damages against the Surety.**

____ (a) Some courts recognize the owner's right to collect liquidated damages against the surety.

____ (b) The owner may want to recite in the performance bond that liquidated damages are recoverable in the event of breach or default.

____ (c) The owner should put the surety on notice that it intends to recover liquidated damages in the notice of default.

____ 6. **Implementation of Clause as Evidence to Prove Enforceability.** Many courts still look at actual damages to determine whether to enforce a liquidated damages clause.

____ (a) **What costs were incurred as a result of delayed completion?**

____ (i) Proof of the types of actual damages suffered weigh in favor of the clause being reasonable.

____ (ii) The owner likely does not need to prove these with certainty but should give the fact finder examples of real damage suffered by the owner as a result of the breach.

____ (b) **How was the clause calculated?**

____ (i) Prepare and preserve the estimate of actual damages as calculated at the beginning of the project. Ultimately, this estimate will be discoverable, and it will show the reasons for needing the clause.

____ (ii) Prepare the estimate, and backup documentation, with an eye toward withstanding judicial or arbitral scrutiny. It will be evidence of the thoughts and intentions of the parties at the time of contracting.

____ (c) **Calculating delay.** Calculating days of delay can be another issue in enforcing liquidated damages clauses. Some of these issues can be avoided by carefully drafting the clause.

____ (i) Does the clause deal with concurrent delays caused by multiple subcontractors?

____ (ii) Delays should probably be measured or calculated from the project's CPM schedule.

____ (iii) Owner should request schedule of days and distribute copies to subcontractors.

____ (d) **Is there an actual cap or limitation to liability under liquidated damages?**

____ (i) A cap might be an indication of the clause's reasonable nature. Delays after a certain point may not cause additional damages.

____ (ii) If damages such as lost profits or fixed costs continue to accrue with delay, a cap might not be appropriate. The owner should offer evidence that damages continued to accrue with extended delays.

____ (e) **Record of the negotiation of the damages.**

____ (i) Some courts will not enforce the liquidated damages clause unless there is evidence that the parties actually bargained for the clause.

____ (ii) Prepare and preserve a record of your negotiations of the clause whether through daily logs, e-mails, or correspondence.

____ 7. **How to Calculate Liquidated Damages.**

____ (a) **When do liquidated damages start to accrue?**

____ (i) **Substantial completion.** Sometimes substantial completion is specifically defined in the contract.

____ (ii) **Final completion.** If the contract specified that liquidated damages accrue until final completion, then an owner can likely recover liquidated damages until all punchlist work is complete.

____ (iii) If an owner intends to enforce a liquidated damages clause, it should strive to be reasonable during the completion phase of the project so as not to create evidence that will disfavor enforcement of the clause.

____ (b) **How to adjust liquidated damages for changes or excusable delay.**

____ (i) The owner can only recover liquidated damages for delays that were not excusable.

____ (ii) Some types of delay are considered excusable including the following: weather, onset of winter, act or neglect by the owner or architect or other prime contractors, labor disputes, fire, unusual delay in deliveries, unavoidable casualties, other causes beyond the contractor's control, and *force majeure.* These excusable delays can be adjusted according to the contract terms.

____ (c) **Did the contractor follow the requests for time extension provisions in the contract?**

____ (i) To receive a time extension, the contractor normally has to give notice of the need for extension within a specified period of time.

____ (ii) Lack of requests for extension can be evidence of poor contract execution and management. It can also discount a contractor's attempt to avoid responsibility for delay.

____ (iii) The lack of a formal request may be overlooked when actual knowledge of the delay existed. If the owner had actual knowledge of a delay, then the contractor may be excused from failing to give the owner notice.

____ (d) **Actual notice should not be presumed to be adequate.**

____ (i) Formal contract requirements should be observed. Failure to follow them can result in a denial of time extensions and assessment of damages.

____ (ii) The owner should always attempt to show whether the notice provisions of the contract were followed.

____ 8. **Multiple Causes of Delay.**

____ (a) When both the owner and contractor caused the delay, the contractor is generally held to be excused from liquidated damages.

____ (b) Delays that are not precisely concurrent can frequently be apportioned between the parties or multiple contractors according to the degree of contribution.

____ (c) A minority of jurisdictions preclude an owner that has contributed to any delay on the project from recovering liquidated damages against the contractor.

____ 9. **Who Has the Burden of Proof?**

____ (a) **Burden to prove unenforceable.** The contractor generally has the burden to prove that a liquidated damage clause is unenforceable.[1]

____ (b) **Burden to prove fault for delay.**

____ (i) The majority view holds that to avoid liquidated damages, the contractor has the burden to prove that the owner caused the delay.[2]

____ (ii) Several older cases place the burden on the owner trying to enforce the clause. Many of these cases come from the time period during which liquidated damages clauses were generally disfavored. Look carefully to determine whether these cases are still good law.

____ 10. **Liquidated Damages versus Waiver of Consequential Damages.** Ambiguities may exist in contracts that include both a liquidated damages clause and a waiver of consequential damages.[3]

____ (a) Some form contracts, such as the 1997 AIA A201 and AGC contracts, include mutual waiver of consequential damages clauses or a clause that allows recovery only for "direct liquidated damages."

____ (i) In these cases, the owner might be limited to liquidated damages as a measure for direct damages.

____ (ii) The meaning of these "direct liquidated damages" clauses is uncertain and enforcement of such clauses should be approached cautiously to determine whether the liquidated sum is for direct or consequential damages.

## *Notes*

1. *Bair v. Axiom Design, LLC*, 20 P.3d 388, 394 (Utah 2001) (trial court erred by placing burden of proof on party seeking to enforce liquidated damages clause; shifting the burden of proof in this manner goes against the principle that liquidated damage clauses are enforceable by reason of their economic efficiency). See also, e.g., *First Nat'l Bank of Chicago v. Atlantic Tele-Network Co.*, 946 F.2d 516, 522 (7th Cir. 1991); *Rodriguez v. Learjet, Inc.*, 946 P.2d 1010, 1014 (Kan. Ct. App. 1997); *Shallow Brook Assocs. v. Dube*, 135 N.H. 40, 599 A.2d 132, 138 (N.H. 1991); *Metlife Capital Fin. Corp. v. Washington Ave. Assocs. L.P.*, 732 A.2d 493, 499 (N.J. 1999); *P.J. Carlin Constr. Co. v. City of New York*, 399 N.Y.S.2d 13, 14 (1977); *R. Conrad Moore & Assocs., Inc. v. Lerma*, 946 S.W.2d 90, 95 (Tex. Ct. App. 1997).

2. See e.g., *George Sollitt Constr. Co. v. United States*, 64 Fed. Cl. 229, 243 (Ct. Cl. 2005) (The government has the initial burden of showing late completion, and the contractor then has the burden to show that the delay was excusable).

3. See e.g., *City of Milford v. Coppola*, 891 A.2d 31, 38 (Conn. App. 2006) (applying liquidated damages clause in contract with mutual waiver of consequential damages).

# Checklist 35: Considerations in Suing an Architect

The factors that should be taken into consideration when evaluating a potential claim against an architect depend on the claimant's relationship to the architect and the project in question. The most advantageous way for the claimant to prosecute its claim will vary depending on whether it was a participant in the project that contracted with the architect, a project participant that lacks contractual privity with the architect, or a third party that was uninvolved in the development of the project. Regardless of whether or not it contracted with the architect, the potential claimant should still obtain a copy of the architect's contract. The scope of work that the architect agreed to perform will serve to define not just its contractual duties, but will also affect the tort duties that may be imposed upon the architect.

This checklist is based largely on the 1997 edition of the American Institute of Architects' (AIA) Document B141, the Standard Form of Agreement Between Owner and Architect. Over the past 100 years, the AIA has published some 90 contract forms that have become the standard for contracting with architects. While generally fair, AIA forms are written with the intent of limiting the architect's potential liability. AIA forms are frequently customized to suit the needs of a particular project and should be carefully read when considering claims against architects.

In October 2007, the AIA introduced a series of new contract forms to replace the one-size-fits-all B141. Documents B101 and B102 serve as the new standard form of agreement between owner and architect. Documents B103, B104, and B105 are alternative forms designed for projects of either greater or lesser scope and complexity than B101 and B102. This recent proliferation of AIA forms has made it more important than ever for parties that are considering stating claims against architects to carefully consider the actual contract documents that are relevant to the project that gave rise to the potential claim.

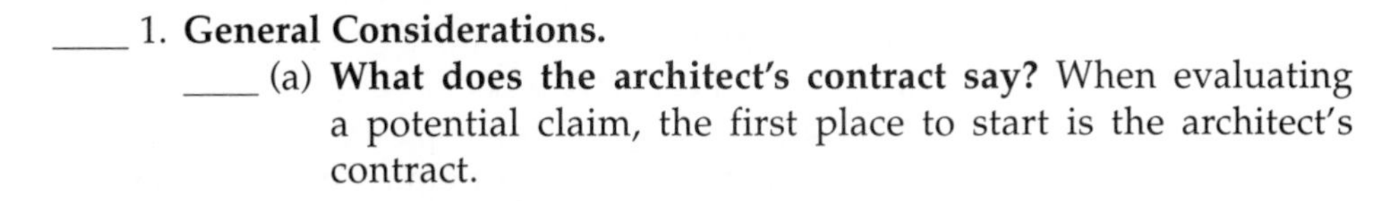

____ 1. **General Considerations.**

____ (a) **What does the architect's contract say?** When evaluating a potential claim, the first place to start is the architect's contract.

**Jeremy S. Baker** is an associate attorney with Schiff Hardin LLP and a member of the firm's Construction Law Group. His practice is focused on representing property owners and developers, as well as contractors, architects, and engineers in a wide variety of construction-related disputes and transactions.

____ (i) An architect's contractual scope of work is often narrower than potential claimants expect.

____ (ii) Identify what duties, if any, were imposed on the architect that relate to the subject matter of the potential claim.

____ (b) **Have all relevant contract documents been identified?** Construction projects are typically governed by numerous contract documents that, while interrelated, are entered into between a wide variety of project participants to address distinct issues of logistics, timing, and differing work. Contract documents other than the owner–architect agreement frequently contain language that can affect an architect's potential liability.

____ (i) Identify all contract documents that serve to define the architect's rights, responsibilities, and scope of work.

____ (ii) AIA A201, the General Conditions of the Contract for Construction, is frequently incorporated by reference into an architect's contract and can affect its potential liability.

____ (iii) Architects often issue comprehensive specifications that set forth the kind and quality of materials to be used during construction.

____ (iv) Architectural drawings frequently contain notes and disclaimers that can affect the architect's potential liability.

____ (c) **Is the architect's liability limited by contract?**

____ (i) Architects' contracts frequently include provisions that seek to limit their maximum liability to parties with whom they contract to:

____ a. The amount of their available insurance coverage;

____ b. The fee that they contracted to receive for the project; or

____ c. A stipulated sum.

____ (ii) Many AIA documents contain mutual waivers of consequential damages that seem to benefit the parties equally, but are in fact more favorable to architects. Property owners and contractors are more likely to incur consequential damages than architects, who sue most frequently to recover fees for professional services rendered.

____ (d) **Is alternative dispute resolution (ADR) required?** Since 1997, AIA forms have required nonbinding mediation as

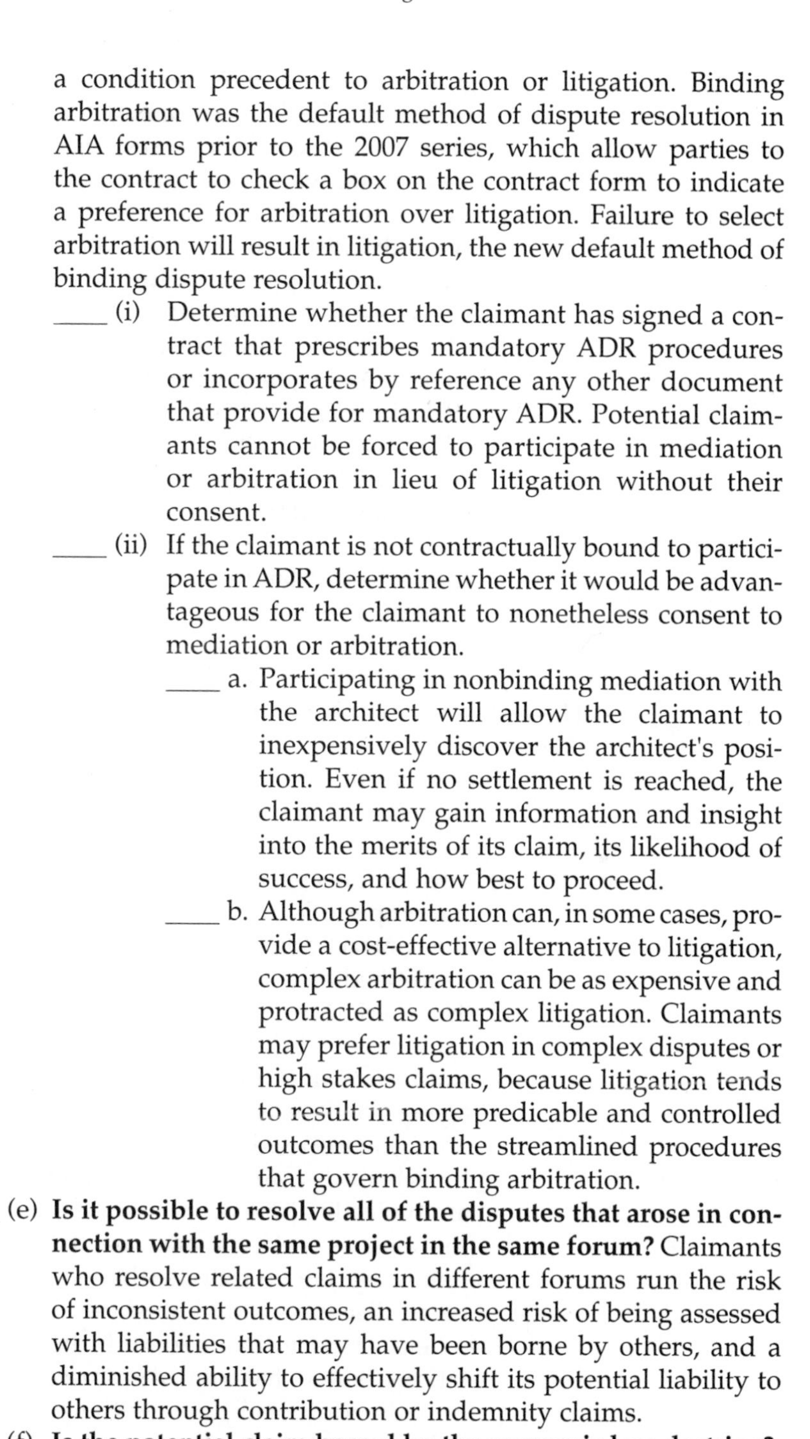

a condition precedent to arbitration or litigation. Binding arbitration was the default method of dispute resolution in AIA forms prior to the 2007 series, which allow parties to the contract to check a box on the contract form to indicate a preference for arbitration over litigation. Failure to select arbitration will result in litigation, the new default method of binding dispute resolution.

____ (i) Determine whether the claimant has signed a contract that prescribes mandatory ADR procedures or incorporates by reference any other document that provide for mandatory ADR. Potential claimants cannot be forced to participate in mediation or arbitration in lieu of litigation without their consent.

____ (ii) If the claimant is not contractually bound to participate in ADR, determine whether it would be advantageous for the claimant to nonetheless consent to mediation or arbitration.

____ a. Participating in nonbinding mediation with the architect will allow the claimant to inexpensively discover the architect's position. Even if no settlement is reached, the claimant may gain information and insight into the merits of its claim, its likelihood of success, and how best to proceed.

____ b. Although arbitration can, in some cases, provide a cost-effective alternative to litigation, complex arbitration can be as expensive and protracted as complex litigation. Claimants may prefer litigation in complex disputes or high stakes claims, because litigation tends to result in more predicable and controlled outcomes than the streamlined procedures that govern binding arbitration.

____ (e) **Is it possible to resolve all of the disputes that arose in connection with the same project in the same forum?** Claimants who resolve related claims in different forums run the risk of inconsistent outcomes, an increased risk of being assessed with liabilities that may have been borne by others, and a diminished ability to effectively shift its potential liability to others through contribution or indemnity claims.

____ (f) **Is the potential claim barred by the economic loss doctrine?**

____ (i) Although application of the economic loss doctrine varies from state to state, economic damages cannot,

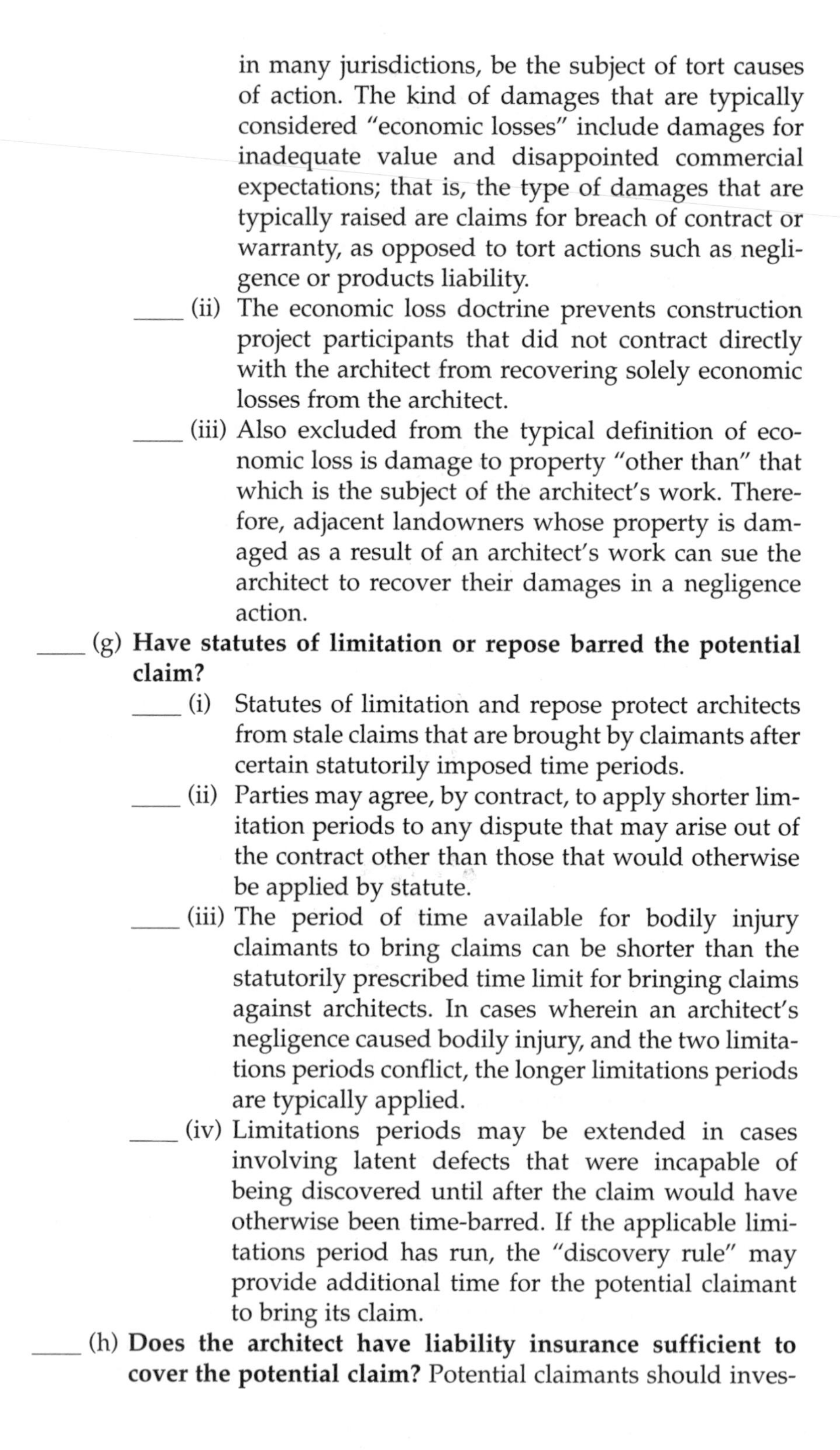

in many jurisdictions, be the subject of tort causes of action. The kind of damages that are typically considered "economic losses" include damages for inadequate value and disappointed commercial expectations; that is, the type of damages that are typically raised are claims for breach of contract or warranty, as opposed to tort actions such as negligence or products liability.

____ (ii) The economic loss doctrine prevents construction project participants that did not contract directly with the architect from recovering solely economic losses from the architect.

____ (iii) Also excluded from the typical definition of economic loss is damage to property "other than" that which is the subject of the architect's work. Therefore, adjacent landowners whose property is damaged as a result of an architect's work can sue the architect to recover their damages in a negligence action.

____ (g) **Have statutes of limitation or repose barred the potential claim?**

____ (i) Statutes of limitation and repose protect architects from stale claims that are brought by claimants after certain statutorily imposed time periods.

____ (ii) Parties may agree, by contract, to apply shorter limitation periods to any dispute that may arise out of the contract other than those that would otherwise be applied by statute.

____ (iii) The period of time available for bodily injury claimants to bring claims can be shorter than the statutorily prescribed time limit for bringing claims against architects. In cases wherein an architect's negligence caused bodily injury, and the two limitations periods conflict, the longer limitations periods are typically applied.

____ (iv) Limitations periods may be extended in cases involving latent defects that were incapable of being discovered until after the claim would have otherwise been time-barred. If the applicable limitations period has run, the "discovery rule" may provide additional time for the potential claimant to bring its claim.

____ (h) **Does the architect have liability insurance sufficient to cover the potential claim?** Potential claimants should investigate whether the architect has coverage under its professional liability or commercial general liability insurance policies that would be sufficient to fund a verdict, settlement, or decision in the potential claimant's favor.

____ (i) **Is a certificate of merit required by the jurisdiction in which the claim will be tried or arbitrated?** Failure to provide a certificate of merit when required by law is typically grounds for dismissal of the claimant's cause of action.

____ (j) **Has the architect complied with applicable licensure laws?** Failure of the architect to be licensed may prevent it from bringing counterclaims or enforcing unfavorable contract terms against the potential claimant.

____ 2. **The Professional Standard of Care.**

____ (a) **Did the architect violate the professional standard of care?**

____ (i) As with all professionals, people have the right to expect that an architect will possess a standard minimum of special knowledge and ability that rises above that possessed by laypeople. People can also expect that it will exercise care and skill that is reasonable under the circumstances. If the architect failed to possess and use the requisite knowledge in a reasonable manner, and that failure has caused damages, the architect may be liable to the claimant for professional negligence.

____ (ii) The professional standard of care does not, however, require the architect to deliver perfect plans or satisfactory results. Absent a special agreement to provide such results or impose a higher standard of care, the architect will be liable only if it fails to exercise the reasonable care and skill that a reasonably well-qualified architect would use under the circumstances.

____ 3. **Considerations for Project Owners That Have Potential Claims against the Project Architect.**

____ (a) **Is the owner in privity of contract with the architect?** The existence or lack of contractual privity with the architect will affect the causes of action available to the owner and the defenses available to the architect.

____ (b) **Does the claim involve disappointed expectations in the architect's finished product?**

____ (i) Determine whether the potential claim involves subjective considerations, such as aesthetic disappointment, or some objective fault that prevents the finished product from fulfilling its essential purpose.

____ a. Subjective disappointment may be insufficient to support the owner's potential claim. Potential claimants should strive to link their disappointment to a specific provision of the owner–architect agreement that may have been violated.

____ b. Architects seldom guarantee that owners will be satisfied with their work once the project is completed. Review the architect's contract to determine what guarantees, if any, have been made.

____ (ii) Architects are professionals that are expected to possess sufficient knowledge to avoid critical errors that, objectively viewed, defeat the functionality of the finished project. That knowledge and experience, along with the obligation to draw upon it with reasonable care in the performance of the duties, is an implied term of the owner–architect agreement.

____ (c) **Did the architect underestimate the cost of construction?** Architects are traditionally required to perform cost estimates, evaluate the owner's budget, and compare that budget against the anticipated cost of work.

____ (i) Architects seldom warrant the accuracy of cost estimates because the actual cost of construction depends on factors beyond their control.

____ (ii) Review the owner–architect agreement to see whether the architect was obligated to provide the owner with periodically updated estimates.

____ a. Failure to provide updated estimates in the face of unanticipated and rising construction costs may have prejudiced the owner's ability to rebid, renegotiate, or terminate the project, and may thus give rise to a breach of contract claim against the architect.

____ b. Review the contract to determine whether monetary damages are available or whether the owner's remedy against the architect is limited to a redesign of the project at no additional cost.

____ (d) **Do the architect's plans and specifications omit necessary items, contain errors, or both?** If the plans omit items that would be necessary to complete the project regardless of whether or not they had been omitted, the act of correcting the mistake may result in a betterment, or a value-adding improvement for which the owner may have to compensate the architect.

____ (i) If the architect was forced to make value-adding improvements at its expense, the owner would receive items that it always needed for free, and thus be unjustly enriched by receiving a better project than it paid for.

____ (ii) The architect may, however, be required to bear the expense of any increased costs that had to be incurred as a result of its omission, such as a price increase or construction inefficiency that could have been avoided.

____ (iii) If a betterment-type situation is presented by the facts, research whether betterment will, in the context of the owner's potential claim, be a valid defense to some or all of that claim.

____ (e) **Did the architect fail to evaluate and warn the owner of defects or deficiencies in the work?**

____ (i) Review the architect's contract to determine whether it had an obligation to evaluate ongoing construction work.

____ a. Architects are at times hired solely to do design work and have no responsibilities related to site observation or administration of the contract between the owner and the prime contractor.

____ b. Architects who contract to perform periodic site observations are typically required to visit the site at intervals appropriate to the stage of construction, at preset intervals (that is, weekly), or upon the request of the owner or contractor.

____ (ii) Determine whether the owner has paid a premium to the architect to expand the traditionally narrow duties to evaluate ongoing work.

____ a. Architects are traditionally tasked to "observe" the progress of construction, a term that denotes a less rigorous level of scrutiny than the term "inspect," which is commonly misapplied to describe the act of an architect observing construction work.

____ b. Architects are typically required only to become generally familiar with the ongoing work to ensure that it will conform to the design intent and the contract documents when completed.

____ c. Architects are not required to make continuous or exhaustive site inspections in order to check the quality of the work.

____ d. Although the architect may be contractually obligated to "endeavor" to guard the owner from defects and deficiencies in the work, no warranties or guarantees of perfect outcomes or results are implied in the absence of special agreements and, usually, additional compensation.

____ (f) **Does the owner's potential claim involve errors in information, calculations, or materials supplied by the architect's subconsultants or other project participants?**

____ (i) Architects are typically obligated to review shop drawings, data, and samples provided by others to determine whether the information provided conforms to the design concept expressed in the contract documents, not to check for dimensions, quantities, or other details.

____ (ii) Failure to catch others' mistakes will not necessarily subject the architect to liability.

____ (iii) However, if the architect hired the party responsible for the error, the architect may be contractually liable to the owner for its consequences.

____ (g) **Does the owner's potential claim involve the architect's failure to comply with laws, codes, or regulations**?

____ (i) Architects are typically obligated by contract to conform to the requirements of the governmental authorities that have jurisdiction over the project.

____ (ii) Building code requirements are often unclear and can be interpreted by local officials in a subjective manner. The architect's contract may protect it from liability related to questionable interpretations of building codes that can lead to allegations of noncompliance against the architect.

____ (h) **Is the potential claimant prosecuting a "pass-through" claim against the architect on behalf of another party that cannot sue the architect directly?**

____ (i) Pass-through agreements can be utilized to resolve disputes in any situation where one construction project participant has contracted with two others that are themselves unable to bring direct claims against one another due to their lack of contractual privity.

____ (ii) In such cases, the owner should join the architect as a defendant in the same forum where the contractor's claim is pending and attempt to pass any liability that the owner may have to the contractor through to the architect that was responsible for causing the damages in question.

____ a. Because the owner may be liable to the project participant for the architect's failures, its allegations against the architect should be couched in terms that do not judicially admit that the architect was negligent.

____ b. The owner's complaint or demand for arbitration should plead that "other parties *have alleged* that the architect was negligent" and, if proven to be true, that owner's liability to the project participant was caused by the architect's negligence.

____ (i) **Has the owner fully compensated the architect for all professional services rendered?** If the owner is holding money that is owed to the architect, the architect may respond to the owner's claim by filing a counterclaim of its own.

____ (i) Determine whether the architect or any of its subconsultants have an unpaid claim for extra work.

____ (ii) Determine whether the architect has the ability to record a mechanic's lien on the property under the laws of the state where the project was developed. If so, determine whether the architect still has time to record a mechanic's lien on the property.

____ (iii) If the architect has potential claims of its own, the potential claimant should weigh the relative merits and dollar value of its claim against the architect's potential claims before deciding whether to initiate a claim against the architect.

____ 4. **Considerations for Parties Other Than Project Owners.**

____ (a) **Considerations for architectural subconsultants**.

____ (i) Does the claim involve an attempt by one of the architect's subconsultants to collect fees from the architect for professional services rendered?

____ a. Determine whether the architect has received payment for the subconsultant's services from the project owner.

____ b. If the architect has received payment from the owner, but has paid the subconsultant with a portion of those funds, consider bringing a breach of contract action against the architect.

____ c. If the architect has not received payment, determine whether the contract between the subconsultant and the architect has a "pay-when-paid" clause. If such a clause is present, and is not barred by applicable law, the owner's nonpayment of funds to the architect may excuse its nonpayment of funds to the subconsultant.

____ d. Determine whether the subconsultant can record a mechanic's lien against the property where the project is being developed.

____ (b) **Considerations for injury and property damage claimants.**

____ (i) Does the personal injury or property damage claim involve permanent features of the building or temporary implements of construction?

____ a. Architects are not responsible for the means, methods, and procedures employed during the construction process. They typically have no duty to reject the temporary equipment and construction techniques utilized by contractors when making site observations.

____ b. Unless the potential claim relates to a permanent building feature that was detailed in the architectural drawings that were issued for construction, it should probably be brought against the prime contractor, not the project architect.

____ (ii) Who controls the site where the injury or damage occurred? If the potential claimant controls evidence that appears material to a potential lawsuit, it may owe a duty to other potential litigants to preserve that evidence. Failure to do so may prejudice their ability to mount a defense and, accordingly, could subject the potential claimant to sanctions that could defeat its claim.

____ a. Take steps to secure the loss scene and preserve all of the evidence necessary to prove the potential claim.

____ b. Refrain from touching, moving, or removing artifacts from the loss scene, if possible.

____ c. Notify any insurance carriers that may provide coverage for the injuries or damage.

____ d. Hire forensic consultants with expertise in all disciplines related to the errors, objects, and events that precipitated the injury or damage.

____ e. Place all potentially interested parties on written notice of the potential claim.

____ f. Facilitate an inspection of the loss scene with the other interested parties in order to recover or document any evidence necessary to prove the potential claim.

____ (iii) Potential claimants that do not control the loss scene should send written notice of their potential claim to the controlling party without delay. The notice should ask that party to place its liability carrier on notice of a potential claim and demand that the scene be maintained intact until the potential claimant's forensic consultants can make an inspection.

____ (c) **Considerations for insurers.**

____ (i) Does a waiver of subrogation bar the insurer's potential claim? Waivers of subrogation are generally enforced by courts to bar claims by insurers that are subrogated to the rights of their insureds for property damage.

____ (ii) Is the architect named as an additional insured on the relevant insurance policy? If so, the anti-subrogation doctrine—which prevents insurers from suing their own insureds—may bar the potential claim.

____ (iii) Is the insurer a worker's compensation carrier that paid benefits to an injured employee of its insured company? If so, it may have a lien against the proceeds of any recovery that the employee may make against the architect.

# Checklist 36: Replevin and Recovery of Materials from the Jobsite

This checklist discusses issues involving a contractor, subcontractor, or supplier's right to recover materials from a job site. A replevin action is a speedy remedy designed to allow the recovery of possession of property wrongfully held or detained as well as any damages incidental to detention. Replevin proceedings may be required when a party is faced with nonpayment by another party. If substantial amounts of monies are tied up in materials located on the jobsite, a party's best option may be to seek recovery of those materials. Replevin actions generally require immediate action. Materials on a jobsite that have not been paid for may be incorporated into the work or may disappear from the jobsite. This restricts the ability to recover damages against the nonpaying party. Replevin deals only with personal property, not real property.

____ 1. **Is replevin the best option available?** Do other avenues of recovery exist?

 ____ (a) **Lien rights or stop-notice claim.** As replevin is a harsh and costly remedy, will lien rights or a stop-notice claim accomplish your purpose rather than proceeding with a replevin action?

 ____ (b) **Payment bond claim.** Is there a payment bond in place, and are you within the class of claimants entitled to recover under a payment bond?

____ 2. **Is possession an issue?**

 ____ (a) **Who has possession of the materials?** Actual or constructive possession of the materials is required for a successful replevin action. Constructive possession of materials simply means that although the injured party may not have actual, physical possession of the materials, the materials are under the injured party's control. Constructive possession usually exists when a third party has actual possession of the materials, but one party has the ability to direct the third party to deliver possession of the materials to him. The controlling person has constructive possession.

**Ellie B. Word** is a partner with the law firm of Krebs, Farley & Pelleteri PLLC and is located in the firm's Jackson, Mississippi office. She regularly represents sureties in a variety of construction disputes, claims, and litigation.

____ (b) **Are the materials secured such that they cannot be replevied without a breach of peace?**

____ (c) **Does anyone else have a claim of possession?** To successfully replevin materials, there must not be another party or person that has rights of possession or any claim to possession of the materials. For instance, does anyone else have a lien on the materials that must first be satisfied? If so, then replevin may be unsuccessful due to the existence of the lien. Once the lien is satisfied, however, the replevin proceedings may continue.

____ 3. **Necessary Elements for a Replevin Action.** Replevin actions are state statute specific. It is imperative to check the applicable statute. Generally, in order to recover in an action for replevin, the claimant must prove:

____ (a) **Title.** The claimant has title or right to possession.

____ (b) **Unlawful detainment.** The claimant must show that the property has been unlawfully detained.

____ (c) **Wrongful possession.** The claimant must show that the defendant wrongfully holds possession.

____ 4. **Jurisdictional Requirements.** Replevin actions are generally created by statute. It is imperative to follow the statutory guidelines. You must review the applicable statute prior to proceeding with an action for replevin. Numerous items must be considered, including conditions precedent.

____ (a) **Conditions precedent.** Does your jurisdiction have any conditions precedent that must be met? Some jurisdictions may require that certain conditions be met or satisfied prior to replevin of the materials. For instance, some jurisdictions require, as a condition precedent to recovery, that a demand for the materials or property be made before a replevin action may be commenced. Check your state's statutes and/or case law for any conditions precedent that may exist.

____ (b) **Demand.** Is a demand for the materials required? If demand is required, has it been waived or would it be futile? If demand is required by your state, you should consider whether the requirement for demand has been waived or would be futile. For example, demand is not necessary when the original taking of the materials, or the holding of the materials, was wrongful or fraudulent. In addition, demand may be waived or may be futile when the other party claims title to the property. Demand may also be waived by the other party's actions or conduct.

____ (c) **Waiver.** If demand is required, has it been waived? Can it be waived?

____ (d) **Due process requirements.** What are the due process requirements of the applicable jurisdiction? What are the due process requirements of your jurisdiction? Some jurisdictions allow for the preliminary seizure of materials without a hearing if certain procedural guidelines of that jurisdiction are met, such as the procurement of a bond that covers the cost of the materials to be seized. Some statutes, however, require that notice be given to the other party prior to the seizure and/or that an emergency hearing be conducted.

____ (e) **Defenses to replevin actions**. Are there any defenses to be considered that would negate your replevin rights? Generally speaking, only a defense that disputes the injured party's right to possession is relevant. For example, abandonment of the materials by the injured party or the rights of third parties would be defenses that dispute the injured party's right to the materials. The merits and sufficiency of any such defenses should be considered before commencing a replevin proceeding. The following are *not* proper defenses to a replevin action: that the defendant made repairs or improvements to the property (if property rather than materials are at issue), that the materials and/or property are security for a debt owed to another party, and that the injured party was also negligent.

____ (f) **Affidavit or verified complaint requirements.** Is an affidavit or verified complaint required to commence a replevin procedure? Usually, an affidavit or a verified complaint must state that the injured party is the owner of the materials or, for a preliminary seizure, that it has the right to immediate possession of the materials. It must also adequately describe the materials to be seized so that an officer can identify and seize it. The affidavit or verified complaint should contain language that discusses the reason that the materials were taken or detained, to the best knowledge, information and belief of the person making the affidavit or verifying the complaint. Some statutes require that the affidavit or verified complaint state the value of the materials.

____ 5. **Replevin Proceedings.** Generally, replevin proceedings can be with notice or without notice.

____ (a) **Prejudgment or preliminary replevin.**

____ (i) **Do you fear that the materials may be removed from the jobsite before you can recover?** If so, you may want to seek immediate possession by way of a preliminary procedure. A preliminary procedure, prior to an actual trial on the merits, is available in many jurisdictions if there is a real and imminent fear that the materials will be moved, sold, or otherwise diminished. Certain statutory guidelines on preliminary seizure often exist, and they should be consulted before commencing a preliminary action. If a preliminary seizure occurs, then a final hearing or trial on the merits must take place afterward. There are usually severe penalties if the preliminary seizure was groundless.

____ (ii) **Have the statutory guidelines of your jurisdiction been met for a preliminary seizure?**

____ a. **Has the necessary showing of the probability of prevailing danger of losing the materials been met?** The injured party, in order to obtain an order for preliminary seizure, must present facts that show that there is a great probability that it will prevail at the final hearing on the merits of the case; that there is a great probability or a fear that the materials will be lost, moved, or sold; and that the injured party will therefore have no possibility of seizing the materials at a later time.

____ b. **Has the injured party shown that it has a right to the materials?** The injured party must also show that it has an actual and valid right to the materials before an order for a preliminary seizure will be granted.

____ c. **Is a replevin bond required?** A replevin bond is designed to protect the defendant if, after preliminarily seizing the property, the injured party is not successful on the final hearing or trial on the merits. The amount required for the replevin bond usually depends on the jurisdiction, but is generally based on the value of the materials to be seized.

____ (iii) **Final adjudication.** A post-seizure hearing is required to ensure that the plaintiff (the injured party) is properly entitled to recover the materials that were seized.

____ (b) **With notice.**

____ (i) **Is the claimant required to be the owner or claim some interest, usually through a security agreement, in order to utilize a replevin statute?**

____ (ii) **Does the statute allow the secured creditor or owner of property to obtain possession from a third party other than a defendant, if the third party is in possession?** This prevents the debtor from transferring the property to a third party in an effort to avoid a creditor's right to possession.

____ (iii) **Can the claimant, at the inception of a replevin action or any time before final judgment, claim immediate delivery of property?** If so, what must be shown?

____ (iv) **Pleading and practical tips for replevin with notice.** In pursuing replevin with notice, the following pleadings may be necessary:

____ a. Complaint.

____ b. Summons.

____ c. Motion for pre-judgment order.

____ d. Affidavit of delivery.

____ e. Order setting hearing and to show cause why plaintiff should not be given pre-judgment possession.

____ f. Order setting amount of bond.

____ g. Bond approved by court.

____ h. Order for prejudgment possession.

____ i. Final judgment for possession (if the defendant fails to appear at a hearing on pre-judgment possession).

____ (v) **Practice tip.** Does the statute contemplate that the affidavit of delivery be made by someone on behalf of plaintiff such that an attorney can file a verified complaint and within the complaint set forth the information necessary to be included in the affidavit in order to meet statutory requirements?

____ (c) **Without notice**. Does the applicable statute provide this extraordinary remedy to creditors under extraordinary circumstances? By this remedy, a creditor can obtain an order for possession without notice to the defendant.

____ (i) **Potential ramifications of replevin without notice.** Due to the special nature of replevin without notice, extreme caution should be employed when using this remedy. The claimant must understand the potential ramifications of using this remedy unwisely.

____ (ii) **Potential elements that must be set forth in an affidavit to establish replevin without notice.**

____ a. Defendant gained possession of the property by theft or criminal conversion.

____ b. The property is perishable and will perish before any notice and hearing can be held.

____ c. There is immediate danger of destruction, serious harm, concealment, or removal from the jurisdiction or sale to an innocent purchaser.

____ d. The holder of the property threatens to destroy, harm, conceal, remove from the state, or sell the property to an innocent purchaser.

____ (iii) **Evidence to present to the court to obtain a replevin without notice.**

____ a. Is testimony required at an *ex parte* hearing, or can the court review the complaint and affidavits to grant relief?

____ b. Is a bond or written undertaking required in order to obtain relief? If so, is it necessary for the court to determine the amount of written undertaking and form of undertaking to be filed?

____ (iv) **Necessary documents to obtain replevin without notice.** What are the necessary documents required to be filed with the court? They may include:

____ a. Complaint for replevin.

____ b. A summons.

____ c. Affidavit for delivery prior to hearing.

____ d. Motion for pre-judgment order without notice.

____ e. Preliminary pre-judgment order for possession without notice to defendant.

____ f. Plaintiff replevin bond and court approval of bond.

____ (v) **Practical tips for utilization of replevin without notice**. This remedy usually requires a practitioner to act with immediate speed. The following are beneficial in pursuing this remedy:

____ a. Verify all facts with the client because of the extreme harshness of the remedy.

____ b. Call the court to determine whether the court will be available that day for the issuance of any orders.

____ c. Make arrangements with the sheriff so that an executed order can be immediately carried out.

____ d. Arrange for pick-up and storage of materials. While a sheriff will maintain possession of property until further order of the court, the sheriff rarely has the facilities available for pick-up and storage. Therefore, arrangements should be made for a bonded warehouse for storage and for trucks or other vehicles to pick up the property.

____ 6. **Post-Hearing Considerations.**

____ (a) **Seizure of the materials.** After a hearing, a writ of replevin will be issued, allowing the sheriff to seize the materials. A "writ of replevin" is merely a legal document that directs the sheriff or other officer to seize the materials and deliver them to the injured party seeking the replevin. If a writ of replevin is issued based on a preliminary seizure request, then the final adjudication will occur after the actual seizure.

____ (b) **Final adjudication.** A post-seizure hearing is usually conducted to ensure that the plaintiff is properly entitled to recover the materials that were seized.

____ 7. **Uniform Commercial Code Considerations.** The Uniform Commercial Code does provide a replevin remedy.

____ (a) **Buyer's right to specific performance or replevin.**

____ (i) **Buyer's remedy.** The legal remedy of replevin is given to the buyer in cases in which cover (finding alternative goods in the marketplace because of seller's failure to deliver) is reasonably unavailable and the goods have been identified in the contract.

# Checklist 37: General Mechanic's Lien Procedure and Protection

The statutory mechanism created by state legislatures that allows a contractor to place a lien on real property for labor and materials furnished on credit to a construction project is a mechanic's lien. Perfection and foreclosure procedures vary from state to state.

Failure to strictly comply with any of these procedural requirements typically invalidates the lien. Equally important, an incorrect, invalid, false, or fraudulent lien clouds the title to the property and encumbers an owner from free disposition of that property. In certain instances an improper lien can interfere with a potential sale. For these reasons, an invalid lien may subject the claimant and/or the attorney to slander of title or tortuous interference with contract claims, and the potential for not only actual but also punitive damages exposure.

The following checklist is designed to help the practitioner, regardless of state, address key issues regarding the preparation, filing, and perfection of a mechanic's lien. As a word of caution, the mechanic's lien statutes are state specific, so the particulars of the applicable state statute must be reviewed.

____ 1. **Mechanic's Liens Are Strictly Construed.** In general, the provisions relating to the creation, existence, and persons entitled to liens are strictly construed. A claimant must comply with the statute in detail. A mechanic's lien that does not strictly comply with the statute could be found invalid on its face.

____ 2. **Claimants Entitled to Assert Mechanic's Liens.**

____ (a) **Contractors and subcontractors.** Generally, lien coverage is afforded to contractors and subcontractors.

____ (b) **Suppliers.** Suppliers are generally treated differently under lien statutes and are more narrowly protected. In some jurisdictions, a supplier to a material supplier may be too remote and outside the scope of lien coverage.

____ (c) **Laborers.** Many jurisdictions allow laborers to lien for wages and associated fringe benefits. However, while some states recognize the right of a claimant to acquire a lien for direct

**Daniel P. King** practices in the Indianapolis, Indiana law firm of Locke Reynolds LLP. He concentrates his practice in the area of construction law, representing contractors, sureties, and owners in commercial construction disputes over design defects, defective construction, and contract/payment issues.

supervisory labor at the site of construction, off-site supervising developers may not have rights to a lien.

____ (d) **Engineers, surveyors, and architects.** Does the applicable state statute allow an engineer, surveyor, or architect mechanic's lien protection? If so, does the claimant have to be registered with the state?

____ 3. **The Labor and Materials That Are Lienable.**

____ (a) **Labor.** Is the labor or service performed lienable? In some instances, a developer's claim involving only supervisory services has been rejected.

____ (b) **Materials and equipment.** Generally, persons furnishing machinery and materials to the owner of the property are protected. Under the applicable state law, a claimant must determine whether lessors of construction equipment are provided lien rights. Also, are those who merely provide parts for equipment belonging to and used by the contractor allowed to pursue a lien?

____ (c) **Owner's consent.** Does the jurisdiction require more than inactive consent by the owner in order to lien the owner's interest? This arises in improvements on leaseholds wherein a contractor has provided services at the request of a lessee.

____ 4. **Notice and Perfection Requirements for Mechanic's Lien Claimants.**

____ (a) Is a notice of furnishing or pre-lien notice required? If so, follow statutory provisions on such notices.

____ (b) Are there different notice requirements on commercial versus residential?

____ (c) General notice requirements vary from state to state, but the following are issues to be considered:

____ (i) **Lien requirements.**

____ a. **Identification of property owner.** A mechanic's lien must typically list the correct legal name of the property owner and may also require that the property owner's latest address be included as well. State law varies as to where the correct property owner and last address is to be located.

____ b. **Identification of claimant.** Typically, the actual party to the contract with the owner has the right to enforce a mechanic's lien. Failure to identify the proper claimant can result in a facially invalid lien.

____ c. **Legal description of property.** Properly identifying the property being liened tends to prove more difficult than initially expected. Securing the proper identification often merits the services of a title company and often takes several business days.

____ d. **Amount of claim.** In some states, the intentional or negligent overstatement of the lien amount can invalidate the lien.

____ (ii) **How is the notice to be filed and served?**

____ a. Is there a state registry for liens?

____ b. Is it filed in the county where the property is located?

____ c. To whom must the notice be served and how?

____ d. What is required for proof of service?

____ e. What is the consequence for failure to properly follow the foregoing?

____ f. Do the requirements differ for contractors versus subcontractors or suppliers?

____ g. Can an attorney sign the lien notice? Oftentimes, lawyers will receive calls from a client on the last day a lien can be recorded. Does the applicable statute allow for the attorney to sign the notice in order to record the lien as quickly as possible?

____ (iii) **Issues to be considered.** A number of issues arise concerning the intricacy of lien statutes. The following is not meant to be an exhaustive list but are items to be considered.

____ a. **Lien notice defects.** Does the applicable statute allow trivial errors in a lien notice so as not to defeat the lien? Must there be a showing that the owner is not misled by the error?

____ b. **Lien amendments.** Once a lien notice has been filed, can the notice be reformed to make it conform to statutory requirements? If so, must it be reformed during the time period allowed for filing of the lien or can it be amended after the time period has run?

____ c. **Time limit for filing lien notice.**

____ (1) Does the time period differ as to the type of project involved, for example, residential construction or commercial construction?

____ (2) When does the time limit run?

____ (3) How is the last date of work or furnishing materials determined?

____ (4) Is there additional, extra, or remedial work to be performed? If additional, extra, or remedial work is required to complete the contract work, or has been requested by the owner, the time period for filing a lien is generally extended.

____ (5) Has separate work been "tacked" on? Where labor or materials are furnished under separate contracts, even though the contracts are between the same persons and relate to the same building or improvements, can contracts be tacked together to enlarge the time for filing a lien for what was done or furnished under either contract?

____ (6) Are there owner-caused delays? In some instances, an owner may be estopped from challenging the time limits of a mechanic's lien when the owner has refused to accept construction work as complete, withholds final payment, and requires corrective work to be performed before payment will be made to the contractor.

____ 5. **Real Property Interests Subject to Mechanic's Liens.**

____ (a) **Private property.** Mechanic's liens are allowed to be placed upon private property.

____ (b) **Publicly owned property.** Historically, mechanic's liens cannot be filed or enforced against public property that is held for public use.

____ (i) Is there a payment bond remedy?

____ (ii) Is there a claim available as to the funds held by the public entity by those not in privity with the public owner?

____ (c) **Quasi-public projects.** The issue of whether a mechanic's lien can be asserted on a quasi-public project is fact sensitive. Although property may be held for public use, if it is clearly privately owned, it may be subject to a mechanic's lien. For example, a privately owned, quasi-public corporation that supplies natural gas may have its property subject to a mechanic's lien as the utility's ownership of a facility may not be central to public use, thus defeating the public use exception.

____ 6. **Contractual and Statutory Defenses to Lien Claims.** The applicable statutes may provide a means by which an owner may insulate itself and its property against mechanic's liens. The following are some of these defenses:

____ (a) No-lien agreement.

____ (b) Contractual waiver clauses.

____ (c) Partial and final lien waivers.

____ (d) Contingent payment clause.

____ (e) Bonding off or discharge of mechanic's liens.

____ 7. **Enforcing Mechanic's Liens.**

____ (a) **Foreclosure.** Enforcing a mechanic's lien typically requires the lien claimant to file a foreclosure suit. Some states require the foreclosure lawsuit to be filed within a certain period of time.

____ (b) **Choice of law.** Does the applicable statute prohibit application of foreign law?

____ (c) **Choice of forum.** Does the applicable statute require the foreclosure action to be filed in a particular forum, such as the county where the property is located? Does the applicable statute preclude enforcement of the mechanic's lien in a foreign jurisdiction?

# Pre-Trial/Discovery

# Checklist 38: Preparing for an Architect's Deposition

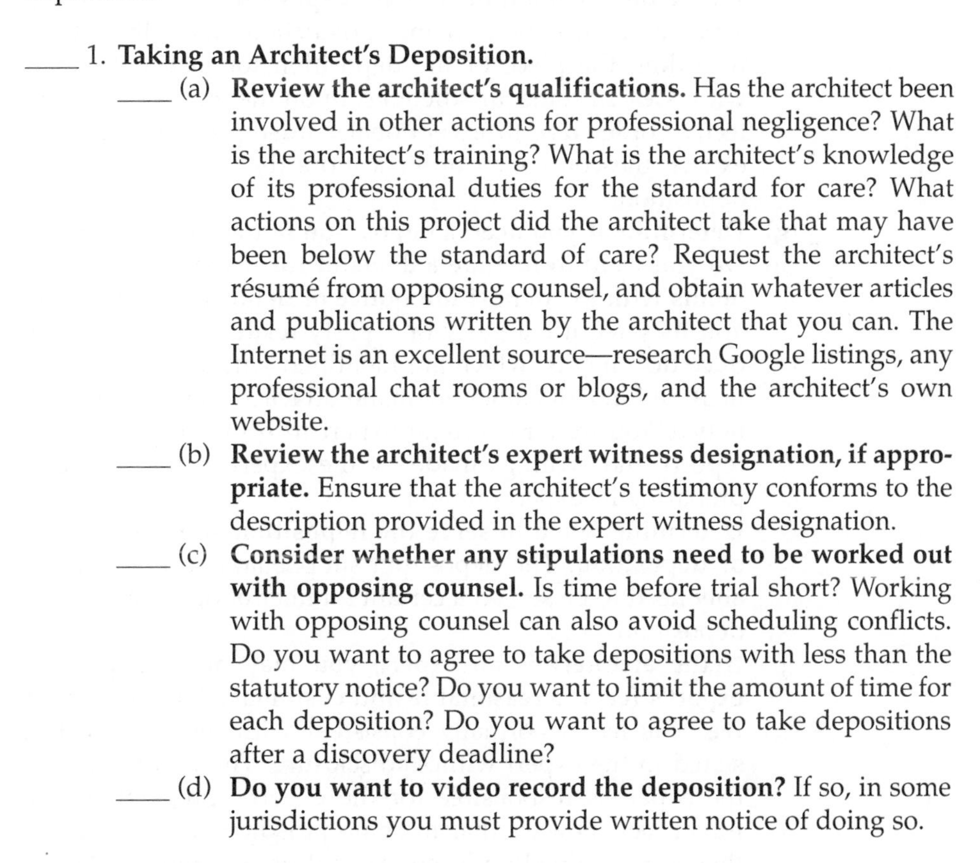

If representing an architect, or litigating against an architect, that is involved in a construction project, that architect's deposition will almost certainly be critical to the outcome of the action. The following checklist addresses the approaches that can be taken for both taking and defending an architect's deposition.

____ 1. **Taking an Architect's Deposition.**

____ (a) **Review the architect's qualifications.** Has the architect been involved in other actions for professional negligence? What is the architect's training? What is the architect's knowledge of its professional duties for the standard for care? What actions on this project did the architect take that may have been below the standard of care? Request the architect's résumé from opposing counsel, and obtain whatever articles and publications written by the architect that you can. The Internet is an excellent source—research Google listings, any professional chat rooms or blogs, and the architect's own website.

____ (b) **Review the architect's expert witness designation, if appropriate.** Ensure that the architect's testimony conforms to the description provided in the expert witness designation.

____ (c) **Consider whether any stipulations need to be worked out with opposing counsel.** Is time before trial short? Working with opposing counsel can also avoid scheduling conflicts. Do you want to agree to take depositions with less than the statutory notice? Do you want to limit the amount of time for each deposition? Do you want to agree to take depositions after a discovery deadline?

____ (d) **Do you want to video record the deposition?** If so, in some jurisdictions you must provide written notice of doing so.

**Theodore D. Levin** is a partner at Morris, Polich & Purdy LLP. He represents design professionals, contractors, construction managers, and owners in all aspects of construction law, including those involving breach of contract, defective design and construction, and delay and disruption claims.

**Christian A. Carrillo** is an associate at Morris, Polich & Purdy LLP. His construction law practice has focused on the representation of contractors, owners, and designers in termination, delay, and breach of contract disputes.

____ (i) If required, and you do not include written notice of your intent to video record the deposition, any attempt to introduce the deposition at trial may be successfully opposed by a protective order.

____ (ii) If the video is to be offered into evidence later, you might need to provide sufficient time for objections to be resolved and for editing.

____ (e) **When do you want to take the deposition?** In what sequence do you want to take the architect(s) deposition(s)? The role of the owner, contractor, subcontractors, structural engineer, and any other design consultants must be considered.

____ (f) **Where do you want to take the deposition?** Is the architect a party or an expert? Some jurisdictions have limitations regarding the place of the deposition for fact and expert witnesses. In some jurisdictions, upon the motion for a protective order due to exceptional hardship of the architect-expert, the court may order a more distant venue for the deposition.

____ (g) **Determine if you need a deposition notice or a subpoena.**

____ (h) **Do you want to include a demand for inspection of documents with the deposition notice or deposition subpoena?** You may require a party or a party-related witness to produce documents, which are identified with reasonable particularity in a document demand attached to the deposition notice. You may require an expert to bring "discoverable" reports and writings made by the expert in the course of preparing its expert opinion.

____ (i) **Determine when to serve the deposition subpoena/notice of deposition.** The deposition subpoena/notice will probably need to be served a certain number of days prior to the deposition.

____ (j) **If the architect is an expert, you may need to pay the expert's fee at a reasonable and customary hourly or daily fee.** The fee is normally consistent with the fee schedule stated in the expert witness disclosure. The party retaining the expert is responsible for the expert's preparation and travel fees. Beware that in some jurisdictions, an architect that was involved with the original project and is asked to express an opinion may be considered to be an expert witness and entitled to expert witness fees. If you believe the fees are unreasonable, then, after a meet-and-confer attempt with opposing counsel to reach an informal agreement, you may be able to move the court for an order setting the fee. This will depend on the jurisdiction.

____ (k) **Causes of action.** What causes of action are present in the case and relevant to the architect?

____ (l) **What are the facts and theories of the case?** A persuasive story must account for all undisputed facts, be supported by the action's details, and explain why the architect or others acted as they did. It must also be plausible. What are your theories and facts?

- ____ (i) What are your opponent's legal theories?
- ____ (ii) What are your opponent's factual claims?
- ____ (iii) You must reconcile your factual theory with your legal theory and identify any missing information/details/evidence that the architect can provide.

____ (m) **Brainstorm questions**. What information/admissions/details do you want to get out of the architect?

____ (n) **Review all pleadings, documents, and depositions.** With whom did the architect have a contract? To whom did the architect owe any contractual obligations or legal duties?

____ (o) **Confer with your architectural expert and client for further information.** Are the architect's actions at issue? Did the architect fulfill its contract obligations? According to your architectural expert, what is the relevant standard of care? Did the architect's actions meet the relevant standard of care? Can the architectural expert work with you to develop a hypothetical question that will overcome any objections? Does your architectural expert know of any authority with which to impeach the deponent? Remember to spend enough time with your architectural expert to understand any technical issues present in the action.

____ (p) **Background information.**

- ____ (i) If the architect is an expert, ask about its fee arrangement and how much the fee is for each part of the action.
- ____ (ii) If the architect is an expert, ask when it was hired.
- ____ (iii) If the architect is an expert, ask what on what topics it was hired to opine, and how much time it has spent on formulating its opinion.
- ____ (iv) Does the architect have an engagement letter?

____ (q) **What materials or documents has the deponent used, referenced, or observed in preparing for the deposition?** With whom has the deponent spoken?

____ (r) **If the architect is an expert, ask for all of its opinions and conclusions reached and the grounds to support them.** Does the expert intend to offer any other opinions at trial? If not, then a court should exclude any expert testimony that goes beyond what is offered at deposition.

____ (i) If the architect is not an expert, beware of asking for testimony that calls for an expert opinion.

____ (ii) If the architect is an expert, ask about any other actions that it should have undertaken but could not, and why not.

____ (s) **Consider any contract issues that affect your case.** Who prepared the contract? What was the architect's role in preparing the contract?

____ (t) **What were the architect's contract administration duties?** Did they change through the phases of the contract? What did the architect do to fulfill each contract administration duty?

____ (u) **Does the case involve delay and impact issues?** If so, make sure you spend enough time with your scheduling consultant to understand how those issues developed. Identify any requests for information or change order requests that you need to review with the architect to determine their role in any delay claim.

____ (v) **Does the case involve allegations of defective plans?** Familiarize yourself with the plans the architect drafted, and, if there are allegations of defective plans, spend enough time with your experts to understand them and be able to question the architect about them.

____ (i) Does the owner allege defective plans?

____ (ii) Does a contractor assert *Spearin* arguments?

____ (w) **Review the architect's license and professional organizations, such as the AIA.**

____ (i) What are the architect's qualifications?

____ (ii) Has the architect's license ever been suspended?

____ (iii) Has the architect ever been subject to disciplinary action?

____ (x) **What does the architect do to keep up with the latest developments in the architecture field?** Does it take seminars or classes? Has it taken any that relate to the issues in your lawsuit?

____ 2. **Defending an Architect's Deposition.** Most of the same issues identified in part 1 apply to defending an architect's deposition.

____ (a) **Deposition procedures.** You must review deposition procedures with your deponent, the probable questions that will be asked, and any documents or other matters that may affect the architect's testimony. Work with your architect to ensure its demeanor is appropriate.

____ (b) **Objections.** What objections does the jurisdiction allow you to make?

____ (c) **Length of deposition.** Does the jurisdiction have a time limit on the length of the deposition?

____ (d) **Discussions with expert.**

  ____ (i) There is probably little protection from the discovery of discussions unless the architect is the client.

  ____ (ii) Does the jurisdiction allow side bar conferences with the architect during the deposition or during breaks?

____ (e) **File materials.** What materials in the architect's files are protected from discovery?

# Checklist 39: Preparing a Witness for a Deposition

Although depositions become routine for attorneys, they can be frightening for witnesses, especially witnesses who have never been deposed before. A few hours preparing a witness can help him or her know what to expect and how to handle what otherwise might be difficult situations. The following is a list of suggestions to use when preparing a witness for a deposition.

____ 1. **What is the purpose of a deposition?**

____ (a) A deposition is the opportunity for a party in litigation to obtain oral evidence from a witness taken under oath, before trial.

____ (b) The deposition allows the opposing lawyer to "discover" all facts the witness may know that will assist that lawyer in preparing his case for trial.

____ (c) A witness also commits him- or herself to a story under oath that he or she cannot change at trial.

____ (d) Opposing counsel will also evaluate the witness to determine how effective that witness will be at trial.

____ 2. **Where is the deposition?** It often takes place in a conference room or office, and the setting is somewhat informal. It is important, however, to take the event seriously.

____ 3. **What does the court reporter do?** Although practices will vary somewhat from jurisdiction to jurisdiction, court reporters record the deposition testimony.

____ (a) To begin the deposition, the court reporter administers the oath to the witness.

____ (b) The court reporter prepares a transcript during the deposition that records every word said during the deposition and finalizes the transcript after the deposition.

____ (c) The witness will have an opportunity to review and sign the transcript.

____ (d) If the case goes to court, the lawyers will use the transcript and may read deposition testimony back to the witness

**Melissa A. Orien** is in the Salt Lake City office of Holland & Hart LLP. Her practice focuses on construction, design, and real estate litigation. She represents owners, contractors, and subcontractors on a variety of public and private construction-related disputes.

during the trial to impeach the witness's credibility if answers at trial are different from answers given at the deposition.

____ 4. **Who attends the deposition?** In addition to the witness, the witness's attorney, and the court reporter, an attorney and a representative for each party may attend.

____ 5. **Who asks questions during the deposition?** One attorney for each party may ask questions. Each attorney will completely finish asking questions before the next attorney starts.

____ 6. **Should the witness bring documents?** Unless the deposition notice that the witness was served with included a "subpoena duces tecum," the witness should not bring documents to the deposition.

____ 7. **Dress for depositions.** It is customary to dress in business attire. A deposition is a formal proceeding, and it is part of the judicial process.

____ 8. **Deposition Do's and Don'ts.**

____ (a) **Deposition do's.**

____ (i) Treat all persons in the deposition room with respect.

____ (ii) Tell the truth. Never attempt to misrepresent facts to protect yourself or help your employer.

____ (iii) Answer out loud with words such as "yes" or "no," not by gestures or with answers such as "uh-huh" or "uh-uh."

____ (iv) Wait until the lawyer finishes asking the question before beginning to answer. The court reporter can only record one person talking at a time.

____ (v) Be humble and respectful.

____ (vi) Speak slowly and clearly.

____ (vii) Understand the question before answering. If the witness does not understand the question, he or she should ask the lawyer to repeat or restate the question, or simply say he or she does not understand the question.

____ (viii) Give the questions and answers as much time and thought as necessary. Pausing for a moment before answering each question allows the witness to better formulate a concise and articulate answer.

____ (ix) Answer all questions directly and as concisely as possible.

____ (x) If the questioning lawyer remains silent after the witness has completed his or her answer, the witness should stop talking. He or she need not feel persuaded to continue answering.

____ (xi) Stick to the facts. A witness should only testify to things he or she personally knows.

____ (xii) A witness should not offer opinions or estimates (distance, dates, times, etc.) unless he or she has a good basis for knowing the estimate is accurate.

____ (xiii) A witness cannot know all the facts and does him- or herself a disservice if he or she attempts to testify to facts with which he or she does not have personal knowledge.

____ (xiv) Sometimes "I don't know" or "I would be speculating" is the perfect answer.

____ (xv) A witness can take a break any time he or she feels tired or needs to relax.

____ (xvi) The witness can talk to his or her lawyer at any time a question is not pending. If the witness has a question for you, he or she should ask to take a break.

____ (b) **Deposition don'ts.** Tell your witness not to do the following:

____ (i) Don't guess.

____ (ii) Don't argue or get angry even if opposing counsel is rude or overbearing.

____ (iii) Don't ramble. Rather, be concise and avoid narrative answers.

____ (iv) Don't chew gum.

____ (v) Don't volunteer information. Answer the questions truthfully, but answer only the questions.

____ (vi) Don't take notes during the deposition. Opposing counsel may ask the witness to see what he has written.

____ (vii) Don't be sarcastic. The record cannot interpret sarcasm.

____ (viii) Don't argue.

____ (ix) Don't fight the easy questions. If a witness is adversarial on foundational or background questions, he or she comes across as completely biased and loses credibility on the important questions.

____ 9. **What questions will be asked at the deposition?**

____ (a) **General questions.** It is customary for the attorney to ask some preliminary questions in virtually all depositions of all types of witnesses. These may cover the following:

____ (i) Full name.

____ (ii) Address.

____ (iii) Education.

____ (iv) Current employment.

____ (v) Employment history.
____ (vi) Employment responsibilities.
____ (b) **Questions related to subjects of litigation.**
____ (i) Complete factual recollection of incidents or issues that are the subject of litigation.
____ (ii) Conversations with others regarding the same.
____ (iii) Recollection of documents regarding the same.
____ (iv) Lay person opinions regarding the same.
____ (c) **Privileged communications.** Make sure your witness understands how to respond to a question that calls for privileged communications.
____ (i) If the answer to a question requires the witness to disclose information that his or her attorney told him or her or would otherwise require the witness to disclose some conversation with his or her attorney, the witness should not answer.
____ (ii) Explain to the witness that if you believe a question calls for privileged information, you will object on the grounds of privilege and instruct your witness not to answer the question.

____ 10. **Is a question fair?**
____ (a) **Fair question, fair answer.** A witness is required to give a fair answer to a fair question. But the witness does not always get fair questions. Objections help the witness understand when a question is not fair.
____ (b) **Witness competence.**
____ (i) A witness should only testify to things he or she saw, heard, did, said, believed, and understood.
____ (ii) If a witness is questioned about an event or subject he or she did not see, hear, do, say, believe, or understand, the witness is not required to answer and can say, "I don't know."

____ 11. **Posture and Presentation.**
____ (a) **Body language.** What a witness does with his or her body during a deposition can send signals of the level of comfort that witness has about his or her answer. It also signals to the opposing lawyer how credible the witness will be. Reminding your witness to make simple adjustments will make him or her a more effective witness.
____ (i) **Sit up straight.** If a witness is slumped over or leaning back in his or her chair, it gives the impression that he or she is either not as confident or not prepared.

____ (ii) **Don't swing in the chair.** Instruct the witness to resist the urge to swing back and forth in his or her chair.

____ (iii) **Body position.** The witness should lean slightly forward and put both feet on the ground. This position is the most likely to prevent subconscious fidgeting. By leaning slightly forward, the witness sends the message that he or she is engaged in the deposition.

____ (iv) **Chair height.** Assist the witness to adjust the chair height, if possible, so that he or she can look opposing counsel directly in the eye.

____ (v) **Monitor body position.** As your witness starts to get tired, his or her body language may become sloppy. If you see this start to happen, take a break and remind him or her to use good posture.

____ (b) **Voice.**

____ (i) **Speak clearly.** The witness should speak clearly and slow enough that people can understand him or her.

____ (ii) **Avoid fillers.** Help your witness become conscious of fillers like "um." Practice with the witness so he or she becomes comfortable with silence between questions and answers.

____ (iii) **Finishing answers.** Train your witness to finish his or her answer completely, even if opposing counsel starts talking before he or she is finished.

____ 12. **Documents.** Inevitably, the witness will be questioned about documents. The witness should understand how to use documents when questioned about them.

____ (a) **Take the time to read the entire document.**

____ (i) Resist attempts to rush through a document. The witness has the right to review the entire document before testifying about it.

____ (ii) The witness should understand that a question might be asked about a portion of a document out of context. The witness should beware of this and add context when appropriate.

____ (iii) Practice with the witness. A few practice rounds of questioning him or her on documents will increase the witness's comfort about testifying with documents.

____ (b) **Unfamiliar documents.** The witness should not interpret a document he or she is not familiar with or has not been given an opportunity to read.

____ (c) **Retaining documents.** The witness should insist on keeping a document in his or her hands when he or she is testifying about it. If later asked about the same document, when it is not in front of him or her, the witness should ask for the document back.

____ (d) **Representations about documents.** A witness should not believe representations about what a document says but check for him- or herself what the document says.

____ (e) **Requesting a document.** A witness can request to see a document if it will help his or her testimony. For example, the witness can say, "I could better testify to the contents of the lease agreement if you showed me a copy of it." Or, "I can't remember specifically what happened that day, but I know I kept daily records in my daily log."

____ 13. **Objections.** Witnesses are easily distracted by objections. Make sure your witness understands the purpose for objections and is comfortable with how to react to them. You can use objections to communicate with your witness and warn him or her about unfair questions. Discuss generally the reasons you will use a specific objection and what the objection says about the question.

____ (a) **General purpose.**

____ (i) Explain that you will object if you feel like a question is not fair.

____ (ii) Explain that the objection is also to preserve the record and that the witness is still required to answer the pending question (unless the objection called for privileged information).

____ (iii) The witness should pause to allow you to finish your objection.

____ (b) **Common objections.** Here are some examples of the common objections you can use to both preserve the record and protect your witness against unfair questions. These objections may not be available in all forums.

____ (i) **Asked and answered.** A witness is only required to give an answer once. Many times opposing counsel won't like the answer to the question so she or he will ask it again immediately or at a different time during a deposition. This objection reminds the witness he or she has already answered the question and does not need to change his or her answer.

____ (ii) **Calls for speculation.** Remind your witness that he or she does not have to guess if he or she does not know the answer to a question.

____ (iii) **Vague.** Remind your witness that he or she can ask for clarification if a question is vague.

____ (iv) **Lack of foundation.** Warn your witness that you believe additional foundation is necessary or that opposing counsel is making representations about a fact that has not yet been established.

____ (v) **Incomplete hypothetical.** Warn your witness against agreeing to a principle in the abstract when not enough facts exist. This objection signals to the witness that lack of facts in the question may make the answer unreliable.

____ (vi) **Compound.** Warn your witness that he or she is being asked two separate questions. A "yes" or "no" answer could later be applied to the wrong part of a compound question.

____ (vii) **Ambiguous.** Warn your witness that the question is unclear. The witness can ask for clarification or answer if he or she is comfortable.

____ (viii) **Calls for legal conclusion.** Your witness is not a lawyer is and not required to interpret contract language or apply the law.

____ (ix) **Calls for expert testimony.** Your witness only has to testify to facts in his or her personal knowledge. He or she does not have to hypothesize about how things normally happen or should happen.

____ 14. **Common Trick Questions.** Teach your witness about some common questioning tactics used by lawyers to help him or her recognize these tactics during the deposition.

____ (a) **Misinterpreting prior testimony.** The opposing lawyer might misrepresent earlier testimony as part of a question to trick the witness into buying into the representation. Witnesses need to listen carefully and correct any misrepresentations.

____ (b) **Open-ended comparisons.** Similar to hypothetical questions. Witnesses should avoid comparing two things in the abstract.

____ (c) **Have you stopped beating your wife?** This is a classic example of a question that lacks foundation. This question assumes that the witness was beating his wife at some point. Neither a "yes" or "no" answer would be appropriate (if the witness had never beat his wife). The witness should correct incorrect assumptions in questions.

____ (d) **Suggesting that the witness could have done better.** Witnesses should avoid using their 20-20 hindsight to agree that they could have handled a situation better. Rather, the witness should view the situation as he or she did at the time it occurred and determine whether, under those circumstances, the course of action was reasonable.

____ (e) **Something was impossible.** Avoid agreeing to absolutes like "never," "impossible," "always," "forever," etc. Rather, the witness should answer the question using a more accurate modifier like "most of the time" or "usually not."

____ (f) **Double negatives.** Questions with double negatives are difficult to answer correctly off the cuff and can be misinterpreted later. The witness should watch for questions with double negatives and ask for the question to be rephrased.

____ (g) **"To your knowledge" or "as far as you know."** If a witness is unsure of the exact result, he or she should not say something did not happen. Rather, the witness should say he or she doesn't know whether it happened.

____ (h) **"Is that all?"** When questioned about a list of items, opposing counsel will often follow up the question, "Is that all?" Witnesses should answer, "That is all that comes to mind," or "That's all I can remember right now," to leave flexibility to include another item later.

____ (i) **Silent treatment.** Witnesses should beware of this tactic and stop talking when they have finished an answer.

____ (j) **Use your own words.** Witnesses don't have to use the lawyer's words to describe something in an answer. Rather, they should answer in their own words. This makes testimony sound more accurate and more natural.

____ (k) **Rapid fire.** The lawyer might start asking questions rapidly to force a witness to give an answer without thinking it through. The witness should resist this and take necessary time to breathe or think between questions. Either you or a witness can ask for a break as well.

____ (l) **Questions that paraphrase the testimony.** The witness should make sure that his or her comment is being properly applied when quoted by the lawyer.

____ (m) **Beware of the nice guy.** The opposing lawyer is not the witness's friend. Even if she or he is nice or acting friendly, the witness should beware that the deposition is part of an adversarial proceeding and the lawyer represents another party.

____ 15. **Practice.** Take a few minutes to practice some questions with the witness. Help him or her to become comfortable with the process after you explain what to expect. Help him or her with the form of his or her answers (but don't change the substance). A few minutes of practice can allay a witness's fear about giving deposition testimony and help him or her to be more comfortable and confident during his or her deposition.

# Checklist 40: Joint Defense Agreements

Once litigation of a dispute has commenced, it may become beneficial for two or more of the parties to enter into a joint defense agreement. The creation of a joint defense agreement is not necessary when attorneys represent the same client or clients who have parallel interests in the litigation. This is because communications between the attorneys in this situation are privileged, and information may be freely shared without the worry of having to later disclose the substance or the content of those communications. However, if the parties have opposing interests in the litigation, then communications between their attorneys are not privileged. A joint defense agreement, in this instance, will allow the attorneys to freely communicate. This checklist assists with determining the propriety of such an agreement, as well as some of the legal implications.

____ 1. **What are the legal implications of a joint defense agreement?**

____ (a) **Is the maintenance of the attorney–client privilege necessary to your litigation?** Whether a joint defense agreement should be entered into should be determined as soon as possible to prevent the disclosure of privileged information. Unless a joint defense agreement is entered into, communications between attorneys are not privileged, unless the attorneys represent the same client or a client with parallel interests. This means that if attorneys for two different clients, who have opposing legal interests in the litigation, discuss various aspects of the litigation, such as legal defenses, legal strategy, potential witnesses, etc., these communications may have to be disclosed to the attorneys on the other side, unless a joint defense agreement is entered into. In addition, if a client speaks with an attorney for another party, and there is no joint defense agreement in place, then the communications between the client and the attorney for the other party are subject to disclosure. In some instances, depending on the complexity and nature of the litigation, the disclosure of such communications could have an adverse affect on your representation.

**Ellie B. Word** is a partner with the law firm of Krebs, Farley & Pelleteri PLLC and is located in the firm's Jackson, Mississippi office. She regularly represents sureties in a variety of construction disputes, claims, and litigation.

____ (b) **Would nondisclosure of communications benefit your litigation?** In some instances, such as in cases of great complexity or where there are multiple co-defendants, the ability to freely communicate with others sharing common legal interests would be beneficial. This ability is helpful in fact development as well as strategy planning in that the parties can share information, ideas, and documentation without the worry of whether their communications will have to be disclosed at a later time during the litigation.

____ (c) **What is your jurisdiction's view on attorney–client privilege in regards to joint defense agreements?** Many jurisdictions differ on what communications are privileged and what communications are not. In some instances, the federal courts in a jurisdiction may differ from what the states in their district hold. Many different views may exist as to how far the privilege extends as to control groups, agents, employees, etc. You should consult your jurisdiction's recent case law to determine what views are followed in your area.

____ 2. **When is a joint defense agreement available?**

____ (a) **Do the parties have a common legal interest in the dispute in question?** If a joint defense agreement is to be valid, the parties who enter into the agreement must have a common legal interest in the dispute. In other words, although the parties do not have to have parallel interests, if their interests are opposing, but they have a common legal interest—that is, they both seek a dismissal of the plaintiff's claims and do not have cross-claims against one another—then a joint defense agreement would be appropriate. If one co-defendant has filed a cross-claim against another co-defendant, then they would not have a common legal interest, and thus, a joint defense agreement would not be available to them.

____ (b) **Would the parties benefit from a sharing of legal resources?** If a joint defense agreement is established, then the attorneys for the parties to the agreement can work together in many respects. For example, they can work together to secure an expert witness and share the cost of the expert witness. They can split up the investigation and fact development of the case and compare notes in the end, thereby eliminating much of the initial cost.

____ (c) **Would the parties benefit from an extended attorney–client privilege?** As discussed previously, if the sharing of communications without the worry of having to later disclose those communications to the plaintiff would be beneficial, then a joint defense agreement should be considered.

____ 3. **What terms should the joint defense agreement contain?**

____ (a) **The agreement should be in writing.** Rather than a verbal agreement that will be disputed later and probably would not be enforced in court, the parties should draft a written joint defense agreement.

____ (b) **Identification of parties and the case.** The agreement should clearly identify the parties to the agreement and the case that they are agreeing to jointly defend.

____ (c) **Intended purpose.** The agreement should generally state that the parties intend to enter into the joint defense agreement for the purpose of aiding and promoting adequate representation, to achieve cost reductions, and for the purpose of freely communicating without waiving any attorney–client privilege (as discussed earlier).

____ (d) **Limitation on use and disclosure of shared information.** The agreement should contain a paragraph that sets forth the agreement of the parties concerning what information will be shared, the limitations on the use of the information shared, and when the information can and cannot be disclosed to third parties.

____ (e) **Limitation on party's disclosure of its own information.** The agreement should state that the parties to the agreement can use and can disclose to anyone information that is not shared information, that is, information that was obtained independently and not in connection with the joint defense agreement.

____ (f) **Work product protection.** The agreement should specifically state that all documents and materials created by or among counsel for any party to the agreement will be attorney work product of each of the attorneys who assisted in its creation. In other words, if the attorneys for both of the parties to the joint defense agreement work together to create a chart of the various issues to be addressed at trial, that chart is attorney work product of both of the attorneys, and neither attorney can disclose the chart to someone who is not a party to the agreement.

____ (g) **Nonwaiver of privilege.** The agreement should state that the attorney–client privilege is not waived as to any shared information disclosed by and between the parties to the agreement, even if the information is disclosed when the disclosing party was not a party to the agreement.

____ (h) **Notice before disclosure.** If, during the course of discovery, another person, who is not a party to the joint defense agreement, requests, through any formal or informal discovery request, that a person who is a party to the joint defense agreement disclose shared information, then the person who is requested to disclose the information must give notice of the request to all parties to the joint defense agreement. At that time, the parties to the joint defense agreement must work together to assert all applicable privileges to the shared information and take whatever steps are necessary to protect the confidentiality of the shared information.

____ (i) **Withdrawal.** The agreement should provide for a means for any party to the agreement to withdraw from the agreement. However, a specific notice period should be included in the agreement. For example, the agreement should provide that any party can withdraw from the agreement upon 10 days' written notice to the other parties to the agreement. If one party withdraws, the agreement should state that the withdrawing party must return all documents containing shared information, without retaining any copies, summaries, or extracts thereof or provide written certification that all shared information was destroyed.

____ (j) **Shared information in other proceedings.** The agreement should specify that none of the shared information would be used by any of the parties to the agreement in any other proceeding, unless there is written consent by the party that disclosed the information.

____ (k) **Confidentiality of agreement.** The agreement should specifically state that the agreement itself is confidential unless it becomes necessary to disclose the agreement for the purpose of proving that the agreement exists or when necessary to enforce the agreement.

____ (l) **Injunctive relief.** The parties to the agreement should acknowledge in the agreement that immediate injunctive relief will be afforded the parties if any party should violate any of the terms of the agreement.

____ (m) **Continuation of confidentiality obligations.** The agreement should state that the confidentiality requirement of the agreement will remain in full force and effect—even if a party withdraws from the agreement and even after the resolution or conclusion of the litigation that gave rise to the entry and creation of the agreement.

____ (n) **Specific waiver.** The agreement should state that if any privilege is waived in a particular instance, it is not deemed to waive the privilege in every instance.

____ (o) **No admissions.** The parties should acknowledge in the agreement that nothing in the agreement constitutes or should be interpreted to be an admission of any liability.

____ (p) **No agency.** A provision stating that the agreement does not create an agency relationship between any of the parties should be included.

____ (q) **Settlement.** A detailed paragraph pertaining to settlement issues should be addressed in the agreement. This term of the agreement should state that each party is free to seek dismissal from the lawsuit and that each party retains the right to seek a settlement with the plaintiff at any time. However, notice should be given to the other parties to the agreement immediately, and the parties should agree and stipulate that none of the shared information will be disclosed to the plaintiff during or following settlement negotiations.

____ (r) **Miscellaneous provisions.** Any other provisions that the parties deem appropriate should be included, such as what law governs any dispute pertaining to the agreement, how the agreement can be executed, the effect of facsimile signatures, and where notice should be given to the parties.

# Trial/Hearing

# Checklist 41: Opening Statements in Construction Cases

The opening statement is, to many commentators, the most important part of the case. The particular style of an attorney's opening is subject to much debate and presents too many variables and subjective choices for a checklist format. However, when preparing for the opening statement in a case, there are several considerations that can be itemized and considered. Many of these considerations are common to all disputes but, where applicable, the peculiarities of construction disputes are noted.

____ 1. **Logistical Considerations.**

____ (a) **Who is your audience?** The audience could span a broad spectrum of legal and technical knowledge. The presentation of an opening statement in a construction dispute could be made to a judge, jury, arbitrator, arbitration panel, mediator, opposing parties, or others. An appreciation of who is the target of the opening statement will affect the style significantly—and perhaps the substance as well. For example, if you are not presenting your opening to a lawyer, avoid the legalese. If you are presenting an opening to a jury comprised of bus drivers, waitresses, and factory workers, then use language and terminology that makes sense to them. If you are in a bench trial, avoid the theatrics that may impress a jury, and appeal to the sensibilities of a judge. If your case is being tried before an arbitrator with construction law experience, industry jargon may be perfectly acceptable and even preferred.

____ (b) **Should you waive or postpone your opening?** An opening statement should be waived only under extraordinary circumstances. If you waive or postpone your opening, you are leaving more time for the finder of fact to understand, digest, and adopt your opponent's view of the case.

____ (c) **What is your venue?** Once you have determined to whom you will make your opening statement, you should consider when, where, and how your opening will proceed.

**Clifford F. Kinney, Jr.** is a member of the law firm of Spilman Thomas & Battle PLLC in its Charleston, West Virginia office. He practices in the areas of construction litigation and insurance disputes and also serves as a mediator and arbitrator.

____ (i) Will you be in a courtroom, a conference room, or some other location?
____ (ii) Where will you be placed physically?
____ (iii) Who goes first, and how is the time divided?
____ (iv) Who can be present in the room?
____ (v) Who are the parties' representatives?
____ (vi) May others, such as expert witnesses, be present at opening statements?

____ 2. **Advocating Your Case.**

____ (a) **First impressions are lasting!** Create a favorable first impression.

____ (b) **Clearly explain the theory of your case.** Present your theory of the case early, late, and often in your opening statement.

____ (c) **Have a theme that connects your case to the evidence and your expected closing.**

____ (d) **Quickly catch the fact-finder's attention.** Your first words will be heard by all. Make sure they have impact. Give a 2-minute summary of your position, including your theme and, if appropriate, human elements.

____ (e) **How will you present your client and the other parties in the proceeding?**

____ (f) **What can you say, and how can you present it?** Is it really an opening "statement," or is it an opening "argument"? What techniques can you employ to present argument in the name of an opening statement?

____ (g) **What exhibits, deposition excerpts, and other potential evidence should you use in the opening statement?** If there is a particularly good piece of evidence, begin stressing it. If there is a particularly dangerous piece of evidence, begin to defuse it.

____ (i) Are you certain the evidence will be admitted?
____ (ii) What visual aids and courtroom technology can you use as a matter of style and courtroom capability?
____ (iii) What visual aids and courtroom technology can you use from an evidentiary standpoint?

____ (h) **What rules apply to objections during the openings, and under what circumstances should you object?** Generally, unless the opponent's transgression is extreme, an objection to an opponent's opening will only serve to highlight the issue to the jury.

____ (i) **What is your theme?**

____ (i) Tell a story that explains your facts. Don't just provide a pile of facts.

____ (ii) What is the human element of your case?

____ (iii) The strict enforcement of construction contract terms has public policy behind it. If this argument is in your favor, use it to your advantage.

____ (iv) The established exceptions to strictly enforcing contractual terms also have public policy support. Use this to your advantage.

____ (j) **Consider the style in which you will present your opening statement.** Most commentators suggest the following:

____ (i) Use plain English. Don't argue.

____ (ii) Be fluid and conversational. Openings that are read or recited from memory are seen as overly rehearsed and do not permit you to adapt to the feedback you will take in from the judge, jury, and opponent.

____ (iii) Opening statements that are purely chronological or proceed witness by witness can also be too static. Focus your opening statement around your theme, and let that serve as the guide for explaining what the witness testimony will be and how the project unfolded chronologically.

____ (iv) Avoid the warm-up language. If you are before a judge or arbitrator, you will not need to explain the legal process. If you are before a jury, let the judge explain the process. Concentrate on your theme, and explain how the evidence supports your cause.

____ (k) **Do not over-promise.** The fact-finder will punish a party who cannot uphold commitments made in an opening statement.

____ 3. **The Content and Structure of Your Opening Statement.** Get quickly to the issues at hand. Don't delay in telling the fact-finder what the case is about.

____ (a) **What will you prove to the finder of fact?**

____ (b) **How will you present the factual and legal issues necessary to prevail?** Don't overwhelm with details but provide enough information so the fact-finder can understand the case.

____ (c) **What factual issues will be your focus?**

____ (i) Are there contractual provisions and documentary evidence you will use? What can you use to make this presentation interesting for the finder of fact?

____ (ii) What testimony and statements will you use? This form of evidence can be just as persuasive and convincing as documents.

____ (iii) Construction cases are document intensive. How will you make them manageable for the fact-finder to understand?

____ (d) **What will you seek to disprove?** There are generally three methods to deal with the case being presented against your client.

____ (i) Co-opt or adopt the seemingly bad facts, and use them to support your case and theme.

____ (ii) Address and defuse the weaknesses. Negate or marginalize the bad facts by making them irrelevant to the dispute.

____ (iii) Attack and discredit the adverse evidence or the persons presenting the adverse evidence such that the finder of fact does not believe the adverse evidence.

____ (e) **Cover the use of expert witnesses.** Explain who and why you are using experts.

____ (f) **Address the use of depositions if you are presenting the case to a jury.**

____ (g) **Tell the finder of fact what you want it to find and why.**

____ (i) If, as a claimant, you cannot directly ask the finder of fact to award you the damages you seek, it is unlikely you will receive them. If you want an award, ask for it.

____ (ii) If, as a respondent, you cannot directly ask the finder of fact to award find against the claimant, it is unlikely you will obtain that outcome.

____ (iii) If you can, use a sense of injustice. Tell about the injustice done to your client.

# Checklist 42: Closing Arguments in Construction Cases

Some commentators contend that the opening statement is the most important part of the case; others believe that closing argument is the key to a successful trial. Both are important. Above all, they must be consistent. When preparing for the closing argument in a case, there are several practical and stylistic considerations that can be itemized and considered. Many of these considerations are common to all disputes but, where applicable, the peculiarities of construction disputes are noted.

____ 1. **Logistical Considerations.**

____ (a) **Who is your audience?** Your audience could span a broad spectrum of legal and technical knowledge. The presentation of closing argument in a construction dispute could be made to a judge, jury, arbitrator, arbitration panel, mediator, opposing parties, or others. An appreciation of who is the target of the closing argument will affect the style significantly. For example, if you are not presenting your closing to a lawyer, avoid the legalese. If you are presenting a closing to a jury comprised of bus drivers, waitresses, and factory workers, then use language and terminology that makes sense to them. If you are in a bench trial, avoid the theatrics that may impress a jury, and appeal to the sensibilities of a judge who is looking to get your case off the docket and move on to the next one. If your case is being tried before an arbitrator with construction law experience, industry jargon may be perfectly acceptable and even preferred.

____ (b) **Who goes first, and how is the time divided?** Must multiple defendants split the time?

____ (c) **How much time is permitted per side?**

____ (d) **Who gets rebuttal?**

____ (e) **Are jury instructions read before or after closing arguments?**

---

**Clifford F. Kinney, Jr.** is a member of the law firm of Spilman Thomas & Battle PLLC in its Charleston, West Virginia office. He practices in the areas of construction litigation and insurance disputes and also serves as a mediator and arbitrator.

____ (f) **If you are in a court proceeding, are you required to receive training prior to trial on the court's trial room equipment?** Can you bring your own computer equipment to the courtroom?

____ (g) **What are the tribunal's rules about moving around the room?** Are you limited to the podium? Can you approach the jury box?

____ (h) **How do you work most comfortably?** At a podium? Moving around? At counsel's table?

____ 2. **Advocating Your Case.**

____ (a) **Anticipate the closing as a part of your pre-trial preparation.** But be prepared to make adaptations to closing as trial progresses.

____ (b) **What will you use to augment your presentation?**

____ (i) What exhibits, deposition excerpts, and other potential evidence can you rely on? If there is a particularly good piece of evidence, stress it.

____ (ii) What visual aids and courtroom technology will you use? Never assume technology will work. Test it thoroughly. Have a support techie present. Have a physical backup plan.

____ (iii) Should you use the jury instructions in your closing argument? How? If you have a key definition or jury instruction, use graphics to highlight it.

____ (c) **What rules apply to objections during closing arguments, and under what circumstances should you object?** Objections during closing arguments should be made sparingly. Do not object unless you are certain the objection will be sustained.

____ (d) **What is your theme?** Use a theme that has been developed and that has been integrated into *voir dire* and an opening statement.

____ (i) Integrating the theme in this manner jogs jurors' memories and impresses them with your organization.

____ (ii) Reference your opening statement to show how you have proven your case.

____ (iii) Reference your opponent's opening statement to show how it has not proven its case.

____ (iv) The strict enforcement of construction contract terms has public policy behind it. If this argument is in your favor, use it to your advantage.

____ (v) The established exceptions to strictly enforcing contractual terms also have public policy support. Use this to your advantage.

____ (e) **Consider the style in which you will present your closing argument.**

____ (i) Be fluid and conversational. Closings that are read or recited from memory are seen as overly rehearsed and do not permit you to adapt to the feedback you will take in from the judge, jury, and opponent.

____ (ii) Closing statements that are purely chronological or witness by witness can also be too static. Focus your closing argument around your theme, and let that serve as the guide for explaining how the exhibits and testimony separate your theory of the case.

____ (iii) Arm the finder of fact, or your supporters on a jury, with the tools necessary to find in your client's favor and to argue to others to find in your client's favor. Jurors need to know how you want them to rule.

____ (f) **Remember the rule of primacy and recency.** What you say first and what you say last will be that which the fact-finder remembers most. Make your key points first and last.

____ (g) **Waiving closing arguments.** In an arbitration or court trial, it may be beneficial to suggest to the fact-finder that closing arguments be waived and instead, the parties submit post-trial briefs on those issues that the fact-finder identifies. Otherwise, closing argument should be waived only under extraordinary circumstances.

____ 3. **The Content of Your Closing Argument.**

____ (a) **If you thank the jury, do so quickly and move on.**

____ (b) **Clearly define the parties and the issues.** This is especially true in multi-party construction cases. Do not assume the jury can readily distinguish amongst the parties or the issues.

____ (c) **Tell the finder of fact what you proved.**

____ (d) **Emphasize that you lived up to commitments made in your opening statement.**

____ (e) **Emphasize any important failures to live up to commitments made by your opponent.**

____ (f) **What factual issues are your focus?**

____ (i) What contractual provisions and documentary evidence did you use?

____ (ii) How can you make contractual provisions and documents understandable and interesting to the finder of fact?

____ (iii) What testimony should you reference? This form of evidence can be just as persuasive and convincing as documents.

____ (g) **Emphasize the strong points and corroborating testimony, but do not avoid the bad.**

____ (i) Never exaggerate or misstate testimony. Doing so may cause a lawyer, and therefore the client, to lose credibility with the jury.

____ (h) **How will you refute harmful evidence?** There are generally three methods to deal with the case being presented against your client.

____ (i) Co-opt or adopt the seemingly bad facts, and use them to support your case and theme.

____ (ii) Negate the bad facts by making them irrelevant to the dispute.

____ (iii) Attack and discredit the adverse evidence or the persons presenting the adverse evidence such that the finder of fact does not believe the adverse evidence.

____ (i) **Tell the finder of fact what you want it to find and why.** Do not assume the fact-finder (particularly a jury) will figure it out.

____ (i) Show how you proved your case (even if the burden of proof is on the opponent). Show how you told the truth, and your opponent did not.

____ (ii) If, as a claimant, you cannot directly ask the finder of fact to award you the damages you seek, it is unlikely you will receive them. Ask for the damages you seek. Do not exaggerate damages.

____ (iii) If, as a respondent, you cannot directly ask the finder of fact to find against the claimant, it is unlikely you will obtain that outcome.

____ 4. **Closing Argument "Don'ts."**

____ (a) **Never speak down to the jury or fact-finder.**

____ (b) **Never tell the jury what it must do.**

____ (c) **It is improper to ask the jury to place itself in the position of the plaintiff.**

____ (d) **Do not appeal to prejudices.**

# Checklist 43: Electronic Demonstrative Exhibits and Presentations

Electronic presentation technology is a pervasive force in the world today. This is especially true in the field of law and more so in document intensive and multi-issue construction disputes. An exceptional oral advocate has always had a powerful advantage in the courtroom, but today, presentation technology brings an intensity and flexibility of its own to court. Carefully planned legal strategy and strong content remain the hallmark of a solid case. Carefully planned visual strategies and compelling graphics are the hallmark of a persuasive electronic trial presentation. It is the combination of the two that wins arguments. This checklist will explore the formulation and design of electronic exhibits and presentations.

____ 1. **Misuse of Slides.** Are you using the right technology to present your case? It is important to choose the technology that is best suited to the material being presented.

____ (a) Are you using electronic presentation software (for example, PowerPoint) to display documents?

____ (b) Are you displaying a full-page document on the screen without any enhancement? This is not conducive to learning.

____ (c) Have you identified which portions of the documents should be enlarged?

____ (d) Will jurors, mediators, or arbitrators be able to read what you are projecting? Pull out the text or passage that is important to your case, enlarge, highlight, and animate it. Your audience will read and remember a phrase that is enlarged on the screen. Bigger is definitely better.

____ (e) Are you using the slides as electronic versions of blow-up boards? There is a difference. It's all in the timing. Tell your audience about the document so that they understand its significance; then use the power of presentation software to emphasize key concepts or points.

---

**Edward M. Josiah** is Director of Nautilus Consulting, LLC's Demonstrative Evidence Practice Group, located in Commack, New York. He is one of the nation's leading demonstrative evidence specialists, immediate past president of the Demonstrative Evidence Specialists Association, and graphics consultant to the American Bar Association's Forum on the Construction Industry.

____ 2. **Confusing Slides.** The purpose of presentation slides is to communicate facts efficiently.

____ (a) How many issues does an individual slide address? A slide that attempts to focus on more than one issue will confuse the viewers.

____ (b) Do your slides contain charts? If so, the title of the slide should define the question that you intend to answer.

____ (c) Do your slides contain too many colors? Using too many colors distracts the viewer from the point you are trying to make. Use a neutral color for the background (shades of gray, black, or blue) and save the brighter color(s) for accentuating the portion of the exhibit that is significant.

____ 3. **Wordy Text Slides.** When words are necessary to assist in graphically conveying a message, brevity is best. Electronic exhibits are like road signs. They should be clean, short on words, and simple.

____ (a) Are your slides too wordy? Electronic exhibits should give direction and get to the point. Extra words waste time and blur the memory. Too much reading is a distraction.

____ (i) What font are you using? Use sans serif fonts (all one thickness), such as Ariel or Tahoma. These are clear and comfortable to the eyes. Don't use decorative font styles.

____ (ii) What size font are you using? Your viewers will have difficulty reading anything smaller than 18 point.

____ (b) Does your electronic presentation tell the story without explanation? If it does, there are way too many words. There should be a happy median between the attorney and the graphics. It is a combination of the two that makes for a persuasive presentation.

____ 4. **Digital Video.** A common misconception is that an event or testimony recorded using a digital video recorder is in a format that is ready to play back at trial. In most cases the video will have to be translated or converted to a format that computer software can accept.

____ (a) What is the output format of your recorder?

____ (b) Do you have the appropriate software to convert the original video to an MPEG file?

____ (c) Does the video need to be edited?

____ (d) Is the video source a DVD; if so, does your laptop have DVD capabilities? Do you need to edit the DVD? This will require some additional effort.

____ 5. **Story Building.** One of the most powerful features of electronic presentations is the ability to tell a story slowly and methodically.

____ (a) Does your story unfold one fact at a time?

____ (b) Does each new fact build on the credibility of the last?

____ (c) Does each new fact support the overall theme of your case?

____ (d) Are your slides designed and animated to reveal one new point or fact at a time, thereby controlling the flow of information and how you want the viewers to learn the case and your arguments?

____ 6. **Information Overload**. Technology-based exhibits should influence the decision making process and facilitate memorization of key facts and issues.

____ (a) Do your electronic exhibits enhance the message content?

____ (b) Do your electronic exhibits work well as memory-recall devices? After being exposed to the presentation, your audience should be able to close its eyes and recall information by remembering one of the visual exhibits.

____ (c) Have you decided what information is important enough to present? Once this decision is made, the principle known as the "smallest effective difference" should be applied. This basically holds that content is king. Anything that appears on a chart or graph, such as lines or color, should be inferior to the content.

____ (d) Are your slides crowded with too many words, have too many heavy or bold lines, or have a complex design for the background? These things compete with the information that the slide was designed to convey in the first place and compromise the overall message. Content should work hand in hand with the design.

____ 7. **Technology Overkill**. When approached in the correct manner, electronic presentations are one of the most powerful and persuasive tools available today. Avoid the temptation to use fancy animations and effects just because the technology allows you do so.

____ (a) Have you thought about your exhibit presentation strategy? As the case begins to unfold, it is important to establish a well-mapped strategy that integrates case materials with trial presentation options. Plan the use of demonstrative evidence, presentation tools, and graphics as carefully as your closing argument.

____ (i) Have you considered a multimedia presentation? Many times a particular computer generated exhibit is so important that it becomes necessary to produce it as a large demonstrative board. The exhibit will then serve as a point of reference during the trail or hearing. These exhibits are referred to as "anchors" because they establish essential information in the minds of the viewer, by means of repetition.

____ (ii) Have you thought about your opening and closing? Generally, electronic presentations (PowerPoint, for example) are used during opening statements and closing arguments, with conventional boards and animations being used during direct and cross-examination.

____ (iii) Have you thought about the technological "sweet spot"? This is a comfortable balance among persuasive technology, effective oratory, and demonstrative boards.

____ 8. **Computer Animation.** Are you sure that the use of computer-generated animation is necessary to explain your case?

____ (a) What are the potential benefits, and do they outweigh the overall production costs?

____ (b) Will the jurors find the animation too theatrical?

____ (c) Will the animation be admissible?

____ (d) Who is going to testify as to the accuracy of the animation? Is the animation a re-creation of an event or your expert's opinion?

____ (e) Is there an alternative to computer animation that might work just as well, but at a fraction of the cost (for example, illustrations, scale models, or an existing video)?

____ 9. **4D Computer Animation.** What is this? A 4D animation is a three-dimensional illustration animated over time. It can be used to compare and contrast the planned versus actual progress of the construction of just about anything. Some questions to ask before setting off in this direction:

____ (a) Will a 4D animation make a difference in how the judge and/or jury view and understand the facts?

____ (b) Did the contractor, owner's representative, architect, or engineer keep records with the level of detail necessary to put the animation together?

____ (i) Do you have accurate planned and actual completion dates for site work, concrete, steel erection, mechanical, electrical, and finish work, etc.? Without these dates, you cannot construct a 4D animation.

____ (ii) Is it necessary to animate the construction of the entire structure, or will animating an area of the structure work just as well? Keep in mind that the larger the structure, the smaller the 3D illustration will be.

____ 10. **Rehearsal/Testing**. Is the presentation sensitive to your style of speaking and presenting a case? It is necessary to synchronize technique with technology, and this takes practice.

____ (a) Rehearsal will give you an opportunity to refine these problem areas, as well as to get more comfortable with the presentation as a whole.

____ (b) A technology-based presentation affects where the attorney stands and how he or she interacts with witnesses, the judge, and/or the facilitator. These are issues that might seem like technicalities, but they definitely affect the overall feel of the presentation.

____ 11. **Rooms Have Limitation.** Where are you presenting your case? A court room, meeting room in a hotel, conference room? Reviewing and planning for the physical size of the room is critical to the success of a presentation.

____ (a) How big or small is the room?

____ (b) Where will the monitors, projector, and screen(s) be located?

____ (c) Are there enough outlets to support your equipment? Is there adequate power in the room?

____ (d) If you are providing your own screen, what size screen will the room accommodate?

____ (e) Will everyone in attendance be able to see what you are projecting? Will your exhibits have the same impact when viewed on a small monitor, or should they be viewed on a large screen?

____ (f) How well does your LCD projector project in a well-lit room? The brightness of the projector should be at least 2,000 lumens.

____ (g) Have you determined what equipment or hardware (LCD projector, screen, laptops, speakers, etc.) will be necessary for this presentation?

____ (h) Have you secured the rental of this equipment? Is it possible to share the cost with opposing counsel?

____ (i) Does the trial judge require her or his own monitor and kill switch?

____ 12. **Murphy's Law Will Rule**. While the reliability of technology has dramatically improved over the past few years, an attorney should always prepare for the worst.

____ (a) Have you arranged for electronic backup?

____ (i) Back up CDs containing all exhibits using extra blank CDs or flash drives.

____ (ii) Duplicate or back up hardware, such as laptops, extension cords, LCD projectors, and have extra bulbs for the projector, audio speakers, etc., on hand.

____ (iii) Have you installed the newest version of the software you are using on backup laptops? Older versions of software may not open files created in later versions.

____ (iv) If you are using a program such as Summation, do you have the correct licenses for nondesktop use?

____ (b) Are you going to employ a litigation technologist to facilitate your presentation?

____ (i) If using a member of your staff to run the equipment and presentation, he or she will have to be trained on how to operate the hardware devices and presentation software.

____ (ii) Do you have emergency technical support available, either by phone or in person? Keep in mind, you cannot wear two hats here. You are either an attorney or the technology expert.

____ (c) Have you arranged for physical backup of your exhibits? This is plan B and can be used in the event that your electronic backup fails.

____ (i) Do you have enlargements (boards) of your key exhibits?

____ (ii) Are your witnesses or experts prepared to use either the electronic or blow-up version of the exhibits?

____ (iii) Have you made color handouts or copies of all of your exhibits? If the original is prepared in color, the reduced size copies should be in color as well.

____ (d) Have you prepared for the worst-case scenario (that is, the rehearsal of the presentation as if there were to be no visual aids whatsoever)? At worst, an exercise such as this can only strengthen the delivery of the presentation.

# Checklist 44: Settlement Agreements for Construction Disputes

This checklist covers important issues encountered in drafting a written settlement agreement for decision makers or counsel involved in negotiating the settlement of a dispute. The issues listed here are general considerations for any person or entity that wishes to memorialize a settlement and include specific considerations that apply to some particular types of disputes.

A settlement agreement is a binding legal contract that should be drafted with the same consideration as any other contract signed in the course of business. In another sense, a settlement agreement documents the transition of the parties from disputants to former disputants. The settlement should be concluded in a detailed writing to memorialize the agreement so nothing is left in question.

____ 1. **What client interests are satisfied by this settlement agreement?** Is this settlement the termination of a one-time (usually accidental) event, or would the parties possibly do business again? The interests in play will drive the details of the settlement agreement.

____ 2. **Specific Considerations.**

____ (a) **Identify the parties released, affected, and bound by the agreement.** Settlement agreements often affect the rights, duties, and interests of multiple individuals, such as insured parties, insurers, spouses, lenders, indemnitees, affiliates, officers and directors, and owners. List all claimants and potential claimants. Identify all parties, obtaining the protection of the release with the same precision. Be sure the agreement extends to each party's heirs, executors, successors, or assignees.

____ (b) **Recite the consideration supporting the release, whether it be cash, performance, or other meaningful exchange that represents the price of the promise.** Affirm that the form and sufficiency of the consideration is acknowledged, and affirm any details regarding time and manner of exchange.

____ (c) **Identify the subject matter of the agreement, the address or other descriptive location of the property, and the name of**

**Jeffrey R. Jury** is a partner in the Austin, Texas law firm of Burns Anderson Jury & Brenner LLP. He represents contractors and subcontractors in all types of construction and land use matters and applies the knowledge and experience he has gained to serve as mediator and arbitrator of construction disputes.

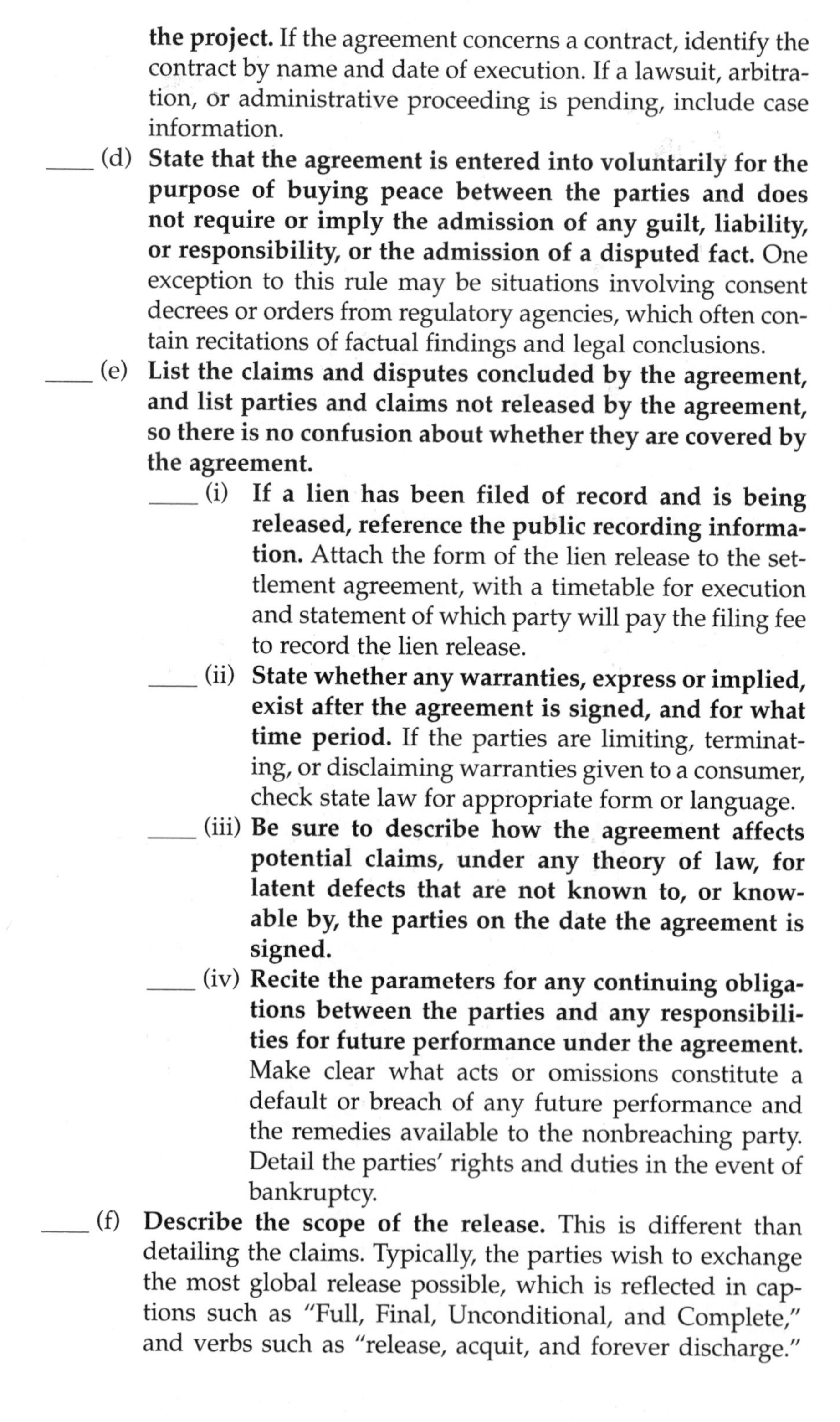

**the project.** If the agreement concerns a contract, identify the contract by name and date of execution. If a lawsuit, arbitration, or administrative proceeding is pending, include case information.

____ (d) **State that the agreement is entered into voluntarily for the purpose of buying peace between the parties and does not require or imply the admission of any guilt, liability, or responsibility, or the admission of a disputed fact.** One exception to this rule may be situations involving consent decrees or orders from regulatory agencies, which often contain recitations of factual findings and legal conclusions.

____ (e) **List the claims and disputes concluded by the agreement, and list parties and claims not released by the agreement, so there is no confusion about whether they are covered by the agreement.**

  ____ (i) **If a lien has been filed of record and is being released, reference the public recording information.** Attach the form of the lien release to the settlement agreement, with a timetable for execution and statement of which party will pay the filing fee to record the lien release.

  ____ (ii) **State whether any warranties, express or implied, exist after the agreement is signed, and for what time period.** If the parties are limiting, terminating, or disclaiming warranties given to a consumer, check state law for appropriate form or language.

  ____ (iii) **Be sure to describe how the agreement affects potential claims, under any theory of law, for latent defects that are not known to, or knowable by, the parties on the date the agreement is signed.**

  ____ (iv) **Recite the parameters for any continuing obligations between the parties and any responsibilities for future performance under the agreement.** Make clear what acts or omissions constitute a default or breach of any future performance and the remedies available to the nonbreaching party. Detail the parties' rights and duties in the event of bankruptcy.

____ (f) **Describe the scope of the release.** This is different than detailing the claims. Typically, the parties wish to exchange the most global release possible, which is reflected in captions such as "Full, Final, Unconditional, and Complete," and verbs such as "release, acquit, and forever discharge."

Add any limiting language that is necessary to constrict the scope of the agreement.

____ (g) **Indemnification is probably the most difficult and controversial aspect of a settlement agreement.** The indemnity paragraphs of many releases have grown longer; are sometimes centered on the page; and often appear in bold, italicized, or bold and italicized font. Some of the potential traps include:

____ (i) **State anti-indemnification statutes.** Be aware of the statutory limitations on the creation of indemnity obligations and any phrasing or document formatting requirements.

____ (ii) **State common-law indemnification decisions.** Courts throughout the land have specific, sometimes exacting, requirements for valid indemnity clauses. Consider checking with local counsel if the governing law of the agreement is unfamiliar to you.

____ (iii) **Indemnification for a party's own negligence.** This is a subset of extra, often onerous, requirements to enforce an indemnification that covers the indemnitor's own negligence. It is imperative that you be familiar with applicable state law on this issue.

____ (iv) **Generally, an indemnification clause should extend to all claims made "by, through, or under" the releasing party.** This ensures that no one else can assert the releasing party's rights against a party released by the agreement. It also helps to include language affirming that the releasing parties have not assigned or pledged their claims, so the releasing party is conveying "all of the sticks in the bundle."

____ (v) **For personal injury cases, address potential claims by third-party payers that arise through subrogation.** Typically, subrogation rights arise in favor of those who pay medical and income benefits, permitting the subrogation interest holder to stand in the shoes of the injured party and seek reimbursement.

____ a. **"First money" liens.** If the injured party received benefits through a federal benefits program, the claim of the United States often has a super-priority that must be satisfied, subject to narrow limitations. In many states, worker's compensation carriers have a "first money" lien, in the amount of medical and income benefits paid, on the injured worker's monetary recovery that cannot be circumvented. In both of these instances, if the lien is not paid as part of the settlement, the government and/or the worker's compensation carrier may have a separate right to recovery against the injured worker and the paying party.

____ b. **Subrogation interests.** Similar liens and subrogation interests are found in many state statutes in favor of hospitals and governmental entities, and the laws among the states vary regarding the contractual subrogation rights of private health insurance providers. If you represent the party paying settlement funds, consider issuing joint checks to the injured party and the subrogation interest holder.

____ c. **Attorney's interests in proceeds.** Depending on the contractual relationship between the claimant and its attorney, the attorney may have an interest in the proceeds of the settlement, either for fees or expenses. This may become important if the claimant was represented by another attorney who asserts an interest in the settlement. Joint checks naming the injured party and the attorney, with recitations in the settlement agreement that there are no other interests, or that any such interest will be satisfied from the proceeds of the settlement, should provide protection from other claims.

____ (vi) **Indemnification encompasses two different obligations, namely, the obligation to pay for the defense of a claim made against the indemnitee and the obligation to pay or reimburse any settlement or judgment against the indemnitee.** The defense payment obligation typically has more profuse detail about how the event activates the defense obligation; how, and by whom, the defense will be managed; and who selects counsel. Any person receiving a defense should be required to cooperate reasonably in the defense. The payment obligation is narrower and arises only when the indemnitee is called upon to pay a settlement or judgment. Insist that the person paying the bill at the end of the day have the exclusive right to make negotiation, settlement, and trial decisions. *CAVEAT:* In some states, an insurance carrier can assert a right of recoupment for claim payments made when it has reserved its rights. The practical effect is that an insurance carrier may be able to settle a claim, then seek reimbursement from the policyholder. Be sure that you have a clear understanding of any rights the insurance carrier may have to collect against your company as policyholder.

____ (h) **Specify the effects of the release on additional claims against third parties.** This is usually accomplished by reciting the claims that either survive, or are not covered by, the settlement agreement. The objective here is to avoid, for example, the inadvertent settlement of claims against defendants two through five by settling with defendant one.

____ (i) **Detail the timing of performance**. If there is a nonfraudulent accounting or tax interest in paying or receiving settlement funds with a certain timeframe, specify the timing of the payment accordingly. If the agreement includes additional work, transfer of goods, or conveyance of realty, consider attaching a schedule of deadlines. Where time is of the essence, state so.

____ (j) **If a settlement agreement includes future performance, call out the performance metrics to assist the parties, or a trier of fact, in determining whether the agreement has been performed.** Detail any technical studies, inspections, certifications, or testing reports that will be used to document performance. Keep in mind that the language you choose may create a condition precedent to future performance, especially if the performance occurs in phases, and be cautious about creating such conditions unintentionally.

____ (k) **Many concerns about transfer of consideration can be alleviated by using a third-party escrow agent, who is in the business of handling other people's money.** Use care in selecting an escrow agent with a strong reputation for neutrality.

____ (l) **The settlement agreement should include a traditional merger clause that affirms there are no oral or side agreements regarding the subject matter of the release and a section detailing representations, warranties, and covenants between the parties.** These sections serve the dual purposes of clarifying the promises that support the agreement and strengthening the agreement from attacks based on misrepresentation. Some examples of the matters that should be detailed are:

____ (i) **That the party executing the agreement has the legal capacity and authority to enter into the contract.** If an entity is a party to the agreement, recite in the body of the agreement, and any attached affidavit, that the person has the specific authority to sign the agreement as an official act of the entity. Entity authority can also be documented by attaching a copy of a corporate resolution or other document authorizing the officer to execute the agreement. Negotiating with a governmental entity sometimes requires approval by a person in higher authority or governing body, so include appropriate language about the authority of the government to enter into the agreement.

____ (ii) **Recite that all persons signing the agreement have read and understood the agreement; have had the opportunity to seek the advice of counsel, and accounting and tax professionals, before signing the agreement; and that neither party has furnished legal, accounting, or tax advice that the other party relied on in deciding to enter into the settlement agreement.** Include some conspicuous language above the signature lines that calls attention to the fact that the agreement is an important legal document affecting each party's rights, so it must be read before signing.

____ (iii) **Protect the agreement from misrepresentation and duress challenges by stating that the parties are entering into the agreement as a voluntary act and that each side has been given access to all information necessary to make an informed decision about settling the dispute.**

____ (iv) **One of the important interests advanced by settlement is finality, so have the settlement agreement**

**reflect the final nature of the agreement throughout.** Acknowledge the parties' understanding and agreement that the settlement is final and that no one will have the right to seek further recovery for any matter covered by the settlement agreement. This is particularly true in the event of a settlement involving a minor or a person under a legal disability to contract.

____ (v) **Recite the parties' agreement regarding how any pending legal action will be concluded, either by voluntary dismissal with prejudice to refiling, a take-nothing judgment, or other procedure that is customary in the jurisdiction.** Consider a covenant of no further action that prohibits any further legal proceedings arising out of the subject matter of the agreement.

____ (m) **If the settlement agreement includes remodel or repair work, be sure to state the responsibilities of each party regarding demolition, removal of debris and spoils, and compliance with any local permit requirements.** Detail how, and by whom, final approval and acceptance of the work will be determined and how any disputes arising out of the work will be resolved. Consider terms for the ownership and disposal of "attic stock"—extra quantities of material ordered and in place for the project.

____ (n) **Allocate duties and describe the sequence of compliance with environmental regulations, including handling and removal of hazardous waste and abatement of materials such as asbestos and lead paint.**

____ (o) **Sometimes parties have an interest in making the existence, terms, and amount of settlements confidential.** The requirements to make a settlement confidential vary among the states and can be cumbersome procedurally. They must be checked. In any event, the parties should be permitted to disclose information to third-party accountants, tax advisors, internal audit committees, and other persons who have a need to know. Even a strong confidentiality provision will not protect a settlement agreement from a criminal investigation, disciplinary proceeding against a lawyer, or use in a subsequent proceeding regarding the agreement.

____ (p) **Include important boilerplate provisions, such as specifying the governing law, providing severability for portions of the agreement found unenforceable, noting that the**

**agreement may be changed only in writing, and listing the venue for disputes.** Make it clear if the agreement may be enforced by declaratory and injunctive relief.

____ (q) **People sometimes disagree about their agreements.** Consider a dispute resolution clause that establishes a sequence of dispute resolution efforts, from negotiation through litigation or arbitration. An arbitration clause should specify the relief available from the arbitrator, such as forum fees and attorneys' fees, and should specify a procedure for choosing a neutral party, whether it be through an arbitration service provider or mutual agreement of the parties. Make it clear that the parties specifically waive a jury trial in favor of arbitration, if that is the ultimate resolution process.

# Checklist 45: Litigating Intellectual Property Claims

The following checklist may be used by those seeking to protect the intellectual property rights that they have in construction-related assets such as architectural designs, as well as those facing allegations of the improper use of such assets.

____ 1. **Protected Construction-Related Intellectual Assets.**

____ (a) **Are intellectual property rights at issue?** Intellectual property rights must be distinguished from personal property rights, as well as from intellectual property that is free for the world to borrow from, to use, or even to exploit. In the construction realm, it is critical to make the distinction to understand what rights, if any, are at issue.

____ (i) **Does the issue relate to drawings or the designs embodied therein?** Ownership of any material object in which a protected work is embodied (such as architectural drawings) is distinct from ownership of a copyright. Transfer of ownership of any material object does not of itself convey any rights in the copyrighted work embodied in the object.

____ (b) **Is the work claimed to be infringed upon registered?** Patents must be registered before they will be recognized; copyrights must be registered before they can be enforced; trademark rights may be enforced without registration.

____ (i) **Were the copyrights at issue registered before the infringement occurred?** Unless the copyright has been registered before the commencement of the infringement, the copyright holder will not be entitled to recover statutory damages or attorney's fees for (a) any infringement of copyright in an unpublished work commenced before the effective date of its registration or (b) any infringement of copyright commenced after first publication of the work and before the effective date of its registration, unless

---

**Clark T. Thiel** is a partner in the law firm of Thelen Reid Brown Raysman & Steiner LLP, San Francisco. He is both an attorney and an architect, and he represents owners, contractors, and design professionals in matters concerning the protection of intellectual property rights.

such registration is made within 3 months after the first publication of the work.

____ (ii) **Were the copyrights at issue registered before the suit was filed?** No action for infringement of the copyright in any work can be instituted until the copyright registration has been submitted to the Copyright Office.

____ 2. **Improper Use of Another's Intellectual Property.** Anyone, including any state and any officer or employee of a state acting in his or her official capacity, who violates any of the exclusive rights of the copyright owner is an infringer of the copyright. The owner of any exclusive right under a copyright is entitled to institute an action for any infringement of that particular right committed while he or she is the owner of it.

____ (a) **Was the building at issue simply altered?** The owners of a building embodying an architectural work may, without the consent of the author or copyright owner of the architectural work, make alterations to the building and destroy the building. The use of another's plans for an addition to the building—even to only facilitate the preparation of comparable plans by another—may constitute copyright infringement.

____ (b) **Was the work inappropriately duplicated?** Copyright protection exists in a design or drawing if the author has introduced *any* element of novelty into the overall arrangement and configuration of spaces, elements, and details. Copying of those aspects original to the author, without regard to the amount of additional material introduced by the copier, will constitute copyright infringement if an "ordinary observer," unless set out to detect disparities, would be disposed to overlook them and regard the aesthetic appeal of the two works as the same.

____ (i) **Were protected aspects of the work copied?** If the only material that has been copied are those elements of the copyright holder's work that are not protectable, the resulting "copy" does not constitute an infringement. For example, if the similarities are traceable to common sources, themes, styles, or material that was otherwise not original to the author, there is no copyright infringement. Likewise, simply employing another's ideas or techniques will not subject one to liability for copyright infringement.

____ a. **Have only "scenes a faire" (that is, scene which must be done) been copied?** Elements of a work of authorship are not entitled to protection against infringement if they are standard, stock, or common to a topic, or if they necessarily follow from a common unprotectible theme or setting. As such, individual elements specific to a particular style of architecture are not subject to copyright protection.

____ (ii) **Was the second work independently created?** The Copyright Act forbids only copying; there is no copyright infringement if even an identical work resulted from independent creation. As such, although striking similarity alone can raise an inference of copying, that inference must be reasonable and will not survive if there is a reasonable possibility that the two works were independently created rather than copied.

____ (iii) **Did the defendant have access to the copyrighted work?** Copying may be established inferentially by showing that a defendant had a reasonable opportunity to access the copyrighted work and that the defendant's work is substantially similar to copyrighted work.

____ (iv) **Would an ordinary observer find the two works substantially similar?** Once access to copyrighted work can be established, copying can be proven by demonstrating "substantial similarity" among the two works. "Substantial similarity" is regarded as sufficient similarity of a second work to the protected work to support a reasoned inference by an ordinary observer that more probably than not the second work was copied from the copyrighted work. Although the focus is on overall similarities rather than minute differences between the works, general impressions of similarity are not enough to make out a copyright infringement case; the use of another's ideas alone is not copyright infringement.

____ a. **Are the ideas found in the two works substantially similar?** One claiming copyright infringement must first meet the "extrinsic" test to determine whether the ideas found in the two works are substantially similar. To establish substantial similarity, the claimant must first demonstrate, through analytic dissection and expert testimony, resting upon specific objective criteria that can be listed and analyzed, that individual features of the two works share specific similarities in theme, character, mood, setting, and sequence.

____ b. **Are the expressions of those ideas substantially similar?** Because the copying of ideas alone is insufficient to constitute copyright infringement, the "intrinsic" test is then employed to compare the forms of expression among the two works. The intrinsic test gauges the more subjective response of the ordinary, reasonable observer regarding the substantial similarity of the total concept and feel of the two works.

____ (v) **Are the two works strikingly similar?** Where the designer has contributed very little to the work that is truly original, its copyright in that work is considered "thin" and is protected only from nearly verbatim copying or a showing of "striking" or "super-substantial" similarity. When most of the similarities between the two works can be attributed to a particular architectural style or to standard construction details and materials, the remaining aspects will be subjected to a heightened, "more discerning observer" test, which requires striking similarity to establish copying.

____ (vi) **Were only small portions of the original work copied?** That the copying may have been only *de minimus* does not alleviate liability. Duplication of every detail or exact reproduction is not necessary to establish infringement. Rather, if the usurped work is material and substantial, copyright infringement can be found where even only a small portion of original work is copied or where the copied work comprises only a small piece of the second work.

____ (vii) **Is the allegedly infringing work a photograph or sketch?** The copyright in an architectural work that has been constructed does not include the right to prevent the making, distributing, or public display of pictures, paintings, photographs, or other pictorial representations of the work, if the building in which the work is embodied is located in or ordinarily visible from a public place. Two-dimensional copies of such a building, therefore, cannot constitute copyright infringement.

____ (c) **Was the copyright violated by other infringing activity?** The owner of a copyright has the exclusive rights to not only reproduce the copyrighted work, but also to prepare derivative works and to distribute copies to the public. As such, although it is not common in the construction context, copyright infringement may occur as a result of activities other than copying.

____ (d) **Was the purportedly infringing activity authorized?** An owner of a copyright may implicitly or expressly authorize others to use or copy the protected work for certain purposes. If the scope of that authorization is not exceeded, such use or duplication is not infringement.

____ (i) **Was ownership of the copyrights transferred?** Copyright ownership may be transferred by sale, assignment, or mortgage so long as such a change in ownership is in writing and signed by the owner of the copyright. Contracts can operate to transfer copyrights in designs, even without using the term "copyright," if they evidence the intent of the parties to transfer such rights. For example, a contract stating that designs and drawings were the "sole property" of the developer and could not be reproduced by the architect without the developer's consent may be interpreted as a transfer of copyright ownership.

____ (ii) **Does the subsequent use fall within an express license?** Like a transfer of ownership, the granting of an exclusive license must be in writing. A nonexclusive license, however, can be granted orally. As such, a builder with copyright rights can grant an express, nonexclusive license to use copyrighted home plans by giving its subcontractor oral permission to use the plans, even notwithstanding that each page of the drawings prohibited reproduction without written permission.

____ (iii) **Was the subsequent use implicitly licensed?** Just as a nonexclusive license for use of copyrighted material can be granted orally, it may also be implied from conduct. A nonexclusive license will be implied when a person (the licensee) requests the creation of a work, the creator (the licensor) makes that particular work and delivers it to the licensee who requested it, and the licensor intends that the licensee-requestor copy and distribute the work. Accordingly, an owner of copyrighted plans may have impliedly granted a nonexclusive license to the one who requested that those plans be created, even though it had not been fully paid for its work. The use of those plans by a replacement design firm will not be infringement so long as its use is within the scope of the implied license.

____ (e) **Is the purportedly infringing activity permitted by law?** The primary objective of the Copyright Act is to encourage the production of original artistic expression for the good of the public, and this objective is promoted by discouraging infringement as well as by the successful defense of copyright infringement actions. Certain activities involving certain works are therefore excluded from copyright protection.

____ (i) **Has the original work fallen into the public domain?** If the exclusive rights granted by the copyright laws expired or never attached, there can be no copyright infringement.

____ (ii) **Does the subsequent use constitute "fair use"?** A copyrighted work may be displayed, reproduced, and distributed without infringement for purposes such as criticism, comment, news reporting, teaching, scholarship, or research. Factors considered when determining whether such use in any particular case is a fair use include (a) the purpose and character of the use, including whether such use is of a commercial nature or is for nonprofit educational purposes; (b) the nature of the copyrighted work; (c) the amount and substantiality of the portion used in relation to the copyrighted work as a whole; and (d) the effect of the use upon the potential market for or value of the copyrighted work.

____ (iii) **Does the assertion of copyright rights constitute misuse?** The doctrine of "copyright misuse" forbids the use of the copyright to secure an exclusive right or limited monopoly not granted by the copyright laws and that is contrary to public policy. As such, copyright infringement will not lie where the copy-

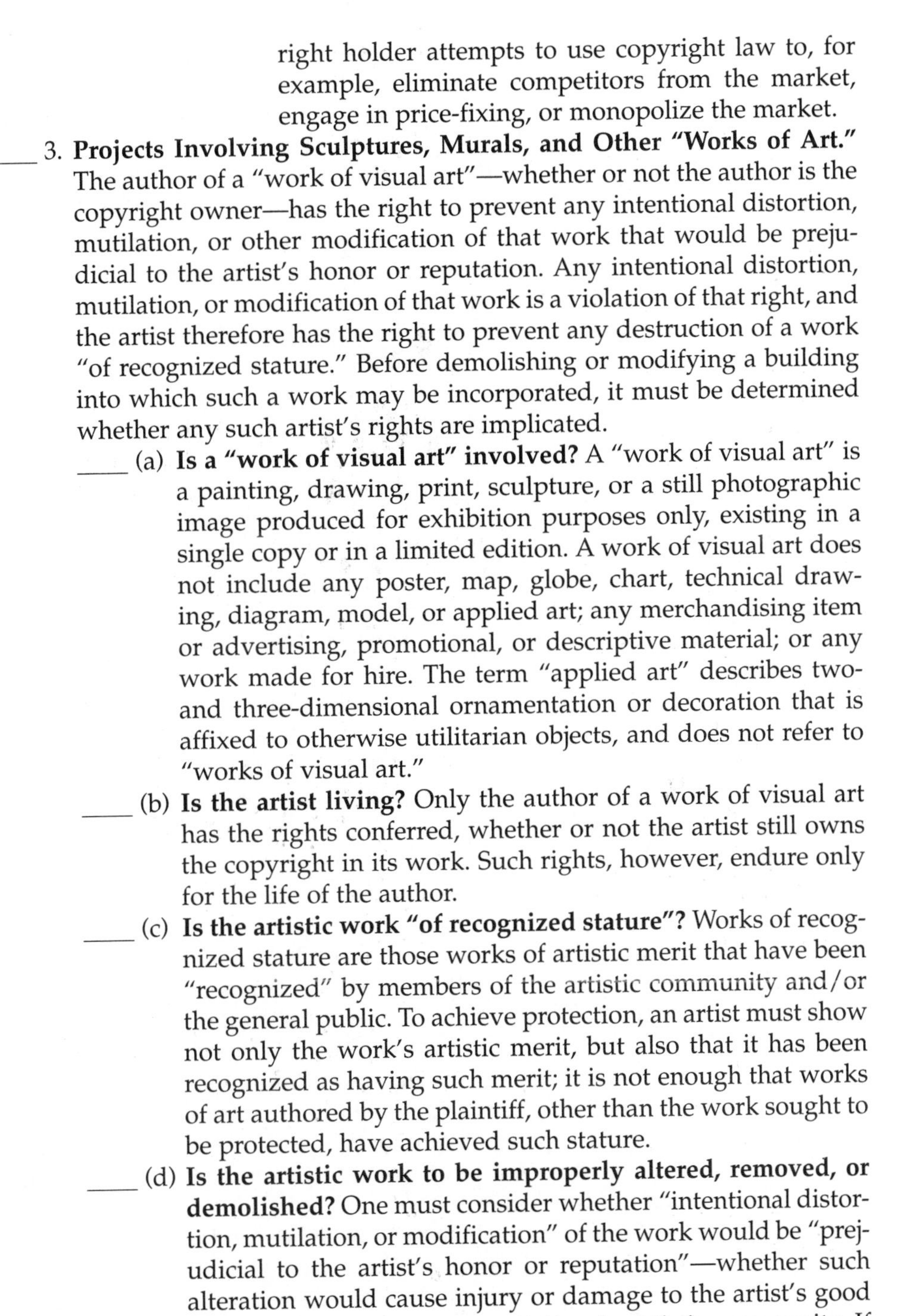

right holder attempts to use copyright law to, for example, eliminate competitors from the market, engage in price-fixing, or monopolize the market.

____ 3. **Projects Involving Sculptures, Murals, and Other "Works of Art."** The author of a "work of visual art"—whether or not the author is the copyright owner—has the right to prevent any intentional distortion, mutilation, or other modification of that work that would be prejudicial to the artist's honor or reputation. Any intentional distortion, mutilation, or modification of that work is a violation of that right, and the artist therefore has the right to prevent any destruction of a work "of recognized stature." Before demolishing or modifying a building into which such a work may be incorporated, it must be determined whether any such artist's rights are implicated.

____ (a) **Is a "work of visual art" involved?** A "work of visual art" is a painting, drawing, print, sculpture, or a still photographic image produced for exhibition purposes only, existing in a single copy or in a limited edition. A work of visual art does not include any poster, map, globe, chart, technical drawing, diagram, model, or applied art; any merchandising item or advertising, promotional, or descriptive material; or any work made for hire. The term "applied art" describes two- and three-dimensional ornamentation or decoration that is affixed to otherwise utilitarian objects, and does not refer to "works of visual art."

____ (b) **Is the artist living?** Only the author of a work of visual art has the rights conferred, whether or not the artist still owns the copyright in its work. Such rights, however, endure only for the life of the author.

____ (c) **Is the artistic work "of recognized stature"?** Works of recognized stature are those works of artistic merit that have been "recognized" by members of the artistic community and/or the general public. To achieve protection, an artist must show not only the work's artistic merit, but also that it has been recognized as having such merit; it is not enough that works of art authored by the plaintiff, other than the work sought to be protected, have achieved such stature.

____ (d) **Is the artistic work to be improperly altered, removed, or demolished?** One must consider whether "intentional distortion, mutilation, or modification" of the work would be "prejudicial to the artist's honor or reputation"—whether such alteration would cause injury or damage to the artist's good name, public esteem, or reputation in artistic community. If so, the work cannot be modified or demolished without the artist's consent.

____ (i) **Did the artist consent?** When a work of visual art has been incorporated in or made part of a building in such a way that removing the work from the building will cause the destruction, distortion, mutilation, or other modification of the work, and the artist consented to the installation of the work in the building as well as the destruction or other modification of the work, the artist no longer has standing to object.

____ (ii) **Can the work be removed without destruction?** If the owner of a building wishes to remove a work of visual art that is a part of its building and that can be removed from the building without the destruction, distortion, mutilation, or other modification of the work, the author's rights are nevertheless implicated unless the owner has made a diligent, good-faith attempt without success to notify the artist of the owner's intended action, or the owner did provide such notice and the artist failed either to remove the work or to pay for its removal.

____ 4. **Filing Suit.**

____ (a) **Is the action filed in federal court?** The federal copyright laws preempt all state and local regulations, and federal courts have original and exclusive jurisdiction over copyright actions. No equivalent right in any copyrighted work exists under the common law or statutes of any state, but the copyright laws do not supersede the common law or statutes of the various states with respect to state and local landmarks, historic preservation, zoning, or building codes.

____ (b) **Is the plaintiff a proper party?** An action for copyright infringement may be brought by the beneficial ownership of the copyright rights that were infringed. Such beneficial owner may be the original author, co-author, assignee, or exclusive licensee. Agents and employees, however, cannot maintain on their own behalf an action for infringement of their principal's or employer's work, and a nonexclusive licensee does not have standing to sue another for infringement of the licensed work.

____ (c) **Is the action against the proper defendant?** Anyone who trespasses into a copyright owner's exclusive domain by using or authorizing use of the copyrighted work is an infringer of the copyright. The infringer is not merely the one who uses work without the copyright owner's authorization, but also the one who authorizes or enables another's use of copyrighted work without actual authority from the copyright owner.

____ (i) **Is there contributory infringement or vicarious liability?** One infringes a copyright contributorily by intentionally inducing or encouraging direct infringement, and infringes vicariously by profiting from direct infringement while declining to exercise a right to stop or limit the infringement. Actual knowledge of particular instances of copyright infringement is not necessary, because constructive knowledge is sufficient to establish liability for contributory infringement.

____ (ii) **Does the defendant claim to have unknowingly infringed?** Liability for copyright infringement is independent of the intent with which the infringer acted. The defendant's intent is therefore irrelevant to copyright infringement and defendant is liable for even innocent or accidental infringements. Although no *scienter* need be shown to prove infringement, a finding of willful infringement permits the court to increase statutory damages.

____ 5. **Remedies Available for Infringement.**

____ (a) **Is an injunction appropriate?** Any court having jurisdiction of a civil action arising under the Copyright Act may grant temporary and final injunctions to prevent or restrain infringement of a copyright.

____ (b) **Can the infringing articles be impounded and/or disposed of?** The court may order the impounding, on such terms as it may deem reasonable, of all copies claimed to have been made or used in violation of the copyright owner's exclusive rights and of all means by which such copies may be reproduced. The court may also order the destruction or other reasonable disposition of all copies found to have been made in violation of the copyright owner's exclusive rights.

____ (c) **What damages and profits are recoverable?** One found to have infringed the copyrights of another is liable for either the copyright owner's actual damages and any additional profits of the infringer or statutory damages.

____ (i) **What actual damages and profits are available?** The copyright owner is entitled to recover the actual damages suffered as a result of the infringement, and any profits of the infringer that are attributable to the infringement and are not taken into account in computing the actual damages. In establishing the infringer's profits, the copyright owner needs to present proof only of the infringer's gross revenues from the infringing activity, and the infringer is required to prove his or her deductible expenses and the elements of profit attributable to factors other than the copyrighted work.

____ (ii) **What damages are provided by statute?** The copyright owner may elect, at any time before final judgment is rendered, to recover, instead of actual damages and profits, an award of statutory damages in a sum of not less than $750 or more than $30,000 per infringement. If it is proven that the infringement was committed willfully, the court may increase the award of statutory damages to not more than $150,000 per infringement. Conversely, where the infringer establishes that it was not aware and had no reason to believe that it was infringing on another's copyrights, the award of statutory damages may be reduced to not less than $200 per infringement.

____ (d) **Are attorney's fees and costs available?** The court in its discretion may allow the recovery of full costs by or against any party other than the United States or an officer thereof. The court may also award a reasonable attorney's fee to the prevailing party in an action regarding post-registration infringement.

____ (e) **What criminal penalties are implicated?** Any person who willfully infringes a copyright may be imprisoned and/or fined if the infringement was committed for purposes of commercial advantage or private financial gain. Moreover, all copies, and all devices used in making those copies, may be seized and forfeited to the United States.

____ 6. **Limitations on Actions.**

____ (a) **When must civil actions be filed?** A civil action must be commenced within 3 years after the claim accrued. A cause of action for copyright infringement accrues when one has knowledge of a violation or is chargeable with such knowledge. In case of continuing copyright infringements, an action may be brought for all acts that accrued within 3 years preceding filing of suit.

____ (b) **When must criminal actions be initiated?** No criminal proceeding can be maintained unless it is commenced within 5 years after the cause of action arose.

# Checklist 46: Pursuing ADR

When representing a party involved in a construction project and considering alternative dispute resolution (ADR), there are several issues to keep in mind. The following checklist should be helpful in considering some of the issues affecting this important decision.

____ 1. **What does your contract say?** Typically, construction projects entail contracts (if the parties are prudent), and those contracts (if the parties' lawyers are prudent) will describe what dispute resolution processes the parties have agreed to.

____ 2. **Does the contract require negotiation?** Many contracts will require that parties engage in good-faith negotiations as a precursor, if not an explicit prerequisite, to later stages of dispute resolution. Sometimes negotiations involve "steps;" for example, the parties' project representatives must meet and attempt to resolve the dispute, and, failing that, the parties' executive-level representatives must meet. The types of negotiation required in the contract are limited only by the parties' imagination. The American Institute of Architects' (AIA) Contract Documents require a determination by an "Initial Decision Maker," such as the architect, as a necessary step before proceeding to mediation.

____ 3. **Does the contract require mediation?** Laypeople are typically confused by the terms "mediation" and "arbitration," so it is important to describe them to your client. Mediation involves a neutral third-party who listens to both sides make their case and then works with each party one-on-one in order to achieve a negotiated settlement. Mediation is typically nonbinding and is part of the AIA requirements before the parties may proceed to binding dispute resolution, such as arbitration.

____ 4. **Does the contract require arbitration?** Arbitration differs from mediation in that it typically involves sworn testimony from live witnesses, cross-examination of those witnesses, and the introduction of documentary and demonstrative evidence. Arbitration is typically binding; that is, arbitrators' rulings are routinely confirmed by the trial court. The contract dictates the degree to which arbitrators are granted authority. In many cases, the contract simply states that the arbitration will be held

**Eric A. Berg** is a shareholder with the law firm of Vedder Price PC in its Chicago office. He has represented owners, developers, contractors and designers in mediations and arbitrations.

according to a particular set of rules (for example, the American Arbitration Association's Construction Industry Rules, which in this particular instance give an arbitrator a significant degree of autonomy regarding issuing subpoenas and admitting evidence). Arbitration is typically not appealable, because it is usually intended to be a prompt, final disposition of parties' disputes.

____ 5. **What if the contract is silent?** If the contract contains no provision regarding ADR, the parties can always decide to undertake ADR, usually a choice of mediation or arbitration.

____ (a) **When is mediation a good idea?** Mediation has many advantages. If all goes well, and the parties approach it in a good-faith attempt to resolve their differences in lieu of litigation, it is worthwhile. Mediation should also be attempted even if the parties feel that there is too much "emotion" involved to permit resolution; if the parties do not ultimately resolve the disputes, preparing for mediation is still a good exercise in itself and can help the parties concentrate on the main elements of their case. Good mediators can also point out the primary areas on which a fact-finder is ultimately going to focus. The drawbacks of mediation are the time and attorneys' fees expended in creating the mediation agreement; the expense of searching for, agreeing on, and hiring the mediator; and the futility of the process if one or both parties pursue mediation in bad faith.

____ (b) **When is arbitration a good idea?** Sensible minds can differ on whether arbitration is worthwhile, and many excellent articles and book chapters have been written on the topic.

____ (i) **The advantages of arbitration are many.** It is not appealable, so it provides finality. Arbitrators are, typically, lawyers, retired judges, and industry professionals, much more experienced than the typical jury or trial-court judge is in sophisticated, technical, construction-related topics such as defects and delays. The amount of discovery permitted in arbitration is a function of the parties' agreement or the arbitrators' discretion, or some combination of both. Because discovery is typically more limited than in litigation, it can reduce the parties' legal expenses significantly. Lastly, arbitrators act at the sufferance of the parties' and their lawyers' schedules, not vice versa as in litigation. As a result, a final ruling will be issued in less time than in litigation.

____ (ii) **Arbitration's disadvantages are numerous.** Because the parties pay for their arbitrators' time, the expenses can add up, even if divided among the parties. Finality has a dark side: arbitrators can be overruled by trial courts in only the most limited of circumstances, usually upon a clear and convincing showing of bias or a gross misapplication of the applicable law. Some courts have noted that an agreement to arbitrate is a conscious decision to relinquish the trappings of due process and therefore should not be taken lightly. Lastly, arbitrators have "real" lives, too, and it is not easy for them to block out several weeks at one time for an arbitration. Consequently, arbitrations frequently are held piecemeal, which adds to the parties' legal fees due to ramp-up time.

____ 6. **What if the parties opt for mediation?**

____ (a) **When to mediate?** An initial question is when to mediate: early or after discovery? The advantages of either are patent: mediation is intended to avoid the expenditure of legal fees, but without discovery, parties may be approaching mediation "blind" (and thus may not be as willing to reach settlement). At the absolute minimum, the parties should individually develop a project accounting—reflecting the amounts owed, the amounts not owed, and the amounts in dispute—and exchange that project accounting information sufficiently in advance of mediation.

____ (b) **How to mediate?** Essential to a mediation is a clear, concise mediation agreement. Under the mediation agreement, the parties agree on length of the mediation; the place of the mediation; the identity of the mediator, or at least the mechanism by which the mediator will be selected; the sharing of the mediation costs; and a confidentiality agreement regarding the information to be exchanged at the mediation. The parties must decide whether to present the mediator with a pre-mediation brief and whether to exchange copies of that brief or submit it in confidence to the mediator. Parties should also decide whether the mediation will commence with an opening session in which all parties are present. (This invites the risk of arousing the parties' emotions and impeding settlement.) Parties should be careful not to allow mediation to take on a life of its own and needlessly burn up legal fees.

____ (c) **Who will mediate?** Participants in the mediation must include party representatives (not just attorneys) with genuine decision-making authority. Do not hesitate to press the

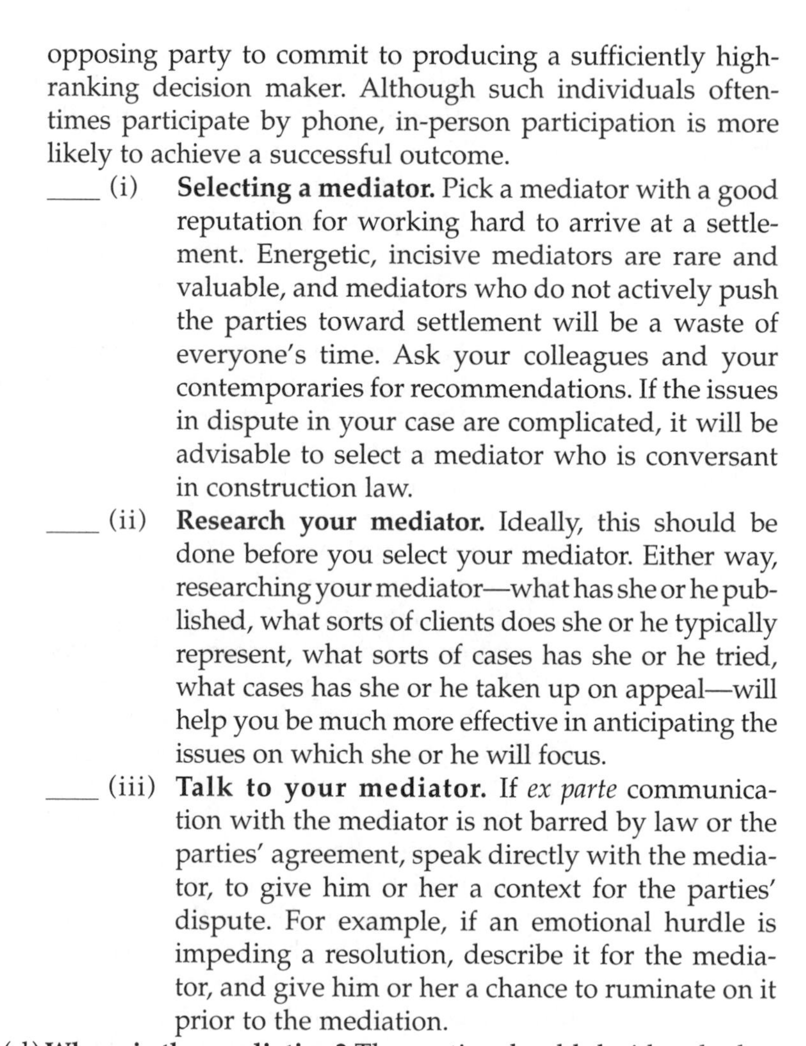

opposing party to commit to producing a sufficiently high-ranking decision maker. Although such individuals oftentimes participate by phone, in-person participation is more likely to achieve a successful outcome.

____ (i) **Selecting a mediator.** Pick a mediator with a good reputation for working hard to arrive at a settlement. Energetic, incisive mediators are rare and valuable, and mediators who do not actively push the parties toward settlement will be a waste of everyone's time. Ask your colleagues and your contemporaries for recommendations. If the issues in dispute in your case are complicated, it will be advisable to select a mediator who is conversant in construction law.

____ (ii) **Research your mediator.** Ideally, this should be done before you select your mediator. Either way, researching your mediator—what has she or he published, what sorts of clients does she or he typically represent, what sorts of cases has she or he tried, what cases has she or he taken up on appeal—will help you be much more effective in anticipating the issues on which she or he will focus.

____ (iii) **Talk to your mediator.** If *ex parte* communication with the mediator is not barred by law or the parties' agreement, speak directly with the mediator, to give him or her a context for the parties' dispute. For example, if an emotional hurdle is impeding a resolution, describe it for the mediator, and give him or her a chance to ruminate on it prior to the mediation.

____ (d) **Where is the mediation?** The parties should decide whether the mediation will be held in person, via telephone, or via videophone, based on the relative costs and benefits of each medium. If the mediation is held in a state in which a party's attorney is not licensed to practice law, the attorney may be in violation of that state's laws. Many states consider the mere participation in even a half-day mediation to rise to the level of practicing law in that jurisdiction. Local counsel should be secured in such instances.

____ (e) **Do you really want to waste everyone's time?** Once you have committed to mediate, do not waste the opportunity to achieve a good outcome for your client. A good outcome is not limited solely to settlement. If you prepare for the mediation with a presentation that resembles your opening statement, emphasizing your case's strengths and the other party's case's weaknesses, you will show opposing counsel (and her or his client) that you are prepared, and will set the tone of the case. Mediation is one of your and your client's only opportunities to communicate with the opposing party's decision-maker in an unfiltered manner (that is, not through counsel). Although you may not settle the case at mediation, you will at least narrow the gap and improve your odds of favorably settling the case later.

____ (f) **In the absence of complete settlement, can you resolve anything else?** The vast majority of cases settle before trial, and mediation can at least reduce the gap between the parties. It can also lead to resolution of other relevant issues, such as discovery parameters.

____ (g) **Did mediation produce a settlement agreement?** If so, the parties should be careful to memorialize the agreement at the end of the mediation, even if they have to do so in a handwritten agreement to be typed later. Otherwise, the parties run the risk of seeing the agreement unravel and result in colossal waste of their time.

____ (i) If the parties reach a settlement and an agreement is drafted (by hand or on a laptop computer), the parties should read the agreement language in its entirety—aloud if necessary—to confirm the case's resolution. (Sometimes counsel could use a second opinion on tricky settlement agreement language and should feel no compunction about conferring with colleagues by phone on such issues.)

____ (ii) One possible way to avoid the hazard of an unraveling settlement would be to exchange proposed settlement agreement language in advance of the mediation (many, if not most, settlement agreements are comprised of standard language), with the settlement amount to be inserted upon the parties' agreement.

____ 7. **What if the parties opt for arbitration?** As with mediation, arbitration is a function of the parties' agreement to arbitrate. If the contract is silent on the issue, the parties are free to agree to whatever form of arbitration they want.

____ (a) **How many arbitrators?** One is typical for small disputes; three for larger (high six- to seven-figure) disputes.

____ (b) **Whose rules?** The American Arbitration Association (AAA) has been in this business for years and has several different sets of rules, including several for construction-related disputes. The efficiency derived from taking an off-the-shelf set of rules must be balanced against the downside of a one-size-fits-all approach.

____ (c) **How much discovery?** AAA rules allow discovery decisions to be made by the parties' mutual consent and, absent that, by the arbitrators themselves. Some arbitrators will take a Spartan approach: no depositions and a basic exchange of project files before proceeding to arbitration. Other arbitrators have been known to allow full discovery in conformity with the federal rules of civil procedure (but this diminishes arbitration's efficiency and low cost). Although it is possible to take too many depositions, depositions are often helpful in reducing the amount of time needed for testimony at the arbitration itself (and thus reduces the amount of money charged by the arbitrators).

____ (d) **Who participates?** A thornier question than it might seem! Parties with arbitration provisions in their contracts are obligated to arbitrate. But if there is no express agreement to consolidate arbitrations (see the AIA architects' agreements, for example, B151—1997), an owner may find itself in parallel proceedings. Also, if a contractor has agreed to arbitrate but has not passed that requirement down to its subs, there can be two parallel proceedings, one in arbitration and one in litigation. This obviously can be very costly.[1]

____ 8. **Hire an Expert.** Chances are, your case involves technical questions; if it ultimately proceeds to trial or arbitration, you will need expert guidance on those issues. Good experts will help organize and simplify your case in a way that will make you more effective in mediation or at arbitration.

## *Note*

1. See, for example, *Board of Managers of the Courtyards at the Woodlands Condominium Assoc. v. IKO Chicago, Inc.*, 183 Ill. 2d 66, 75, 697 N.E.2d 727, 731 (1998).

# General Claims/Disputes

# Checklist 47: Perfecting or Pursuing a Payment Bond Claim

A payment bond is financial security provided by a contractor or subcontractor on a construction contract that gives protection to those who supply labor or materials to the project if the contractor, or bond principal, fails to make payment for the labor or materials. In that event, the surety on the bond will make payment subject to suretyship defenses or defenses of the principal. A payment bond claim is a demand made to the surety that issued the payment bond for payment for the labor and materials supplied to the bonded project, which the principal on the bond has failed or refused to pay. The bond principal is the entity that procures the bond for the security of persons supplying labor or materials to the project. A claim is usually submitted as a letter to the surety and/or a lawsuit filed against a surety.

____ 1. **How do you ascertain what, if any, rights your client has under a payment bond?** First, determine whether there is a payment bond on the project. A payment bond will usually be required if the project uses public funds or is built on publicly owned property.

____ (a) **Federal construction projects.** All federal construction contracts in excess of $100,000 require payment bonds under the Miller Act. The Miller Act establishes notice, limitations on filing suit, venue and other factors.

____ (b) **State or local municipal construction projects.** Most state or local municipal projects are governed by state procurement laws, which require payment bonds. Many states have adopted "Little Miller Acts," which are very similar to the federal Miller Act. There may be a state-mandated bond form in place, and statutes will govern notice, limitations on filing suit, venue and other factors.

____ (c) **Private construction projects.** Payment bonds are sometimes employed on large private projects. If bonds were required, it is imperative to obtain a copy of the bond form because it will dictate many issues regarding who can file a claim, what can be included in the claim, notice, suit limitations, and other issues.

---

**Shannon J. Briglia** is a partner in the McLean, Virginia, office of the national construction law firm of Moore & Lee LLP. She regularly represents sureties and contractors in a variety of construction disputes, claims, and litigation.

____ (d) **Bond form.** Obtain a copy of the bond and review its terms and conditions carefully. Compare the bond form with any applicable statutes.

____ (i) The Miller Act requires the contracting officer to provide a copy of a payment bond provided by a prime contractor on a federal construction project upon proper request.

____ (ii) Many Little Miller Acts have a similar requirement that a copy of the bond must be given to anyone who asks for it.

____ (iii) On private projects, the construction contract may contain a provision requiring the contractor or owner to provide a copy of the bond. If not, your client may ask for a copy of any bond provided for the project but may not have an enforceable right to obtain a copy of the bond.

____ 2. **Does your client have the right to file a payment bond claim? Is it a proper "claimant"?** Either applicable legislation or the terms of the bond will define who may be a claimant.

____ (a) **Claimants on federal projects.** The Miller Act provides that only subcontractors or suppliers that have a contract with the party supplying the bond or with someone in privity with the party supplying the bond may be a claimant. This definition has given rise to the terms first- and second-tier claimants, both of which are eligible to pursue payment bond claims.

____ (b) **Claimants on state or local municipal projects.** State procurement law defines who may be a claimant.

____ (c) **Potential multiple sources of recovery for subcontractors or suppliers.** If your client is a subcontractor or supplier, there may be more than one payment bond under which your client can pursue a claim. The Miller Act and most Little Miller Acts do not require a subcontractor or supplier to pursue one bond over another.

____ (d) **Bond language limitation on definition of claimant.** On private projects, the bond form will usually define who may be a claimant under the bond.

____ 3. **Are there any written notices that must be given to pursue a payment bond claim?**

____ (a) **Claimants in privity with the bond principal.** Claimants in contractual privity with the bond principal do not usually have to give notice of their claim to the surety or any other party before filing suit. Giving notice is frequently done, however, and may result in the surety or principal resolving the claim without the necessity of filing suit.

____ (b) **Claimants not in privity with the bond principal.** Claimants that are not in direct contractual privity with the principal on the bond usually have to give written notice of their claim to the surety before filing suit.

____ (i) Federal construction contracts require a second-tier claimant to give written notice of its claim to the bond principal and owner in advance of filing suit. Written notice is a condition precedent to filing suit.

____ (ii) **State construction contracts.**

____ a. Some Little Miller Acts require a claimant to give notice of furnishing of labor or materials in advance of providing labor or materials (called a "front-end notice") as a condition precedent to filing suit.

____ b. Most Little Miller Acts require a claimant to give notice after providing labor or materials as a condition precedent to filing suit (called "back-end notice").

____ c. Some Little Miller Acts require both a notice of furnishing or front-end notice and a back-end notice as a condition precedent to filing suit.

____ (c) **Surety's response to a notice of claim.** Upon receipt of the claim letter, a surety will usually send an acknowledgment letter and ask the claimant to submit a sworn statement (sometimes called a "Proof of Loss" or "Affidavit of Claim") and copies of all pertinent documents supporting the claim. The claimant should respond as completely as possible to this request.

____ (d) **Time limit on surety's response.** Some payment bond forms require a surety to act within a set period of time, often 45 days from receipt of the notice of claim, to specify any undisputed amounts and make arrangement for payment and to identify and explain the dispute over the remaining claim amounts. Several courts have held that the surety's failure to act within the mandated period may constitute a waiver of all defenses to the disputed portion of the claim.

____ 4. **What are the time limits for filing a payment bond claim or lawsuit?**

____ (a) **Federal construction projects.**

____ (i) Under the Miller Act, claimants must wait 90 days from the date they last supplied labor or materials to give notice and/or to file suit. This waiting period allows the primary debtor the opportunity to make payment in the ordinary course.

____ (ii) Suit must be filed within 1 year of the date the claimant last supplied labor or materials to the project.

____ a. Provision of the last labor or materials is typically defined to mean base contract work, not corrective work (punch list work) or *de minimus* work.

____ b. Change order work or extra work will count as work for purposes of determining the one year limitation.

____ (b) **State or local municipal construction contracts.**

____ (i) Little Miller Acts typically define whether the claimant must wait 90 days or some other time period before filing suit.

____ (ii) Little Miller Acts typically define the last day for filing suit. Usually the suit limitation is the same 1-year period as the Miller Act.

____ (c) **Private construction contracts.** The terms of the bond will establish any waiting period before filing suit and the deadline for filing suit on the bond.

____ 5. **How do you price or value a payment bond claim?**

____ (a) **Determining and verifying the value of the claim.** Gather relevant documents and confirm what components can be included in the claim. As a general rule, the cost of labor, equipment, or materials normally and ordinarily totally consumed by the project, such as boilers, air handlers, sprinkler systems, pipes, bricks, lumber, nails, concrete, tile, grout, insulation, or other generic or specialty building materials, are recoverable. Fair rental charge for use of equipment necessary to prosecute the work on the project, and fuels such as gas, diesel, oil, or coal used for generating power are typically recoverable.

____ (i) **Review legal documents.**

____ a. **Contract.** It is axiomatic that you can recover under a payment bond claim only what is recoverable under the underlying contract.

____ b. **Bond.** The bond may eliminate or enhance the ability to recover interest, attorney's fees or other claim components.

____ c. **Pertinent statutes or regulations.** There may be limitations on recovery in the statute.

____ (ii) **Financial documents.**

____ a. **Payment applications.** It is important to ascertain what the adjusted contract value is, what amount has been invoiced by the client, and what percentage of work has been confirmed by the architect/engineer.

____ b. **Payments.** Account for all payments to the claimant to determine what amount is due under the contract.

____ c. **Change orders.** Extra work performed at the request or direction of the prime contractor or owner is generally recoverable under a payment bond.

____ (iii) **Other costs.**

____ a. Other claims, such as claims for delay, may be sought under a payment bond claim if provided for under the contract and law.

____ b. Claims for consequential damages may be sought if not waived in the contract.

____ (b) **Recovery of interest or legal fees.** Determine whether interest or legal fees are recoverable under the contract, bond, or applicable statute.

____ (i) Identify pertinent interest rate and calculate amount.

____ (ii) Obtain legal invoices.

____ 6. **Where do you pursue or file a payment bond claim?**

____ (a) **Federal construction contracts.** On federal construction contracts, the Miller Act gives federal district courts having jurisdiction over the place the project is located jurisdiction to hear payment bond claims.

____ (b) **State or municipal construction contracts.** Little Miller Acts typically establish the place of the project as the proper venue for payment bond suits for state or other municipal construction contracts. The statute may limit suit to state court, but, in some jurisdictions, suit on a payment bond for a state project can be filed in federal court if diversity jurisdiction exists under 42 U.S.C. § 1334.

____ (c) **Private construction contracts.** On private construction contracts, the bond will usually state where and in what court suit may be brought.

____ 7. **Can you file suit against just the surety, or must you also name the bond principal in the suit?**

____ (a) **Federal construction contracts.** Nothing in the Miller Act requires a claimant to sue both surety and principal. The claimant has the option of including the principal but is not required to do so.

____ (b) **State and local municipality construction contracts.** Some states' laws require suit to be brought against both principal and surety or to require suit to be pursued against the principal first.

____ (c) **Contracts containing arbitration provisions.** If the underlying contract requires arbitration of disputes, a surety who is the only defendant in a suit may move to stay the litigation pending arbitration between the claimant and bond principal under the contract. A surety cannot be compelled to participate in an arbitration between the claimant and bond principal.

____ 8. **What happens if the bond principal files for bankruptcy?** Suit against the surety is not stayed by its principal's bankruptcy.

# Checklist 48: Owner's Enforcement of a Performance Bond

The following is a checklist for use by an owner for the enforcement of a performance bond claim against a surety.

____ 1. **Before a Performance Bond Is Issued**. An owner has an obligation to disclose to a surety any information that the owner has reason to know about the principal or the project that would be material to the surety's decision to undertake the risk of issuing the bond. For example, if the owner knows the principal is in financial difficulty or already in default on other projects with the owner, but conceals that information from the surety, then the bond may be declared void for fraud. If the owner knows the principal is the low bidder because it has obviously failed to appreciate the complexity of the project, perhaps through its inexperience or unilateral mistake, but conceals that fact from the surety, the surety's liability under the bond may be discharged.

____ 2. **Read the Bond**. The owner must, repeatedly, throughout the project and certainly before any performance issues arise, *read the bond.* Not all performance bonds are the same. An owner's claim under a performance bond may be defeated by its failure to comply with the simply stated terms of the bond. Too often, an owner misunderstands the extent of a surety's liability under a bond. Be sure to obtain a complete, fully executed copy of the bond, together with any riders or endorsements—and then ascertain the following:

____ (a) **Owner's obligations.** What are the obligations of the owner enumerated in the bond that may be conditions precedent to enforcement of the bond or that may become the owner's responsibility upon the surety's performance of its duties under the bond?

____ (b) **What does the bond provide concerning the extent of the surety's liability?** Is the surety liable only for performing the defaulted contractor's work? Does the bond expressly provide that the surety may have liability for

**Patricia H. Thompson** is a shareholder in the Miami, Florida, office of Carlton Fields P.A. She is past chair of the Fidelity Surety Law Committee, of the Tort Trial and Insurance Practice Section, and past co-chair of the Construction Litigation Committee of the Litigation Section of the American Bar Association.

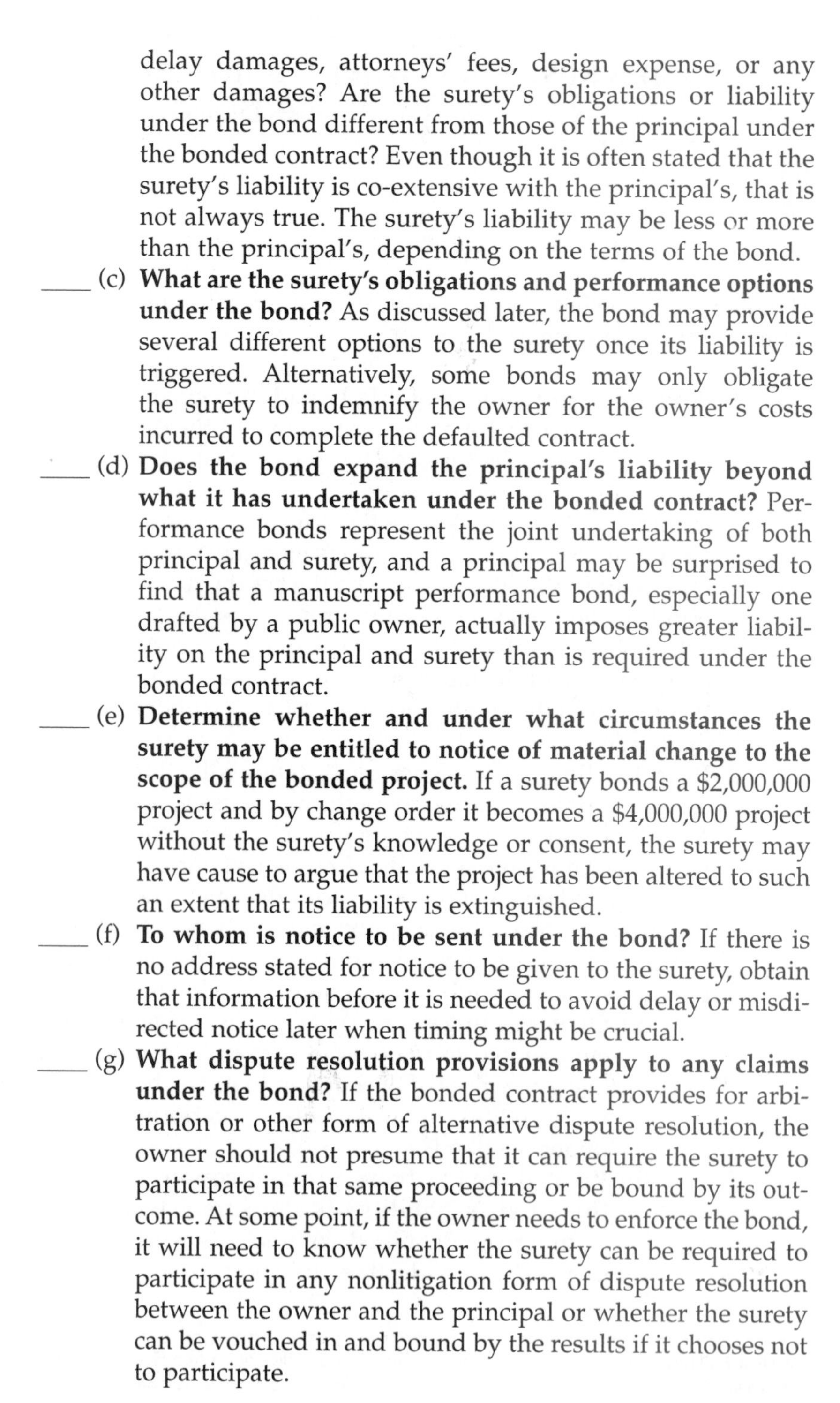

delay damages, attorneys' fees, design expense, or any other damages? Are the surety's obligations or liability under the bond different from those of the principal under the bonded contract? Even though it is often stated that the surety's liability is co-extensive with the principal's, that is not always true. The surety's liability may be less or more than the principal's, depending on the terms of the bond.

____ (c) **What are the surety's obligations and performance options under the bond?** As discussed later, the bond may provide several different options to the surety once its liability is triggered. Alternatively, some bonds may only obligate the surety to indemnify the owner for the owner's costs incurred to complete the defaulted contract.

____ (d) **Does the bond expand the principal's liability beyond what it has undertaken under the bonded contract?** Performance bonds represent the joint undertaking of both principal and surety, and a principal may be surprised to find that a manuscript performance bond, especially one drafted by a public owner, actually imposes greater liability on the principal and surety than is required under the bonded contract.

____ (e) **Determine whether and under what circumstances the surety may be entitled to notice of material change to the scope of the bonded project.** If a surety bonds a $2,000,000 project and by change order it becomes a $4,000,000 project without the surety's knowledge or consent, the surety may have cause to argue that the project has been altered to such an extent that its liability is extinguished.

____ (f) **To whom is notice to be sent under the bond?** If there is no address stated for notice to be given to the surety, obtain that information before it is needed to avoid delay or misdirected notice later when timing might be crucial.

____ (g) **What dispute resolution provisions apply to any claims under the bond?** If the bonded contract provides for arbitration or other form of alternative dispute resolution, the owner should not presume that it can require the surety to participate in that same proceeding or be bound by its outcome. At some point, if the owner needs to enforce the bond, it will need to know whether the surety can be required to participate in any nonlitigation form of dispute resolution between the owner and the principal or whether the surety can be vouched in and bound by the results if it chooses not to participate.

____ (h) **What are the applicable statute(s) of limitation for actions to enforce the surety's liability?** Too often, an owner may engage in a long-lasting performance dispute with the principal, without realizing that the statute of limitations for a related claim under the bond has expired in the meantime. The statute of limitations applicable to an owner's claims under the bond may be different—and shorter—than that applicable to the owner's claims against the contractor.

____ 3. **Check the Law.** Research the applicable law to determine to what extent it varies the owner's rights and obligations from those stated in the bond. While this research need not be done at the beginning of a project, it is important to know at some point before the owner needs to enforce a bond whether all of the terms and conditions of the bond are enforceable. Additionally, the owner should determine whether surety bonds are subject to the insurance "bad-faith" statutes in the state in which the project is located.

____ 4. **Read the Contract.** Read the bonded contract to determine what it says, if anything, about the bond, any notices to be given concerning the bond, and, most importantly, what must be done in order to declare the principal in default and terminate the principal. As is discussed later, if the contractor is not properly terminated, that may constitute a defense for the surety.

____ 5. **Keep the Surety Informed.** During construction, respond timely and accurately to any inquiries or requests for status reports from the surety. The surety may make periodic inquiries to determine whether any change orders have expanded the cost, scope, or length of the project; the percentage of work completed; the amount of contract funds paid to the contractor and the amount of retainage withheld; whether the owner knows of any unpaid suppliers or subcontractors; and whether the owner is experiencing any specific performance problems. This information is important to a surety for several reasons. Additionally, an owner may benefit by keeping a surety well apprised of issues as they arise in a troubled project. An owner may include in its responses to such inquiries disclaimers as to the accuracy of such information provided in good faith, but such disclaimers may not protect an owner who knowingly, recklessly, or negligently provides misleading information upon which the surety relies.

____ 6. **Proper Payments.** At all times, be mindful of the surety's interest in the contract's balances. Under certain circumstances, a surety may be excused from performance, in whole or in part, to the extent the owner fails to ensure that it makes only such payments to the principal as are properly due under the bonded contract or as required by applicable proper payment laws. During a construction project, the surety has an equitable interest in the contract balance. Upon the default of the principal, the surety's rights to the contract balance are triggered, and it is entitled to use the contract balance to complete the bonded contract. To the extent the contract balance is less than it should be, because the owner has paid for work not performed or for defective work or because the owner has not ensured that subcontractors and suppliers are being properly paid, the surety may require the owner to replenish the contract balance to the extent of such improper payments, or the surety's liability may be excused to the extent of the improper payments.

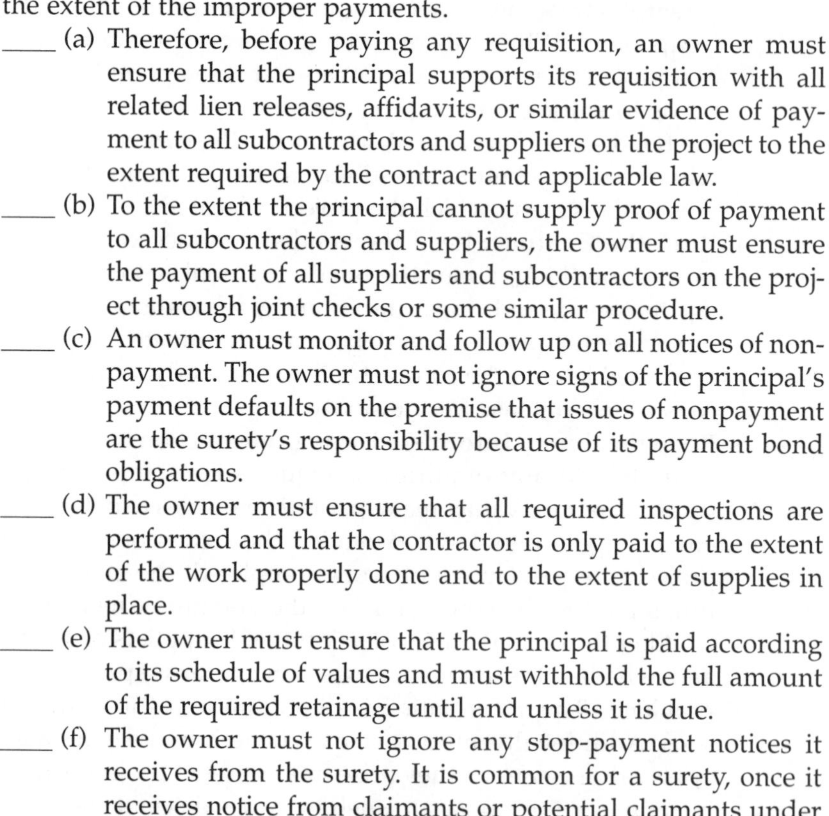

____ (a) Therefore, before paying any requisition, an owner must ensure that the principal supports its requisition with all related lien releases, affidavits, or similar evidence of payment to all subcontractors and suppliers on the project to the extent required by the contract and applicable law.

____ (b) To the extent the principal cannot supply proof of payment to all subcontractors and suppliers, the owner must ensure the payment of all suppliers and subcontractors on the project through joint checks or some similar procedure.

____ (c) An owner must monitor and follow up on all notices of nonpayment. The owner must not ignore signs of the principal's payment defaults on the premise that issues of nonpayment are the surety's responsibility because of its payment bond obligations.

____ (d) The owner must ensure that all required inspections are performed and that the contractor is only paid to the extent of the work properly done and to the extent of supplies in place.

____ (e) The owner must ensure that the principal is paid according to its schedule of values and must withhold the full amount of the required retainage until and unless it is due.

____ (f) The owner must not ignore any stop-payment notices it receives from the surety. It is common for a surety, once it receives notice from claimants or potential claimants under its payment bond for a given project, to notify the owner of this fact and to request that the owner stop making payment to the principal until the surety is able to determine why the principal is not using the contract funds to pay its subcontractors and suppliers on the project. If an owner ignores a stop-payment notice, it may have to replenish the contract balance due to the surety, in effect having to pay twice for the same work.

____ (g) The owner may need to take reasonable steps to determine that a principal has the capacity and intention to complete a job, if it receives sufficient warnings from the surety or lienors on the project that the principal is in default of its obligations under the contract, especially its payment obligations.

___ 7. **Notice of Disputes.** Err on the side of providing the surety notice of material disputes with the contractor that may give rise to grounds for termination, and when giving notice, be sure to fully comply with every aspect of every notice requirement of the bond, the bonded contract, and the applicable law. If the performance bond has a notice of dispute provision, such as that in the standard AIA A312 performance bond (1987 ed.), then the owner must not fail to provide the notice required thereby, exactly as required. If the notice is to be in writing, that is how it should be provided. If it is to be provided to both the surety and the principal, they both must receive notice. The requirement of notice to a surety is not a technicality and must not be taken lightly or ignored.

___ 8. **Pre-default Conference.** Following notice of potential default, follow the rest of the procedures required by the bond and the bonded contract prior to a formal declaration of default. For example, the standard 1987 A312 performance bond requires the owner attempt to schedule a conference with the surety and contractor within 15 days of the notice of potential default to discuss the owner's performance concerns about the principal.

___ 9. **Default and Termination.** Timely and properly declare a default of the contractor, and, if appropriate, terminate its right to perform thereunder. A surety's liability usually does not arise until the principal is declared in default under its contract and the principal's right to perform the contract is terminated. Not every breach of contract justifies termination of a contactor. Therefore, it is important that an owner determine whether it has a right to terminate the contractor and then properly follow the provisions of the bonded contract concerning termination, including notice and opportunities to cure, architect's certification, etc. To trigger the surety's liability under the bond, the termination of the contractor must comply with any other bond requirements in a timely fashion. If the owner gives notice of potential default under the 1987 A312 bond, and then waits a year before terminating the general contractor, the surety may persuasively defend its liability under the bond by arguing that the earlier notice of default was untimely and ineffective. Consequently, as soon as an owner determines it is ready to terminate a contractor for default, even if it gave prior notice or otherwise tried to comply with the conditions of the bond, if too much time as passed, the owner should consider whether or not it must again comply with any notice or other conditions precedent arising under the bond, the bonded contract, or other applicable law.

____ 10. **Notice of Default and Termination.** Timely notify the surety in writing of the principal's default and termination and make timely demand on the surety to perform under the bond. To the extent required by the bond, a surety must be given notice of the principal's default and termination so the surety can then investigate the termination and determine whether and, if so, how it will cure the principal's default and complete the principal's contract. If the bond requires that an additional notice of default be given to the surety, as does the 1987 A312 bond, then the owner must comply therewith. If an owner attempts to cure the principal's default itself, without first allowing the surety the opportunity to perform the principal's contractual obligations, the owner may find itself without recourse against the surety.

____ 11. **Cooperate with the Surety's Investigation.** Comply with all reasonable requests for information from the surety as it investigates the principal's default, and be prepared to explain and document for the surety the basis for declaring the principal in default and terminating the contract. Typically, following notice of default, a surety will request that the owner provide the surety with copies of the bonded contract; any change orders; and pending pay requests, information about contact balances and retainage, the reasons for the principal's default and termination, any inspection or experts' reports substantiating any defective work, the status of payment to subs and suppliers, and other information that will enable the surety to determine how it should proceed in response to the notice of default. Indeed, it is often stated that a surety has a duty to investigate the owner's termination of its principal to ensure that there is a basis therefor and that the owner itself is not in default under the bonded contract. Most bonds condition the surety's performance obligations on the owner *not* being in default. Also, because most bonds give the surety options as to whether and how it will perform under the bond, the surety must be provided the information that will enable it to make an informed decision as to which option it should undertake.

____ 12. **Surety's Performance Options.** Determine what options are available to the surety under the applicable law, the particular bond, and the facts of the default, and be ready to negotiate with the surety toward the option the owner finds most preferable. A performance bond may provide the surety with a choice among several performance options upon the principal's termination, or the bond may be silent concerning the surety's manner of performance.

____ (a) **The 1987 AIA A312 bond.** For example, the 1987 A312 bond allows the surety to arrange for the principal to complete the project, with the owner's consent; undertake to perform the contract itself, usually through the use of a consulting contractor; tender a new completing contractor to the owner; or agree to have the owner cure the default and complete the contract, paying the owner an agreed-upon amount, up to the penal sum of the bond. There are advantages and disadvantages to each of these options, and the owner must be ready to give or withhold consent or negotiate the terms under which the surety undertakes whichever choice the surety makes.

____ (b) **The 1970 AIA A311 bond.** The 1970 A311 bond requires the surety to "complete" the contract or to obtain bids and award the contract to the lowest conforming bidder. Similarly, the law of the jurisdiction may require the surety under a public works bond to comply with the public bid laws.

____ (c) **No bond provisions concerning surety's manner of performance.** The bond may say very little about the options available to the surety, in which case the surety's options will depend on the applicable law and the negotiations between it and the owner.

____ 13. **Completion Agreement.** If the surety elects to complete performance, the owner must decide whether to enter into a takeover agreement with the surety and, if so, what terms to include in that agreement.

____ (a) **Takeover agreement.** Some owners refuse to enter into takeover agreements, reasoning that the bond and the underlying contract are sufficient to define the responsibilities of the owner and surety. However, most sureties want a takeover agreement, usually so any issues in dispute can be identified and, if possible, resolved at the outset rather than letting them fester and cause unnecessary litigation. Any issues that are identified but unresolved can be specifically preserved in the takeover agreement so no one's rights or defenses are waived by either party's performance or delay in litigating those rights. Furthermore, the agreement may preserve the surety's rights against the principal, indemnitors, and any potentially liable third parties.

____ (b) **Takeover agreement issues.** There are a number of commonly used takeover agreement forms, but they must always be adapted to the facts of a given contract default. It is typical for a takeover agreement to address the following issues:

____ (i) The owner should recite its termination of the principal, its request to have the surety cure the principal's default, and its promise to dedicate the contract balance to the surety for completion of the work, less any specifically reserved sums claimed by the owner for stated reasons.

____ (ii) The surety should agree to cure the principal's default, the agreement should define scope of work to be performed, and the agreement should specify which option the surety will use to perform the work.

____ (iii) To the extent required, the owner should consent to the surety's chosen method of completion.

____ (iv) The amount of contract balance available to complete the project should be defined, as should its component parts, by line item, including unpaid but earned payments due the principal, all retainage, and any potential increases due to pending but not yet approved change orders.

____ (v) The parties should agree on the time left under the contract to substantial performance and whether the surety is entitled to an extension of time and/or waiver of liquidated damages, for the time it took the surety to investigate the default and prepare to complete the work or for any delays caused by the owner.

____ (vi) The parties should state whether or not the surety's liability will be limited to the amount of the bond penalty. This provision may need to be supported by new consideration, because some courts have held that once a surety undertakes to complete the contract, its liability is not limited to its bond penalty and any effort to reduce its liability must be supported by sufficient consideration.

____ (vii) The underlying contract should be reinstated, or preserved, so the surety can possibly retain the underlying subcontracts and any warranties related thereto.

____ (viii) Each party must preserve all equitable and legal claims and defenses it may have against the other parties, as well as others such as the principal, indemnitors, or design professionals.

____ (ix) Any special role or rights of the surety's consultants on the project or the surety's completing contractor should be defined.

____ (x) The manner and frequency of the owner's payments to the surety and the surety's payment to its performing contractors should be defined.

____ 14. **Performance by the Owner.** If the surety does not respond to the notice of default or notice of termination, or elects not to perform, then the owner should undertake to perform the contract itself, taking care to document its costs incurred in doing so.

____ 15. **Actions to Enforce the Owner's Rights.** In the event the surety wrongfully fails to perform and cure the contractor's default, the owner should decide where, how, and when it wants to enforce its rights against the contractor or the surety, or both, for their respective breaches of contract and the bond.

____ 16. **Statutory Claims-Handling Requirements.** Additionally, if the surety is subject to the insurance bad-faith statutes, the owner should provide whatever notice is required as a condition precedent to suing the surety for bad faith.

# Checklist 49: Performance Bond Claims—Surety's Considerations

If a performance bond surety receives a claim on its performance bond, the following items should be considered in processing the notice of claim, gathering information, and responding to the claim.

____ 1. **Has the principal been declared in default?** Not every breach is a material default that triggers the surety's liability and obligations under a bond. The declaration of default must be made in clear, direct, and unequivocal language.

____ (a) **AIA A312 performance bond.** In paragraph 3.1, the owner must notify the contractor and the surety that the owner is considering declaring a contract default which gives rise to the surety's obligation to attend a pre-default conference that might be requested.

____ (b) **Other bond forms.** Was proper default notice provided? If not, the failure to provide such notice may relieve the surety of its performance bond obligations.

____ (c) **Prompt acknowledgment of receipt.** When a surety receives notice of default of its principal on a bonded project, the surety should promptly acknowledge receipt of the obligee's notice and initiate investigation to determine the validity of the claim.

____ (d) **Initiate prompt investigation.** The failure to investigate the claim may lead to a claim of extra contractual damages against the surety.

____ 2. **Review the Performance Bond Form.** There may be certain time periods for both the obligee and the surety to consider, depending on the bond form. For example, the AIA A312 performance bond sets forth several time periods which must be considered by a surety in responding to a claim on the performance bond, including conditions precedent to the surety's elections under that particular bond form.

____ (a) **AIA A311 performance bond.** The AIA A311 performance bond is relatively straightforward.

**Wm. Cary Wright** is a shareholder in the Tampa, Florida, office of Carlton Fields PA. He focuses exclusively on construction law, and as part of his practice he represents owners, contractors, and subcontractors with construction claims, construction liens, insurance coverage matters, and bond claims.

____ (b) **AIA A312 performance bond.** The AIA A312 performance bond is more detailed and contains conditions precedent to recovery; specifies alternatives from which the surety can choose, provided the obligee satisfies conditions of the bond; contains specific time limits and suit limitations; and addresses damages that the obligee may recover.

____ 3. **If a default was declared, was the principal properly terminated pursuant to its contract with the obligee?** Typically, in order to properly terminate a contract, the termination provisions of a contract must be strictly followed. The failure to follow the termination provisions of a contract can result in a wrongful termination of the principal and relieve the surety of its obligations under the bond.

____ 4. **Has the principal been notified of the claim against the bond?** The principal should be notified of the claim, reminded of its indemnity obligations, and encouraged to cooperate with the surety's investigation.

____ 5. **Does the principal acknowledge the default?** If the principal acknowledges the default and it is of the principal's making, the surety's course of action is clear. Depending on the terms of the bond, it can engage the principal to complete the work, complete the work with another contractor, or pay the obligee to complete the work with a contractor of its selection. If the principal does not acknowledge the default, then the surety must perform its independent analysis of the claim.

____ 6. **Compile the Information to Assess the Claim.** To properly investigate the claim, the surety must compile the relevant information. This includes, but is not limited to, documents related to:

____ (a) The bond and contract documents.

____ (b) The principal and its records.

____ (c) Relevant project documents.

____ (d) Subcontractors and suppliers.

____ (e) Underwriting information.

____ (f) Current financial and credit reports on the principal.

____ 7. **Review the Principal's Records.** A thorough review of the principal's records should be conducted in order to assess the status of the project. This includes a review of the initial bid estimate file, change orders, progress payments, and job correspondence.

____ 8. **Review the Obligee's Records.** A thorough review of the obligee's records should be conducted to assess the project from the obligee's perspective. This includes a review of the contract documents, change orders, back-charges, pay applications, job schedules, original bids from all contractors, and job correspondence.

____ 9. **Interview Representatives of the Principal and Owner.** Conducting interviews with representatives of both the principal and obligee will greatly assist in the information gathering process and will add context to the review of the project documents.

____ 10. **Conduct a Site Visit if Necessary.** If appropriate, the surety or a consultant should visit the project site to ascertain the physical status of the project and to document the existing conditions at the time of default.

____ 11. **Consider the Use of Consultants to Assist in Investigating the Claim.** Depending on the type of claim, the surety may need the services of consultants in order to investigate and evaluate the claim.

____ (a) **Types of consultants:**

____ (i) Legal consultants.

____ (ii) Accounting consultants.

____ (iii) Construction consultants.

____ (iv) Scheduling consultants.

____ (v) Other consultants.

____ 12. **Protect the Surety's Equity Interest in the Contract Balance as to Other Creditors.** Upon receipt of notice of a default, the surety should consider several steps to protect itself.

____ (a) **UCC filing.** The surety should consider filing the general indemnity agreement (GIA) as a financing statement to secure its interest in contract balance.

____ (b) **Notice to obligee to withhold funds.** The surety should immediately send a notice to the obligee to withhold payment of any remaining contract balances from the principal. If the obligee disregards the notice, the surety may be able to assert a claim against the obligee to recover payments made to the principal after the date of the notice.

____ 13. **If the surety concludes that the principal is in default, it should first consider whether it has any defenses that would relieve it of its obligations under the bond.** These defenses include, but are not limited to:

____ (a) **Contractor's defenses.** The surety can assert the defenses of the contractor to contest default or termination.

____ (i) The obligee's failure

____ a. to make payment under the contract.

____ b. to grant time extensions under the contract.

____ c. to issue change orders under the contract.

____ (ii) The obligee's cardinal change in the contract.

____ (iii) The obligee's failure to follow the termination provisions of the contract.

____ a. Were the proper "cure" notices given by the obligee?

____ (iv) The contract was "substantially performed" by the principal.
____ (v) The obligee waived contract completion dates or requirements upon which it relied to support its termination.
____ (vi) The owner/obligee's implied warranty of constructability.
____ (vii) The owner/obligee's implied warranty of commercial availability of specified construction materials.
____ (viii) The owner/obligee's implied duty to disclose information material to the principal's performance of the work.
____ (ix) The owner/obligee's implied duty of cooperation.
____ (x) Impossibility of performance.
____ (xi) Commercial impracticality of performance.
____ (xii) The obligee's failure to timely file suit.

____ (b) **Surety's defenses.** A surety may have independent defenses in addition to any defenses of its principal.
____ (i) The obligee's failure to provide adequate notice under the bond.
____ (ii) The obligee's failure to provide timely notice under the bond.
____ (iii) Material alteration of the bonded contract.
____ (iv) Improper payment of contract funds by the obligee.
____ (v) Fraud or misrepresentation by the obligee that induces the surety to issue the bond.
____ (vi) Statutory defenses, including statute of limitations.

____ 14. **Lack of Surety Defenses.** If no surety defenses exist, the surety must determine how to perform its obligations under the bond.

# Checklist 50: A Surety's Pursuit of Coverage through the Principal's Insurance Policies

A surety faces a number of challenges when evaluating a bond claim. In addition to the direct question of whether a performance or payment bond claim is valid, a surety can pursue other options to redirect or offset potential losses. One of these tools is pursuit of a claim on commercial general liability (CGL) policies or other insurance policies. Many construction disputes involve both bond claims of failure to perform a contract or pay a subcontractor or supplier and the issues involving defects in the work. This checklist addresses considerations for the surety in seeking to secure coverage through its principal's insurance policies.

____ 1. **Identify All Applicable Insurance Policies.**

____ (a) **Sources of information.** The surety should check with several sources for obtaining its principal's insurance information.

____ (i) The surety underwriter.

____ (ii) The underwriting files.

____ (iii) The surety's agent that provided bonds. The agent may also be the principal's agent for insurance purposes.

____ (iv) The principal. The surety should obtain copies of declaration pages and copies of the policies themselves, if available.

____ (v) The obligee on the bond.

____ 2. **Review the Contract between Principal and Obligee.** The contract should indicate what insurance was required on the project. Other sources include the suppliers and subcontractors to the principal.

____ (a) **Practice tip.** It is important to act quickly to obtain this information. Parties are generally more cooperative at the beginning of an event than after disputes arise over the event.

____ 3. **Check the General Indemnity Agreement (GIA).** The general indemnity agreement may include language wherein the principal assigns

**Alfred A. Malena, Jr.** is a partner with Thompson, Slagle & Hannan LLC. He represents sureties, developers, contractors, and others in a wide array of commercial and residential construction matters. He also represents parties in commercial litigation, business formation, and estate planning matters.

certain rights under insurance policies to the surety. Generally, the GIA contains a provision allowing the surety reasonable access to the books and records of the principal.

____ 4. **Types of Available Insurance.** It is important to determine what insurance coverage is available.

____ (a) **Commercial general liability (CGL) policies.** CGL policies provide contractors third-party coverage for property damage and personal injury.

____ (b) **Builder's risk policies.** Builder's risk policies provide first-party coverage insuring a contractor for damages to materials and equipment at the job site.

____ 5. **Overlap between the Performance Bond and a CGL Policy.**

____ (a) **Principal fails to obtain insurance coverage.** In the event the principal fails to obtain CGL coverage required by a contract, the surety may find itself acting as an insurer for purposes of paying losses.

____ (b) **Inadequate policy limits.** In the event the CGL policy limits are not high enough to cover the loss, a surety may be liable for the remainder of the loss.

____ (c) **Damages resulting from poor workmanship performed by subcontractors.** In some instances, a surety and a CGL insurer may both be liable for damages resulting from poor workmanship performed by subcontractors if there is coverage under the CGL policy. To the extent that the poor workmanship is the responsibility of the general contractor under its contract with the owner, the surety may be liable under its bond.

____ 6. **Builder's Risk Insurance.** Under certain circumstances, the builder's risk insurer may defend the insured's performance bond surety.

____ (a) **Election to defend in builder's risk policy.** The builder's risk policy may contain language whereby the builder's risk insurer can elect to defend the insured against suits arising from claims of owners of property.

____ (b) **Surety's subrogation rights.** As a surety is subrogated to the rights of its insureds by reason of payment, all rights of the principal inure to the benefit of the surety. The builder's risk carrier may elect to defend the surety, at least under a reservation of rights.

____ 7. **Surety's Subrogation Rights.** The surety's rights of subrogation may allow the surety to be subrogated to the principal's rights under the principal's insurance policies.

____ (a) **Payment by surety.** The surety's subrogation rights do not arise until the surety has performed by reason of payment. By reason of payment, the surety stands in the place of its principal and becomes subrogated to the rights of the principal.

____ (b) **Defenses available to the insurer.** As the surety stands in the principal's shoes by reason of subrogation, the surety is subject to all defenses that the insurer may have against the principal.

# TOPICAL LISTS

## Labor & Employment

# Checklist 51: Dealing with an OSHA Inspection and Citation

The following checklist provides considerations in dealing with an Occupational Safety and Health Administration (OSHA) inspection and citation.

____ 1. **General.**

____ (a) The inspection is OSHA's opportunity to gather information and facts to support a citation, and the employer's challenge to provide sufficient information to satisfy the compliance officer (CO) without "giving the store away."

____ (b) A key role for the lawyer is to facilitate the flow of good information and to impede the flow of information other than the minimum amount necessary to satisfy the CO.

____ (c) The employer's lawyer should "run" the inspection. The general contractor owns the site. The CO is a visitor and should not be given unfettered access to either the employees or the geography of the site.

____ 2. **Site Control.**

____ (a) No party can prevent OSHA from photographing or videotaping a project from a public right-of-way or adjacent project or building.

____ (b) COs will generally stop at the jobsite trailer before performing an inspection; however, they may begin gathering information in the form of photographs or talking to employees on their way to the trailer.

____ (c) An owner and the general contractor have the ability to limit OSHA's access to the site. A subcontractor does not have that ability.

____ (d) If you are the owner or general contractor, in almost all cases you should limit OSHA's access until the proper people can attend the inspection.

____ (e) If you are a subcontractor or other noncontrolling party, you should encourage the owner or general contractor to likewise limit access.

**Michael G. Murphy, P.E.,** is a shareholder with Greenberg Traurig in its Orlando, Florida, office. His main area of practice is general construction litigation on behalf of owners, contractors, and subcontractors. Over the past 9 years he has developed a subspecialty of representing clients in their dealings with the Occupational Safety and Health Administration, ranging from inspections to contest of citations through trial.

____ (f) In theory, the owner or general contractor can require OSHA to get a warrant. Requiring a warrant is rarely done, and the timing of the inspection is usually a matter of agreement.

____ (g) If the CO is resistant to delay the inspection, consider speaking to the area director, who may be more accommodating. In the case of a fatality, if your requested delay is reasonable (for instance, timed with the next available flight), if the site is secure, if no changes to the condition of the site will take place, and if the area director still resists your request, you may exercise the right of refusal to entry until you arrive.

____ 3. **Who should be present for the inspection?**

____ (a) For a regular inspection, the lawyer should be present if possible.

____ (b) In a fatality situation, it is almost certain that someone will be receiving an OSHA citation, someone will be subject to a worker's compensation claim, and multiple parties may be subject to a wrongful death suit. The attendance of the lawyer should be considered mandatory. See the Dealing with OSHA Regarding Fatalities checklist.

____ (c) As few people as possible is always recommended.

____ (d) For cases in which the lawyer will not attend, the attendance of a lead safety professional may have the advantage of previous experience with OSHA. The safety professional, however, may present a liability in that it has an investment in the safety program and may tend to defend or offer information when the correct course of action may be simply to listen.

____ (e) A senior management person who is not on the site on a day-to-day basis provides some unique advantages. The presence of a senior person shows the company is concerned about the situation. The senior person can probably speak generally about the company's commitment to safety, etc., but will not have the specific knowledge of the jobsite to offer any comments that could be admissions. When confronted with direct questions about a perceived hazard, the senior management person may honestly answer that he or she does not know if it is a hazard or not.

____ (f) Having the lawyer present and doing most of the talking may also work to limit inadvertent admissions by the employer. Most citations rely only upon statements by employees and management.

____ (g) The employees, and union, have a right to have a representative present at the inspection.

____ 4. **Limit Planned Scope of Inspection.**

____ (a) The scope of the inspection is usually agreed upon at the opening conference, and should be related to the purpose of the inspection and no broader than the minimum required to satisfy the CO.

____ (b) Resist turning the inspection into a comprehensive, wall-to-wall inspection.

____ (c) There is no requirement that the contractor continue working while OSHA is performing its inspection. Shutting down operations limits OSHA's ability to see employees exposed to hazards.

____ (d) The planned scope of inspection may be expanded by the CO if it observes employees exposed to a hazard. Therefore, limit the CO's observation of employees and the site as discussed below.

____ 5. **Limit Access to Employees.**

____ (a) There is no requirement that all employees must remain on site during the inspection.

____ (b) Employees standing around or walking up to the CO and the group of people conducting the inspection are often sources of information that can support a citation.

____ (c) OSHA has a right to conduct private interviews with nonmanagement employees. The employer has a right to have counsel present during an interview of management personnel.

____ (d) Identify specific individuals for interview by the CO and conduct employee interviews at the job trailer.

____ 6. **Prepare Employees for Interview by OSHA.**

____ (a) Prepare nonmanagement employees for interview by OSHA as you would a friendly nonparty for a deposition. Ask them the questions that OSHA will likely ask so they are prepared for the questions. Recognize that you will not be present at the interview and that inquiry into any preparation for the interview may be explored.

____ (b) When first asked, many employees simply forget that they have a safety program, that they received a copy of it when they hired on, that a copy of the safety manual is in their truck or the trailer, that they had generalized safety training, that the equipment provider was out at the beginning of the job and trained them on the use of fall protection, that they attended an OSHA 10-hour course, that quarterly safety meetings are held at the main office, that weekly safety meetings and tool box talks qualify as safety training, that safety people do visit the site, and that the company has an enforcement policy for safety violations.

____ (c) The hazard communication standard is perennially one of the most-cited standards. When asked about a hazard communication program, many employees blank out. Refresh their memory that they did receive hazard communication training dealing with the material safety data sheets (MSDS).

____ (d) Many employees are hesitant to identify specifics of their discipline program for fear that it admits that there are violations. Having an effective graduated system of enforcement of the company's safety policy is an element in the employee misconduct defense.

____ (e) After completing an interview, the CO will generally write out a statement in its own words and ask the employee to sign it. Employees should be advised prior to the interview that they do not have to sign anything and that they are entitled to receive a copy of anything they do sign. If the employee receives a copy of his or her statement, the employer may ask but should not pressure the employee to obtain a copy.

____ (f) Management should never sign a statement that has been written out by the CO.

____ 7. **Prepare the Site for Inspection.**

____ (a) Ensure that OSHA paperwork, including the MSDS binder and OSHA 300 logs, are up to date.

____ (b) With the exception of the area surrounding the scene of an accident that OSHA will be arriving to investigate, or other instances where OSHA has indicated an area that it intends to inspect, there is no prohibition on the employer preparing the site for inspection.

____ (c) Focus on the area to be inspected, adjacent areas, and those areas that must be passed in order to get to the site of the inspection.

____ (d) Consider dismantling problematic equipment or scaffolding, and red tag problematic equipment or scaffolding that cannot be removed.

____ (e) Dispatch an advance team to walk the path likely to be taken in conducting the inspection, if known, to identify any hazards.

____ 8. **Limit Visual Observations.**

____ (a) Proceed to the area to be inspected by the best route, which is not necessarily the most direct route. The best route limits the CO's observations of employees; work in progress generally; and sensitive work such as steel erection, leading edge work, and roofing operations.

____ (b) Consider also how you are going to get to the area to be inspected. Driving may shorten the amount of time required to get to the area. Driving also somewhat limits the ability to stop and look around. Driving can also overcome taking the long way around to stay on the best route.

____ 9. **Identification and Correction of Hazards.**

____ (a) During the inspection, the CO may identify hazards and request that they be corrected. Immediately correcting hazards is a two-edged sword in that a citation may not be issued based upon the immediate correction, but agreeing to correct the hazard may be an admission that a violation existed.

____ (b) Avoid confusion in admitting the existence of a violation. The CO may say, "Do you see that handrail missing"? The answer, "Yes," may be interpreted many different ways. At trial the CO may testify that the employer knew of the hazard ("he said he knew the handrail was missing"), the employer knew it was a violation ("he said he knew it was missing and needed to be replaced"), or a host of other incriminating admissions.

____ (c) At the outset of the inspection, make clear that the employer is not agreeing that any hazards or violations exist. Come to an understanding that the employer may acknowledge the condition that the CO is pointing out, but simply acknowledging the observation is not an agreement with the CO's evaluation of the condition.

____ (d) Create a one-for-one documentation of all photographs, videos, or other recordings created by OSHA.

____ 10. **Post-Inspection Communication.**

____ (a) Inform the CO that all post-inspection communication should be directed to the lawyer.

____ (b) Prepare a letter to the area director, following up on the request for communications to be directed to the lawyer.

____ (c) Gather all documents requested by OSHA, and forward copies of same. Bates label all documents produced.

____ (d) Begin gathering documents that may support the employer's affirmative defenses, including records related to enforcement of its safety policy.

____ 11. **Informal Settlement.**

____ (a) After receipt of the citation, there is a 15-working-day window in which to meet with OSHA and possibly reach a negotiated settlement.

____ (b) Some practitioners report success at the informal hearing in having OSHA completely dismiss particular citation items when presented with a compelling argument.

____ (c) Reasonable expectations for settlement at the informal conference should include a reduction of the penalty amount ranging up to 40%, but in general do not include reduction in the seriousness or complete dismissal of any of the individual items in the citation.

____ (d) There is no requirement to attend an informal conference, and the employer is free to proceed directly to notice of contest upon receipt of the citation.

____ 12. **Contest of Citation.**

____ (a) The employer has 15 working days after the date of the citation to contest the citation. After 15 days, the citation becomes a final order, and attempting to "undo" this default is practically impossible.

____ (b) The notice of contest is directed to the area office that issued the citation. Although not strictly required, certified mail with return receipt and copy by facsimile is recommended.

____ (c) There are no strict form requirements for the notice of contest. It should indicate the inspection number and that the employer is contesting one or more of the citations, penalty amount, and/or abatement.

____ (d) The recommended notice of contest would simply say: "Please consider this notice of contest of the above-referenced citation. The employer contests the citation, penalty, and abatement."

____ 13. **Administrative Hearing.**

____ (a) After receiving the contest of citation, OSHA forwards the case file to its lawyer, the Regional Solicitor. The Regional Solicitor then has 20 days to file a complaint with the Occupational Safety and Health Review Commission (OSHRC).

____ (b) The OSHRC is an independent government agency comprised of 13 administrative law judges (ALJs), whose sole job is to hear contests of OSHA citations. They operate under their own rules of evidence similar to and supplemented by the federal rules.

____ (c) The OSHRC has a simplified proceeding that purports to offer the employer necessary due process without pleadings, without formal rules of evidence, and with only limited discovery. In short, the rules are eliminated to accommodate the trial of the case by unrepresented employers. Simplified proceedings should be avoided if a lawyer is going to handle the matter.

____ (d) The case will be assigned to an ALJ and set for final hearing to occur usually within about 6 months.

____ (e) The OSHRC rules of procedure provide for requests for production, requests for admission, interrogatories, and depositions upon agreement of the parties.

____ (f) As in many cases, the best settlements may be obtained by forcing the other side to spend money prosecuting its case. The effective use of discovery can aid in this effort.

____ (g) The first interrogatory to OSHA should ask for an identification of the people with knowledge. The answer to this interrogatory will most likely include the CO, its boss, the assistant area director, and the area director. This answer can then be used to establish the need to depose each of these people.

____ (h) Settlement is possible at any time during this proceeding and can include up to complete dismissal by the government.

# Checklist 52: Dealing with OSHA Regarding Fatalities

The Occupational Safety and Health Administration (OSHA) aims to ensure employee safety and health in the United States by working with employers and employees to create better working environments. According to OSHA statistics, there are close to 6,000 employee deaths each year. Because OSHA penalties range from $0 to $70,000, depending on how likely the violation is to result in serious harm to employees, it is important for employers to follow all requirements of the Occupational Safety and Health Act (OSHAct) in dealing with a fatality. The following checklist will help employers to navigate OSHAct requirements when dealing with a fatality.

____ 1. **General.**

____ (a) In a fatality situation, the employer is faced with the requirement to give notice to OSHA and its carriers, as well as issues of evidence preservation.

____ (b) Because of the requirement to notify OSHA, there will almost always be an inspection. The inspection procedures covered in the "Dealing with an OSHA Inspection and Citation" checklist apply equally in the case of a fatality.

____ 2. **Requirement to Notify OSHA.**

____ (a) The requirement to notify OSHA rests with the employer only. An owner, general contractor, subcontractor, or other employer that is not the direct employer of the person involved in the accident, does not have an obligation to notify OSHA.

____ (b) The requirement to notify OSHA arises if there is either a fatality or three or more hospitalizations that occur within 30 days of an accident. For example, if there is an accident and an employee dies from his or her injuries 30 days after the accident, the employer must notify OSHA. Similarly, if there is an accident in which two employees are immediately hospitalized and the third employee is hospitalized 1 week later, the employer must notify OSHA.

**Michael G. Murphy, P.E.,** is a shareholder with Greenberg Traurig in its Orlando, Florida, office. His main area of practice is general construction litigation on behalf of owners, contractors, and subcontractors. Over the past 9 years he has developed a subspecialty of representing clients in their dealings with the Occupational Safety and Health Administration ranging from inspections to contest of citations through trial.

____ (c) The employer has 8 hours from learning of the fatality or three or more hospitalizations to inform OSHA. There is not an obligation to call OSHA immediately upon learning of the incident. However, there are no legal justifications for delaying beyond the 8 hours.

____ (d) OSHA can be notified by telephone to the local area office or by calling 1-800-321-OSHA. You must speak to a person, and notice by voicemail, fax, or e-mail is not acceptable.

____ (e) On-the-job heart attacks resulting in fatality are a reportable incident. Motor vehicle accidents on public streets outside the work zone do not have to be reported.

____ (f) The occurrence of a reportable event is one of the rare instances in which the employer knows in advance that an inspection will occur and to some extent may be able to control when the inspection occurs. OSHA may learn of the fatality through news reports; reporting by police, fire, or other emergency response units; or by someone other than the employer calling OSHA.

____ (g) To the extent the employer can control when OSHA becomes aware of the incident, the employer should use the 8-hour notification window to its advantage to prepare for the inspection. For details on how to prepare for the inspection, see the Dealing with an OSHA Inspection and Citation checklist.

____ 3. **Accident/Incident Reports.**

____ (a) Particularly in fatality situations, there is often pressure on the employer to create an accident report. This pressure comes from owners, the general contractor, in-house safety departments and various carriers. Do not allow your client to fill out an accident report without your involvement.

____ (b) Most accident report forms have been created for two purposes: (i) to create a record of the accident for worker's compensation and (ii) to provide feedback to the safety department. The importance of these purposes is overshadowed by the potential liability inherent in a fatality situation, and standard forms should not be used.

____ (c) Standard forms often contain questions that require subjective information and evaluation. They will often ask what caused the accident and what can be done to prevent a similar occurrence in the future. These questions are well and good for minor accidents; however, for most fatalities, "why the fatality occurred" and "what can be done to prevent another one in the future" are not easily ascertainable. A site person's guess as to these answers can form the basis of an admission and should be avoided.

____ (d) Accident reports should only contain what will be undisputed issues of fact in any subsequent proceeding. It should contain only those facts that you would "admit" when served with a complaint: date of accident, name of employee, location of the accident, time of accident (if known), location on project, etc.

____ 4. **Secure the Area of the Incident.**

____ (a) The employer and emergency response personnel may partially disturb the site of the accident in order to aid any injured persons. Also, action should be taken to safeguard the area to prevent any further accidents. After these initial actions are taken, the site should be secured from further disturbance.

____ (b) Generally, the police will have initial control of the area. After the police have released the site, it will be the contractor's responsibility to preserve the site until other parties have had a chance to make their own observations.

____ (c) After the police, the next people in line to perform their inspection would be OSHA, and the contractor should ensure that the site is not disturbed until OSHA has released the site. If the OSHA inspection will not occur until the next day, security should be hired.

____ (d) The inspection by the police and OSHA prior to disturbing the site should be considered mandatory. Inspections by other parties are discretionary and should be based upon notice, opportunity to inspect, and negotiation with the interested parties. See item 5, "Notice to Other Parties."

____ 5. **Notice to Other Parties.**

____ (a) An insured has an obligation to notify its carrier of a loss or potential loss. Both the worker's compensation carrier and the general liability carrier should be put on notice.

____ (b) Carriers should be put on notice almost immediately by phone, with written notice to follow, within an hour or so.

____ (c) The notice to the carrier is two-pronged: notice of the loss and notice of opportunity to inspect the scene of the accident.

____ 6. **Inspection by Other Parties.**

____ (a) After the site is released by OSHA, the general contractor has the ability to clean up the site of the accident and continue work in the area. The clean-up and continuing work should not be completed until inspection by other parties is completed and preservation of evidence issues are addressed.

____ (b) To avoid spoliation issues being raised by other parties and their carriers as a defense, they should be given opportunity to inspect the scene. In some cases, the carriers can be helpful in securing and paying for experts to inspect and take photographs of the scene.

____ 7. **Preservation of Evidence.**

____ (a) Consider preserving as much evidence as possible. In building construction, there may be some portion of what could be physical evidence that is incorporated into or covered up by the final work. However, to the extent there is physical evidence that is not part of the work, it should be preserved.

____ (b) Ownership of the physical evidence may be an issue. For instance, scaffold rental agreements may speak to the rental company obtaining possession after an accident.

____ (c) To the extent that someone other than your client is taking possession of physical evidence, immediately write a letter to the party taking possession requesting that it preserve all evidence and prevent any spoliation.

____ (d) To the extent your client is taking possession of physical evidence, ensure that it takes all due diligence to preserve it. The evidence should be properly stored. It should not simply be placed in the equipment yard where it may undergo degradation or be mistakenly reused.

# Checklist 53: Handling a "Salting" Campaign

Nonunion employers confronted with the reality of having to deal with a union salting campaign or other similar organizing effort should use the following checklist to assist in the identification and evaluation of some of the issues and options that may arise.

____ 1. **Definition.** "Salting" is a prominent labor union organizing tactic, particularly in the construction industry, in which unions send paid or unpaid organizers, or "salts," to apply for jobs with nonunion companies in an attempt to organize or force these companies to enter into a union contract. Upon application for a job with a nonunion company, salts will either conceal or openly announce their union membership and/or intent to organize the nonunion company.

____ 2. **Methods of Union Salting.** A union may use one of the following methods to "salt" the employer:

____ (a) **Unlawful termination of salt.**

____ (i) **Firing of salt—ULP charge.** A union may send out a member to apply for a job with a construction company, all the while hiding the member's union membership. If and when the member (aka "salt") is hired by the company, the salt will attempt to organize the other employees. In so doing, the salt may try to claim that the company is unfair to its employees (for example, by picketing the jobsite). Typically, the salt's actions will result in violations of company policy, forcing the company to fire the salt or forcing the salt to quit voluntarily. At that point, the union will file an unfair labor practice (ULP) charge with the National Labor Relations Board (NLRB), charging that the company discriminated against the salt because of his or her union affiliation.

____ (ii) **Solicitation of employees.** A union may solicit a current employee of the construction company to

**Robert J. Orelup** is a partner in the Indianapolis, Indiana, construction law firm of Drewry Simmons Vornehm LLP. He frequently counsels and represents construction industry employers in a wide variety of employment and labor-related matters, including union-management matters.

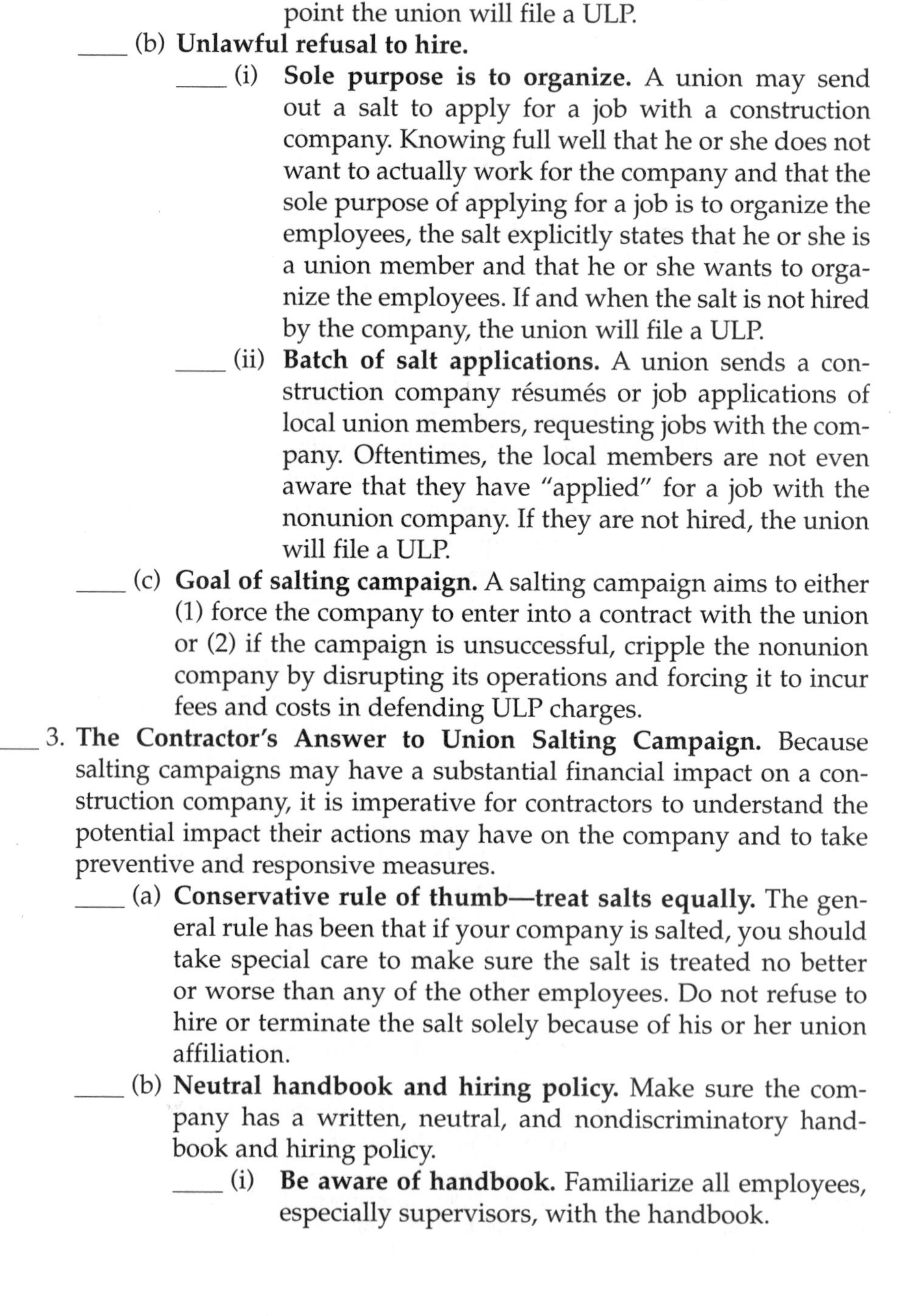

become a salt, paying such employee to attempt to organize the company. As with other examples, the salt will then purposely violate company rules and will either be fired or voluntarily quit, at which point the union will file a ULP.

____ (b) **Unlawful refusal to hire.**

____ (i) **Sole purpose is to organize.** A union may send out a salt to apply for a job with a construction company. Knowing full well that he or she does not want to actually work for the company and that the sole purpose of applying for a job is to organize the employees, the salt explicitly states that he or she is a union member and that he or she wants to organize the employees. If and when the salt is not hired by the company, the union will file a ULP.

____ (ii) **Batch of salt applications.** A union sends a construction company résumés or job applications of local union members, requesting jobs with the company. Oftentimes, the local members are not even aware that they have "applied" for a job with the nonunion company. If they are not hired, the union will file a ULP.

____ (c) **Goal of salting campaign.** A salting campaign aims to either (1) force the company to enter into a contract with the union or (2) if the campaign is unsuccessful, cripple the nonunion company by disrupting its operations and forcing it to incur fees and costs in defending ULP charges.

____ 3. **The Contractor's Answer to Union Salting Campaign.** Because salting campaigns may have a substantial financial impact on a construction company, it is imperative for contractors to understand the potential impact their actions may have on the company and to take preventive and responsive measures.

____ (a) **Conservative rule of thumb—treat salts equally.** The general rule has been that if your company is salted, you should take special care to make sure the salt is treated no better or worse than any of the other employees. Do not refuse to hire or terminate the salt solely because of his or her union affiliation.

____ (b) **Neutral handbook and hiring policy.** Make sure the company has a written, neutral, and nondiscriminatory handbook and hiring policy.

____ (i) **Be aware of handbook.** Familiarize all employees, especially supervisors, with the handbook.

____ (ii) **Consistently apply rules.** Make sure that all rules are uniformly and consistently applied to both union and nonunion applicants and employees.

____ (iii) **Require complete applications and tests.** Require that all applicants complete the employment application and take the necessary tests prior to being hired.

____ (iv) **Check references for each applicant.**

____ (c) **"Genuinely interested" in employment.** The NLRB has recently held that a union salt must be "genuinely interested" in employment with nonunion company for protection under the National Labor Relations Act (NLRA).

____ (d) **Refusing to hire a salt because of lack of genuine interest.**

____ (i) **Documented evidence.** A company should exercise caution and make sure that it has sufficient and well-documented evidence of an applicant's lack of genuine interest before refusing to hire an applicant because he or she is a union salt.

____ (ii) **Indication of lack of genuine interest.** The employer can attempt to create a reasonable question of genuine interest in employment through evidence that:

____ a. The applicant rejected a prior employer's job offer.

____ b. The applicant included offensive or belligerent language on application.

____ c. The applicant engaged in disruptive or antagonistic behavior during application process.

____ d. The application contained incomplete or out-of-date information.

____ 4. **Communications with the Union.** In the event a union organizer arrives at the construction company's offices or contacts the company by telephone to discuss unionization of the company's employees, the following is a list of items important to keep in mind:

____ (a) **What should be done upon realizing that the company is a target for union organizing?** Advise the company that it should immediately contact its labor attorney or other counsel knowledgeable in the area of labor law.

____ (b) **What should be done when the union offers to give the company something to look over?** The company should *not* look over anything that is offered by the union, especially authorization cards signed by employees. Doing so could create a presumption of union recognition.

____ (c) **What if the union attempts to discuss any term or condition of employment?** The company is *not* required to enter into discussions regarding any labor contract proposals, employment benefits, or personnel policies.

____ (d) **What should the company say instead of entering into such discussions?** The company may say that it has a good-faith doubt that the union represents an uncoerced majority of the employees in an appropriate bargaining unit.

____ (e) **Insist on an election.** Advise the company to insist on the holding of an election administered by the NLRB prior to any recognition of the union as the employee's bargaining representative.

____ (f) **What if the company receives a letter from the union during a salting/organizing campaign?** Advise the company of the following steps:

____ (i) **Don't open a union package.** If the envelope or package is thick (that is, it possibly contains authorization cards), do *not* open it, and call your labor attorney immediately.

____ (ii) **Don't look at cards.** In the event the letter was inadvertently opened and it does contain authorization cards, do *not* look at the cards. Explain that the letter was opened by mistake and that the cards were not looked at. Then, place the cards back in the envelope, seal it, and call your labor attorney immediately.

____ (iii) **Communicate a good-faith doubt of union representation.** If the letter does not contain authorization cards or any other evidence that the employees have selected the union as their representative, but merely claims that the union represents the employees, the company or its counsel should write a response to the union in which it expresses good-faith doubt of the union's claim. It is advisable to have an attorney at least review the letter prior to sending it to the union.

____ 5. **Communications among Management and Supervisors.**

____ (a) **What should be done upon realizing that the union is seeking to organize the employees?**

____ (i) **Meet with senior management.** The company's chief executive should meet with senior management in an effort to determine exactly why the union is looking to organize the employees and to determine what organizing activity has already taken place.

____ (ii) **Meet with all supervisors.** It is also advisable that the chief executive meet, either individually or collectively, with all front-line supervisory personnel, with an attorney present, to brief them on the organizing campaign and to determine what the supervisors know. It is important to note that this meeting should *not* include any personnel who may be eligible to vote in a union election.

____ (iii) **Determine company "supervisors."** The company's labor attorney needs to determine who is considered a "supervisor" under the NLRA. Supervisors are not eligible to vote in union elections and can commit ULPs as agents of management.

____ (b) **What should be said to the supervisors?** It is important to clearly and effectively state the company's position to all supervisors. Explain the following:

____ (i) **No need for union representation.** Provided management is doing its job well, there is no need for union representation of the employees.

____ (ii) **Discourage through legitimate means.** The company will attempt, by legitimate means, to discourage employees from signing authorization cards and voting for a union.

____ (iii) **No discrimination.** Perhaps most importantly, the company will not discriminate against employees on the basis of union activity or affiliation.

____ 6. **Employee Communications—"TIPS" to Follow.** Generally speaking, it is important for supervisors and management to follow TIPS, a convenient acronym to remember things that should *not* be said or done to employees during a salting or other organizing campaign.

____ (a) **"T" is for *threaten.*** Do *not* threaten individuals participating in union activities with reprisals such as reducing their benefits, terminating their employment, or any other form of retaliation. Needless to say, do *not* commit the threatened acts.

____ (b) **"I" is for *interrogate.*** Do *not* question employees as to whether they signed union cards or whether they support the organizing effort, how they intend to vote, or how they feel about union representation.

____ (c) **"P" is for *promise.*** Do *not* promise wage or benefit increases, promotions, or future benefits to employees for opposing the union. Also, do *not* grant the promised benefits.

____ (d) **"S" is for *spy.*** Do *not* spy on union activities to determine who is attending meetings, signing cards, or supporting the union, regardless of whether it applies to on- and off-work time and on- and off-work premises.

____ 7. **Employee Communications—Do's and Don'ts.** In addition to following the aforementioned TIPS, supervisors and management should be made aware of the following do's and don'ts in handling salting or other organizational campaigns:

____ (a) *Do* increase personal contacts with the workers and have informal conversations with them as often as possible. But *don't* interrogate or question workers about how they feel about union representation or whether they support the organizing effort.

____ (b) *Do* have all supervisors forward any information discovered about the organizing campaign to the chief executive, as well as any noticed changes in employee attitude, evidence of union coercion, employee huddles, and rumors. But *don't* threaten, interrogate, or spy on employees to obtain such information.

____ (c) *Do* talk with employees about unions, individually or in groups, at any time in any public place or open work area. But *don't* talk with employees about unions in any private management office.

____ (d) *Do* tell the employees of the company's disapproval of unions and union policies, including sharing any bad experiences with unions that happened either to the company or to others. But *don't* make false statements or untruthful statements.

____ (e) *Do* truthfully rebut union propaganda, arguments, or claims by disclosing facts about the company's operation. But *don't* base such statements on incorrect or untruthful facts.

____ (f) *Do* be positive and emphasize that the company's history with its employees and the outlook for the future shows that a union is not necessary, while also pointing out any problem areas or mistakes the company has made and how the company is working on improving those areas. But *don't* make promises that certain problems or issues will be resolved if the company is not unionized.

____ (g) *Do* point out the negative aspects of having a union, such as the following: (i) hiring restrictions which may require the company to replace workers and/or hire less productive ones, (ii) decreased functionality of the "team," (iii) placing the company's competitiveness in jeopardy, (iv) loss of flexibility in work rules and discipline, (v) more formal communications with management, and (vi) the possibility of union fines. But *don't* say that bad things about a union will automatically happen if the company is unionized.

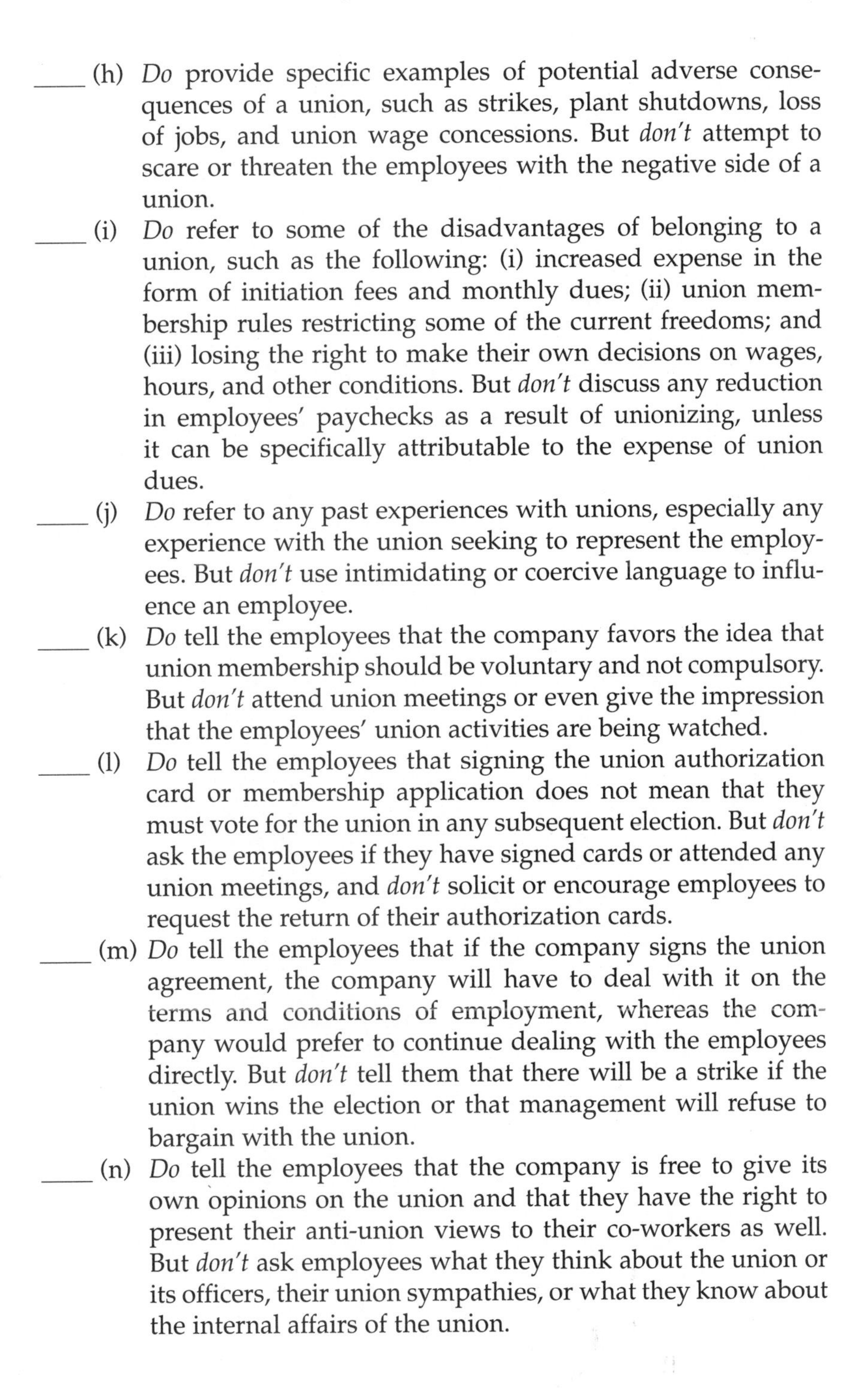

____ (h) *Do* provide specific examples of potential adverse consequences of a union, such as strikes, plant shutdowns, loss of jobs, and union wage concessions. But *don't* attempt to scare or threaten the employees with the negative side of a union.

____ (i) *Do* refer to some of the disadvantages of belonging to a union, such as the following: (i) increased expense in the form of initiation fees and monthly dues; (ii) union membership rules restricting some of the current freedoms; and (iii) losing the right to make their own decisions on wages, hours, and other conditions. But *don't* discuss any reduction in employees' paychecks as a result of unionizing, unless it can be specifically attributable to the expense of union dues.

____ (j) *Do* refer to any past experiences with unions, especially any experience with the union seeking to represent the employees. But *don't* use intimidating or coercive language to influence an employee.

____ (k) *Do* tell the employees that the company favors the idea that union membership should be voluntary and not compulsory. But *don't* attend union meetings or even give the impression that the employees' union activities are being watched.

____ (l) *Do* tell the employees that signing the union authorization card or membership application does not mean that they must vote for the union in any subsequent election. But *don't* ask the employees if they have signed cards or attended any union meetings, and *don't* solicit or encourage employees to request the return of their authorization cards.

____ (m) *Do* tell the employees that if the company signs the union agreement, the company will have to deal with it on the terms and conditions of employment, whereas the company would prefer to continue dealing with the employees directly. But *don't* tell them that there will be a strike if the union wins the election or that management will refuse to bargain with the union.

____ (n) *Do* tell the employees that the company is free to give its own opinions on the union and that they have the right to present their anti-union views to their co-workers as well. But *don't* ask employees what they think about the union or its officers, their union sympathies, or what they know about the internal affairs of the union.

# Checklist 54: Employer Compliance with Federal Labor and Employment Laws

An employer that considers taking any type of employment action with regard to an employee that may be construed as "adverse" should understand that such actions may be covered by and trigger any number of federal employment and labor laws. Virtually every employee is protected by the federal antidiscrimination laws, and employers must take care to ensure that actions taken are consistent and in compliance with all laws.

Employers should be aware of and must pay close attention to the existence and provisions of these laws and ensure that their practices and actions are in accordance and in compliance with all federal law. Following is a checklist and survey of important federal laws and obligations of employers and rights of employees for employers to consider prior to taking perceived adverse actions against an employee or applicant. Importantly, an employer's failure to follow its own policies, practices, or contracts may also translate into inferences of discrimination and potential violations of federal law.

____ 1. **Before disciplining or terminating an employee, ask the following questions:**

- ____ (a) Do we have a policy that covers this situation and the employee's behavior?
- ____ (b) Are we following the policy?
- ____ (c) If not, why not?
- ____ (d) Is this a valid reason to make an exception?
- ____ (e) Do we have a company practice that covers this behavior?
- ____ (f) Are we following it?
- ____ (g) If not, why not?
- ____ (h) Have other employees demonstrated this or similar behavior?
- ____ (i) Have we treated those employees as we plan to treat this employee?
- ____ (j) Are we treating this employee differently than others who have acted similarly?
- ____ (k) Is there a contract, collective bargaining agreement, or written document which discusses or covers this behavior or the company's planned action?

**Kristine L. Cato** is a partner in the Columbia, South Carolina, law firm of McAngus Goudelock & Courie, where she leads the firm's employment law practice group. She is a certified specialist in labor and employment law.

____ (l) Are we following it?

____ (m) By taking the planned action, will we be in compliance with all applicable company documents and verbal assurances?

____ 2. **National Labor Relations Act (NLRA).**

____ (a) The NLRA provides all employees:

____ (i) The right to organize and join a union.

____ (ii) The right to bargain collectively.

____ (iii) The right to engage in strikes, picketing, and other concerted activities.

____ (b) It covers virtually all employers engaged in commerce. However, the NLRA specifically excludes the U.S. government or wholly owned government corporations, Federal Reserve banks, any state or its political subsidiaries, employers subject to the Railway Labor Act, and labor organizations.

____ (c) The NLRA also excludes from coverage agricultural laborers, domestic employees, supervisors, independent contractors, and employees of employers subject to the Railway Labor Act.

____ (d) The NLRA covers employees *and* applicants. It prohibits employers from taking adverse actions based on union or nonunion actions or interests.

____ (e) The NLRA specifically prohibits employers from interfering with, restraining, or coercing employees in the exercise of these rights.

____ (f) Employers are prohibited from interrogating employees, which may simply be asking their opinions about unions.

____ (g) Employers are also prohibited from making threats or promises to employees to deter them from union interest or sympathy, or engaging in surveillance of union activity.

____ (h) Employers are further prohibited from discriminating or retaliating against employees because of their involvement with a union or union activity.

____ (i) For all employers, even those without a union representing their employees, the protections of the NLRA exist at all times, not just when the threat of union activity is imminent.

____ (j) Employees are entitled to engage in "protected concerted activity without fear of termination." If employees act in concert to complain about a term or condition of employment, they may not be terminated for such activity.

____ (k) Employers may not prohibit employees from talking to or about a union.

____ (l) Employers should ensure that they have an enforceable "solicitation/distribution" policy in effect to deal with unwanted propaganda.

____ (m) Employers should communicate their desire and intent to maintain a union-free environment, both verbally and in writing.

____ (n) Employers should train their managers and supervisors regarding employee rights and employer obligations.

____ (o) Employers should train their managers and supervisors regarding signs of union activity.

(See the "Handling a 'Salting' Campaign" checklist for further details.)

____ 3. **Fair Labor Standards Act (FLSA).**

____ (a) The FLSA establishes minimum wage, overtime pay, record-keeping, and child labor standards for covered private employers and for federal, state, and local governments.

____ (b) The FLSA requires employers to pay employees who are not exempt from the overtime provisions of the FLSA at least $5.15 per hour. It also requires employers to pay overtime pay for each hour worked over 40 hours in a workweek, at a rate of one-and-a-half times the regular rate of pay.

____ (c) The FLSA provides exemptions from the payment of overtime for employees who fall into an executive, administrative, professional, outside sales, or computer-related (programming and systems analysis) categories.

____ (d) Employers should analyze their jobs and create job descriptions for all positions. Employers should ensure they have accurately characterized their employees as exempt or nonexempt.

____ (e) To qualify for any exemption, employees must meet the "salary" and "duties" test. To meet the "salary" test for all exemptions, employees must be compensated at a rate of no less than $455 per week.

____ (f) To qualify for the executive exemption and meet the "duties" test, the employee's primary duty must be that of a manager of a department or customarily recognized subdivision, who customarily and regularly directs the work of two or more other employees; and who has the authority to hire or fire other employees, or whose suggestions and recommendations as to the hiring, firing, advancement, promotion, or any other change in status of other employees are given particular weight.

____ (g) To qualify for the professional exemption and meet the "duties" test, the employee's primary duty must be a performance of work that requires knowledge of an advanced type in a field of science or learning customarily acquired by a prolonged course of specialized intellectual instruction;

or required invention, imagination, originality, or talent in a recognized field of artistic or creative endeavor.

____ (h) To qualify for the administrative exemption and meet the "duties" test, the employee's primary duty must be the performance of office or nonmanual work directly related to the management and general business operations of the employer or the employer's customer, which includes the exercise of discretion and independent judgment with respect to matters of significance.

____ (i) Employers that make improper deductions from the pay of employees they classify as exempt may inadvertently lose the protection of the exemption. In general, exempt employees should not have any deductions made from their salaries for missed time in any week in which they work.

____ (j) If employers do make such improper deductions, they could be liable for all overtime the employee and others in the same classification have worked.

____ (k) If the employer fails to reimburse employees for improper deductions or continues to make improper deductions after receiving employee complaints, the exemption is lost during the time period in which the improper deductions were made for employees in the same job classification working with the same managers responsible for the actual improper deductions.

____ (l) Employers should review their payroll practices for exempt employees to ensure that they are not making improper deductions and inadvertently lose the protection of the exemption for those employees and others similarly situated.

____ (m) Employers who have improperly classified their employees as exempt are liable for all unpaid overtime, attorney's fees, and liquidated damages.

____ (n) The FLSA requires that employers maintain employee payroll records for at least 3 years, including name, address, pay by pay period, hours worked, overtime (for nonexempt employees), and deductions.

____ 4. **Title VII of the Civil Rights Act and the Age Discrimination in Employment Act (ADEA).**

____ (a) Title VII and the ADEA prohibit discrimination in employment on the basis of race, gender, religion, national origin, and age.

____ (b) Employers with 15 or more employees are covered.

____ (c) Employers are also prohibited from harassing and allowing harassment to occur based on those factors.

____ (d) Employers may not retaliate against employees complaining of harassment or discrimination.

____ (e) Employers should ensure that employment decisions are not made based on race, gender, religion, national origin, or age.

____ (f) Employers must have a policy in place prohibiting discrimination and harassment based on race, gender, religion, national origin, and age. The policy should also prohibit retaliation.

____ (g) The policy should provide an avenue for employees to complain and a commitment to investigate all complaints quickly and thoroughly and to take appropriate remedial action.

____ (h) Employers should train all managers and supervisors regarding this policy and the law.

____ (i) Employers should communicate the policy to all employees.

____ (j) Employers should regularly monitor all disciplinary action to ensure consistent administration and implementation of policies and procedures.

____ 5. **Americans with Disabilities Act (ADA).**

____ (a) The ADA prohibits discrimination in all employment actions against individuals who are disabled but still capable of performing the essential functions of the job in question.

____ (b) Employers with 15 or more employees are covered.

____ (c) Employers may not take adverse action against an employee because of his or her disability, perceived disability, or history of disability.

____ (d) The ADA requires employers to make certain accommodations if needed by the disabled individual to perform the essential functions of his or her job.

____ (e) Employers are prohibited from seeking medical information from employees or using it as a basis for any employment decision.

____ (f) The ADA defines "disability" to include a physical or mental impairment that substantially limits one or more major life activities. It also includes "having a record" of a substantially limiting impairment or "being regarded" as having a substantially limiting impairment.

____ (g) Employers are also prohibited from harassing and allowing harassment based on an individual's disability, perceived disability, or record of a disability.

____ (h) Employers may not retaliate against employees complaining of harassment or discrimination.

____ (i) Employers should ensure that employment decisions are not made based on a person's disability, perceived disability, or record of disability.

____ (j) Employers must have a policy in place prohibiting discrimination and harassment based on a person's disability, perceived disability, or record of disability. The policy should also prohibit retaliation.

____ (k) The policy should provide an avenue for employees to complain and a commitment to investigate all complaints quickly and thoroughly and to take appropriate remedial action.

____ (l) Employers should do all the same training, communications, and monitoring they would do under Title VII and the ADEA.

____ (m) Damages that can be awarded against an employer to a successful complainant may be actual damages, such as back-pay and/or reinstatement, as well as punitive or compensatory damages up to $300,000 per violation.

____ 6. **Family and Medical Leave Act (FMLA).**

____ (a) The FMLA requires employers that have 50 employees within a 75-mile radius to provide up to 12 weeks of unpaid leave in any 12-month period to eligible employees for the birth or placement of a child or for the serious health condition of the employee or a member of the employee's immediate family.

____ (b) To be eligible, an employee must have 1 year of service and have worked 1,250 hours within the previous 12-month period.

____ (c) A "serious health condition" means an illness, injury, impairment, or physical or mental condition that involves: (i) inpatient care in a hospital, hospice, or residential medical care facility, including any period of incapacity or any subsequent treatment in connection with such inpatient care; or (ii) continuing treatment by a health care provider.

____ (d) Eligible employees may be entitled to leave in blocks of time, or on an intermittent or reduced leave schedule, based on the nature of their condition and treatment.

____ (e) Employers are entitled to have FMLA leave run concurrently with any other leave to which the employee may be entitled, and may require employees to take vacation or other paid leave before taking the unpaid leave.

____ (f) If an employee has been out of work for more than 3 consecutive days, he or she may be entitled to protected leave. This may trigger "notice" to the employer to notify the employee of his or her rights and/or offer leave.

____ (g) *Beware!* Employees are generally not required to affirmatively assert a specific request for FMLA leave in order to be entitled to it.

____ (h) Employers are prohibited from interfering with, restraining or denying an employee's right to exercise his or her rights granted by the FMLA.

____ (i) Employers should have a written policy complying with the regulations accompanying the FMLA.

____ (j) Once employers have any notice that eligible employees have a condition covered by the FMLA or any absence covered by the FMLA, they should provisionally cover that time as FMLA and require the employee to have the appropriate medical certification form completed by a health care provider to confirm its coverage under the FMLA.

# Checklist 55: Ensuring Jobsite Harmony

A contractor may find itself agreeing to a contract containing a "Peace and Harmony" clause. These clauses attempt to ensure that a contractor will do nothing to disrupt peace and harmony on the jobsite. The following checklist will help contractors understand the contract ramifications of such clauses.

____ 1. **What are "Peace and Harmony" clauses?**

- ____ (a) There are different types of "Peace and Harmony" requirements. Peace and Harmony clauses typically attempt to ensure that the contractor will do nothing to disrupt the performance of work on a jobsite.
- ____ (b) Peace and Harmony requirements are typically buried in other miscellaneous contract provisions.
- ____ (c) Many contractors sign Peace and Harmony clauses, mistakenly assuming that they or their employees will do nothing to disrupt the jobsite.
- ____ (d) Many Peace and Harmony clauses are written so broadly that if the owner (or general contractor) decides that the cause of the disruption means the mere presence of contractor or its (nonunion) employees, the general contractor or owner may declare a breach of the Peace and Harmony clause. Before agreeing to a Peace and Harmony clause, the following should be analyzed:
  - ____ (i) Who is responsible for Peace and Harmony?
    - ____ a. Is it the project manager? Is it the general contractor? Is it the construction manager? Is it the owner?
    - ____ b. Even if the project manager or the general contractor is technically "responsible," who else should be prepared to take charge of the situation before it boils over?
  - ____ (ii) Is the Peace and Harmony requirement too broad or onerous to assume the risk?

**Frank T. Mamat** is a shareholder in the Farmington Hills, Michigan firm of Foster, Swift, Collins & Smith, P.C. As part of his construction practice, he frequently represents construction owners, contractors, and subcontractors facing labor, union, Employee Retirement Income Security Act, and Occupational Safety and Health Administration issues.

____ 2. **Is the jobsite dispute labor-related? What are the potential consequences of a labor dispute?**

____ (a) Is the labor dispute a jurisdictional issue between local unions?

____ (b) Does the labor dispute involve traditional jobsite picketing of a nonunion project by union labor?

____ (c) What are the available legal rights in case the Peace and Harmony clause is invoked?

____ (d) What are the available legal rights and options to respond to a jobsite disruption?

____ (i) Can a dual gate be set up at a picketed jobsite?

____ (ii) If not, can a reserved time system be established?

____ (iii) Can the "troublesome" union causing the disharmony at the jobsite be enticed to sign a "job-only" labor agreement?

____ (e) Penalties to contractors in breach of a Peace and Harmony clause can range from daily fines and damages to removal from the job and suspension of payments. Ultimately, legal action may be initiated against the contractor for higher costs incurred by the new contractors and consequential damages and costs.

____ (f) Is there a "Termination for Convenience" provision in the contract? Some owners and contractors use Termination for Convenience provisions to resolve jobsite labor disputes by removing the contractor that is the target of a labor dispute.

____ 3. **Keys to jobsite harmony.**

____ (a) **What kind of jobsite is it?**

____ (i) Who is the owner? Is the owner supportive of union labor? Is the owner against union labor? What is the owner's reputation with the local unions? How has the owner handled past jobsite disputes?

____ (ii) Who is the general contractor? Is the general contractor a union contractor? Is the general contractor anti-union? How has the general contractor handled past jobsite disputes?

____ (iii) Is the construction manager a union contractor? Is the construction manager anti-union? How has the construction manager handled past jobsite disputes?

____ (iv) What are the local governmental labor requirements and restrictions (for example, prevailing wage requirements; project labor agreement statutes).

____ (b) **Know your workforce.**

____ (i) Is the general contractor a union signatory?

____ (ii) Are current employees union members?
____ a. Did they ever join a union?
____ b. If so, are they still members in good standing?
____ c. Did they (properly) resign from a union?
____ d. Were their union benefits vested?
____ e. Would they cross a picket line?
____ f. Would they be fined by the union if they did?
____ g. Would they lose their benefits if they had to cross a picket line?

____ 4. **What to do in case of a picket line.**
____ (a) Setting up a dual gate or reserved gate system will not make pickets go away—it will only allow union employees to avoid having to cross a picket line and allow a secondary boycott charge to be filed against the union.
____ (i) Identify which company on the jobsite the union is targeting.
____ (ii) Identify which union is leading the pickets.
____ (iii) Document (with photographs) the language on the picket signs.
____ (iv) Decide which "entrance" you will reserve for the targeted company.
____ (v) Notify the union in writing which is "Gate 1" and which is "Gate 2," and when the dual-gate system starts.
____ (vi) Make sure that the gate reserved for the non-targeted companies is not used by employees, suppliers, visitors, or owners of the targeted company.
____ (vii) Use proper language at your gate signs that is legible and readable (two-sided, at least 3 feet by 3 feet). Examples of language for signs include:
____ a. THIS GATE IS RESERVED FOR THE SOLE AND EXCLUSIVE USE OF ALL EMPLOYEES, VISITORS, AND SUPPLIERS OF XYZ CO. ALL OTHER PERSONS **MUST** USE GATE 2, WHICH IS LOCATED THIRTY (30) FEET TO THE WEST ON EAST FLINT STREET.
____ b. THIS GATE IS RESERVED FOR THE SOLE AND EXCLUSIVE USE OF **ALL** EMPLOYEES, VISITORS, AND SUPPLIERS OF ALL CONTRACTORS **EXCEPT** XYZ CO. ALL

EMPLOYEES, VISITORS, AND SUPPLIERS OF XYZ CO. MUST USE GATE 1, WHICH IS LOCATED THIRTY (30) FEET TO THE WEST ON EAST FLINT STREET.

____ (viii) Have as many gates as needed. If a targeted company makes an honest mistake using the wrong gate, the mistake can be lawfully cured.

____ (ix) Are there at least two entrances to the jobsite? The unions do not get to choose which entrance (gate) they want to picket.

____ (b) Can a reserved schedule system be implemented? Will the general contractor allow a reserved schedule system instead of a dual-gate system (or in combination with a dual-gate system)?

____ (i) Does the general contractor's scheduling require the targeted nonunion company to work at same time as union companies?

____ (ii) When is the targeted subcontractor allowed to work? When are the nontargeted subcontractors allowed to work?

____ (iii) Other points to remember:

____ a. Notify union in advance of specifics of reserved schedule.

____ b. Make sure the targeted company (and its owners, suppliers, employees, and visitors) strictly abide by the published schedule.

____ c. Upon advance notice to union, schedule can be changed.

____ (c) Can picketing be ignored with work proceeding as normal?

____ (d) Should a federal (NLRA) injunction, or state court injunction, be initiated?

____ (e) Should a Section 8(b)(4) ("secondary boycott") action be filed with NLRB?

____ (f) Should a lawsuit, either state or federal, be initiated?

# Government Contracting

# Checklist 56: Obtaining Federal Government Work

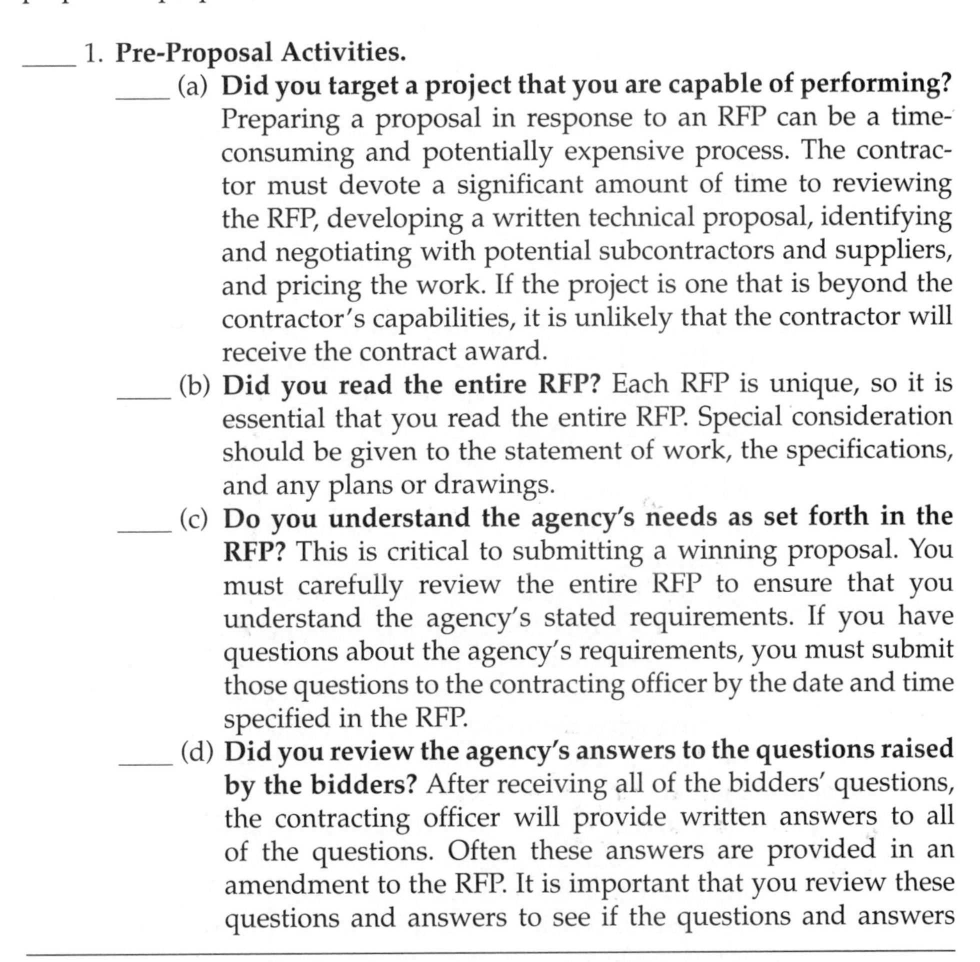

For contractors submitting a proposal to a federal government agency in response to a request for proposals (RFP), there are various strategies to keep in mind when developing the proposal and participating in the procurement process. This checklist provides guidance on what a contractor should do to prepare its proposal.

____ 1. **Pre-Proposal Activities.**

____ (a) **Did you target a project that you are capable of performing?** Preparing a proposal in response to an RFP can be a time-consuming and potentially expensive process. The contractor must devote a significant amount of time to reviewing the RFP, developing a written technical proposal, identifying and negotiating with potential subcontractors and suppliers, and pricing the work. If the project is one that is beyond the contractor's capabilities, it is unlikely that the contractor will receive the contract award.

____ (b) **Did you read the entire RFP?** Each RFP is unique, so it is essential that you read the entire RFP. Special consideration should be given to the statement of work, the specifications, and any plans or drawings.

____ (c) **Do you understand the agency's needs as set forth in the RFP?** This is critical to submitting a winning proposal. You must carefully review the entire RFP to ensure that you understand the agency's stated requirements. If you have questions about the agency's requirements, you must submit those questions to the contracting officer by the date and time specified in the RFP.

____ (d) **Did you review the agency's answers to the questions raised by the bidders?** After receiving all of the bidders' questions, the contracting officer will provide written answers to all of the questions. Often these answers are provided in an amendment to the RFP. It is important that you review these questions and answers to see if the questions and answers

**Lori Ann Lange** is an attorney at Peckar & Abramson, Washington, D.C., focusing on government contracts and construction contracts counseling and litigation. She received both her bachelor of arts degree and her law degree from George Washington University.

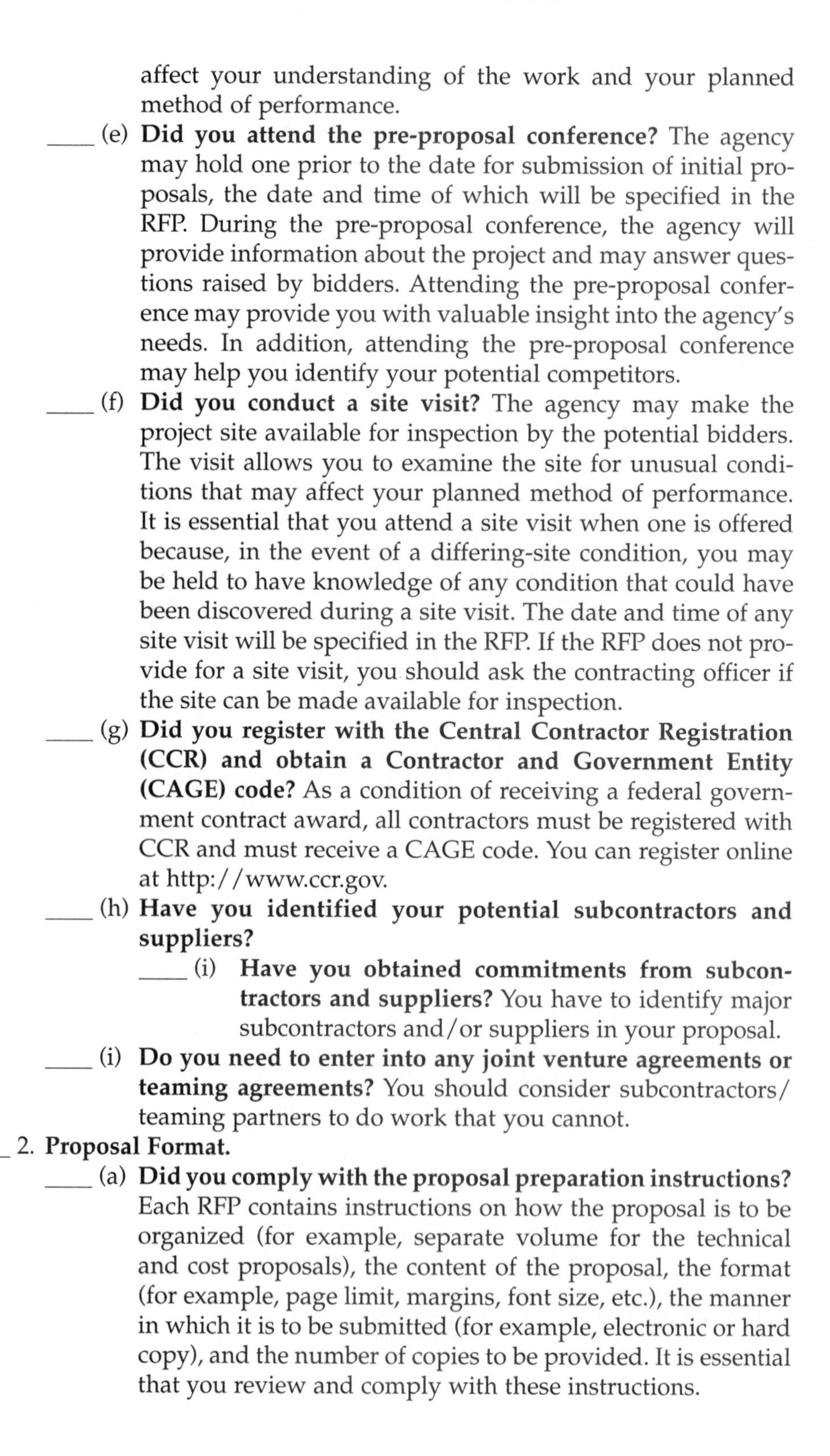

affect your understanding of the work and your planned method of performance.

____ (e) **Did you attend the pre-proposal conference?** The agency may hold one prior to the date for submission of initial proposals, the date and time of which will be specified in the RFP. During the pre-proposal conference, the agency will provide information about the project and may answer questions raised by bidders. Attending the pre-proposal conference may provide you with valuable insight into the agency's needs. In addition, attending the pre-proposal conference may help you identify your potential competitors.

____ (f) **Did you conduct a site visit?** The agency may make the project site available for inspection by the potential bidders. The visit allows you to examine the site for unusual conditions that may affect your planned method of performance. It is essential that you attend a site visit when one is offered because, in the event of a differing-site condition, you may be held to have knowledge of any condition that could have been discovered during a site visit. The date and time of any site visit will be specified in the RFP. If the RFP does not provide for a site visit, you should ask the contracting officer if the site can be made available for inspection.

____ (g) **Did you register with the Central Contractor Registration (CCR) and obtain a Contractor and Government Entity (CAGE) code?** As a condition of receiving a federal government contract award, all contractors must be registered with CCR and must receive a CAGE code. You can register online at http://www.ccr.gov.

____ (h) **Have you identified your potential subcontractors and suppliers?**

____ (i) **Have you obtained commitments from subcontractors and suppliers?** You have to identify major subcontractors and/or suppliers in your proposal.

____ (i) **Do you need to enter into any joint venture agreements or teaming agreements?** You should consider subcontractors/teaming partners to do work that you cannot.

____ 2. **Proposal Format.**

____ (a) **Did you comply with the proposal preparation instructions?** Each RFP contains instructions on how the proposal is to be organized (for example, separate volume for the technical and cost proposals), the content of the proposal, the format (for example, page limit, margins, font size, etc.), the manner in which it is to be submitted (for example, electronic or hard copy), and the number of copies to be provided. It is essential that you review and comply with these instructions.

____ (b) **Is your proposal well organized?** You should organize your proposal so that the evaluator reading it can easily find the information.

____ (i) **Did you include a table of contents in your proposal?** Do not make the evaluators reading your proposal hunt for the information. The evaluators may miss the information and your proposal may be down-scored as a result.

____ (ii) **Did you use section and subsection numbers and titles as appropriate?** Doing so will assist the evaluators in finding information in your proposal.

____ (c) **Is your proposal concise and well written?**

____ (i) **Did you avoid using use long sentences?**

____ (ii) **Did you use the active voice rather than the passive voice?**

____ (iii) **Did you avoid using equivocal words?** Whenever possible, you should avoid equivocal words such as "might," "could," and "may." These types of words can lead to confusion as to whether you will actually satisfy a requirement. You should affirmatively state what you *will* do to meet the agency's needs.

____ (iv) **Did you check for grammatical mistakes and spelling errors?**

____ (v) **Does your proposal contain charts, tables, and graphics (as appropriate) to emphasize key points?** These can provide a way to present the evaluator with a significant amount of information in a condensed format, important when the RFP restricts the maximum number of pages for the technical proposal. Charts, tables, and graphics, however, cannot be used in isolation. There must be accompanying text that puts the charts, tables, and graphics in context.

____ (vi) **Did you put your company name and/or logo on each page of the proposal?**

____ (d) **Did you put a restrictive-use legend on your proposal?** You should put language on the cover page of your proposal limiting the federal government's right to disclose or use the information contained in your proposal to the evaluation of the proposal and the administration of any resulting contract. Each subsequent page should contain a notation that the use or disclosure of information contained on the page is subject to the restriction on the cover page.

____ (e) **Did you submit the proposal on time?** Proposals must be received by the contracting officer by the date and time set forth in the RFP. Generally speaking, contracting officers cannot accept late proposals.

____ 3. **Proposal Contents—General.**

____ (a) **Did you sign and include the Standard Form 1449 cover sheet?**

____ (b) **Did you sign and include Standard Form 30 for each of the amendments to the RFP, or otherwise acknowledge the amendments in your proposal?**

____ (c) **Did you execute the required certifications and representations?** Each federal government RFP contains representations and certifications that the contractor must execute. These certifications and representations generally cover such issues as suspension and debarment, small-business status, independent pricing, equal opportunity and affirmative action compliance, and previous contracts and compliance reports. Some RFPs require the contractor to register and complete these certifications on-line via the Online Representations and Certifications Application (ORCA). Contractors can register with ORCA at http://orca.bpn.gov.

____ (d) **Did you complete the contract clauses requiring contractor information, such as the Buy American Act—Construction Materials clause (FAR 52.225-9) and the Hazardous Material Identification and Material Safety Data clause (FAR 52.223-3)?**

____ (e) **Did you provide properly completed and executed bid guarantees and performance and payment bonds (if required by the RFP)?**

____ (f) **Did you include any other required forms, such as past-performance questionnaires?**

____ 4. **Technical Proposal.**

____ (a) **Does your technical proposal describe how you intend to perform the work requirements set forth in the specifications?** Your technical proposal is your opportunity to explain in detail how you intend to perform the work if you are awarded the contract. Thus, you need to demonstrate a good understanding of the procuring agency's requirements. You also need to explain the benefits of your proposed method of performing the work. Mere statements that you will comply with the specifications are insufficient.

____ (b) **Does your technical proposal describe your company's technical capabilities and translate those capabilities to the project requirements?** Each proposal is evaluated based on its own content. In drafting technical proposals, contractors often make the mistake of failing to adequately discuss their capabilities because they believe that the procuring agency already knows their reputation and capabilities.

____ (c) **Is your technical proposal tailored to the specific project?** Just as each project is unique, so should each proposal be unique. Avoid the use of boilerplate language when addressing how you will perform the contract if you receive the award.

____ (d) **Does your proposal identify any foreseeable performance issues?** If you anticipate that there may be problems with performing the work, your proposal should identify those problems and discuss your proposed solutions.

____ (e) **Does your proposal offer a technical solution that exceeds the procuring agency's minimum requirements as set forth in the RFP?** For example, if the specifications require a minimum heating, ventilating, and air conditioning standard efficiency and your proposed technical solution exceeds that minimum, you should clearly state so. Proposing solutions that exceed the agency's minimum requirements can result in your proposal receiving a higher technical score. Be careful, however, that you do not "gold plate" your technical proposal such that your proposed price is no longer competitive.

____ (f) **Does your technical proposal address each of the evaluation factors and subfactors?** The RFP sets forth the factors and significant subfactors that the evaluators will use to score your proposal. It is critical that your proposal addresses each of them.

____ (g) **Does your technical proposal clearly address the roles of your subcontractors and how you will coordinate those subcontractors?** Virtually all construction projects require the use of subcontractors to perform significant portions of the work. Your technical proposal should address the role of your proposed subcontractors, their qualifications, and how you will coordinate subcontractor work to ensure that the project is not delayed.

____ (h) **Does your company have an adequate small-business subcontracting plan?** Generally speaking, under FAR 19.702, contractors that receive contract awards or modifications that are expected to exceed $1 million must submit a small-business subcontracting plan. There are some exceptions to this requirement, such as when there are no subcontracting opportunities, when the contractor itself is a small business, and when the work is to be performed entirely outside of the United States.

____ (i) **Does your technical proposal identify by name your key personnel, such as your project manager, supervisors, inspectors, etc.?** Most federal government construction RFPs require the contractor to identify its proposed key personnel and provide their résumés. In selecting your proposed key personnel, it is imperative that those people meet any requirements in the RFP, such as years of experience, training, and certifications. In addition, their duties and responsibilities, as well as the lines of communication, should be addressed.

____ 5. **Past Performance.**

____ (a) **Does your proposal adequately discuss your past performance?** Some RFPs require the contractor to submit a past performance proposal or otherwise address its past performance. Past performance is viewed by the federal government as an indicator of the contractor's ability to perform the contract successfully and is a significant evaluation factor in RFPs for construction services. Any write-up should correlate the contractor's experience from past projects to the work to be performed under the RFP. Relevant awards, certifications, and letters of commendation can be included. If you have some negative past performance, such as a show-cause notice or threat of termination for default on a federal government project, it may be beneficial to identify the negative past performance, explain the circumstances in which it arose, and describe any measures you have subsequently taken to ensure that similar circumstances will not occur on this project.

____ (b) **Have you selected relevant references that will provide you with a strong reference?** The procuring agency usually will require the contractor to identify a set number of references that will be asked to complete a questionnaire rating your performance on previous jobs. In determining which references to use, you should select references for previous projects that are the same or similar type of work and are of similar or higher dollar value. Obviously, you also want to select references that you believe will give you an excellent evaluation.

____ 6. **Proposed Pricing.**

____ (a) **Is your proposed pricing realistic?** Any price proposal you submit should be realistic for the work to be performed. It also should be competitive. Many construction contracts are being awarded on the basis of best value, as opposed to lowest price. Although you do not need to submit the lowest price in a best-value procurement to receive the contract award, your price still must be realistic and competitive with the other bidders.

____ (b) **Did you complete all of the contract line item numbers (CLINs)?** When the RFP requires CLIN pricing, you need to ensure that all of the CLINs are filled out.

____ (c) **Did you check for mathematical errors?** Prior to submitting your proposal, you should check your pricing to make sure that you have not made any errors.

____ 7. **Discussions, Clarifications, and Oral Presentations.**

____ (a) **Did you answer all discussion questions and requests for clarifications?** The procuring agency may have discussions with you regarding any aspect of your proposal. Discussions can either be in writing or face to face. Alternatively, the agency may request that you clarify an aspect of your proposal. Regardless of whether you have discussions or clarifications, it is imperative that you answer all of the questions raised by the agency and provide any additional information as necessary. Remember, the purpose of responding to the discussion questions and requests for clarifications is to increase your evaluation score and thus your chance of receiving the contract award.

____ (b) **Did you revise your proposal as necessary in response to the discussion questions?** If you engage in discussions with the procuring agency, you will be given an opportunity to revise your proposal to address the concerns raised by the agency. When the concerns go to performance issues, you should revise your technical proposal to address the agency's concerns. You also should review your pricing proposal to determine if the changes you have made affect your proposed pricing.

____ (c) **Are you prepared for your oral presentation?** Some RFPs provide for oral presentations to be given by the contractor to the procuring agency. The purpose of the oral presentation is for the contractor to explain its proposed method of meeting the agency's needs and the benefits of the contractor's proposal. It also provides the agency with the opportunity to ask questions. It is important that you properly prepare for the presentation. The person(s) giving the oral presentation must understand the RFP and the proposal and be able to communicate effectively.

____ 8. **Debriefings.**

____ (a) **Did you receive notice from the agency that the contract has been awarded to another bidder?** The procuring agency will give the unsuccessful bidders notice of award within 3 days after the date of contract award, identifying the successful bidder and the contract price [FAR 15.503(b)(1)].

____ (b) **Did you request a timely debriefing?** Within 3 days of receiving a notice of award, you should submit a written request for a debriefing to the contracting officer. If you do not submit a debriefing request within 3 days, the procuring agency is not required to give you a debriefing [FAR 15.506(a)].

____ (c) **Did you attend the debriefing?** A debriefing can provide you with helpful information about why you did not receive the contract award. During the debriefing, the procuring agency will provide you with its evaluation of your proposal and your overall ranking. You should use the debriefing as an opportunity to understand why the agency evaluated your proposal as it did and what you can do to improve in the future. The information provided in the debriefing may also help you determine if there are potential bases for filing a bid protest challenging the agency's award decision.

# Checklist 57: Government Bid Protests

The following is a checklist for use by construction industry professionals in determining whether and how to protest a public-sector procurement.

____ 1. **Identify All Applicable Dates and Deadlines.** The most common mistake in government bid protests is not acting soon enough. Bid protests are subject to short time frames, and you can lose significant rights by even a few days of delay. In particular, you should identify the deadlines for:

____ (a) **Protest to the terms of the solicitation.** This is typically due before the date for submission of bids or proposals. Find out how many days in advance, which is frequently set forth in the solicitation itself.

____ (b) **Bid or proposal submission.** Consider if there is any ground to protest based on the date, time, and location of bid or proposal submissions.

____ (c) **Bid or proposal opening and award.** Bids are usually opened immediately after time for submission; proposals may not be opened immediately.

____ (d) **Filing of the protest and any supporting documentation.** Such filing usually takes place within a few days after bid opening or announcement of intent to award.

____ (e) **Requesting a hearing or appearance before the public agency.** This may automatically appear on the agency's meeting agenda, or you may have to request a hearing.

____ (f) **Filing suit.** You must act quickly, typically after exhausting your administrative remedies.

____ 2. **Standing.** Determine whether you have standing to protest.

____ (a) **In line for award if protest sustained?** In general, in order to protest you have to be in a position to receive the award if the protest is sustained. Thus, a fifth-low bidder may not have standing to protest, unless it can demonstrate that there is something wrong with all four lower bids. Similarly, prospective subcontractors and suppliers generally do not have

**W. Samuel Niece** and **John W. Ralls** practice construction law with Thelen Reid Brown Raysman & Steiner LLP in the firm's San Francisco, California, office. Both have prosecuted and defended bid protests before a variety of agencies, commissions, boards, and courts.

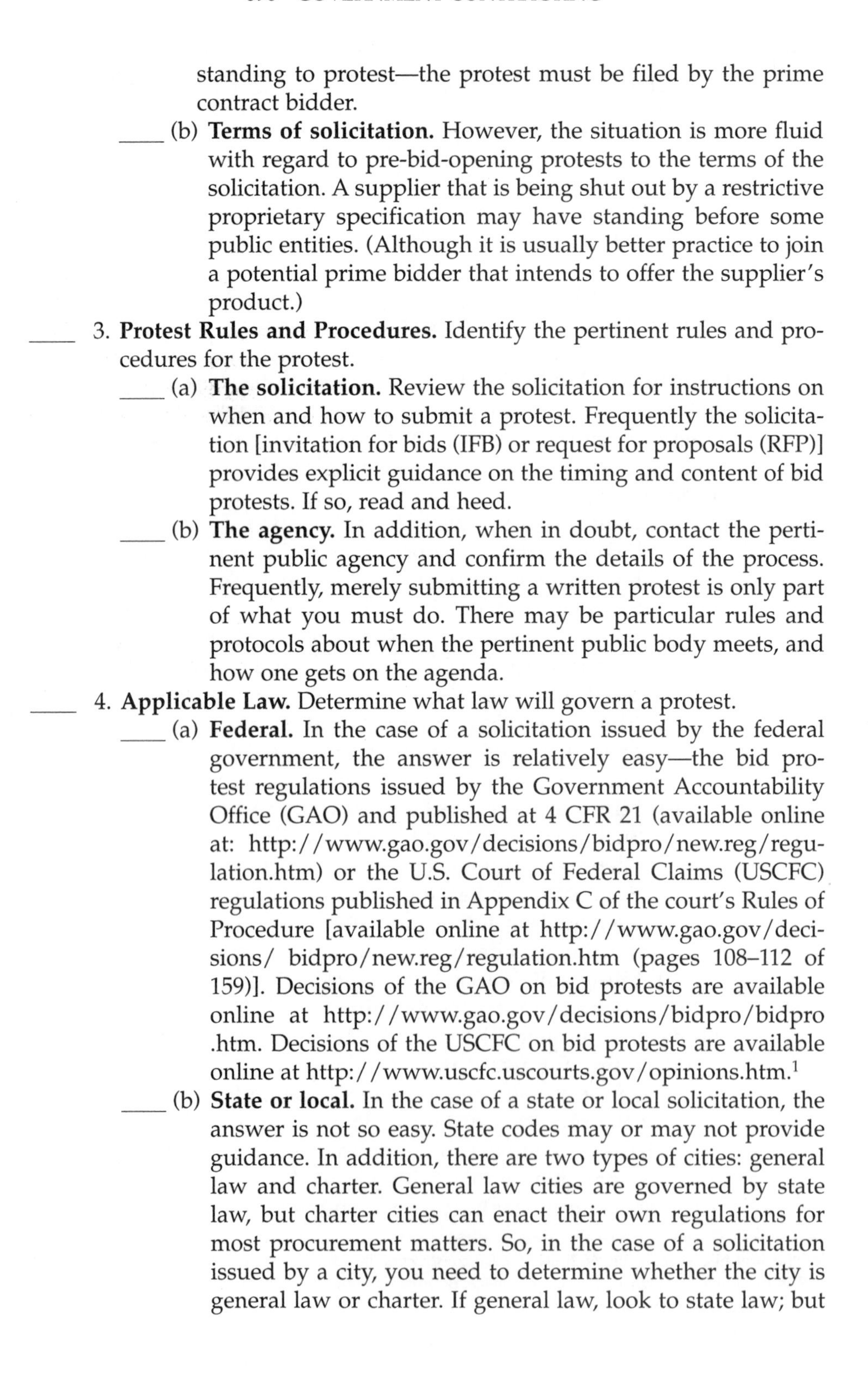

standing to protest—the protest must be filed by the prime contract bidder.

____ (b) **Terms of solicitation.** However, the situation is more fluid with regard to pre-bid-opening protests to the terms of the solicitation. A supplier that is being shut out by a restrictive proprietary specification may have standing before some public entities. (Although it is usually better practice to join a potential prime bidder that intends to offer the supplier's product.)

____ 3. **Protest Rules and Procedures.** Identify the pertinent rules and procedures for the protest.

____ (a) **The solicitation.** Review the solicitation for instructions on when and how to submit a protest. Frequently the solicitation [invitation for bids (IFB) or request for proposals (RFP)] provides explicit guidance on the timing and content of bid protests. If so, read and heed.

____ (b) **The agency.** In addition, when in doubt, contact the pertinent public agency and confirm the details of the process. Frequently, merely submitting a written protest is only part of what you must do. There may be particular rules and protocols about when the pertinent public body meets, and how one gets on the agenda.

____ 4. **Applicable Law.** Determine what law will govern a protest.

____ (a) **Federal.** In the case of a solicitation issued by the federal government, the answer is relatively easy—the bid protest regulations issued by the Government Accountability Office (GAO) and published at 4 CFR 21 (available online at: http://www.gao.gov/decisions/bidpro/new.reg/regulation.htm) or the U.S. Court of Federal Claims (USCFC) regulations published in Appendix C of the court's Rules of Procedure [available online at http://www.gao.gov/decisions/ bidpro/new.reg/regulation.htm (pages 108–112 of 159)]. Decisions of the GAO on bid protests are available online at http://www.gao.gov/decisions/bidpro/bidpro.htm. Decisions of the USCFC on bid protests are available online at http://www.uscfc.uscourts.gov/opinions.htm.[1]

____ (b) **State or local.** In the case of a state or local solicitation, the answer is not so easy. State codes may or may not provide guidance. In addition, there are two types of cities: general law and charter. General law cities are governed by state law, but charter cities can enact their own regulations for most procurement matters. So, in the case of a solicitation issued by a city, you need to determine whether the city is general law or charter. If general law, look to state law; but if charter, examine the city's charter and municipal codes for provisions governing bid protests. When in doubt, call the city or state agency and ask. Federal procurement law is frequently useful and persuasive in the absence of controlling state authority.

____ 5. **Grounds for Protest.** Consider whether you take exception to the terms of the solicitation (as opposed to the public agency's evaluation of the bids or proposals).

____ (a) **Terms of the solicitation.** Many solicitations (and the GAO regulations and USCFC case law) require that any objection to the terms of the solicitation be submitted prior to the time set for opening of bids or receipt of proposals. Even in the absence of specific guidance on this point, courts do not look with favor on a bidder that waits until after it is not selected for award to protest a term of the solicitation that was apparent prior to bid or proposal submission (the forbidden or disfavored "two bites at the apple").

____ (b) **Before bid opening or receipt of proposals.** If you believe that the solicitation is unfair or stacks the deck against you (for example, by specifying a proprietary product or favoring your competitors based on geography or sociological factors), then you should submit a strong protest well before the time set for opening of bids or receipt of proposals. (The agency may ignore you, but a court will be hard-pressed to take you to task later for not raising the issue in a timely manner.)

____ (c) **Amendments.** Immediately upon receiving a solicitation or amendment, you need to review it for requirements that you may want to protest. The day before the bid or proposal is due is not the time to be deciding whether or not to protest a term of the solicitation.

____ 6. **Responsiveness, Responsibility, or Evaluation.** Decide whether to protest based on responsiveness, responsibility, and/or evaluation.

____ (a) **The basic rule.** A general principle of public contracting is that award should be made to that *responsible* bidder submitting the lowest, *responsive* bid.

____ (i) **Responsibility.** Bidders are responsible (or not). Responsibility goes to the bidder's capacity (personnel, equipment, working capital) to accomplish the work. Agencies generally can consider matters outside the bid (for example, references) in making a responsibility determination, and many jurisdictions conduct a due process hearing before they make a finding of nonresponsibility.

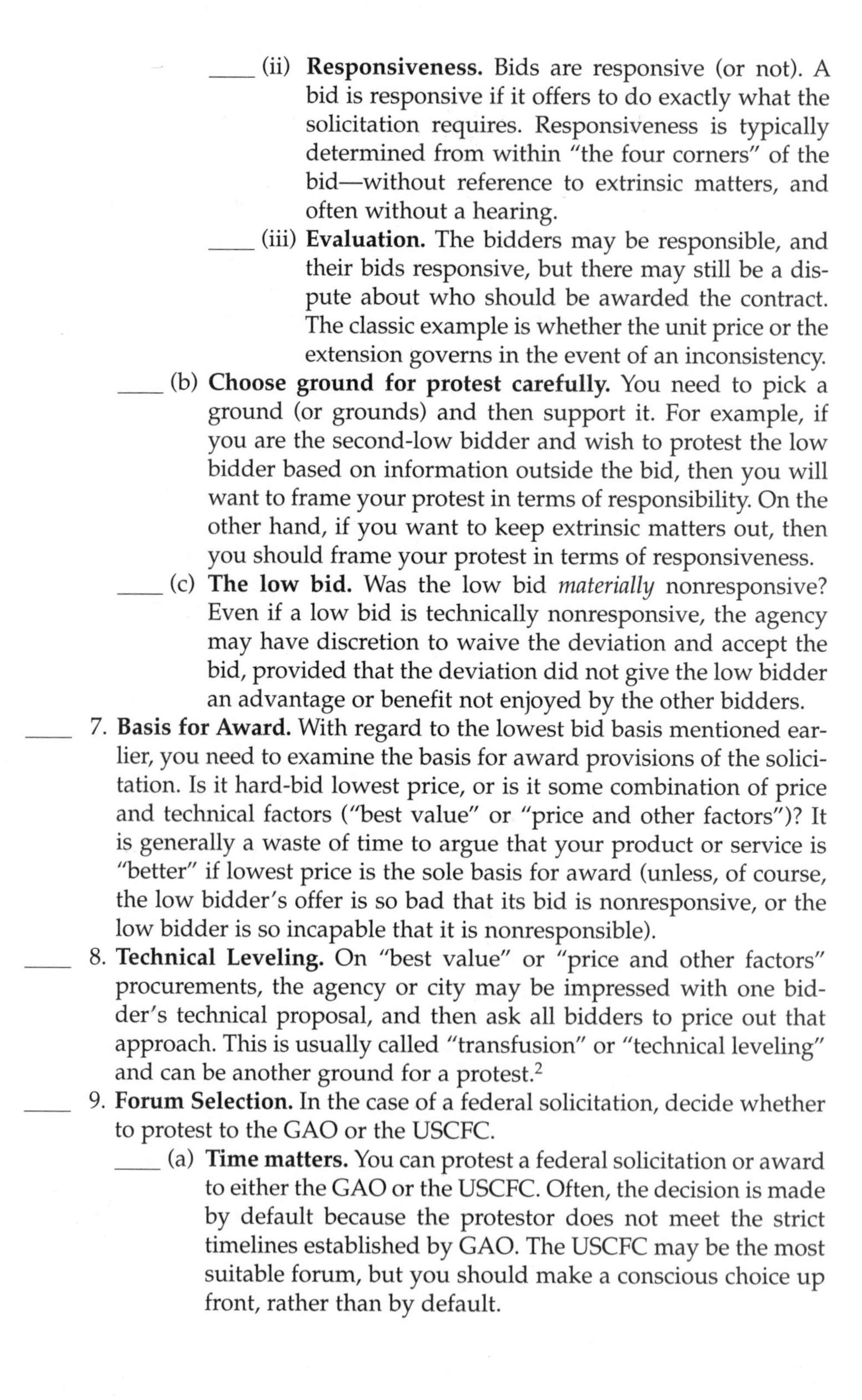

____ (ii) **Responsiveness.** Bids are responsive (or not). A bid is responsive if it offers to do exactly what the solicitation requires. Responsiveness is typically determined from within "the four corners" of the bid—without reference to extrinsic matters, and often without a hearing.

____ (iii) **Evaluation.** The bidders may be responsible, and their bids responsive, but there may still be a dispute about who should be awarded the contract. The classic example is whether the unit price or the extension governs in the event of an inconsistency.

____ (b) **Choose ground for protest carefully.** You need to pick a ground (or grounds) and then support it. For example, if you are the second-low bidder and wish to protest the low bidder based on information outside the bid, then you will want to frame your protest in terms of responsibility. On the other hand, if you want to keep extrinsic matters out, then you should frame your protest in terms of responsiveness.

____ (c) **The low bid.** Was the low bid *materially* nonresponsive? Even if a low bid is technically nonresponsive, the agency may have discretion to waive the deviation and accept the bid, provided that the deviation did not give the low bidder an advantage or benefit not enjoyed by the other bidders.

____ 7. **Basis for Award.** With regard to the lowest bid basis mentioned earlier, you need to examine the basis for award provisions of the solicitation. Is it hard-bid lowest price, or is it some combination of price and technical factors ("best value" or "price and other factors")? It is generally a waste of time to argue that your product or service is "better" if lowest price is the sole basis for award (unless, of course, the low bidder's offer is so bad that its bid is nonresponsive, or the low bidder is so incapable that it is nonresponsible).

____ 8. **Technical Leveling.** On "best value" or "price and other factors" procurements, the agency or city may be impressed with one bidder's technical proposal, and then ask all bidders to price out that approach. This is usually called "transfusion" or "technical leveling" and can be another ground for a protest.[2]

____ 9. **Forum Selection.** In the case of a federal solicitation, decide whether to protest to the GAO or the USCFC.

____ (a) **Time matters.** You can protest a federal solicitation or award to either the GAO or the USCFC. Often, the decision is made by default because the protestor does not meet the strict timelines established by GAO. The USCFC may be the most suitable forum, but you should make a conscious choice up front, rather than by default.

____ (b) **Factors to consider.** The factors affecting this decision are beyond the scope of this brief checklist. However, as a general rule, GAO provides a more expeditious forum for the resolution of run-of-the-mill protests on smaller projects. An attorney is not absolutely required for a GAO protest. But large protests on major projects often land at the USCFC.

____ 10. **Consider Whether a Defensive Protest Is Necessary.** Even if you are the low bidder, you may need to file a protest of your own.

____ (a) **Possibly, on a state or local project.** If you are the low bidder and in line for award on a state or local project, and you think that another bidder has protested or may protest the award to you, you should consider submitting a protest (within the time specified for receipt of protests) against award to anyone other than you—on the basis that you are the responsible bidder submitting the lowest, responsive bid. Otherwise, the agency may grant the protest against you, and then reject your counterprotest as untimely.

____ (b) **But, not on a federal project.** On a federal procurement, the apparent low bidder must be notified of a protest filed by another bidder and afforded an opportunity to weigh in against the protest.[3]

____ 11. **Exhaust Administrative Remedies.** Review the applicable law, and determine whether and how you must exhaust administrative remedies.

____ (a) **Federal.** In the case of a federal procurement, you can submit a protest to the agency, and then protest to GAO if you are not satisfied with the agency's response. However, you are not required to submit an agency protest; you can go directly to the GAO.

____ (b) **State or local.** In the case of state or local procurements, you can bring a court action (generally styled a "petition for writ of mandate") to have an award to your competitor stopped or reversed. However, you generally need to exhaust administrative remedies (for example, by submitting a protest to the procuring city or state agency and pursuing that protest to decision) before going to court.

____ 12. **Litigation.** After exhausting your administrative remedies (or determining that you need not do so), the next step is litigation.

____ (a) **Federal.** A protestor (or real party in interest) that is dissatisfied with a GAO determination may appeal to the USCFC. A protestor or real party in interest that loses at the USCFC may appeal to the Court of Appeals for the Federal Circuit.

____ (b) **State or local.** State or local protests are usually litigated by bringing a petition for writ of mandate in the state trial court, typically with a right of appeal to the state intermediate courts of appeal or the state supreme court.

____ 13. **Consider the Standard of Review.** The courts are inclined to defer to the procuring agency's decisions.

____ (a) **Review the administrative record.** The court will attempt to base its decision on the administrative record, so you should confirm that the procuring agency's record is complete, and supplement it if necessary.

____ (b) **Typically, deferential standard applies.** Federal protests are generally reviewed under the Administrative Procedures Act (5 U.S.C. §706), and a court will uphold the agency action unless the protestor can show that the agency action was arbitrary or capricious. This is an extremely deferential standard. Most state courts follow a similar standard when reviewing the procurement decisions of state and local agencies.

____ (c) **Case law.** Look for previous cases arising from a similar factual situation. The best case law is from a court in your jurisdiction interpreting your jurisdiction's bidding law. There may be no state case on point. There is, however, likely to be a federal (GAO or USCFC) case on point, and state courts can be persuaded to follow (or at least consider) federal case law.

## *Notes*

1. For an excellent discussion of the law concerning bid protests on federal projects, see A. Bastianelli III, A. Ness & J. West, eds., *Federal Government Construction Contracts*, Chapter 8, "Bid Protests" by J. Nagle and L. Kleisle (2003).

2. See FAR 15.306(e)(2).

3. See GAO Bid Protest Regulations at 4 CFR 21.3(a); USCFC Procedure in Procurement Protest Cases, Appendix C, Paragraph 2.

# Checklist 58: Avoiding Common Mistakes in Government Claims

The following checklist should be helpful in identifying, documenting, and preparing claims against the government for contractors on federal construction projects. The checklist will address issues that arise during the bidding and construction stage, as well as during the preparation of the claim itself. It includes references to the Contract Disputes Act of 1978 (CDA) (41 U.S.C. §§601-613) and the Federal Acquisition Regulation (FAR).

____ 1. **Pre-Bid Considerations.**

____ (a) **Attend the pre-bid conference.** Thoroughly review the contract documents, specifications, drawings, borings, or other data that the government reasonably makes available. Notify the government of any obvious conflicts, omissions, inconsistencies, or errors in the contract documents and request clarification.

____ (b) **Inspect the construction site.** Perform a site investigation, and review the surface and subsurface conditions. Become familiar with local weather conditions, site access, area transportation, local construction practices, local labor practices, etc. Under the Investigation and Conditions Affecting the Work clause (FAR 52.236-3), the contractor is responsible for information that would be determined by a reasonable site investigation.

____ (c) **Keep a copy of your bid estimate file.** Keep all quotes and/or bids received from subcontractors and suppliers. Your bid price should include all of the work required to perform the contract, even if it is not included in specific pay items.

____ (d) **Subcontract flow-down provision.** All subcontracts should include a provision incorporating the requirements of the prime contract. In particular, subcontracts should incorporate (that is, flow down) the provisions of the Disputes clause in the prime contract. This means that subcontractor claims based on actions or omissions of the government will be submitted to the contracting officer for a decision. The

**Donald A. Tobin** is a partner in the Washington, D.C., office of Peckar & Abramson P.C. As part of his construction practice, he regularly advises construction contractors who have claims on government projects.

subcontractor would be bound by that decision and any resulting appeal.

____ 2. **Claim Identification, Notice, and Management.**

____ (a) **Relevant contract clauses.** Government contracts require that contractors provide timely notice of events giving rise to claims. Examples include the Differing Site Conditions (FAR 52.236-2), Changes (FAR 52.243-4), and Suspension of Work (FAR 52.242-14) clauses. In addition, the Default clause (FAR 52.249-10) requires the contractor to give notice of "excusable delays."

____ (b) **Prompt notice.** Notify the appropriate government representatives as soon as you encounter events (such as defective specifications, design defects, extra work directives, differing site conditions, delays, acceleration orders, etc.) that will result in claims. If a subcontractor notifies you of a potential claim, promptly forward that notice to the contracting officer.

____ (c) **Confirm any oral directions in writing.** Promptly advise the government of corrective action taken to resolve potential claims. Provide status reports on progress in resolving problems.

____ (d) **Monitor costs**. Establish systems to monitor and record costs, equipment usage, additional personnel, etc. Establish cost codes for added or extra work.

____ (e) **Reporting requirements.** Comply with all contract reporting requirements; keep critical path method (CPM) schedules current. Include in daily/weekly reports a description of problems, status of open claims, extra work directives, delays, etc.

____ (f) **Demonstrative evidence.** Take photographs and videos of affected construction areas on a regular basis. This will assist in claim preparation, as well as settlement negotiations and/or litigation.

____ (g) **Get technical experts involved early.** As soon as problems are encountered on a construction project, consider retaining the appropriate technical expertise. Bring the experts to the site before you take corrective action (as soon as possible) so that they can review and document problems first hand.

____ (h) **Do not waive claim rights.** Review all contract modifications to ensure that potential claims are not waived; reserve contractor's rights to assert impact and delay claims. When submitting requests for final payment, contractors should identify all outstanding claims and change orders and ensure that such claims are not released. Be careful not to release any potential subcontractor claims without first settling with the subcontractor.

____ 3. **Contract Disputes Act Requirements.**

____ (a) **The Contract Disputes Act of 1978.** The CDA requires that (i) contractor claims "shall be in writing and submitted to contracting officer for a decision" and (ii) all contractor claims over $100,000 must be certified [41 U.S.C. §§605(a), 605(c)].

____ (b) **Claim defined.** The Disputes clause defines a claim as a "written demand or written assertion by one of the contracting parties, seeking, as a matter of right, the payment of money in a sum certain, the adjustment or interpretation of contract terms, or other relief under or relating to this contract" [FAR 52.233-1(c); see also FAR 33.201].

____ (c) **Sum certain.** In general, construction claims should include a clear and easily understandable statement of the basis and amount of the claim. The amount of the claim should be a "sum certain"; however, a contractor may calculate the amount of its claim by preparing good-faith (and supportable) estimates.

____ (d) **Certification requirements.** For claims of more than $100,000, the CDA [41 U.S.C. §601(c) (1)] imposes the following certification requirement:

> For claims of more than $100,000, the contractor shall certify that the claim is made in good faith, that the supporting data is accurate and complete to the best of his knowledge and belief, that the amount requested accurately reflects the contract adjustment for which the contractor believes the government is liable, and that the individual executing the certification is duly authorized to certify the claim on behalf of the contractor.

____ (e) **FAR sample certification**. Contractors should use the sample certification set forth in FAR 33.207(c). Use of this form will avoid challenges to the sufficiency of the certification. A claim does not qualify as a CDA claim until it is properly certified. The person certifying the claim must be authorized by the company to execute the certification.

____ (f) **Effect of certification.** By certifying that the claim is prepared in good faith, the contractor is agreeing that the claim has not been improperly or artificially increased for negotiation purposes or artificially inflated by the inclusion of meritless claims. By certifying that the claim is accurate and complete, the contractor is certifying that the information is accurate as of the date of the certification and that the contractor has provided enough information so that the contracting officer can

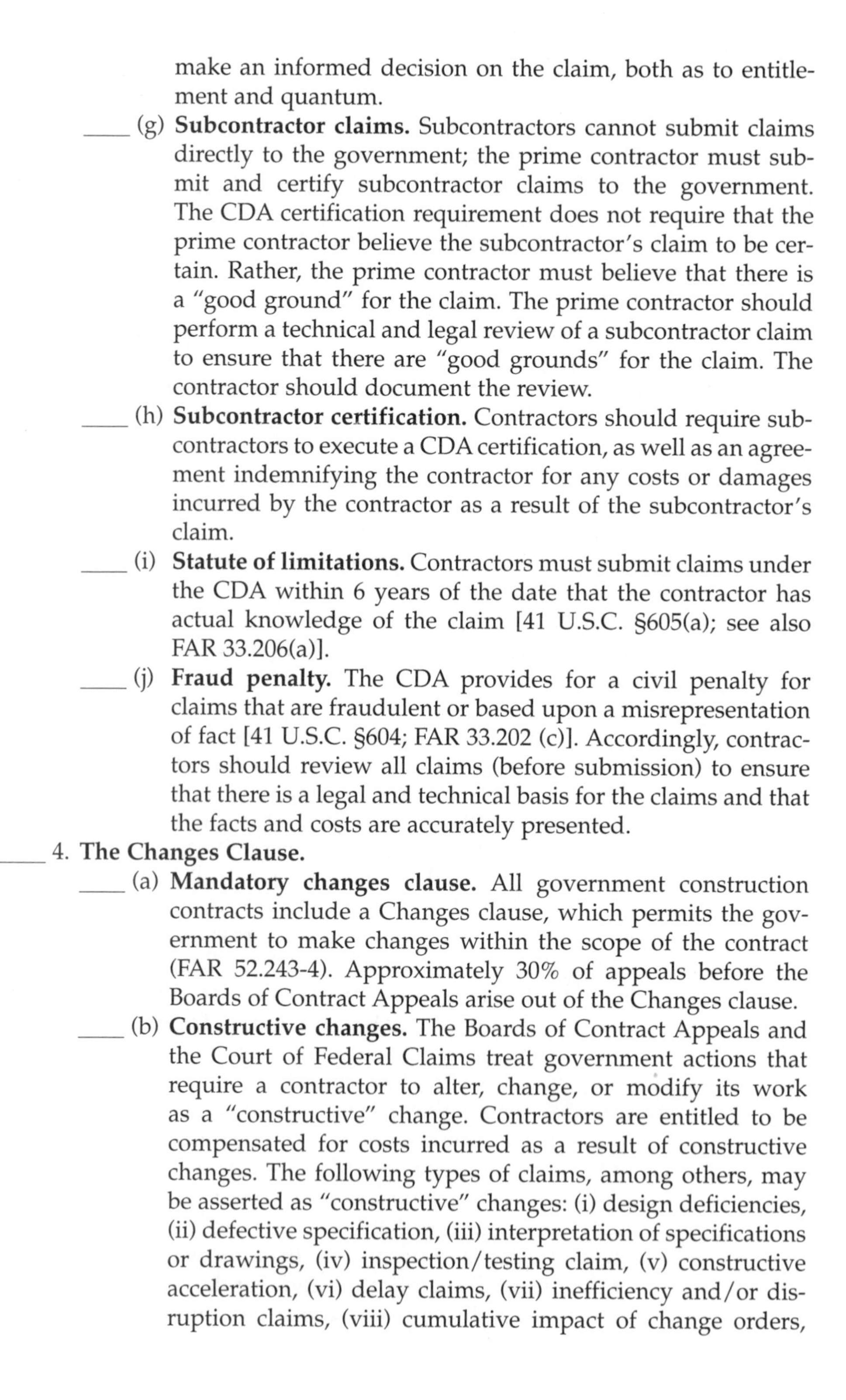

make an informed decision on the claim, both as to entitlement and quantum.

____ (g) **Subcontractor claims.** Subcontractors cannot submit claims directly to the government; the prime contractor must submit and certify subcontractor claims to the government. The CDA certification requirement does not require that the prime contractor believe the subcontractor's claim to be certain. Rather, the prime contractor must believe that there is a "good ground" for the claim. The prime contractor should perform a technical and legal review of a subcontractor claim to ensure that there are "good grounds" for the claim. The contractor should document the review.

____ (h) **Subcontractor certification.** Contractors should require subcontractors to execute a CDA certification, as well as an agreement indemnifying the contractor for any costs or damages incurred by the contractor as a result of the subcontractor's claim.

____ (i) **Statute of limitations.** Contractors must submit claims under the CDA within 6 years of the date that the contractor has actual knowledge of the claim [41 U.S.C. §605(a); see also FAR 33.206(a)].

____ (j) **Fraud penalty.** The CDA provides for a civil penalty for claims that are fraudulent or based upon a misrepresentation of fact [41 U.S.C. §604; FAR 33.202 (c)]. Accordingly, contractors should review all claims (before submission) to ensure that there is a legal and technical basis for the claims and that the facts and costs are accurately presented.

____ 4. **The Changes Clause.**

____ (a) **Mandatory changes clause.** All government construction contracts include a Changes clause, which permits the government to make changes within the scope of the contract (FAR 52.243-4). Approximately 30% of appeals before the Boards of Contract Appeals arise out of the Changes clause.

____ (b) **Constructive changes.** The Boards of Contract Appeals and the Court of Federal Claims treat government actions that require a contractor to alter, change, or modify its work as a "constructive" change. Contractors are entitled to be compensated for costs incurred as a result of constructive changes. The following types of claims, among others, may be asserted as "constructive" changes: (i) design deficiencies, (ii) defective specification, (iii) interpretation of specifications or drawings, (iv) inspection/testing claim, (v) constructive acceleration, (vi) delay claims, (vii) inefficiency and/or disruption claims, (viii) cumulative impact of change orders,

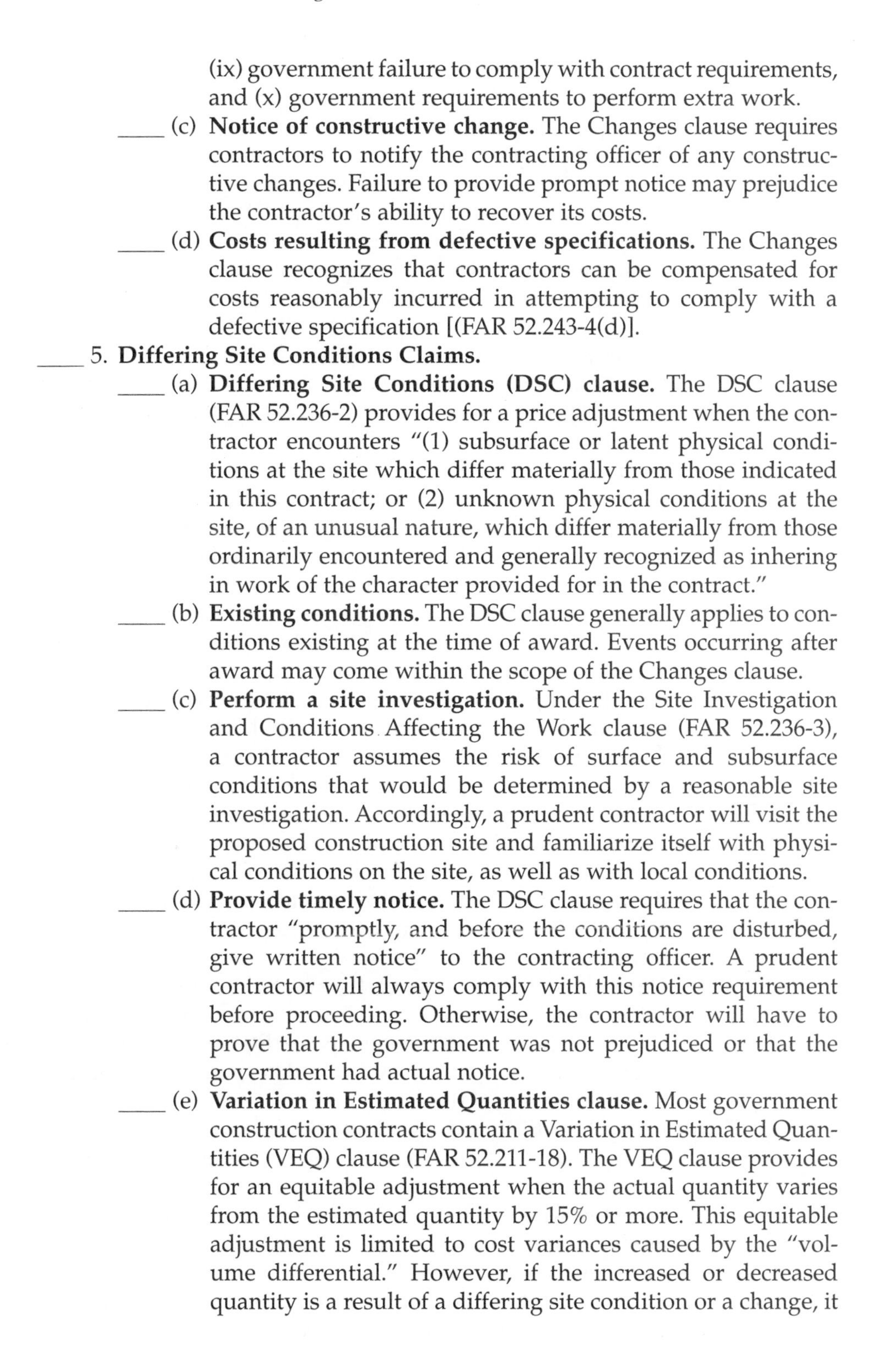



(ix) government failure to comply with contract requirements, and (x) government requirements to perform extra work.

____ (c) **Notice of constructive change.** The Changes clause requires contractors to notify the contracting officer of any constructive changes. Failure to provide prompt notice may prejudice the contractor's ability to recover its costs.

____ (d) **Costs resulting from defective specifications.** The Changes clause recognizes that contractors can be compensated for costs reasonably incurred in attempting to comply with a defective specification [(FAR 52.243-4(d)].

____ 5. **Differing Site Conditions Claims.**

____ (a) **Differing Site Conditions (DSC) clause.** The DSC clause (FAR 52.236-2) provides for a price adjustment when the contractor encounters "(1) subsurface or latent physical conditions at the site which differ materially from those indicated in this contract; or (2) unknown physical conditions at the site, of an unusual nature, which differ materially from those ordinarily encountered and generally recognized as inhering in work of the character provided for in the contract."

____ (b) **Existing conditions.** The DSC clause generally applies to conditions existing at the time of award. Events occurring after award may come within the scope of the Changes clause.

____ (c) **Perform a site investigation.** Under the Site Investigation and Conditions Affecting the Work clause (FAR 52.236-3), a contractor assumes the risk of surface and subsurface conditions that would be determined by a reasonable site investigation. Accordingly, a prudent contractor will visit the proposed construction site and familiarize itself with physical conditions on the site, as well as with local conditions.

____ (d) **Provide timely notice.** The DSC clause requires that the contractor "promptly, and before the conditions are disturbed, give written notice" to the contracting officer. A prudent contractor will always comply with this notice requirement before proceeding. Otherwise, the contractor will have to prove that the government was not prejudiced or that the government had actual notice.

____ (e) **Variation in Estimated Quantities clause.** Most government construction contracts contain a Variation in Estimated Quantities (VEQ) clause (FAR 52.211-18). The VEQ clause provides for an equitable adjustment when the actual quantity varies from the estimated quantity by 15% or more. This equitable adjustment is limited to cost variances caused by the "volume differential." However, if the increased or decreased quantity is a result of a differing site condition or a change, it may be to a contractor's advantage to file a claim under the DSC or Changes clause, rather than under the VEQ clause.

____ 6. **Delay, Disruption, and Inefficiency Claims.**

____ (a) **Types of delays.** Delays maybe characterized as follows:

____ (i) Government-caused: time, money.

____ (ii) Excusable: time, no money.

____ (iii) Contractor-caused: no time, no money.

____ (b) **Compensable delays.** Examples of compensable delays include: (i) lack of access, (ii) late approvals, (iii) defective design, (iv) late response to RFIs, (v) overinspection, (vi) improper rejection, (vii) differing site conditions, (viii) nondisclosure of superior knowledge, (ix) failure to coordinate multiple prime contractors, (x) active interference, and/or (xi) acceleration.

____ (c) **Excusable delays.** Excusable (but not compensable) delays include: (i) acts of God, (ii) unusually severe weather, (iii) strikes, (iv) acts of third parties, etc. However, if a government-caused delay pushes performance into an otherwise excusable delay period, the "excusable delay" can be compensable. For example, if a defective specification delays performance into bad weather or a labor strike, the weather or strike delays become compensable.

____ (d) **Schedule updates.** During the delay period, the contractor should prepare updates to its CPM schedule, depicting current conditions. A CPM schedule that is updated during contract performance and used for project scheduling is more persuasive evidence than one prepared for litigation only.

____ (e) **Proving delays.** To prove delay, a contractor will be expected to present a delay analysis. Types of delay analysis include (i) impacted as-planned, (ii) as-built critical path, (iii) collapsed as-built/but for, and (iv) time impact analysis (windows analysis).

____ (f) **Delay damages based on early completion.** A contractor can calculate delay damages based on an early completion date; however, there must be solid proof that (i) the contractor planned upon an early completion date, and (ii) the contractor could have met the earlier date.

____ (g) **Lost productivity.** Causes of lost productivity include (i) out-of-sequence work, (ii) stacking of trades, (iii) restricted or congested work areas, (iv) lack of access, (v) excessive overtime, (vi) weather, (vii) multiple changes and/or cumulative impact, and (viii) poor morale.

____ 7. **Recovery of Construction Costs.**

____ (a) **Establish cost codes.** Contractors are entitled to recover the actual costs of changed or extra work, plus overhead and profit. Establish cost codes for extra or changed work. Once such cost accounts are established, contractors should be careful that all applicable costs are charged to that account.

____ (b) **FAR Part 31.** On claims arising under the contract, costs are subject to FAR Part 31, Contract Cost Principles and Procedures. This means that certain costs will not be allowed as part of the claim, such as interest on borrowing (FAR 31.205-20), entertainment (FAR 31.205-14), and fines (FAR 31.205-15).

____ (c) **Recoverable delay and disruption costs.** Recoverable delay and disruption costs include (i) extended field overhead, (ii) labor and material escalation, (iii) extended equipment costs, (iv) unabsorbed home office overhead, (v) mobilization and demobilization costs, (vi) lost productivity costs, (vii) additional bond premiums, and (viii) profit.

____ (d) **Computing inefficiency costs.** Methods of computing disruption or inefficiency costs include (i) measured mile, (ii) industry manuals, (iii) expert estimates, and (iv) comparison with previous projects. There are numerous studies showing the effect of overtime and severe weather on labor productivity.

____ (e) **Field overhead.** General conditions or field overhead costs are allowable as either a direct or indirect cost, provided that the accounting method used complies with the contractor's established and consistently followed accounting practice for all work [FAR 31.105(d)(ii)(3)].

____ (f) **Owned equipment.** To the extent possible, equipment costs should be based on actual ownership and operating costs. The individual agencies may specify schedules of predetermined rates, to be used when actual equipment costs cannot be calculated [FAR 31.105(d)(2)(i)(A)].

____ (g) **Rented equipment.** Contractors may charge projects for the use of rented equipment. However, rental charges between related companies cannot exceed the actual costs of ownership [FAR 31.105(d)(2)(ii)(C); 31.205-36(b)(3)].

____ (h) **Total cost claims.** A total cost claim is one in which a contractor seeks to recover all of its costs in excess of the contract price. However, total cost claims are the least favored approach. The use of total cost claims require a showing that:

____ (i) It is impossible to prove damages any other way.

____ (ii) The contractor's bid is reasonable.

____ (iii) The contractor's costs are reasonable and accurately recorded.

____ (iv) The contractor is not responsible for any of the cost overruns.

____ (i) **Claim preparation costs.** The costs of preparing a claim are recoverable in requests for equitable adjustment; however, once the contractor submits a certified CDA claim, claim preparation costs are no longer recoverable.

____ (j) **CDA interest.** Interest is recoverable under the CDA, from the date of certification.

____ (k) **Profit.** Generally speaking, contractors can recover profit as an element of a request for equitable adjustment or claim. Contractors can support profit calculations by reference to similar projects. Generally, profit is not allowed on deleted or terminated work.

# Checklist 59: Avoiding False Claims on Federal Projects—Contractor

Because of recent fraud, waste and abuse initiatives by the U.S. Department of Justice, and existing and recently proposed regulatory requirements, federal contractors would be well advised to institute comprehensive compliance programs or perform a thorough review of existing compliance programs to determine whether they are adequate and fully operational. Only by instituting an effective compliance program can the potential for false claims be minimized.

____ 1. **What is a false claim?** The federal False Claims Act (FCA), 31 U.S.C. § 3729, 18 U.S.C. § 287, punishes the submission of false or fraudulent claims to the government. Civil penalties include treble the amount of the false claim, plus fines of $5,500 to $11,000 for each violation. Intentional violations can lead to criminal penalties of up to 5 years' imprisonment. The company may also be suspended or debarred from government work.

____ 2. **What are common types of false claims?** A common source of false claims is false or fraudulent progress payment requests. However, a false claim can also arise when the contract requires the use of certain materials, but the contractor instead uses different materials and then invoices the government for the materials specified in the contract. This is called "product substitution." Even if the contractor believes that the substituted materials are equal to or better than the specified materials, a false claim may have been committed because the government is entitled to receive exactly what it pays for. By the same token, a contractor cannot invoice the government for quality assurance testing that has not been performed or for work that is known to be defective. The FCA covers not only the intentional submission of a false claim, but also claims that are submitted with deliberate ignorance or reckless disregard for the falsity of the claim.

____ 3. **Does the FCA apply to federally funded projects?** Generally, yes. The courts are split on the question of whether a claim must be "presented" to the federal government for payment or approval on

**William W. Thompson, Jr.** is a partner in the Washington, D.C., office of Peckar & Abramson PC, specializing in government contracts, corporate ethics and compliance, and construction law. His compliance practice includes defending clients in false claims and debarment actions, conducting internal investigations, and assisting clients in structuring and implementing compliance programs.

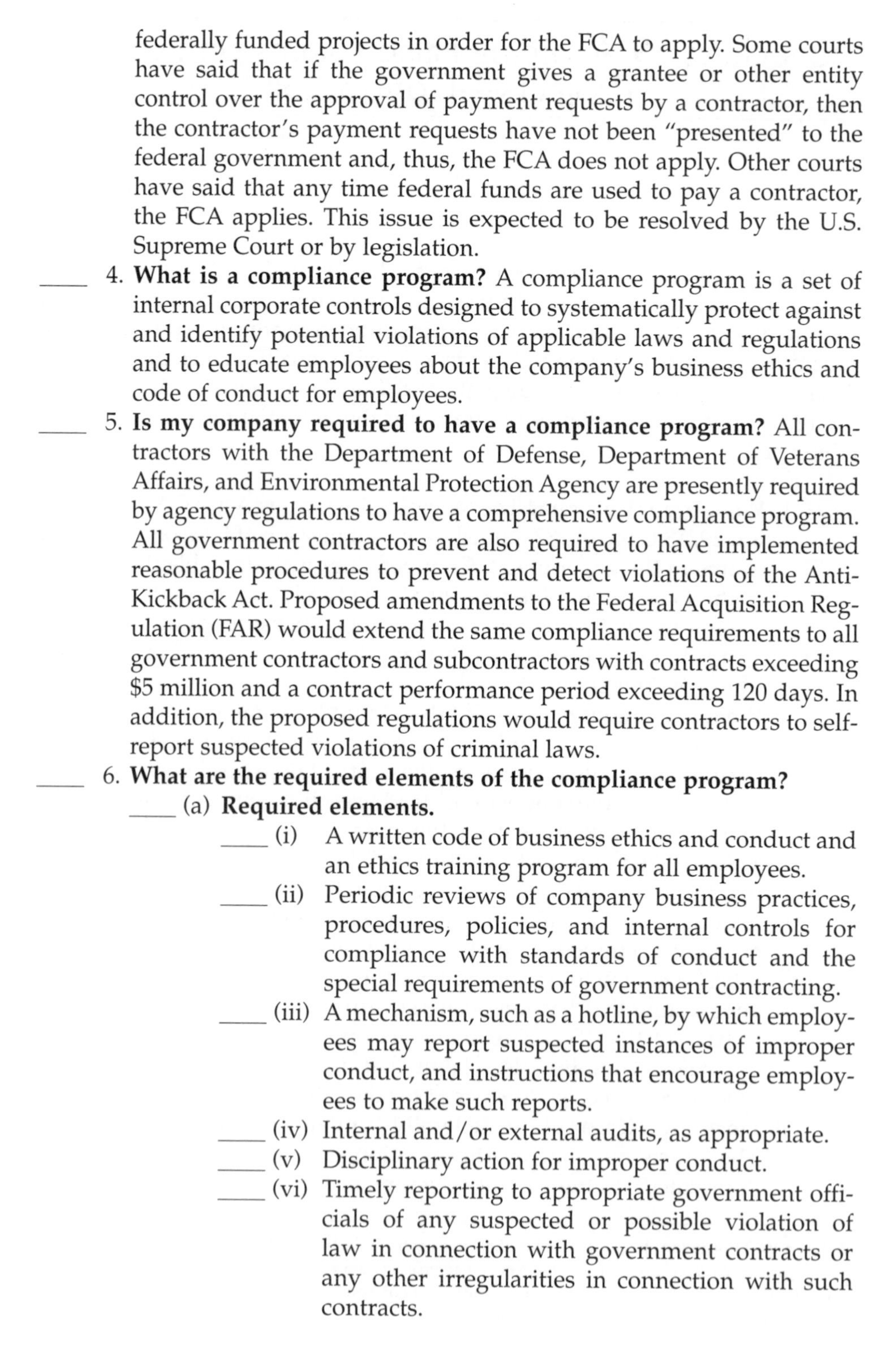

federally funded projects in order for the FCA to apply. Some courts have said that if the government gives a grantee or other entity control over the approval of payment requests by a contractor, then the contractor's payment requests have not been "presented" to the federal government and, thus, the FCA does not apply. Other courts have said that any time federal funds are used to pay a contractor, the FCA applies. This issue is expected to be resolved by the U.S. Supreme Court or by legislation.

____ 4. **What is a compliance program?** A compliance program is a set of internal corporate controls designed to systematically protect against and identify potential violations of applicable laws and regulations and to educate employees about the company's business ethics and code of conduct for employees.

____ 5. **Is my company required to have a compliance program?** All contractors with the Department of Defense, Department of Veterans Affairs, and Environmental Protection Agency are presently required by agency regulations to have a comprehensive compliance program. All government contractors are also required to have implemented reasonable procedures to prevent and detect violations of the Anti-Kickback Act. Proposed amendments to the Federal Acquisition Regulation (FAR) would extend the same compliance requirements to all government contractors and subcontractors with contracts exceeding $5 million and a contract performance period exceeding 120 days. In addition, the proposed regulations would require contractors to self-report suspected violations of criminal laws.

____ 6. **What are the required elements of the compliance program?**

____ (a) **Required elements.**

____ (i) A written code of business ethics and conduct and an ethics training program for all employees.

____ (ii) Periodic reviews of company business practices, procedures, policies, and internal controls for compliance with standards of conduct and the special requirements of government contracting.

____ (iii) A mechanism, such as a hotline, by which employees may report suspected instances of improper conduct, and instructions that encourage employees to make such reports.

____ (iv) Internal and/or external audits, as appropriate.

____ (v) Disciplinary action for improper conduct.

____ (vi) Timely reporting to appropriate government officials of any suspected or possible violation of law in connection with government contracts or any other irregularities in connection with such contracts.

____ (vii) Full cooperation with any government agencies responsible for either investigation or corrective actions.

____ (b) **Suggestions.** In addition, the Guidelines of the U.S. Sentencing Commission suggest that a company should appoint a management official or officials (often called an ethics officer or compliance committee) to exercise day-to-day operational control over the company's compliance program. To carry out this operational responsibility, the appointed individual(s) should be given "adequate resources, appropriate authority, and direct access to the governing authority or an appropriate subgroup of the governing authority." Consequently, the implementation of a compliance program must have the full support of the senior management of the company.

____ 7. **How can my company meet all of these requirements?** Although contractors must implement procedures and internal controls that address *each* of the required elements of the compliance program previously described, the level of complexity and sophistication of a given contractor's compliance program should be scaled according to:

____ (a) The size of the company.

____ (b) The volume of the company's federal contracts.

____ (c) Standard industry practice.

____ (d) Whether the contractor has had fraud, waste, and abuse problems in the past.

Thus, as an example, a small contractor might conduct periodic site visits to review progress payment requests as a form of internal auditing, as opposed to hiring outside consultants to perform such audits.

____ 8. **What is a "written code of business ethics and conduct"?** This code of business ethics and conduct consists of two basic components.

____ (a) **Statement of ethical principles.** A brief statement of the ethical principles that govern the company's business activities should be included.

____ (b) **Detailed description of laws and regulations.** A more detailed description of the various laws and regulations with which the company must comply should be included. For example, the False Claims Act should be described and examples of potential violations should be provided. It is critically important that these descriptive materials cover the specific risks that are common to the business areas in which a particular contract operates. Thus, contractors that sell manufactured products to the government that include materials of foreign origin should include a discussion of the Trade Agreements Act, whereas construction contractors should be more concerned with the Buy America Act. At a minimum, the code of conduct should explain the legal elements and consequences of false claims, false statements, kickbacks, gratuities and bribes, and collusive bidding. Employees should be advised of their responsibility to report suspected fraud, waste, and abuse and should be told how to anonymously report such suspected violations. This employee code of conduct should be provided to all employees as part of the company's employee manual and should be placed on the company's employee-accessed website.

____ 9. **What types of internal and external audits are required?**

____ (a) **Internal audits.** Contractors should conduct periodic (quarterly, if possible) internal audits of their compliance controls to ensure that they are operating effectively and that no new controls should be implemented because of changes in legal requirements. Typically, this means conducting a sampling of progress payment requests, certifications, purchasing department activities, and management controls for the contracts of all business units. Contractors should consider utilizing a written checklist that records the specific compliance controls that were sampled in each internal audit.

____ (b) **External audits.** Periodic external audits by outside counsel are also advisable to confirm that the contractor's compliance controls are fully operational. Internal and external audits should be conducted with greater frequency if systemic problems are discovered.

____ 10. **Who should oversee a contractor's compliance program?** Contractors should appoint an ethics officer or compliance committee, duly authorized by the board of directors or senior management, to fully and independently investigate reports of ethics violations.

____ 11. **What are my company's options for providing an anonymous mechanism for reporting violations?** Larger companies often find that it is efficient and cost effective to hire a private-service provider to operate a toll-free hotline or e-mail address to initially field questions or complaints. A less costly approach is to provide employees with a toll-free number that will be answered by a compliance officer of the company or a telephone number with voice mail requesting a number to promptly return the call. The advantage of using a private-service provider is that it distances the company from the complainant and makes it easier to ensure that anonymity is maintained, at least in the initial interview. Depending on the seriousness of the issues raised by the complainant, the ethics officer may conduct a preliminary internal investigation. If the complaint raises issues that suggest the possibility of criminal or civil liability for the company or its employees, the compliance officer often will recommend to senior management that the company retain outside counsel to conduct an independent investigation.

____ 12. **If there is a credible report of potentially serious wrongdoing, who should conduct an internal investigation?** Internal investigations are normally conducted by the company's in-house or outside counsel. Nonlawyer company employees (such as Human Resources) should not investigate potentially serious wrongdoing because no legal privilege will attach to the investigation, and any information gathered in the investigation would have to be disgorged to the government in the event of a government investigation. Although in-house counsel can conduct an investigation, preservation of the attorney–client privilege is more difficult because the government may later argue that the recommendations of in-house counsel are in the nature of business advice rather than legal advice. Using outside counsel is usually preferable because of outside counsel's independence and its ability to better protect the attorney–client privilege. In addition, counsel that specializes in compliance will normally be experienced in conducting internal investigations and, thus, will understand the techniques for conducting witness interviews and the relevant considerations in developing and delivering recommendations to senior management at the conclusion of the investigation.

____ 13. **What are the consequences of failing to institute a required compliance program?** Contractors that fail to implement required compliance programs are at risk on many different levels. First, and most obviously, the absence of a compliance program makes it less likely that a contractor will prevent or identify ethics violations. Second, if a contractor has established an effective, fully operational compliance program, the Department of Justice (DOJ) may look more favorably upon the company if it has committed an ethics violation, notwithstanding its compliance program. For example, the DOJ may decide to prosecute the offending employee but not the company. Third, a recent federal district court decision indicated that a company's failure to institute a required compliance program may be *prima facie* evidence of intent to defraud under the False Claims Act. Finally, as many privately held companies have found after voluntarily implementing Sarbanes-Oxley financial controls, compliance programs are considered a "best practice" that may enhance a company's standing and value in the marketplace.

____ 14. **How can a compliance program detect and prevent false claims?**

____ (a) **Institute and audit internal controls.** By instituting internal controls that ensure the accuracy of payment requests and other certifications to the government, and then auditing those controls, a contractor should be able to minimize the potential for false claims.

____ (b) **Types of internal controls to implement.** Among the controls that a contractor should consider implementing include the following:

____ (i) Before submitting a progress payment request to the government or to the owner on a federally funded project, ensure that all of the information is truthful and accurate, including the status of payments to subcontractors, and that invoiced work has been performed in accordance with the requirements of the contract.

____ (ii) The government should never be invoiced for work that has not been performed or for subcontractor work before an invoice has been submitted by the subcontractor to the company.

____ (iii) Special care should be devoted to progress payment requests on cost reimbursement or guaranteed maximum price (GMP) projects to ensure that only reimbursable costs that have been paid or incurred are invoiced.

____ (iv) Only allowable, allocable, and reasonable costs may be charged to the government on a cost reimbursement or GMP contract. The same is true on change orders that are issued and performed before agreement on price, and the contractor's price adjustment is based upon such incurred costs.

____ (v) Only bond premiums that have been actually paid may be invoiced to the government on fixed price contracts.

____ (vi) Progress payment requests should be consistent with certified payrolls and the schedule of values.

____ (vii) Payments should be made to subcontractors within 7 days in accordance with the Prompt Payment Act.

# International Contracting

# Checklist 60: Common Issues in Drafting International Dispute Resolution Clauses

Anticipating how disputes will be resolved on a construction project prior to commencement of work will greatly assist in effective resolution and potentially save all parties significant time and expense. This checklist discusses issues that arise for drafters of a dispute resolution clause in the international context.

____ 1. **What type of disputes are covered?** In drafting a dispute resolution clause, an initial decision should be made considering what types of disputes will be governed by the clause. For example, the parties may wish to resolve payment-related claims or construction defect claims through some form of alternative dispute resolution process, while allowing claims related to personal injury to be resolved in court.

____ 2. **Opportunity for Nonbinding Negotiation or Mediation.** To facilitate cooperation and to keep the contentious nature of disputes at a minimum as well as saving the parties time and expense, it may be advisable to create a tiered or "step" dispute resolution process that utilizes negotiation, mediation or both prior to arbitration or litigation. The American Arbitration Association has recommended the following examples to provide for a tiered process:

> In the event of any controversy or claim arising out of or relating to this contract, the parties hereto shall consult and negotiate with each other and, recognizing their mutual interests, attempt to reach a solution satisfactory to both parties. If they do not reach settlement within a period of 60 days, then either party may, by notice to the other party and the International Centre for Dispute Resolution, demand mediation under the International Mediation Rules of the International Centre for Dispute Resolution. If settlement is not reached within 60 days after service of a written demand for mediation, any unresolved controversy or claim arising out of or relating to this contract shall be settled by arbitration in accordance with the International Arbitration Rules of the International Centre for Dispute Resolution.
>
> In the event of any controversy or claim arising out of or relating to this contract, the parties hereto agree first to try and settle the dispute

**R. Carson Fisk** is an attorney at Ford Nassen & Baldwin P.C. in the Austin, Texas, office. Mr. Fisk represents owners, general contractors, and subcontractors in both contentious and noncontentious matters. He regularly assists clients in drafting contract documents and represents them in litigation, arbitration, administrative actions, and mediation.

by mediation administered by the International Centre for Dispute Resolution under its rules before resorting to arbitration, litigation, or some other dispute resolution technique.[1]

The Dispute Resolution Services division of the International Chamber of Commerce suggests the following clauses, which may be adapted to suit the specific needs of the parties:

> The parties may at any time, without prejudice to any other proceedings, seek to settle any dispute arising out of or in connection with the present contract in accordance with the ICC ADR Rules.
>
> In the event of any dispute arising out of or in connection with the present contract, the parties agree in the first instance to discuss and consider submitting the matter to settlement proceedings under the ICC ADR Rules.
>
> In the event of any dispute arising out of or in connection with the present contract, the parties agree to submit the matter to settlement proceedings under the ICC ADR Rules. If the dispute has not been settled pursuant to the said Rules within 45 days following the filing of a Request for ADR or within such other period as the parties may agree in writing, the parties shall have no further obligations under this paragraph.
>
> In the event of any dispute arising out of or in connection with the present contract, the parties agree to submit the matter to settlement proceedings under the ICC ADR Rules. If the dispute has not been settled pursuant to the said Rules within 45 days following the filing of a Request for ADR or within such other period as the parties may agree in writing, such dispute shall be finally settled under the Rules of Arbitration of the International Chamber of Commerce by one or more arbitrators appointed in accordance with the said Rules of Arbitration.[2]

____ 3. **What parties sign or are otherwise bound by the agreement?** Depending on the applicable law, there may be some basis to require nonsignatories to participate in the dispute resolution process. The parties can address the issue by including flow-down clauses in the subcontracts, requiring multiple parties to sign the agreement, or otherwise incorporating the dispute resolution agreement or clause in the relevant contract.

____ 4. **Number of Arbitrators.** As in domestic arbitration, the parties may wish to have disputes resolved by a single arbitrator or perhaps a panel of multiple arbitrators of different nationalities or specialties such as attorneys, contractors, or design professionals.

____ 5. **Nationality of Third-Party Neutral or Arbitrator.** The parties may wish to consider requiring that any mediator or arbitrator be a national of a specific country or, conversely, not a national of a specific country. This may be particularly advisable if the parties wish to avoid the appearance of bias or unfair advantage. The American

Arbitration Association has recommended the following examples: (a) "The arbitrator(s) shall be a national of [country]"; (b) "[t]he arbitrator(s) shall not be a national of either [country A] or [country B]"; and (c) "[t]he arbitrator(s) shall not be of the nationality of either of the parties."[3]

____ 6. **Language of the Proceedings.** If the parties are of different nationalities or otherwise multilingual, the language in which any dispute resolution proceeding will be conducted may be one of the more practical, yet critical, considerations for the parties. A party to a dispute may feel at a significant disadvantage if a dispute resolution proceeding is conducted in a foreign language of which the party has no or limited understanding. The American Arbitration Association has recommended the following examples: (a) "The language(s) of the arbitration shall be [specify]" and (b) "[t]he arbitration shall be conducted in the language in which the contract was written."[4]

____ 7. **Selection and Cost Allocation for Interpreter.** If necessary, the parties could consider how the services of an interpreter will be obtained and how any costs will be allocated.

____ 8. **Venue.** Another important practical consideration is where any dispute resolution procedure will occur. Perhaps the most common place would be the location of the project, although where one of the parties is located may also be preferable. Alternatively, the parties may elect to conduct any proceedings in a neutral location.

____ 9. **Choice of Law.** Certain institutions, such as the American Arbitration Association, provide procedural rules to determine the governing law in the event the choice of law is not specified. This may be a critical consideration depending on where the project is located.

____ 10. **Governing Rules.** This issue is more fully addressed in the International Arbitration Rules and Procedures checklist. The American Arbitration Association has recommended the following examples for determining the governing rules:

> Any controversy or claim arising out of or relating to this contract shall be determined by arbitration in accordance with the International Arbitration Rules of the International Centre for Dispute Resolution.
>
> Any dispute, controversy, or claim arising out of or relating to this contract, or the breach thereof, shall be finally settled by arbitration administered by the Commercial Arbitration and Mediation Center for the Americas in accordance with its rules, and judgment on the award rendered by the arbitrator(s) may be entered in any court having jurisdiction thereof.
>
> Any dispute, controversy, or claim arising from or relating to this contract, or the breach, termination, or invalidity thereof, shall be settled by arbitration in accordance with the Rules of Procedure of the Inter-American Commercial Arbitration Commission in effect on the date of this agreement.

> Any dispute, controversy, or claim arising out of or relating to this contract, or the breach, termination, or invalidity thereof, shall be settled by arbitration under the UNCITRAL Arbitration Rules in effect on the date of this contract. The appointing authority shall be the International Centre for Dispute Resolution. The case shall be administered by the International Centre for Dispute Resolution under its Procedures for Cases under the UNCITRAL Arbitration Rules.[5]

The Dispute Resolution Services division of the International Chamber of Commerce suggests the following clause:

> All disputes arising out of or in connection with the present contract shall be finally settled under the Rules of Arbitration of the International Chamber of Commerce by one or more arbitrators appointed in accordance with the said Rules.[6]

____ 11. **Time Limit for Rendering Award.** Including a timeframe within which an award is rendered may help the parties avoid disputes concerning when final resolution will be attained.

____ 12. **Enforcement of Settlement Agreement or Award.** It is certainly advisable to fully research and address the enforceability of an arbitration award or settlement agreement under the governing law. The successful resolution of a dispute obviously means nothing if the resulting award or agreement cannot be enforced.

____ 13. **Recovery of Fees, Costs, and Expenses.** The parties can expressly provide for the recovery of fees, costs, or expenses. However, this would generally require a prevailing party, something absent in mediated or other types of settlement agreements.

## *Notes*

1. Drafting Dispute Resolution Clauses—A Practical Guide (American Arbitration Association, 2004), p. 15.

2. See http://www.iccwbo.org/court/.

3. The AAA Guide to Drafting Alternative Dispute Resolution Clauses for Construction Contract (National Construction Dispute Resolution Committee), p. 19.

4. *Id.* at 20.

5. Drafting Dispute Resolution Clauses—A Practical Guide (American Arbitration Association, 2004), pp. 13-14.

6. See http://www.iccwbo.org/court/.

# Checklist 61: International Arbitration Rules and Procedures

The following checklist is intended to assist lawyers whose clients face disputes on international projects that are subject to either mandatory or voluntary arbitration. It is important to draft a workable and clear arbitration clause in the contract documents, before a dispute has arisen (see preceding checklist, "Common Issues in Drafting International Dispute Resolution Clauses.") This checklist endeavors to address the essential considerations for international commercial arbitrations, but does not provide an exhaustive list of the issues or available resources. When advising clients, it is recommended that foreign local counsel be consulted.

___ 1. **Have the parties agreed to submit disputes to arbitration?**

____ (a) **Contract review.** Parties can refer disputes to arbitration in two ways:

____ (i) By agreement after the dispute has arisen ("ad hoc agreements").

____ (ii) By agreement to refer disputes arising in the future to arbitration ("future disputes agreements"). Such agreements typically form part of much larger agreements governing the relationship between the parties.

If there is an arbitration clause but a party does not wish to participate, the New York Convention, if applicable, will compel that party to take part in the arbitration provided it is an arbitrable dispute.

____ (b) **Definition of "dispute" by parties.** Parties must define the actual dispute submitted to arbitration in an ad hoc clause or define the type of disputes to be referred to arbitration in the future in a future disputes clause. In either case, care and accuracy during the drafting stage are required to avoid

**Wendy J. Earle** and **Matthew R. Alter** are partners in the Toronto office of the Canadian law firm, Borden Ladner Gervais LLP. Earle practices in the area of commercial litigation and provides advice on all types of arbitration and ADR agreements. She is the author of the first Canadian text on drafting ADR and arbitration clauses, *Drafting ADR and Arbitration Clauses for Commercial Contracts*, published by Carswell Co. in 2001. Alter is a certified specialist in construction law with the Law Society of Upper Canada, a fellow of the Canadian College of Construction Lawyers, and member of the Steering Committee for Division 8 of the ABA Forum on the Construction Industry. His practice involves representing parties at the front end of domestic and international projects and in all types of construction-related disputes.

lengthy procedural wrangling over whether a particular dispute is or is not included in the reference to arbitration.

____ 2. **Is the dispute arbitrable?** A dispute is generally not arbitrable if it is not arbitrable under the law governing the arbitration agreement or the law of the arbitration venue. Issues that are arbitrable or not arbitrable differ from country to country (typically issues that are not arbitrable involve issues of a public nature such as labor relations, employment standards, family relations, consumer protection, etc.). Intellectual property disputes are also not arbitrable in some countries. Consider also that some jurisdictions do not permit future-dispute clauses in arbitration agreements to be used to avoid class actions.

____ 3. **What should the arbitration agreement specifically address?**

____ (a) **Law governing the arbitration.**

____ (i) Parties should explicitly state which law will govern the interpretation of the contract.

____ (ii) The law of the jurisdiction where the arbitration is heard also determines the interpretation of the arbitration agreement.

____ (iii) The procedure will be determined by the jurisdiction in which the arbitration is heard. If this is not desirable, parties can stipulate which jurisdiction's procedure they want to govern their arbitration, but must also dictate which jurisdiction will handle procedural disputes.

____ (b) **Place of arbitration.** See Section 11 for further discussion.

____ (c) **Treaty/legislation governing arbitration.** These should be specified in the arbitration agreement. New York United Nations Commission on International Trade Law (UNCITRAL) Convention and the Model Law are frequently referenced for this purpose, along with the domestic legislation in the place of arbitration which implements the UNCITRAL Model Law. However, parties can agree to have their arbitration governed by domestic arbitration legislation unrelated to the UNCITRAL Model Law (if available).

____ (d) **Binding all relevant parties by the agreement.** The arbitration agreement should contemplate who will need to be a party to the arbitration to avoid settling part of the dispute through arbitration and another part through the court system or a parallel adjudication process. Commonly forgotten parties in construction contract disputes include subcontractors, suppliers, and design consultants. Many alternatives exist to bind all relevant parties, including:

____ (i) Require that all further contracts the main parties enter into contain the same arbitration agreement

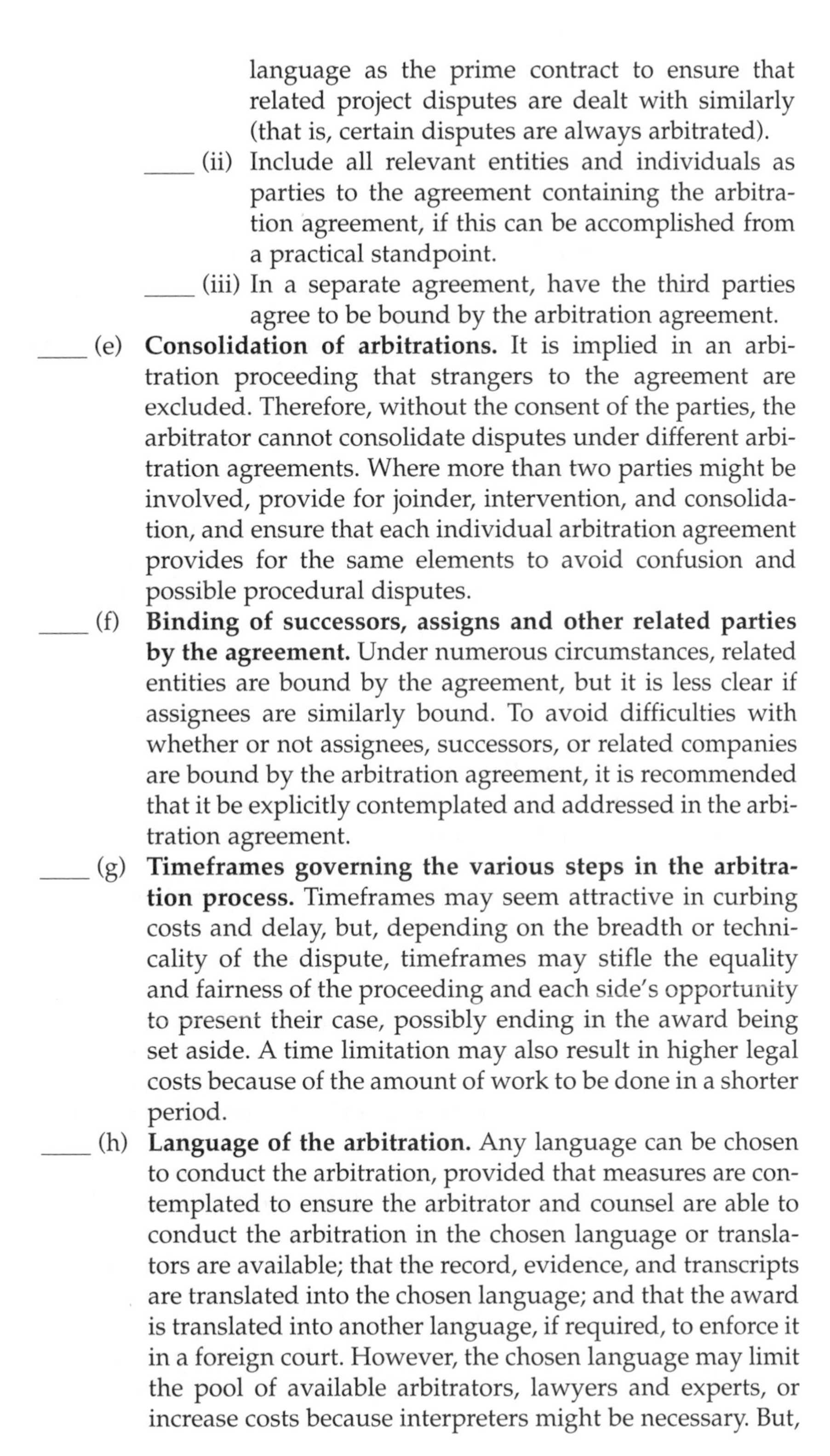

language as the prime contract to ensure that related project disputes are dealt with similarly (that is, certain disputes are always arbitrated).

____ (ii) Include all relevant entities and individuals as parties to the agreement containing the arbitration agreement, if this can be accomplished from a practical standpoint.

____ (iii) In a separate agreement, have the third parties agree to be bound by the arbitration agreement.

____ (e) **Consolidation of arbitrations.** It is implied in an arbitration proceeding that strangers to the agreement are excluded. Therefore, without the consent of the parties, the arbitrator cannot consolidate disputes under different arbitration agreements. Where more than two parties might be involved, provide for joinder, intervention, and consolidation, and ensure that each individual arbitration agreement provides for the same elements to avoid confusion and possible procedural disputes.

____ (f) **Binding of successors, assigns and other related parties by the agreement.** Under numerous circumstances, related entities are bound by the agreement, but it is less clear if assignees are similarly bound. To avoid difficulties with whether or not assignees, successors, or related companies are bound by the arbitration agreement, it is recommended that it be explicitly contemplated and addressed in the arbitration agreement.

____ (g) **Timeframes governing the various steps in the arbitration process.** Timeframes may seem attractive in curbing costs and delay, but, depending on the breadth or technicality of the dispute, timeframes may stifle the equality and fairness of the proceeding and each side's opportunity to present their case, possibly ending in the award being set aside. A time limitation may also result in higher legal costs because of the amount of work to be done in a shorter period.

____ (h) **Language of the arbitration.** Any language can be chosen to conduct the arbitration, provided that measures are contemplated to ensure the arbitrator and counsel are able to conduct the arbitration in the chosen language or translators are available; that the record, evidence, and transcripts are translated into the chosen language; and that the award is translated into another language, if required, to enforce it in a foreign court. However, the chosen language may limit the pool of available arbitrators, lawyers and experts, or increase costs because interpreters might be necessary. But, certain countries require the arbitration to be conducted in their language.

____ (i) **Survival of the arbitration agreement beyond termination or expiry of the contract.** Once the contract has expired or been terminated, it may be necessary to have a specific provision keeping alive the arbitration agreement in order to arbitrate disputes under that agreement.

____ (j) **Continued performance of contract while arbitration proceedings are ongoing.** In some cases, the continuation of the contract during arbitration is advantageous. It can minimize disruption and economic loss, but its effectiveness is dependent on the circumstances of the dispute. In cases of repudiation or abandonment, fundamental breach, or noncompetition clauses, continuation may not be wanted or feasible.

____ (k) **Continuance of arbitration where one party abandons or refuses to participate.** Arbitration legislation does not always contemplate continuing proceedings when one party does not participate in the arbitration (for example, a party fails to deliver a statement or documents on time or even fails to attend). To enjoy the option of continuing the arbitration, it is necessary to explicitly address the issue.

____ (l) **Opposing party is a sovereign state or entity owned or controlled by a sovereign state.** Consider whether the opposing party is protected by sovereign immunity laws and whether the sovereign state can waive immunity.

____ (m) **Confidentiality/publicity issues.** Confidentiality used to be an implied obligation of an arbitration, but now, where it may be a matter of public interest, it cannot be assumed that confidentiality will be upheld. Parties should take care to provide for confidentiality in the agreement. Conversely, negative publicity can be a powerful threat in an arbitration and confidentiality may be a hindrance to this effective tool.

____ (i) **Pleadings, evidence, and other underlying materials.** These documents—the materials used by the arbitrator prior to award—have been held by the English courts to be confidential by the implied obligation.

____ (ii) **The arbitrator's award and reasons.** In subsequent proceedings (for example, enforcement of the award), the parties, regardless of their choice to maintain confidentiality, may have to disclose confidential documents to aid the proceeding.

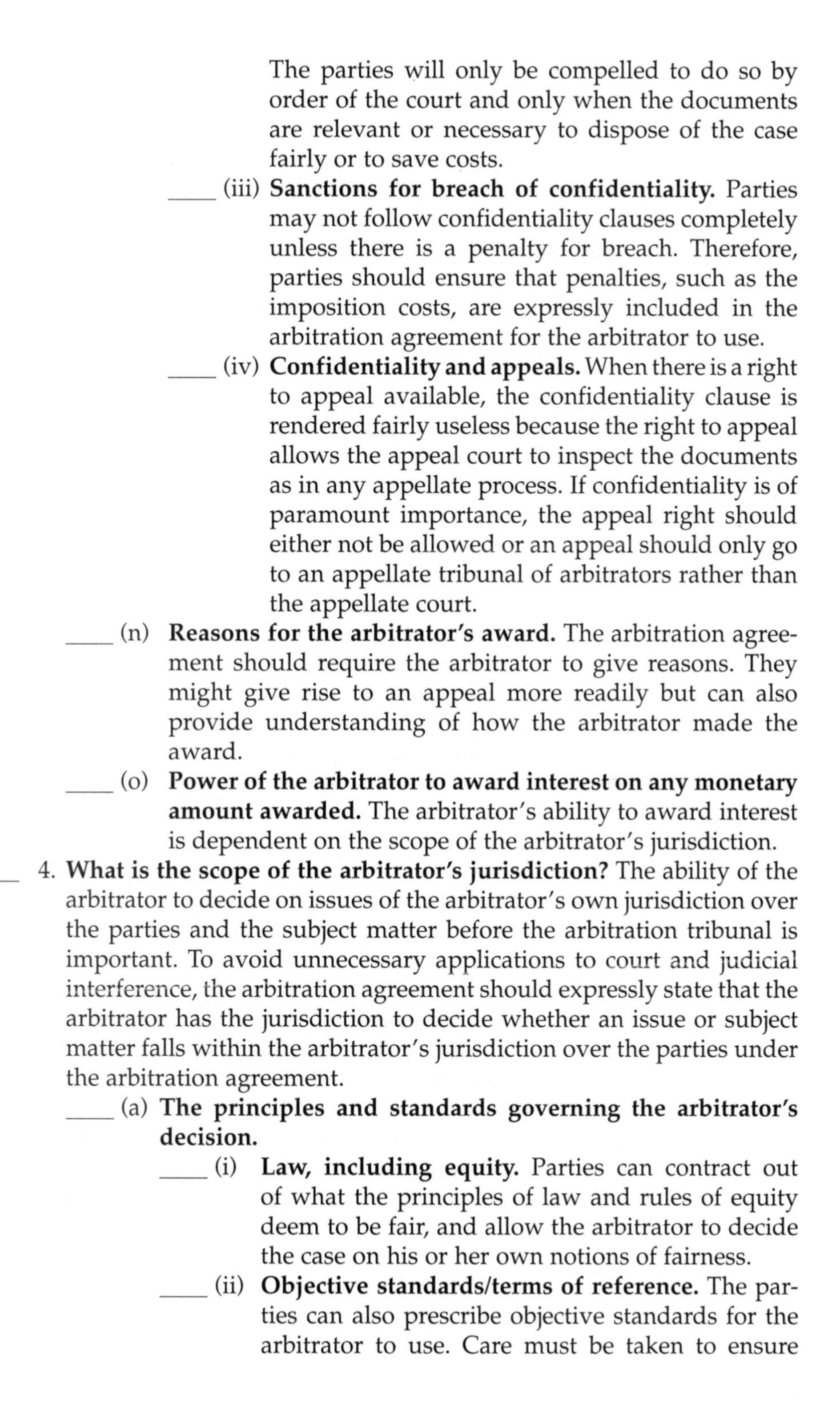

The parties will only be compelled to do so by order of the court and only when the documents are relevant or necessary to dispose of the case fairly or to save costs.

____ (iii) **Sanctions for breach of confidentiality.** Parties may not follow confidentiality clauses completely unless there is a penalty for breach. Therefore, parties should ensure that penalties, such as the imposition costs, are expressly included in the arbitration agreement for the arbitrator to use.

____ (iv) **Confidentiality and appeals.** When there is a right to appeal available, the confidentiality clause is rendered fairly useless because the right to appeal allows the appeal court to inspect the documents as in any appellate process. If confidentiality is of paramount importance, the appeal right should either not be allowed or an appeal should only go to an appellate tribunal of arbitrators rather than the appellate court.

____ (n) **Reasons for the arbitrator's award.** The arbitration agreement should require the arbitrator to give reasons. They might give rise to an appeal more readily but can also provide understanding of how the arbitrator made the award.

____ (o) **Power of the arbitrator to award interest on any monetary amount awarded.** The arbitrator's ability to award interest is dependent on the scope of the arbitrator's jurisdiction.

____ 4. **What is the scope of the arbitrator's jurisdiction?** The ability of the arbitrator to decide on issues of the arbitrator's own jurisdiction over the parties and the subject matter before the arbitration tribunal is important. To avoid unnecessary applications to court and judicial interference, the arbitration agreement should expressly state that the arbitrator has the jurisdiction to decide whether an issue or subject matter falls within the arbitrator's jurisdiction over the parties under the arbitration agreement.

____ (a) **The principles and standards governing the arbitrator's decision.**

____ (i) **Law, including equity.** Parties can contract out of what the principles of law and rules of equity deem to be fair, and allow the arbitrator to decide the case on his or her own notions of fairness.

____ (ii) **Objective standards/terms of reference.** The parties can also prescribe objective standards for the arbitrator to use. Care must be taken to ensure that the desired standards are referred to in the arbitration agreement, and that they are clear and comprehensive enough to be useful and avoid hiring experts to comment on the chosen objective standards.

____ (b) **The range of remedies that the arbitrator can award.** Parties may wish to limit the range of remedies available to the arbitrator (for example, nonprofit corporations may not want monetary remedies). Parties should ensure their intention as to the breadth of remedies is explicitly stated in the arbitration agreement. Typical remedies include:

____ (i) **Damages.**

____ (ii) **Punitive, aggravated, triple damages.**

____ (iii) **Injunctive relief (interlocutory and permanent).** Courts in some jurisdictions may grant asset preserving orders and/or other interim relief, which are the judicial "seat" of the arbitration. While an arbitrator can award an injunction, the arbitrator cannot enforce it, which will force the parties to go to court to get the injunction enforced if the party refuses to comply.

____ (iv) **Mandatory orders/specific performance.**

____ (v) **Is remedy provided intended to exclude other remedies?** In specifying a particular remedy, it must also be specified if that remedy is to preclude all others or if other remedies are still available.

____ (vi) **Should there be limitations on the arbitrator's remedies?** The parties can limit which remedies it wants the arbitrator to award for various reasons, such as the goals of the parties and the nature of the dispute.

____ (vii) **Does law governing the agreement or the arbitration prohibit the parties agreeing to certain limits on the remedies which the arbitrator can award?**

____ (c) **Costs and expenses.** In the arbitration agreement, the award of costs and expenses should be considered. Parties should take into account the types of costs and expenses the arbitrator can award and to whom, and on what basis. Many different arrangements can be made, including:

____ (i) Having each party bear its own costs and share the arbitrator's expense.

____ (ii) Having the arbitrator award costs and expenses against the unsuccessful party.

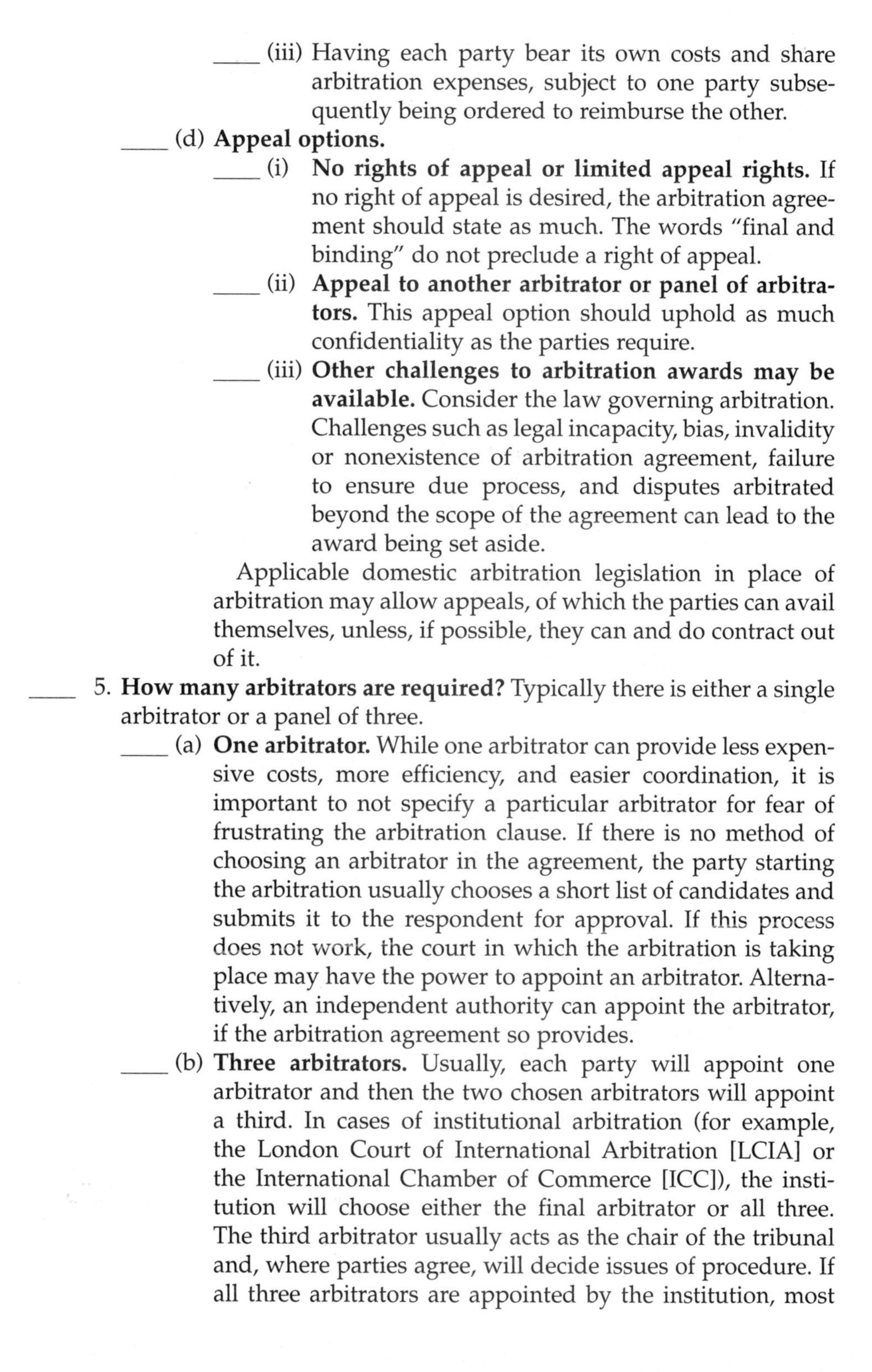

____ (iii) Having each party bear its own costs and share arbitration expenses, subject to one party subsequently being ordered to reimburse the other.

____ (d) **Appeal options.**

____ (i) **No rights of appeal or limited appeal rights.** If no right of appeal is desired, the arbitration agreement should state as much. The words "final and binding" do not preclude a right of appeal.

____ (ii) **Appeal to another arbitrator or panel of arbitrators.** This appeal option should uphold as much confidentiality as the parties require.

____ (iii) **Other challenges to arbitration awards may be available.** Consider the law governing arbitration. Challenges such as legal incapacity, bias, invalidity or nonexistence of arbitration agreement, failure to ensure due process, and disputes arbitrated beyond the scope of the agreement can lead to the award being set aside.

Applicable domestic arbitration legislation in place of arbitration may allow appeals, of which the parties can avail themselves, unless, if possible, they can and do contract out of it.

____ 5. **How many arbitrators are required?** Typically there is either a single arbitrator or a panel of three.

____ (a) **One arbitrator.** While one arbitrator can provide less expensive costs, more efficiency, and easier coordination, it is important to not specify a particular arbitrator for fear of frustrating the arbitration clause. If there is no method of choosing an arbitrator in the agreement, the party starting the arbitration usually chooses a short list of candidates and submits it to the respondent for approval. If this process does not work, the court in which the arbitration is taking place may have the power to appoint an arbitrator. Alternatively, an independent authority can appoint the arbitrator, if the arbitration agreement so provides.

____ (b) **Three arbitrators.** Usually, each party will appoint one arbitrator and then the two chosen arbitrators will appoint a third. In cases of institutional arbitration (for example, the London Court of International Arbitration [LCIA] or the International Chamber of Commerce [ICC]), the institution will choose either the final arbitrator or all three. The third arbitrator usually acts as the chair of the tribunal and, where parties agree, will decide issues of procedure. If all three arbitrators are appointed by the institution, most issues of independence and impartiality (because a party-appointed arbitrator may feel affinity toward its appointer) are resolved.

____ 6. **Which procedure should be chosen?** The parties have the following choices with regard to the procedure to be adopted:

____ (a) To say nothing, in which case the arbitral tribunal will (subject to the domestic law of the place of the arbitration) be free to determine the rules of procedure.

____ (b) To adopt the rules of procedure of the domestic law of the place of arbitration.

____ (c) To adopt the rules of procedure of another jurisdiction (to the extent permitted by the law of the place of arbitration).

____ (d) To adopt the rules of procedure established by a body other than a national legislature.

____ (e) To set out specific rules of procedure in the arbitration agreement clause itself.

If the nature or frequency of possible disputes is difficult to predict, parties should consider not detailing procedure in the arbitration agreement. Instead, an experienced arbitrator can decide the best procedure with regard to the circumstances of the specific dispute.

____ 7. **What rules are required regarding evidence?** Consider whether it is desirable to agree in advance to prescribed rules of evidence that arbitrators must follow (for example, only admit such evidence as would be permitted in a particular jurisdiction's Superior Court, adopt those of chosen arbitration rules, or rely on national arbitration laws to determine evidentiary limits). National arbitration laws come into play when the parties have not chosen rules or when evidence from nonparty persons is required. Both the UNCITRAL and the Federal Arbitration Act (FAA) invest arbitrators with the U.S. FAA, 9 USC § 1, discretionary powers to compel third parties to produce evidence.

____ 8. **Deposition options.** The range of possibilities can extend from no depositions to the range of depositions as found in the U.S. Federal Rules of Civil Procedure. When drafting the deposition rules desired, attention must be made to the type of disputes that might arise and the probability that the parties will comply with the deposition process provided.

____ (a) **When depositions are not specifically dealt with in the arbitration clause.** In this situation, the arbitration rules chosen will give the arbitral tribunal the power to require deposition. Generally, the rules do not require deposition, but instead provide a discretionary power for the arbitral tribunal to order depositions in a limited manner. The ICC

Rules provide the least opportunity for depositions while the LCIA and UNCITRAL provide greater powers for the arbitral tribunal. The arbitral tribunal generally takes into account the parties' expectations and background and the nature of the transaction in dispute when exercising its discretion.

____ (b) **IBA rules.** To supplement any party-chosen or institutional discovery rules, the International Bar Association (IBA) provides a middle ground between civil and common law procedures. Under the IBA rules, each party is required to submit to both the arbitral tribunal and the other parties all documents that are relied on and available. Also, a party can request, through the tribunal, that another party produce a document provided they explain why it is necessary to be produced. The AAA, International Arbitration Rules, provide that the tribunal may order a party to deliver to the tribunal and to the other parties a summary of the documents and other evidence which that party intends to present in support of its claim, counterclaim, or defense.

____ 9. **Is the arbitration well suited to having an institution administer it?**

____ (a) **Review the fee structure of proposed arbitration institution**. Is it acceptable? Is it reasonable in light of amount in issue? Sometimes an institutional arbitration's fee can be based on a percentage of the value of the dispute, which can cost more than an ad hoc arbitration.

____ (b) **Multiple parties, large numbers of documents, or other circumstances.** Institutional arbitration provides an administrative structure that can be helpful when multiple parties and documents are involved, because the structure is predictable. Even though an ad hoc arbitration provides flexibility, with multiple parties involved the flexibility may become cumbersome, leading to increased costs and procedural disputes.

____ (c) **Review the rules of the proposed arbitration institution.**

____ (i) **Do they permit the arbitral tribunal to decide its own jurisdiction?**

____ (ii) **Do the rules require the arbitrators to be neutral and have the necessary expertise?** It is preferable for the parties to have access to well-established arbitrators, qualified in the subject matter of the dispute?

____ (iii) **What standards of disclosure does the arbitral institution require of the arbitrator so that the**

**parties can evaluate neutrality as needed?** Do the rules provide for a challenge to a proposed arbitrator for lack of neutrality?

____ (iv) **Do the arbitration rules provide a procedure to appoint an arbitrator if one party fails to appoint one?**

____ (v) **Do the arbitration institution's rules permit the arbitrator to authorize disclosure of documents prior to the hearing?** If so, do they permit the arbitrator to determine in advance the type of documents to be disclosed in the absence of an agreement between the parties?

____ (vi) **Do the arbitration institution's rules permit arbitrators to appoint their own experts?** There is a growing trend, particularly in international arbitrations in the United Kingdom and Europe, toward permitting the arbitration tribunal to appoint its own experts and thereby reduce the costs of a "battle of experts," which often occurs.

____ (vii) **Do the arbitration institution's rules permit hearings with oral evidence?** Civil law court procedures are often based only on documents and written statements, while common law jurisdictions place more emphasis on oral evidence. A hearing with written submissions and oral evidence may not be the norm in international arbitrations, so parties who want it should ensure that the rules provide for it.

____ (viii) **Do the arbitration institution's rules provide a procedure for the hearing to proceed in the absence of a party, provided that the party has been given reasonable and appropriate notice?** Such a provision precludes an arbitration from floundering because one party chooses not to appear.

____ (ix) **Do the arbitration institution's rules allow a party to apply for security for costs?** If so, what is the test?

____ (x) **Does the arbitration institution require that awards be reasoned and in writing?** The existence of a written award may well be significant if there is an appeal to a court or another level of arbitration.

____ (xi) **How does the institution select its arbitrators?**

____ (xii) **How long does it take the arbitration institution to form an arbitration tribunal?** This could be very significant where a party requires the appointment of an arbitration tribunal in circumstances of urgency because a party needs an interim injunction or other emergency relief.

____ (xiii) **What standards of review does the arbitration institution exercise over its roster of arbitrators?** Does it review the awards (as in the case of the ICC)? Does it conduct evaluations of the performance of its roster of arbitrators?

____ (xiv) **What appeal rights does the arbitration institution afford to the parties?** Are the appeal rights satisfactory to the parties or should the parties agree on different appeal rights or no appeal rights?

____ 10. **How do you select the arbitrator(s)?** The arbitration agreement should specify how the arbitrator is selected.

____ (a) **Selection options.**

____ (i) Court in place of arbitration appoints arbitrator.

____ (ii) Designated appointing authority (for example, arbitration institution) appoints arbitrator. If so, the arbitration agreement needs reference to the Designated Appointing Authority or to the Rules of the Arbitration Institution.

____ (iii) Parties agree on roster of arbitrators before dispute arises (the more names the better).

____ (iv) Parties agree on a process to appoint arbitrator (for example, coin toss between nominees).

____ (b) **Selection considerations.**

____ (i) Do parties require arbitrators with technical expertise? If so, qualifications should be specified.

____ (ii) Ensure no conflict of interest or reasonable apprehension of bias.

____ 11. **Where should the arbitration take place?**

____ (a) **Does the proposed place of arbitration have a modern arbitration law that respects the principle of party autonomy, restricts the role of the local courts, and minimizes the grounds upon which an award can be set aside?** This question is often best answered by ascertaining whether or not jurisdiction has adopted in whole or in part the UNCITRAL Model Law.

____ (b) **Where are the opposing party's assets located?** Are the opposing party's assets capable of being seized to satisfy an award under the laws of the place where the arbitration is to take place or arbitration award to be enforced? Are they in a country that has ratified and implemented New York Convention and the UNCITRAL Model Law? This will maximize the potential for enforceability of the award. Are the assets located in a jurisdiction that will grant interim relief (for example, asset-preserving orders in aid of proposed or pending arbitration proceedings in other jurisdictions)?

____ (c) **Where is the contract being performed?** It is convenient for the law governing the contract to match that of the forum, which may avoid the need for the appointment of lawyers experienced in two legal systems.

____ (d) **How practical and effective is the legal regime in the place of arbitration?**

____ (e) **What is the domestic arbitration regime?** Would it make sense to waive rights under the international arbitration regime and adopt the domestic one?

____ (f) **Is there a functioning arbitration infrastructure in the proposed jurisdiction?** Is the proposed jurisdiction supportive of international arbitration? Do the courts in the jurisdiction issue interim orders in support of proposed or pending arbitration?

____ (g) **Are there circumstances that would make arbitration in the proposed country impractical or difficult?** Civil war, restrictions on travel, and human rights issues may render certain countries difficult to arbitrate in.

____ (h) **Are qualified arbitrators readily available in the proposed jurisdiction?**

____ (i) **What are the costs involved in arbitrating in a foreign jurisdiction?** Major arbitration centers may be costly to accommodate the parties, but can readily provide support services.

____ (j) **In what circumstances can a court in the proposed jurisdiction give interlocutory injunctive relief, if required?**

____ (k) **What process is available for judicial review in the proposed jurisdiction?** What steps are involved?

____ 12. **Where will the arbitral award likely be enforced?**

____ (a) **Is the place(s) where the arbitral award will likely be enforced (the Enforcing State) party to the UNCITRAL Convention with the result that the Enforcing State will recognize the arbitral award?** If not, does the Enforcing State recognize foreign arbitral awards? In what circumstances? What procedural steps are involved? What opportunities will there be for a disappointed party to challenge either recognition of the arbitral award or its enforcement?

____ (b) **Even if the Enforcing State is party to the UNCITRAL Convention, ascertain what procedural steps are necessary for the arbitral award to be recognized by the courts in the Enforcing State and the status of a judgment which can be enforced.** Has the Enforcing State implemented by legislation the UNCITRAL Model Law which sets out, in Article 36, the grounds on which the Enforcing State's court may apply or refuse recognition for enforcement of a foreign arbitral award? If so, is there case law on how the Enforcing State's courts have interpreted Article 36 of the Model Law? This is particularly significant in light of the fact that Article 36 of the Model Law provides, among other things, as grounds for refusing enforcement, that:

> (b) (i) the subject matter of the dispute is not capable of settlement by arbitration under the law of this State, or
>
> (ii) the recognition or enforcement of the award would be contrary to the public policy of this State.

On these issues, the opinions of local counsel in the Enforcing State would be highly significant at the very outset when arbitration as a dispute resolution method is being considered and the arbitration clause is in preparation.

# Checklist 62: United Nations Convention on Contracts for the International Sale of Goods (1980)

The United Nations Convention on Contracts for the International Sale of Goods (CISG) was prepared by the United Nations Commission on International Trade Law (UNCITRAL) and adopted by a diplomatic conference on April 11, 1980.[1] There were 11 original signatories[2] to the CISG, which came into force on January 1, 1998. As of July 1, 2008, 71 States are parties to the CISG.[3]

This checklist considers the applicability of the CISG to various contracts and the implication of the application of the CISG to a contract. This is not an exhaustive review of the provisions of the CISG or its implications to any particular contract.

The CISG is divided into four parts:

- Part One deals with the scope of application of the CISG and the general provisions.
- Part Two contains the rules governing the formation of contracts for the international sale of goods.
- Part Three deals with the substantive rights and obligations of buyer and seller arising from the contract.
- Part Four contains the final clauses of the CISG concerning such matters as how and when it comes into force, the reservations and declarations that are permitted, and the application of the CISG to international sales where both States concerned have the same or similar law on the subject.

The CISG refers to countries as "States" and refers to countries that are parties to the CISG as "Contracting States." These terms are also used in this checklist in that context.

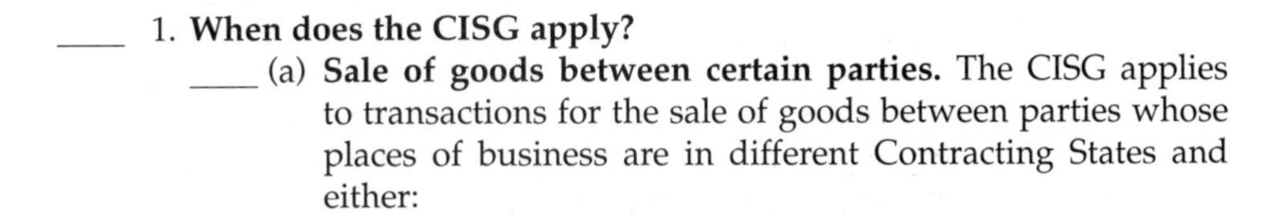

____ 1. **When does the CISG apply?**

____ (a) **Sale of goods between certain parties.** The CISG applies to transactions for the sale of goods between parties whose places of business are in different Contracting States and either:

**E. Jane Sidnell** is a partner with the firm of Fraser Milner Casgrain LLP, in its Calgary, Canada, office. She is a former chair of the Canadian Bar Association's national construction law section and practices construction law, drafting agreements, and resolving disputes.

____ (i) Both are Contracting States.
____ (ii) The rules of private international law lead to the law of a Contracting State.

____ (b) **Article 95 exception.** A few Contracting States have availed themselves of the authorization in Article 95 to declare that they will apply the CISG only where the places of business of both parties are in Contracting States. The United States is one of the countries that has availed itself of this exception.

____ 2. **What types of transactions does the CISG not apply to?** The CISG does not apply to the following transactions:

____ (a) Where the buyer has undertaken to supply a substantial part of the materials necessary for their manufacture or production of the goods in question.

____ (b) When the majority of the seller's obligations consists of the supply of labor or other services.[4]

____ (c) The following types of sales:

____ (i) Goods bought for personal, family or household use.
____ (ii) Sales by auction, on execution, or otherwise by law.
____ (iii) Stocks, shares, investment securities, negotiable instructions, money, ships, vessels, hovercraft, aircraft, or electricity.

____ (d) Where a party is resident in a State that is a signatory to another international agreement that contains provisions concerning matters governed by the CISG.

____ (e) Where the States in which the parties are resident have the same or similar domestic law of sales and such States have declared that the CISG does not apply between them.

____ 3. **What are the implications of the application of the CISG?**

____ (a) **The CISG is restricted to the formation of the contract and the rights and duties of the buyer and seller arising from such a contract.** The CISG does not deal with the validity of the contract, the effect the contract may have on the property in the goods sold, or the liability of the seller for death or personal injury caused by the goods to any person.

____ (b) **Expectation of the parties.** Given that the purpose of the CISG is to unify the law governing the international sale of goods, where disputes arise as to its meaning and application, all parties, including domestic courts and arbitral tribunals, are expected to observe its international character and to promote uniformity in its application and the observance of good faith in international trade. When the CISG does not expressly deal with a matter governed by it, then the issue should be settled by conformity with the general principles on which the CISG is based. Private international law should only be a last resort in interpreting a contract governed by the CISG.

____ (c) **The CISG deals with how statements and conduct of a party are to be interpreted in the context of the formation of the contract and its implementation.** Practices established between the parties to a contract or use of language that the parties knew or ought to have known and that are widely known to, and regularly observed by, parties to contracts of the type involved in the particular trade concerned, may all be binding on the parties to the contract of sale.

____ 4. **Does the contract have to be in writing?**

____ (a) **The CISG does not require a contract to be written.** The CISG does not require any specific form of contract. In particular, Article 11 provides that no written agreement is necessary for the conclusion of a contract. However, if a contract is in writing and it contains a provision requiring any modification or termination by agreement to be in writing, Article 29 provides that the contract must only be modified or terminated as stipulated. The only exception to this is that a party may be precluded by that party's conduct from asserting such a provision to the extent that the other person has relied on that conduct.

____ (b) **Exceptions for Contracting States that require contracts of sale to be in writing.** To accommodate those Contracting States whose legislation requires contracts of sale to be in writing, Article 96 entitles those Contracting States to declare that Articles 11 and 29 do not apply where any party to the contract has a place of business in that Contracting State.[5]

____ 5. **Has there been an offer and acceptance?** Where the formation of a contract arises by the exchange of an offer and an acceptance, then a contract under the CISG is concluded when the acceptance of the offer becomes effective.

____ (a) **When does a proposal constitute an offer?** For a proposal to constitute an offer, it must be:

____ (i) Addressed to one or more specific persons.

____ (ii) Sufficiently definite, which means it must indicate the goods and expressly or implicitly fix or make provision for determining the quantity and the price.

____ (b) **Revocation of offer.** The CISG provides that an offer may be revoked by the offeror if the revocation reaches the offeree before the offeree has sent an acceptance. However, an offer cannot be revoked if:

____ (i) It indicates that it is irrevocable, which includes a provision setting a fixed time for acceptance.

____ (ii) In all the circumstances it was reasonable for the offeree to rely on the offer as being irrevocable and the offeree has acted in reliance on the offer.

____ (c) **How is an acceptance made?** Acceptance of an offer may be made by:

____ (i) A statement or other conduct of the offeree indicating acceptance of the offer that is communicated to the offeror.

____ (ii) The offeree performing an act, such as sending the goods or paying for the goods, which would normally be effective as an acceptance the moment the act was performed.

____ (iii) Replying to an offer, even where the reply is an acceptance and contains additional or different terms, so long as:

____ a. The additional or different terms do not materially alter the terms of the offer.

____ b. The offeror does not, within a reasonable time, object to those terms, in which case, the terms of the contract are the terms of the offer with the modifications contained in the acceptance.

____ (d) **Battle of the forms.** If the reply to an offer does contain terms that materially alter the terms of the contract, the reply constitutes a counteroffer that must in turn be accepted for a contract to be concluded. Material terms include the price, payment, quality, and quantity of the goods; place and time of delivery; extent of one party's liability to the other; or settlement of disputes.

____ 6. **What are the seller's obligations under the CISG?**

____ (a) **Obligations of seller.** The seller must:

____ (i) Deliver the goods.

____ (ii) Hand over any documents relating to the goods.

____ (iii) Transfer the property in the goods, as required by the contract and the CISG.

The CISG provides supplementary rules for use in the absence of an agreement as to when, where and how the seller must perform these obligations.

____ (b) **Seller's delivery obligations.** The seller must deliver goods that are:

____ (i) Of the quantity, quality, and description required by the contract.

____ (ii) Contained or packaged in the manner required by the contract.

____ (iii) Free from any right or claim of a third party, including rights based on industrial property or other intellectual property.

____ 7. **What are the buyer's obligations under the CISG?**

____ (a) **Inspection of goods.** The buyer must inspect the goods and give notice of any lack of their conformity with the contract within a reasonable time after the buyer has discovered it, or ought to have discovered it, and at the latest 2 years from the date on which the goods were actually delivered to the buyer, unless this time limit is inconsistent with a contractual period of guarantee.

____ (b) **Payment and acceptance of delivery.** The buyer must:

____ (i) Pay the price for the goods.

____ (ii) Take delivery of the goods as required by the contract and the CISG.

The CISG provides supplementary rules for use in the absence of an agreement as to how the price is to be determined and where and when the buyer should perform the buyer's obligation to pay the price.

____ 8. **What remedies are available under the CISG?**

____ (a) **General remedies.** The CISG provides for remedies in connection with the parties' respective obligations.

____ (i) Where one party has fulfilled its obligations, that party may require performance of the other party's obligations, claim damages, or avoid the contract.

____ (ii) In addition, the buyer has the right to reduce the price when the goods delivered do not conform to the contract.

____ (b) **Fundamental breach.** In the case of a fundamental breach[6] by one of the parties, the aggrieved party can make a declaration of avoidance of the contract.

____ (i) Where the fundamental breach is alleged to have been committed by the seller, the buyer can require the delivery of substitute goods only if the goods delivered were not in conformity with the contract and the lack of conformity constituted a fundamental breach of contract.

____ (ii) A declaration of avoidance of the contract may be made where the party in breach fails to perform, in a reasonable time fixed by the aggrieved party:

____ a. Delivery of the goods by the seller.
____ b. Payment of the price or failure to take delivery by the buyer.

____ (c) **Anticipated breach.** In the case of anticipated breach, where it becomes apparent that one of the parties will not perform a substantial part of that party's obligations, or will commit a fundamental breach of contract, then:

____ (i) The other party may suspend its own performance of the contract, but the contract remains in existence awaiting future events.

____ (ii) The other party may declare the contract avoided.

____ (d) **Nonconforming goods.** Where the goods do not conform to the contract, the buyer may require the seller to repair the goods, unless this is unreasonable in regard to all the circumstances.

____ (e) **Duty to mitigate.** A party cannot recover damages that the party could have mitigated by taking the proper measures.

____ (f) **Events beyond a party's control.** A party may be exempted from paying damages if that party fails to perform any of its obligations due to an impediment beyond that party's control that:

____ (i) The party could not reasonably have been expected to take into account at the time of the conclusion of the contract.

____ (ii) The party could not have avoided or overcome.

This exemption from paying damages may also apply if the failure is due to the failure of a third person engaged by a party to perform the whole or a part of the contract. However, that party is subject to any other remedy, including reduction of the price, if the goods were defective in some way.

____ (g) **Duty to preserve goods.** The CISG imposes on both parties the duty to preserve any goods in their possession belonging to the other party. This duty is of great importance in an international sale of goods in which the other party is from a foreign country and may not have agents in the country where the goods are located. Under certain circumstances, the party in possession of the goods may sell them, or may even be required to sell them.[7]

____ 9. **How is the transfer of risk of loss dealt with under the CISG?** The parties may regulate the exact moment when the risk of loss or damage to the goods passes from the seller to the buyer in the contract either by an express provision or by the use of an INCOTERM.[8] However, where the contract does not contain such a provision, the CISG sets out the following rules:

____ (a) Except as provided later, the risk passes to the buyer when the buyer takes over the goods, or from the time when the goods are placed at the buyer's disposal and the buyer commits a breach of contract by failing to take delivery, whichever comes first.[9]

____ (b) When the contract of sale involves carriage of the goods.

____ (c) When the goods are sold while in transit.

____ 10. **Can the CISG be excluded from a transaction?**

____ (a). **Parties can contract to exclude the CISG.** The principle of contractual freedom is recognized by Article 6, which permits the parties to exclude the application of the CISG or to depart from or vary the effect of any of its provisions.

____ (b) **How to exclude the CISG.** The exclusion of the CISG can be implemented by the parties by specifically stating that the CISG does not apply; the parties would then normally state that the law of another State will be the law applicable to the contract.

____ (c) **Exclusion of CISG when contract provisions differ from CISG.** Departure from the CISG occurs whenever a provision in the contract provides a different rule from that found in the CISG.

## *Notes*

1. The United Nations Convention on Contracts for the International Sale of Goods can be found at 52 Federal Register 6262, 6264-6280 (March 2, 1987); United States Code Annotated, Title 15, Appendix (Supp. 1987).

2. Argentina, China, Egypt, France, Hungary, Italy, Lesotho, Syria, United States, Yugoslavia, and Zambia.

3. Argentina, Australia, Austria, Belarus, Belgium, Bosnia and Herzegovina, Bulgaria, Burundi, Canada, Chile, China, Colombia, Croatia, Cuba, Cyprus, Czech Republic, Denmark, Ecuador, Egypt, El Salvador, Estonia, Finland, France, Gabon, Georgia, Germany, Greece, Guinea, Honduras, Hungary, Iceland, Iraq, Israel, Italy, Japan, Kyrgyzstan, Latvia, Lesotho, Liberia, Lithuania, Luxembourg, Macedonia (former Yugoslav Republic of), Mauritania, Mexico, Moldova, Mongolia, Montenegro, Netherlands, New Zealand, Norway, Paraguay, Peru, Poland, Republic of Korea, Romania, Russian Federation, Saint Vincent and the Grenadines, Serbia, Singapore, Slovakia, Slovenia, Spain, Sweden, Switzerland, Syrian Arab Republic, Uganda, Ukraine, United States of America, Uruguay, Uzbekistan, and Zambia.

4. CISG Article 3.

5. Argentina, Belarus, Chile, Hungary, Latria, Lithuania, Paraguay, Russian Federation, and Ukraine.

6. For a breach of contract to be fundamental, it must result in such detriment to the other party as to substantially deprive that other party of the benefit of the contract, unless the result was neither foreseen by the party in breach, nor foreseeable by a reasonable person of the same kind in the same circumstances.

7. A party selling the goods has the right to retain out of the proceeds of sale an amount equal to the reasonable expenses of preserving and selling the goods, but must account to the other party for the balance.

8. INCOTERMs are standard trade definitions commonly used in international sales contracts and are published by the International Chamber of Commerce (http://www.icewbo.org/index_incoterms.asp).

9. When the contract relates to goods that are not identified when the contract is formed, the goods must be identified before they can be considered to be placed at the disposal of the buyer and the risk of their loss can be considered to have passed to the buyer.

# Checklist 63: International Corruption Laws

American organizations doing business overseas can face a variety of cultural and political challenges, not the least of which may be that key decision makers in the foreign country will expect to be bribed. Organizations that regularly engage in international business transactions often have compliance programs and know where the land mines lie. For organizations with "one-off" deals or otherwise new to doing business across borders, there are features of both the U.S. Foreign Corrupt Practices Act (FCPA) and the Convention on Combating Bribery of Foreign Public Officials in International Business Transactions of the Organization of Economic and Cooperative Development (OECD Convention) of which they should be aware. This checklist addresses both the basic elements of the FCPA and the OECD Convention and elements of a typical compliance program.

____ 1. **Issues Under the FCPA and the OECD Convention.**

____ (a) **No payments for improper advantage.** The FCPA anti-bribery provisions prohibit U.S. persons from directly or indirectly offering or paying anything of value to a foreign official to gain an improper advantage.

____ (i) Is there anyone in the organization who has contact with officials from the foreign jurisdiction in connection with the transaction at issue?

____ (ii) Is there an individual in any related organization (for example, marketing representatives, sales agents, affiliates, joint venture partners) who has contact with officials from the foreign jurisdiction in connection with the transaction at issue?

____ (iii) Have any of the above persons paid (or offered to pay) anything of value to such officials? If so, what was paid (or offered)?

____ (b) **Are any payments allowed?** The FCPA permits some payments to foreign officials: (1) lawful political contributions and (2) payments for bona fide services rendered.

**Troy L. Harris,** King & Spalding LLP, Atlanta, Georgia, is a fellow of the Chartered Institute of Arbitrators and an adjunct professor at Emory Law School. He is a member of the Steering Committee for Division 8 (International Contracting) of the ABA's Forum on the Construction Industry.

____ (i) If any payments have been made, can they legitimately be characterized as political contributions or for bona fide services rendered?

____ (c) **Are there any affirmative defenses?** The FCPA also provides affirmative defenses: (1) where the payment is legal under the foreign law or (2) where the payment is in reimbursement of the foreign official's reasonable expenses in connection with demonstration of products or services.

____ (i) If any payments have been made, can they legitimately be characterized as legal under the foreign law or as permitted reimbursement?

____ (d) **Has a Department of Justice advisory opinion been sought?** The FCPA permits organizations to seek an advisory opinion concerning a proposed transaction from the U.S. Department of Justice (DOJ).

____ (e) **Are there other accounting requirements?** In addition to anti-bribery provisions, the FCPA also has certain accounting requirements designed to prohibit off-book transactions facilitating bribes by ensuring transparency in record keeping.

____ (i) Have the organization's accounting practices been reviewed for compliance with FCPA requirements?

____ (ii) Have the accounting practices of any related organization (for example, marketing representatives, sales agents, affiliates, joint venture partners) been reviewed for compliance with FCPA requirements?

____ (f) **Local laws.** The OECD Convention requires signatory states to have local laws against corruption meeting standards set forth in the Convention, which are similar to the FCPA in prohibiting bribes and requiring accounting standards that facilitate transparency.

____ (i) Has local counsel in the foreign country reviewed and advised upon the applicable anti-corruption laws?

____ (ii) Have all personnel within the organization and any related organization (e.g., marketing representatives, sales agents, affiliates, joint venture partners) been advised of the requirements of any country-specific anti-corruption laws?

____ (g) **Are any payments permitted under the OECD?** Like the FCPA, the OECD Convention permits certain payments: (1) "facilitation payments" to induce officials to perform routine functions (for example, issuing permits) and (2) payments for advantages permitted or required under the law of the country of the foreign official.

____ (i) Have any organization personnel or personnel of related organizations made payments of any kind to any officials?

____ (ii) If payments have been made, what was their purpose?

____ (iii) May any such payment reasonably be characterized as a "facilitation payment"? Note that issuing permits may not be a routine function in many construction projects. Accordingly, care should be taken that the exception for facilitation payments not be abused.

____ (h) **Payments to political parties or candidates.** Unlike the FCPA, the OECD Convention permits payments to foreign political parties or candidates for foreign political office.

____ (i) If any payments to foreign officials have been made, may they reasonably be characterized as payments to political parties or candidates for political office?

____ (ii) Does the local law of the foreign jurisdiction restrict such payments?

____ (i) **Do any other anti-corruption laws apply?** Depending on the location of the project or related transactions actions, other anti-corruption laws may apply, including the Organization of American States' Inter-American Convention Against Corruption (1997), the European Union Council's "Convention in the fight against corruption involving officials of the European Communities or officials of the Member State of the European Union" (1997), and the World Bank's guidelines regarding ethics in procurement.

____ (i) Has local counsel provided an opinion concerning what laws or rules apply to the transactions involved?

____ (ii) What steps have been taken to ensure compliance with the applicable laws or rules?

____(j) **Corruption Perceptions Index.** Transparency International publishes a Corruption Perceptions Index, which purports to rank countries according to the level of corruption present in each.

____ (i) Where does the country in which the organization is doing business rank in the Corruption Perceptions Index?

____ (ii) How does the perceived level of corruption in that country compare with other countries in which the organization does business?

____ 2. **Elements of a Compliance Program.** For organizations that anticipate engaging in overseas transactions on a regular basis, it is advisable to have a formal program to ensure compliance with applicable anti-corruption laws. Such programs typically have several elements:

____ (a) **Corporate policy statements.** Does the organization have a policy statement clearly prohibiting the payment of bribes or other forms of unlawful remuneration to foreign officials? Note that some corporate policy statements also prohibit bribes to private-sector parties.

____ (b) **Accounting procedures.** Has the organization's accounting system been audited for compliance with anti-corruption laws?

____ (c) **Personnel compliance.**

____ (i) What training programs does the organization offer or require for personnel who deal with foreign officials?

____ (ii) Does the organization require such personnel to certify that they are familiar with applicable anti-corruption laws and have engaged in no prohibited activity? If so, how frequently are such certifications required (that is, annually? quarterly? for each transaction over a threshold dollar value?)?

____ (iii) Is adherence to the organization's compliance program a factor considered in personnel reviews?

____ (d) **Independent audits.**

____ (i) Does the organization commission independent audits of its compliance program to identify areas of improvement?

____ 3. **Third-Party Compliance.** As previously noted, organizations are often exposed to liability under anti-corruption laws not only for their own acts but also for the acts of their representatives and partners (for example, agents, subsidiaries, joint venture partners). Accordingly, organizations should conduct due diligence into prospective third-party associates and require appropriate protections in their contracts with such associates.

____ (a) **Screening of third-party partners.**

____ (i) Has the organization developed a standard questionnaire to provide to prospective partners? Among other things, such a questionnaire should seek information about the candidate's previous experience, its own compliance program, and any investigations or enforcement actions to which it has been subject.

____ (ii) Does the organization conduct candidate interviews?

____ (iii) Does the organization perform its own due diligence investigation of candidates (for example, background checks or Dun & Bradstreet reports)?

____ (iv) Does the organization require opinion letters from candidates' outside advisors (that is, lawyers and accountants) confirming the accuracy of information submitted by candidates?

____ (b) **Contractual protections.**

____ (i) Has local counsel provided an opinion regarding the anti-corruption laws applicable to the third-party partner?

____ (ii) Does the organization's contracts with third-party partners require periodic certification that the partner has complied with all applicable anti-bribery laws, including any unique accounting requirements?

____ (iii) Does the organization's contracts require the partner to indemnify the organization against any claims that the organization has violated applicable anti-corruption laws as a result of the activities of the partner?

____ (iv) Does the organization have a right to terminate the third-party partner's contract if credible evidence suggests that the partner has breached the contract's anti-corruption provisions?

____ (v) Does the contract specify that no payments may be made to the partner in cash, to number-only bank accounts, or to bank accounts outside the country where the services will be rendered?

____ (vi) Does the contract provide for random audit rights?

____ (vii) Does the contract include documentation requirements for reimbursement of the partner's expenses?

____ (viii) Does the contract prohibit assignment by the third-party partner?

# Checklist 64: International Discovery

The following checklist addresses issues for counsel engaged in matters involving international discovery. Taking a deposition in a foreign country is covered in Checklist 68.

____ 1. **Discovery from Foreign Nonparties to U.S. International Discovery.**

____ (a) **U.S. style discovery.** Does the foreign nonparty's country preclude the taking of U.S. style discovery? If no, then consider voluntary cooperative discovery.

____ (i) **Rules for discovery.** Does the country allow the parties to stipulate to such discovery at a time and location of mutual convenience? If yes, then the discovery is conducted by American attorneys in the offices of a foreign attorney or solicitor who has the power to administer oaths in the foreign country. Discovery may also be conducted in hotel conference rooms or another venue.

____ (ii) **Contacting the U.S. Embassy.** If not allowed to stipulate to discovery, then the U.S. litigant may be required to arrange for the production of evidence through a U.S. consulate. The U.S. attorney must contact the U.S. Embassy or the U.S. Consulate of the country in which the evidence is sought. The U.S. Consulate will then assist in arranging for the discovery to be produced in accordance with the foreign country's rules and regulations.

____ (iii) **Transcript.** Is there a signed agreement of the parties agreeing to allow the stenographer/court reporter to distribute the deposition transcript once it is prepared without further involvement of the Consulate or Embassy? If not, then once the transcript is finished the stenographer/court reporter forwards the original transcript to the Consulate General, who holds the transcript until the witnesses go back to the Consulate or Embassy and

**John S. Vento** is a shareholder at the firm of Trenam Kemker P.A. in Tampa, Florida. He is a trial lawyer and certified construction lawyer.

make any errata corrections and sign the transcript. Once the witnesses have signed the transcript, then the Consulate General transmits the transcript and exhibits to the clerk of the court that issued the order for the deposition. If the parties stipulate, copies of the materials can also be sent to the attorneys.

____ (b) **Involuntary discovery.** If voluntary discovery is not available, is involuntary discovery an option?

____ (i) **Hague Convention member.** Is the country in which the discovery is sought a member of the Hague Convention? If yes, then a "Letter of Request" can be sent from the judicial authority of another contracting country to ask the foreign state to allow evidence to be obtained in conformance with the foreign state's laws and regulations. If approved, the requesting state will have an opportunity to obtain the sought-after evidence from the foreign nonparty.

____ 2. **Discovery from a Nonparty Who Is a U.S. National or Resident Located in a Foreign Country.**

____ (a) **Subpoena.** Are the prerequisites for a court order authorizing a subpoena under 28 U.S.C. § 1783(a) satisfied?

____ (i) **Resident of the United States.** The subpoenaed person is a national or resident of the United States.

____ (ii) **Necessary in the interest of justice.** The testimony or production of the document or thing "is necessary in the interest of justice" considered in light of the circumstances of the particular case and in the posture of the case when the issue arises.

____ (iii) **Personal appearance of witnesses.** In civil cases, it is not possible to obtain the witness's testimony in admissible form without his or her personal appearance or to obtain the production of the document or other thing in any other means.

____ (b) **Federal Rule of Civil Procedure 45.** Is the subpoena under property served pursuant to Federal Rule of Civil Procedure 45?

____ (c) **Sanctions.** Are sanctions for failure to comply with the subpoena appropriate after a hearing upon an order to show cause?

____ 3. **Foreign Legal Impediments to Discovery of Foreigners Who Are Parties in U.S. Litigation.** Obtaining evidence that is located outside the United States is easiest when the party controlling the evidence

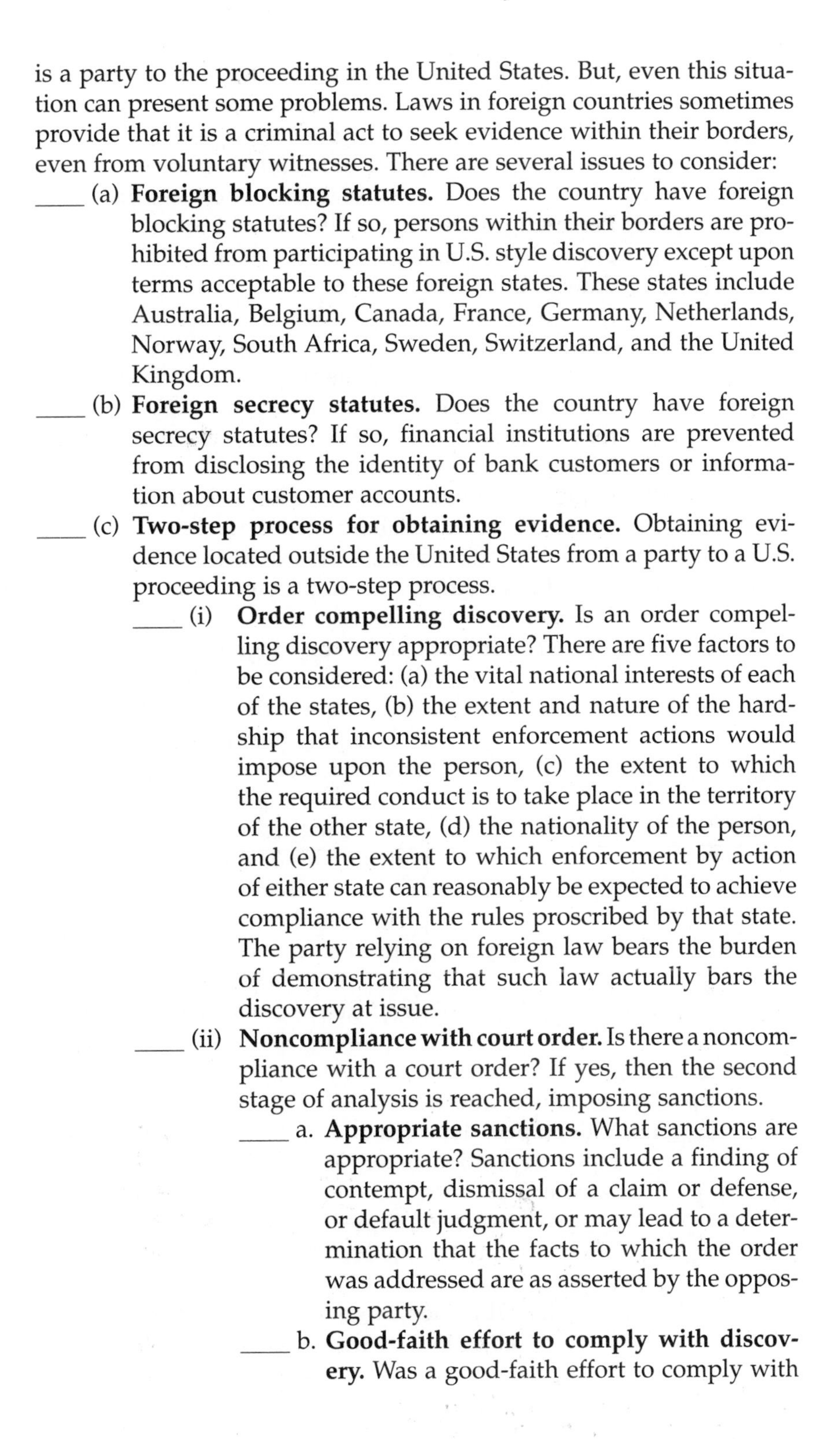

is a party to the proceeding in the United States. But, even this situation can present some problems. Laws in foreign countries sometimes provide that it is a criminal act to seek evidence within their borders, even from voluntary witnesses. There are several issues to consider:

____ (a) **Foreign blocking statutes.** Does the country have foreign blocking statutes? If so, persons within their borders are prohibited from participating in U.S. style discovery except upon terms acceptable to these foreign states. These states include Australia, Belgium, Canada, France, Germany, Netherlands, Norway, South Africa, Sweden, Switzerland, and the United Kingdom.

____ (b) **Foreign secrecy statutes.** Does the country have foreign secrecy statutes? If so, financial institutions are prevented from disclosing the identity of bank customers or information about customer accounts.

____ (c) **Two-step process for obtaining evidence.** Obtaining evidence located outside the United States from a party to a U.S. proceeding is a two-step process.

____ (i) **Order compelling discovery.** Is an order compelling discovery appropriate? There are five factors to be considered: (a) the vital national interests of each of the states, (b) the extent and nature of the hardship that inconsistent enforcement actions would impose upon the person, (c) the extent to which the required conduct is to take place in the territory of the other state, (d) the nationality of the person, and (e) the extent to which enforcement by action of either state can reasonably be expected to achieve compliance with the rules proscribed by that state. The party relying on foreign law bears the burden of demonstrating that such law actually bars the discovery at issue.

____ (ii) **Noncompliance with court order.** Is there a noncompliance with a court order? If yes, then the second stage of analysis is reached, imposing sanctions.

____ a. **Appropriate sanctions.** What sanctions are appropriate? Sanctions include a finding of contempt, dismissal of a claim or defense, or default judgment, or may lead to a determination that the facts to which the order was addressed are as asserted by the opposing party.

____ b. **Good-faith effort to comply with discovery.** Was a good-faith effort to comply with the discovery order made? If so, then the sanctions of contempt, dismissal or default should not be imposed. The more appropriate sanction would be findings of fact adverse to the noncomplying party.

____ (d) **Personal jurisdiction by the United States.** Does the United States have personal jurisdiction over the foreign defendants? U.S. courts have sustained discovery against the foreign defendant on jurisdictional issues. The U.S. Supreme Court has held that the concept of international comity requires an analysis of the respective interests of the foreign nation and the requesting nation in discovery disputes. Factors include (1) the importance of the documents or other information requested, (2) the degree of specificity of the request, (3) whether the information originated in the United States, (4) the availability of alternative means of securing the information, and (5) the extent to which noncompliance would undermine the important interests of the United States or of the foreign country.

____ (i) **Limitations of the Hague Convention.** There are two key limitations of the Hague Convention. Do you fall within one of the limitations?

____ a. **Sovereignty issues.** A Letter of Request may be refused on two grounds: (1) in the State of Execution, the execution of the Letter does not fall within the functions of the judiciary; or (2) the State addressed considers that its sovereignty or security would be prejudiced thereby.

____ b. **Pretrial discovery.** A signatory of the Hague Convention may refuse to execute a Letter of Request that has been issued for the purpose of obtaining pretrial discovery of documents.

____ 4. **Special Procedures and Issues.**

____ (a) **Videotaped deposition.** Are the prerequisites for a videotaped deposition under Rule 30(b)(2) and 28 U.S.C. § 1783 satisfied?

____ (i) **Notice of deposition.** Does the notice of deposition state the method by which the deposition shall be recorded?

____ (ii) **Objection to nonstenographic recording.** Has any objection to the nonstenographic recording of a deposition been presented to court by motion for a protective order?

____ (iii) **Compliance with requirements.** During the deposition, has the officer complied with the requirements?

____ a. **Officer's name and address.** Have the officer's name and business address been repeated at the beginning of each tape?

____ b. **Date, time, and place of deposition.** Have the date, time, and place of the deposition been repeated at the beginning of each tape?

____ c. **Name of deponent.** Has the name of the deponent been repeated at the beginning of each tape?

____ (b) **Any stipulations?** Have the parties entered into a written stipulation to allow a deposition to be taken by telephone or other remote electronic means, or has a court order been entered?

____ 5. **Discovery Outside the United States.**

____ (a) **Evidence.** Determine the evidence that you might need outside the United States and start measures to obtain that evidence as soon as possible. Include ample time for obtaining evidence in any scheduling orders.

____ (b) **Technical requirements.** Comply with all technical requirements.

____ (c) **Discovery.** Research what discovery actions are permitted under the country's laws.

____ (d) **Preclude evidence.** Does the foreign nonparty's country preclude the taking of evidence? If not, consider voluntary discovery by stipulation.

____ (e) **U.S. resident.** Is the nonparty controlling evidence a U.S. citizen or U.S. resident? If so, U.S. courts may have the power to force that person to provide requested information under 28 U.S.C. § 1783(a).

____ (f) **Deposition.** Can you persuade the witness to voluntarily come to the United States for a deposition? If so, even if you have to pay the expenses, this might be the easiest and least expensive method to obtain evidence in a deposition.

____ (g) **U.S. Embassy.** Visit the website for the U.S. Embassy in the country in which the evidence is sought for information on how to gather evidence in that country and for lists of resources available.

____ (h) **Hague Convention.** Has the foreign nonparty's country joined the Hague Convention? If so, the U.S. litigant can use the Hague Convention as a tool to obtain evidence from the foreign nonparty.

____ (i) **Electronic discovery.** Can you conduct the foreign party deposition by telephonic or other electronic means? If so, this may reduce the costs of deposing persons in foreign countries.

____ (j) **International arbitration.** If choosing international arbitration, be familiar with the country's laws and procedures in which the arbitration will be held because that law will most likely govern the procedure.

____ (k) **Institutional rules.** Adopt a recognized set of institutional rules to govern the arbitration to avoid inconsistency.

# Checklist 65: Pre-Trial Discovery Procedure in Canadian Litigation

While there are a number of similarities between Canadian and American civil procedure, there are also important differences between the processes of the two countries, particularly in relation to the discovery process. The following checklist is intended to highlight the most significant issues and differences between U.S. and Canadian discovery procedure and processes.[1]

____ 1. **What are the documentary obligations?**

____ (a) The first step of discovery, disclosure, is the preparation and service of an "affidavit of documents."[2] After the completion of the pleadings, each party must make a sworn statement listing all documents related to the proceedings that they have, or formerly had, in their control. The written statement listing a party's records or documents is called, variously in different provinces, an "affidavit of documents," "list of documents," or "affidavit of records." The basic test for inclusion of documents in this list is whether documents are relevant to the material issues in the pleadings. Canadian courts have generally interpreted "relevance" very broadly.

____ 2. **How and when should the affidavit of documents be served?**

____ (a) A party to an action is required to serve the affidavit of documents on every other party within 10 days after the close of pleadings.

____ 3. **What must the affidavit of documents contain?**

____ (a) An affidavit of documents must list and describe, in separate schedules, all documents relating to any matter at issue in an action:

____ (i) That are in the party's possession, control or power and that the party does not object to producing (Schedule A).

____ (ii) That are or were in the party's possession, control, or power, and for which the party claims privilege, and the grounds for the claim (Schedule B). The

---

**Paul A. Ivanoff** is a partner in Osler, Hoskin & Harcourt LLP's litigation department and is a member of the firm's Construction and Infrastructure Specialty Group. He is certified as a specialist in construction law by the Law Society of Upper Canada and is listed in The Best Lawyers in Canada in the area of construction law.

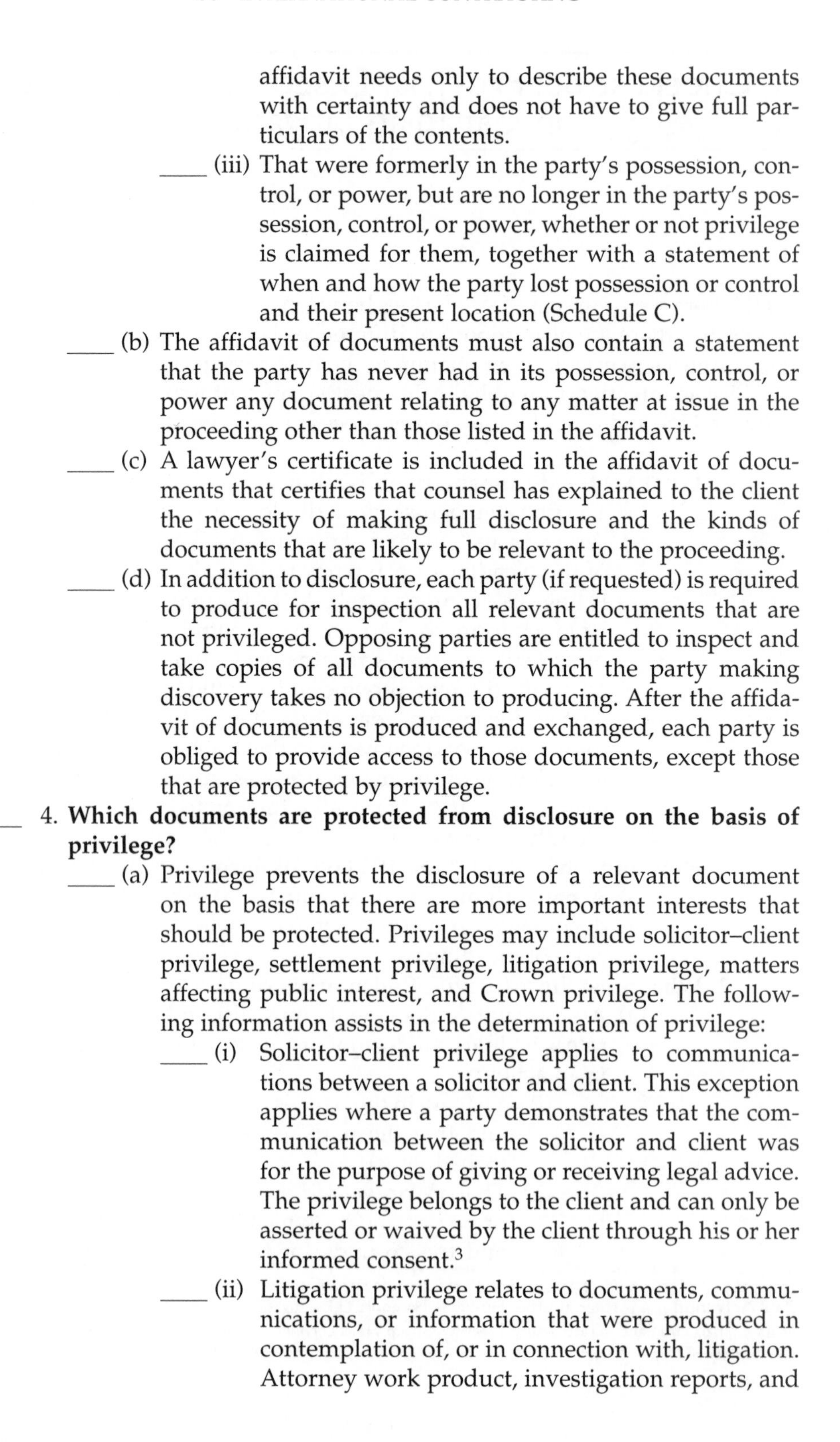

affidavit needs only to describe these documents with certainty and does not have to give full particulars of the contents.

____ (iii) That were formerly in the party's possession, control, or power, but are no longer in the party's possession, control, or power, whether or not privilege is claimed for them, together with a statement of when and how the party lost possession or control and their present location (Schedule C).

____ (b) The affidavit of documents must also contain a statement that the party has never had in its possession, control, or power any document relating to any matter at issue in the proceeding other than those listed in the affidavit.

____ (c) A lawyer's certificate is included in the affidavit of documents that certifies that counsel has explained to the client the necessity of making full disclosure and the kinds of documents that are likely to be relevant to the proceeding.

____ (d) In addition to disclosure, each party (if requested) is required to produce for inspection all relevant documents that are not privileged. Opposing parties are entitled to inspect and take copies of all documents to which the party making discovery takes no objection to producing. After the affidavit of documents is produced and exchanged, each party is obliged to provide access to those documents, except those that are protected by privilege.

____ 4. **Which documents are protected from disclosure on the basis of privilege?**

____ (a) Privilege prevents the disclosure of a relevant document on the basis that there are more important interests that should be protected. Privileges may include solicitor–client privilege, settlement privilege, litigation privilege, matters affecting public interest, and Crown privilege. The following information assists in the determination of privilege:

____ (i) Solicitor–client privilege applies to communications between a solicitor and client. This exception applies where a party demonstrates that the communication between the solicitor and client was for the purpose of giving or receiving legal advice. The privilege belongs to the client and can only be asserted or waived by the client through his or her informed consent.[3]

____ (ii) Litigation privilege relates to documents, communications, or information that were produced in contemplation of, or in connection with, litigation. Attorney work product, investigation reports, and communications with experts generally fall within this exemption. The general test is whether the document was prepared for the dominant purpose of litigation. A party may, on an examination for discovery, obtain disclosure of the findings, opinions, and conclusions of an expert engaged by or on behalf of the party being examined that relate to a matter in issue in the action. The party being examined need not disclose the information or the name and address of the expert where (a) the findings, opinions, and conclusions of the expert relating to any matter in issue in the action were made or formed in preparation for contemplated or pending litigation and for no other purpose; and (b) the party being examined undertakes not to call the expert as a witness at the trial.

____ (iii) Settlement negotiation privilege applies to discussions or negotiations prior to, or during the course of, litigation. The main qualifier is that the statements must have been made for the purpose of settling the dispute. It is not an absolute rule that communications made bona fide to induce settlement of litigation are never to be disclosed. Exceptions may include circumstances where fraud or threats involving the negotiations are in issue.

____ 5. **Can a party be examined by both written questions and then by oral examination?**

____ (a) Although examination of a witness can be fulfilled through written interrogatories, a party may not be examined by both written questions and oral examination without leave of the court.

____ (b) However, examinations for discovery by written question can be conducted by delivery of written questions that must be answered in writing by the affidavit of the person being examined. The use of written interrogatories as a means of discovery in Canada is relatively infrequent.

____ 6. **How do oral examinations for discovery differ in Canada from those conducted under the U.S. Federal Rules of Civil Procedure?**

____ (a) The rules for Canadian examinations for discovery vary significantly from the American deposition rules.

____ (b) The most important distinction between the systems is that Canadian jurisdictions permit the examination of each individual party to the litigation. In the case of a corporation, only one representative from the party may be examined, unless leave of the court is obtained to examine additional witnesses. This is generally difficult to obtain. In addition, under Canadian rules the choice of the individual to be examined on behalf of the corporation is made by the examining party. There is no obligation on the corporate party to be examined to put forward someone with the most knowledge of the issues in dispute, and there is no principle that the court must select who between two people has the most knowledge.

____ 7. **If you can only examine one representative from a corporation, how can you be sure to get the information you need from that one corporate representative?**

____ (a) In Canada, a corporate representative is responsible for obtaining and providing relevant information from others in the company, including all relevant information not within his or her personal knowledge. In addition to the obligation to inform him- or herself in advance of oral examination of relevant information, the corporate representative might also have to make an "undertaking" to obtain relevant information from others in the company, corporate group, or nonparties who were connected in some way to the corporate party in the situation surrounding the litigation.

____ (b) No specific limits for the length of examinations are imposed under Ontario's rules. Where the right to examine is being abused by an excess of improper questions or objections, or is being conducted in an unreasonable manner so as to oppress the person being examined, an order can be sought terminating the examination or limiting its scope.

____ 8. **What is the test for substituting an officer/director/employee for examination for discovery?**

____ (a) As stated earlier, Canadian rules permit the examining party to select the corporate representative. The corporation may seek an order substituting another individual in appropriate circumstances in order to ensure that an individual with sufficient knowledge and involvement in the issues in dispute is examined.

____ (b) In Ontario, although there is no general right to examine the former officers or former employees of a corporation, the courts have on occasion ordered the examination of such persons upon a showing that they left the corporation in order to frustrate the opposite party's discovery.

____ 9. **Can a witness refuse to answer questions at an oral examination for discovery?**

____ (a) Unlike the American process of noting objections to questions and answering on examinations, the Canadian rules

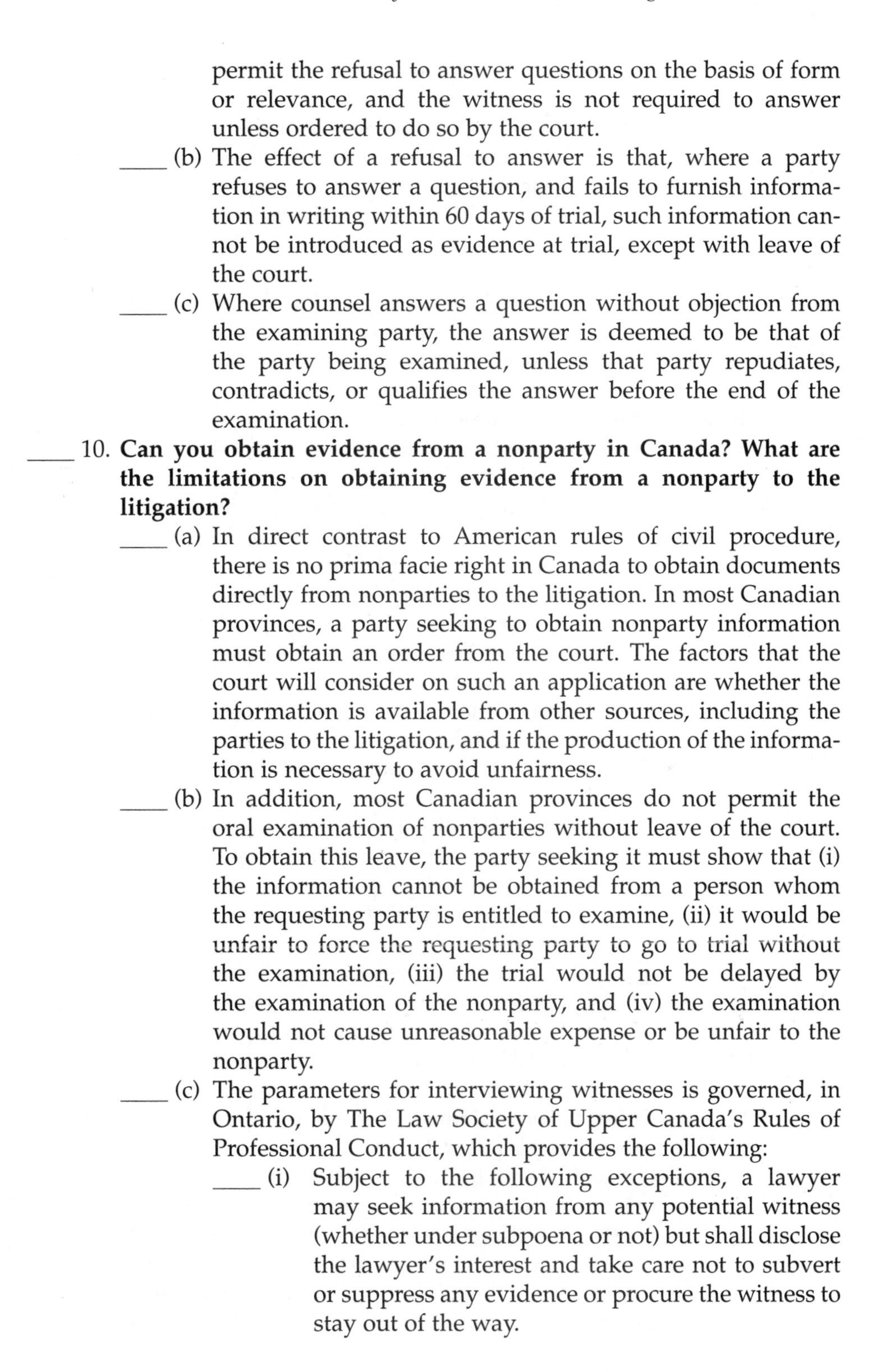

permit the refusal to answer questions on the basis of form or relevance, and the witness is not required to answer unless ordered to do so by the court.

____ (b) The effect of a refusal to answer is that, where a party refuses to answer a question, and fails to furnish information in writing within 60 days of trial, such information cannot be introduced as evidence at trial, except with leave of the court.

____ (c) Where counsel answers a question without objection from the examining party, the answer is deemed to be that of the party being examined, unless that party repudiates, contradicts, or qualifies the answer before the end of the examination.

____ 10. **Can you obtain evidence from a nonparty in Canada? What are the limitations on obtaining evidence from a nonparty to the litigation?**

____ (a) In direct contrast to American rules of civil procedure, there is no prima facie right in Canada to obtain documents directly from nonparties to the litigation. In most Canadian provinces, a party seeking to obtain nonparty information must obtain an order from the court. The factors that the court will consider on such an application are whether the information is available from other sources, including the parties to the litigation, and if the production of the information is necessary to avoid unfairness.

____ (b) In addition, most Canadian provinces do not permit the oral examination of nonparties without leave of the court. To obtain this leave, the party seeking it must show that (i) the information cannot be obtained from a person whom the requesting party is entitled to examine, (ii) it would be unfair to force the requesting party to go to trial without the examination, (iii) the trial would not be delayed by the examination of the nonparty, and (iv) the examination would not cause unreasonable expense or be unfair to the nonparty.

____ (c) The parameters for interviewing witnesses is governed, in Ontario, by The Law Society of Upper Canada's Rules of Professional Conduct, which provides the following:

____ (i) Subject to the following exceptions, a lawyer may seek information from any potential witness (whether under subpoena or not) but shall disclose the lawyer's interest and take care not to subvert or suppress any evidence or procure the witness to stay out of the way.

____ (ii) A lawyer may not approach or deal with a person who is represented by another lawyer, save through or with the consent of that party's lawyer.

____ (iii) A lawyer retained to act on a matter involving a corporation that is represented by another lawyer shall not approach: (a) directors, officers, or persons likely involved in the decision-making process for the corporation; or (b) employees and agents of the corporation whose acts may expose the corporation to liability, unless the lawyer representing the corporation consents, or unless otherwise authorized or required by law.

____ 11. **How is information obtained from discovery used at trial?**

____ (a) There are two basic ways in which an examination for discovery may be used at trial:

____ (i) A party may read into evidence any part of the examination for discovery of an adverse party (if otherwise admissible).

____ (ii) The evidence given on discovery may be used for the purposes of impeaching the deponent as a witness in the same manner as any prior inconsistent statement.

____ (b) In addition, Canadian rules permit the transcript of the discovery to be taken as evidence at trial in extraordinary circumstances that preclude the availability of the witness at trial.

____ (c) The ability to use discovery information at trial affects the conduct of the examination in the following ways:

____ (i) Counsel will seek to obtain answers that can be used as admissions and hence read into evidence at trial.

____ (ii) Counsel will seek to exhaust the recollection of the witness and tie the witness down to a story so that, if the witness changes his or her story at trial, the discovery transcript can be used to impeach the witness.

____ 12. **Can the information obtained through the discovery process be used for any other purpose?**

____ (a) Unlike in the United States, discovery obtained in a proceeding in Canada cannot be freely used in other proceedings. Most jurisdictions in Canada impose an express or implied undertaking on the parties to the litigation and their counsel that prohibits the disclosure or use of evidence or information provided during discovery for any purpose other than the prosecution or defense of that action. Violations of these undertakings can result in contempt-of-court orders. The effect of this undertaking prohibits information-sharing between plaintiffs' lawyers in Canada.

## *Notes*

1. The particular requirements of Canadian discovery procedure and processes vary across each of the Canadian provincial jurisdictions. The following is intended to be an overview of some of the discovery procedures and processes applicable to some or all such jurisdictions. For the requirements of a particular Canadian jurisdiction, the rules of procedure for such jurisdiction should be consulted.

2. See, for example, Rule 30.03 in Ontario's Rules of Civil Procedure, but similar rules exist across most Canadian provincial jurisdictions.

3. See, for example, *R. V. McClure,* [2001] 1 S.C.R. 445.

# Checklist 66: Advising a Foreign National Doing Business in the United States

The following checklist is intended for lawyers asked to represent a foreign national seeking to do business in the United States as a major supplier, equipment manufacturer, general contractor, subcontractor, or design professional on a construction project or to establish a U.S. office or presence. The following is by no means all-encompassing or exhaustive. For many areas, consider associating or consulting with lawyers within the firm or outside with specific expertise in the practice areas or potential issues noted.

____ 1. **Familiarize Yourself with the Culture.** While it is not necessary (but helpful) to speak the language, it is necessary to be sensitive to cultural differences. There are basic mind-set differences and ways of viewing things (that is, the Eastern mind vs. the Western mind; Mandarin vs. Sichuan; Spanish vs. Mexican) that affect purchasing, contract negotiations, dispute resolution, methods of dealing with governmental entities, and virtually every aspect of your representation. But total immersion is not necessary. Remember that your client is appreciative of your (even awkward) attempts to understand his or her culture just as you when traveling abroad appreciate a native's attempts to give you directions in English.

____ 2. **Be Patient.** With the exception of perhaps Germany and Great Britain, no country or nationality is as obsessed with time and schedules as Americans'. You can anticipate long lead times and long periods without contact or answers to important or basic questions. Plan for this and do your best to mask your frustrations. Obviously, without prior planning and your client's understanding, delays in communication can cause problems with project schedules. Take time to convince your client that the concepts of "on time" and "within budget" result in more work and opportunities. You may be surprised to learn that those concepts are not commonly embraced by even more advanced or sophisticated cultures.

____ 3. **Maintain a Working Knowledge of U.S. Laws and Regulations Affecting Construction Issues.** Recognize that knowing everything about all the myriad disciplines that affect the construction industry is

**Robert W. Wachsmuth** is with Glast, Phillips & Murray P.C. in San Antonio, Texas. His practice consists of business litigation, construction law, antitrust law, intellectual property law, sports and entertainment law, as well as arbitration and mediation and all other forms of alternative dispute resolution.

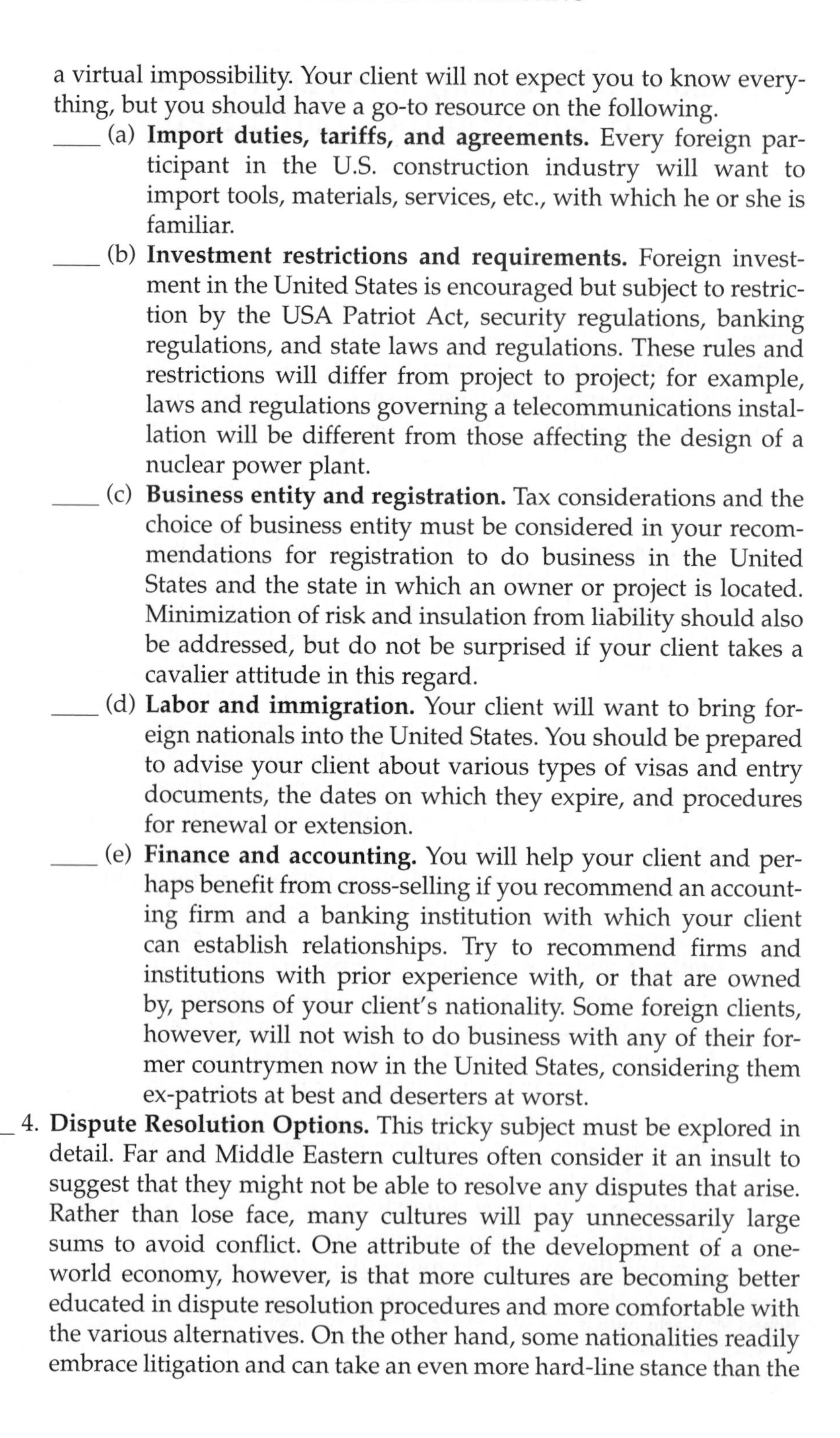

a virtual impossibility. Your client will not expect you to know everything, but you should have a go-to resource on the following.

____ (a) **Import duties, tariffs, and agreements.** Every foreign participant in the U.S. construction industry will want to import tools, materials, services, etc., with which he or she is familiar.

____ (b) **Investment restrictions and requirements.** Foreign investment in the United States is encouraged but subject to restriction by the USA Patriot Act, security regulations, banking regulations, and state laws and regulations. These rules and restrictions will differ from project to project; for example, laws and regulations governing a telecommunications installation will be different from those affecting the design of a nuclear power plant.

____ (c) **Business entity and registration.** Tax considerations and the choice of business entity must be considered in your recommendations for registration to do business in the United States and the state in which an owner or project is located. Minimization of risk and insulation from liability should also be addressed, but do not be surprised if your client takes a cavalier attitude in this regard.

____ (d) **Labor and immigration.** Your client will want to bring foreign nationals into the United States. You should be prepared to advise your client about various types of visas and entry documents, the dates on which they expire, and procedures for renewal or extension.

____ (e) **Finance and accounting.** You will help your client and perhaps benefit from cross-selling if you recommend an accounting firm and a banking institution with which your client can establish relationships. Try to recommend firms and institutions with prior experience with, or that are owned by, persons of your client's nationality. Some foreign clients, however, will not wish to do business with any of their former countrymen now in the United States, considering them ex-patriots at best and deserters at worst.

____ 4. **Dispute Resolution Options.** This tricky subject must be explored in detail. Far and Middle Eastern cultures often consider it an insult to suggest that they might not be able to resolve any disputes that arise. Rather than lose face, many cultures will pay unnecessarily large sums to avoid conflict. One attribute of the development of a one-world economy, however, is that more cultures are becoming better educated in dispute resolution procedures and more comfortable with the various alternatives. On the other hand, some nationalities readily embrace litigation and can take an even more hard-line stance than the most Rambo-like practitioner. Be careful to explore all options, including potential forums and locations outside the United States and dispute resolution processes with which your client may be familiar (for example, conciliation, fact finding, and quasi-judicial determinations). Make sure your client understands the end game to any dispute resolution process, including costs, appeals, collection of judgments, bankruptcies, guarantees, bonds and other security interests, and discovery and disclosure concepts with which your client may not be familiar.

____ 5. **Insurance and Other Risk-Shifting Devices.** Unless your client is from Western Europe or has done business there, he or she may not be familiar with complex insurance programs, security bonds, guarantees, indemnity agreements, warranties, and related concepts. For example, even though letters of credit have been used in international business transactions for more than a century, secured transactions have only been recognized and enforced in Mexico in the last decade.

____ 6. **Personal Injury, Business Torts, Fraud, and Bribery.** Your client will not be familiar with many of our most commonly litigated and prosecuted legal theories. In many cultures, what we deem bribery is just a normal way of doing business. In some countries, injured parties are compensated on a sliding scale. Your client may be completely ignorant of the types of representations or agreements for which he or she could be sued.

# Checklist 67: Service of Process under the Hague Convention

If contemplating a lawsuit against a foreign defendant, this checklist should help navigate the various steps to complete service of a complaint on the foreign defendant through the Hague Convention on the Service Abroad of Judicial and Extrajudicial Documents ("Hague Convention").[1]

____ 1. **Is the Hague Convention applicable to your situation?** Two steps are required for this determination: (a) decide whether you will bring the lawsuit in state or federal court, and (b) determine whether the country in which your foreign defendant resides is a signatory to the Hague Convention.

____ 2. **Are you in federal court?** If so, under Federal Rule of Civil Procedure 4(f), service upon an individual or a corporation may be effected in a place not within any judicial district of the United States:

- ____ (a) By any internationally agreed means reasonably calculated to give notice, such as those means authorized by the Hague Convention on the Service Abroad of Judicial and Extrajudicial Documents.
- ____ (b) If there is no internationally agreed means of service, or the applicable international agreement allows other means of service, provided that service is reasonably calculated to give notice:
  - ____ (i) In the manner prescribed by the law of the foreign country for service in that country in an action in any of its courts of general jurisdiction.
  - ____ (ii) As directed by the foreign authority in response to a letter rogatory or a letter of request.
  - ____ (iii) Unless prohibited by the law of the foreign country, by delivery to the individual personally


**George Anthony Smith,** a partner in the Atlanta office of Kilpatrick Stockton LLP, has more than 30 years of experience in litigating and arbitrating matters around the globe. He is a member of the firm's Construction and Infrastructure Projects practice group and the International Disputes Resolution team. Special thanks to Kilpatrick Stockton colleague Hayley Ambler for all of her hard work and assistance with this project.

**Stephen D. Butler** was formerly the managing counsel of Bechtel Corporation and recently joined Parsons Brinckerhoff as its interim general counsel. He has more than 35 years of experience in managing complex legal cases involving major projects, as well as litigating and arbitrating such matters around the world. Among other construction-related organizations he is active in, he is a member of the American College of Construction Lawyers and a Director of the American Arbitration Association.

(not applicable for corporation), or any form of mail requiring a signed receipt.

____ (c) By other means not prohibited by international agreement as may be directed by the federal court.

____ 3. **Are you in state court?** If so, you will need to research the methods of service recognized by that state. However, the manner of service permitted in a state may be superseded by international agreements. Thus, even if you are in state court, you must serve a foreign defendant pursuant to the Hague Convention, if the Hague Convention is applicable. See Section 4 for a list of signatory countries.

____ 4. **Is the country a signatory to the Hague Convention?** Once you have determined that the federal or the state court will allow service pursuant to the Hague Convention, you must determine whether the country in which your foreign defendant resides is a signatory to the Hague Convention.[2]

____ 5. **How do you perfect service?** Now that you have determined that the Hague Convention is applicable, how do you perfect service in accordance with the terms of the Hague Convention? The Hague Convention generally allows service of process by:

____ (a) International registered mail.

____ (b) Agent.

____ (c) Central Authority of the country in which the defendant resides.

____ 6. **Can you serve by international registered mail or agent?** A country that is a signatory to the Hague Convention has the option of objecting to service of process by international registered mail or by agent.[3]

____ 7. **Should you serve by international registered mail or agent?** Even if your foreign defendant resides in a signatory country that allows service of process by international registered mail or by agent, the courts of the United States are not in agreement that service by these means is proper and effective. To ensure that service on your foreign defendant is proper and effective, it is best to serve that defendant through the Central Authority of the country in which the defendant resides.

____ 8. **What is the Central Authority?** Each signatory country has designated a Central Authority to process requests for service. A list of each country's Central Authority can be found at www.travel.state .gov. The U.S. Central Authority is located at Office of International Judicial Assistance, Civil Division, Department of Justice, 1100 L Street, NW, Room 11006, Washington, D.C. 20530.

____ 9. **How do you serve a foreign defendant through the Central Authority of the country in which the defendant resides?** The following steps must be taken:

____ (a) Completion of the Request for Service form USM-94, which is available at the office of any U.S. Marshal or which can be found online at www.usmarshals.gov/forms/usm94.

____ (b) Translation of USM-94 and the documents to be served into the official language of the foreign country.

____ (c) Two copies of USM-94 and the documents to be served, with accompanying translations.

____ (d) Transmittal, by the authority or judicial officer, of the two copies of USM-94, the documents to be served, and the accompanying translations directly to the foreign Central Authority.

____ (i) The attorney representing the party seeking service or an international process server is the "authority or judicial officer" who should transmit the documents just listed to the foreign Central Authority. No type of transmittal is specified by the Hague Convention; however, transmittal by registered mail or federal express will allow the party requesting service to track the documents being sent.

____ 10. **How do you complete Request for Service form USM-94?**

____ (a) **"Identity and Address of the Applicant."** This section should be executed by the attorney representing the party seeking service or by an international process server.

____ (b) **"Address of Receiving Authority."** See Section 8.

____ (c) **The identity and address of the individual or entity to be served.**

____ (d) **A designation of the method of service to be used by the foreign Central Authority.**

____ (i) Paragraph (a) of USM-94 should be selected if formal service is desired, whereby the Central Authority itself serves or arranges to have served "by a method prescribed by its internal law for the service of documents in domestic actions upon persons who are within its territory" (Article 3 of the Hague Convention). Formal service is preferred.

____ (ii) Paragraph (b) of USM-94 should be selected if personal service is required.

____ (iii) Paragraph (c) of USM-94 should be selected if the person or entity to be served will accept service voluntarily.

____ (e) **List of documents to be served.**

____ (f) **"Summary of Documents to Be Served."** This is a form to be completed, indicating the nature of the documents (such as "complaint for damages"), the purpose of the proceedings (such as "to recover damages"), and the date and place for entering an appearance.

____ (g) A reference to Federal Rule of Civil Procedure 4(c)2(A) must appear on the request. If you are in state court, specify that the request is made pursuant to Rule 4(c)2(A) of the Federal Rules of Civil Procedure and any pertinent state law. See Section 3.

____ 11. **What are the costs?** There are generally no costs associated with service through a foreign Central Authority.

____ 12. **Can you hire someone to perfect service**? International process servers specializing in the Hague Convention are available to complete USM-94 and transmit the form and documents to the foreign Central Authority. Fees for such process servers are in the range of $300 to $500 per individual or entity to be served.

____ 13. **How long does service take?** There is no specific time frame required by the Hague Convention for the foreign Central Authority to complete service. Service is generally accomplished, however, within 2 to 3 months, depending on the country in which service is to be effected.

____ 14. **Can you get proof of service?** The foreign Central Authority will provide proof of service. On UMS-94, there is a Certificate of Service form. The foreign Central Authority will complete the certificate and mail it directly to the requesting party after service has been effected.

## *Notes*

1. 20 UST 361; TIAS 6638. You can also access the text of the Hague Convention at www.travel.state.gov, in the judicial assistance section.

2. The following countries are signatories to the Hague Convention: Anguilla, Antigua and Barbuda, Argentina, Aruba, Bahamas, Barbados, Belarus, Belgium, Bermuda, Botswana, British Virgin Islands, Bulgaria, Canada, Cayman Islands, People's Republic of China, Croatia, Cyprus, Czech Republic, Denmark, Egypt, Estonia, Falkland Islands and Dependencies, Finland, France, French Polynesia, Germany, Gibraltar, Greece, Guernsey, Hong Kong Sar, Hungary, India, Ireland, Isle of Man, Israel, Italy, Japan, Jersey, Republic of South Korea, Kuwait, Latvia, Lithuania, Luxembourg, Macau Sar, Malawi, Mexico, Montserrat, Netherlands, Norway, Pakistan, Pitcairn, Poland, Portugal, Romania, Russian

Federation, San Marino, St. Helena and Dependencies, St. Vincent and the Grenadines, Seychelles, Slovakia, Slovenia, Spain, Sri Lanka, Sweden, Switzerland, Turkey, Turks and Caicos Islands, Ukraine, United Kingdom, United States of America, and Venezuela.

3. The following countries have opted out of allowing service by international registered mail or by agent: Argentina, China, Czech Republic, Egypt, Germany, Greece, Hungary, Latvia, Lithuania, Luxembourg, Norway, Poland, Republic of South Korea, Slovakia, Sri Lanka, Switzerland, Turkey, Ukraine, and Venezuela.

# Checklist 68: Taking a Deposition in a Foreign Country

Procuring deposition testimony in a foreign country can be a complicated, time-consuming, and expensive task. This checklist provides general guidance for those considering or seeking foreign depositions. It highlights general considerations to be kept in mind when contemplating depositions abroad and delineates specific procedures and options potentially available to a party seeking foreign depositions. It also addresses a series of practical questions and logistical considerations for actually taking a deposition overseas.

____ 1. **General Considerations.**

____ (a) **Under what circumstances might a foreign deposition be required?** Foreign depositions may be required in:

____ (i) U.S. litigation, where one or more of the parties and/or witnesses are located in another country.

____ (ii) U.S. government contract litigation, where the project is overseas.

____ (iii) International arbitration, where the parties are permitted (by rule or agreement) to conduct foreign depositions.

____ (b) **Who requires knowledge of foreign discovery rules?**

____ (i) Clients who are parties or witnesses.

____ (ii) Counsel in U.S. litigation—both corporate and outside counsel.

____ (iii) Counsel in international arbitration.

____ (iv) Local counsel retained in foreign nations.

____ (c) **When foreign depositions are necessary, how does this affect the timing of the overall proceeding?**

____ (i) Depositions overseas, if allowed by the foreign nation, can take several months to arrange. Parties should initiate contact with the U.S. Department of State, Office of American Citizen Services and relevant foreign authorities early in the litigation/

**Lisa K. Virani** is an associate at Eisner & Frank in Beverly Hills, California. Her practice focuses on the resolution of complex commercial disputes for domestic and international clients. She would like to thank Ronan J. McHugh, a partner at Thelen Reid Brown Raysman & Steiner LLP, for his guidance and assistance with this checklist, and Byron L. Pickard, an associate at Thelen Reid Brown Raysman & Steiner LLP, for recounting tales of recent depositions in India.

arbitration process to avoid delay of the proceedings and/or exceeding discovery cut-off dates.

____ a. Contacting the Department of State, Office of American Citizens Services:

Mailing address: Room 4811A, 2201 C Street, N.W., Washington, D.C. 20520; Telephone: (202) 647-5225 or (202) 647-5226.

Information regarding discovery overseas is available at the Department of State's Bureau of Consular Affairs website: http://travel.state.gov/law/info/judicial/judicial_702.html.

____ b. Contacting foreign authorities:

The State Department Bureau of Consular Services issues circulars regarding obtaining evidence abroad, on a country-specific basis. These circulars can be found at http://travel.state.gov/law/info/judicial/judicial_2510.html.

The circulars include contact information for the appropriate foreign agency with authority to receive and address discovery requests, if permitted by the foreign nation, and offer helpful advice on the necessary steps in obtaining evidence abroad.

____ (d) **Is it necessary to retain local counsel in the relevant foreign nation?**

____ (i) The assistance of local counsel is recommended. Foreign local counsel can provide invaluable assistance in navigating the complex local procedures governing discovery in a foreign nation. It is advisable to retain local counsel early in the litigation. The State Department's country-specific circulars often include lists of foreign attorneys willing to act as local counsel for U.S. litigants. See http://travel.state.gov/law/info/judicial/judicial_2510.html for available contact information.

____ (e) **Will the deponent appear voluntarily?**

____ (i) An important threshold consideration in deciding to pursue depositions overseas is whether or not the deponent will appear voluntarily. Can the witness's voluntary appearance be arranged by opposing counsel? If not, it can be difficult, time-consuming, and expensive to procure testimony under compulsion in a foreign country. In fact, some of the means and methods for procuring depositions overseas discussed later, such as notice and commission, are only permitted where there is a willing deponent.[1] If the deponent agrees to appear voluntarily, it may be more cost effective to pay for the deponent's expenses for a trip to the United States for the deposition, rather than navigate the complex and lengthy procedures for obtaining discovery in a foreign country.[2] If travel is not a viable option, issuing a subpoena for the voluntary witness is still advisable to protect the party seeking the deposition if the witness suddenly decides not to appear. For each of the discovery methods discussed in the procedures section (Section 2), the deponent's willingness to appear should be kept in mind.

____ 2. **Procedures for Procuring Foreign Deposition Testimony.**

____ (a) **The applicable rules.** In the United States, court procedures governing foreign discovery vary, depending on which court, federal or state, has jurisdiction over the action and the applicable local court rules. The procedures applicable to a foreign deposition also vary depending on the relevant foreign nation's law. This checklist is based on an original action pending in U.S. federal court, under the Federal Rules of Civil Procedure (FRCP). If discovery abroad is necessary in a state court action, the applicable state civil procedure rules should be consulted and, in all cases, parties should review the applicable local court rules.

____ (b) **The Hague Convention and other relevant treaties.** Depositions abroad, if permitted by foreign law, can be procured from foreign parties and nonparty foreign witnesses who are prepared to appear for deposition voluntarily, under Federal Rules of Civil Procedure 28(b), 29, 30, 45(b)(2); 28 U.S.C. § 1783; the Hague Convention on Taking of Evidence Abroad in Civil or Commercial Matters ("Hague Convention");[3] the Inter-American Convention on Letters Rogatory and Additional Protocol ("Inter-American Convention");[4] and/or the Vienna Convention on Consular Relations ("Vienna Convention").[5]

If the deponent is a nonparty, foreign national who will not voluntarily consent to a deposition, the Hague Convention, or a foreign treaty, may offer a basis to compel a deposition.

The United States, along with numerous other nations, has acceded to the Hague Convention.[6] The Hague Convention sets forth certain procedures by which a judicial authority in one contracting state may request evidence located in another contracting state.[7] The Inter-American Convention provides a mechanism for service of documents by a foreign central authority, although this treaty does not offer a basis to compel a deposition.[8]

____ 3. **What are the options for procuring foreign deposition testimony?**

____ (a) **FRCP 30: Is the foreign deponent a party to the action?**

____ (i) If the deponent is a party to the action, located in a foreign country, the deposition(s) of the party deponent may be noticed as a typical party deposition under FRCP 30.[9] However, if the deposition is set to take place in the foreign country in which that party is located, it may still be necessary or appropriate to follow the protocol set forth in the Hague Convention, the Inter-American Convention, or the Vienna Convention, as applicable.

For example, although parties may agree to a Rule 30 deposition of a party deponent in, for example, India, in order for the deposition to occur in India, the party seeking the deposition must follow the procedures set forth under the Vienna Convention to obtain a commission from an Indian court. This requires a letter rogatory, issued by the U.S. court, which seeks a commission from the appropriate Indian court allowing the deposition to occur in India. The Indian Court has the ultimate authority to decide if the deposition will be allowed to proceed and to decide whether the commission will be issued.

____ (b) **FRCP 29: Will the other side agree to foreign depositions by stipulation?**

____ (i) Rule 29 allows parties to stipulate to depositions under circumstances agreed to by the parties. Rule 29 states, in relevant part:

> Unless otherwise directed by the court, the parties may by written stipulation (1) provide that depositions may be taken before any person, at any time or place, upon any notice, and in any manner and when so taken may be used like other depositions.

Rule 29 is useful insofar as the parties can agree on the terms and conditions of the deposition and the admissibility of the resulting testimony.[10] Rule 29 may only be employed in situations where the deponent will appear voluntarily.[11] Additionally, the parties should ensure that the testimony is given under an enforceable oath, administered according to the laws of the foreign nation.[12]

Parties employing Rule 29 should also consult the law of the foreign country where the deposition will be held to ensure that the deposition will not be viewed as a usurpation of the function of the judiciary in the host country and, therefore, an infringement of its sovereignty.[13] To avoid such a scenario, foreign local counsel and U.S. consular offices can provide helpful advice on the procedures required by law in the foreign nation to ensure that the deposition is conducted with permission and lawfully.

____ (c) **FRCP 28(b): Additional ways to seek depositions abroad.**

____ (i) If a stipulation is not possible, Rule 28 provides various mechanisms for procuring depositions overseas. Rule 28(b) states that depositions may be taken in a foreign country:

____ a. Pursuant to any applicable treaty or convention, that is, the Hague Convention, the Vienna Convention, or the Intra-American Convention (discussed later).

____ b. Pursuant to a letter of request (whether or not captioned as a letter rogatory):

____ (1) A letter of request is a request to a foreign judicial authority asking for its assistance in obtaining evidence in connection with a U.S. proceeding.[14]

____ (2) A letter rogatory is a formal request from a court in one country to "the appropriate judicial authorities" in another country requesting compulsion of testimony or documentary or other evidence or to effect service of process.[15]

Although statutory authority generally refers to the instrument as a "letter rogatory," the terms "letter rogatory" and "letter of request" (which is used specifically in the

Hague Evidence Convention) are virtually synonymous in practice.[16] In some countries, which do not permit the taking of depositions of willing witnesses, letters rogatory are the only method of obtaining evidence or serving process. This process via letter rogatory is the best methodology for obtaining the deposition overseas of a witness unwilling to appear voluntarily.

____ c. On notice before a person authorized to administer oaths in the place where the examination is held, either by the law thereof or by the law of the United States.

____ (1) Depositions by notice do not require the party seeking the deposition to submit an application to the U.S. court.[17] However, deposition by notice may require the voluntary participation of the parties and the deponent.[18]

Be sure to determine if the law of the foreign nation permits depositions by notice.[19] Local counsel and the State Department should be consulted to ensure that the process being considered is proper and permissible in the applicable jurisdiction.[20]

____ d. Before a person commissioned by the court, with the power to administer any necessary oath and take testimony.

____ (1) Depositions by commission require the party seeking the deposition to apply to the U.S. court to have a particular person commissioned to take the deposition testimony. It is important to note that depositions by commission can only be conducted with deponents who will appear voluntarily. If the deponent is unwilling to appear voluntarily, the letter of request procedures, under the Federal Rules or the Hague Convention, should be used.[21]

____ (d) **Is the deponent a U.S. citizen or resident living abroad?**

____ (i) A U.S. court can compel a U.S. citizen or resident to testify in a U.S. federal lawsuit, which is considered a civic duty, even when the person is living abroad. FRCP 45(b)(2) permits the service of a subpoena directed to a witness in a foreign country who is a national or resident of the United States. 28 U.S.C. § 1783 governs the issuance and service of a subpoena to a U.S. national or resident living abroad. Pursuant to 28 U.S.C.§ 1783:

> A court in the United States may order the issuance of a subpoena requiring the appearance as a witness before it, or before a person or body designated by it, of a national or resident of the United States who is in a foreign country...if the court finds that particular testimony...is necessary in the interest of justice.[22]

____ (ii) Will the U.S. national or resident appear for deposition voluntarily? Although a U.S. court can compel a U.S. national or resident living abroad to testify at a deposition, if the U.S. national is unwilling to testify, the appropriate procedures for compulsion of testimony must be followed. Under the Hague Convention, this requires the issuance of a letter of request by the U.S. court, which is then sent to the appropriate foreign authority.

____ (e) **Is the deponent's country a signatory to the Hague Convention?**

____ (i) If so, the Hague Convention will govern the service of the deposition subpoena. Both the discovery rules set forth in the FRCP and the Hague Convention are the law of the United States.[23] The Hague Convention is, consistent with the law of many foreign countries, limited to the taking of evidence.[24]

____ (ii) What is the designated Central Authority in the relevant nation?

____ a. Article 2 of the Hague Convention provides that each contracting state shall designate a Central Authority that will undertake to receive letters of request.[25] In the United States, the Department of State is the designated Central Authority.[26] The State Department country-specific circulars provide information on each contracting state's Central Authority and often include links to their websites.

____ (iii) Has the Contracting Nation made reservations and declarations regarding the procedures set forth in the Hague Convention?

____ a. Each nation participant or "Contracting Nation" is permitted to make reservations and declarations that change or limit the availability of certain procedures under the Hague Convention. Be sure to review any reservations or declarations issued by the relevant nation that limit or change the procedures set forth in the Hague Convention. For example, in a reservation made at the time of ratification of the treaty, Switzerland declared that letters of request issued for the purpose of obtaining pre-trial discovery of documents will not be executed if:[27]

____ (1) The request has no direct and necessary link with the proceedings in question.

____ (2) A person is required to indicate what documents relating to the case are or were in his or her possession or keeping or at his or her disposal.

____ (3) A person is required to produce documents, other than those mentioned in the request for legal assistance, which are probably in his or her possession or keeping at his or her disposal.

____ (4) Interests worthy of protection of the concerned persons are endangered.

____ (iv) **Procedures under the Hague Convention for setting a deposition:**

____ a. By notice and before a U.S. consular official or local official authorized to administer oaths.

____ b. By a commission issued by a U.S. court appointing a local commissioner to take the deposition.

____ c. By a letter of request issued by a U.S. court to the foreign nation's designated central authority. (This is the only method available, under the Hague Convention, for seeking the testimony of an unwilling deponent. The letter of request should be used if the witness is not cooperative or if there is some reasonable possibility that the witness may object to some portion of the deposition after its commencement.)

____ (f) **Is the deponent's country a signatory to the Inter-American Convention?**

____ (i) If so, the Inter-American Convention will govern the service of the deposition subpoena. The Inter-American Convention covers letters rogatory in connection with civil and commercial matters that seek the performance of "procedural acts" (for example, service of subpoenas, summons, etc.).[28] Similar to the Hague Convention, letters rogatory are issued to a designated Central Authority.[29] In the United States, the Department of State is the designated Central Authority.[30]

____ (ii) **Are you seeking deposition testimony from a voluntary witness?**

____ a. The procedures available under the Inter-American Convention are applicable only where the deposition testimony is sought from a willing witness.

____ b. If not, Article 3 of Inter-American Convention provides that the treaty cannot be used to compel the production of evidence.[31] Accordingly, in this situation, if available, the letters rogatory process under the Hague Convention should be used instead to obtain the deposition testimony.

____ (iii) **Procedures under the Inter-American Convention for setting a deposition:**[32]

____ a. A letter rogatory must be issued by a competent consular or diplomatic agent.

____ b. A letter rogatory and any appendices attached thereto must be translated into the official language of the country of destination.

____ c. When the process, summons, or subpoena is being served on a person, the letter rogatory should be accompanied by: (1) an authenticated copy of the complaint and supporting documents that serve as a basis for the deposition; (2) a written informational document identifying the judicial authority issuing the letter, the time limits within which to respond to the request, and warnings of the consequences for failure to do so; and (3) information on the existence and address of court appointed defense or competent legal aid societies in the state of origin.

____ (g) **If the foreign nation is not signatory to the Hague Convention or the Inter-American Convention, is there another treaty between the U.S. and the relevant nation governing discovery/depositions?**

____ (i) The State Department and the State Department country-specific circulars may provide information regarding other bilateral treaties, if they exist. If another treaty is applicable, the specific terms of that treaty regarding the issuance and service of a subpoena or other process will govern.

____ (h) **Are there applicable local rules of foreign courts?**

____ (i) Always check the local rules of the foreign court involved in the request for a foreign deposition. Local counsel should be consulted. Information is also available via the State Department and the State Department country-specific circulars. Reviewing the foreign nation or court's website may provide additional guidance as well.

____ (i) **What if there is no treaty or convention governing discovery between the U.S. and the relevant nation?** If that is the case, consider the following:

____ (i) Will the witness appear voluntarily (that is, without a subpoena)?

____ (ii) Is the deponent subject to the jurisdiction of a U.S. court (that is, a party to the action)? Look to the FRCP and/or any applicable state and local rules.

____ (iii) Is the deponent a U.S. national or resident living abroad? If so, look to 28 U.S.C. § 1783, discussed earlier.

____ (iv) Can the deposition be held in a third nation covered by a treaty, where the rules on depositions are flexible and favorable? For example, attorneys from abroad are allowed to depose anyone in the United Kingdom provided they are willing witnesses. No commission from a court is necessary.[33]

____ (v) Have you checked for relevant domestic local rules and applicable rules/laws of the foreign nation?

Ultimately, if the witness will not appear voluntarily and no treaty covers the foreign nation, it is unlikely that a deposition will be possible.

____ 4. **What are the logistics of taking a deposition overseas?**

____ (a) **A party seeking foreign depositions should review the applicable rules and requirements of the relevant foreign nation.** Carefully check all requirements of the foreign nation to avoid unnecessary delay in obtaining foreign discovery.

____ (i) **Who may take the deposition?**

____ a. Each nation has its own requirements for who may take a deposition in that nation. For example, the law of Brazil does not permit American attorneys to take depositions for use in a U.S. court before a U.S. consular officer, with the assistance of a Brazilian attorney, or in any other manner. Brazilian law views the taking of depositions for use in foreign courts as an act that may be undertaken in Brazil only by Brazilian judicial authorities.

Consult with the State Department, U.S. Consular offices, the appropriate foreign embassy, and/or local counsel to determine who may properly take the deposition.

____ (ii) **Are immigration specific visas necessary?**

____ a. Consult with the State Department, U.S. Consular offices, the appropriate foreign embassy, and/or local counsel to determine if temporary work/business visas are required to enter the host nation and conduct the deposition. For example, Japan requires that persons from the United States wishing to participate in a deposition of a witness in Japan must apply for a Japanese "special deposition visa."[34]

____ (iii) **Where does the foreign nation permit depositions to be taken?**

____ a. Be sure to review the host nation's rules on where a deposition can be taken within the confines of the host nation. For example, Japan will only allow a deposition to take place at the U.S. Embassy and the U.S. Consular offices. Conversely, the United Kingdom permits any location to be used for a deposition.

____ (iv) **Who will administer the oath?**

____ a. It is important to have the oath administered to the deponent according to the law of the host nation to ensure the admissibility of the deposition testimony in the U.S. court proceeding.

____ (v) **Are court reporters available?**

____ a. American attorneys are used to having a wealth of available court reporters to transcribe a deposition; however, in many foreign nations, court reporters are difficult to find.[35] For example, in Belgium, stenographers are few and far between. As a result, the State Department urges litigants to consider using a stenographer from another country.[36] Be sure to consider the additional costs associated with hiring a court reporter from another country as well.

____ (vi) **Interpreter needed? Translated transcript? Additional time needed?**

____ a. Remember to consider whether additional services will be needed for the deposition such as an interpreter to translate the questions or the answers depending on the language(s) spoken by the stenographer. Depositions requiring an interpreter often run at a much slower pace than the typical deposition. Consider whether or not additional days of testimony will be required in order to accommodate the interpretation.

Also, translating the transcript will have additional cost and time implications.

____ (vii) **Video/telephone depositions?**

____ a. FRCP 30(b)(2) and 30(b)(7) permit depositions conducted by video and telephone, respectively. However, holding a video or telephone deposition with a deponent located abroad is considered a foreign deposition. Although seemingly convenient, depositions of persons overseas taken by video or telephone may result in communication problems, delays, and difficulty in establishing a clear transcript/record of the testimony. Also, many countries prohibit video and/or telephone depositions. Be sure to consult local counsel and foreign authorities to ensure compliance with the foreign nation's law.

____ (j) **Standards applied by U.S. federal courts in allowing overseas depositions.**

____ (i) FRCP 28, 29, 30 and 45, discussed earlier, are construed by U.S. federal courts in deciding to allow foreign depositions.

____ (ii) Is a foreign deposition admissible in a U.S. court? Federal Rule of Evidence 804(b)(1) provides for the admissibility of deposition testimony under the former testimony exception to the hearsay rule. FRCP 28, which delineates persons before whom a deposition may be taken, must be complied with as well for the deposition testimony to be admissible. Finally, all applicable foreign laws regarding the oath administration and governing the deposition conduct must be followed to ensure admissibility.

## *Notes*

1. See Baker, William H., "Obtaining Evidence: International Discovery Techniques—The Taking of Evidence Abroad for Use in American Courts," p. 8, *International Business Litigation & Arbitration,* Vo1. 1, 173, 184, (Practising Law Institute, 2003).

2. *Id.* at p. 4.

3. Hague Convention on Taking of Evidence Abroad in Civil or Commercial Matters, 23 U.S.T. 2555; 1970 U.S.T. LEXIS 497; TIAS 7444.

4. Inter-American Convention on Letters Rogatory and Additional Protocol, January 30, 1975, S. TREATY DOC. No. 27, 98th Cong., 2d Sess. (1984).

5. Vienna Convention on Consular Relations, 21 U.S.T. 77, 596 UNTS 261; TIAS 6820 (where applicable).

6. See *Societe Nationale Industrielle Aerospatiale v. U.S. Dist. Ct. for the So. Dist. of Iowa*, 482 U.S. 522, 524 (1987); for country-specific information regarding the various contracting states, visit http://travel.state.gov/ law/info/judicial/judicial_2510.html.

7. See *Societe Nationale* at p. 524.

8. Inter-American Convention on Letters Rogatory and Additional Protocol, Department of State Bureau of Consular Affairs Circular, http://travel.state.gov/law/info/judicial/judicial_687.html.

9. See *Societe Nationale* at p. 541 (stating that the Federal Rules of Civil Procedure provide ample means for obtaining discovery from parties who are subject to the court's jurisdiction; when a litigant is subject to the jurisdiction of the district court, arguably the evidence it is required to produce is not "abroad" within the meaning of the [Hague] Convention, even though it is in fact located in a foreign country at the time of the discovery request).

10. See Baker at pp. 6-7.

11. *Id.*

12. *Id.*

13. *Id.*

14. See Baker at p. 9.

15. Preparation of Letters Rogatory, Department of State Bureau of Consular Affairs Circular, http://travel.state.gov/ law/info/judicial/judicial_683.html.

16. Preparation of Letters Rogatory, Department of State Bureau of Consular Affairs Circular, http://travel.state.gov/law/info/judicial/judicial_683.html [citing Epstein & Snyder, *International Litigation: A Guide to Jurisdiction, Practice & Strategy*, 2nd. Sec. 10.09, p. 10.13–10.14.; *Black's Law Dictionary* (6th ed., 1994), Fed. R. Civ. P. 4(f)(2)(B) Advisory Committee's Note (West Supp. 1993)].

17. See Baker at p. 15.

18. *Id.*

19. See State Department country-specific circulars, http://travel.state.gov/law/info/judicial/judicial_2510.html; see also Baker at 19.

20. See Baker at 15.

21. See *id.* at 19.

22. 28 U.S.C.S. § 1783(a) (2007).

23. See *Societe Nationale*, 482 U.S. at 533.

24. Simpson, Regean Wm., *Civil Discovery and Depositions*, § 8.17 Discovery Pursuant to a Treaty, p. 496 (2nd ed., 1994).

25. See Baker at p. 23.

26. 28 U.S.C.S. § 1781 (2007).

27. Switzerland Judicial Assistance, Department of State Bureau of Consular Affairs Circular, http://travel.state.gov/law/info/judicial/judicial_668.html.

28. See Baker at p. 30.

29. *Id.*

30. 28 U.S.C.S. § 1781 (2007).

31. See Baker at p. 31.

32. *Id.*

33. United Kingdom Judicial Assistance, Department of State Bureau of Consular Affairs Circular, http://travel.state. gov/law/info/judicial/judicial_671.html.

34. Japan Judicial Assistance, Department of State Bureau of Consular Affairs Circular, http://travel.state.gov/law/info/judicial/judicial_678.html#japanesevisas.

35. See Baker at pp. 17-18.

36. Belgium Judicial Assistance, Department of State Bureau of Consular Affairs Circular, http://travel.state.gov/law/info/judicial/judicial_666.html.

# General Lists

# Checklist 69: Bankruptcy Considerations on the Construction Project

A bankruptcy can disrupt a construction project at several levels. There are many issues in common, although they are somewhat different depending on the player that is forced into bankruptcy. This checklist analyzes issues that arise for the owner, surety, and downstream parties in the event of a general contractor bankruptcy. Fundamental to any bankruptcy considerations are the automatic stay under 11 U.S.C. § 362 that arises upon filing, and the right of the debtor to assume or reject executory (partially performed) contracts under 11 U.S.C. § 365.

Because a number of bankruptcy issues are common to all creditors, a general bankruptcy considerations checklist that applies to the owner, surety, and downstream claimants precedes the checklists that apply to each.

____ 1. **General Considerations** (applies to owner, surety, subcontractor, and supplier).

____ (a) **Attend the first meeting of creditors under 11 U.S.C. § 341.**

____ (i) **Debtor is under oath.** Testimony is recorded on tape, and a copy of the tape can be obtained.

____ (ii) **Details explained as to what triggered the bankruptcy.**

____ (iii) **Ask questions.** Can ask debtor's representative questions regarding the most significant details about claimant's debt. Should not be confused with a deposition; however, 5 to 10 minutes of questions can glean very significant information.

____ (b) **Proof of claim issues.**

____ (i) **Is a proof of claim necessary?** If debt is properly scheduled and not disputed or listed as contingent in a Chapter 11, a proof of claim may not be necessary. If the case is filed in or converted to a Chapter 7, a proof of claim must be filed. Otherwise, no proof of claim means no chance to share in any distribution.

____ (ii) **Jurisdiction.** Filing is a consent to jurisdiction for disputes in the bankruptcy court.

**Fred D. Wilshusen** is a partner in the Dallas, Texas, law firm of Thomas, Feldman & Wilshusen, LLP. As part of his construction practice, he has frequently represented construction interests in the bankruptcy courts.

____ (iii) **Jury trial not generally available in bankruptcy court.**

____ a. Is there already a jury trial waiver in the contract?

____ (iv) **Jury or nonjury trial?** Is a trial before the judge better than a trial before a jury?

____ a. Complex legal or factual issues?

____ b. Very strong legal position?

____ (c) **Evaluate the bankruptcy estate by reviewing the statement of assets and liabilities.**

____ (i) **Not usually filed until some weeks after the petition.**

____ (ii) **Discloses assets and liabilities.** Discloses a fairly accurate listing of the debtor's assets and the outstanding claims against the debtor. In the case of a contractor, the substantial assets are accounts receivables and contract rights, and the substantial creditor is usually the secured lender.

____ (d) **Motion to Lift Stay.**

____ (i) **Automatic stay.** Upon filing of bankruptcy, all commencement and continuation of efforts to collect from the debtor or its property are automatically stayed under the risk of contempt.

____ (ii) **Notice issues**. Many contractual notice requirements regarding rights against the debtor may require a Motion to Lift Stay.

____ a. Declaring default of the contractor to trigger performance bond obligations.

____ b. Claims for extra money or time.

____ c. Other contractual rights requiring notice?

____ (iii) **Comply with local rules.** Motions to Lift Stay are often subject to local procedural rules regarding filing of preliminary evidence, designations of witnesses, etc.

____ (iv) **Automatic stay in contractor's bankruptcy does not protect its bonding company from claim or suit.**

____ 2. **Owner Considerations.**

____ (a) **Read the contract with the contractor.** Many of the rights stated therein drive the rights in the bankruptcy.

____ (i) **Offset rights.** Does the owner have the right to offset against amounts claimed by the debtor?

____ (ii) **Insurance.**

____ a. Is the owner an additional insured on any of contractor's policies?

____ b. If not, is the contractor maintaining the various insurance policies required by the contract?

____ (b) **Initial cash collateral hearing and order.**

____ (i) **Timing.** Happens shortly after filing of a Chapter 11 to arrange continued financing, usually from general secured lender. The lender often seeks a super-priority lien to protect its post-bankruptcy financing. The court is strongly inclined to grant some relief to the lender because the lack of post-petition financing will usually doom the bankruptcy. The super-priority lien can trump legal rights of other parties. Attend the hearing.

____ (ii) **Miss the hearing?** Most parties miss the hearing. Protection is still available.

____ a. Read the order to determine what the court ordered.

____ b. Challenge provisions that compromise the client's rights prior to the final cash collateral hearing some weeks later.

____ (c) **Motion to compel assumption or rejection of contract.**

____ (i) **Assumption of contract.** In a Chapter 7, the Bankruptcy Code allows the debtor 60 days to assume or reject a contract, which can be an eternity on a construction project. In a Chapter 11, the debtor can assume or reject any time before the confirmation of the plan. This time limit can be lengthened or shortened by court order. Consider moving the court to require a prompt decision by the debtor to accept or reject the contract. (There are different rules for executing contracts dealing with real property.)

____ (ii) **If the contract is rejected.**

____ a. Is there an assignment of the subcontracts to the owner?

____ b. Who will schedule, coordinate and manage the subcontractors?

____ (d) **Does the contractor have colorable claims against the owner?**

____ (i) **Evaluate the quality of the claim.** Does the claim have merit?

____ (ii) **Other options.** Consider options to have the case converted to Chapter 7 or have a trustee appointed. If there is a lack of funds, trustees rarely want to pursue unliquidated or fact-intensive claims for the debtor, even good and substantial claims.

____ 3. **Surety Considerations.**

____ (a) **Protecting the surety's superior claims on contract proceeds is the first priority.**

____ (i) **Educate the bankruptcy judge at every opportunity about the surety's equitable rights.**

____ (ii) **Prevent owner from compromising collateral.**

____ a. Warning owners to withhold payment on the project will not be appreciated by the bankruptcy judge.

____ b. Consider a Motion to Lift Stay to protect surety's collateral in the possession of the project owners.

____ (b) **Initial cash collateral hearing and order.**

____ (i) **Timing.** Happens shortly after filing of a Chapter 11 to arrange continued financing, usually from general secured lender. The lender often seeks a super-priority lien to protect its post-bankruptcy financing. The court is strongly inclined to grant some relief to the lender because the lack of post-petition financing will usually doom the bankruptcy. The super-priority lien can trump legal rights of other parties.

____ a. Attend the hearing.

____ b. Educate the judge about equitable rights.

____ c. Evaluate protections requested by the lender. Do they invade the equitable rights of the surety to the contract proceeds?

____ (ii) **Miss the hearing?** Most parties miss the hearing. Protection is still available.

____ a. Read the order to determine what the court ordered.

____ b. Challenge provisions that compromise the client's rights prior to the final cash collateral hearing some weeks later.

____ (c) **Can the surety terminate its bond or refuse to accept the annual renewal premium?** Although this issue is periodically analyzed under the theory that the bonds constitute "financial accommodations," which are contracts that cannot be assumed under 11 USC § 365, most agree that the surety cannot refuse to honor a bond that it has already issued and for which it has received a premium. On the other hand, the bonding company is not obligated to issue bonds for new projects under most circumstances.

____ (d) **Preserving documents and witnesses.**

____ (i) **Documents and files.** Many crucial files have been lost in bankruptcy. The debtor has a duty to preserve records as long as it is in Chapter 11. Once the case is converted to Chapter 7, the debtor rapidly loses interest in old records. The trustee has a responsibility to maintain records, but the actual maintenance of the records and their accessibility is often questionable. They are often stored in mini-warehouses and are vulnerable to the elements.

____ a. Copies are cheap. Copy all project documents, including time sheets, payroll records, bank statements, and checks for the relevant time.

____ b. Index documents. Having a knowledgeable contractor employee organize, label, and index documents so they are easier to work with in the future is a benefit.

____ (ii) **Witnesses.** Former employees of the debtor are often well intentioned but rapidly put emphasis on their new job and usually do not start with strong loyalties to the bonding company.

____ (iii) **Employees**. The bonding company is significantly dependent on debtor's employees to defend against claims of unpaid subcontractors and suppliers or offsets alleged by the owner.

____ (iv) **Sureties.** Sureties often hire key employees as consultants to assist in completing jobs, including resolving claims. Also consider allowing the estate to pay for an employee to stay employed by the debtor in order to act as a fact witness and to assist in recovering assets and avoidable transfers. Usually there will need to be an incentive including a "stay bonus" to offer to the employee.

____ 4. **Subcontractor and Supplier Considerations.**

____ (a) **Read the contract with the contractor.** Many of the rights stated therein drive the rights in the bankruptcy.

____ (b) **Initial cash collateral hearing and order.**

____ (i) **Timing.** Happens shortly after filing of a Chapter 11 to arrange continued financing, usually from general secured lender. The lender often seeks a super-priority lien to protect its post-bankruptcy financing. The court is strongly inclined to grant some relief to the lender because the lack of post-petition financing will usually doom the bankruptcy. The super-priority lien can trump legal rights of other parties. Attend the hearing.

____ (ii) **Miss the hearing?** Most parties miss the hearing. Protection is still available.

____ a. Read the order to determine what the court ordered.

____ b. Challenge provisions that compromise the client's rights prior to the final cash collateral hearing some weeks later.

____ (c) **Lien and bond claims.**

____ (i) **Perfecting lien rights.** Does perfecting lien and bond rights violate the automatic stay in the relevant jurisdiction?

____ a. If the claim relates back to the pre-petition period, it has been held not to violate the stay.

____ (ii) **Secured or unsecured?** Liens can create a "secured" status for the creditor, which is always superior to being unsecured.

____ (iii) **Perfected lien/bond claim.** A properly perfected lien or bond claim can help in defending against a preference action brought in the future by the trustee.

____ (iv) **Collection rights.** The lien or bond claims give collection rights against third parties other than the debtor.

____ (d) **Preference issues.**

____ (i) **What constitutes a preference payment?** All payments received within 90 days before the bankruptcy are potentially preferences.

____ (ii) **Evaluate claim.** Typically preceded by demand letters from the trustee or its representatives. Do not pay until after consulting an attorney and evaluating the legitimacy of the claim. Often the claim is overstated and subject to defenses and negotiation.

____ (iii) **Timing.** Trustee can sue up to 2 years later.

____ (iv) **Collection efforts.** As a policy, diligently collect accounts receivable or perfect lien and bond claims as a defense against future preference actions.

____ (e) **Guaranties.** Many suppliers have clients fill out a credit report that includes personal guaranties by the principals of the purchaser. Claims against the guarantors are not stayed by the bankruptcy of the company. Sue on the guaranty.

____ (f) **Exception or objection to discharge?**

____ (i) **Fairly short deadline after filing a bankruptcy.**

____ (ii) **Exception to discharge.**

____ a. Grounds for exception listed under 11 USC § 523.

____ b. Excepts a specific debt from the bankruptcy discharge.

____ c. Diversion of trust funds? Possible if contractor has wrongly diverted trust funds, however, the particular state's trust fund statute must create an express trust in favor of the claimant. Many do not.

____ d. Difficult to prove an exception for a traditional commercial creditor.

____ (iii) **Objection to discharge.**

____ a. Grounds for objection listed under 11 USC § 727.

____ b. Applies to all debts of the debtor.

____ c. Creditors usually should not use § 727 to gain leverage for a single debt.

____ d. Movant represents the interest of all unsecured creditors.

____ e. Cannot dismiss an objection without court approval, even when the debtor agrees.

____ (g) **Post-petition work.**

____ (i) **Administrative claim.** The debtor will make all manner of assurances about continued payment to keep subcontractors and suppliers working. This work constitutes an administrative claim, which is given priority for payment, but only if the estate has money.

____ (ii) **Payment of pre-petition debt.** The bankruptcy petition is usually filed in the middle of a pay period. Any payment of pre-petition debt must be approved by the court or violates the bankruptcy laws even if the debtor agrees.

____ (iii) **The safest policy is prepayment or C.O.D.**

____ (h) **Service on the unsecured creditors' committee.**

____ (i) Has the inside information about events in the bankruptcy.

____ (ii) The committee is consulted on most major decisions.

____ (iii) Represents all unsecured creditors' interests.
____ (iv) Time consuming, without pay.

____ (i) **If the debtor rejects the subcontract.**

____ (i) Did the subcontractor agree to an assignment of the subcontract to the owner?
____ (ii) Does the assignment provide for the owner to pay amounts unpaid by the debtor?

____ (j) **Reclamation.**

____ (i) A seller of goods is entitled to a bankruptcy court order requiring that the debtor return any goods received by the debtor within 45 days of the filing of the bankruptcy. However, the notice of reclamation must be filed with the bankruptcy court within 20 days of filing. This is the best chance to get full reimbursement on those goods.

# Checklist 70: Responding to a Catastrophic Construction Event

This checklist identifies many of the issues faced by a contractor, or an attorney representing a contractor, that has experienced a catastrophic accident on a construction project over the short term. The checklist indicates those issues that must be addressed.

____ 1. **Crisis Management Plan.** Does the company have a crisis management plan? If yes, it should be immediately reviewed and implemented. All contractors should consider designing a plan, and training employees with respect to its implementation, to be prepared for such an event.

____ 2. **Designate Key Individuals**. Immediately designate individuals responsible for specific tasks, particularly those that will inevitably arise in the first several days following the event.

  ____ (a) **Specific tasks for individuals.** The following identifies the key individuals and tasks:

    ____ (i) An overall "commander-in-chief" with the authority to make critical decisions on behalf of the company.

    ____ (ii) An individual who will be the face of the company in communicating with third parties about the event, including, but not limited to, the media, which may or may not be the same person as the overall commander-in-chief.

    ____ (iii) An individual responsible for the project site, to undertake the tasks discussed in Section 3.

    ____ (iv) Individuals responsible for the other tasks outlined in the following sections.

  ____ (b) **Communication among individuals.** Establish 24/7 communication ability with all individuals having responsibilities in connection with the event. Consider the need for support groups to back up the individuals having designated responsibilities.

---

**José M. Pienknagura** graduated from the Indiana University Business and Law School and is the vice president, risk manager, and general counsel of Hunt Construction Group Inc. He is responsible for overseeing and directing legal affairs, risk management, and personnel matters for Hunt Construction Group, including the preparation, negotiation, and administration of more than $2.0 billion of contract work each year.

____ 3. **Responsibility at the Site of the Accident.** Shortly after a catastrophic accident, local government agencies (generally, police or fire) will likely assume control of the site. Nonetheless, the contractor should have a high-level representative(s) present at all times, able to undertake the tasks and responsibilities described further later.

  ____ (a) **Initial contact.** Shortly after the accident (often that day), investigators from state and/or federal OSHA, FEMA, and other agencies may arrive. They will expect to conduct interviews and to investigate the cause of the accident. Who is prepared to interact with these individuals on behalf of the contractor?

  ____ (b) **Criminal investigations.** There may be separate or parallel criminal investigations, especially if there have been deaths. Ultimately, these could encompass a wide range of forensic investigations, as well as employee interviews. Again, who will represent the contractor in dealing with the investigators? Will you allow employees to be interviewed without counsel present? These kinds of issues must be considered promptly.

  ____ (c) **Control of site.** The contractor must be prepared to accept control of the site when responsibility is returned from local authorities to the owner (and then to the contractor) or directly to the contractor. This could be within a day, or not for weeks, but the contractor must be prepared whenever it occurs.

____ 4. **Make Safe Efforts.** One of the contractor's first obligations will be to undertake itself, or to assist others in undertaking, efforts to make the site safe (that is, to prevent further accidents, injuries, or damages). Simply as an example, if part of a structure has collapsed, it may be necessary to shore the remainder to prevent a further collapse. This may necessitate the retention of outside engineering assistance and other specialists.

____ 5. **Evidence Preservation.** The failure to preserve critical evidence can have civil and criminal implications.

  ____ (a) **Immediate protocols.** Protocols must be established quickly to preserve all potentially relevant evidence.

    ____ (i) For a major construction project this may require, as but one example, the leasing of a secure site upon which construction debris can be stored.

    ____ (ii) Debris should not be discarded unless and until it is clear that it can have no relevance to investigations of the cause or scope of the damages.

  ____ (b) **Going-forward protocols.** Going-forward protocols will be needed with respect to who has access to the evidence, and in what circumstances, for inspection, testing, etc.

____ (i) All interested parties should be given advance notice of any destructive testing and an opportunity to participate at some level. Generally this would include, at a minimum, the right to comment on the nature and conduct of anticipated tests, observe the tests, and obtain the results of such testing.

____ (ii) Who might constitute interested parties (for example, potentially responsible subcontractors, design professionals, sureties, insurers)?

____ 6. **Media Relations.** Consider how to handle inquiries from the media.

____ (a) **Approach with the media.** Some contractors believe that efforts should be made to aggressively manage the media, while others have concluded that the less said the better.

____ (i) Your best approach may depend on the nature of the event and the extent of the initial media interest.

____ (b) **Use of outside consultant.** Should you engage an outside consultant?

____ (i) Various outside firms specialize in assisting contractors with media relations.

____ (ii) On the first day, it should be clear that the contractor's principal concern is for any victims and safety.

____ (iii) The contractor should avoid finger-pointing and discussion of causation, if at all possible, and assure the public that appropriate steps are being taken in response to the accident.

____ (c) **Going-forward strategy.** Going forward, you will need a strategy for dealing with the media that also considers, among other things, whether all project participants will agree to a single spokesman who will be the face of the company or project participants generally, and the substance of the messages to be conveyed.

____ 7. **Family and Friends of Victims.** Efforts should be undertaken immediately to reach out to families and friends of any victims. This would include immediate, frank communications, as well as aid and comfort at the site if individuals are still missing or in the process of being rescued. Do not have family and friends standing alone at the site, without the support of the contractor, or others, or material information. Later, consider offering professional, monetary, and other assistance to the victims and their families, independent of (and without prejudice to) any type of damages claims. In many cases, victims will be employees of subcontractors, so these efforts should be undertaken in coordination with the direct employer. Acting humanely and establishing as good relations as possible in the circumstances is both the right thing to do and can pay dividends in the future.

____ 8. **Employee Communications and Relations.** It is important to promptly communicate with your employees about a significant accident.

____ (a) Include not only project employees—who need to know when and where to report, expectations, etc.—but all employees of the company. A significant accident will lead to widespread questions and concerns.

____ (b) How will the contractor's message be communicated (e-mail, phone chains, etc.), and what is the substance of that message?

____ (c) Also consider giving individual employees a way to help, even in a very limited way, as many will want to do so.

____ 9. **Communications with Other Project Participants.** Owners, contractors, subcontractors, design professionals, and other project participants will need to undertake prompt and frequent communications with respect to the accident, the status of the project, expectations, and other issues.

____ (a) **With whom?** Immediately consider who should be the parties to those communications. Generally, it should not be counsel.

____ (b) **Confidentiality agreement.** There is a benefit to developing a level of trust, cooperation, and coordination at an early stage among decision makers. Confidentiality and non-waiver agreements can help promote a more open level of dialog.

____ 10. **Communications with Neighbors.** If adjacent properties are at any risk, then there is a need to communicate promptly with owners, tenants, residents, and others who are potentially affected. Consider the substance of the initial message to be conveyed and by whom and how it will be conveyed. Frequent, ongoing communication thereafter is critical, until "make-safe" efforts eliminate any risks presented.

____ 11. **Provide Required Notices.** Owner, contractor, subcontractor, design, and other project agreements typically contain claim provisions, indemnity clauses, and other provisions potentially implicated by the accident. In many agreements, notices are required within specified timeframes.

____ (a) **Review agreements.** Review relevant agreements and ensure that required notices have been given. At the same time, consider whether notices can be given in a manner that does not immediately engender war.

____ (b) **Agreements among parties.** Consider also the benefits of negotiating agreements among potentially responsible and potentially affected parties deeming all relevant notices to have been given, tolling contractual and other time periods, establishing confidentiality for certain communications among project participants, preserving privileges, designating individual media spokespersons, and so on.

____ 12. **Communications with Insurers.** Prompt notice must be provided to all insurers potentially responsible for losses or damages arising from the event; provide them with an opportunity to participate in investigations, claims resolution, and other matters from a very early stage. Insurance issues are discussed further later.

____ 13. **Notice to Sureties.** Consider whether to provide notice of the event to sureties for potentially responsible contractors or subcontractors. The goal, of course, is to avoid a late notice or similar defense down the road by the surety for a party later found to be in "default" by reason of the accident.

____ 14. **Project Recovery Efforts.** Quickly begin to consider how to repair damaged work, resequence the work, continue with undamaged work to the extent possible, and similar issues to minimize the impact of the accident on schedule, costs, and so on. Coordination with other project participants will become important.

____ 15. **Forensic Analysis of Causation.** In most cases, it will be necessary to undertake an examination of the cause of the accident.

____ (a) **Investigation.** Who will conduct that investigation on behalf of the contractor?

____ (b) **Use of experts.** Do you have the right experts involved?

____ (i) Give consideration to whether numerous project participants will conduct their own separate investigations, or whether there will be some level of coordination and transparency.

____ (ii) There will be a tendency to circle the wagons and become defensive, but it is not necessarily beneficial to have dueling expert reports and/or finger pointing from an early stage.

____ (iii) In some situations, government agencies will need to approve a proposed repair or, ultimately, a certificate of occupancy. If there are dueling expert reports, whom will government agencies trust?

____ (iv) Will competing expert reports delay getting the project back on track and/or help third-party plaintiffs pursue claims against potentially responsible parties?

____ 16. **Will all parties immediately attempt to downstream losses?** The contractor must preserve its ability to downstream losses to responsible subcontractors and to pursue recoveries from the owner and/or its design professionals in appropriate circumstances. At the same time, there are benefits to cooperation, with respect to governmental investigations, potential bodily injury/wrongful death claims, getting the project back on track, and in other respects. Do not automatically initiate war.

____ 17. **What insurance coverages will potentially respond to losses and damages flowing from the accident?**

- ____ (a) **Worker's compensation.** Injury to or death of employees. Who is covered by the exclusive remedy rule (in some states, where an employee of a subcontractor is injured, the general contractor in addition to the subcontractor)?
- ____ (b) **Commercial general liability.** Bodily injury/wrongful death claims, damage to adjacent property, potentially some damages to or arising in connection with the project itself (for example, certain damages not covered by the project builder's risk policy). General liability policies typically require an insured to provide notice of an occurrence likely to give rise to a claim, which a catastrophe accident likely is. Also consider whether the contactor is an additional insured on policies procured by subcontractors or other potentially responsible parties.
- ____ (c) **Builder's risk.** Repair of physical damage to the work. In addition, if the policy contains "coverage extensions," then certain soft costs, delay-related damages, extra expense, expediting costs, increased costs by reason of changes in the law, professional fees, and other losses may be covered. It is critical to (i) involve the builder's risk carrier from as early a stage as possible; (ii) distinguish losses caused by the accident from base contract work, and to implement a system allowing base contract work to be easily differentiated; and (iii) manage coverage extensions and policy sublimits from an early stage, which includes the submission of claims tailored to maximize available limits. If possible, obtain the builder's risk carrier's approval of intended means of repair and recovery and seek to have it fund the repair effort on an ongoing basis, in whole or in part.
- ____ (d) **Professional/error or omission.** If a design, engineering, or other professional error or omission (E&O) potentially caused or contributed to the accident, then any professional

liability insurance covering the responsible professional may be implicated. These are likely to be claims made policies, and appropriate notices should be given.

____ (e) **Pollution.** If the accident caused any kind of pollution exposure or loss, then the availability of CPL, PLL, or other pollution coverages should be explored.

____ (f) **Equipment floaters and other property policies.** Equipment, tools, and similar property destroyed in the accident (typically, property that is not intended to become part of the final work) will not be covered by the project builder's risk policy, but should be insured by equipment floaters or other property policies.

____ (g) **Force majeure and other coverages.** Parties sometimes obtain force majeure or other specialty coverages in connection with significant construction projects. Their availability should be explored.

____ 18. **Who provided potentially implicated insurance coverages? Does the project have a CIP?** If so, then it will be necessary to work closely with the CIP Administrator, and CIP policies will be the first place to turn. Nonetheless, consideration should still be given to what non-CIP policies are potentially implicated (equipment floaters being a simple, but not exclusive, example). If no CIP is in place, then insurance certificates provided by project participants should give a partial, but rarely complete, picture of the coverages potentially available. Efforts must be undertaken to obtain a complete picture of the coverages available to each potentially responsible party.

____ 19. **Claim Preparation.** Even on a project in which the parties proceed in a relatively cooperative fashion to address the consequences of an accident, there is a strong possibility of litigation, particularly if deaths were involved.

____ (a) **Claims.** While we recommend exploring a more cooperative model in the first instance, unilateral steps should also be taken to prepare for claims.

____ (b) **Claims steps.** A comprehensive listing of such steps is not possible in this context, but they include:

____ (i) Dissemination of an internal directive forbidding the destruction of potentially relevant evidence (including documents and electronic communications).

____ (ii) The retention of experts if narrow technical issues will predominate (particularly if it is an area with few leading practitioners, you may want to tie-up one or more as quickly as possible).

____ (iii) Witness interviews.
____ (iv) Forensic examinations.

____ 20. **Consider the Possibility of Negotiating a "Funding Agreement" with Potentially Responsible Parties and Their Insurers.** Pursuant to such an agreement, the parties agree to jointly determine whether wrongful death and bodily injury claims can be settled before litigation is filed, or at a very early stage of litigation. Relative contributions are negotiated in advance of an approach being made to the prospective plaintiffs. This process is easier in states with caps on pain and suffering, punitive, and similar awards, because the maximum possible award can be calculated with more accuracy. Of course, insurance carrier participation and approval must be obtained in advance.

# Checklist 71: Time and Schedule Issues

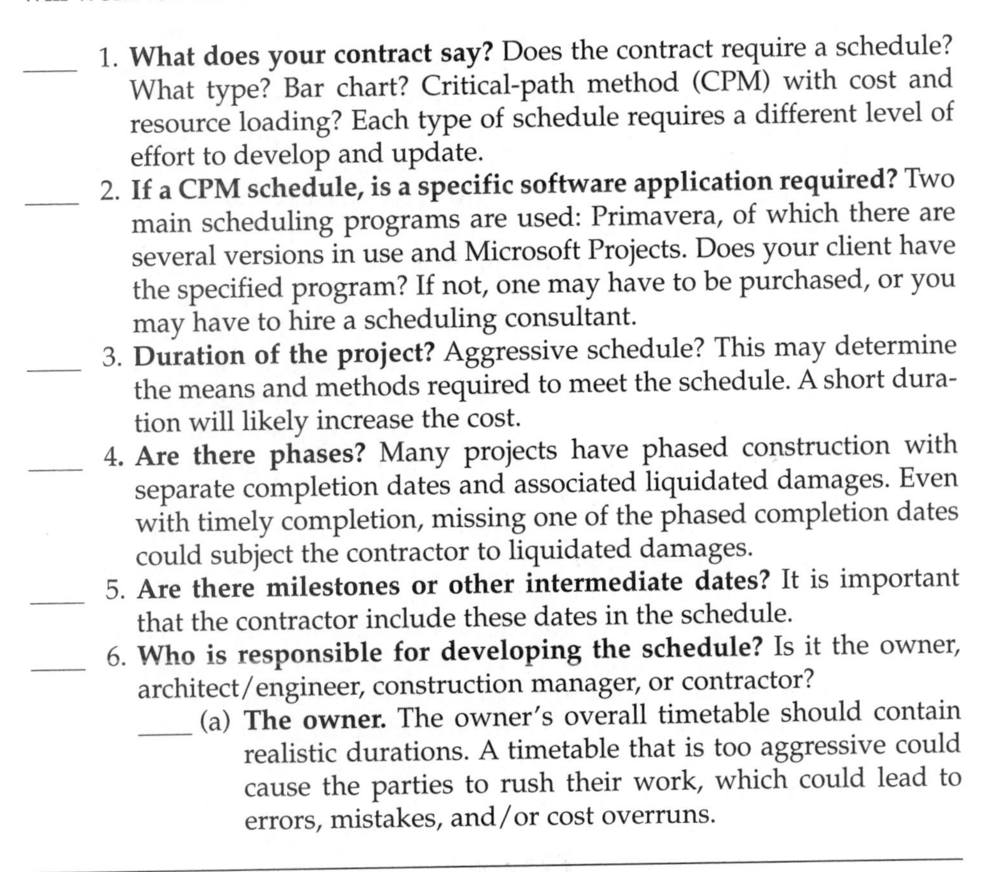

The following checklist should be helpful for counsel for owners or contractors when reviewing or developing the contract and when considering the scheduling and/or time requirements on the project. Much of this checklist will work for either the owner or contractor.

____ 1. **What does your contract say?** Does the contract require a schedule? What type? Bar chart? Critical-path method (CPM) with cost and resource loading? Each type of schedule requires a different level of effort to develop and update.

____ 2. **If a CPM schedule, is a specific software application required?** Two main scheduling programs are used: Primavera, of which there are several versions in use and Microsoft Projects. Does your client have the specified program? If not, one may have to be purchased, or you may have to hire a scheduling consultant.

____ 3. **Duration of the project?** Aggressive schedule? This may determine the means and methods required to meet the schedule. A short duration will likely increase the cost.

____ 4. **Are there phases?** Many projects have phased construction with separate completion dates and associated liquidated damages. Even with timely completion, missing one of the phased completion dates could subject the contractor to liquidated damages.

____ 5. **Are there milestones or other intermediate dates?** It is important that the contractor include these dates in the schedule.

____ 6. **Who is responsible for developing the schedule?** Is it the owner, architect/engineer, construction manager, or contractor?

____ (a) **The owner.** The owner's overall timetable should contain realistic durations. A timetable that is too aggressive could cause the parties to rush their work, which could lead to errors, mistakes, and/or cost overruns.

**John C. Livengood** is a registered architect and attorney at PinnacleOne in its Washington, D.C., office. He has more than 30 years of experience in project management, design, construction litigation, claims, and schedule analysis. He has testified numerous times as an expert in court proceedings, arbitrations, and mediations.

**Christopher R. Bryant** is a construction consultant at Warner Construction Consultants, Inc. He has more than 31 years of experience in the construction industry. His expertise includes the fields of cost control, estimating, contract negotiations, claim preparation, owner's representative, construction management, project controls, general contracting, and construction dispute resolution.

____ (b) **The architect/engineer, construction manager, or contractor.** The owner needs to confirm that the party with scheduling responsibility has the capacity and expertise in-house or available.

____ 7. **How much time is allowed to produce baseline or initial schedule?** The specifications usually identify the requirements. Many owners require a detailed schedule 30 days after notice to proceed. While sufficient for a small project, it may not allow sufficient time to gather all of the information necessary to produce an accurate schedule for a larger project.

____ 8. **Is a short-term schedule required?** Some specifications for large projects require a short-term schedule to identify an overall schedule framework and establish a work plan for the first few months of the project, prior to submission of a more comprehensive schedule.

____ 9. **Does the schedule have to be approved by the owner?** If yes, then there may be several submissions before it is approved by the owner. If the approved schedule is the basis for progress payments, then the contractor must be financially prepared to carry the project until the schedule is approved.

____ 10. **If owner approval is required, then allow adequate time for analysis.** If necessary, a scheduling expert should be retained.

____ 11. **Which schedules are required to be approved?** Preliminary schedule? Full baseline schedule, which identifies all elements of the work, including logic and duration? Are schedule updates required to be approved by the owner or architect? Are revised schedules, developed as a result of major changes in the work, required to be approved?

____ 12. **How much time is the contractor allowed for resubmittal of the schedule once disapproved?** Late resubmittal may cause progress payments to be withheld.

____ 13. **Are there penalties in the contract for late submission?** Many contracts contain clauses that preclude a contractor from being paid until contractor submits the required schedule or updates.

____ 14. **What are the requirements that the schedule must meet?** Most contracts have a scheduling specification that identifies what is required. For example:

____ (a) Schedule must be "full term," starting at notice to proceed through to final completion.

____ (b) Activity durations should be no more than 20 work days.

____ (c) Have only one start activity and one completion activity.

____ (d) Include all of the work in the project.

____ (e) Include resource and cost-loaded activities.

____ (f) Include owner milestone dates.

____ (g) Have a data date no later than the notice to proceed date.
____ (h) Include all activities coded by area, responsibility, floor, etc.

____ 15. **Who is responsible for updates?** Most contracts require that the schedule be updated by the party that has scheduling responsibility. It is important that the update be accurate because it may be used as a basis for progress payments and is essential for the submission of time extension requests.

____ 16. **Are joint schedule updates required?** Some contracts require the party responsible for the schedule to meet with the owner periodically in a joint meeting to review the requested percent complete for actual progress achieved through the update period. The meeting also reviews accuracy regarding actual start and finish dates and percent complete.

____ 17. **How often is the schedule required to be updated?** Updating once a month is generally the standard. More frequent updates will mean additional expense.

____ 18. **Does a report have to accompany the schedule update?** If yes, the more complicated the submission, the more costly the schedule update. These costs need to be included in the estimate. Generally, schedule reports are issued at each update period. Examples of items include:

____ (a) Full-color, time-scaled network prints.
____ (b) Set of tabular reports by activity ID.
____ (c) Cost report sorted by responsibility.
____ (d) Cost loading graphic charts (that is, S-curve).
____ (e) Manpower histogram showing weekly manpower usage.
____ (f) Set of tabular reports by total float.

____ 19. **Does the schedule have to be resource-loaded?** These resources could include manpower, materials, and equipment usage. It is relatively expensive and time-consuming to perform this work. The contractor will need appropriate information from its subcontractors. At the early stages of the project, when the schedule is being developed, many of the subcontracts will not be sufficiently developed to accurately estimate the resources for that portion of the work.

____ 20. **Does the schedule have to be cost-loaded?** If yes, then generally every work activity is loaded with the value of the work to be performed by that activity. Material delivery can be separately cost-loaded. This requirement is time-consuming because the total value of all the costs loaded are generally required to equal the contract price.

____ 21. **Will the schedule be used as a payment mechanism?** If yes, it can affect the contractor's cash flow and progress payments. Using the schedule for payment reduces its value as a project management and scheduling tool. Contractors will be more concerned statusing activities for payment purposes, rather than for scheduling the project.

____ 22. **How much detail is required?** A number of factors are relevant:

____ (a) **How complex is the project?** Generally, the more complex a project, the more detail is needed in the schedule in order to properly control the project.

____ (b) **What do the specifications require?** Some specifications state that activity durations must be 20 work days or less and have a value of less than $20,000. On large projects, this requirement creates a very large schedule.

____ (c) **How many areas is the project divided into?** The more areas, the more detailed the schedule.

____ (d) **What type of project is it?** A petrochemical plant will require more detail activities than a highway project.

____ (e) **How many phases is the project divided into?** The more phases, the more activity detail required.

____ 23. **Is there a limitation on activity durations?** If yes, this requirement will increase the number of activities in the schedule.

____ 24. **Must project milestones be included?** The project specifications will generally state what milestones are to be included. Addressing these milestones during the schedule development will help in defining the level of detail.

____ 25. **Are there multiple prime contractors?** If yes, has the owner assumed the overall scheduling responsibility, or has the owner assigned the overall scheduling and coordination responsibility? Responsibility could be with the owner, construction manager, architect/engineer, one of the prime contractors, or a scheduling consultant. It is critical that the overall scheduling and coordination responsibility be assigned. If the contract documents are silent, then, by default, the owner assumes that responsibility.

____ 26. **Is the project phased or fast-track construction?** If yes, then the owner generally assumes the responsibility for the scheduling and overall coordination.

____ 27. **Is the project design-build?** These projects generally impose scheduling requirements on both the design and construction phases under one contract. Owners must not assume that the contractor will perform to all of the contract milestone dates. This assumption can cause the owner to ignore the contractor's plan and schedule for performing the work, with disastrous consequences when the contractor has performance problems.

____ 28. **Are there any provisions that require notice of delays?** Most contracts contain notice provisions. Some only require notice of the occurrence of a delaying event, while others additionally require submission of details. Many contracts have additional notice requirements such as details regarding the amount of delay or potential costs. Pay attention to and abide by these requirements. It is possible that any future request for additional contract time or compensation will be barred if you have not complied with these contractual requirements.

____ 29. **Is there a scheduling clause that defines how delays must be established?** Any request for additional contract time or additional compensation resulting from a delaying event may be summarily rejected if the request does not comply with the requirements of the scheduling clause.

____ 30. **What is the effect for failure to give notice?** Does such failure prejudice the other party's opportunity to mitigate damages? Even absent any actual or constructive notice, all still may not be lost. Notice provisions are intended to give the delaying party a fair opportunity to avoid or mitigate the cost and time effects for which it may be responsible. If the delaying party did not lose that opportunity because of the lack of notice, then the claim may still proceed.

____ 31. **What options are available to recover time if the project falls behind schedule?**

____ (a) Is the contractor required to provide more manpower to recover for delays? Does that requirement apply to both contractor and force majeure delays, as well as owner-caused delays?

____ (b) Is the use of overtime allowed? Is permission for any overtime required?

____ (c) Is the contractor allowed to bring on a second shift of workers?

____ 32. **Who owns the float?** Float allows both the owner and the contractor to have some flexibility in planning and performing its work. Many contracts are silent on float ownership. In that case the general rule is, the float is owned by the project and is available to either party—whoever uses it first. Some contracts specifically state that the float belongs to the project. However some contracts state that the float belongs to the owner. It is important that whoever develops the schedule be aware of this requirement and plan the work accordingly. It seldom does the owner much good to own the float, because contractors can minimize the available float as they plan the project.

____ 33. **Are there specific requirements regarding major revisions to the schedule?** Many contracts require that the owner give consent to any major schedule revisions. Listed here are conditions under which a schedule revision may be necessary:

____ (a) If there is significant change to contractor's operations that affect the critical path.

____ (b) If there are additions, deletions, or revisions to the work as a result of contract change orders.

____ (c) If actual prosecution of the work differs from that represented in the latest schedule update.

____ (d) If the contractor significantly changes its planned sequence of work.

____ 34. **What input do the parties of the contract have to provide to the schedule during its development and or updating?**

____ (a) The following is a general list of information required to develop the schedule by participant:

____ (i) Owner.

____ a. Scope of work—contract plans and specifications.

____ b. Overall planned duration.

____ c. Required milestone dates.

____ d. Owner-furnished material and equipment with delivery dates.

____ e. Level of detail required in schedule.

____ (ii) Contractor.

____ a. Work breakdown structure.

____ b. Activity and task information.

____ c. Estimated activity durations.

____ d. Planned flow of work through the project (activity sequencing).

____ e. Cost and resource information.

____ f. Estimated quantities.

____ g. Production rates.

____ h. Subcontractor input.

____ i. Expected weather days.

____ (b) The following information is required for schedule updating:

____ (i) Owner.

____ a. Actual delivery dates for owner-furnished material and equipment.

____ b. Any changes in milestone dates.

____ (ii) Contractor.

____ a. Actual start/finish dates.

____ b. Percent complete of activities in progress.

____ c. Any minor logic changes.

____ 35. **What are the requirements for accurate reporting?** It is important that the project schedule accurately portray the status of a project at any point in time. To accomplish this, the following items must be verified:

____ (a) Actual start/finish dates are confirmed.
____ (b) Percentage completion of an activity.
____ (c) Contractor is following the plan to complete the work.
____ (d) Contractor has included changed work in the schedule.

# Checklist 72: Contractor's Delay and Acceleration Claims

This checklist is for contractors that believe that progress has been delayed such that they are (1) entitled to additional contract time and additional compensation for extended jobsite overhead or (2) entitled to additional compensation for extraordinary efforts employed to accelerate the work in order to make up for lost time. This checklist will help preserve the contractor's rights and present a recoverable claim. (Note: This checklist also is applicable to a subcontractor at any tier making a request for equitable adjustment or a claim to the next higher tier contractor.)

____ 1. **Carefully Read Your Contract.** Look for procedural requirements with which you must comply in order to preserve your rights to recover. Some provisions limit your rights for recovery. Even if you believe that you are thoroughly familiar with your contract, read it again. Do not risk being denied a recovery simply because you failed to comply with a simple procedural requirement.

____ (a) **Are there notice provisions?** Most contracts contain notice provisions. Some only require notice of the occurrence of delay while others require additional details.

____ (i) **Timely notice of delay.** Most contracts have a provision that requires the delayed party to give notice of the delaying event within a stated period of time. This allows the other party an opportunity to reduce the impacts of the delay. Failure to give the required notice may jeopardize a contract time extension or additional compensation. Even in the absence of a contractual notice provision, always notify the other party as soon as you believe that a delaying

**Mark I. Anderson** is executive vice president of Warner Construction Consultants, Inc. with more than 25 years of experience in the preparation, analysis, and resolution of construction disputes. His clients include many of the world's largest and best known participants in the construction industry. He has testified as an expert in CPM scheduling and cost and damage analysis in various forums including federal courts and boards of contract appeals, state courts, and arbitrations.

**Fred J. Bush** is a licensed professional engineer, attorney, and accountant with Warner Construction Consultants, Inc. He has more than 30 years of experience in the avoidance, resolution, and management of construction claims, construction and project management, and quality control and risk avoidance. His experience has covered transportation, buildings, hospitals, hotels, housing, water and wastewater treatment plants, as well as steam generation and power generation projects.

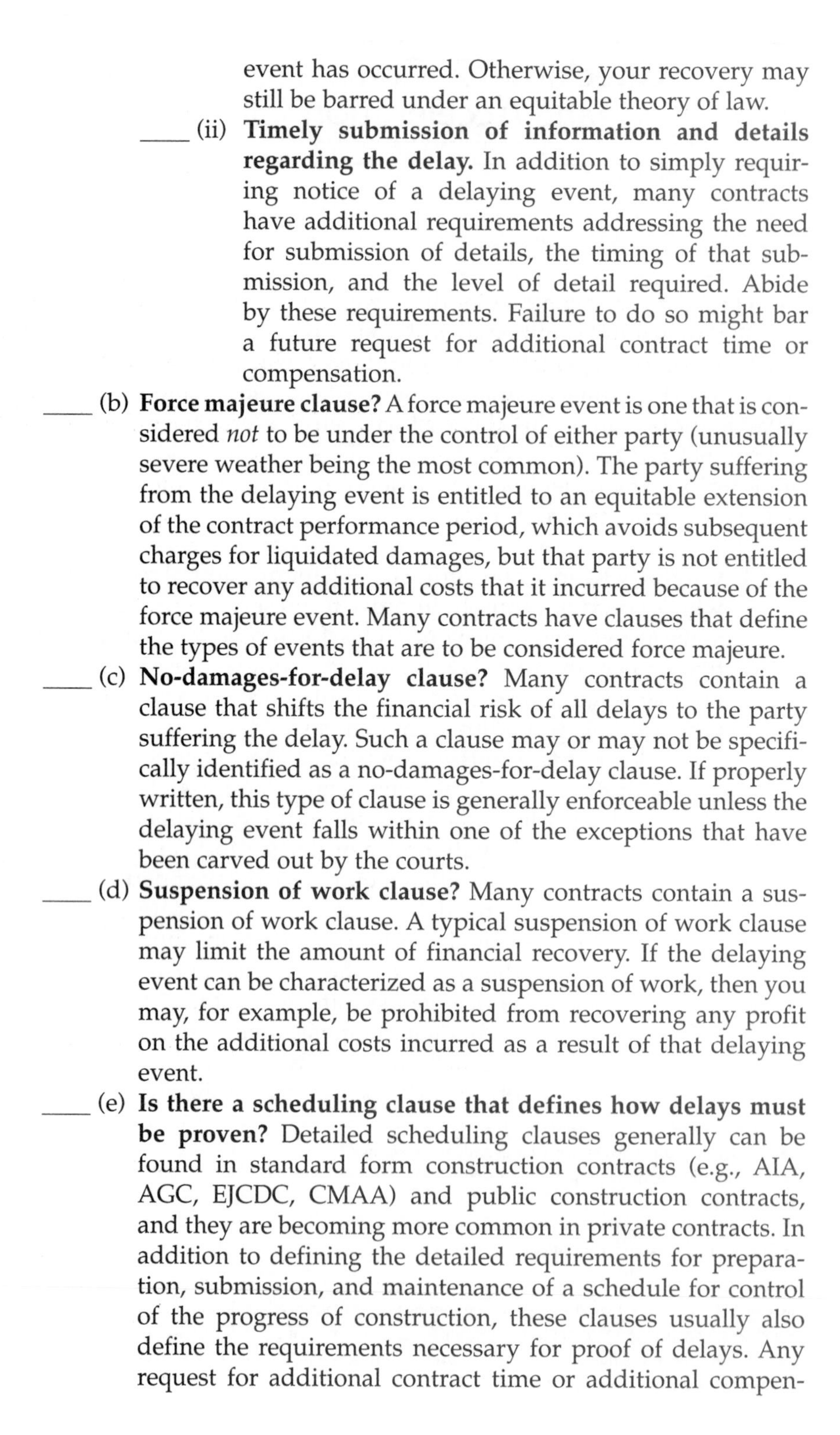

event has occurred. Otherwise, your recovery may still be barred under an equitable theory of law.

____ (ii) **Timely submission of information and details regarding the delay.** In addition to simply requiring notice of a delaying event, many contracts have additional requirements addressing the need for submission of details, the timing of that submission, and the level of detail required. Abide by these requirements. Failure to do so might bar a future request for additional contract time or compensation.

____ (b) **Force majeure clause?** A force majeure event is one that is considered *not* to be under the control of either party (unusually severe weather being the most common). The party suffering from the delaying event is entitled to an equitable extension of the contract performance period, which avoids subsequent charges for liquidated damages, but that party is not entitled to recover any additional costs that it incurred because of the force majeure event. Many contracts have clauses that define the types of events that are to be considered force majeure.

____ (c) **No-damages-for-delay clause?** Many contracts contain a clause that shifts the financial risk of all delays to the party suffering the delay. Such a clause may or may not be specifically identified as a no-damages-for-delay clause. If properly written, this type of clause is generally enforceable unless the delaying event falls within one of the exceptions that have been carved out by the courts.

____ (d) **Suspension of work clause?** Many contracts contain a suspension of work clause. A typical suspension of work clause may limit the amount of financial recovery. If the delaying event can be characterized as a suspension of work, then you may, for example, be prohibited from recovering any profit on the additional costs incurred as a result of that delaying event.

____ (e) **Is there a scheduling clause that defines how delays must be proven?** Detailed scheduling clauses generally can be found in standard form construction contracts (e.g., AIA, AGC, EJCDC, CMAA) and public construction contracts, and they are becoming more common in private contracts. In addition to defining the detailed requirements for preparation, submission, and maintenance of a schedule for control of the progress of construction, these clauses usually also define the requirements necessary for proof of delays. Any request for additional contract time or additional compensation resulting from a delaying event may be summarily rejected if the request does not comply with the requirements of the scheduling clause.

____ 2. **Is there a project schedule?** For proof of any allegations of delay or acceleration to be successful, some form of a project schedule will be required. All federal forums and many state forums require that the schedule be in CPM (critical-path method) format.

____ (a) **Does the project schedule comply with contractual requirements?** If not, the other party may have a valid argument that your schedule is not reasonable as the basis of proof of a delay or acceleration allegation.

____ (b) **Has the project schedule been accepted by both parties?** Use of that schedule for your delay analysis may be unpersuasive if the other party believes that the schedule does not accurately reflect the scope, timing, duration, and relationship of work activities.

____ (c) **Is the project schedule being used to manage the work?** A schedule analysis may be unpersuasive if it is based on a schedule that had been prepared as required by contract but not actively used for management of the work.

____ (d) **Has the project schedule been regularly updated and revised?** Failure to properly update and revise the schedule on a regular basis will be strong evidence that the schedule was not actively used for management of the work.

____ 3. **Is the delay claim being submitted contemporaneously with the delaying event?** It is always best to try to resolve delay issues at the time the delaying event occurs.

____ (a) **Have you established a fragnet (small part of a CPM) of the activities that define the delaying event?** This may be only a single activity or it may be many activities to define the work of a major change.

____ (b) **Have you properly incorporated the delay fragnet into the project schedule?** The best method for proving the delay is to create a fragnet of the activities that define the delaying event, properly incorporate the fragnet into your schedule, and recalculate the schedule to demonstrate the delay impact.

____ (c) **Do not ignore your own concurrent delays.** Ignoring or even inadvertently overlooking your own delays will hamper and may prevent early settlement of delay issues. Show that you have considered your own delays even if they would not have caused critical-path delay of the project.

____ (d) **Reasonable efforts to mitigate.** You have a legal obligation to make reasonable efforts to minimize damages caused by another party. Failure to mitigate may prevent recovery for damages that could have been otherwise avoided.

____ (e) **Have you established cost accounting procedures to segregate and accumulate all additional costs caused by the delaying event?** Even if you are successful in establishing the fact of delay for which the other party is responsible, you still must directly link additional expense to the delaying event. Your success in overcoming this element of your burden of proof begins with an established, company-wide cost accounting system in conformance with generally accepted accounting principles. It continues with detailed records of your bid estimate and regular cost reporting that identifies cost variances. And it finishes with your timely establishment of new cost accounts into which all costs related to the delay are recorded. Keep all supporting documents in a separate file folder.

____ 4. **Is the delay/acceleration claim being submitted after completion?** Many parties may prefer to wait until project completion to evaluate a delay claim because the damages will be more certain. However, it is more challenging for the claimant to prove its allegation retrospectively.

____ (a) **Did you comply with the contractual notice provisions?** Your first consideration is whether or not the other party received timely notice of your claim.

____ (i) **Written notice.** If you complied with contractual notice provisions, include a copy of the notice with your claim submission.

____ (ii) **Was there constructive notice?** If you did not provide timely written notice, constructive notice may be considered adequate. Constructive notice means that the alleged delaying party knew or should have known of the delaying events and their potential effects on contract time and costs.

____ (iii) **Did failure to give timely notice cause prejudice?** Even absent any actual or constructive notice, all still may not be lost. Notice provisions are intended to give the delaying party a fair opportunity to avoid or mitigate the cost and time effects for which it may be responsible. If the delaying party did not lose that opportunity because of the lack of notice, then the claim may still proceed.

____ (b) **Was the project performance period extended by the delaying event?** Most forums will allow your recovery only to the extent that you can demonstrate that the delaying event actually delayed the completion date of the project.

____ (i) **Schedule analysis.** A schedule analysis is fundamental to demonstrate the effect of the delaying event on the progress of the work. The law of the forum must be researched to determine what type of schedule analysis is considered acceptable.

____ (ii) **Did you account for your own concurrent delays?** Do not overlook your own delays. Include your own delays in your analysis whether or not they would have affected the critical path of the project.

____ (iii) **Did you make every reasonable effort to mitigate?** If you fail to minimize the impacts of any delaying events for which you consider the other party responsible, you may be denied recovery of your damages despite a finding that the delay is compensable.

____ (iv) **Identify and tabulate all additional costs.** You will be required to prove with reasonable certainty that every element of cost for which you are requesting compensation is reasonable and is factual.

____ (v) **Causation.** In addition to proving that your costs are reasonable and factual, to recover them on a delay claim you will have to prove that they were incurred solely as a result of the alleged delaying event.

____ 5. **Does your claim include an element for acceleration of your work?**

____ (a) **Did you request an extension of the contract performance period?** If your claim is for the costs of acceleration, you must first demonstrate that at the time of the delay you were entitled to an extension of the contract performance period.

____ (b) **Did the other party demand completion within the contract performance period?** You must show that the other party denied your request for a time extension or otherwise made it abundantly clear that you were expected to finish on time despite any delays that had occurred.

____ (i) **Did you receive a written denial of your request or a request that you accelerate your remaining work, such as to complete on time?**

____ (ii) **Did the other party otherwise demand timely completion?** For example, the other party may have threatened to impose liquidated damages for late completion.

____ (c) **Did you employ extraordinary efforts to accelerate your work?** For example, overtime, extra shifts, added crews, hiring subcontractors.

____ (d) **Did you incur additional costs due to your extraordinary efforts?** You will need to prove the reasonableness of those costs and the causal connection of the costs to the acceleration.

____ (i) **Did you prepare a contemporaneous schedule delay analysis to show your reasonable belief that the project would be delayed?** If not, do so now. It will not be as effective, but it is still necessary to establish the need for acceleration.

____ (ii) **Schedule analysis.** A detailed schedule analysis is necessary to demonstrate that you did, in fact, accelerate your work in an effort to recover lost time.

____ (iii) **Have you identified all extraordinary efforts that you employed?**

____ (iv) **Have you identified and tabulated all additional costs actually incurred?**

# Checklist 73: Owner's Defense of Delay and Acceleration Claims

This checklist is intended to help owners defend against a request or claim received for equitable adjustment or a claim, demanding (1) additional contract time for project delay and additional compensation for extended jobsite overhead or (2) additional compensation for extraordinary efforts employed by the contractor to accelerate its work in order to make up for lost time, (Note: This checklist also is applicable to the contractor or a subcontractor at any tier defending a request for equitable adjustment or a claim from the next lower tier contractor.)

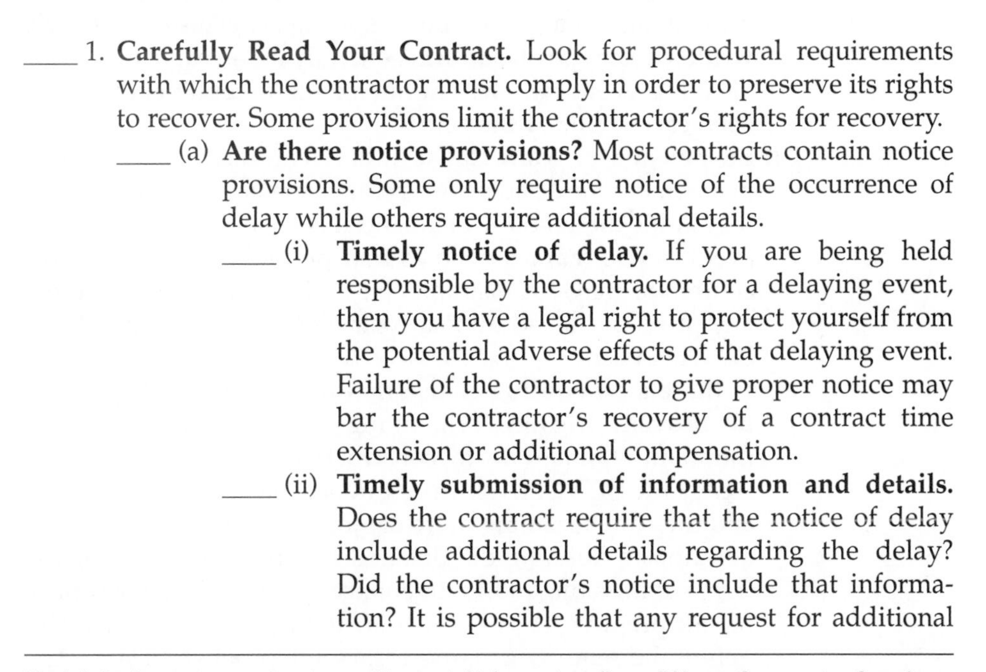

____ 1. **Carefully Read Your Contract.** Look for procedural requirements with which the contractor must comply in order to preserve its rights to recover. Some provisions limit the contractor's rights for recovery.

____ (a) **Are there notice provisions?** Most contracts contain notice provisions. Some only require notice of the occurrence of delay while others require additional details.

____ (i) **Timely notice of delay.** If you are being held responsible by the contractor for a delaying event, then you have a legal right to protect yourself from the potential adverse effects of that delaying event. Failure of the contractor to give proper notice may bar the contractor's recovery of a contract time extension or additional compensation.

____ (ii) **Timely submission of information and details.** Does the contract require that the notice of delay include additional details regarding the delay? Did the contractor's notice include that information? It is possible that any request for additional

**Mark I. Anderson** is executive vice president and chief operating officer of Warner Construction Consultants, Inc. with more than 25 years of experience in the preparation, analysis, and resolution of construction disputes. His clients include many of the world's largest and best known participants in the construction industry. He has testified as an expert in CPM scheduling and cost and damage analysis in various forums including federal courts and boards of contract appeals, state courts, and arbitrations.

**Fred J. Bush** is a licensed professional engineer, attorney, and accountant with Warner Construction Consultants, Inc. He has more than 30 years of experience in the avoidance, resolution, and management of construction claims, construction and project management, and quality control and risk avoidance. His experience has covered transportation, buildings, hospitals, hotels, housing, water and wastewater treatment plants, as well as steam generation and power generation projects.

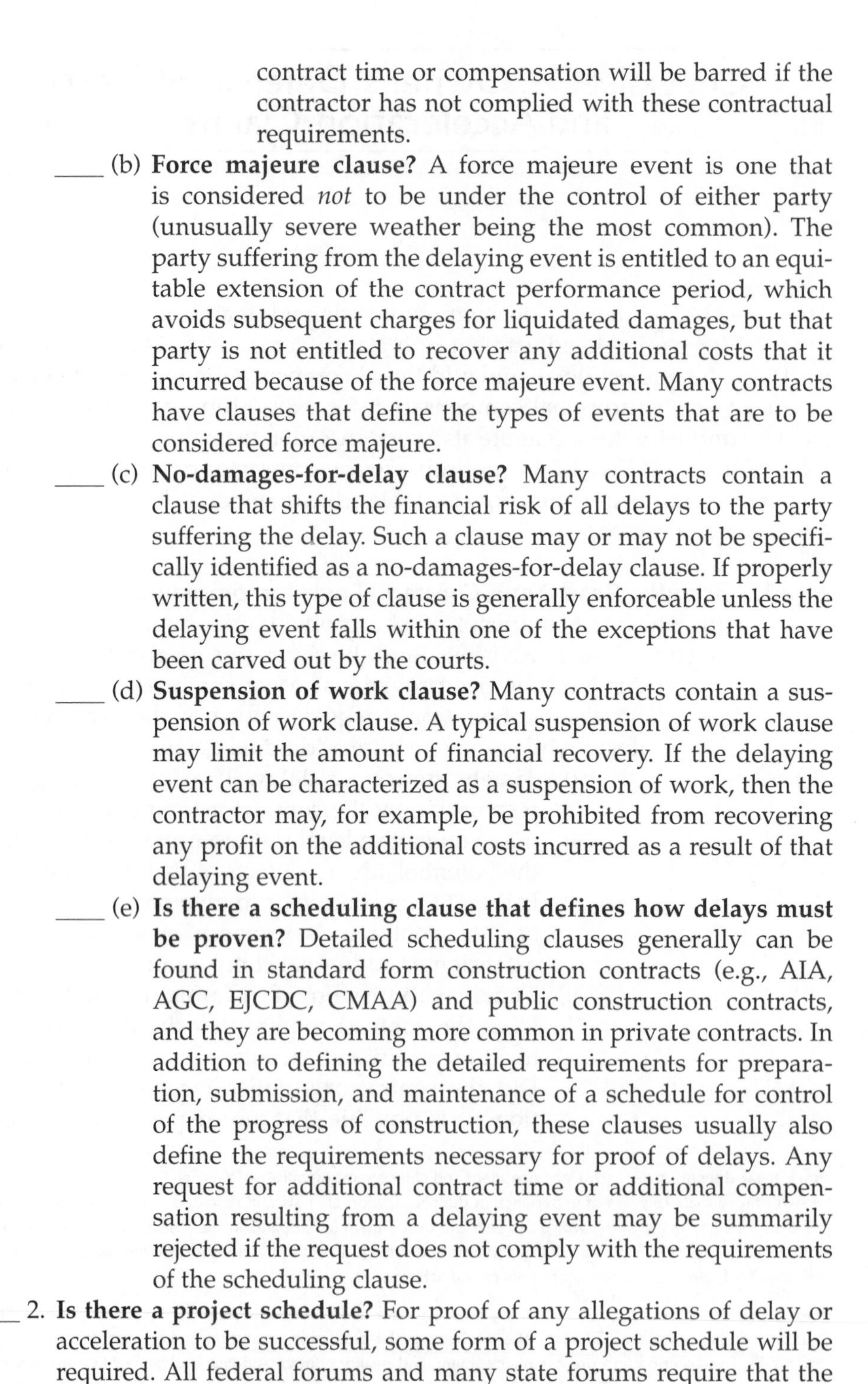

contract time or compensation will be barred if the contractor has not complied with these contractual requirements.

____ (b) **Force majeure clause?** A force majeure event is one that is considered *not* to be under the control of either party (unusually severe weather being the most common). The party suffering from the delaying event is entitled to an equitable extension of the contract performance period, which avoids subsequent charges for liquidated damages, but that party is not entitled to recover any additional costs that it incurred because of the force majeure event. Many contracts have clauses that define the types of events that are to be considered force majeure.

____ (c) **No-damages-for-delay clause?** Many contracts contain a clause that shifts the financial risk of all delays to the party suffering the delay. Such a clause may or may not be specifically identified as a no-damages-for-delay clause. If properly written, this type of clause is generally enforceable unless the delaying event falls within one of the exceptions that have been carved out by the courts.

____ (d) **Suspension of work clause?** Many contracts contain a suspension of work clause. A typical suspension of work clause may limit the amount of financial recovery. If the delaying event can be characterized as a suspension of work, then the contractor may, for example, be prohibited from recovering any profit on the additional costs incurred as a result of that delaying event.

____ (e) **Is there a scheduling clause that defines how delays must be proven?** Detailed scheduling clauses generally can be found in standard form construction contracts (e.g., AIA, AGC, EJCDC, CMAA) and public construction contracts, and they are becoming more common in private contracts. In addition to defining the detailed requirements for preparation, submission, and maintenance of a schedule for control of the progress of construction, these clauses usually also define the requirements necessary for proof of delays. Any request for additional contract time or additional compensation resulting from a delaying event may be summarily rejected if the request does not comply with the requirements of the scheduling clause.

____ 2. **Is there a project schedule?** For proof of any allegations of delay or acceleration to be successful, some form of a project schedule will be required. All federal forums and many state forums require that the schedule be in CPM (critical-path method) format.

____ (a) **Does the project schedule comply with contractual requirements?** If not, then you may have a valid argument that the schedule is not reasonable as the basis of proof of a delay or acceleration allegation.

____ (b) **Has the project schedule been accepted by both parties?** The contractor's delay analysis may be unpersuasive if your nonacceptance is based on your belief that the schedule is unreasonable or is not in conformity with the contract.

____ (c) **Is the project schedule being used to manage the work?** A schedule analysis may be unpersuasive if it is based on a schedule that had been submitted as required by contract but not actively used for management of the work.

____ (d) **Has the project schedule been regularly updated and revised?** Failure to properly update and revise the schedule on a regular basis will be strong evidence that the schedule was not actively used for management of the work.

____ 3. **Is the delay claim being submitted contemporaneously with the delaying event?** It is always best to try to resolve delay issues at the time the delaying event occurs.

____ (a) **Has the contractor established a fragnet (small part of a CPM) of the activities that define the delaying event?** This may be only a single activity or it may be many activities to define the work of a major change.

____ (b) **Has the contractor properly incorporated the delay fragnet into the project schedule?** The contractor has the burden of proving its allegations. The best method for proving the delay is to create a fragnet of the activities that define the delaying event, properly incorporate the fragnet into the schedule, and recalculate the schedule to demonstrate the delay impact.

____ (c) **Has the contractor accounted for its own concurrent delays?** If the contractor is responsible for delays that would have delayed the project absent your delays, then at best the contractor may be entitled to additional time but not additional compensation.

____ (d) **Reasonable effort to mitigate?** The contractor has a legal obligation to make reasonable efforts to minimize damages it is suffering. Failure to mitigate may prevent the contractor from recovering the damages it could have avoided.

____ (e) **Has the contractor established cost accounting procedures to segregate and accumulate all additional costs caused by the delaying event?** Even if the contractor is successful in establishing the fact of delay for which you are responsible, the contractor still may not recover any additional expense if it cannot directly link that expense to the delaying event. The contractor should have an established, company-wide cost accounting system in conformance with generally accepted accounting principles. It should maintain detailed records of its bid estimate and have regular cost reporting that identifies cost variances. And it should timely establish new cost accounts into which all costs related to the delay are recorded.

____ 4. **Is the delay/acceleration claim being submitted after completion?** Many parties may prefer to wait until project completion to evaluate a delay claim because the damages will be more certain. However, it is more challenging for the claimant to prove his allegations retrospectively.

____ (a) **Did the contractor comply with the contractual notice provisions?** Failure of notice may be your opportunity for summary dismissal of the claim.

____ (i) **Did you get timely written notice as required by the contract?**

____ (ii) **Did you have constructive notice?** Constructive notice means that you knew or should have known of the delaying events and their potential effects on contract time and costs. Even if the contractor failed to provide written notice, its delay or acceleration claim may still be valid if you had constructive notice.

____ (iii) **Did failure to get timely notice cause prejudice?** Even complete failure of notice may not bar a contractor's delay or acceleration claim if you would have had no opportunity to mitigate the effects of the delaying event had you received notice.

____ (b) **Was the project performance period extended by the delaying event?** Most forums will allow recovery to the contractor only to the extent that it can demonstrate that the delaying event actually delayed the completion date of the project.

____ (i) **Schedule analysis.** A schedule analysis is fundamental to demonstrate the effect of the delaying event on the progress of the work. The law of the forum must be researched to determine what type of schedule analysis is considered acceptable.

____ (ii) **Concurrent delays of the contractor?** Failure of the contractor to consider its own delays may render its analysis of delay unconvincing for proof of its allegations.

____ (iii) **Did the contractor make every reasonable effort to mitigate?** If the contractor fails to mitigate, it may be denied recovery of its damages despite a finding that the delay is compensable.

____ (iv) **Did the contractor identify and tabulate all additional costs?** The contractor will be required to prove with reasonable certainty that every element of cost for which it is requesting compensation is reasonable and is factual.

____ (v) **Causation?** In addition to proving that its costs are reasonable and factual, to recover them on a delay claim the contractor will have to prove that they were incurred solely as a result of the alleged delaying event.

____ 5. **Does the contractor's claim include an element for acceleration of its work?**

____ (a) **Did the contractor request an extension of the contract performance period?** If the contractor's claim is for the costs of acceleration, then it must first demonstrate that at the time of the delay it was entitled to an extension of the contract performance period.

____ (b) **Did you demand completion within the contract performance period?** The contractor must show that you denied the request for a time extension or otherwise made it abundantly clear that the contractor was expected to finish on time despite any delays that had occurred.

____ (c) **Did the contractor accelerate?** This may be evidenced by the contractor working overtime or extra shifts or by the contractor employing additional crews or subcontractors.

____ (i) **Had the contractor previously submitted a contemporaneous schedule analysis to demonstrate that the delaying event would delay the project?** This would establish the contractor's reasonable belief at the time of the delaying event that it was entitled to a contract time extension.

____ (ii) **Did the contractor identify all extraordinary efforts employed?**

____ (iii) **Did the contractor identify and tabulate all additional costs actually incurred?**

# Checklist 74: Representing the Construction Lender

For lawyers representing construction lenders in design and construction transactions, the following checklist should be helpful in recognizing items of unique concern to their clients. Lender's counsel should bear in mind that the documents reviewed in the transaction must be assessed in light of credit risk perspectives while also considering the reality that the lender may ultimately become the project owner. The checklist concerns the most common documents considered by lender's counsel, but does not deal with loan agreements or their equivalents, which are beyond the scope of this article.

____ 1. **Lender Consents and Conditional Assignments.**

____ (a) **What are lender consents and conditional assignments?** Lender consents and conditional assignments are mechanisms by which a lender accedes to the rights of the owner with respect to various agreements when such owner defaults on the owner's obligations under the loan agreement or the applicable underlying agreement (for example, owner/general contractor agreement).

____ (i) Lender consent is an agreement whereby the counterparty (for example, the architect in the architect–owner agreement) consents to the lender taking the place of the owner in the event of the owner's default under the loan agreement.

____ (ii) A conditional assignment is where the owner actually assigns the applicable agreement to the lender, but such assignment is not effective until the occurrence of certain conditions (for example, owner's default under the loan agreement).

____ (b) **What are the goals for a lender?** Securing the rights of the owner and the ability to force completion of the project at current prices is the aim. Unwittingly accepting liabilities or being forced to cure monetary (and other) owner defaults prior to taking over the project is the risk.

---

**Christopher S. Dunn** is a partner in the Nashville, Tennessee, office of Waller Lansden Dortch & Davis, LLP. His practice is focused on construction transactions and disputes, and he frequently represents the interests of construction owners, developers, and lenders.

____ (c) **What are the typical characteristics of a lender consent or conditional assignment?**

____ (i) Recitation of contractual provisions, representations, and warranties.

____ (ii) Consent of counterparty to assignment and acknowledgment of limitation on some of lender's duties.

____ (iii) Acknowledgment of lender's right to approve change orders or alterations to character of the improvements or work exceeding construction loan agreement thresholds.

____ (iv) Certification of construction, zoning, restrictions, laws, and no departures from the plans and specs.

____ (v) Corporate authority to execute and bind the counterparty.

____ (vi) Estoppel provision regarding enforceability of the contract and certification of no pending legal actions.

____ (vii) Waiver of setoff rights.

____ (viii) Express authorization of lender's ability to use plans and specifications without charge.

____ (ix) Consider arbitration clause of Owner-Architect Agreement could be invoked if assignment is contested and typical AIA form is used.

____ (d) **What is a tri-party agreement?** A tri-party agreement is an agreement among the contractor, the lender and the owner, which generally tracks a conditional assignment structure but may include additional terms in favor of the contractor, such as requiring the lender to use the contractor to finish the project or requiring payment for pre-default work.

____ (e) **What are some of the pitfalls of lender consents and conditional assignments?**

____ (i) Failure to file a financing statement in the appropriate jurisdiction(s) could leave lender's interests (generally intangible) unperfected.

____ (ii) Often difficult to enforce because of posture of case when they are invoked—serious disruption (for example, receivership)—so lender may need to remain flexible and be willing to modify terms in order to get cooperation.

____ (iii) Failure to include an option for the lender to terminate the applicable agreement can remove the option to terminate construction of the project.

____ (iv) Failure to provide a grace period, or time between owner's default and lender's decision to take over the project (or terminate the construction), can force a lender to make a hasty decision. Consider fronting costs to counterparty during grace period to allow for a reasonable time to make a decision on whether to accept the assignment.

____ 2. **Credit Enhancements.**

____ (a) **What are some enhancement vehicles for a lender?** There are various forms of credit enhancements that may be available to a lender, depending on the situation. Because defaults are unpredictable and the exact situation cannot be predicted, some enhancement vehicles may work well and others may fail, depending on the circumstances. Such options include:

____ (i) **Letters of credit.**

____ a. **Unconditional versus documentary.** Unconditional letters of credit are paid upon request by the beneficiary, while documentary letters of credit are paid upon the bank's receipt of certain documents in a required form. Most letters of credit are documentary.

____ b. **Precision is the guiding principle.** Inclusion of a sample of the required document is paramount so that no dispute arises as to whether the conditions for payment have been met. An expiration date is typical.

____ c. Inclusion of vague circumstances or debatable requirements for payment can transform a letter of credit into a guaranty and cloud the usual clarity with which letters of credit are paid.

____ d. Typically very expensive and banks usually require cash reserves in the amount of the letter to be maintained at all times.

____ (ii) **Guaranties.**

____ a. **Guaranty of payment versus collection.** Guaranty of payment typically does not require the beneficiary to exhaust remedies against the principal obligor while guaranty of collection typically does. Require specificity that any guaranty is a guaranty of payment.

____ b. **Absolute guaranty versus conditional.** Self-explanatory.

____ c. **Completion guaranty.** Guaranty that construction will be completed. Unless very specifically stated, this type of guaranty is likely to be the subject of extensive litigation, especially regarding consequential-type issues such as cost overruns as a result of delay from a breach by the principal, etc. Make sure reference to specific performance is included. Key question: does surety law apply? Seek counsel for local law.

____ d. Beware of notice requirements in guaranties to trigger payment or performance.

____ e. Consideration can be an issue with guaranties, so include statement that guaranty is being furnished to induce entry into other documents and specify guarantor's benefit (for example, benefit as a result of being a shareholder of the owner).

____ f. Set out how payments are to be applied.

____ g. Set out the term of the guaranty, or indicate that it is a continuing guaranty.

____ h. Include assignability language from the lender's perspective.

____ i. Consider periodic reporting requirements of guarantor as well as financial covenants of guarantor to ensure liquidity and collectibility.

____ (iii) **Cash balance.** Requiring a particular cash balance on hand or on deposit.

____ (iv) **Bank guaranty.** Bank guarantys performance upon owner's actual nonperformance.

____ (b) **What should a lender look for generally in performance and payment surety bonds?**

____ (i) **Lender as "dual obligee."**

____ a. Surety obligated to complete construction upon contractor's default.

____ b. Beware of savings clauses (conditions precedent) that could obviate or potentially reduce surety's liability under certain circumstances, such as owner default, continued performance by owner, etc.

____ (ii) **Beware of limitations on the assignment of right to enforce performance bond.**
____ a. Is consent of contractor (principal) and/or surety required?
____ b. Is assignment prohibited?
____ (iii) **Subrogees of performance bond obligees.** Last resort that can be contractually waived.

____ (c) **What should a lender look for in performance bonds in particular?**
____ (i) Carefully examine the escape clauses.
____ (ii) Confirm form of bond with statutory requirements, if any.
____ (iii) Confirm recordation if required.
____ (iv) Make a note of enforcement deadlines and notice requirements.
____ (v) Require subcontract bonds to name the owner and lender as dual obligees, but double-check to make sure owner default does not impair payment to lender.
____ (vi) **Completion bonds.** "Continuing flow of money" clauses and tying construction lender to owner performance can equate to a lender guaranty of owner's performance.

____ (d) **When should a lender be concerned about collecting from enhancement vehicles?** From the beginning. But ultimately the question is determined by the lender's goal after a default. Is it to collect or is it really to force completion of the project? Such goals are not necessarily mutually exclusive, but often a particular goal can drive a strategy.
____ (i) Completion of the project will generally treat the payment guaranties and other non-performance-based enhancements as leverage points to force completion.
____ (ii) Collection of the amounts outstanding will seek to recover from deep-pocketed guarantors and will place less emphasis on performance. The ease of recovery often drives this decision.
____ (iii) **What strategies are available to a lender?**
____ a. **Foreclosure.** Gives a lender title free and clear of junior interests and is generally a strategy for completion, but it can be expensive, can be slow in certain jurisdictions, can cut off contractual obligations of counterparties in

some cases, can create negative publicity, or can subject the lender to possible environmental liability by stepping into the chain of title (but check local statutes regarding statutes providing immunity or limitations on a lender's liability for tort and other issues after a foreclosure or takeover situation).

____ b. **Receivership.** Provides a layer of protection between the lender and the counterparties and lender does not step into chain of title, but can be difficult to implement in an orderly fashion.

____ c. **Mortgagee in possession status.**

____ d. **Deed in lieu of foreclosure.** It is fast, cheap, and nonpublic, but there are significant bankruptcy concerns regarding fraudulent transfers and preferences.

____ e. Tax consequences of each of these avenues should not be ignored but are beyond the scope of this article.

____ 3. **Owner–Architect Agreement.**

____ (a) **Does the agreement cover all design phases?** Failure to cover all possible design phases could hinder a lender's ability to complete construction in the event of a takeover situation prior to the completion of design and/or implementation of design. The following design phases should be covered:

____ (i) Schematic design.

____ (ii) Design development.

____ (iii) Construction documents.

____ (iv) Bidding/negotiation.

____ (v) Construction contract administration.

____ (b) **What are the architect's responsibilities for the drawings?** The owner–architect agreement should place the full responsibility for drawings and specifications on the architect without conditions and without requiring owner demand. Basic payment should be contingent upon reaching the required levels of completion of each phase.

____ (i) Beware of conditional responsibility or requirements for owners to request/demand performance.

____ (ii) Definitional issues can erode an architect's obligations. When and under what circumstances is each phase deemed completed (for example, temporary certificate of occupancy issued versus punchlist finished)?

____ (c) **When can an architect terminate the contract?** Beware of architect's rights to terminate contract, which can arise as a result of an owner default or under other circumstances. Lenders should require notice of such defaults or the intent to terminate with an opportunity to either cure or obtain cure from the owner.

____ (d) **How can a lender create defenses to claims by architects?** A lender should consider including an architect's express acknowledgment of lender's role in the deal in the owner–architect agreement, such as:

____ (i) Limitation of effect of lender's approval of plans. Architect agrees that lender's approval is simply a determination that a condition of the funding is met and that such approval is not intended or to be construed to benefit any third party, including architect.

____ (ii) Architect agrees and acknowledges that lender and owner are not partners, joint venturers, or co-owners.

____ (e) **Who owns the drawings and other documents?** The U.S. Copyright Act vests ownership of the drawings and instruments of service in the architect, but in event of a default by owner and if lender takes over construction, not having access to such drawings may provide the architect with excessive leverage. In addition, a default or termination by architect after a lender takeover resulting in architect ownership of the plans could affect the lender's ability to finish the project. Thus, lender should carefully consider negotiation to adjust default ownership in architect (for example, joint ownership of drawings or a perpetual, royalty fee license).

____ (f) **What should the architect's certifications say?**

____ (i) Beware of qualification of certification "in architect's opinion or professional judgment," which could work to restrict architect's liability to situations in which certification is negligently given.

____ (ii) To be provided to lender and specify the required contents, including:

____ a. Certification with regard to zoning or utility issues.

____ b. Status reports regarding progress of construction.

____ c. Certification that hard-cost budget will cover hard-cost expenses.

____ d. Reaffirmation of representations and warranties given in any consent.
____ e. Certification of work performed.
____ f. Certification of timely payment.
____ g. Certification of no hard-cost changes.
____ h. Certification of no adjustment of completion date.

____ (iii) Consider including reaffirmation of terms of consent agreement or conditional assignment of owner–architect agreement to lender, including:
____ a. Consent to assignment.
____ b. Recognition of lender's right to complete project by requiring architect's performance under the architect agreement.
____ c. Agreement to cooperate with lender on owner default and lender's completion of project.
____ d. Grant of license for lender to use plans without charge, whether or not original architect is completing the project.

____ (g) **What other items should concern a lender?**

____ (i) Convoluted or architect-friendly expense reimbursement terms.

____ (ii) Liquidated damages provisions in favor of architect (termination fee).

____ (iii) Anti-assignment provisions are troublesome, because the ultimate effect of the provision is unclear in the event of an assignment. The assignment could be:
____ a. Effective but treated as a breach of the provision.
____ b. Ineffective, essentially preventing a lender from stepping into the owner's shoes (in an event of default) and taking over the contracts.

____ (iv) Any assignment provisions that are inconsistent with a consent or conditional assignment, such as providing for lender's liability for default or obligations arising prior to takeover or preventing a lender from further assigning the owner–architect agreement in a workout situation.

____ (v) Indemnification clauses that do not expressly indemnify lender for architect's negligence.

____ (vi) Limitations of liability, waivers of so-called consequential damages.

____ (vii) **Timing.** Often the agreement will be executed prior to lender being included in discussions, thus amendments will usually need to be incorporated in the consent.

____ (viii) Assignment of the owner–architect agreement should require the lender's consent.

____ (ix) **Acceleration clauses.** Any provision that shortens the period in which the owner or lender can assert claims versus the architect.

____ 4. **Owner/General Contractor Agreement.**

____ (a) **What is the key issue?** Are the owner obligations something that the lender is willing to provide if or when owner defaults? If the answer is no, then lender should reconsider making the loan, as termination of construction may be the only option in a default situation.

____ (b) **How involved should the lender be?** Very involved. The lender should review the owner/general contractor agreement from a point of view as if the lender is itself the owner. Lender's approval of contractor, major subcontractors, or construction manager should include analysis of the following categories for each approval:

____ (i) Experience/track record.

____ (ii) Work load.

____ (iii) Reputation.

____ (iv) Efficiency.

____ (v) Integrity.

____ (vi) Sufficient resources/labor.

____ (c) **What should the contract say?**

____ (i) Include clear scope and specificity of:

____ a. Plans.

____ b. Conditions.

____ c. Bonds.

____ d. Quality of construction.

____ e. Location of improvements.

____ f. Related amenities (parking, landscaping, etc.).

____ (ii) Lender should make both a technical review and a cost-analysis perspective.

____ (iii) Include clear delineation of Contract Documents and how those documents interact with each other (can be a daunting task in this age of forms).

____ (iv) Include clear representation that contractor has inspected the work site and is responsible for all work despite unexpected conditions surfacing.

____ (v) Check the requirements of any permanent loan commitment, and make sure plans fit within such framework.

____ (vi) Verify plan compliance with local, state, and federal laws.

____ (vii) Include work site information with complete legal description.

  ____ a. If possible, consider delineation of the smallest tract, including the improvements location, so as to limit potential construction liens to that particular parcel.

____ (viii) Provide consistency of costs with budget and loan agreement.

  ____ a. Beware of difficulties arising from "cost-plus" or other payment arrangement without a maximum compensation amount.

____ (ix) Include payment terms/timing.

  ____ a. Consistent with loan agreement.

  ____ b. Retainage requirements.

____ (x) **Cross-check.** Deadlines must be consistent with loan agreement!

  ____ a. Consider liquidated damages provisions for failure to meet timing requirements.

____ (xi) Include change orders or contractor's claims for additional compensation.

  ____ a. Detailed (but realistic) procedures.

  ____ b. Require lender approval for changes over a threshold.

  ____ c. Consider consent form disclaiming lender's recognition of any nonapproved change orders.

____ (xii) Confirm owner's right to cure defaults after notice from contractor.

  ____ a. Lender should be a notice party.

____ (xiii) Dovetail the effects of owner's default under the loan agreement to protect lender in the context of the owner/general contractor agreement.

____ (xiv) Extend contractor's indemnification of owner to lender.

____ (xv) Limit the effect of lender's approval of any work.

  ____ a. Approval is simply a determination that a condition of the funding is met.

____ b. Approval is not intended to benefit any third party, including contractor.

____ (xvi) Include specific agreement from contractor that it is not third-party beneficiary of the loan agreement.

____ a. Beware that direct payment or other actions could vitiate this provision.

____ (xvii) Include recognition by contractor that joint check arrangements create no liability from lender to contractor.

____ (xviii) Include statement that general contractor agrees that lender and owner are not partners, joint venturers, or co-owners.

____ (xix) **Role of architect.** Make sure it is consistent with the owner–architect agreement.

____ (xx) List stored materials.

____ a. Require that title passes to owner.

____ b. Confirm lender lien on any such materials.

____ c. Require secure storage and insurance.

____ (xxi) List warranty issues.

____ a. Require warranty from contractor.

____ b. Require contractor to furnish any applicable manufacturer/supplier warranties and to build so as to maintain warranty.

____ (xxii) Contractor default should result in owner's option to:

____ a. Terminate the agreement.

____ b. Assume possession of project (with very limited notice or a quick procedure).

____ c. Enforce contractor's contracts with subcontractors.

____ (xxiii) **Dispute clauses.** Require the contractor to continue work pending resolution of a dispute.

____ (xxiv) Anti-assignment provisions are troublesome, as the ultimate effect of the provision is unclear in the event of an assignment. The assignment could be:

____ a. Effective, but treated as a breach of the provision.

____ b. Ineffective, essentially preventing a lender from stepping into the owner's shoes (in an event of default) and taking over the contracts.

____ (xxv) Include any assignment provisions that are inconsistent with a consent or conditional assignment, such as providing for lender's liability for default or obligations arising prior to takeover or preventing a lender from further assigning the owner–architect agreement in a workout situation.

____ (xxvi) No assignment of contractor's rights under the contract is permitted without lender consent.

____ a. Similar provisions for major subcontracts.

____ b. Consider specific prohibition of pledging such rights as security.

____ (d) **How should a lender act?**

____ (i) Respond promptly, clearly, and affirmatively to requests for payment or guaranty from a contractor.

____ (ii) Demanding discharge of a contractor could give rise to a tortious interference claim.

____ (iii) Provide for equitable estoppel issues if lender induces contractor activity.

____ (e) **In a fast-track project, what should the lender be most concerned about?**

____ (i) Strong objective benchmarks.

____ (ii) Quick dispute-resolution procedures.

____ (iii) Analysis of benefits and burdens.

____ (iv) Stronger requirements of lender notice, inspections, and progress reports.

____ (f) **How can a lender protect against the contractor "getting ahead"?** Getting ahead implies that the contractor is seeking funds to pay for subcontracts prior to such subcontracts being finished, allowing a cash balance to build up that may be improperly used by the contractor (for example, to fund other projects).

____ (i) Require substantial completion of a subcontract prior to release of funds.

____ (ii) Perform periodic audit/review of contractor's books and records.

____ (g) **How can a lender protect against mechanic's liens?** Mechanic's liens statutes and case law vary from state to state; therefore, counsel should be sought to advise on the peculiarities of a particular jurisdiction. Some general guidelines include the following:

____ (i) Make use of first-in-time rule.

____ a. Record and do not allow construction to begin (material delivery may be significant) until after loan closing; consult local counsel for state-specific guidance.

____ b. Require representations from contractor and owner, plus site investigation on closing date.

____ (ii) Consider the following options, or a combination thereof:

____ a. "No lien" contract.

____ b. Contractor's interim lien waivers or subordination agreements.

____ c. Contractor responsibility for liens (for example, by payment or bond).

____ (1) Ability to withhold payments until resolved.

____ (2) Indemnity of both owner and lender.

____ d. List of subcontractors/materialmen and contractor required to obtain lien releases from all listed parties upon payment.

____ (h) **What are the insurance issues facing a lender in the owner/general contractor agreement?**

____ (i) Typical insurance requirements include:

____ a. Worker's compensation and disability benefits.

____ b. Bodily injury claims.

____ c. Occupational sickness/disease/death of contractor's employees.

____ d. Same as before, for those other than contractor's employees.

____ e. Personal injury.

____ f. General property loss.

____ g. General auto liability.

____ h. Builder's risk (loss to buildings during construction, alteration, or repair).

____ i. Loss of use of property (fire, flood, or other hazards).

____ j. Business interruption insurance.

____ k. Comprehensive general liability.

____ l. Contractual liability insurance (to cover assumptions of liability and indemnity covenants in the contract).

____ (ii) Require certificates at a minimum, but actual endorsements and policies preferred (deductible, insurer's termination rights, etc.).

____ (iii) Determine if insurer licensed for state of project and adequate limits.

____ 5. **Insurance Issues.**

____ (a) **Which agreements should address insurance?** All of them. Require specific recognition in each and every construction document that construction lender's lien on insurance proceeds comes first.

____ (b) **What is the difference in a standard mortgage clause versus loss payee versus additional insured?**

____ (i) Lender as "loss payee" and insurance payable to lender "as his interest may appear" can be negated by other insured's negligence.

____ (ii) **Mortgagee (standard mortgage clause):**

____ a. Mortgagee's right of recovery not negated by mortgagor or any other insured's negligence (that is, contractor or subcontractor).

____ b. Consider waiver of subrogation rights by insurer.

____ (iii) **Additional insured.** Right to receive payment of proceeds.

____ a. Cold comfort if this covenant is breached (no action against insurer).

____ b. Require lender to be named additional insured on any and all insurance policies associated with the project, but provide that contractor and subcontractors shall not be included as joint payees.

____ (c) **What is an agreement to insure?** Agreement from owner to insure the project.

____ (i) Enforceable if oral (no problem with the statute of frauds), but generally should be written and precise as to what insurance is being procured.

____ (ii) There may be implied indemnity and may be implied waiver of claims against other contracting party, but there are obvious collection issues.

# Index

## A

## D

## O



## P

**R**

## U



## V



## W